TOWARD UNDERSTANDING POWER AND ITS USE

Machiavelli, Jesus, I-Thou

Norman Wood Beck

VANTAGE PRESS
New York / Atlanta
Los Angeles / Chicago

FIRST EDITION

Published by Vantage Press, Inc.
516 West 34th Street, New York, New York 10001

Manufactured in the United States of America
ISBN: 0-533-07292-1

Library of Congress Catalog Card No.: 86-91474

To
Evelyn and Peter

ad amorem fontem veritatis

CONTENTS

The perennial question: Can humans derive from experience a science of politics? The arms race as indication of inadequate leadership. Testimonies from the past. Machiavelli's approach: recognition of the difficulty; deliberate innovation; active participation as key to understanding; renewal through re-evaluating original principles in light of subsequent experience. Methods of dealing with change: science, fiction. Conceptions of human nature: the organismic process; recognition of human diversity; social circulation of energies; persistent questions; relation to the cosmos. The question restated.

Factors accelerating change in the wake of the Crusades. Impact of nation-forming on Machiavelli. Chronic strife over relation of force to power: Cain; the territorial state; Jesus' affirmation of "the kingdom of heaven" on earth. Attempt at compromise: the new community's growth and organization of power; proliferation of kingdoms. Signs of obsolescence of Machiavelli's concept of requisited authority; review of assumption of "evil" in human nature; unaddressed current needs; limited availability of nationhood; "Great Powers' " obstruction of effective control over military policies; diminution of peoples' confidence in political process.

Is the political process itself flawed? Some general basic fictions: assumption of "leader-follower" relationship; assumption of knowledge of self-interest; assumption of "the collective" as source of essential supplementary aid; various additional assumptions as fictions. Fictions in Machiavelli's writings (note: special obligation that fictions used by Machiavelli be identified and evaluated): the founder-reformer; "history"; no place for every-body; security through power over others; effective force against others; public purpose transmuting power; force ingenerate in states; knowledge of cause and effect in human affairs; supernal sanction for control over others; "selfhood" through organized membership; therapeutic political surgery; assimilation of artifice into reality; effectiveness of power despite untruth; power through stunning action; "evidence" of "history"; successful achievement of war aims. Classification of fictions according to degree of Machiavelli's endorsement. Current cultural developments which exposed additional fictions; impact on Machiavelli, personally; impact on his as-sumptions buttressed by force.

own resources. Universal interdependency of citizenship. Increasing opportunity for individual choice with undiminished need to identify oneself with others in like need. Experimentation for governmental processes more effective for serving the common good with Machiavelli as guide; contributions from seventeenth and eighteenth centuries; contributions from American experience with development towards self-government. Summons of individual awareness that in one's own resources dare to be found one's best possibilities—an emphasis common to Jesus and Machiavelli. War as parasite at expense of resources vital for human survival.

Ancient conceptions of power consonant with universal order realizable on earth. Machiavelli's conception of power in terms of militant pluralism. Perennial civic qualities recognized by Machiavelli. Prospect of progress for the common good and diminished violence. Enhanced need for political science to be renewed by re-examination of its origins. Implication for the present of appropriate response according to the "principle of proportionate duty." Qualities requisite for effective government, according to Machiavelli; evaluation of their current relevance.

Universally, open-ended, unprejudiced attentiveness to intentional behavior and its verifiable recording. Experimental exploration of all scales of human relationships through typical models. Informed, responsible participatory but unbiased action. The individual as unit of operation. Consensus as unit of valuation. Political science as individual living out courageous prudence.

APPENDIXES

FOREWORD

Norman Wood Beck has spent a lifetime thinking, teaching, and writing about the nature and use of political power. *Toward Understanding Power and Its Use—Machiavelli, Jesus, I-Thou* is the capstone of a truly remarkable scholarly career during which Professor Beck taught almost three generations of students to seek their own understanding of politics, not through the opinions of others, but by becoming "participant-observers" in the world of practical politics.

True to his own teachings, Professor Beck's study breaks new ground in its approach to understanding the essential teachings of both Machiavelli and Jesus on the subject of power and its use. Although the focus of his book is not centered upon the life and thought of either, the insights of each into the nature of power required him to examine their contributions in penetrating and telling detail. Avoiding the diverse interpretations of what each said and meant and the debates among the entrenched schools of thought on these subjects, Professor Beck allows Machiavelli and Jesus each to speak for himself by providing the reader with the direct quotations relevant to the sometimes unique points of view which he proposes.

There is little doubt that Machiavelli scholars and other historians, political scientists, and theologians will find much more to argue with in this work. I am certain that nothing could please the author more. His own belief that, "the source of 'authority' and power may be found in interpersonal understanding expressed in 'courageous initiative,' " is nowhere better demonstrated than in his singular approach to scholarship; which makes this study distinctive among the many works which have appeared since the 1969 quincentenary celebration of Machiavelli's birth.

Professor Beck spares the reader and himself from wading through the more than 500 scholarly items that have appeared since 1969. This is not to say that his book is not informed by the findings of these works, for he has been meticulous in surveying the relevant literature in both English and Italian. But having done so, he does not feel obliged to demonstrate his virtuosity for the reader or try to provide a mechanical chart for traversing the complex topography of Machiavelli's life and work.

Instead, the author provides the insights of the participant-observer's approach to understanding the apparent conflicts between the secular Machiavelli of *The Prince* and the Christian Machiavelli of "An Exhortation to Penitence." And, he does so in a way that will likely cause the partisans of both schools of thought on the "essential Machiavelli" to criticize the author as "idealistic" when he is, in fact, the most practical of men.

Professor Beck's starting point and touchstone for understanding the nature and use of political power is the individual, not the state. His belief in, "the fact of inherent individuality as contrasted with the *myths* of leadership and corporate entity," is a signal contribution to the debate about the inevitable need for deception, force, and exploitation by states and their political leaders.

Both the individual's "creative uniqueness and constructive potentiality" (described by Jesus) and his "inevitable capacity for vengeful retaliation" (indicated by Machiavelli) insure that "force proves transitory, however ingeniously contrived the fiction in which it is clothed."

In the author's view both Machiavelli and Jesus cut through the myths and rejected the fiction of the militantly nationalistic state as the source and guardian of security and human freedom.

Machiavelli's aim was to detect the "effectual truth" in the poilitical process and to communicate it to those willing to accept the responsibility for acting in the light of it. Machiavelli, like Jesus, personifies Beck's "participant-observer" in demonstrating that "courageous manhood (*virtù*) could be practiced regardless of changes in fortune," and by his recognition that man had "direct personal access to creative power," a perception contributed to him by his religious heritage.

In the face of a global-system approach and a resurgence of nationalistic myth in place of informed analysis, Professor Beck calls for no less than a "new political science," divorced from "state policy" and renewed through a reexamination of its origins. *Toward Understanding Power and Its Use* is Norman Wood Beck's unique and lifelong contribution to that renewal.

December 1986
William J. Maxwell, President
Jersey City State College

ACKNOWLEDGMENTS

The author would like to thank the following for graciously granting permission to quote from previously published works:

Abingdon Press, for permission to reprint material from *Christian Attitudes toward War and Peace*, by Roland Bainton, copyright © 1960, and excerpts from *Interpreter's Bible* vol. 7, copyright renewal © 1979, *Interpreter's Bible* vol. 8, copyright renewal © 1980, *Interpreter's Bible* vol. 9, copyright renewal © 1982, *Interpreter's Bible* vol. 10, copyright renewal © 1981, *Interpreter's Bible* vol. 11, copyright renewal © 1983, and *Interpreter's Bible* vol. 12, copyright renewal © 1985.

American Heritage Publishing Co., Inc., for permission to reprint from English language edition of *The Horizon Book of the Renaissance*, by J. H. Plumb. Copyright © 1961.

Cornell University Press, for permission to reprint material from *Machiavelli's New Modes and Orders: A Study of the "Discourses on Livy,"* by Harvey C. Mansfield, Jr. Copyright © 1979.

Duke University Press, for permission to reprint material from *Machiavelli, The Chief Works and Others*, by Allan Gilbert.

Martin Fleischer, excerpted from *Machiavelli and The Nature of Political Thought*. Copyright © 1972 by Martin Fleischer. Reprinted with the permission of Atheneum Publishers, Inc.

Felix Gilbert, for permission to quote from *Machiavelli and Guicciardini: Politics and History in Sixteenth Century Florence*. Copyright © 1965 by Princeton University Press.

Harcourt Brace Jovanovich, Inc., for permission to reprint excerpts from *Machiavelli: A Dissection*, copyright © 1969 by Sydney Anglo; from *On Aggression*, by Konrad Lorenz, copyright © 1963 by Dr. G. Barotha-Schoeler Verlag, Wien; English translation copyright © 1966 by Konrad Lorenz; and from *Alexander Hamilton and the Constitution*, copyright © 1964 by Clinton Rossiter.

Greenvale Press, for permission to reprint material from *Niccolo Machiavelli and the United States of America* by Anthony J. Pansini. Copyright © 1969.

Harper and Row Publishers, Inc. for permission to reprint material from

Alexander Hamilton, Portrait in Paradox by John C. Miller, copyright © 1959, and from *The Columbia History of the World*, edited by John A. Garaty and Peter Gay. Copyright © 1972.

W. Heffer and Sons Ltd., Cambridge, England, for permission to reprint material from *Discourses on Machiavelli*, by J. H. Whitfield. Copyright © 1969.

Northwestern University Press, for permission to reprint material from *Florentine Studies*, edited by Nicolai Rubenstein. Copyright © 1968.

Oxford University Press, for permission to reprint material from *The Growth of the American Republic*, by Samuel Eliot Morison, Henry Steele Commager, and William E. Leuchtenburg. Copyright © 1969.

J. G. A. Pocock, for permmission to reprint scattered excerpts from *The Machiavellian Moment: Florentine Political Thought and the Atlantic Republican Tradition*. Copyright © 1975 by Princeton University Press.

Random House, Inc., for permission to reprint material from *The Medici*, by G. F. Young. Copyright © 1930.

Routledge and Kegan Paul Inc., for permission to reprint material from *Machiavellism*, by Friedrich Meinecke. Copyright © 1957.

George B. Sabine and Janet V. Kelbleg, for permission to reprint from *A History of Political Theory*, by their father, George H. Sabine.

James Schevill, for permission to reprint material from *History of Florence from the Founding of the City through the Renaissance*, by Ferdinand Schevill. The copyright is currently held by James Schevill.

The estate of Leo Strauss, for permission to reprint material from his *Thoughts on Machiavelli*.

Kenyon College and Robert Horwitz for permission to reprint quotations from Professor Horwitz's *Moral Foundations of the American Republic*, published by The University Press of Virginia. Copyright © 1977.

The University of California Press, for permission to reprint material from *Corruption, Conflict, and Power*, by Alfredo Bonadeo. Copyright © 1973.

The University of Chicago Press, for permission to reprint material from *The Life of Niccolo Machiavelli*, by Roberto Ridolfi. Copyright © 1963.

Yale University Press, for permission to reprint material from *Quaker Experiences in International Conciliation*, by C. H. Mike Yarrow. Copyright ©

In addition, the author would like to express appreciation for the timely encouragement and expert advice given by Elizabeth and John Beveridge Robinson and by Donald Henry Hinkle in the preparation of the manuscript for submission to the publisher.

*Toward Understanding
Power and Its Use*

Chapter One

HISTORIC QUEST FOR WISDOM IN SECURING POWER

By generating prudence, can the violence attendant upon the quirks of chance be curbed? Is the prospect encouraging? Is it within human competence to work out a way toward freedom, justice, security, peace, and to progress with understanding? Can people develop a method by which to distill out of experience guidance adequate for making constructive decisions, for manifesting and realizing their potentialities? Can any positive ingredients for a process of political inquiry truly responsible to observable human experience in its entirety, be detected and registered?

Although it is conceivable that applied science might make available for all mankind consumers' goods in abundance sufficient to meet human material needs, in fact, in the service of systematically nourished fear, the most powerful governments themselves, with tax-derived public subsidies, aggressively induce their creatures, multi-national corporations, to dedicate their energies and resources to produce in unmanageable quantities ever-more-lethal instruments for mutual destruction and thereby, in reality, to diminish freedom, security and the prospects for peace.

Long before Niccolo Machiavelli set modern man on the quest for a science of politics, sages and saints had confronted the question. Solomon prayed:

Give thy servant . . . a heart with skill to listen, so that he may govern thy people justly and distinguish good from evil.[1]

Yet the wisdom of Solomon was not sufficient to prevent, following his death, the rift between his sons, the civil war, and the division of the kingdom.

Somberly, the author of Ecclesiastes, at the conclusion of his search, recorded:

I applied my mind to acquire wisdom and observe the business which goes on upon the earth, when man never closes an eye in sleep day or night;

1

and always I perceived that God has so ordered it that man should not be able to discover what is happening here under the sun. However hard a man may try, he will not find out; the wise man may think that he knows, but he will be unable to find the truth of it.[2]

The "wise men of the East" who, following the Star, were seeking "the new born king" to worship him and give him gifts, did not obey the ruler Herod's orders and make available to him the results of their search, since they perceived that he sought only to preserve his violent control. Instead, they "returned home by another way."[3] And Herod, frustrated, in his ignorant rage, had Bethlehem's children, two years of age and under, slaughtered.[4]

Although to Pilate's question, "What is truth?" Jesus made no reply, yet, according to John, Jesus had said to his disciples:

If you dwell within the revelation I have brought . . . you shall know the truth, and the truth will set you free.[5]

In his first letter to the Corinthians, Paul wrote:

Scripture says, 'I will destroy the wisdom of the wise and bring to nothing the cleverness of the clever.' Where is your wise man now, your man of learning, or your subtle debater—limited, all of them, to this passing age? God has made the wisdom of this world look foolish. As God in his wisdom ordained, the world failed to find him by its wisdom.[6]

A recognition of the difficulty of making understandable the processes of government but a determination through doing so to diminish the violent role of Fortune, began to appear early in Machiavelli's writings. In the period of his official service as an officer of his city in its foreign intelligence, through his private correspondence, and through the *Prince* and the *Discourses on Livy* can be observed the genesis of his approach to the consideration of decision-making. From the Court of Pope Julius II he reported to the Florentine Signoria:

I know it is a presumption to make a judgment of events, and especially of those which change every hour; none the less it appears to me never to err in writing to Your Lordships what opinions the wise men have of events here, so that you can with the usual prudence always make a better judgment;[7]

and later,

It is difficult to judge matters of this nature, and of all those which remain to the discretion and the will of men.[8]

Shortly after the fall of the Florentine republic in 1513, but before his own imprisonment and torture, he responded to a letter from the exiled former head of the republic:

> the reason why different ways of working are sometimes equally effective and equally damaging I do not know, but I should much like to know. So in order to get your opinion I shall be so presuming as to give mine.[9]

Just a month after his release from prison, Machiavelli wrote his friend, Francesco Vettori, the Florentine ambassador to the papal court of Leo X (Giovanni de'Medici):

> Fortune has determined that since I don't know how to talk about the silk business or the wool business or about profits and losses, I must talk about the government; I must either make a vow of silence or discuss that;[10]

and later, in that same month,

> in these matters I do not intend that any authority should move me without reason.[11]

And, to Vettori, after some twenty months:

> I try always to keep my judgment firm, especially in these things and not let it be corrupted by a vain contest, as do many others.[12]

Of his motive and perspective, he wrote in the *Prince:*

> since my purpose is to write something useful to him who comprehends it, I have decided that I must concern myself with the truth of the matter as facts show it rather than any fanciful notion;[13]

and in *Discourses* when introducing consideration of the possibility for free government in corrupt cities:

> although to give rules for it is almost impossible . . . nevertheless, since it is well to reason about everything, I do not wish to omit this;[14]

and, later, when supporting his position that "the multitude is wiser and more consistent than a prince,"

> I do not know whether I am undertaking a task so hard and full of difficulties that I shall be forced to defend something that, as I have said, has been

condemned by all the writers. But however that may be, I do not judge and I shall never judge it a sin to defend any opinion with arguments, without trying to use either authority or force.[15]

To Machiavelli himself may well be applied a criterion for quality which he expressed in *The Art of War* when he wrote:

No man without inventiveness was ever great in his profession.[16]

Of the many and diverse contributions accredited to him, none is more generally recognized and better substantiated than that of his having laid a new basis for a science of politics. J. H. Whitfield has noted:

It was Croce who spoke of Machiavelli as the discoverer of the *anatomy of politics*[17]

and Count Sforza has written:

he was truthful, wise and unmistakeably clear, a diagnostician of modern scope, more, the very first scholar of political science, and its discoverer.[18]

Referring to the *Prince* and the *Discourses*, Max Kemmerich has written:

Zwei Schriften, die zusammen den Grundstein der Staatswissenschaften legen sollten, sind es, die ihn zuerst und gleichzeitig beschäftigten und durch die er der Vater der theoretischen Staatskunst und-Wissenschaft wurde.[19]

They are two works which, taken together, were to lay the foundation for political science, which occupied him first and at the same time and through which he became the father of theoretical statecraft and political science.

Arnoldo Mondadori has referred to him as

lo scrittore che aveva rivendicato alla politica una sua autonomia di contenuti e metodi e quindi una sua moralità laica piú valida della morale di tradizione.[20]

The writer who had reclaimed for politics an autonomy of contents and methods and thence a secular morality of its own sounder than the morale of tradition.

That active participation gives the opportunity for understanding was, for Machiavelli, a cardinal principle. In the draft of his letter of January 1513 to ex-Gonfalonier Soderini, he wrote:

Non consigliar persona, ne pigliar consiglio da persona, eccetto che un consiglio generale: che ognuno faccia quello che gli getta l'animo, e con audacia.[21]

I do not give advice to anyone, nor take advice from anyone, except this general advice: that each man do what his spirit dictates to him, and with boldness.

and to his friend Vettori:

I believe, have believed, and will always believe that it is true, as Boccaccio said, that it is better to act and repent than not to act and repent.[22]

In the *Discourses* he observed:

About courage in important matters, no one without experience can promise himself certainty.[23]

In "The (Golden) Ass," he warned:

To believe that without effort on your part God fights for you while you are idle and on your knees, has ruined many kingdoms and many states.[24]

In a similar vein, when considering the power of Fortune, he wrote:

I assert, indeed, once more that it is very true, according to what we see in all the histories, that men are able to assist Fortune but not to thwart her. They can weave her designs but cannot destroy them. They ought, then, never to give up as beaten, because, since they do not know her purpose, and she goes through crooked and unknown roads, they can always hope, and hoping are not to give up, in whatever fortune and whatever affliction they may be;[25]

and in his account of Francesco Sforza's rise to power:

Still he determined to show his face to Fortune, and according to her shifts to make his plans; for often when a man is doing something, plans reveal themselves to him which, if he stood still, would forever hide themselves.[26]

Likewise, regarding the time at which a general should engage in battle, he advised:

Necessity comes when you see that if you do not fight you must surely lose, that, for instance, you lack money and therefore your army is certain to go to pieces; or that hunger is going to attack you; or that your enemy is expecting to increase his army with new men. In these instances you should always fight, even if you are at a disadvantage, because it is much better to tempt Fortune when she possibly will favor you than, not tempting her, to face certain ruin.[27]

In the *Prince*, he laid down as a general rule for his own conduct:

As for me, I believe this: it is better to be impetuous than cautious, because Fortune is a woman . . . always, like a woman, she is the friend of young men, because they are less cautious, more spirited, and with more boldness master her.[28]

When removed from his official position, his name stricken from the list of those eligible to serve in the government, exiled from the city, he wrote in his dedication of the *Prince* to Lorenzo de'Medici, the Duke of Nemours:

I have found among my treasures nothing I hold dearer or value so high as my understanding of great men's actions, gained in my lengthy experience with recent matters and my continual reading on ancient ones.[29]

With directness and clarity he set forth his reasons for writing: in the *Prince* as already noted;[30] and in the *Discourses:*

driven by the natural eagerness I have always felt for doing without any hesitation the things that I believe will bring benefit common to everybody, I have determined to enter upon a path not yet trodden by anyone; though it may bring me trouble and difficulty, it can also bring me reward, by means of those who kindly consider the purpose of these my labors.[31]

It was his expressed conviction that

men never do anything good except by necessity.[32]

Oreste Tommasini, whose work along with that of Pasquali Vallari ranks as one of the two greatest studies of Machiavelli, has truly observed:

Può scrivere ma il suo pensiero è all'azione, il suo scritto è un tentativo per riguadagnare la via e la carriera sua.[33]

He is able to write but his thought is for action, his writing is an attempt to get back on the track and his career.

The practical necessity to find himself restored to participation in public affairs where he would again receive nourishment from that food which only is mine and which I was born for,[34]

drove him to make use of those insights gained through his past official experience and his reading of history and to write those two books which, as a by-product, gave rise to modern political science. Whitfield has well concluded:

> The whole *oeuvre* of Machiavelli is all a *grido di dolere* for the conditions in which his country finds itself, and the attempt to find the clue which will allow escape into a more bearable atmosphere. Certainly, Machiavelli wishes to ascertain the facts, but in order to change them.[35]

That principle which Machiavelli recommended as salutary for religions, republics and kingdoms may as profitably be related to political science. In the *Discourses* he wrote:

> those are best organized and have longest life that through their institutions can often renew themselves or that by some accident outside their organization come to such renewal. And it is clearer than light that if those bodies are not renewed they do not last. The way to renew them, as I have said, is to carry them back to their beginnings; because all the beginnings of religions and of republics and of kingdoms must possess some goodness by means of which they gain their first reputation and their first growth. Since in the process of time that goodness is corrupted, if something does not happen that takes it back to the right position, such corruption necessarily kills that body.[36]

The benefit worked in carrying the institutions "back to their beginnings" results from the fresh and deeper insights prompted by taking into account the subsequent experience. Twice, Machiavelli adjudged

Time . . . the father of Truth.[37]

Recent scholarship has facilitated the re-study and re-evaluation of Machiavelli's presentation of "the truth of the matter as facts show it"[38] and wherein it continues to be "useful to him who comprehends it." Moreover, profound cultural, and especially technological, changes of the past four to five centuries have generated insights and perspectives which condition the continuing relevance of his findings.

In responding to the challenge of change, two methods contrast sharply: that of science and that of fiction.

The essence of the scientific method is the process of exploring further the way toward which all of the relevant evidence taken together points. Konrad Lorenz has written:

7

nobody knows as well as the scientist that there are limits to human understanding, but he is always aware that we do not know where these limits lie. Kant said, "Our observation and analysis of its phenomena penetrate to the depth of nature. We do not know how far this will lead us in time."[39]

The discipline which commitment to the search toward truth requires has been well set forth in the words of W.E.H. Lecky:

> To love truth sincerely means to pursue it with an earnest, conscientious, unflagging zeal. It means to be prepared to follow the light of evidence even to the most unwelcome conclusions; to labor earnestly to emancipate the mind from early prejudices; to resist the current of desires, and the refracting influence of the passions; to proportion on all occasions conviction to evidence, and to be ready, if need be, to exchange the calm of assurance for all the suffering of a perplexed and disturbed mind. To do this is very difficult and very painful; but it is clearly involved in the notion of earnest love of truth.[40]

Sometimes the formulation and projection of a basis for procedure seems to demand the use not only of hypotheses but also of imaginary elements as factors: as, in mathematics with the introduction of minus numbers; and, in architecture, with the employment of scaffolding. However, before the process is considered as completed, the minus numbers have to be cancelled out and the scaffolding removed rather than incorporated as an integral part of the final product. "Something accepted as fact for the sake of convenience, although not necessarily true" is a "fiction."[41] In the foregoing examples, the establishing of the reality requires the sacrificing of the fictions used in the process.

In human relations, however, the assumption has had widespread acceptance that "imaginary nothing" can be given "a local habitation and a name,"[42] thereby be made a part of reality and, with duress, be assimilated as such.

Caught and wrenched to the core in processes of change, men have availed themselves of one of two responses. When perceiving the breaking up and dissolution of their institutions and values upon which they had relied and in terms of which they had felt themselves living meaningfully, some, taking offense at their fellowmen, have, through the force of imagination, formulated instrumentalities as preservers of those values and accorded them a higher validity than they were willing to recognize in those other human beings whom they held in opposition. Others, by contrast, have taken into themselves the costs of facing the change and, by spending whatever of the cherished values the preservation of the human relationship required, have purchased thereby deeper and broader understanding. Personality, thereby, spending itself through compassionate consciousness transforms, enlarges and deepens the foundation of its structure of significant relations.

In order that thinking about political processes might become a science of politics, fictions have to be identified and evaluated in light of progress in the understanding of human behavior. Any attempt to treat the imaginary element as an integral part of the given reality or to employ it as a substitute for a part of that reality always gives itself away by the emergence of an element of force being used to sacrifice existing relationships as means toward altering the reality as given.

The study of politics inescapably involves the study of human nature. In his years-long clinical observation of the rebuilding of the organisms of men who in World War I had suffered brain injuries and were convalescing under his care from 1918–1933, Dr. Kurt Goldstein established that the processes of the human organism are wholistic interactions of all of its parts and that its health is dependent upon the degree of freedom of circulation among them. Characteristic of organismic behavior is the fact that each one always expresses a drive for the best performance of which the given organism is capable under the given circumstances. The healthy organism gives a diversified, innovative, creative response expressive of its latent potentialities: the healthier the organism, the more individualized the response and the more representative of the entire organism; however, the more severe the injury, the more mechanical and violent are the reactions to stimuli. When a part operates as if it is in itself the whole, a component of violent mechanicality emerges as the surrogate for the missing elements of the more inclusive whole to which the part belongs. The pathological behavior of the injured organism signifies merely the organismic response under the inhibiting conditions—not a more fundamental feature characteristic of the organism itself when in a state of health.[43]

The approach to the understanding of human behavior requires at the outset the recognition that the concern is with the interrelationships of individuals as organisms and that the phenomena are, therefore, always organismic in character. A fertilized egg nourished into growth, aggregated out by preponderantly congenial experiences, has generated each individual as a unique, exploring and patterning process toward, and through, encounters which give at once strength and direction. Each organism is a kind of dynamic puzzle-in-process which, under the impetus of its positive experiences, is obligated to work itself out according to the unique pattern of its highest potential. The living process continually develops a potentiality for such varied alternatives of combinations of past associations and new impulse that one can profitably pursue with active choice the inclination towards the best and contribute to the realization of a more harmonious ambience. Moreover, as a social being, each, through his sympathetic nervous system, spontaneously mobilizes an inner reserve of energy to respond to each other's need. So, regardless of parentage and condition of up-bringing, each develops a sense of rightful claim to survival, an obligation of respect for himself and for the development of his own adequate articulateness through his own potentialities, and a full and equal title to the fruits of the good earth and, among his fellow men, to authentic dignity. This authentic dignity belongs to each human being most deeply, as a most natural property right—an organically functioning necessity for an equal opportunity for the full development of his potentialities without any shadow of inferiority. All alike propelled or invited involuntarily into living, each is impelled to avail himself of whatever presents itself as essential for securing his development in greater freedom, be it access to: food, a share in the making of decisions affecting himself, education, gainful employment, family, land. One's perception and understanding of himself becomes clarified through his more responsible participation in the largest group in which he functions as a member. The more inclusive the social relationship, the more sensitive and finely functioning the mutuality, the more diverse and flexible the resources for more creatively appropriate expression, the less mechanical, violent and destructive the responses or reactions encountered in the effort at survival and right conduct. Basic regard for and loyalty to all who have contributed to his well-being renders him incapable of reconciling himself to any lesser status. Such is the "natural right" to "the pursuit of happiness." In order to secure, maintain and advance this position, he merges his energies into such a social relationship and process which promises to prove congenial and in its terms he identifies and defines his freedom.

The resulting ultimate diversity between human beings has received ancient and widespread acknowledgment. The prophet Jeremiah (627–586 B.C.) seems to have been the first to have affirmed clearly that it is in the individual that moral responsibility resides:

> This is the very word of the Lord. In those days it shall no longer be said, 'The fathers have eaten sour grapes and the children's teeth are set on edge'; for a man shall die for his own wrongdoing; the man who eats sour grapes shall have his own teeth set on edge.[44]

Later, similarly, the prophet Ezekiel (597–582 B.C.):

> It is the soul that sins, and no other, that shall die. . . .The righteous man shall reap the fruit of his own righteousness and the wicked man the fruit of his own wickedness.[45]

The ultimate value of the individual was one of Jesus' major teachings:

> As for you, even the hairs of your head have all been counted. So have no fear;[46]

> anything you did for one of my brothers here, however humble, you did for me;[47]

10

and he made it the point of the parable of the lost sheep[48] and of the lost piece of silver.[49] In his first letter to the Corinthians, Paul wrote:

Among men, who knows what a man is but the man's own spirit within him?[50]

Machiavelli, in his writings, repeatedly recognized that inherently human beings differ from one another: thus, in the draft of his letter to Piero Soderini:

Ciascuno secundo la sua fantasia si governa.[51]

Each one governs himself according to his own fancy.

Further, in the same letter, Machiavelli affirmed:

I believe that as Nature has given each man an individual face, so she has given him an individual disposition and an individual imagination. From this it results that each man conducts himself according to his disposition and his imagination.[52]

Furthermore, he recognized in human individuality a power of self-defense and a threshold, transgressions of which incur consequences unpredictable. Both in the *Discourses* and in the *Prince* he attested to the individual's ultimate resource of violent reaction:

a man who is threatened and knows himself forced by necessity to act or to suffer becomes very dangerous to the prince;[53]

whoever governs . . . ought never to esteem anyone so lightly as to believe that, when injury is piled on injury, an injured man will not decide on getting revenge, in spite of all danger and personal harm to himself;[54]

If a man is greatly injured either by the state or by a single person, and is not avenged to his satisfaction, if he lives in a republic, he seeks, even with its ruin, to get his revenge. If he lives under a prince and has any nobility in himself, he is never quiet until in some way he has avenged himself on him, even though he sees therein his own injury;[55]

above all, he [the wise prince] refrains from the property of others, because men forget more quickly the death of a father than the loss of a father's estate. [N.4. Men feel more sorrow for a farm taken away from them than for a brother or a father put to death, because sometimes death is forgotten, but property never. The reason is close to the surface, for everyone knows that a brother cannot rise up again because of a change of government, but there is a possibility of getting back a farm.];[56]

11

it makes him [any prince] hated above all, as I have said, to be rapacious and to seize upon the property and the women of his subjects; from this he [the wise prince] abstains;[57]

a prince . . . cannot plunder a man so completely as not to leave him a dagger for revenging himself; a man cannot be so dishonored as not to retain a spirit determined on revenge;[58]

a prince . . . should never bring them [men] to a condition in which they are convinced that either they must die or the prince must die;[59]

he who seizes a tyranny and does not kill Brutus, and he who sets a state free and does not kill Brutus' sons, maintains himself but a little while;[60]

deaths, resulting from the decision of one determined mind, princes cannot avoid, because any man not afraid to die can harm them;[61]

Still another cause—a very great one—makes men conspire against a prince: this is the desire for liberating their native land which he has conquered. This cause moved Brutus and Cassius against Caesar. . . . From this passion no tyrant can protect himself except by laying down his tyranny. But because no one will do that, there are few tyrants who do not come to a bad end;[62]

The energies which the individual releases into the social relationship are replenished and indeed augmented to the degree to which he finds his experience expressed in the making of its decisions and his participation involved in the carrying out and the evaluating of the programs which affect him. Any persistent malfunction in the interrelationship gives rise to strain which develops into exploitation and coercion of the parts in the name of the fictional "whole." The order of freedom is nourished and replenished through the service given to the common welfare which in turn re-defines, re-invigorates and ennobles the individual member. The health of the relationship requires of the member a continuous weighing and/or judging as to whether his membership is becoming one which undermines his own experienced standards of validity and also as to whether he or any other is trying to extract from the whole a special private advantage. Inherently the resort to force against another betokens action in ignorance.

Persistently, questions such as the following arise: Whence come those goods which one has regarded as "one's own?" Does the nature of their origin make them vulnerable to others' demand as callable loans rather than as indeed one's own? By what process can they be made one's own? Where is one along that road? What is, therefore, to be exacted or intentionally voluntarily contributed if one is to make valid his claim as heir, effectively entitled to use it for his own purposes and so not be guilty as a corrupter or as a misuser of public resources for private purposes by bribery or betrayal of others' trust or of one's own conscience? What does one owe to whom? Why? For the promotion of what objectives is it suitable to make available what kind and amount of one's energies or resources?

An ancient perspective on the order of nature and man's place in it was portrayed in the name of Moses as reported by the Deuteronomist:

> To the Lord your God belong heaven itself, the highest heaven, the earth and everything in it,[63]

reaffirmed by the Psalmist, David:

> The earth is the Lord's and all that is in it, the world and those who dwell therein[64]

and repeated by Paul,

> The earth is the Lord's and everything in it.[65]

And Paul asks:

> Who makes you, my friend, so important? What do you possess that was not given you? If then you really received it all as a gift why take the credit to yourself?[66]

Announced with the message:

> Do not be afraid; I have good news for you: there is great joy coming to the whole people,[67]

Jesus affirmed that human beings are created by and in the spirit of love: such is the reading of the letter of I John:

> love is from God. Everyone who loves is a child of God and knows God. . . . For God is love; and his love was disclosed in this, that he sent his only Son into the world to bring us life. . . . If God thus loved us, dear friends, we in turn are bound to love one another. . . . God is love; he who dwells in love is dwelling in God, and God in him. . . . There is no room for fear in love; perfect love banishes fear.[68]

> We love because he loved us first.[69]

To the Athenians, Paul declared:

> he [God] is not far from each one of us, for in him we live and move, in him we exist; as some of your own poets have said, "We are also his offspring."[70]

13

Jesus offered to show a way adequate for meeting the needs of men as children of God:

I have come that man may have life, and may have it in all its fullness;[71]

Therefore I bid you put away anxious thoughts about food and drink to keep you alive, and clothes to cover your body. Surely life is more than food, the body more than clothes. . . . All these are things for the heathen to run after, not for you, because your heavenly Father knows that you need them all. Set your mind on God's kingdom and his justice before everything else, and all the rest will come to you as well.[72]

In sincere awareness of one's own shortcomings and needs,[73] responding through their own spontaneous impulses, people meet one another's needs[74] and release energies for courageous freedom in the quest for truth.[75] Jesus taught that, through forgiveness of others, one found release from his own inner blockages and tensions:

Forgive us the wrong we have done, as we have forgiven those who have wronged us. . . . For if you forgive others the wrongs they have done, your heavenly Father will also forgive you; but if you do not forgive others, then the wrongs you have done will not be forgiven by your Father,[76]

and through recognizing and helping meet another's need one finds the way.[77] Hence, endowed with the potentiality for manifesting love, the human being can reach beneath and beyond fear and/or the encounter of rage and the impulse to react for revenge and can through love stir a sense of mutuality.

A sharply contrasting perspective finds emphasis in much of the writings of Machiavelli. In his life of Machiavelli, Tommasini has made the observation:

la certezza è cara agli uomini più della verità, e quanta la verità necessaria.[78]

certainty is dearer to men than truth, in spite of however necessary is the truth.

Is not "necessity" a fear-born sense of inner anxiety? That such an attitude appeared to Machiavelli to be basic in human affairs, becomes clear in the response which, in *The Art of War,* he had his spokesman, Fabrizio Colonna, make to the interlocutor, Cosimo Rucellai:

Cosimo: Hence it seems to me that there is a place, in time of peace, for everybody.
Fabrizio: I do not believe that you believe that in time of peace everyone has his place, because, supposing that no other reason could be brought forward, the small number of all who remain in the places mentioned by

14

you would answer you. What fraction of the infantry needed in war are those used in time of peace? . . . So hereafter you will not say that in peace there is a place for every man.[79]

Upon this assumption, it follows, as asserted in the *Discourses:*

Men cannot make themselves safe except with power,[80]

insecurity is elemental and in the general alienation with no basis for mutual understanding, one, in his time, is more prudent if he acts on the consideration that it is "much safer . . . to be feared than loved."[81]

Could there be a starker contrast with the proclamation by "the Prince of Peace"[82] "who has led the way to life"[83] that each is created, sustained, strengthened by creative love[84] and, through it, one shall come to know the liberating truth?[85] Significant, also, is Dr. Kurt Goldstein's conclusion from his study of emotions in the human organism:

Our discussion has led us to realize not only how pertinent are emotions for human behavior, that they are inherent in it, but it also points to *an essential character of man, his not being primarily concerned with security.* The search for security is neither the only nor the highest form of self-realization of man. At least there are other forms which do not lack emotion, when we live in insecurity, when we take over deliberately insecurity, because only then we can realize ourselves in the highest form. There we are correct to speak of purpose of emotions.[86]

Between a tradition of elemental insecurity and a tradition of original and authentic entitlement, the dialogue continues throughout this study, even as in experience. Is one tradition more than the other inclined to give rise to fictions and the other to prove in accord with scientific procedure? Can the fictions be identified, their origins tracked down, their consequences evaluated, and their further influences be constructively managed? Can proved data be discerned as valid ground for Machiavelli's hope that there can arise those able to detect the lessons to be found in human experience and so institute them as to establish a periodically self-renewing order of security and freedom among men?

Chapter Two

THE CHALLENGE OF CHANGE: VIOLENT CHANGE VERSUS INNOVATIVE ORDER

Changes in power and levels of influence greatly alter perspective both of individuals and whole cultures. In time, these changes may become so numerous, profound and pervasive that it becomes important to differentiate the obsolete from the still significant and essential.

Stimulated by the Crusades and then by reactions against exploitive practices by the ecclesiastical-financial-commercial-industrial complex, nation-states consolidated in England, France, Spain and, beginning in 1494, wreaked havoc in an unprepared Italy. An insatiable curiosity invaded compartment after compartment of European civilization. Through new techniques of scholarship, John Wycliffe in fourteenth century England, John Hus in Bohemia and, in Italy, Lorenzo Valla—*both* in the fifteenth century—exploded venerable, sanctified claims of biblical authority for institutional beliefs and practices and rediscovered and proclaimed Jesus' imperative for dynamic personal compassion. Machiavelli himself alluded to the unconventional understanding to be gained by him "who reads the Bible intelligently."[1] During Machiavelli's own lifetime, the Reformation was splitting the western Church and Martin Luther delineated the freedom of the Christian man. Recovery of great bodies of classical literature provided alternative perspectives on human relations, exemplified in Machiavelli's study and advocacy of the civic virtues of republican Rome. Introduction of moveable type for the printing of books, in the middle of fifteenth century, made their ownership and circulation available to a much larger public. In geographic exploration, Machiavelli's contemporaries, the Genoese, Christopher Columbus, and the Florentines, Amerigo Vespucci and Giovanni Verrazzano, discovered "the new world."

That period in which Machiavelli lived his life was the one in which the greatness of the "universal Empire" and the "universal Church" seemed with increasing rapidity to be receding into a distant past. The once brash young city states were proving decreasingly competent for directing or managing forces stirring within them. Rising nation-states roused in Italians the initial flushes of a yet-distant dawn. The more inclusive unit to membership into which Machiavelli felt himself drawn, vacillated between his city—the freest which men had known since ancient Athens—and, the object of nascent patriotism, the Italian nation. Before his very eyes he was seeing the transformation of political units into great states and the attendant metamorphosis in the citizens of the respective nations. Involved in the diplomacy of his city, from time to time he was encountering their representatives animated by a new identity and awakened to a new aware-ness.[2] In the *Discourses* he wrote:

> truly no region is ever united or happy if all of it is not under the sway of one republic or one prince, as happened to France and to Spain.[3]

He saw these newly consolidated countries, in shifting arrangements with the ever-elusive Papacy,[4] testing their emerging strength at the expense of the peoples of Italy, the prey of whoever has wished to overrun this land.[5] With deep conviction he wrote:

> Among all famous men . . . next after [those who have been heads and organizers of religions] are those who have founded either republics or kingdoms;[6]

And to Pope Leo:

> no man is so much exalted by any act of his as are those men who have with laws and with institutions remodeled republics and kingdoms; these are, after those who have been gods, the first to be praised.[7]

Again, in the *Discourses:*

> Nor will a prudent intellect ever censure anyone for any unlawful action used in organizing a kingdom or setting up a republic. It is at any rate fitting that though the deed accuses him, the result should excuse him; and when it is good, like that of Romulus, it will always excuse him, because he who is violent to destroy, not he who is violent to restore, ought to be censured.[8]

In the *Art of War* he declared:

> where political powers are many, many able men appear; where such powers are few, few.[9]

18

The bearing on personal worth due to one's relation to his country constitutes a principal theme throughout Machiavelli's writings. In the *History of Florence,* to the leader of Florentine exiles in 1435 he gave the words:

"No good man will ever censure any citizen who strives to defend his native city, in whatever way he defends her."[10]

In a chapter in the *Discourses* entitled

One's Country Should Be Defended Whether with Disgrace or with Glory; She Is Properly Defended in Any Way Whatsoever,

he declared:

when it is absolutely a question of the safety of one's country, there must be no consideration of just or unjust, or merciful or cruel, of praiseworthy or disgraceful; instead, setting aside every scruple, one must follow to the utmost any plan that will save her life and keep her liberty.[11]

He began his "Discorso o Dialogo intorno alla Nostra Lingua" with a personal testimonial:

Sempre che io ho potuto onorare la patria mia, eziandio con mio carico e pericolo, l'ho fatto volentieri; perchè l'uomo non ha maggiore obligo nella vita sua che con quella, dependendo prima da essa l'essere e, di poi, tutto quello che di buono la fortuna e la natura ci hanno conceduto; e tanto viene a esser maggiore in coloro che hanno sortito patria più nobile. E veramente colui il quale con l'animo e con le opere si fa nimico della sua patria, meritamente si può chiamare parricida, ancora che da quella fosse suto offeso. Perchè, se battere il padre e la madre, per qualunque cagione, è cosa nefanda, di necessità ne seguita il lacerare la patria essere cosa, nefandissima, perchè da lei mai si patisce alcuna persecuzione per la quale possa meritar di essere da te ingiuriata, avendo a riconoscere da quella ogni tuo bene; tal che, se ella si priva di parte de'suoi cittadini, sei piuttosto obbligato ringraziarla di quelli che la si lascia, che infamarla di quelli che la si toglie. E quando questo sia vero (che è verissimo) io non dubito mai di ingannarmi per difenderla e venire contro a quelli che troppo presuntuosamente cercano di privarla dell'onor suo.[12]

Always when I have been able to honor my country, even though with personal hardship and peril, I have done so willingly; because a man has no greater duty in life than that, being dependent on it, first, for his being, and, then, for all of the good which fortune and nature have granted him and as much greater it comes to be in those whose country of origin is more noble. And truly whoever in spirit and works makes himself an enemy of his country, justly may be called a parricide, even if he had been offended by her. Because, if to strike one's father and one's mother, for whatever reason, is an infamous thing, it follows that inflicting pain on one's country is the most infamous thing, because from her never is there any persecution suffered which justifies her being injured by you, in light of the fact that from her comes all your good; so that if she deprives herself of some of her citizens, you are duty-bound to be grateful to her for those whom she has left rather than to condemn her for those whom she has taken away. And since this is true (and it is most true) I do not doubt that ever I am in danger of deceiving myself in defending her and opposing those who too presumptuously seek to deprive her of her honor.

One chapter in the *Discourses* bears as heading:

A Good Citizen for Love of his Native City Will Forget Private Injuries.[13]

Machiavelli's appraisal of the significance of one's city or country as intrinsic for the citizen is implicit in the tribute he paid to certain Florentines. Of the leaders of the city's resistance to the hostilities carried on under Pope Gregory XI, Machiavelli wrote:

This war undertaken against the Pope . . . lasted three years, ending only with the Pope's death. The Eight [citizens appointed to take charge of the war] managed it with such effectiveness and satisfaction to the citizens generally that every year their term of office was extended. They were called saints, even though they had little regard for the Censures, stripped the churches of their property, and forced the clergy to celebrate the offices. So much higher did those citizens then value their city than their souls![14]

Similarly, in "The Natures of Florentine Men," in praise of Francesco Valori, he wrote:

no country ever had a citizen who more desired her good then he did or who was so much and with fewer scruples her defender. This, because it was not understood by many, made him hated by many. As a result, his special enemies determined to kill him.[15]

That Machiavelli held such dedication to his city as a standard for himself becomes clearly evident in his letter of 16 April 1527, less than ten weeks before his death, in which he summarized for his friend, Francesco Vettori, the anguishing crisis in public affairs:

I love my native city more than my soul.[16]

Although there is no indication, or probability, that he did so, Machiavelli might have found Scriptural precedents for expressions of such a priority. At Mount Sinai, after the people had turned aside and worshipped the golden calf which Aaron, his brother, had had made, Moses prayed:

> O hear me! This people has committed a great sin; they have made themselves gods of gold. If thou wilt forgive them, forgive. But if not, blot out my name, I pray, from thy book which thou has written.[17]

And Paul, in his yearning that his fellow Jews would perceive and follow the truth of his conviction:

> in my heart there is great grief and unceasing sorrow. For I could even pray to be outcast from Christ myself for the sake of my brothers, my natural kinsfolk. They are Israelites: they were made God's sons; theirs is the splendour of the divine presence, theirs the covenants, the law, the temple worship, and the promises. Theirs are the patriarchs, and from them, in natural descent, sprang the Messiah who is supreme above all.[18]

All three affirmations of unity—that by Machiavelli, by Moses and by Paul—imply allegiance to a value considered by each, respectively, as being more authentic than the highest conventionally symbolized by tradition.

For Jesus, the Cross was his payment for holding and manifesting clearly and steadily the unique priority: above land and possessions;[19] above family and kindred;[20] above his own will.[21] He called to attention the sense of responsibility within each person to know and do the will of one's creator, when he proclaimed the standard:

> Whoever cares for his own safety is lost. . . . What does a man gain by winning the whole world at the cost of his true self? What can he give to buy that self back?[22]

Following Herod's execution of John from whom Jesus had accepted baptism during which he had received confirmation of his identity as son of God, he perceived that thenceforth his disciples could begin to realize the inherently, irrationally violent character of the behavior of the claimants of political authority in society. From then on, he instructed the disciples closest to him (and more able to understand) the imminent necessity that his mission involved his own death and resurrection. Perceiving that one's grounding in love is more elemental and adequate than any in land or physical heritage, he knew for himself and sought to make manifest to others a sense of security immune to any pressure of mechanical claims by which others might attempt to entrap him.

21

Did Machiavelli, also, value being "born again"[23]—but in a political and civic sense? Machiavelli grew to realize that a more immediate commitment between the bodies, emotions, attitudes and aims of the inhabitants of the land and their government was essential if an order of freedom was to be attained and secured; and, as an exponent of the use of the vernacular, he nourished an incipient patriotism for both his city and country. Because of his observations, reflections, his especially arresting style in expressing them and the subsequent widespread use made of his prescriptions, the period of his activity as public official and writer has been referred to as "The Age of Machiavelli."[24]

Deep in human psychology and the history of institutions, and recurrent in the Scriptures, runs the condemnation of dominance sought through the use of force. Genesis recounts that Cain who had dared to kill his brother tried to parry the searching question put to him—"Where is your brother Abel?"—by answering:

I do not know. Am I my brother's keeper?[25]

He thus set the precedent for those who by force presume to interpose their means of control between individuals and their creator, but by their words evade accountability. Moreover, it is notable that the question, "Am I my brother's keeper?," was the murderer Cain's effort to parry the question put to him by his own conscience and that the answer, as the Quaker Henry Haviland pointed out, is:

No! The Maker has placed in each one the Keeper, The Inner Light. For one to presume to be another's keeper, or leader, is personal imperialism and the source of all other imperialisms, including "the white man's burden." What, then, is one's responsibility to his brother? First, to get out of his way; and second, if way opens, to help him mind that Light which is his own in him.[26]

Through observation, understanding and cooperation with the seasonal rhythms of the Nile and making use of the products of the land for refreshing the energies of the laborers in the process, the ancient Egyptians led the way in structuring the territorial state, as the system of timely irrigation ensured for more people a stable supply of food. After Amenhotep III (c. 1411–1375 B.C.) when the Egyptian Empire reached its greatest extent, his son—the religious reformer Ikhnaton (Amenhotep IV, c. 1375–1358?)—with his motto "Living in Truth,"[27] adopted, as the symbol of his authority, the orb of the sun with rays, each terminating in a human hand extended open for helping the inhabitants in all parts of the land. Nevertheless, however benevolently portrayed, the authoritarian rule by the pharaoh required that the meaning of the existence of all the people center in endeavoring to make the reigning pharaoh an immortal god.

Eventually reacting against exploitation in the service of the ruler's monopolistic sanction, acclaiming an unseen God as the source of their strength for conquering a land for themselves in which to exemplify justice, the twelve tribes of the Hebrews, under the leadership of Moses and the judges, formed themselves into a patriotic nation rooted in "the promised land."

Moreover, a recognition of the dignity of the individual had been derived, even prior to their Egyptian history, from Sumeria—the middle-class, commercial cities of the Plain of Shinar and the originators of forms of business contract and commercial paper. Abraham, raised in the city of Ur, son of a craftsman of religious images, thought in terms of God as a being not made by human hands, of contract as being the basic characteristic of human relationship and, hence, of the relation to God as being contractual in nature. The process of contract through which he and God are reported to have come to terms, has certain specific implications. For a contract to be valid, each of the contracting powers has to be acting freely and of his own volition. Since, in their tradition, the Hebrews considered Abraham to have been a man—not a god or, as a prototype in Greek mythology, a superhuman being—there was, in Abraham, affirmed for the human individual a freedom of will which the Creator of the whole universe considered himself bound to respect.[28] Again, later, in the account of God's and Abraham's conversation prior to the destruction of the cities Sodom and Gomorrah, there is manifested in the individual man, Abraham, a sense of justice with respect to which even the Creator recognized an obligation not to disregard.[29] The historical books of the Old Testament trace the development of the descendants of Abraham in terms of a record of periodic reminders of the consequences of forgetting or disregarding the provisions of the contract between Abraham and God. Through time and the circumstances of taking possession of "the promised land," the Hebrew people, led by "the elders of Israel," petitioned the judge Samuel (c. 1025 B.C.):

appoint us a king to govern us, like other nations.[30]

And Samuel, presenting their request, received the response:

'Listen to the people . . . they have not rejected you, it is I whom they have rejected, I whom they will not have to be their king . . . Hear what they have to say now, but give them a solemn warning and tell them what sort of a king will govern them.' Samuel told the people who were asking him for a king all that the Lord had said to him. 'This will be the sort of king who will govern you,' he said, 'he will take your sons and make them serve in his chariots and with his cavalry, and will make them run before his chariot. Some he will appoint officers over units of a thousand and units of fifty. Others will plough his fields and reap his harvest; others again will make weapons of war and equipment for mounted troops. He will make your daughters for perfumers, cooks, and confectioners, and he will seize the best of your cornfields, vineyards, and olive-yards, and give them to his lackeys. He will take a tenth of your grain and your vintage to give to his eunuchs and lackeys. Your slaves, both men and women, and the best of your cattle and your asses he will seize and put to his own use. He will take a tenth of your flocks, and you yourselves will become his slaves. When that day comes, you will cry out against the king whom you have chosen; but it will be too late, the Lord will not answer you.' The people refused to listen to Samuel: 'No,' they said, 'We will have a king over us, to lead us out to war and fight out battles.' So Samuel, when he had heard what the people said, told the Lord; and he answered, 'Take them at their word and appoint them a king.'[31]

Experiences of responsibilities of government, the failures in performance, the frustration of hopes, the ordeals of civil war and division, refined, among the Hebrews, a conception of conscience—the roots and early development of which are traceable in the pyramid and coffin texts of Egypt.[32] The guide to conduct, the prophet Micah (c. 750–700 B.C.) summarized in the following formulation and brought it clearly within the framework of the individual's own competence enlightened by his own respective experiences:

What is it that the Lord asks of you? Only to act justly, to love loyalty, to walk wisely before your God.[33]

The Deuteronomist (693–639 B.C.) whose manuscript was brought to light in 621 B.C., while mindful of the centuries-long achievements by students of the law, placed even the law itself as discoverable by each one in his relations with others. In his concluding charge to the people, "Moses" is there recorded as saying:

If you turn back to him and obey him heart and soul in all that I command you this day, then the Lord your God will show you compassion and restore your fortunes. He will gather you again from all the countries to which he has scattered you . . . The Lord your God will circumcise your hearts and the hearts of your descendants, so that you will love him with all your heart and soul and you will live . . . The commandment that I lay on you this day is not too difficult for you, it is not too remote. It is not in heaven, that you should say, 'Who will go up to heaven for us to fetch it and tell it to us, so that we can keep it?' Nor is it beyond the sea, that you should say, 'Who will cross the sea for us to fetch it and tell it to us, so that we can keep it?' It is a thing very near to you, upon your lips and in your heart ready to be kept.[34]

Confronted by the experience of harrowing conquests by Babylon, Assyria, Chaldea, Persia, the Hebrew prophets expanded the implications of the contract into an outlook on history which came to include events shaping up in the foreign lands as indications of God's impending wrath caused by "the chosen people's" forgetting their part under the terms of the contract. After having foreseen, warned against and endured the destruction of Jerusalem (the capital city, 586 B.C.), the kingdom and the temple, and having witnessed the scattering of the priesthood, the dissipation of the rites and ceremonies and the dispersion of the people, Jeremiah (c. 630–585 B.C.)—alone, in exile—discovered that however helpful the material symbols had been, there was available to each one a surer and deeper access to the Creator: i.e., through true individual prayer:

> If you invoke me and pray to me, I will listen to you: when you seek me, you shall find me; if you search with all your heart, I will let you find me, says the Lord.[35]

Furthermore, the Eternal declares that each individual is valued in terms of his own choices (his own decision-making) and there are no alibis:

> The time is coming, says the Lord, when I will make a new covenant with Israel and Judah. It will not be like the covenant I made with their forefathers . . . But this is the covenant I will make with Israel after those days, says the Lord; I will set my law within them and write it on their hearts; I will become their God and they shall become my people. No longer need they teach one another to know the Lord; all of them, high and low alike, shall know me, says the Lord;[36]

and Ezekiel (597–556 B.C.):

> When they see that I reveal my holiness through you, the nations will know that I am the Lord, says the Lord God. I will take you out of the nations and gather you from every land and bring you to your own soil . . . I will take the heart of stone from your body and give you a heart of flesh. I will put my spirit into you and make you conform to my statutes, keep my laws and live by them. You shall live in the land which I gave to your ancestors; you shall become my people, and I will become your God;[37]

Isaiah (c. 549–538 B.C.) of the Babylonian exile, proclaimed:

> Thus speaks the high and exalted one
> whose name is holy, who lives for ever;
> I dwell in a high and holy place
> with him who is broken and humble in spirit,
> to revive the spirit of the humble
> to revive the courage of the broken.[38]

Thus, the seeker, "broken and humble in spirit," fulfills all of the requirements of liturgy, ritual and mediator. Moreover, Isaiah interpreted God's plan as encompassing the salvation of all nations[39]—with the Jewish people serving as the special interpreters of the realization of the purposes and nature of the Eternal within terms of time, the temporal. Experiencing the rise and fall of the great military empires, whether in exile or in the land of their fathers tenaciously remembering their land, the people drew present strength and confident hope in their future from the cherished messages that God is just, concerned, compassionate and has a plan for their deliverance.

Meanwhile, through the conquests by Alexander and then by the Romans, the state, as idea and institution with unprecedented military power and led by the ruler glorified as divine emperor, was coming to claim omnipotence. In the reigns of Augustus and Tiberius, it sought by force and crucifixion to extirpate nationalistic opponents, such as the Galilean patriots of Sepphoris (about four miles from Nazareth), two thousand of whom were nailed to crosses which lined the roads as an indication of Rome's vengeance against rebels.[40] This atrocity took place when Jesus was, perhaps, between five and ten years of age.[41]

A new voice began to confront the rulership with a different perception of authority. In the Wilderness, Jesus had faced and rejected the temptation of seeking a political career as his way; as it is recorded:

> Once again the devil took him to a very high mountain, and showed him all the kingdoms of the world in their glory. 'All these', he said, 'I will give you, if you will only fall down and do me homage.' But Jesus said, 'Begone Satan; Scripture says, "You shall do homage to the Lord your God and worship him alone." '[42]

Toward the end of his ministry, on the way to Jerusalem, Jesus said to the Twelve:

> You know that in the world, rulers lord it over their subjects, and their great men make them feel the weight of authority; but it shall not be so with you. Among you, whoever wants to be great must be your servant, and whoever would be first must be the willing slave of all—like the Son of Man: he did not come to be served, but to serve, and to surrender his life as a ransom for many.[43]

Repeatedly Jesus reaffirmed recognition of human incapacity for valid interpersonal judgment. Long before, the Psalmist had declared:

> God is judge.[44]

Now Jesus said:

> 'Pass no judgment and you will not be judged. For as you judge others,

so you will yourselves be judged, and whatever measure you deal out to others will be dealt back to you. Why do you look at the speck of sawdust in your brother's eye, with never a thought for the great plank in your own? Or how can you say to your brother, "Let me take the speck out of your eye", when all the time there is that plank in your own? You hypocrite! First take the plank out of your own eye, and then you will see clearly to take the speck out of your brother's.'[45]

That it is presumptuous for humans to arrogate to themselves judgment of others is the point of two parables: that of the wheat and the tares[46] and that of the net full of fishes, edible and inedible.[47] Mark recorded:

As he [Jesus] was starting out on a journey, a stranger ran up, and, kneeling before him, asked, 'Good Master, what must I do to win eternal life?' Jesus said to him, 'Why do you call me good? No one is good except God alone.'[48]

To that same question, Luke gave Jesus' endorsement of the answer:

Love the Lord your God with all your heart, with all your soul, with all your strength, and with all your mind; and your neighbour as yourself;[49]

and his definition of "neighbor" as one who showed kindness to another in need.[50] Derived from the same perception are: his precept:

Love your enemies and pray for your persecutors; only so can you be children of your heavenly Father, who makes his sun rise on the good and bad alike, and sends the rain on the honest and the dishonest;[51]

the petition included in the prayer given as the model:

Forgive us the wrong we have done, as we have forgiven those who have wronged us;[52]

and, as the all-inclusive summary:

Always treat others as you would like them to treat you: that is the Law and the prophets.[53]

Paul, likewise, underscored the invalidity of one's passing judgment upon another:

Who are you to pass judgment on someone else's [God's] servant? Whether he stands or falls is his own Master's business . . . And you, sir, why do you hold your brother in contempt? We shall all stand before God's tribunal.

For Scripture says, 'As I live, says the Lord, to me every knee shall bow and every tongue acknowledge God.' So, you see, each of us will have to answer for himself;[54]

and again:

My dear friends, do not seek revenge, but leave a place for divine retribution; for there is a text which reads, 'Justice is mine, says the Lord, I will repay.'[55]

James, in his letter on practical religion, wrote:

Brothers, you must never disparage one another. He who disparages a brother or passes judgement on his brother, disparages the law and judges the law. But if you judge the law, you are not keeping it but sitting in judgement upon it. There is only one lawgiver and judge, the One who is able to save life and destroy it. So who are you to judge your neighbour?[56]

At last, in light of the centuries-long and repeated shocks suffered by the Jewish people through trust in kingship, came the illumination of another way: the affirmation that ours is a moral universe formed by the power of love, that each one has his origin in a loving Creator and hence has a right to inner security, that through not passing judgment upon others but in mutual respect through the process of reconciliation and forgiveness in interpersonal behavior and responsive readiness to assist others in meeting their needs, arises reciprocal communion, release from fear, the refreshment of living in truth. Thereby the law and the order is brought into being.[57]

Thus, the law and the order is a living process brought into being by individuals transforming their conflicts into mutually creative endeavors. From the Judaeo-Christian point of view there had developed a standpoint which was in the individual himself and, while not identified with his citizenship in the state, was inextricably dependent upon and realizable only through more adequate fulfilment of interpersonal responsibilities.

Jesus felt the necessity to manifest anew the living reality of the meaning of the Covenant not only in his own relation with the Creator and with his fellow men but also in the relationship between people and those assuming and claiming authority over them. Convinced that John the Baptist had ushered in the time, that henceforth the "kingdom of Heaven" is characterized by men manifesting it through direct action,[58] Jesus was, and he was showing and teaching others how to be, no longer fearfully responsive to those accustomed to control through attempting to implant and exploit a sense of original sin. In his own contacts with others, Jesus, characteristically, exacted nothing for himself but, rather, confirmed the other in perceiving and acting through the unique authority of his own innermost potentiality. Jesus summoned each to discover, through needful service, himself as a son of God who is as a loving father, and to take his place among his fellow men as a member of a loving and sharing family. Through experiencing such membership and coming to see and fulfill one's unique role in defining it, comes awareness of right and worth proved in a crucible of straining, rupturing, dissolving all the most conventionally cherished personal relations. In the words of Jesus:

> You must not think that I have come to bring peace to the earth; I have not come to bring peace, but a sword. I have come to set a man against his father, a daughter against her mother, a young wife against her mother-in-law; and a man will find his enemies under his own roof . . . no man is worthy of me who does not take up his cross and walk in my footsteps. By gaining his life a man will lose it; by losing his life for my sake, he will gain it.[59]

In explanation, George A. Buttrick has commented that Jesus came to bring strife and peace, not through compromise, but through "the regnancy of his spirit"[60] and, in commenting on Romans 4:16, Gerald R. Cragg has affirmed:

> Within that new community, all find their place, not because of any condescending gesture, but as rightful descendants of all true believers.[61]

In holding to his course, as recorded in the earliest Gospel, Mark, Jesus was sending shock waves through habit-and-ritual-bound contemporaries.[62] At length, Jesus felt impelled to make manifest the living Covenant at Jerusalem, the center, and at the very time of the celebration of the Passover—the time in which conventional authority claimed, in the name of the Covenant, customarily to affirm itself most impressively and powerfully.[63] With the direct action of the entry into Jerusalem,[64] with the driving of the money changers out of the temple,[65] and with his holding discourses within the temple,[66] the confrontation became unendurable for those attempting to conduct the conventional procedures. The conflict is always profound between one holding himself open to perceive and make known new intimations of truth on the one hand and, on the other, those aiming and endeavoring to gain and maintain influence over other men. Under the jealous eye of imperial Rome, the High Priest, Caiaphas, could sense in Jesus' approach a profound disregard for all formalized force-based rule. Seeing his prerogatives threatened and identifying them with the nation itself, fearing lest any course other than that of silencing Jesus would weaken his and the state's influence in the eyes of the Romans under the ruthless emperor, Tiberius, Caiaphas rallied behind himself the support of the Council by berating them and challenging them to action:

> You know nothing whatever: you do not use your judgement; it is more

to your interest that one man should die for the people, than that the whole nation should be destroyed.[67]

Paul was to write,

Those who live on the level of the spirit have the spiritual outlook, and that is life and peace;[68]

upon which Gerald Cragg has commented:

The heart of the gospel is a conviction that God has used the concreteness of our human life as the medium for the revelation of his love.[69]

Jesus so realistically preceived the personal and social ills and he himself so directly, truthfully, though non-violently, confronted and dealt with them that by undergoing crucifixion as one among robbers and outlaws—as viewed by those who identified themselves and their values in terms of security and survival with respect to dehumanizing conventional institutions—that he gave objective evidence of the way for human beings to come to consciousness of themselves, the nature of their relationships, their place in them, and the obligation to affirm it vitally. In the words of R. H. Strachen,

He "was numbered with the transgressors" in order that he might offer them his friendship and his filial consciousness of the friendship of God and thus redeem them.[70]

Jesus gave his life: in the process he showed to men the way of discovering or creating one's real self; and showed that the life of reason consists of interpersonal understanding in love. That in mankind which, neither by use of the name of the Assyrian war-god Marduk nor through the combination of the priestly hierarchy of Jerusalem and the authority of the Roman court could be vanquished, came to be recognized as reincarnated in each individual perfected in awareness of himself as one elected to his office by the Eternal. The blessed forgiven, living forth personal and social construction through encountering and confronting corruption as occasions not for resort to the sword but as co-creative moments, generate order in truth. The great Jewish philosopher Claude Joseph Goldschmid Montefiore wrote:

It was left to Jesus to turn this picture of divine activity into an ideal of human activity; and it is amazing to think what marvelous and fruitful results have followed the dozen or score of verses in which this ideal is set forth and driven home.[71]

As Jesus lived forth the Covenant publicly in the civil and religious capital of

30

his country, so Paul of Tarsus, a Roman citizen, through his appeal of his case to Caesar,[72] carried his challenging affirmation into the imperial capital

A power grew which aggressive policies proved unable to thwart. With its increasing strength and the recognition it won, there arose within it concern for the conduct of operations on the expanding scale and resort to conventional organs of administration and defense. The heightened influence attracted attention, concern, periodic persecution and offers of adjustment on the part of traditional institutions until, beginning in 312 A.D. with the emperor Constantine, the imperial authority espoused the Christian Church in return for its sanctioning the enforcement of order.

Confronted by the sack and destruction of Rome by the "barbarian Goths" (410 A.D.) and the general discouragement and disorganization, the classically educated Augustine perceived the whole of human history past and present as a drama taking place within each person who himself always plays the leading role. Augustine portrayed the individual as citizen both of the city of man (the temporal) and of the city of God (the eternal) and projected for every individual a program of significant action in living out the present responsibility of one's membership in the city of man to engage in decision-making in accord with the responsibility of his membership in the city of God. As a citizen of both orders simultaneously, at each moment one has freedom of will to fulfill in the framework of time his role as a particle of the eternal in accord with the prayer

Thy will be done
On earth as in heaven [author's emphasis].[73]

Thereby one is

in the world but not of it,

as Paul exhorted[74] and in the beginning is the deed[75]—the act of intelligent will. As in the Greek city and the Roman state, virtue still was considered to consist in the fulfilling of the obligation of membership and the way was prepared for the transition from one's secular citizenship to one's church membership as the source of one's value; yet, according to Augustine, one does not in his entirety, belong to the organization: the value of the individual is not fully comprehended in terms of membership in it. In fact, the value of any organization is itself measured in terms of the use available, and that which the individual makes of it in carrying forward his development in the city of God. Membership in a group or institution is not an end in itself—either for the sake of the group or the individual—however intensely some in the group or institution might seek so to interpret and represent it. Rather, it is an instrumentality for facilitating the emergence of the individual's more authentic service as a living being. Out

31

of this evaluation arises the tension between conscience and membership which characterizes Western civilization.

Besides the Jewish heritage, antiquity had bequeathed another factor which, with the fall of Constantinople (1453 A.D.) and the revival of ancient Greek influence in fifteenth century Europe, operated as a powerful solvent. The Delphic oracle's "Know Thyself," Anaxagoras' (c. 500–428 B.C.) affirmation that "ours is a mind-ordered universe," Socrates' (c. 470–399 B.C.) that "the life unexamined is not worth living," the Aristotelian view that a man is that which he can become at his best through responsible citizenship and "who can foresee with his mind is intended to be lord and master,"[76] again aroused and released new energies.

In time, the attempt to exact recognition and tribute in the name of either the "universal" Church or Empire led the inhabitants of different lands to apply to themselves the attitudes of the ancient Israelites to their land, as recorded in the Scriptures common to all Christendom, and to express themselves as patriots under kings of their own; and kings began to see in the inhabitants of their respective realms the most effective recruits and conscripts for their national forces.

Openings provided by the Crusades, overseas discoveries, the Protestant Reformation, scientific inquiry, the accelerating and ever-more-widespread communications through print, the hopes stimulated by the cultural and political revolutions being implemented with new programs and structures—all were awakening and increasingly strengthening peoples' affirmations of their right of access to the earth and its resources and to government as the instrument for maximizing guaranteed recognition and protection of the rights of men, women, children everywhere to the release and cultivation of their talents. Repeatedly the nation-state proved itself as the medium through which different peoples were able to appropriate to themselves the benefits of these openings and thereby to enhance the quality of their living and the prospects for their future.

While the flaunting of national pride provoked, in the downtrodden and disregarded, a determination to attain equivalent status and resulted in the multiplication of nation states—each eagerly ready to prove to the world its claim to absolute authority—both in number and in degree of seriousness, grew evidence of interests, desires, needs and claims which even the most powerful and resourceful political units were incapable of securing for themselves.

Ever more pressing, the question posed itself: is there an inherent insufficiency in the nation-state, as a concept, which impels it to elicit from individuals generous energies, devotes them to inadequately generous obejctives, masks the misapplication with the myth of "national security" implemented as militant foreign policy and domestic police action for effectuating programs and policies conceived as "top secrets" to be protected against the very individuals and groups of people whose energies are being drawn upon in the name of loyalty and conscience?

May cultural changes during the past four and one-half centuries have rendered decreasingly tolerable certain of the features which in its beginning were adjudged indispensable for the establishment of the state? Analogously, Aristotle, early in the first book of his *Politics,* wrote:

> If every instrument could accomplish its own work, obeying or anticipating the will of others, like the statues of Daedalus, or the tripods of Hephaestus, which, says the poet,
>
>> of their own accord entered the assembly of the Gods;
>> (Homer, II, xviii, 376)
>
> if, in like manner, the shuttle would weave and the plectrum touch the lyre without a hand to guide them, chief workmen would not want servants, nor masters slaves.[77]

and thus he reconciled himself to the persistence, in human society, of slavery, economic classes and war on the ground that it was impractical to consider that machinery for the production of economic goods would be automated; consequently he concluded, as had Plato, that the affluence considered indispensable for "the good life" could be available only for the few and that poverty had to be the lot of the masses for whose subjugation military force would always be necessary in the conduct of both domestic and foreign affairs. Subsequently, the operation of increasingly complex power-driven machinery has required better trained and more resourceful workmen so that slavery became uneconomic and systems of education for the general public were instituted.

Likewise, while expressing in life and writings the faith that by objective study of human endeavor to establish the order of freedom men could find adequate guidance if they pursued it with intelligent will, Machiavelli rejected as impractical reliance upon a quality of goodness in human nature and, instead, directed men's thoughts toward violent competitive struggle as the way for political man according to the lessons to be derived from the study of history and the observation of contemporary practice:

> As is demonstrated by all those who discuss life in a well-ordered state—and history is full of examples—it is necessary for him who lays out a state and arranges laws for it to presume that all men are evil and that they are always going to act according to the wickedness of their spirits whenever they have free scope; and when any wickedness remains hidden for a time, the reason is some hidden cause which, in the lack of any experience of the contrary, is not recognized, but then its discovery is brought about by Time, which they say is the father of every Truth . . . men never do anything good except by necessity, but where there is plenty of choice and excessive freedom is possible, everything is

at once filled with confusion and disorder. Hence it is said that hunger and poverty make men industrious, and the laws make them good;[78]

Every man hopes to climb higher by crushing now one, now another, rather than through his own wisdom and goodness. To each of us, another's success is always vexatious; and therefore always, with effort and trouble, for another's ill we are watchful and alert.
To this our natural instinct draws us, by our own motion and our own feeling, if laws or greater forces do not restrain us;[79]

men are more prone to evil than to good;[80]

Men always turn out bad for you unless some necessity makes them good;[81]

I believe it very true that rarely or never do men of humble fortune come to high rank without force and without fraud, except that a rank which another has attained may be given to such men or left them by inheritance. Nor do I believe that force alone will ever be enough, but fraud alone certainly will be enough . . . a prince who wishes to do great things must learn to deceive . . . I do not believe that ever any man originally placed in humble fortune has come to great authority only by open force and honestly, but I firmly believe they have done it by fraud alone . . . And what princes are obliged to do when they begin to grow great, republics are also obliged to do, until they have become powerful, and force alone is enough;[82]

the generality of men feed themselves as much on what seems to be as on what is; still more, many times they are moved more by the things that seem than by the things that are;[83]

so simple-minded are men and so controlled by immediate necessities that a prince who deceives always finds men who let themselves be deceived;[84]

experience in our time shows that those princes have done great things who have valued their promises little, and who have understood how to addle the brains of men with trickery; and in the end they have vanquished those who have stood upon their honesty;[85]

by no means can a prudent ruler keep his word—and he does not—when to keep it works against himself and when the reasons that made him promise are annulled. If all men were good, that maxim would not be good, but because they are bad and do not keep their promises to you, you likewise do not have to keep yours to them. Never has a shrewd prince lacked justifying reasons to make his promise-breaking appear honorable . . . The one who knows best how to play the fox comes out best, but he must understand well how to disguise the animal's nature and must be a great simulator and dissimulator.[86]

34

Experience through subsequent centuries has been proving for mankind that no part of the earth in itself has the resources adequate for instituting and maintaining social stability. Machiavelli, already in the sixteenth century, convinced that such adequacy is not to be found or achieved, based his judgment upon his interpretation of human nature:

> human wants are insatiable, since man has from Nature the power and wish to desire everything, and from Fortune the power to attain but little; the result is unending discontent in human minds and weariness with what is attained. Hence the present is blamed, the past is praised, and the future is desired, even though men are not moved to act in this way by any reasonable cause;[87]

> men . . . do not know how to put limits to their hopes. And when they rely on these and do not make an estimate of themselves, they fall;[88]

> men are slower to take what they can have than they are to want what they cannot get;[89]

> men are so eager for changes that most of the time there is as much desire for change among those who are well off as among those who are badly off, because, as I have said—and it is true—men are bored in good times and complain in bad ones;[90]

> very great disturbances . . . most of the time . . . are caused by those who already possess, because the fear of loss produces in them the same desires as exist in those who wish to gain, because it is generally held that a man is not in secure possession of what he has if he does not gain something new in addition. And, besides, there is this, that since they have great possessions, they can use greater power and greater force in causing revolutions. And there is still this besides, that their unrestrained and ambitious conduct kindles, in the breasts of those who do not possess, the wish to possess, either in order to get revenge on the rich by plundering them or in order to be able themselves to enter upon those riches and those offices that they see badly used by others;[91]

> To a great extent the ambition of the rich, if by various means and in various ways a city does not crush it, is what quickly brings her to ruin;[92]

> so much more ready the crowd is to take the property of others than to protect its own, and so much more are men moved by the hope of gain than by the fear of loss. Loss, except when it is close to them, they do not imagine; gain, even though distant, they hope for;[93]

> Ancient writers say that men usually worry in bad conditions and get bored in good ones, and that either of these afflictions produces the same results.

Whenever men cease fighting through necessity, they go to fighting through ambition, which is so powerful in human breasts that, whatever high rank men climb to, never does ambition abandon them. The cause is that Nature has made men able to crave everything, but unable to attain everything. Hence, since men's craving is always greater than their power to attain, they are discontented with their acquirements and get slight satisfaction from them. Men's fortunes therefore vary because, since some strive to get more and others fear to lose what they have gained, they indulge in enmity and war. These cause the ruin of one province and the prosperity of another;[94]

we can say this about men in general: they are ungrateful, changeable, simulators and dissimulators, runaways in danger, eager for gain; while you do well by them they are all yours; they offer you their blood, their property, their lives, their children, as was said above, when need is far off; but when it comes near you, they turn about;[95]

Oh human spirit insatiable, arrogant, crafty, and shifting, and above all else malignant, iniquitous, violent, and savage, because through your longing so ambitious, the first violent death was seen in the world, and the first grass red with blood! Since this evil seed is now mature, since evil's cause is multiplied, there is no reason for men to repent of doing evil.[96]

"Exhortation to Penitence" is his description in religious terms of the human condition:

all the sins of men . . . for the most part can be divided into two groups: one is to be ungrateful to God, the second is to be unfriendly to one's neighbor.
But in order to realize our ingratitude, it is necessary to consider how many and of what sort are the benefits we have received from God . . . You see first of all the huge extent of the land . . . Do you not see how much toil the sun undertakes to cause us to share in his light, to cause to live, through his energy, both ourselves and those things that have been created by God for us? So every object is created for the good and glory of man, and man is alone in being created for the good and glory of God, who gave him speech that he might praise him, gave him sight, not turned to the ground as for the other animals but turned to the sky, in order that he might always see it, gave him hands in order that he might build temples, offer sacrifices in his Honor, gave him reason and intellect inorder that he might consider and understand the greatness of God. See, then, with how much ingratitude man rises against such a great benefactor! And how much punishment he deserves when he perverts that use of these things and turns them toward evil! That tongue made to glorify God blasphemes him; that mouth, through which he must be fed, he makes into a sewer and a way for satisfying the appetite and the belly with luxurious and excessive food;

those thoughts about God he changes into thoughts about the world; that desire to preserve the human species turns into lust and many other dissipations. Thus with these brutish deeds man changes himself from a rational animal into a brute animal. Man changes, therefore, by practising this ingratitude to God, from angel to devil, from master to servant, from man to beast. Those who are ungrateful to God—it is impossible that they are not unfriendly to their neighbors . . . Because into these vices we often fall, God the gracious creator has showed us the way for raising ourselves up, which is penitence . . . But, because it is not enough to repent and weep (for it is necessary to prepare oneself by means of the actions opposed to the sin), in order not to sin further, to take away opportunity for evil . . . we must resort to penitence and cry out with David: "Have mercy upon me oh God!" and with Saint Peter weep bitterly, and for all the misdeeds we have committed feel shame

> and repent and understand clearly
> that as much as pleases the world is a short dream
>
> [Petrarch, Sonnet 1][97]

The ever-more-complex rivalry among political units for power to control means for satisfying the basic needs of their inhabitants, has made clear certain concerns with respect to which all share special vulnerability. Among these are:

the protection of basic human rights: religion, communications, assembly, participation in elections, employment, education, privacy;

the protection of the quality of the atmosphere, the seas, the soil, the ground water against atomic and chemical emissions and waste materials;

the coordination of agricultural programs with a world-wide system of weather monitoring and reporting;

the equitable articulation between producers, processors, and consumers of raw materials to their mutual benefit;

the preservation of endangered species of wild life and the world's most ecologically-sensitive areas.

Significant, dramatic and splendid as have been, and are, many of the contributions through the institution of the nation-state in enhancing the quality of life for a great proportion of mankind, certain limitations in its capacity to serve mankind appear to be inherent. For some groups, the nation-state system still holds faint prospect for their ever achieving satisfactory status, for example: Native Americans in the United States and Canada; the aborigines in Australia;

the Palestinians; the Kurds; the Blacks of South Africa; the Macedonians. Second, the great military powers, through intervention or its threat, through "aid" and affiliated "intelligence" systems and practices, through preferential arrangements with multi-national corporations, hold subject many small countries, especially in Eastern Europe, Central America, the Caribbean, the Middle East, Africa. Third, in other regions in which great military powers checkmate one another, the tension has split nations into two states: East and West Germany, North and South Korea, North and South Yemen, the Peoples Republic of China and Nationalist China, the spheres of influence in Lebanon; and the special case of Eire and North Ireland. Meanwhile, fourth, the number of persons who are refugees from their homelands or displaced within them, according to the U.S. Committee for Refugees, a non-profit, private organization, far exceeds ten million.[98] Fifth, the attempts to reverse the drift toward ever-more-destructive wars appears yet far from adequate for achieving the goal. Shocked by World War I, although still unwilling to sacrifice the claims of ultimate national sovereignty, the "victors" set up the League of Nations in the hope of dispelling or controlling factors tending towards future wars; but with the "victors" failing to find a way, through competition for advantage, to economic recovery or to relinquish rivalry in their rates of increasing armaments, the defeated populations, suffering unequal treatment (both political and economic), responded to leadership in protesting, negotiating away and bursting through the limiting agreements. The League collapsed and the still-more-devastating World War II ensued. Again, impelled by shock, the "victors" instituted "the United Nations;" but yet again the most powerful states reserved for themselves ultimate autonomy as sovereign nation-states with their right of veto in the Security Council. However, the use, in World War II, by one country of the atomic bomb had served to challenge citizens of other countries to seek a way to achieve an equal status. As a countermeasure, the first user continually augmented and diversified its destructive power. Again, economic recovery lagged and found stimulus primarily in the rivalry of accelerating production for military purposes. Awareness of dangers inherent in the growing destructive power of the developing weaponry and in its availability to more countries, together with mounting investment in conventional weapons, prompted national leaders to cultivate in their respective citizenry a climate of fear, as a means by which to extract increasing tax funds, to spend more on "defense," and to leave less available for education, health, welfare, the production and purchase of consumer goods, and protection of the quality of the environment. Sixth, citizens began to show less confidence in the constructive contribution and usefulness of the political processes and to take less interest in them. Even in the most stable and prosperous countries, signs of alienation grew more apparent. Among minority groups unrelenting economic retrogression dispelled hopes nourished by token recognition and accompanied rise in the use of drugs and in the incidence of violent crimes. Even in the United States, with

38

such traditions as: Penn's "Holy Experiment;" the principles of popular sovereignty enunciated in the Declaration of Independence; the republican institutions established through its Constitution; the expanding system of "universal education;" the unprecedented expansion of the suffrage; the many on-going voluntary civic crusades for participatory democracy; the reforms in Congressional and political party procedures; the widespread changes to make the governments of the states and localities more accountable to their constituencies; despite the unparallelled coverage of the campaign by television and radio, 47.4% of the eligible voters failed to participate in the presidential election of 1980 and 48.6% in that of 1984; moreover, the mode of participation was significantly characterized by the increase in effectiveness of private contributions to candidates' campaign funds and the newly-elected administration (having a "mandate" from slightly under 26.5% (1980) to slightly under 26% (1984) of the eligible electorate) fueled the dismantling of the non-military public service aspects of government. Throughout the world, hi-jacking of planes, increase of political kidnapping, assassination of officials, further denote lowering regard for the state and its established processes.

Raised in the belief that people do not belong to governments but that governments belong to them as instruments to promote their life, liberty, equality of opportunity to discover, cultivate and express their diverse talents, were the citizens coming to a view that conditions had changed in such a way that the traditional state is no longer serving to liberate and empower individuals stirred to venture forth seeking to respond appropriately to the needs of mankind but, instead, is bent upon conditioning the people into elements of a war-machine geared, in the name of "defense," for suicidal combat against other segments of mankind similarly conditioned? Is the reduction of educational opportunities and the continuing high rate of unemployment transforming the young people from becoming competent self-reliant individuals prepared for self-government into instruments for the designs of insatiably power-demanding "leaders?" Do the "leaders" increasingly tend to pursue goals different from the people's sense of needs and welfare? Do they consider essential the use of covert methods which they know would be unacceptable if subjected to public scrutiny and are of dubious constitutionality? Do they use the accumulated power to enlist and sustain in positions of influence in other countries men of like mind and purpose?

Five centuries of expanding opportunities have nourished private hopes—and implemented them with public institutions—that through conscientious endeavors one can live his life meaningfully. With advances in the development of discriminating judgment through education and with the diminution of economic and psychologic necessity through self-discipline, more people have become less vulnerable to others' manipulation. In the struggle for the release of people's civic energies, claims for leadership are coming to be searched into more thoroughly in the effort to discriminate between those aiming to use the powers of office in the public's service and those inclined to use them in the promotion of some special private interest. Methods adopted and employed for the former are recognized as those of openness to all relevant information for the process of decision-making, regard for due process and freedom of judgment as contrasted with those of secrecy, restrictions on receptivity of data, and resort to force and violence. When, however, the country which affirmed and still professes as its basic principle that "governments derive their just powers from the consent of the governed" and that they are "instituted to promote life, liberty, and the pursuit of happiness," takes the lead in the development and spread of weaponry and nuclear capabilities directed toward warfare, when it undertakes to subvert foreign governments, even if democratically structured and operated, and to support with military aid and advisers regimes using torture against dissidents, when it not only lets continue unexposed and unrepudiated, but actually gives aid and encouragement to, powerful domestically-based multi-national corporations which advance their aggressive designs by means of bribery, when domestically it subverts constitutionally-guaranteed rights by use of wire-tapping and entrapment—all such practices betray, erode and corrupt in the people the sense of public integrity and disintegrate the will and courage for public initiative, endeavor and endurance.

Recognizing that the fulfilment of one's potentialities proceeds through the scale of decision-making in which one shares effective participation, brings into focus the growing imperative that the traditional conception of political science be reexamined and revised to accord more truly with all of the data and the assurance for each participant of the availability of meaningful membership.

Chapter Three

CRITIQUE OF FICTIONS

May there be detected a radical flaw in the political process? May it be found in the role of fictions?

Although, as previously noted (pp. 9–12), the uniqueness of individuals is generally acknowledged, yet conventionally it is taken for granted that some are competent, and indeed even are obligated, to try to control others.

May, perhaps, the psychological basis for this assumption be found in a misinterpretation of the dynamics of compassion? Impulsively, imitatively, one, observing another's falling physically or even making an obvious mistake, experiences through his sympathetic nervous system a corresponding inner motion. Not having to be used for his own recovery, the surplus energy released could be made available to assist the other's recovery of his equilibrium. If, instead, it is let explode as in laughter, it gives offense as "conspicuous waste" of a vitally needed social resource. Or, the observer feeling a summons for action, reacting impulsively, may take it as an opportunity to give vent to some of his own pent up tensions and behave as if the other's need is identical with his own and is able to be similarly compensated. The irrelevant projection on the one hand reveals specific insecurity in the respondent and on the other hand produces in the injured one, instead of appreciation for assistance, a shocked realization of alienation. Continued behavior as if the other's need is fully understood and being adequately met by the proffered response and that an appreciative expression of unity should be forthcoming on the other's part, misses the mark and provokes in the sufferer defensive reactions of increasing violence.

Or, again, the observer may become so deeply moved, carried away, impressed by what he interprets as his own compassion and readiness for service for the "common good" that he declares willingness to sacrifice for it "his own soul." Such valuation, Machiavelli, as noted above (pp. 20–24), deemed most admirable for a citizen with respect to his native city or country; and Moses and

Paul felt the tension of such an impulse. Through expressing such readiness for "self-sacrifice," one may stir others to the dedication of their courageous energies and to the commission of deeds outside of, or even in conflict with, habitual patterns and, indeed, institutional taboos. In this way the "leader" makes himself a magnetic foundation for the building of "a people." Inherent in such initiative is the hazard of an arrogance wherein he assumes that his perception for assuaging his own personality-need is salutary for other's conditions also; that the "services" which he himself actually gives are commensurate with those sacrifices which he tries to arouse his followers to make. Protecting himself against their potential demands for accountability, he accumulates power divested of effectual responsibility and elaborates rationalizations permissive of conduct freed from any standards of humane considerations.

Holding back the power, denying the needed assistance except on self-serving terms, blinds one to the other's diversity and in the name of fictitious unity uses up the power in combatting the engendered violence. The temptation to indulge oneself in holding on to, and exercising, a power and leadership over others on grounds that one is more competent to serve their welfare than they would be with shared power, depends on the fiction that one can attain a true perspective of that which is within the life-experience of another. If one tries to attribute to himself the power released in himself and claim it as evidence of the obligation of others to accept his control as sanctioned by some transcendent or superhuman authority, one encounters an equivalent resistance on their part and the social energy, deflected from enunciating and serving the common good, becomes spent in both internal and external destructive conflict. So love-initiated-and-generated structures, commenced for the service of each with and through the service of all, corrode when the powerful ones vest themselves in a fictional "whole" in order to secure for themselves special advantage at others' expense. This robbery is the great graft. In interpreting the position of the "civic humanists" of the Renaissance and thereafter, J.B.A. Pocock wrote:

> Any form of government in which the good of a particular group was treated as identical with the good of the whole was despotic, even though the particular good might be, at least initially, a real good in itself; perverted government consisted essentially in the dictatorship of the particular over the universal, and led toward the corruption of the good which had assumed dictatorial power.[1]

Zealous pretensions of service and protestations of loyalty may blind followers to a more mutually considerate course perceivable through more open communication. Thus Luke recorded that James and John were ready to invoke from heaven fire to consume the Samaritans whose indifference or opposition they felt was impeding Jesus' progress; but Jesus rebuked those disciples and said:

You do not know to what spirit you belong; for the Son of Man did not come to destroy men's lives but to save them.[2]

He schooled himself in facing and dealing constructively with individuals in confusion and distress, for, he said:

It is not the healthy that need a doctor, but the sick. Go and learn what the text means, "I require mercy, not sacrifice." I did not come to invite virtuous people, but sinners.[3]

He became known as "a friend of sinners."[4] With respect to himself,[5] he became able to accept crucifixion and that in the company of transgressors.[6] Jesus did not indulge himself in self pride and block his associations with the judgment of "evil" in men as an accepted elemental fact to be dealt with by force as the treatment appropriate for the "corrupt" or "corrupted," but, instead, he reached through to the creative core which he perceived to be the original essence of each. Unreservedly, his grace poured out upon not merely some elite or as the reward for some regimen or discipline but upon all[7] so that whoever hungers and thirsts "to see right prevail"[8] receives the full benefit.

Not *just any* action is called for. The experience of the sufferer and that of the observer takes place in the context of different, even if kindred, organisms each of which gives it, respectively, different meaning and implications. Feeling the call for action, one needs, first, to sensitize oneself to its distinctive accent and then, assaying his own potential responses, to make himself available for implementing that which the other finds acceptable as an aid to his recovery. So grows understanding of shared-being-in-truth. The enhancement of the dimensions of one's being, attendant upon participation, is power attuned for service. Transcending one's there-to-fore experienced personality, its advent partakes of the unknown and undefined and is able to be understood only through deeper and more sensitive appreciation of the other members in the relationship involved.

By what process does the fiction of leadership come about and win acceptance? What consequences does it entail?

From the fact, already considered (pp. 9–13), that everyone is unique, it follows that each one's needs and desires, even if externally stimulated and nourished, are structured within and relative to his own organism and the adequacy of any response to his expression of these wants is similarly conditioned. Each one is the only one who can be at the center of his experience and make right valuation for optimum direction. One cannot know from its central core the growing-direction or the pattern of another.[9]

Moreover, people cannot reconcile themselves to unequal treatment; because, since no criterion for superiority, equality or inferiority has been established objectively with respect to human beings, and since no one can see into and know the ultimate truth about another, for one to claim, or to accept, unequal treatment as valid would be to become a party to a groundless prejudice, as well as to betray the confidence with which others' faith in him has been previously strengthening him. The concept that one can be another's leader and validly assume direction of his life involves, therefore, an affirmation beyond the possibility of knowledge; and the attempt to seize or exercise such control over another is an act of presumption, arrogance and ignorance—an aggression which tends to provoke equally mechanical, violent reaction. The conviction that one has knowledge of greater importance for another (or others) than he (they) can know for himself (themselves), or that one senses a deeper, more inclusive relationship for others than that which they can for themselves appreciate, cannot bridge the chasm of irrelevance and enable him to give appropriate leadership and confer benefits to transcend or equal those which they win for themselves to the degree that their understanding supports true consensus.

Insofar as one does not know himself (his aims and their cost in terms of his own energies), insofar as he thinks that others can be brought around to give him that which he wants but does not undertake to get through disciplining himself to achieve through directing his own efforts, so long as, and to the extent that, he thinks that he can get value at others' expense, when he turns toward others for assistance, either through lack of his own right effort or through the inadequacy of his resources, he exposes himself to unforeseen exploitation, even servitude, whether as "leader" or "follower." Through organizing with people, entering into membership, there may be imagined and generated a surrogate-being artificially—but, through the making of myths, seemingly validly—endowed with transcendent personality so that thenceforth through it knowledge of self, self-interest, property, self-defense, security can be subsumed as individualized through membership in the group. There arises a problem of compatability between his own organic process of growing out through the satisfaction of the need felt and the other's organic process in providing the energy supplement being received. A consequence of the inherent uniqueness of individuals is that neither "leaders' " nor "followers' " expectations can ever be in perfect agreement with each others' intentions, expectations and performances.

"Leaders" are those who claim to be able to provide those satisfactions for others; and "followers" are those who hope, through avoiding their own exertions, by availing themselves of others' services to receive the benefits vicariously. Upon him who proffers a readiness and ability to serve, people, half-credulously, project their frustrated hopes and, without providing—indeed, often by obstructing—persistent attention to follow through in finding and carrying out effective procedures, they grant a discretion and excuse for irregular behavior to those whom they endow with all those vices which they deny to themselves through fear of consequence anticipated for breakers of conventions. Much of political history and current practice consists in the effort to invest some with sufficient force and plausibility for them to deliver privileges at others' expense and least cost to themselves.

In human experience, consequences are considered and perceived differently. For some actions, there has come to be established a close, direct, uniform and reliable relationship. With respect to others, as in scientific pursuits, even where the relationship has not been clearly established, methods are considered available through which clarification is being achieved. In the political process, there is a class of consequences the actions prerequisite for which are especially insulated against perception. Here is found a distinction between private and official behavior. Privately, one grasps at something, to obtain or to hold on to which he enlists whatever kind of assistance from another offers the prospect of securing it for him. Nor is he willing to concern himself or hold himself accountable or, if possible, let there be any connection detectable between that which he has grasped and the means used to achieve it. In these matters, the greatest inner psychological and inter-personal barriers are generated to obscure and prevent the establishing of observable consequences. One such barrier is the powerful convention that in public behavior a set of standards is effective different from that perceived as requisite in private relations. People are encouraged to become "leaders" and enter upon public responsiblities for which the public is not stirred to provide the resources either of understanding participation or of adequate finances for meeting the costs of acquiring the office or of carrying through its responsibilities and demands. Thus, vulnerable, candidates for public office, as well as those in office, find pressed upon them offers of "assistance" which conceal that the "benefactors" will later seek, in return, extra- or even il-legal privileges through the diversion of the public power to private advantages.

As a candidate, the would-be leader moves among people with his psychological antennae sensitized and sweeping the field to tune in on gestures, expressions, attitudes, positions on issues which will identify him as the recipient of their wish-projections. Out of these he weaves a fabric of insinuations, and promises, to launch and carry aloft his candidacy and sustain it to victory. In the process, giving higher value to that which is conventionally commendable, he distills or fabricates a perspective which is not only acceptable but passes as the public's truth. The closer candidates ("leaders") feel themselves to grasping power, the more they seek to avoid committing themselves to positive and definite positions. To veil differences with potential supporters, the candidate resorts to deceptive ambiguities which, frequently, the constituents, biased by their own undisciplined and irresponsibly private interests, overlook or hasten to interpret as to their own advantage. Since people's wants are subjectively individual, another can, at best, only approximately satisfy them and in reality his own subjectivity modifies and redirects his perceptions of them. Meanwhile, those who had let themselves believe that governmental or official action was essential for relieving their needs, find the process of the campaign one of obliterating attention to critical needs with a barrage of ambiguous phrases and an exaltation of personalities so that in the end, the victor, uncommitted and irresponsible, holds, as power, the symbol-manipulated energies of a people, confused but committed.

Responsible participation does reveal meaning in relationships otherwise unperceived. Victory elicits sufficient public confidence for the "leader" to have a chance to give his subsequent actions the appearance of conforming with some possible interpretation of the ambiguous terminology of his broadly-phrased campaign promises. It may, indeed, even be true that it is the political leader alone who approximates a realistic understanding of the meaning of the values "honesty" and "integrity." Those who, as private individuals, place demands but try to avoid seeing, or being called upon to pay, the costs, cannot attain such knowledge. The political leader occupies publicly the position of accountability. Ambiguous though his assurances may be, he knows that the endurance of his power depends upon his credibility. Therefore he prizes mindfulness to ensure that the words which he chooses have implications adequate to cover the actions his policy requires, and his on-going experience refines understanding of the words adequate for inspiring sufficiently the hopes and for interpreting acceptably the unanticipated developments. Moreover, as official, deriving power from a constituency more inclusive than any of the respective special interests which selected him as candidate and promoted his campaign, in responsiveness to the interest of the larger whole, he is seen by his special-interest supporters as a betrayer of the expectations for which they had relied upon him as candidate, whereas from his new standpoint as official the use of the office to reward the private interests, as such, would verge on a betrayal of the public trust. When a moment of truly public reckoning threatens, when strained interpretations tend to surface as contradictions, the "leader" senses the possibility that his subtle devices and the tricks by means of which he had bolstered his pretenses are becoming transparent, the loyalties on which he had counted are dissolving into vengeful disillusion on the part of those eager not to be faced with the evidence that they had been "had" due to their own self-indulging and -deluded credulity, and that, with his power on the verge of vanishing away, he is in danger of being left pitifully and abhorrently dispensable. He is then tempted to use the mystic power attributed to "the whole" for his own self-preservation as an official. The "leader" and the "followers," each, may project upon the other a burden of guilt for not producing an acceptably fruitful return for the energy the other has been devoting to the enterprise.

The "leader" attempts to deflect from himself the feared ordeal by seeking to devise and attract attention to a power governing both leader and followers, beyond the followers' knowledge and of which the "leader" presents himself as the interpreter to the people. He identifies his authority with the unity of the organization and treats any questioning or opposition as an attack upon its security and that of each of the members.

Every person having been constituted by the preponderantly favorable impact of internal and external influences feels himself at the same time limited and constricted in and to their terms and yet, due to the fact of his uniqueness, impelled to diverge from and transcend them. Such is the source both of the sense of human bondage and of the sense of a transcendent power of utterly different quality essential for the realization that there can be and is an escape from such bondage. However, the claim of a knowledge of a process or of a power outside of everyone else's experience opens the way for one to claim a superior and more general knowledge of it than that available to others under its influence and, on the basis of that claim, to establish a control expansible into ecclesiastical, political, economic and other such hierarchies. Since the power affirmed is outside of experience through consensus, it cannot be tested as to whether or not the claimant's assertion of its existence and his "superior knowledge" of it is in truth knowledge superior for another for whom he is prescribing it as the way toward security and well-being. Possessed of new insights and momentum for action gained in responsible participation, bearer of relatively unencumbered power entrusted to him by relatively uninformed clients, "the leader" is granted by his supporters an obligation to break faith with restrictive conventions and current endowments of privilege clothed in forms of law, in the hope that he will yet in some extraordinary way fulfill those wishes for the sake of which they gave him supportive power. Attributing to himself the virtue of providing security through using his authority to achieve and preserve unity, "the leader" seeks to give convincing demonstration of his power by some striking and unparalleled show of force. Thus he takes for granted that "the all" can be superseded through the disregard or sacrifice of some in the name of "the whole" and that imagination and the proclamation of "unity" can empower, authorize, sanction the disesteem and exclusion of those non-conforming to the newly defined and enunciated "whole." Accordingly, it has been written:

Not law but lawlessness is the living force of the great empire.[10]

    Conventional politics consists in the determined effort of those grasping for control over others to obtain and secure it and those apparently not in control, to acquire it. Such is the tension occasioned by dividing people so that some are considered specialized as "leaders" and others as "followers," that it has been found "necessary" to resort to artifices by which to amaze, dumbfound, awe, stun and keep poeple in a state of unquestioning acquiescence. "Leaders" reach for "religion" in order, by wrapping themselves about in an aura of sanctity, to acquire for themselves a sphere of irresponsibility unaccountable to the scrutiny and rational judgment of their constituents whose energies provide their suste-nance. Thus, actions prompted by fear, at an accelerating rate, divert "leaders" and "followers" from the application of their mutual resources to understanding and constructively resolving their respectively intrinsic aims,and increasingly

47

subject them to autocracy, secrecy, intolerance of difference, demand for total commitment and blind obedience to "leadership."

Since the motive power of a leader is his attraction to himself of others' expressions of faith in his being capable of implementing their desires—especially, in the case of charismatic "leaders," their unarticulated desires—, but since the uniqueness of human individuality renders such a hope inherently illusory, leadership originates in, builds upon and operates as fiction. Fiction consists in assuming, acting upon and defending as valid a position by disregarding or denying the inadequacy of the evidence for it or by attempting to conceal or destroy weakening or contrary evidence.

The determination and attempt to create the appearance of evidence or reality through demanding of others sacrifice—"in the name of" or "for the sake of" "the Whole,"—of already existent relationships, rather than through deepending understanding by working out articulation of a more inclusive whole, manifests itself in force. In the *Prince*, Machiavelli wrote:

> the people are by nature variable; to convince them of a thing is easy; to hold them to that conviction is hard. Therefore a prophet must be ready, when they no longer believe, to make them believe by force,[11]

and, by way of confirmation, he cited the effectiveness of Moses,[12] the destruction of Savonarola along with his new institutions,[13] and the fall of Piero Soderini.[14]

Leadership policy fosters a sense of personal inadequacy within another (or others), a need to delegate an unalienable responsibility, to vest another with an authority without regard to the fact that in operation it is intrinsically irrelevant in so far as it attempts to make the other responsible for doing for one that of which he only can rightly perceive the nature as he engages himself in the endeavor to work it out. Such "leadership" becomes not merely a debilitating crutch but an actively corroding corruption which masks itself with mystique and affirms itself with violence. Resort to the services of others as authority in order to avoid the painful but potentially creative labor of directly working through inter-personal tensions, generates a fear-born force liable to hold in bondage all whom it "serves." However beneficial the "leaders" may claim their intentions to be, only each person's own responsible participation can disclose or evoke the meaning which has validity for him; faith given to the "leader's" "vision" becomes but the sanctification of the force which in the end exploits, confuses and eventually annihilates the energies of both.

Jesus specifically rebuked men's impulse to accredit superiority to other men or to themselves when he said:

> you must not be called "rabbi"; for you have one Rabbi, and you are all brothers. Do not call any man on earth "father"; for you have one Father, and he is in heaven. Nor must you be called "teacher"; you have one

Teacher, the Messiah. The greatest of you must be your servant. For whoever exalts himself will be humbled; and whoever humbles himself will be exalted,[15]

and to one who addressed him as "Good Master,"

Why do you call me good? No one is good except God alone.[16]

That "leaders" find themselves compelled to put forward myths in the guise of religion for which they demand faith from their followers, Machiavelli held as a basic conviction. Of the use of religion as an instrument of government, Livy's *History of Rome* is replete with examples. Seventeen years of age when the Senate, under Octavian's leadership in 42 A.D., deified Caesar, Livy, in subsequent years, witnessed Augustus' rebuilding of temples, reviving ancient cults, and step-by-step approaching the establishment of emperor worship.[17] Through Livy's *History* the long series of precedents for the political use of religion provided Machiavelli with authoritative evidence for its effectiveness and, in his turn, he repeatedly endorsed the practice:

No quality does a prince more need to possess—in appearance—than this last one [of being religious], because in general men judge more with their eyes then with their hands, since everybody can see but few can perceive. Everybody sees what you appear to be; few perceive what you are, and those few dare not contradict the beliefs of the many, who have the majesty of the government to support them;[18]

[Numa], finding a very savage people and wishing to bring it to obey the laws by means of the arts of peace, turned to religion as something altogether necessary if he wished to maintain a well-ordered state. And he established it in such a way that for many ages there was never so much fear of God as in that republic; this facilitated whatever undertaking the Senate or those great men of Rome planned to carry on. And he who will go over countless actions both of the people of Rome altogether and of many of the Romans for themselves, will see that these citizens feared much more to break an oath than to break the laws, since they respected the power of God more than that of men . . .Thus he who examines Roman history will see how helpful religion was in controlling the armies, in inspiring the people, in keeping men good, in making the wicked ashamed . . . Because where there is religion, it is easy to bring in arms; but where there are arms and not religion, only with difficulty can the latter be brought in. We see that Romulus, in establishing the Senate and making other civil and military provisions, had no need for the authority of God. Yet it was necessary to Numa, who pretended he was intimate with a nymph who advised him about what he was going to advise the people [*Livy I, 19*]. He did so because he planned to introduce new and unwonted laws into the city, but feared that his own authority would not be enough. And truly no one who did not have recourse to God ever gave to a people unusual laws, because without that they would not be accepted. Because many good things are known to a prudent man that are not in themselves so plainly rational that others can be persuaded of them. Therefore wise men, who wish to remove this difficulty, have recourse to God . . . religion caused good laws; good laws make good fortune; and from good fortune came the happy results of the city's endeavors. And as the observance of religious teaching brings about the greatness of states, so contempt for it brings about their ruin. Because, where fear of God is lacking, it is necessary either that a kingdom fall or that it be sustained by fear of a prince which atones for what is missing in religion. And because princes are short-lived, it is probable that a kingdom will quickly fail just as the strength and wisdom of the prince fails . . . It is not, then, the salvation of a republic or a kingdom to have a prince who will rule prudently while he lives, but to have one who will so organize it that even after he dies it can be maintained. And though rude men are more easily won over to a new order or opinion, it is still not for that reason impossible to win over to it also cultured men and those who assume they are not rude . . .

Those princes or those republics that wish to keep themselves uncorrupted must above everything else keep the ceremonies of their religion uncorrupted and hold them always in respect, because one can have no better indication of the ruin of a country than to see divine worship little valued. This is easy to understand if it is known on what the religion of a man's birthplace is founded, because the life of every religion has its foundation in some chief usage of its own . . . It is the duty, then, of the rulers of a republic or of a kingdom to preserve the foundation of the religion they hold. If they do this, it will be an easy thing for them to keep their state religious, and consequently good and united. And whatever comes up in favor of religion, even though they think it false, they are to accept and magnify. And so much the more they are going to do it as they are more prudent and as they have better understanding of natural things.

And because this method has been followed by wise men, there has risen from it the belief in miracles, which are celebrated even in false religions. Because whatever the beginning in which they originate, they are magnified by the prudent, whose authority then gains them credit with everybody;[19]

In theirs [the religion of the people in ancient times] neither pomp nor magnificence was lacking in the ceremonies, and in addition there was the deed of sacrifice, full of blood and ferocity in the slaughter of a multitude of animals; this terrible sight made men resemble it. Ancient religion, besides this, attributed blessedness only to men abounding in worldly glory, such as generals of armies and princes of states;[20]

Though this matter appears in all the Roman histories, yet it is proved more surely by the words that Livy puts in the mouth of Appius Claudius.

On complaining to the plebeians of the arrogance of the Tribunes of the People, and showing that they were allowing the auspices and other things pertaining to religion to become debased, he spoke as follows. "Those who wish may mock at religious ceremonies, saying: 'What does it matter whether chickens eat, whether they come out of their coops slowly, whether a bird chirps?' These are little things, but by not despising these little things, our fathers made this republic great" [*Livy 6.41*]. Indeed in these little things is that force for holding the soldiers united and confident which is the first cause of every victory;[21]

if for every other order of men in cities and kingdoms every diligence should be used to keep them faithful, peaceful, and full of the fear of God, in the army it should be redoubled . . . In whom ought there to be more fear of God than in a man who every day, being exposed to countless perils, has great need for his aid;[22]

Because to control armed men the fear neither of the laws nor of man is enough, the ancients added to them the authority of God; and therefore with very great ceremonies they had their soldiers swear to observe military discipline, in order that if they acted against it, they would have to fear not merely the laws and men but God; and they used every device to give them strong religious feeling;[23]

This condition, mingled with other religious customs, many times made every sort of undertaking easy for the ancient generals, and will always make them so, where religion is feared and observed.[24]

That even God can be swayed by the use of force when it is employed with prudence, Machiavelli seemed to hold when he wrote in the *Prince:*

Princes who follow the first method [of "well-used" cruelties] can before God and before men, make some improvements in their position, as Agathocles could.[25]

Agathocles! of whom in the same chapter he had just written:

It cannot . . . be called virtue to kill one's fellow-citizens, to betray friends, to be without fidelity, without mercy, without religion; such proceedings enable one to gain sovereignty, but not fame . . . his outrageous cruelty and inhumanity together with his countless wicked acts do not permit him to be honored among the noblest men.[26]

According to Sydney Anglo,

Machiavelli's principal view of Roman religion seems to be that it was easily manipulated for political purposes and was especially useful as a means of inculcating military *virtu*—an idea borrowed from Polybius, but much distorted in the process.[27]

Through myths, buttressed with violence, comes into being the theory and practice of holding that good ends require and justify what are recognized as otherwise bad means; however, it has been written:

> It is good to be full of *zeal for God;* but when we begin to assume that we must do for him, by being zealous for his cause, what only he can do for us, then indeed zeal defeats itself and turns into an irreligious solicitude about him, quite incompatible with humble trust and grateful dependence.[28]

Leaders, through the examples set by their extra-, il-legal or ruthless deeds, encourage among the people the sense that, despite institutional taboos, they also rightfully secure for themselves adequate access to whatever natural resources are requisite in their eyes for the full development of their potentialities. So individuals through their citizenship gain a sense of solidity and specificity in relating themselves directly to the good earth and its resources despite social and conventional reservations and prohibitions. "Benefactors" of candidates, finding pliant instruments, continue to support in office, and in future candidacies, the parties and individuals able to amass the votes and manipulate the "democratic" process by which the voters are browbeaten and terrorized into continuing to confer the authority which continues to deceive them into maintaining their own exploitation through psychological, religious, political, economic devices.

However, the quest for power and security through the effort to accumulate preponderant force and ingenious deception encounters the power of the inexorable and irreducible factor which, as already noted (pp. 9–13, 43–44), Machiavelli himself recognized in human individuality: people do not reconcile themselves to unequal or discriminatory treatment; nor does one's knowledge reliably comprehend another's (or others') attitudes or motivations. The "leader's" sense of security for freedom of action is eroded by intimations of its fragility and his accumulated resources become consumed as inadequate for self-defense against the reactions and recriminations of those who had put their trust in him. To some degree "leaders" suffer from the malady which Machiavelli noted when he observed:

> princes who are not good always fear that somebody will do to them what they themselves think they deserve;[29]

> if your conscience is not clear you easily believe you are spoken of; you can hear a word, spoken for another purpose, that disturbs your courage and makes you believe it spoken about your affair;[30]

> almost always the prince of a city, after he is assailed with such a conspiracy,

52

if he is not killed . . . —which seldom happens—rises to greater power. Many times, indeed, having been good, he becomes wicked, because these conspiracies, through their example, give him reasons for being afraid; fear gives him reasons for making himself safe; making himself safe gives him reasons for doing harm. Hence feelings of hatred result from them, and in time often his downfall. So these conspiracies destroy quickly those who carry them on and, in the course of time at least, harm him against whom they are carried on.[31]

"Leadership" is but one of many fictions discernable in the political process as conventionally conceived and exercised.

There is assumed and claimed a knowledge of oneself and self-interest such that in "self-defense" there are generally accepted, excused, even justified, deeds of deceit and violence. With the same apology, statesmen who, for "reasons of state," transgress conventions of legality, morality and ethics, receive indulgence and exoneration from citizens who welcome the examples as nourishment for their own arrogant impulses.

In staking out and defending territorial claims, various wild animals bare their teeth and in various ways display strength but are not given to fighting to the death others of their own species;[32] however, human beings, although not creators of the earth, its resources and those that dwell therein, claiming a God-given and natural right, wrest for themselves freedom to work their will upon whatever they can bring under their control, exploit it for private gain, and join together in such organizations as give endorsement to their claims while they short-sightedly exhaust irreplaceable resources, exterminate other peoples, cultures and creatures in their way, pay less heed to growing domestic tensions than, through fomenting a climate of fear, to stirring up readiness for further and more effective aggression; and, driven by mounting apprehension of challenges, they consume an ever-increasing proportion of their resources (physical, scientific, emotional) in pursuit of an ever more elusively retreating "security." Support of such a fiction of "ownership" (individual and collective) as a natural right, is given status as "fact" only through violent manipulation of reality as encountered.

As a device for attempting to acquire and exercise control over others, perhaps none has been more effectively and frequently employed than that of manipulating a relationship into an entity-by-proclamation. Subtle, pervasive, insidious, resourceful, difficult to find-and-take-one's-stand-against, is the demand for—and attempt at—exaction of control in the name of some relationship as part of a collective.

Although almost utterly dependent upon all kinds of help from outside, at the moment of birth and forever after, the unique human being is the sole ultimate assayer of assimilability of proffered aid. Needed as are the resources of kindred, food, shelter, friendship, country, religious-, economic-, political-culture, they can be received, incorporated, lived with and utilized only insofar as they are proffered in a way, form and flavor which the given being experiences as congenial. Either another's pressure in disregard of the distinguishing uniqueness, or the being's own ostensible compliance under conditions of weakness, generates an alienation which subsequently breaks up and cancels out any claimed progress in constructive achievements. From infancy on, one is engaged in and has ahead the unalienable task of differentiating and filtering out the harmful from the beneficial influences impinging upon him. Members in a need-supply relationship are especially susceptible to manipulation from both ends of it and the fruitful exchange of mutual assistance, while scrupulously refraining from transgression of the sensitive boundary of essential ignorance, requires from both sides an openness to appreciation of the diversity in each other.

When, however, the common involvement is interpreted as a collective—whether as family, tribe, race, faith, country, class, business corporation, organization, *et cetera*—and in its name the attempt is made by any part, despite its lack of understanding of the other parts and its disregard of the lack of the other's consent, to draw upon the relationship of all for support, frequently it proceeds to wrap around its ignorance a mantle of "transcendental" mystery in order to sanctify the use of force in carrying through its program. Especially useful toward that end is the conceit that the participants in the relationship constitute "a whole" of which they function as cells in a living organism. This metaphor with its related concepts of disease and the use of surgery, provides a convenient rationalization for resort to the use of force "for the health of the whole" against some of the members, in disregard of the fact that they also are constituent elements of the real whole and that all alike are neither more nor less than individual human beings. Although the introduction and development of organization in the pursuit of shared interests and goals may be of general benefit, when "for its sake" there occurs discriminatory manipulation and even sacrifice of some of the members, its character changes from one of service into an exploitive instrument of privilege. Thenceforth the maintenance of the appearance of unity grows increasingly subjected to pressure for support of, and involvement in, the force aspect of the organization. Tensions indicative of incipient cleavages are overwhelmed with dramatization of actual or artfully induced threats from outside.

"Corporate" organization serves also as a medium for preserving and cultivating projections of unresolved inner tensions and inter-personal conflicts and transmuting them into hopes of satisfaction through the pooling of energies for calculated aggression. The imputation of qualities to an artificial social aggregate and the exaction of treatment of it as an entity to be accorded regard and rights as if it were another human being, creates the impression of endowing it with powers superior to those of natural human beings and the capacity to override and sacrifice them when challenged in encounter. Thus: in matters of religion, the church is the collective in relation to which the individuals, as souls, are vulnerable to exploitation for the sake of the organization; in matters of governance, the state is the collective in position to exploit the individuals as material bodies for the purposes of the organization; in matters of instruction and education, the school is the collective which too frequently tends to exploit individuals, as minds and skills, for the sake of advancing technology, despite the potential for liberation which Aristotle imagined might accompany the invention of automated machinery (see above, p. 33); in the economy, the business corporation is the collective which exploits individuals as consumers by exciting as "wants" and "needs" the release and expenditure of energies able to be processed for the organization's profit; in the society, the Class is the collective which, identifying people with status, nourishes the organization through mobilization and manipulation of frustration.

The concept that the state is an organism liable to illnesses, responsive to treatment analogous to that used in medicine and, especially, in surgery, and that the inhabitants bear to the state a relationship similar to that of cells to an organism, Machiavelli employed frequently as an explanation for political developments and a justification for recommended policies. The most detailed exposition, he gave in the *Discourses:*

> It is most certain that there is a limit for the existence of all things in the world; but they generally move through the entire course ordained for them by Heaven without getting their bodies into confusion but keeping them in the way ordained; this way either does not change or, if it does, the change is to their advantage, not to their harm. And because I am speaking of mixed bodies, such as republics and religions, I say that those changes are to their advantage that take them back toward their beginnings.

After further developing the analogy, he clinched his argument with the generalization:

> The doctors of medicine say, speaking of the bodies of men, that "daily something is added that now and then needs cure;"[33]

and later,

> It must be, as I have said before, that every day in a large city emergencies will occur that have need of a physician, and in proportion as they are more important, a wiser physician is needed;[34]

> an uncontrolled and rebellious people can be spoken to by a good man and easily led back into a good way. A wicked prince nobody can speak to, and the only remedy is steel. This lets us guess at the seriousness of the diseases both suffer from, since for the curing of the people's disease words are enough, but for the prince's disease steel is required;[35]

the physicians say that when the disease [hectic fever] begins it is easy to cure but hard to recognize, but in the course of time, when not recognized and treated at the beginning, it becomes easy to recognize but hard to cure. So it is in things of state; on early recognition (which is granted only to a prudent man), the maladies that spring up in a state can be healed speedily; but when, not being recognized, they are allowed to increase in such a way that everybody recognizes them, they can no longer be remedied;[36]

there is not time to cure . . . those sicknesses that have to do with the government . . . If they are not cured by a prudent man, they ruin the city.[37]

The collective to which Machiavelli accorded a value above all others was his city, his country. In his "Discourso . . . Lingua," he wrote:

A man has no greater duty in life than that [to honor his country] being dependent on it, first for his being and then for all that good which fortune and nature have granted him;[38]

and to the Medicean pope Leo X:

I believe the greatest honor possible for men to have is that willingly given them by their native cities; I believe the greatest good to be done and the most pleasing to God is that which one does to one's native city.[39]

In *The Art of War,* he declared:

Men become excellent and show their ability only as they are employed and brought forward by their prince or republic or king as it may be;[40]

and in the *Discources*

the methods by which they [citizens] get reputation . . . are two, public and private. The public methods are when a person advising well and acting better, for the common good, gains reputation. To this honor, the way should be opened to citizens, and for their advice and their actions rewards should be set up, with which they will be honored and satisfied;[41]

similarly in *The History of Florence*:

Publicly, [citizens] gain reputation by winning a battle, capturing a town, carrying on an embassy with diligence and prudence, and advising the state wisely and successfully . . . a reputation gained by unselfish conduct benefits the republic, since it is not mixed with partisanship being founded on the common good, not on private favor.[42]

In clearest terms he expressed supremacy for one's country,[43] and finally in his letter of 16 April 1527, just over two months before his death, he valued love of his native city above that for his own soul.[44]

Of the analogy between state and organism found in Machiavelli's writings, Jacob Burkhardt wrote:

> Endlich fasst Machiavelli in seinen fiorentinishen Geschichten seine Vaterstadt vollkomen als ein lebendiges Wesen und ihren Entwicklungsgang als einen individuell naturgemässen auf; der erste unter den Modernen, der dieses so vermocht hat.[45]

In short, Machiavelli in his Florentine History conceived of his home city entirely as a living being and its development as that of an individual in accordance with nature—the first among moderns with the ability to do this.

Besides "leadership," self-conceit and the treatment of the collective as an entity, the company of fictions frequently encountered in the political processes includes:

subordination of experienced reality to plausible appearance;
acceptance of a given part as "the whole" despite relevant elements yet unknown or absent;
subordination of an emergent power of truth to desire for security;
acceptance of apologies for guilty consciences as historiography;
claim of knowledge of cause and effect rather than of only experienced frequency;
identification of individual and civic virtue with apparent success in conquering others and holding control until death.

The myth of effective violence frequently wins credibility through an inadequate relating of original objectives to eventualities. Moreover, passage in time, distance in space, differences in culture, may seemingly successfully veil— and ambiguous interpretations fully preclude—the discovery by the credulous that the artifices for eliciting their support involved even them themselves as victims of covert measures directed to their own disadvantage.

Fictions found in Machiavelli's writings are those assumptions which he sought to endow with validity despite complete disregard of—or even the endorsement of violent sacrifice of—some of the reality so encountered.

Adherence to his expressed determination to explore

> the reason why different ways of working [in gaining kingdoms and sovereignties or falling] are sometimes equally effective and equally damaging[46]

and to

concern myself with the truth of the matter as facts show it rather than with any fanciful notion,[47]

requires that any fictions to which he resorted be discovered, and that their reconcilability with progress in the understanding of human political behavior be assayed.

Fictions found in Machiavelli's writings can be grouped according to the degree of credibility which he gave them. Some of them, he employed as a device subsidiary to the pursuit of a more inclusive purpose. Others, he himself, in light of reiterated undeniably conflicting examples, reluctantly intimated recognition of their inherently fictional character and ultimate inadequacy. Among the fictions are other affirmations which he uncritically endorsed but which subsequent historical and cultural developments have proved no longer tenable.

Perhaps foremost among his fictions, his concept of the founder of a new state or reformer of an old state, needs thorough examination.

For his contemporary Florence, the problem of executive leadership was immediate and crucial. During the period from 1434 to 1492, Cosimo de'Medici and his grandson Lorenzo the Magnificent, through manipulation of the traditional institutions, had, unofficially, concentrated and exercised the economic and decision-making authority of the city and brought it to a position of economic, political and cultural leadership throughout the peninsula. Following Lorenzo's death, the adventurist policy indulged in by his son, Piero, upset the balance in Italy, resulted in the independence of Pisa under French influence, his own exile, and the restoration of the republic with Savonarola in control.[48] Checkmated by enemies at home and abroad, the unarmed prophet,[49] after nearly four years of rule was hanged and burned.[50] In the revived republic, Machiavelli, as Secretary of the Second Chancery, was, to some degree, a participant and always an alert observer of the forming of military decisions and of their execution. Faced by military reverses in the effort to recover Pisa, its major access to the sea held subject from 1406 to 1494,[51] and the looming danger posed by the growing power of the Pope's son and French king's protege, Cesare Borgia, the Grand Council of Florence, in the fall of 1502, elected Piero Soderini as gonfalonier for life.[52] Despite evidence which led Tommasini[53] to conclude that Machiavelli would have preferred that the Grand Council elect either Alamanno Salviati or Tebalducci Antonio Giacomini whose military effectiveness in the field Machiavelli had had occasion to observe, and, with respect to the latter, whose interest in the formation of a citizen militia helped stimulate his own, Machiavelli became Soderini's especially favored aide.[54] With Soderini's fall, in 1512, which Machiavelli attributed to his letting conventional scruples prevail against the need to resort to extraordinary measures for the retention of power,[55] Machiavelli, through his study and writing, undertook to formulate the model for a leader adequate to meet the needs of the city and of Italy, to identify potential candidates,

58

to stir them to accept the mission, and to present himself as available for participating as an adviser in the enterprise.

The concept that, as Machiavelli wrote,

A man must be alone if he is to organize a republic afresh or remodel her with complete annulment of her old laws[56]

may, as Tommasini has pointed out,[57] have had its origin in contemporary suggestions for church reform:

A proposito del rinnovamento di corpi politici il Machiavelli enunciò una massima che, in mezzo agli ardori conciliari per riordinare la Chiesa, era già balenata anche a un frate: cioè che a riformare un'istituzione bisogna che l'uomo, che a tale impressa si accinge, non abbia compagni, sia solo.

With respect to the renewal of political bodies, Machiavelli enunciated a maxim which, in the midst of the conciliar exertions for reforming the Church, had already struck a monk also: that is, that in order to reform an institution, it is necessary that the man who sets for himself such an undertaking should be alone, without having accomplices.

There is, however, indication of a possible derivation from Livy.[58] That one person can validly not only construe the needs and desires of another or of a large number but also define and put in operation the methods appropriate for meeting them effectively, Machiavelli repeated insistently in his prescriptions for the reformer of an old state, the founder of a new, and the periodic restorer of one in decline:

This we must take as a general rule: seldom or never is any republic or kingdom organized well from the beginning, or totally made over, without respect for its old laws, except when organized by one man. Still more, it is necessary that one man alone give the method and that from his mind proceed all such organization. Therefore a prudent organizer of a republic and one whose intention is to advance not his own interests but the general good, not his own posterity but the common fatherland, ought to strive to have authority all to himself;[59]

envy many times prevents men from working well, since it does not permit them to have the authority necessary in things of importance . . . when they are men used to living in a corrupt city, where education has not produced any goodness in them, they cannot because of any emergency reverse themselves; but to gain their desire and to satisfy their perversity of mind, they are content to see the ruin of their country. For subduing this envy there is no other method than the death of those affected with it. When Fortune is so propitious to an able man that the envious die naturally, without contention he becomes famous, since without obstacle and without offense he can show his ability. But when he does not have this good fortune, he has to plan in every way to get the envious out of his path, and before he does anything, he has to adopt methods for overcoming the difficulty. He who reads the Bible intelligently sees that if Moses was to put his laws and regulations into effect, he was forced to kill countless men who, moved by nothing else than envy, were opposed to his plans;[60]

He who seizes a tyranny and does not kill Brutus, and he who sets a state free and does not kill Brutus' sons, maintains himself but a little while;[61]

every prince can learn that he has no lasting security for his princedom so long as they are alive whom he has deprived of it . . . every ruler can be reminded that never have new benefits erased old injuries; and so much the less in so far as the new benefit is less than the injury;[62]

he who undertakes to govern a multitude, whether by the method of freedom or by that of a princedom, and does not secure himself against those who are enemies to the new government, establishes a short-lived state;[63]

in cities many times there are such disorders that a merciful and good citizen, when steel is the necessary remedy, would sin much more in leaving them untreated than in treating them;[64]

There is no other ["method of consolidating a divided city"]—nor can the disease be otherwise cured—than by killing the leaders of the disorders;[65]

such decisive actions have in them something great and noble;[66]

Where [the matter] is corrupt, well-planned laws are of no use, unless, indeed, they are prepared by one who with the utmost power can force their observation, so that the matter will become good;[67]

From all the things explained above comes the difficulty or impossibility of maintaining a government in a corrupt city or of setting up a new government there. Indeed when in such one is to be set up or maintained, necessity demands that it be inclined more toward kingly rule than toward popular rule, in order that those men who, on account of their arrogance, cannot be controlled by law may in some fashion be restrained by a power almost kingly;[68]

where the matter is so corrupt that the laws are not restraint enough, along with them some greater force must of necessity be established, namely, a kingly hand that with absolute and surpassing power puts a check on the over-great ambition and corruption of the powerful;[69]

for the overthrow of those who with various excuses sought by private ways to make themselves great, she [Rome] established the Dictator, who with his kingly arm made those return within bounds who had gone outside them . . . One such case that goes unpunished is enough to ruin a republic, because when she has such an example, she is with difficulty brought back into the right;[70]

all armed prophets win, and unarmed ones fall. Because in addition to what has been said, the people are by nature variable; to convince them of a thing is easy; to hold them to that conviction is hard. Therefore a prophet must be ready, when they no longer believe, to make them believe by force. Moses, Cyrus, Theseus, and Romulus could not have gained long-continued observance for their constitutions if they had been unarmed;[71]

If anyone who becomes prince of a city or of a state, especially when his foundations are weak, cannot move toward constitutional government by way of a kingdom or a republic, the best means he has for keeping that princedom (if he is a new prince) is to make everything in that state anew . . . These methods are very cruel, and enemies to all government not merely Christian but human, and any man ought to avoid them and prefer to live a private life rather than to be a king who brings such ruin on men. Notwithstanding a ruler who does not wish to take that first good way of lawful government, if he wishes to maintain himself, must enter upon this evil one;[72]

Well used we call those [cruelties] (if of what is bad we can use the word *well*) that a conqueror carries out at a single stroke, as a result of his need to secure himself, and then does not persist in, but transmutes it into the greatest possible benefits to his subjects;[73]

When a man of that sort ["a very strong man, devoted to his father and his native city and very respectful to his superiors"] comes to commanding rank, he reckons on finding all men like himself, and his strong spirit makes him command strong things; that same spirit, after they are commanded, expects them to be carried out; otherwise your expectations will be deceived. This teaches that if you expect to be obeyed, you must know how to command. Men who know that compare their capacities with those of the men who are to obey. When they see that such capacities correspond, then they give commands; when they see lack of that correspondence, they refrain from it. Therefore a prudent man was wont to say that if a state is to be held with force, he who uses force must correspond in strength with him who is subject to it. When such correspondence exists, we can believe that such use of force can continue, but when he who is subject to force is stronger than he who is using force, we must fear that any day such use of force will end . . . I say that a man who commands hard things must be hard, and he who is hard and commands hard things cannot let them be carried out with gentleness . . . We should, then, believe that Manlius was forced to proceed so severely by those extraordinary commands to which his nature inclined him. These are useful in a state because they bring back its laws to their beginning and to their ancient vigor. If a state were fortunate enough, as we have said above [3.1], to have frequently a leader who with his example would renovate its laws, and would not merely stop it from running to ruin but would pull it backward, it would be everlasting;[74]

After the Duke had seized the Romagna and found it controlled by weak lords who had plundered their subjects rather than governed them, and had given reason for disunion, not for union, so that the whole province was full of thefts, brawls, and every sort of excess, he judged that if he intended to make it peaceful and obedient to the ruler's arm, he must of necessity give it good government. Hence he put in charge there Messer Remirro de Orco, a man cruel and ready, to whom he gave the most complete authority. This man in a short time rendered the province peaceful and united, gaining enormous prestige. Then the Duke decided there was no further need for such boundless power, because he feared it would become a cause for hatred; so he set up a civil court in the midst of the province, with a distinguished presiding judge, where every city had its lawyer. And because he knew that past severities had made some men hate him, he determined to purge such men's minds and win them over entirely by showing that any cruelty which had gone on did not originate with himself but with the harsh nature of his agent. So getting an opportunity for it, one morning at Cesena he had Messer Remirro laid in two pieces in the public square with a block of wood and a bloody sword near him. The ferocity of this spectacle left those people at the same time gratified and awestruck.[75]

Besides making a prudent use of force and a convincing cultivation of the native religion (above, pp. 49–51), the wise founder or reformer of a state identifies himself with "the common good" (above, p. 59). Service to the "common" or "general good," whether by citizens in a republic or by princes, Machiavelli emphasized as the surest way of securing and increasing influence. In the *Discourses,* he observed:

Nothing makes them [citizens and princes] so much esteemed as to display extraordinary ability in some rare action or saying, in keeping with the common good, that shows the lord as high-minded or liberal or just, and gets to be a sort of proverb among his subjects;[76]

not individual good but common good is what makes cities great;[77]

> All cities and provinces that live in freedom anywhere in the world, as I said above, make very great gains. They do so because their populations are larger, since marriages are freer and more attractive to man, and each man gladly begets those children he thinks he can bring up, without fear that his patrimony will be taken from him; he knows not merely that they are born free and not slaves but that by means of their abilities they can become prominent men. Riches multiply in a free country to a greater extent, both those that come from agriculture and those that come from industry, for each man gladly increases such things and seeks to gain such goods as he believes, when gained, he can enjoy. Thence it comes that men in emulation give thought to private and public advantages; and both kinds keep marvelously increasing.[78]

In *The Art of War,* among the characteristics of the early Romans which he wished to see re-introduced, he included:

> to esteem private less than public good.[79]

As an illustration of the use of the "common good" as a tactic, he suggested:

> it is wise . . . for a general when attacking a town to make every effort . . . showing them [the defenders] that he is acting not against the common good but against a few ambitious men in the city. This plan has many times made easier movements against cities and their capture. And though such pretenses are easily discerned, especially by prudent men, yet they often deceive the people, who, longing for immediate peace, close their eyes to all the traps hidden under such big promises.[80]

A major reason for Machiavelli's principle that for a city to be well-founded or effectively reformed it is necessary that one man concentrate in his own hands all power and exercise it for the general good, was that he assumed that the one securing, holding and exercising power is justified to define the "common-" or "public-good," to use force to compel others' support, and to differentiate reliably between the use of power "to restore" and the use of power "to destroy."[81]

Credence in the possibility that another can have the capacity to define for one, individually or collectively, "the good" and effectively to employ force in establishing it, is radically reinforced by the attitude toward the authority on the part of one who claims the desire to merge himself in subordination to it (above, p. 21).[82] Even so, notwithstanding the claim of voluntary, even enthusiastic, support on the part of some for the leadership, the necessity that force be used to make way for the establishment and maintenance of the authority is proof that it not only disregards existing human reality but proceeds on the assumption that it can overcome, destroy and annihilate the reality of and in another human being.

One additional attribute which Machiavelli considered essential for the wise founder or restorer of a princedom or a republic for the common good, was that he make practical provision for a broad-based government as the successor to his own rule. Thus,

> [The wise founder] ought, moreover, to be so prudent and high-minded that he will not leave to another as a heritage the authority he has seized, because, since men are more prone to evil than to good, his successor might use ambitiously what he had used nobly. Besides this, though one alone is suited for organizing, the government organized is not going to last long if resting on the shoulders of only one; but it is indeed lasting when it is left to the care of many, and when its maintenance rests upon many. The reason is that just as a large number are not suited to organize a government, because they do not understand what is good for it on account of their diverse opinions, so after they become familiar with it they do not agree to abandon it.[83]

As a precedent for such devolution of power, Machiavelli cited Romulus' creation of the Senate (Livy, I.viii, p. 11).[84] Livy wrote of Servius Tullius, also,

> Gentle and moderate as his sway had been, he had nevertheless, according to some authorities, formed the intention of laying it down, because it was vested in a single person, but this purpose of giving freedom to the State was cut short by that domestic crime.[85]

Moreover, when, at the request of Pope Leo X, Machiavelli was invited to offer his recommendations for remodeling the government of Florence, after the death of Lorenzo de'Medici, Duke of Urbino, he proposed that the Pope and Cardinal Giulio De'Medici provide, upon the death of both, just such a transfer of power to a broad popular base and republican institutions.[86]

In his "Life of Castruccio Castracani," Machiavelli perfected the design of the heroic founder through freely modifying the data from history and, according to Tommasini,[87] reviving the style of heroic biography associated with Plutarch and Lucien in his *Storie vere*.

Taking for granted the effectiveness of leadership, in the *Prince* he advocated imitation of ancient leaders:

> a prudent man will always choose to take paths beaten by great men and to imitate those who have been especially admirable, in order that if his ability does not reach theirs, at least it may offer some suggestion of it; and he will act like prudent archers, who, seeing that the mark they plan to hit is too far away and knowing what space can be covered by the power of their bows, take an aim much higher than their mark, not in order to reach with their arrows so great a height, but to be able, with the aid of so high an aim, to attain their purpose.[88]

He recognized an inherent relationship between the nature of "leadership" and military proficiency:

A wise prince, then, has no other object and no other interest and takes as his profession nothing else than war and its laws and discipline; that is the only profession fitting one who commands.[89]

Friedrich Meinecke, in his *Machiavellism, the Doctrine of Raison d'Etat and its Place in Modern History*,[90] has demonstrated the convenience and usefulness during the succeeding centuries of the model for founder and reformer which Machiavelli had delineated.

In Machiavelli's study of the ancients and in the annals of Florence, he perceived examples of such leadership and, at times, with respect to several of his contemporaries he dreamed of their potentialities for achieving it. Thus in the *Discourses* he wrote:

In support of what I have written above, I could give countless examples, such as Moses, Lycurgus, Solon, and other founders of kingdoms and republics, who, because they appropriated to themselves sole power, could form laws adapted to the common good;[91]

[Cleomenes] knew that he could not do this good to his fatherland if he did not become the only one in authority, since he saw that on account of the ambition of men he could not do good to the many against the will of the few;[92]

Duke Valentino, whose works I should always imitate if I were a new prince, realizing this necessity, made Messer Remirro President in Romagna: that decision made those people united, fearful of his authority, fond of his power, and trustful in it; and all the love they felt for him, which was great, considering his newness, resulted from this decision.[93]

Besides Moses, Lycurgus and Solon, from antiquity Machiavelli cited: Romulus,[94] Cyrus,[95] Theseus,[96] Hiero of Syracuse.[97] Hoping to stir young Medicean princes to heroic enterprises on behalf of Florence and Italy, he directed his dream first to Giuliano de'Medici, later Duke of Nemours,[98] and then to Lorenzo de'Medici, Duke of Urbino, to whom he dedicated the *Prince* and who was the object of his "Pastoral: The Ideal Ruler,"[99] and finally to Giovanni de'Medici, of the Black Bands.[100]

Of heroic quality, but peculiarly limited by fortune, was Castruccio Castracani of Lucca.[101]

In the course of his work on *The History of Florence,* he identified yet others who either fully or to a notable degree manifested such leadership: Theodoric,[102] Niccolo di Lorenzo,[103] Michele di Lando.[104]

Despite Machiavelli's emphasis on the necessity that one man alone be the

65

founder[105] or reformer of a state,[106] however clearly he conceptualized, dreamed of, yearned for, interpreted historical figures as examples of such heroic prowess, Machiavelli himself had his doubts. He wrote to his former chief, the exiled Soderini:

> Certainly anybody wise enough to understand the times and the types of affairs and to adapt himself to them would have always good fortune, or he would protect himself always from bad, and it would come to be true that the wise man would rule the stars and the Fates. But because there never are such wise men . . . it follows that Fortune varies and commands men and holds them under her yoke.[107]

Similarly, in his "Tercets on Fortune:"

> That man most luckily forms his plan, among all the persons in Fortune's palace, who chooses a wheel befitting her wish, since the inclinations that make you act, so far as they conform with her doings, are the causes of your good and your ill. Yet you cannot therefore trust yourself to her nor hope to escape her hard bite, her hard blows, violent and cruel, because while you are whirled about by the rim of a wheel that for the moment is lucky and good, she is wont to reverse its course in midcircle
> And since you cannot change your character nor give up the disposition that Heaven endows you with, in the midst of your journey she abandons you.
> Therefore, if this be understood and fixed in his mind, a man who could leap from wheel to wheel would always be happy and fortunate,
> but because to attain this is denied by the occult force that rules us, our condition changes with her course;[108]

and later in the same poem:

> Fortune, not that a man may remain on high carries him up, but that as he plunges down she may delight, and he as he falls may weep . . .
> We see at last that in days gone by few have been successful, and they have died before their wheel reversed itself or in turning carried them down to the bottom.[109]

Thus, only those appear to have their reputations preserved whom fortune had rescued by giving them a timely end. May Machiavelli have come upon Plutarch's comment regarding the actualization of the Stoics' ideal of the wise man:

> He is nowhere on earth nor ever has been?[110]

In the *Discourses* with great insight, Machiavelli analyzed psychological and moral aspects of the problem:

It was necessary, therefore, if Rome when corrupt was to keep herself free, that, just as in the course of her life she formed new laws, she should also form new basic methods, because the methods and ways of living suitable for adoption by a bad subject are not like those for a good one, nor can matter of entirely different sorts have the same form. But since these basic methods must be replaced either all at once, when they evidently are no longer good, or little by little, before they generally are recognized as bad, I say that both these things are almost impossible. The cause of any attempt to replace them little by little must be a prudent man who can see these evils at a great distance as they originate. Yet it can easily be that no man of that sort will ever appear in a city. And if indeed such a man does appear, never will he succeed in persuading others of what he himself understands, because when men are used to living in one way, they do not like to change, and so much the more when they do not look the evil in its face but need to have it indicated to them through reasoning. As to reforming these basic methods at one stroke, when everybody knows they are not good, I say that their injurious quality, then easily recognized, is hard to correct because to accomplish it the use of lawful devices is not enough, since lawful methods are futile, but it is necessary to resort to unlawful ones, such as violence and arms, and before anything else to become prince of that city and have power to manage it in one's own way. To reorganize a city for living under good government assumes a good man, and to become prince of a state by violence assumes an evil man; therefore a good man will seldom attempt to become prince by evil methods, even though his purpose be good; on the other hand, a wicked man, when he has become prince, will seldom try to do what is right, for it never will come into his mind to use rightly the authority he has gained wickedly. From all the things explained above comes the difficulty or impossibility of maintaining a government in a corrupt city or of setting up a new government there.[111]

Regarding the possibility that a man with the requisite qualities would appear when needed, Machiavelli had previously written in the *Discourses*:

I do not know that this has ever happened or if it can happen, because, as I said a little above, evidently when a city has declined by corruption of her matter, if ever she rises, she does so through the virtue of one man who is then living, not through the virtue of the masses in supporting good laws. And as soon as such a man is dead, she goes back to her early habits.[112]

In *The History of Florence* he wrote:

> I allow that when it comes about (and it seldom does come about) that by
> a city's good fortune a wise, good and powerful citizen gains power, who
> establishes laws and represses strife between the nobles and the people or
> so to restrain these parties that they cannot do evil, at such a time a city
> can be called free and her government can be considered firm and solid.[113]

However, even if such a wise, good and powerful citizen should appear
with the

> intention to advance not his own interest but the general good, not his own
> posterity but the common fatherland[114]

Machiavelli had serious doubts that the result would correspond to the good
citizen's original intent:

> Nobody should start a revolution in a city in the belief that later he can
> stop it at will or regulate it as he likes.[115]

Besides the already noted inadequately calculable resourcefulness of others in
plotting and taking revenge,[116] there is the tendency for an inner transformation
of the character and with it the objectives of the leader. In the *Discourses* he wrote:

> often the desire for victory so blinds men's perceptions that they see nothing
> except what appears to their advantage;[117]

> men make this blunder because they do not know how to put limits to their
> hopes. And when they rely on these and do not make an estimate of
> themselves, they fall.[118]

Moreover, as already indicated (above, pp. 52–53), Machiavelli perceived that
a gnawing concern over the unestimated possible consequences of the leader's
actions may seriously deflect his attention and energies.[119]

A general conclusion, expressed in the *Discourses,*

> no one will ever be so foolish or so wise, so bad or so good, that, if there
> is put before him the choice between the two kinds of men, he will not
> praise what is to be praised, and blame what is to be blamed. Yet, in the
> end, almost all, deceived by a false good and a false glory, allow themselves
> to go, either willingly or ignorantly, into the positions of those who deserve
> more blame than praise. And though able to set up a republic or a kingdom,
> they turn to tyranny,[120]

finds reaffirmation in *The History of Florence*:

> almost always . . . the more authority they [men] have, the worse they
> use it and the more overbearing they become.[121]

This tendency, he considered, accelerates, following a ruler's defeat of a conspiracy.[122] And, should there arise such a wise, good and powerful citizen who should have succeeded in concentrating power and using it for the common good to found or reform a state,

> since men are more prone to evil than to good . . . his successor might
> use ambitiously what he had used nobly,[123]

unless the reformer had accomplished leaving the power "to the care of many."[124]

In "history," as employed by Machiavelli to support his positions, may be recognized one of his most serviceable fictions. The weight which he gave to examples drawn from his reading of history requires examination of his attitude toward its validity. To "continual reading" of history along with his own official and personal experience, he attributed his "understanding of great men's actions."[125] Underlying his firm belief in the educative value to be derived from the purposive study of history are his two assumptions: first, that there is basic uniformity in human nature:

> Prudent men are in the habit of saying—and not by chance or without
> basis—that he who wishes to see what is to come should observe what
> has already happened, because all of the affairs of the world, in every age,
> have their individual counterparts in ancient times. The reason for this is
> that since they are carried on by men, who have and always have had the
> same passions, of necessity the same results appear;[126]

and

> men are born, live and die, always, with one and the same nature;[127]

> he who considers present affairs and ancient ones readily understands that
> all cities and all peoples have the same desires and the same traits and that
> they always have had them. He who diligently examines past events easily
> foresees future ones in every country and can apply to them the remedies
> used by the ancients or, not finding any that have been used, can devise
> new ones because of the similarity of the events;[128]

and the second assumption, that, seeing the little ability shown by men to curb the power of Fortune,[129] there is a cyclical pattern in events:

> In their normal variations, countries generally go from order to disorder

and then from disorder move back to order, because—since Nature does not allow worldly things to remain fixed—when they come to their utmost perfection and have no further possibility for rising, they must go down. Likewise, when they have gone down and through their defects have reached their lowest depths, they necessarily rise, since they cannot go lower. So always from good they go down to bad, and from bad rise up to good. Because ability brings forth quiet; quiet, laziness; laziness, disorder; disorder, ruin; likewise from ruin comes order; from order, ability; from the last, glory and good fortune. Therefore the discerning have noted that letters come after arms, and that in countries and cities generals are born earlier than philosophers. Because, after good and well-disciplined armies have brought forth victory, and their victories quiet, the virtue of military courage cannot be corrupted with a more honorable laziness than that of letters; nor with a greater and more dangerous deception can this laziness enter into well-regulated cities . . . By such means, then, countries come to ruin; and when they have suffered it, and their people through afflictions have grown wise, they return to good order, as I have said, unless indeed an unusual force keeps them stifled.[130]

These two assumptions contributed to a further one—that of knowledge of cause and effect which underlies his characteristic use of the conjunction "because." Commenting upon chapter 5 of Book 3 of *The History of Florence*,[131] Sydney Anglo has written:

The rigidly sequential character of Machiavelli's thought is here laid bare: his favorite conjunctions are "because", "by this means", and "whence arose";[132]

and later,

Machiavelli's favorite constructions begin with *because,* or some similar conjunction—*thus, for, therefore, whence,* and *hence*—and . . . these constructions mirror his clear-cut view of historical causation.[133]

Machiavelli saw in the purposeful study of history a power which

kindles free spirits, to imitation, . . .[or] to avoid and get rid of present abuses;[134]

when I see . . . that the most worthy activities which histories show us, which have been carried out in ancient kingdoms and republics by kings, generals, citizens, lawgivers, and others who have labored for their native land, are sooner admired than imitated (rather they are so much avoided by everyone in every least thing that no sign of that ancient worth remains among us) . . . This I believe comes not from the weakness into which the present religion has brought the world, or from the harm done to many

Christian provinces and cities by a conceited laziness, as much as from not having a true understanding of books on history, so that as we read we do not draw from them that sense or taste that flavor which they really have. From this it comes that great numbers who read take pleasure in hearing of the various events they contain, without thinking at all of imitating them, judging that imitation is not merely difficult but impossible, as if the sky, the sun, the elements, men were changed in motion, arrangement, and power from what they were in antiquity. Wishing, then, to get men away from this error, I have decided that on all the books by Titus Livius which the malice of the ages has not taken away from us, it is necessary that I write what, according to my knowledge of ancient and modern affairs, I judge necessary for the better understanding of them, in order that those who read these explanations of mine may more easily get from them that profit for which they sould seek acquaintance with books.[135]

Similarly, in the preface of Book 2:

I shall be bold in saying clearly what I learn about Roman times and the present, in order that the minds of the young men who read these writings of mine may reject the present and be prepared to imitate the past, whenever Fortune gives them opportunity. For it is the duty of a good man to teach others anything of value that through the malice of the times and of Fortune you have been unable to put into effect, in order that since many will know of it, some of them more loved by Heaven may be prepared to put it into effect.[136]

Indeed,

truly not without cause good historians, such as this one of ours, give certain events in detail and clearly, in order that those who come later may learn how in similar emergencies they can defend themselves.[137]

The study of history he considered to be essentially significant for a prince:

as to the training of the mind, the prudent prince reads histories and observes in them the actions of excellent men, sees how they have conducted themselves in wars, observes the causes for their victories and defeats, in order to escape the latter and imitate the former; above all, he does as some excellent men have done in the past; they selected for imitation some man earlier than themselves who was praised and honored, and his actions and heroic deeds they always kept before them;[138]

and also for republics:

If any reading is useful to citizens who govern republics, it is that which shows the causes of the hatreds and factional struggles within the city, in order that such citizens having grown wise through the sufferings of others, can keep themselves united;[139]

If the experiences of any republic are moving, those of a man's own city, when he reads about them, are much more moving and more useful.[140]

The same thesis underlies *The Art of War*. In the dedicatory preface he wrote:

If we consider ancient ways, we shall not find things that are more closely united, more in conformity, and of which one, necessarily, so much loves the other as do these [civil and military life] . . . judging from what I have seen and read. . . . it is not impossible to bring military practice back to ancient methods and to restore some of the forms of earlier excellence.[141]

Machiavelli recognized, however, that surviving records of past events could not be accepted as a pure reflection of them and relied upon as infallible sources for practical wisdom:

about ancient affairs we do not know the whole truth, and usually things are concealed that would bring those times bad repute, and other things that would bring them glory are made splendid and tremendous.[142]

He perceived that destruction of ancient records due to natural and social cataclysms has as a consequence that facts become mixed with fables and myths:

As to the causes that come from Heaven, they are those that wipe out the race of men and bring down to a few the inhabitants of part of the world, either through plagues or through famine or through a flood. The most important is this last, both because it is the most universal and because those who are saved are all mountaineers and ignorant men who, having no knowledge of anything ancient, cannot leave it to posterity. If among them anybody is saved who has any knowledge of antiquity, he conceals and modifies it as suits him, to get himself a reputation and a name, so that for his successors, what he has chosen to write about it remains, and nothing more;[143]

On the rise of a new sect, that is, a new religion, its first effort, in order to give itself reputation, is to extinguish the old, and when the founders of the new sect are of a different language, they blot it out easily . . . But because these sects change two or three times in five or six thousand years, we have lost the record of things done before that time, and if there does remain any trace of them, it is looked upon as fabulous, and no faith is put in it. This applies to the history of Diodorus Siculus, which, though it gives an account of forty or fifty thousand years, yet is reputed—truly I believe—full of lies.[144]

Furthermore, by faulty analysis, letting themselves indulge in contradictions, historians sometimes obscure the implications of the events:

Hannibal's well-known inhuman cruelty . . . together with his numberless abilities, made him always respected and terrible in the soldiers' eyes; without it, his other abilities would not have been enough to get him that result. Yet historians, in this matter not very discerning, on one side admire this achievement of his [keeping united and fit for action "a very large army, a mixture of countless sorts of men, led to service in foreign lands"] and on the other condemn its main cause.[145]

Personal considerations at times render accounts untrustworthy.

If these very noble writers held back in order not to injure the memory of those whom they were going to discuss, they deceived themselves and showed that they did not understand the ambition of men and the desire they have to perpetuate the names of their ancestors and of themselves; these historians did not remember that many who have not had opportunity to gain fame with praiseworthy deeds have striven to gain it with blameworthy actions, nor did they consider that conspicuous actions such as those of government and state, however they are carried on or whatever outcome they have, are always looked upon as bringing their doers honor rather than censure.[146]

To one distortion, he found historians especially prone:

He who considers the continent of Europe, then, finds that it has been full of republics and princedoms . . . And even though in comparison with the Romans few others are named, that results from the malice of historians who follow Fortune; usually they are satisfied to honor the conquerors;[147]

Most writers are so subservient to the fortunes of conquerors as not merely, in order to make their victories splendid, to increase what they have done ably, but also to give such renown to the actions of their enemies that anyone born afterward in either of the two lands, whether the victorious or the defeated, has reason to wonder at those times, and is obliged to praise them and love them to the utmost;[148]

Nor should anyone be deceived by the glory of Caesar, on seeing him especially celebrated by the historians, for those who praise him are bribed by his fortune and awed by the long duration of the Empire, which, being ruled under his name, did not allow writers to speak freely of him. But a reader wishing to know what free historians would say of Caesar, may see what they say of Cataline, for Caesar is so much the more blameworthy in proportion as one is more to blame who has done evil than one who has intended to do it. Let a reader observe too with what great praises they laud Brutus, as though unable to blame Caesar because of his power, they laud his enemy.[149]

Concerning the impact on Machiavelli of the concept of one man as founder or reformer of a state, Tommasini concluded:

Pertanto quel suo ideale di principe nuovo, secondo il logico divisamento ch'ei n'ebbe concepito, non prese mai corpo; e, avesse pur potuto farsi reale ed estrinseco, chi sa se non l'avrebbe la fortuna reietto, come abbandonò e schiantò già il Valentino, che ne parve l'esempio più prossimo; dacchè la natura non tollera dagli uomini la pretensione de mettere giudizio a lei e valere nell'andamento cosmico da più che da coefficienti. E se il Machiavelli sperò che, mercè d'un uomo solo, potesse seguire il risorgimento di tutta la patria decaduta, fu il desiderio ardentissimo del bene, fu la sua fiducia nelle reazioni cicliche per cui dal disordine si torna all'ordine, fu il suo conforto paradossale "che il vero modo ad andare in paradiso è imperare la via dell'inferno" che gli fecero velo a poteron lasciargli per un istante lusinga che l'indipendenza e sicurtà nazionale potesse altronde sorgere che dal consentimento virtuoso, caldo, appassionato della nazione intera.[150]

However, that ideal of his of a new prince, in accordance with the logical arrangement he had conceived for it, never took form; and even if it had been made real and manifest, who knows if fortune would not have rejected it as it already had abandoned and broken Valentino who seemed the nearest example of it; since nature does not tolerate from men the pretension of passing judgment on her and of being worth more in the cosmic scale than a contributing factor. And if Machiavelli hoped that, thanks to one man alone, the resurrection of a whole decadent country might follow, was it his very ardent desire for the good, was it his belief in the cyclical reaction through which from disorder there turns to order, was it his paradoxical encouragement "that the true way for going to paradise is to explore the way to hell," that so placed a veil over him as to enable him for an instant to hope that the independence and security of the nation could be able to arise other than from the virtuous, warm, impassioned consent of the entire nation.

Machiavelli does not appear to relate the admitted historical infrequency, or perhaps total absence, of success on the part of those attempting such leadership to the incongruity and irrationality in the effort of one human being to impose his will and his definition of "good" upon others. Nor does he seem ever to suspect that that process itself, in light of human individuality, inherently and necessarily engenders an intensity of misunderstanding and ignorance which eventuates in mutual recrimination and the attribution of inherent evil to human beings. Insofar as they "follow Fortune" and "honor the conquerors," historians' accounts tend to give the impression that wilful imposition upon others is effective in human affairs and to bring too infrequently the consequences into focus with regard to those apparently successful only because the protagonists

> have died before their wheel reversed itself or in turning carried them down to the bottom.[151]

The failure to register and evaluate the unacceptability of coercion against human beings is observable also in some contemporary presentations of history as a source for role-models for conduct, thus Martin Fleischer:

> It is by regarding history (the arena of politico-military deeds) and not by contemplating themselves that men can come to recognize themselves—to rediscover their capacity for great deeds and also to learn the principles of the sustained greatness of states. For it is in public life that the passions find their most appropriate stage, a stage on which they can act and in turn win public recognition. To know the world of affairs at any time is at the same time to know one's own world and one's self. The Socratic injunction is sharply redirected. If Socrates gave the inquiring mind a new program when he called upon men to turn from the study of natural and cosmological phenomena and to redirect their gaze inward in an examination of the ethical basis of life, Machiavelli's proposal represents the turning to a third tradition which seeks *vera cognizione* in the inspiration and analysis of politico-historical experience.
>
> From the central principle, echoed in all of Machiavelli's writings, that men are the same in all ages, also derives the prudential or realistic element in Machiavelli's hope that Italy can be saved. This hope links *The Prince* and the *Discourses* [author's note: to which might well be added *The Art of War.*] In the last chapter of the former, Machiavelli also tries to dispel the sense of hopelessness that overwhelms people when they are confronted with the enormous task of revitalizing Italy by again arguing that what was possible in the past is possible in the present. The amount of *virtù* and prudence in the world does not change from age to age. (An observation also repeated in *The History of Florence*). The *Animo* remains as expansive and as capable of greatness as ever. Hence political vitality and greatness are not limited to Italy's past. If the Florentines would only recognize themselves in their ancestors they would soon discover their own political energies and talents. The *virtù* and prudence of Machiavelli the writer and advisor is to help revitalize this political *virtù* and prudence. Almost unnoticed, Machiavelli has advanced a highly ambitious claim for the political thinker. And to judge by his longevity, Machiavelli, our man of *grandezza d'animo*, has achieved his end—succeeding generations have turned to him to receive the inspiration of political *virtù* no less than that of political prudence.[152]

Through the sixteenth and the following four centuries, through Machiavelli, Richelieu, Frederick the Great, Hegel, Marx, Hitler, Stalin, Mao, Begin, there developed the fictionalization of the power apparatus into corporate entities each endowed with its own interest, life, will, and a secularized conscience which in the arrogance of the claim of absolute right endeavored by force either to silence or kill off opposition and refashion "reality" to accord with the respective specially conceived pattern. Through resort to, or advocacy of, extreme measures, they considered it possible to establish their artificial structures on the assumption that, as Machiavelli wrote,

> a dead man cannot be concerned with revenge.[153]

History, as a guide and manual for the effective use of force, required, in Machiavelli's hands, repeated editing and even re-creation. Although he dissociated himself from those who

> have fancied for themselves republics and principalities that have never been seen or known to exist in reality

on the grounds that

> since my purpose is to write something useful to him who comprehends it, I have decided that I must concern myself with the truth of the matter as facts show it rather than with any fanciful notion,[154]

and claimed to confine his observations to evidence given by the records of history and his own experience, as Sydney Anglo has noted,[155] he selected, manipulated and reconstructed events and personalities of history into an instrument for putting forward and substantiating his basic principles so that, under the guise of his findings in his search "for the truth of the matter as facts show it," he achieved a new work of art which he valued more highly than the facts which he purported to present. Leo Strauss, in his *Thoughts on Machiavelli,* shows that Machiavelli made a similar use of Livy's *History*[156] and that, for such procedure, Machiavelli recognized that Livy himself had provided a model. In the *Discourses* Machiavelli wrote:

> Among the splendid things that our historian [i.e., Livy] makes Camillus say and do, in order to show what an excellent man is, he puts in his mouth these words . . . [157]

Treatment as known facts of matters requiring further participant observation and systematic research, occasioned some of the most basic fictions encountered in Machiavelli's writings. Examples of such prime assumptions are:

76

1. that in time of peace there is no place for everybody (above, pp. 14–15);[158]

2. that one's security requires power over others (above, pp. 14–15, 33, 36);[159]

3. that the nature of human nature is predictably known, that there is valid basis for adjudging and executing judgment on others as "good" and "evil" and that it is inherently "evil" (above, pp. 33–36);[160]

4. that one man can attain and exercise effective leadership over others (above, pp. 65–67),[161] due to the susceptibility of the generality of men to the pressures of necessity and to appearances (above, pp. 33–34);[162]

5. that force exercised by the one against others can be effective;[163] at times, through exploitation of awe[164] (above pp. 49–51; 54, 65); or through discounting the inclination of the living to avenge the dead[165] (above, p. 76); (Indeed, Felix Gilbert has written:

   the dominating idea in these two works [the *Prince* and the *Discourses*] is an appeal to recognize the crucial importance of force in politics);[166]

6. that public purpose can transmute into benefits behavior which, if indulged in for private ends, would occasion injury and ruin[167] (above, pp. 49–51, 65);

7. that force is ingenerate in the coming-to-be and in the maintenance of states due to their requirements of:

   Love for a man's native land is caused by nature;[168]

   another cause—a very great one—makes men conspire against a prince: this is the desire for liberating their native land which he has conquered . . .From this passion no tyrant can protect himself except by laying down his tyranny;[169]

   An army that is to win a battle must be made so confident as to believe it will win in any case. It becomes confident when well armed and organized and when each man knows the others; such confidence and organization cannot appear except in soldiers who are born and live together;[170]

if we wish to give a rule that anybody will be able to use, we must say every republic and every kingdom must draw its soldiers from its own countries, hot or cold, or temperate as they may be. Because ancient examples show that in every country training can produce good soldiers, because where nature fails, the lack can be supplied by ingenuity, which in this case is more important than nature;[171]

never did anybody establish a republic or a kingdom who did not suppose that the same persons who inhabited it would need with their weapons to defend it;[172]

[the Romans] believed that the inhabitants were not worthy to have those goods they could not protect;[173]

An army evidently cannot be good if it is not trained, and it cannot be trained if it is not made up of your subjects. Because a country is not always at war and cannot be, she must train her army in times of peace, and she cannot apply this training to others than subjects, on account of the expense;[174]

a wise prince takes care to base himself on what is his own not on what is another's;[175]

I shall never hesitate to use as an example Cesare Borgia and his actions . . . never was he esteemed high until everybody saw that he was sole master of his own troops;[176]

I conclude, then, that without her own armies no princedom is secure; on the contrary, she is entirely dependent on Fortune, not having strength that in adversity loyally defends her. Wise men have always said and believed that "nothing is so weak or shaky as the reputation of a power that does not rely on its own strength." [Tacitus, *Annals 13.19*] Armies of your own are those made up of your subjects or of citizens of your state or of dependents;[177]

One can . . . observe . . . how much difference there is between an army that is satisfied and fights for its own glory and an army that is ill disposed and fights for some leader's ambition . . . in these [mercenary] armies where there is no affection for him in whose behalf they fight, so that they do not become his partisans, there never can be enough military vigor to resist an enemy who has a little of that vigor. And because this love and this eagerness to excell cannot spring up in others than your own subjects, it is necessary, if you expect to maintain a republic or a kingdom, to provide yourself an army of your own subjects, as we see they all have done who have gained great advantages with their armies;[178]

Whereas it has been observed by the Magnificent and Exalted Signors that all republics which in times past have preserved and increased themselves have always had as their chief basis two things, to wit, justice and arms, in order to restrain and to govern their subjects, and in order to defend themselves from their enemies . . . and since through long experience, indeed with great expense and danger, she [your republic] has learned how little hope it is possible to place in foreign and hired arms, because when they are numerous and of high repute they are either unendurable or suspected, and if they are few and without reputation, they are of no use, these signors judge it well that she should be armed with her own weapons and with her own men;[179]

It is a contradiction to say that a wise man finds fault with the citizen army . . . I tell you that no military force can be employed that is more useful than one's own, and that one cannot provide one's own army except in this way [i.e., by a citizen army];[180]

Pocock has noted:

Bruni . . . in the *De Militia* [1421] and the *Oratio Funebris* of seven years later, address[ed] himself to the idealization of the citizen as warrior and the warrior as citizen. It was already in the civic tradition to do this—Petrarch had noticed as one of the highest manifestations of the Roman triumph of *virtus* over *fortuna* that any army of citizens was prepared *pro libertate tuenda recta fronte mori*—and it was part of the Periclean ethos which Bruni was adapting to express Florentine values that the supreme good, the supreme devotion of oneself to the public good, might be to embody in one's life as many virtues as one man might display and then offer them all to the city in a sacrificial death.[181]

79

b)   an aggressive posture:

it is impossible for a republic to succeed in standing still and
enjoying its liberties in the narrow confines, because if she
does not molest some other, she will be molested, and from
being molested rises the wish and the necessity for expansion;
and when she does not have an enemy outside, she finds him
at home, as it seems necessarily happens to all great states;[182]

if you try to make a people so numerous and so well-armed
that it can produce a great empire, you make it such that you
cannot manage it as you wish. If you keep it either small or
unarmed, so that you can manage it, when you gain territory
you cannot hold it, or your state becomes so weak that you
are the prey of whoever assails you . . . If anyone sets out,
therefore, to organize a state from the beginning, he needs to
examine whether he wishes it to expand like Rome, in dominion
and power, or whether it is to remain within narrow limits. In
the first case, it is necessary to organize it like Rome and to
give scope to disturbances and discords among the inhabitants,
as well as one can, because without a large number of men,
and well armed, a republic never can grow larger, or, if it does
grow larger, never can maintain itself . . . since all human
affairs are in motion and cannot remain fixed, they must needs
rise up or sink down; to many things to which reason does not
bring you, you are brought by necessity. Hence, if a republic
is so organized that she is adapted to maintaining herself, provided she does not grow, and necessity then forces her to grow,
the process will remove her foundations and make her fall more
speedily. Thus, on the other side, if Heaven is so kind to her
that she does not have to make war, the effect might be that
ease would make her effeminate or divided; these two things
together, or either one alone, would cause her ruin. Therefore,
since I believe it impossible to balance these affairs or to keep
exactly this middle way, it is essential in organizing cities to
think of the most honorable courses, and to organize them in
such a way that if necessity causes them to grow, they can
keep what they have taken. To return to the beginning of our
discussion, then, I believe the Roman method must be followed,
and not that of the other states, because to find a course half
way between one and the other I believe not possible. Those
enmities rising between the people and the Senate must be
borne, being taken as an evil necessary to the establishment
of Roman greatness. Besides the other reasons I brought for-

ward when I showed the authority of the Senate necessary as
a guard for liberty, I easily observe the benefit a republic gains
from the right to make changes.[183]

The originality of Machiavelli's

> impartial advice to all parties and persons to acquire when they
> can

and its significant contribution to the development of the idea of the "impersonality of the modern state," Mansfield has perceptively indicated.[184]

    c)   a sustained, non-violent tension between domestic classes with
        externally-directed aggression:

> nothing makes a republic so firm and solid as to give her such
> an organization that the laws provide her a way for the discharge
> of the partisan hatreds that agitate her;[185]

> It always has been and always will be true that in republics
> great and exceptional men are neglected in times of peace; at
> such times envy of the reputation their ability gives them raises
> in many citizens a desire to be not merely their equals but their
> superiors . . . We see, then, that republics show this defect:
> they pay slight attention to capable men in quiet times. This
> condition makes such men feel injured in two ways: first, they
> fail to attain their proper rank; second, they are obliged to have
> as associates and superiors men who are unworthy and of less
> ability than themselves. This abuse in republics has produced
> much turmoil, because those citizens who see themselves un-
> deservedly rejected, and know that they can be neglected only
> in times that are easy and not perilous, make an effort to disturb
> them by stirring up new wars to the damage of the republic.
> When I consider possible remedies, I find two: the first is to
> keep the citizens poor, so that, when without goodness and
> wisdom, they cannot corrupt themselves or others with riches;
> the second is to arrange that such republics will continually
> make war, and therefore always will need citizens of high
> repute, like the Romans in their early days. Because that city
> always kept armies in the field, she always needed able men.
> Hence she could not take a position from one who deserved it
> and give it to one who did not deserve it;[186]

> every city ought to have methods with which the people can
> express their ambition, and especially those cities that intend
> to make use of the people in important affairs;[187]

The serious and natural enmities between the people and the nobles, caused by the latter's wish to rule and the former's not to be enthralled, bring about all the evils that spring up in cities; by this opposition of parties all the other things that disturb republics are nourished. This kept Rome disunited . . . the enmities that at the outset existed in Rome between the people and the nobles were ended by debating, . . . terminated by law, . . . in Rome always increased military power, . . . in Rome brought that city from an equality of citizens to a very great inequality . . . the people of Rome wished to enjoy supreme honors along with the nobles . . . the Roman people's desire was more reasonable [than the Florentines'], their injuries to the nobles were more endurable, so that the nobility yielded easily and without coming to arms; hence, after some debates, they agreed in making a law with which the people would be satisfied and by which the nobles would remain in their public offices, . . . From this it also resulted that through the people's victories the city of Rome became more excellent, because, along with the nobles, men from the people could be appointed to administer the magistracies, the armies, and the high offices; thus the latter acquired the same ability the former had, and that city, as she increased in excellence, increased in power;[188]

those who condemn the dissensions between the nobility and the people seem to me to be finding fault with what as a first cause kept Rome free, and to be considering the quarrels and the noise that resulted from those dissensions rather than the good effects they brought about; they are not considering that in every republic there are two opposed factions, that of the people and that of the rich, and that all the laws made in favor of liberty result from their discord.[189]

Herein Machiavelli has been considered to have departed furthest from Christian principles. Pocock has written:

perhaps the most disturbing suggestions in all Machiavelli's writings are that the republic cannot rest on a simply Christian morality, that it must pay the price of a high incidence of social conflict at home, and that it must pursue a career of war and conquest abroad.[190]

Through using the tensions generated in domestic discords and diverting them into foreign conflicts, and through deceptively transforming "allies"[191] into what today would be termed "satellites," Rome exemplified for Machiavelli the drive for power which achieves the great state and a citizenry qualified for the magnitude of action essential in human history. Alfredo Bonadeo has pointed out:

> Machiavelli has been credited for "first assigning a positive social and political value to domestic conflicts," and his reflections and emphasis upon conflict are said to represent "a radical break with the classical-medieval tradition of political thought [Neal Wood, "Some Reflections on Sorel and Machiavelli," *Political Science Quarterly,* 83 (1968), p. 85]. Machiavelli did assign positive value to conflicts only under particular circumstances.[192]

> By comparing the failure of Florentine dissensions and conflicts with the success of those of Rome, Machiavelli stressed the vital role dissension and conflict can play, and indeed have played; he, moreover, stressed the necessity of nonviolence and coexistence for opposing classes and parties, for it is only on this basis that the power of a country is maintained and increased, and the common good fulfilled.[193]

> in Machiavelli's thought, dissensions and conflicts differ according to their nature and results. If they are not marked by violence, and if the citizens involved in them endeavor to compromise and to reach some agreement so that the common good is enhanced, they play a useful and essential role in the life of the commonwealth. If, however, dissensions and conflicts do not meet these standards, then they are nothing but manifestations of rivalry for power and wealth among factions, and as such, they disregard the common good.[194]

That this behavior attributed by Machiavelli to the Romans has deep phylogenetic roots seems to be borne out in findings by the natural scientist Konrad Lorenz:

> The principle of the bond formed by having something in common which has to be defended against outsiders remains the same, from cichlids defending a common territory or brood, right up to scientists defending a common opinion and—most dangerous of all—fanatics defending a common ideology. In all these cases, aggression is necessary to enhance the bond;[195]

> it is quite typical of man that his most noble and admirable qualities are brought to the fore in situations involving the killing of other men, just as noble as they are;[196]

> militant enthusiasm is a specialized form of communal aggres-

sion, clearly distinct from and yet functionally related to the more primitive forms of petty individual aggression;[197]

militant enthusiasm is an instinctive response with a phylogenetically determined releasing mechanism . . . Like the triumph ceremony of the greylag goose, militant enthusiasm in man is a true autonomous instinct: it has its own appetitive behavior, its own releasing mechanisms, and, like the sexual urge or any other strong instinct, it engenders a feeling of intense satisfaction;[198]

Militant enthusiasm can be elicited with the predictability of a reflex when the following environmental situations arise. First of all, a social unit with which the subject identifies himself must appear to be threatened by some danger from outside. That which is threatened may be a concrete group of people, the family or a little community of close friends, or else it may be a larger social unit held together and symbolized by its own specific social norms and rites . . . A second key stimulus which contributes enormously to the release of intense militant enthusiasm is the presence of a hated enemy from whom the threat to the above "values" emanates. This enemy, too, can be of a concrete or of an abstract nature . . . A third factor contributing to the environmental situation eliciting the response is an inspiring leader figure . . . A fourth, and perhaps the most important prerequisite for the full eliciting of militant enthusiasm is the presence of many other individuals, all agitated by the same emotion. Their absolute number has a certain influence on the quality of the response. Smaller numbers at issue with a large majority tend to obstinate defense with the emotional value of "making a last stand," while very large numbers inspired by the same enthusiasm feel the urge to conquer the whole world in the name of their sacred cause. Here the laws of mass enthusiasm are strictly analogous to those of flock formation described in Chapter Eight.[199]

d)   manifestation and validation of a "whole" through sacrifice of some of the parts (above, pp. 46–48); elimination of those deprived of actual rule or its anticipation;[200] elimination of leaders of disorders in a divided city;[201] elimination of the envious;[202] political surgery and periodic exemplary punishments;[203]

from one such enforcement of the law to the next, there should be a lapse of not more than ten years, because, when that time has gone by, men change their habits and break the laws, and

84

if something does not happen to bring the penalty back to their memories and renew fear in their minds, so many offenders quickly join together that they cannot be punished without danger;[204]

men individually and a city as a whole sin sometimes against a state, so that, for an example to others, for security to himself, a prince has no other remedy than to destroy them. And honor consists in being able and knowing how to punish such a city, not in being able with a thousand perils to hold her. For that prince who does not punish him who errs, in such a way that he cannot afterward err, is held ignorant or worthless.[205]

e) a good military organization:

all the arts that are provided for in a state for the sake of the common good of men, all the statutes made in it so that men will live in fear of the laws and of God, would be vain if for them there were not provided defenses, which when well ordered, preserve them, even though they themselves are not well ordered. And so . . . good customs, without military support, suffer the same sort of injury as do the rooms of a splendid and kingly palace, even though ornamented with gems and gold, when, not being roofed over, they have nothing to protect them from the rain;[206]

though elsewhere [the *Prince*, chap. 12, Gilbert, I, 47: *Discourses*, 1, 4, ibid., p. 202; 21, ibid., pp. 246–47] I have said that the foundation of all states is good military organization, and that where this does not exist there cannot be good laws or anything else good, I think repetition not superfluous, because at every point in reading Livy's *History* this certainty appears;[207]

Men, steel, money, and bread are the sinews of war; but of these four the most necessary are the first two, because men and steel find money and bread, but bread and money do not find men and steel;[208]

wherever there are good soldiers there must be good government, and it seldom happens that such a city does not also have good Fortune;[209]

among private men laws, writings and agreements, make them keep their word; but among princes nothing but arms makes them keep it;[210]

Force and necessity . . . not writings and obligations, make princes keep their agreements.[211]

f)   a successful war policy:

when power and territory increase, enmity and envy likewise increase; from these things result war and loss;[212]

the Romans did what all wise princes do: these take thought not merely for present discords but also for future ones, and the latter they forestall with every sort of ingenuity; when foreseen far ahead, discords can easily be remedied, but when you wait until they are upon you, the medicine is not in time; they have grown incurable . . . Hence the Romans, seeing their troubles far ahead, always provided against them, and never let them continue in order to avoid a war, because they knew that such a war is not averted but is deferred to the other side's advantage . . . Nor did they ever approve what all day is in the mouths of the wise men of our age: to profit from the help of time; but they did profit from that of their own vigor and prudence. Time indeed drives all things onward and can take with him good as well as bad, bad as well as good;[213]

A wise prince . . . has no other object and no other interest and takes as his profession nothing else than war and its laws and discipline; that is the only profession fitting one who commands, and it is of such effectiveness that it not merely sustains in their rank men who are born princes but many times enables men born in a private station to rise to princely stations . . . A wise prince, then, never withdraws his thought from training for war; in peace he trains himself for it more than in time of war. He does this in two ways, the first with his actions, the second with his mind. As to his actions, besides keeping his subjects well organized and trained, he himself continually goes hunting in order to accustom himself to hardships . . . but as to the training of his mind, the prudent prince reads histories and observes in them the actions of excellent men;[214]

it is truer than any other truth that if where there are men there are not soldiers, the cause is a deficiency in the prince and not a deficiency in the position or nature of the country;[215]

When a prince or a republic is willing to undergo toil and put effort into these methods and this training, always it is true that in his country there are good soldiers. Such princes are superior to their neighbors; they give laws and do not take them from other men;[216]

among the chief privileges the Roman people gave to a citizen was that he would not be forced against his will to serve as a soldier. Rome, then, while she was well governed (which was up to the time of the Gracchi) did not have any soldier who took this pursuit as his profession, and for that reason she had few bad ones, and all of those were severely punished. A well-ordered city will then decree that this practice of warfare shall be used in times of peace for exercise and in times of war for necessity and for glory, and will allow the public alone to practice it as a profession, as did Rome. Any citizen who in such an activity has another purpose is not a good citizen, and any city that conducts itself otherwise is not well governed;[217]

kings, if they wish to live securely, make up their infantry of men who, when it is time to make war, gladly for love of them go into it, and when peace comes, more gladly return home—which will always happen when a king selects men who know how to live by some other profession than this. So he must see to it than when peace comes his chief men return to their people, his gentlemen to the management of their property, and the infantry to their individual occupations. Each one of these will gladly make war in order to have peace, and will not seek to disturb the peace in order to have war;[218]

when men are brought into military service on the demand of the prince, they will come to it not altogether through force nor altogether voluntarily, because free will alone would cause all the difficulties I spoke of above: namely, that there would not be a selection and there would be few who would go; and likewise pure force would produce evil results. Therefore one ought to take a middle course, in which there would not be force alone nor free will alone, but the men will be so influenced by respect for their prince that they will fear his anger more than immediate inconvenience. And it will always happen that this will be a force mixed with free will in such a way that from it will not arise such discontent as to produce bad effects;[219]

It always has been, and it is reasonable that it should be, the object of those who go to war to enrich themselves and to impoverish the enemy, nor is victory sought for any other reason or gains wished for anything else than to make oneself powerful and weaken one's opponent. From this it follows that whenever your victory impoverishes you or your gain weakens you, you must either have passed beyond or not have reached the goal for which wars are made. A prince (and a republic also) is made rich by victories and by wars in which he destroys his enemies and is master of the booty and the ransom money; a prince is impoverished by victories who, though he conquers his enemies, cannot destroy them, and not he but his soldiers get the booty and the ransom money. In defeats, such a prince is unfortunate and in victories very unfortunate; if defeated, he suffers injuries from his enemies; if victorious, from his friends. Injuries from his friends, as less reasonable, are less easily borne, especially since he is obliged to lay upon his subjects the weight of taxes and fresh vexations. If he has in him any humanity, he cannot altogether rejoice in any victory for which all his subjects lament. Ancient and well-ordered republics, as the result of their victories, usually filled their treasuries with silver and gold, distributed gifts to the people, remitted tribute to their subjects, and with games and splendid shows entertained them;[220]

The prince spends either his own money and that of his subjects, or that of others. In the first case the wise prince is economical: in the second he does not omit any sort of liberality. For that prince who goes out with his armies, who lives on plunder, on booty, and on ransom, has his hands on the property of others; for him this liberality is necessary; otherwise he would not be followed by his soldiers. Of wealth that is not yours or your subjects', you can be a very lavish giver, as were Cyrus, Caesar, and Alexander, because to spend what belongs to others does not lessen your reputation but adds to it. Nothing hurts you except to spend your own money;[221]

Whoever makes war through choice or ambition has the intention of making gains and keeping them, and of acting in such a way as to enrich his city and his country and not to make them poor. He must, then, both in the gaining and in the keeping, take care not to spend, but rather to do everything to the profit of the public. He who wishes to do these things must hold to the Roman custom and method. This, first of all, was to make their wars, as the French say, short and big. Coming into the field with large armies, they finished in a very short time their wars . . . On observing all the wars they fought from the founding of Rome to the siege of Veii, we see that they finished them all, some in six, some in ten, some in twenty days . . . As soon as war was declared, they led their armies against the enemy and at once fought a battle. When this was won, the enemy, so that their country would not be completely laid waste, came to terms, and the Romans fined them in land;

this land they changed into private property or assigned to a colony. This colony, placed on the frontiers of the vanquished, became a guard of the Roman boundaries, with profit to the colonists who received those fields and with profit to the Roman public, which without expense kept up this garrison . . . They kept on using this method until they changed their procedure in war. This happened after the siege of Veii, during which, to be able to carry on the war for a long time, they arranged to pay the soldiers, whom before, since it was not necessary because the wars were short, they did not pay.

Though the Romans paid their soldiers, and therefore could make their wars longer, and when they made them at a greater distance necessity kept their armies longer in the field, nevertheless they never varied from their first method of finishing wars quickly, according to the place and the time; nor did they ever vary from sending out colonies. To their first rule, that of making wars short, they were kept not only by natural habit but by the ambition of the Consuls, who, holding office only one year and having to spend six months of that year at Rome, wished to finish a war in order to triumph . . . They [the Romans] did somewhat change their custom about the spoil, with which they were not so liberal as they had been earlier, both because it was not so necessary when the soldiers had their pay and because, since the spoil was greater, they planned so to increase the public funds with it that they would not have to carry on expeditions by means of taxes from the city . . . These two methods, then, that of distributing the booty, and that of sending colonies, caused Rome to grow rich by war, though other princes and unwise republics grow poor;[222]

Only those wars are just that are necessary; and arms are holy when there is no hope apart from them;[223]

arms and force . . . ought to be reserved for the last place, where and when other methods do not suffice.[224]

8. that knowledge of cause and effect in human affairs is available due to: uniformities (above, pp. 69–72);[225] to cycles (above, pp. 69–70);[226] and to such supplementary factors as:

"Accident"—(credited with too many events for listing);

"Chance"—in "The (Golden) Ass," his benefactress consoled him:

Through your own fault this did not overtake you, as it happens to some, but because Chance was opposed to your good conduct. Chance closed upon you the gates of pity above all when she led you into this place so savage and strong;[227]

and in a letter to his nephew:

As in many of my letters I have said to you, Chance, since you left, has done the worst for me that she can, so that I am brought down to a condition enabling me to do little good to myself and less to others.[228]

"Fate(s)"—clearly allied to "Chance," if not interchangeable. His benefactress in "The (Golden) Ass" advised him:

Not yet has Heaven altered its opinion, nor will alter it, while the Fates keep toward you their hard purpose . . . that Providence which supports the human species intends you to bear this affliction for your greater good.[229]

In his most celebrated letter, that of 10 December 1513 to Vettori:

So mixed up with these lice [usually a butcher, a miller, two furnace tenders, at the local inn], I keep my brain from growing mouldy, and satisfy the malice of this fate of mine, being glad to have her drive me along this road, to see if she will be ashamed of it;[230]

However, before disaster had overtaken Machiavelli personally, to the exiled ex-gonfalonier he had written in previous years:

frequently after long prosperity a man who finally loses does not in any way blame himself but acccuses the heavens and the action of the fates.[231]

"Fortune"—a power inverse to a man's ability:

in the world most men let themselves be mastered by Fortune;[232]

As I am well aware, many have believed and now believe human affairs so controlled by Fortune and by God that men with their prudence cannot manage them—yes, more, that men have no recourse against the world's variations.

Such believers therefore decide that they need not sweat much over man's activities but can let Chance govern them . . . Thinking on these variations, I myself now and then incline in some respects to their belief. Nonetheless, in order not to annul our free will, I judge it true that Fortune may be mistress of one half of our actions but that even she leaves the other half, or almost, under our control;[233]

where men have little ability, Fortune shows her power much, and because she is variable, republics and states often vary, and vary they always will until some one arises who is so great a lover of antiquity that he will rule Fortune in such a way that she will not have cause to show in every revolution of the sun how much she can do;[234]

greatly displeasing to Fortune is he who does well;[235]

it is the duty of a good man to teach others anything of value that through the malice of the times and of Fortune you have been unable to put into effect, in order that since many will know of it, some of them more loved by Heaven may be prepared to put it into effect.[236]

"Heaven(s)"

If we observe carefully how human affairs go on, many times we see that things come up and events take place against which the Heavens do not wish any provision to be made. And if this I am going to speak of happened at Rome, where there was such great efficiency, so much religion, and such good organization, it is not strange that such things happen more often in cities or countries which lack the things aforesaid. Because this instance is very noteworthy for showing Heaven's power over human affairs, Titus Livius explains it at length in very effective words, saying that since Heaven for some reason wished the Romans to know its power . . .;[237]

since you cannot change your character nor give up the disposition that Heaven endows you with, in the midst of your journey she [Fortune] abandons you;[238]

Heaven commands (and she is not to be resisted);[239]

Oh proud men, ever you have arrogant faces, you who hold the scepters and the crowns, and of the future do not know a single truth!
So blinded are you by your present greed which over your eyes

holds a thick veil that things remote you cannot see. From this it comes that heaven, shifting from this to that, shifts your states more often than the heat and ice are changed.[240]

"Nature"

Nature has made men able to crave everything but unable to attain everything;[241]

I believe that as Nature has given each man an individual face, so she has given him an individual disposition and an individual imagination;[242]

you always act as Nature inclines you;[243]

the mind of man, ever intent on what is natural to it, grants no protection against either habit or nature;[244]

[Messer Rinaldo degli Albizzi] A man indeed worthy of honor in every fortune, but he would have been still more so if Nature had had him born in a united city, because in a divided city he was damaged by many of his qualities which in a united one would have honored him.[245]

"Necessity"

Those wheels [of Fortune] are ever turning, day and night, because Heaven commands (and she is not to be resisted) that Laziness and Necessity whirl them around.[246]

9. that affirmation of access to a supernal power provides and endows the leader with special sanctions[247] (above, pp. 49–51, 54–55);
10. that organization through membership defines one's essential self[248] (above, pp. 19–21, 41–42, 54–57);
11. that organizations, relating to their membership as an organism to its parts, benefit through the methods analogous to those of medicine and surgery[249] (above, pp. 55–56);
12. that plausible appearance can prevail over experienced reality[250] (above, pp. 8, 34);
13. that power is acquired and security can be preserved despite disregard for truth[251] (above, pp. 8, 34);
14. that a death-grip over others confers individual and/or civic greatness[252] (above, pp. 51, 59–62);
15. that, despite the fragmentary and, at times, distorted character of the records of history (above, pp. 72–74), in them can be found instruction

in the effective and prudent use of violence and models for imitation[253] (above, pp. 70–72);

16. that wars can be beneficial and result in prosperous victors[254] (above, pp. 80–81, 86–89).

Each of the foregoing assumptions in Machiavelli's writings serves as a basis for his acceptance of intervention by force in human affairs.

In several instances, however, he registered, as previously noted, serious reservations; thus, however hard he labored to portray the heroic figure of the founder or restorer of states as historically effective, he was unable to eliminate the possibility that it remained but a hope-inspired fiction for the realization of which even force and fraud still remained insufficient (above, pp. 65–69) and that the records of past events are variously flawed (above, pp. 72–74).

Moreover, seemingly almost to break forth to Machiavelli's full awareness, was the realization that the very history of Rome itself, as he himself traced it, proved that only by drastic distortion of the evidence could the continual warfare be credited with the achievements for which he acclaimed it as worthy of imitation. His thesis that the postponement of acceptable response to economic grievances and inequality at home in deference to the cultivation of an aggressive military policy abroad contributed to the fostering of republican *virtù*, the common good and the well-being of the Roman state (above, pp. 80–82), proves itself essentially fictional and able to be taken as plausible only through his failure to relate his evaluation of Roman warfare to the prolongation of commands and to the emergence of the military as a profession, the reduction in the reservoir of wise and experienced citizens available for public service, the exhaustion of manpower and neighboring resources, the deteriorization of the populace with the increase of wealth and pride, and the acceptance of the loss of freedom under Caesar as "the first tyrant in Rome."[255] Elements of the indictment of the policy can be drawn from various of his own writings:

> we see that Rome's lawgivers needed to do one of two things if Rome was to remain quiet like the republics mentioned above: either not to make use of the populace in war, like the Venetians, or not to open the way to foreigners, like the Spartans. Yet they did both of these. This gave the people power and increase in numbers and countless reasons for rioting. But if the Roman state had become quieter, this difficulty would have followed, namely, that it would have been weaker, because the way to come to the greatness it reached would have been cut off from it. Hence, if Rome had planned to take away the causes of riot, it would also have taken away the causes of growth . . . So then, if you try to make a people so numerous and so well-armed that it can produce a great empire, you make it such that you cannot manage it as you wish;[256]

> Wars are begun at will but not ended at will;[257]

On considering well the course of the Roman republic, we see two causes for that republic's dissolution: first, the struggles provoked by the Agrarian Laws; second, the prolongation of supreme commands . . . Though the prolongation of supreme command apparently never caused rioting in Rome, nevertheless it is evident how much a city is injured by the authority that citizens obtain through such decrees . . . This practice, though begun by the Senate for the public good, in time made Rome a slave, because the farther the Romans went abroad with their armies, the more necessary they thought this extension of command and the more they used it. It resulted in two ills. One was that a smaller number of men had experience in command; therefore reputation became restricted to a few. The other was that when a citizen was for a long time commander of an army, he gained its support and made it his partisan, for that army in time forgot the Senate and considered him its head . . . If the Romans had never prolonged the magistracies and the commands, they might not have come so quickly to great power, for their conquests might have been later, but they would have come later to slavery;[258]

Because Octavian first and then Tiberius, thinking more about their own power than about the public advantage, began to disarm the Roman people in order to command them more easily and to keep those same armies continually on the frontiers of the Empire. And because they still did not judge that they would be enough to hold in check the Roman people and the Senate, they set up an army called Praetorian, which remained near the walls of Rome and was like a castle over that city. Because they then freely began to allow men chosen for those armies to practice soldiering as their profession, these men soon became arrogant, so that they were dangerous to the Senate and harmful to the Emperor;[259]

[war] is a profession by means of which men cannot live virtuously at all times, it cannot be practiced as a profession except by a republic or a kingdom; and neither of these, when they have been well regulated, has ever allowed one of its citizens or subjects to practice it as a profession. Because he will never be reckoned a good man who carries on a profession in which, if he is to endeavor at all times to get income from it, he must be rapacious, fraudulent, violent, and must have many qualities which of necessity make him not good; nor can men who practice it as a profession, the big as well as the little, be of any other sort, because this profession does not support them in times of peace. Hence they are obliged either to hope that there will be no peace, or to become so rich in time of war that in peace they can support themselves. And neither one of these two expectations is to be found in a good man, because from the desire to support themselves at all times come the robberies, the deeds of violence, the murderous acts that such soldiers commit as much against their friends as against their enemies; and from not wishing peace come the deceits that the generals practice against those by whom they are employed, in order

that a war may last; and if peace does come, it often happens that the generals, being deprived of their stipends and their living, lawlessly set up their ensigns as soldiers of fortune and without any mercy plunder a region;[260]

Do you not have a proverb reinforcing my reasons that runs: "War makes thieves and peace hangs them?" Because those who do not know how to live by any other occupation and do not find anybody who will support them in soldiering and do not have so much ability that they can join together to carry out an honorable villainy, are forced by necessity to rob on the highway, and justice is forced to wipe them out;[261]

if a king does not manage in such a way that his infantrymen in times of peace are glad to return home and live by their occupations, he will necessarily be ruined, because there is no more dangerous infantry than that composed of men who carry on war as their profession, because you are obliged either to make war always, or to pay them always, or to be subject to the danger that they will deprive you of your kingdom. To make war always is not possible; to pay them always is not possible; so necessarily you run into danger of losing your power;[262]

conquered territories sometimes do no small damage to the best-organized state, as when she conquers a city or province full of dissipations, from which she borrows some of their bad customs in the course of her dealings with them, as in the conquest of Capua happened first to Rome, later to Hannibal. Indeed if Capua had been more distant, so that the soldiers' dissipation had not had a remedy near at hand, or if Rome had been to any extent corrupt, without doubt that conquest would have been the ruin of the Roman republic . . . Truly such cities or provinces revenge themselves upon the conqueror without combat and without bloodshed, because, filling him with their evil customs, they expose him to be conquered by whoever assails him. Juvenal in his *Satires* could not have dealt better with this matter, saying that because of their conquest of foreign lands, foreign customs had entered the breasts of the Romans, and instead of frugality and other very excellent virtues, "gluttony and luxury fastened upon her and revenged the conquered world." If, then, success in conquest was beginning to destroy the Romans in times when they were acting with such prudence and such vigor, what will happen then to those whose actions are far different from theirs . . .?[263]

after the Romans had conquered Africa and Asia and brought almost all Greece under their rule, they felt sure of their freedom, and believed they had no more enemies who could cause them fear. This security and this weakness of their enemies caused the Roman people, in awarding the consulate, no longer to consider ability, but favor, putting in that office those who knew best how to please men, not those who knew best how to conquer enemies. Then from those who had most favor, they descended to giving it to those who had most power, so that the good, because of the weakness of such a procedure, were wholly excluded from office . . . only the powerful proposed laws, not for the common liberty but for their own power, and for fear of such men no one dared to speak against those laws. Thus the people were either deceived or forced into decreeing their own ruin;[264]

Rome, when that excellence of her citizens was turned into pride, was brought to such a pass that she could not keep going without a prince.[265]

As Pocock has pointed out, already, as early as the 1420's, Leonardo Bruni had charged that the aggressive course of the Roman republic had been at the expense of the civic spirit not only of the regions conquered but of the Roman people themselves:

In the writings of his middle period, Bruni restated the theme that Florence was descended from the Roman republic—in which the temporal and spatial finitude of republics, and their consequent mortality, had been clearly acknowledged—by declaring that there had been many free republics in ancient Etruria (the modern Tuscany) and that their subjugation by the single conquering republic of Rome had been a prime cause of the decay of virtue, in Italy at large and ultimately of Rome herself. Republics needed other republics, because virtue was participatory and relational and required the virtue of others.[266]

In *The Art of War,* Machiavelli developed the same theme:

Since . . . it is true that where there are more states, more strong men rise up, of necessity when states are destroyed competence is destroyed along with them, since the cause disappears that makes men competent. Hence, when the Roman Empire later increased and did away with all the republics and princedoms of Europe and of Africa and for the most part those of Asia, no road to competence was left except in Rome. The result was that competent men became as few in Europe as in Asia. Competence then reached its final decline, because when all competence was brought to Rome, as she was corrupt, soon there was corruption in almost all the world; and the peoples of Scythia could prey upon that Empire, which had destroyed the competence of others but could not maintain her own. Though afterward that Empire, through the inundation of barbarians, was divided into several parts, this competence was not reborn there;[267]

Pondering, then, why it can be that in those ancient times people were greater lovers of freedom than in these . . . I believe that the cause of this is . . . that the Roman Empire with her arms and her greatness wiped out all the republics and the self-governing communities. And though later that Empire was liquidated, the cities have not yet united themselves or reorganized themselves for governing according to law, except in a very few places in that Empire;[268]

the ancient Tuscans . . . were able to gain in Italy the power that their manner of proceeding yielded them. This was for a long time secure with the utmost glory of authority and arms, and with the highest reputation in manners and religion. This power and glory were first decreased by the French, then destroyed by the Romans; it was indeed so completely destroyed that, although two thousand years ago the power of the Tuscans was great, at present there is scarcely any record of it.[269]

Machiavelli recognized that Rome, by destroying *virtù* in those whom it conquered, and itself becoming "corrupt," did not succeed in distributing power and educating the inhabitants in and for civic freedom. Moreover, he perceived that wars were uneconomic for a commercial city. In *The History of Florence* he noted that even as early as Giovanni de'Medici's support of a tax policy which bore more heavily on the rich the realization was growing that wars were unprofitable:

the trouble consisted in something they ["the rich"] did not speak of, because it pained them that they could not start a war without damaging themselves, having to share in its expenses like the others; if this method [*The Castasto*, a graduated direct tax] of taxation had been devised before, there never would have been war with . . . , nor with . . . , for these wars were undertaken to enrich the citizens, and not from necessity;[270]

and in the *The Art of War* he had Fabrizio Colonna say:

I believe you realize, because at other times I have talked with some of you about it, how the present wars make poorer both those rulers who win and those who lose, for if one loses his state, the other loses his money and his goods; in ancient times this did not happen, because the victory in war gained riches. In our day war brings poverty because we do not now manage the booty as the ancients did but we leave it all in the power of the soldiers.[271]

Does not a country's policy of hope and exertion for victory at foreigners' expense and individuals' endeavors to use public power to their own enrichment at others expense provide mutual examples and reciprocally reinforcing stimuli? Does not Machiavelli's praise of the aggressive spirit of republican Rome and his disregard, as its inevitable consequence, of the imperial decadence which he deplored, involve him in an error of judgment similar to that for which he criticized historians of Hannibal's methods and achievements?[272] Conversely, although Machiavelli praised the "cause," he did not relate it to the withering sequel.

Furthermore, notwithstanding his emphasis upon the effectiveness of force (above, pp. 46–51, 59–62), of fraud and disregard of truth (above, pp. 8, 34), he warned of inherent limitations to their employment. His concept of one's ultimate, unalienable defense respecting oneself indicates that he recognized those previously mentioned[273] (above, pp. 11–12, 43–44). One encounters as additional limitations which he perceived:

> it is not disgraceful not to keep promises that you are forced to make. Forced promises in public matters, when the force is removed, will always be broken, without disgrace for him who breaks them;[274]

> Since, then, a prince is necessitated to play the animal well, he chooses among the beasts the fox and the lion, because the lion does not protect himself from the traps; the fox does not protect himself from the wolves. The prince must be a fox, therefore to recognize the traps and a lion to frighten the wolves. Those who rely on the lion alone are not perceptive. By no means can a prudent ruler keep his word—and he does not—when to keep it works against himself and when the reasons that made him promise are annulled . . . Never has a shrewd prince lacked justifying reasons to make his promise-breaking appear honorable. Of this I can give countless modern examples, showing how many treaties of peace and how many promises have been made null and empty through the dishonesty of princes. The one who best knows how to play the fox comes out best, but he must understand well how to disguise the animal's nature and must be a great simulator and dissimulator.[275]

In *The History of Florence* he cautioned against the strength born of desperation. In a confrontation between the nobles and the people in 1295, "the go-betweens"

> reminded the people that it was not prudent always to strive for complete victory and that it was never wise to make men despair, because he who does not hope for good does not fear ill;[276]

and in 1427, in order to calm citizens quarrelling over the new tax levies, Giovanni de'Medici counselled:

> he who is content with half a victory will always come out better for it because those who try to do more than win often lose.[277]

The assumption that religious and political organizations are so analogous to organisms that members can validly be treated as but parts, having value only insofar as they may be useful for the organization—even to the point of being

98

involuntarily sacrificed for its welfare (above, pp. 55–56, 92)—is impaired by the recognition given to the uniqueness of the human individual and the potential for self defense when entrapped (above, pp. 9–13, 43). May it be that it is primarily persistence of would-be state-builders in trying to over-ride human intractability when faced with coercion which has given rise to, and continues to support, the conclusion endorsed by Machiavelli that:

> all men are evil and that they are always going to act according to the wickedness of their spirits whenever they have free scope?[278]

While Machiavelli expressed various degrees of reservation in the following affirmations—that state-building and reform can be successfully achieved by one man (above, pp. 65–69, 74); that history, as recorded, is reliable as a source for political prudence (above, pp. 70–72, 92–93); that the use of force and fraud is effective (above, pp. 48, 93); that wars can accomplish the aims for which they are begun (above, pp. 97–98), as further grounds for the use of force in human affairs he accorded, as already noted, full acceptance to the following assumptions:

1. that in time of peace there is no place for everybody (above, pp. 14–15);
2. that one's security requires exercise of power over others (above, pp. 14–15, 33–36);
3. that the nature of human nature is known to be evil (above, pp. 33–34);
4. that one can exercise effective leadership over others (above, pp. 51, 59–62);
5. that public purpose can transmute into benefits behavior which if engaged in for private ends would occasion injury and ruin (above, pp. 51, 59–63);
6. that resort to the use of force is ingenerate in states (above, pp. 77–80);
7. that knowledge of causation in human affairs is available (above, pp. 69–70, 89–92);
8. that affirmation of access to a supernal power provides and endows the leader with especially effective sanction (above, pp. 49–52);
9. that organization through membership defines essential selfhood (above, pp. 55–57);
10. that organizations benefit through the use of methods analogous to those of medicine and surgery (above, pp. 55–56);
11. that sufficient credulity prevails among people for assimilation of fictions into reality (above, pp. 34–36, 49–52);
12. that stunning actions create power (above, pp. 48, 49–52, 59–65).

Although all of the above assumptions were generally held to be true for long after the Renaissance, and many of them still receive widespread support, their fictional character grows ever more evident.

Already in Machiavelli's own lifetime, in widely different components of European culture, innovations giving rise to long-continuing processes were beginning to reveal the fictional character of some of the assumptions which he had taken for granted. Occasionally traces of these life-enhancing events touched him, significantly influenced his development, or gained his personal attention.

Only nineteen years before his birth, had appeared the first book printed in Europe from moveable type, an art introduced in Mayence.[279] The excitement stirred by the new art of printing—introduced into Florence in 1471—,[280] as first editions began to make ancient literature more generally available, touched the home of young Niccolo. At the request of a local printer, his father prepared the index of place names for a printing of Livy's *History* and, as a reward for the nine months' labor, became the proud possessor of a printed copy which remained, henceforth, a valued treasure in the family's library.[281] At the time, Niccolo was seventeen years of age. As the availability of Livy for the young Machiavelli was the seed which led to the consummate harvest in the *Discourses,* so the crescendo of printed books, pamphlets, newspapers, stimulated and diversified communication and scholarship throughout the western world. The continuing spread of information, the arousing of the under-privileged to participation in expression and exchange of opinion which the introduction of printing facilitated, proved to be revolutionary ferment in succeeding centuries with twentieth century radio, television, satellite communication and computer-adapted duplication growing into a veritable communication explosion.

Machiavelli was twenty-one when Savonarola, for a second time, took up residence in Florence;[282] twenty-three, when Lorenzo, the Magnificent, died; twenty-five, when—with the invasion of Italy by Charles VIII of France and the expulsion of the Medici from Florence—the city lost control of Pisa which had been held as its sea port for eighty-five years, and Savonarola became the city's revered leader. Machiavelli was twenty-nine when, through popular frenzy incited and inflamed by Pope Alexander VI, Savonarola was hanged and his body burned.[283]

That, personally, Machiavelli was appreciative of sincere religious expression, passages from his later writings will make clear. In the Roman Church of Alexander VI and Julius II, however, he observed an institution which had so far departed from the principles of the Founder of the religion that it had become discredited on account of its professed representatives. Deliberately undertaking to arrive at his conclusions through observations of how men behave, he found such contradiction between the conduct of churchmen and both the principles of the religion which they professed and the life of its Founder, that formal religion had lost its access to the minds and hearts of the people. In the *Discourses,* he was to write:

If religion of this sort ["all devout and full of reverence"] had been kept up among the princes of Christendom, in the form in which its giver founded it, Christian states and republics would be more united, much more happy than they are. Nor can a better estimate of its decline be made than by seeing that those people who are nearest to the Roman Church, the head of our religion, have least religion. And he who considers its foundations and sees how different its present habit is from them, will conclude that near at hand, beyond doubt, is its fall or its punishment. And because many are of the opinion that the well-being of the cities of Italy comes from the Roman Church, I am going, in opposition to this, to discuss some reasons that occur to me. And I shall bring forward two very strong ones, that, as I think, are not to be refuted. The first is that through the bad examples of that court this land has lost all piety and all religion. This brings about countless evils and countless disorders, because, just as we assume everything good where we find religion, so when it is lacking we assume the contrary.
We Italians, then, have as our first debt to the Church and to the priests that we have become without religion and wicked. But we have one still greater, which is the second reason for our ruin: this is that the Church has kept and still keeps the region divided. And truly no region is ever united or happy if all of it is not under the sway of one republic or one prince, as happened to France and to Spain. The reason why Italy is not in that same condition and why she too does not have one republic or one prince to govern her is the Church alone; because, though she has dwelt there and possessed temporal power, she has not been so strong or of such ability that she could grasp sole authority in Italy and make herself ruler of the country. Yet on the other hand she has not been so weak that, when she feared to lose dominion over her temporal possessions, she could not summon a powerful man to defend her against anyone who in Italy had become too powerful.[284]

Years later, in a letter to his friend Francesco Guicciardini, then Pope Clement VII's representative as governor of Modena and Reggio, he wrote:

Seeing . . . how much credit a bad man has who conceals himself under the cloak of religion, I can easily conjecture how much of it a good man would have who in truth and not in pretense continued to tread muddy places like St. Francis.[285]

With brilliant irony, throughout his play *Mandragola* he exposed to ridicule the moral weakness, hypocrisy and venality of local priests, the social confusion and the shallow self-delusion provided by mechanical observances of rites and ceremonies.[286] Throughout *The History of Florence* he laid bare the Church's deep-rooted policy of political disruption for the advancement of its own temporal power and/or the personal ambition of its leaders:

> the popes, first with censures, and then with censures and arms at the same time, mixed with indulgences, excited fear and awe, and . . . through bad use of censures and arms they have wholly lost awe, and as to fear, they are in the power of others;[287]

> Thus the pontiffs, now through love for religion, now through their personal ambition, did not cease to provoke new dissensions in Italy and to stir up new wars, and when they had made a prince powerful, they repented of it and sought his ruin; thus that country which through their own weakness they could not hold, they did not permit any other to hold. Yet the princes were afraid of them, because they always won, either fighting or running away;[288]

> The short lives of the popes, the variations among those chosen, the Church's slight fear of the princes, the few scruples she has in making decisions, are reasons why a secular prince cannot wholly rely on a pontiff and cannot securely share his fortune with him. He who is the Pope's friend in wars and in dangers will in victory have a companion but in defeat will be alone, since by his spiritual power and reputation the Pontiff is supported and defended;[289]

> Because the pontiffs always feared any man whose power in Italy had become great, even though it had grown up as a result of the Church's support, and because they tried to reduce it, their policy caused the frequent disturbances and frequent changes that took place in the country. The pontiff's fear of a powerful man caused a weak one to grow, and when he had grown strong, made them fear him, and since they feared him, made them try to bring him low;[290]

> The Heavens (knowing a time would have to come when the French and the Germans would abandon Italy and that land would remain entirely in the hands of the Italians) in order that the Pope, when he lacked opposition from beyond the Alps, might not make his power solid or enjoy it, raised up in Rome two very powerful families, the Colonna and the Orsini; with their power and their proximity these two were to keep the papacy weak. Hence Pope Boniface, who knew this, undertook to get rid of the Colonna; besides excommunicating them, he proclaimed a crusade against them. This, though it somewhat injured them, injured the Church still more, because that weapon which through love of the Faith he might have used effectively, when through personal ambition it was turned against Christians, began to stop cutting. Thus too great a desire to satisfy their own greed caused the popes, little by little, to disarm themselves;[291]

102

[Nicholas III] of the house of Orsini was the first of the popes who openly revealed his personal ambition, and who attempted, under the pretext of aggrandizing the Church to honor and assist his relatives. As before this time no mention had ever been made of any pontiff's nephews or relatives, so in the future they will fill history; and at last we shall come to sons; and there is nothing left for the pontiffs to try except that, as up to our times they have planned to leave their sons as princes, in the future they may strive to leave them the popedom as hereditary. It is indeed true that up to now the princedoms they have established have had short lives, because most of the time the pontiffs, since they lived but a short while, either did not finish setting out their plants, or if they did set them out, left them with so few or so weak roots that, since the strength sustaining them was gone, at the first wind they withered away.[292]

How radically disruptive the papal influence could be, impressed itself upon the young Machiavelli just one week before his seventeenth birthday. The Pazzi family and their partisans, with the complicity of Pope Sixtus IV and the Archbishop, during mass in the Cathedral attacked Lorenzo and killed his brother, Giuliano. In the subsequent tumult, the Archbishop and such leaders of the conspiracy as could be seized were hanged from the windows of the Palace of the Signoria. In Chapter 11 of Book VII of *The History of Florence*, Machiavelli detailed the subsequent propaganda used by each side in the struggle to gain general support throughout Italy:

Then the Florentines prepared for war, getting together men and money to the largest total they could. They sent for help, by virtue of the League, to the Duke of Milan and to the Venetians. And since the Pope had shown himself a wolf and not a shepherd, and they hoped not to be devoured as guilty, they showed in all the ways they could that their cause was just. They filled Italy with reports of the treachery carried on against their city, showing the Pontiff's impiety and his injustice, and declaring that he had obtained the papacy wickedly, he had exercised his office wickedly, sending those he had put in the highest prelacies to commit treachery in the Cathedral, in the company of parricides and traitors, in the midst of the divine office, in the celebration of the Sacrament. Then, because he had not succeeded in killing the citizens, in changing the government of their city and at his will plundering her, he had interdicted her and, with pontifical curses, threatened and wronged her. But if God is just and if acts of violence offend him, those of this vicar of his must offend him, and he must be glad when men who are injured and find no refuge with his vicar turn to himself. Meanwhile the Florentines not merely did not receive the interdict and obey it, but they forced the clergy to celebrate the divine offices, and they called a council in Florence of all the Tuscan prelates who obeyed their authority, in which they appealed from the injuries of the Pope to the coming Council of the Church. The Pope also did not lack

103

arguments for justifying his cause, declaring that it is a Pontiff's part to destroy tyranny, to put down the wicked and raise up the good, and that he ought to carry on these duties with all fitting measures. But it is not the function of secular rulers to arrest cardinals, to hang bishops, to murder, dismember and mangle priests, and to kill the innocent and the guilty without any distinction.[293]

Twice in his writings, Machiavelli gave a more personal tone to his expression of antipathy for churchmen. While on this third mission to France, this time to try to protect the security of his city when its two traditional allies (the papacy and France) were moving toward war with each other, as Ridolfi reports it,

> at the French court fine words are uttered about the spring offensive: 'indeed it will not be a war, but an excursion to Rome.' Machiavelli notes that this would be a desirable thing, 'so that these priests should have to swallow some bitter pill in this world.'[294]

Five years earlier, Machiavelli had been in Perugia as Florentine agent to the same pope, Julius II, when its "tyrant," Giovampagolo Baglioni, failed to seize an unparallelled opportunity for which, later, in the *Discourses,* Machiavelli was to castigate him:

> carried on by that impetuosity with which he [Julius II] conducted everything, with only his bodyguard he put himself in the hands of his enemy, whom then he took off with him, leaving in the city a governor who would execute justice for the Church.
> All the sagacious men with the Pope observed the rashness of the Pope and the cowardice of Giovampagolo, and they could not reckon whence it came that the latter did not, to his everlasting fame, at one stroke put down his enemy and enrich himself with booty, since with the Pope were all the cardinals with all their precious things. Nor can it be believed that he abstained either through goodness or through conscience that held him back, because into the breast of a vicious man, who had taken his sister for himself, who had killed his cousins and nephews in order to rule, no pious scruples could come, but we must conclude that it happened because men cannot be splendidly wicked or perfectly good, and when an evil deed has greatness in itself or is in some part noble, they cannot comprehend it.[295]

Among people ground down by exactions in fees and services by both religious and secular powers, deprived of rights to ownership of the land they worked and of participation in the forming of the policies and the making of the laws which governed them, taught to place their hopes in a kingdom of heaven to be available to them—if obedient to the earthly authorities—only on the other side of the grave, here and there in western Christendom erupted protests that their experience in no way accorded with "the Good News" heralded by Jesus and for affirming which he had given his life. As in the instances of the Orders (Benedictine, Franciscan, and Dominican) and the Crusades, the hierarchy, by institutional devices, commandeered, managed and assimilated many of the impulses to innovative overt action. Machiavelli expressed in the *Discourses* his evaluation of such developments:

> In religious bodies these renewals are also necessary, as we see through the example of our religion, which, if Saint Francis and Saint Dominic had not brought it back toward its beginnings, would have entirely disappeared. They with their poverty and with the example of Christ's life, brought it back into the minds of men when it had disappeared from them. The power of their new orders is the reason why the improbity of the prelates and the heads of our religion does not ruin it; for still living in poverty and having great influence with the people because of hearing confessions and preaching, they give them to understand that it is well to speak evil of what is evil, and that it is good to live under the prelates' control and, if prelates make errors, to leave them to God for punishment. So the prelates do the worst they can, because they do not fear the punishment which they do not see and do not believe in. This renewal, then, has maintained and still maintains our religion.[296]

Affirmations in action continued to break out ever more widely afield among those being alienated by traditional institutional practices. Machiavelli was in the final stages of writing *Discourses* when, in 1517, Martin Luther nailed his Ninety-five Theses to the door of the church in Wittenberg and initiated the Reformation which in succeeding centuries would find expression in the individualism of George Fox affirming that "There is that of God in every man," the political initiative of William Penn in his "Holy Experiment" establishing in the governments of colonial Pennsylvania and New Jersey the Quaker implications of participatory democracy, of Thomas Jefferson leading Virginia to legislate the separation of church and state, and of James Madison getting that principle included as part of the Bill of Rights embedded in the Constitution of the United States—a lethal blow to the legal sanction for that use of religion as an instrument of governmental policy which, through Livy, Machiavelli had considered essential in the founding or reforming of states, and which the treaties of Augsburg (1553) and of Westphalia (1648) came to sanction. The individual conscience was being called up to a new awakening for responsible behavior in daily life.

That the reports of the voyagers who were expanding the horizons of the known world may not have left Machiavelli untouched may be inferred from the initial sentence of the first book of *Discourses* in which he wrote:

> On account of the envious nature of man, it has always been no less dangerous to find ways and methods that are new than it has been to hunt

for seas and lands unknown, since men are more prone to blame than to praise the doings of others.[297]

For three centuries Florence had been as nearly the economic—especially, financial—capital of Europe as existed. In the mid- and late-thirteenth century, the leading bankers for both popes and emperors were Florentine. By the early fourteenth century banking and commerce were becoming more closely interrelated as leading families with their numerous sons developed the precursors of joint stock companies. By mid-fourteenth century, especially in the Florentine wool industry, with the emergence of the central workshop, both the physical structure and social problems characteristic of the later factory system were beginning to emerge in Florence.

Machiavelli's birth occurred at just about the mid-point between that of his fellow Florentine Amerigo Vespucci (1454) and that of Giovanni da Verrazano, born in Greve near Florence, probably in 1485. Like Machiavelli's father, Vespucci was a notary. Amerigo served for some years in the "bank" of Lorenzo and Giovanni de'Medici and then was sent to their branch in Seville which was involved in outfitting ships, participated in outfitting Columbus's second and third voyages, and became personally acquainted with Columbus. Of Vespucci's own voyage to North America, according to *The Encyclopaedia Britannica* (15th edition),[298] still extant are three private letters which he wrote to the Medici and one, dated 4 September 1505 and written in Italian, presumed to have been sent to Gonfalonier Piero Soderini, probably passed through the hands of Machiavelli, the secretary in charge of foreign affairs. News of the intrigues and quarrels attendant upon Columbus's commissions may have reached Machiavelli and impressed him with the extent to which "the envious nature of men" made it "dangerous . . . to hunt for seas and lands unknown." It may be, however, as Felix Gilbert has noted, that the introductory sentence "actually is a classical topos" though "some writers have even seen an allusion to Columbus in this phrase."[299] Vespucci's explorations firmly established that in fact a "new world" had been discovered.

Especially for Europeans in the next four centuries the reports from voyages, expeditions and settlements gave sustenance to individuals' aspirations for ownership of land, exploitation of natural resources, increased freedom of movement, economic individualism and subsequently even choice of national allegiance and citizenship. The opening up of North America together with the encouragement of immigration there, broadened and deepened the message to the peoples of Europe that the new world could be for them the fulfilment of the inbred hope. Eventually, in the United States, the Homestead Act (1862) wrote into law the opportunity for the freehold of a family-size farm. Other laws and judicial decisions were to foster enterprises in finance, commerce and industry.

On an unprecedented scale was being re-enacted the ancient drama. Four thousand years previously, Abraham (c. 2000–1500 B.C.), after renouncing the

106

gods of which his father had crafted images, left the land of his birth and, guided by the hope believed in as a promise of land for his descendants, set forth with his family and dependents. The passionate hunger and love for land which characterized Abraham and which he transmitted to his descendants as rightful heirs of "The Promised Land," has been communicated to all mankind as a sense of a god-given or natural right to a share of the good earth. Heir to ancient Egypt after his father Amenhotep III had extended the empire's boundaries to their farthest reaches, Ikhnaton (Amenhotep IV, 1410?–1375 B.C.) proclaimed all the inhabitants throughout the land as the blessed beneficiaries of the helping hand of the one, concerned Sun God. Emerging from a period of servitude, in the process of invading and conquering for themselves the land of Canaan, the Twelve Tribes of the Hebrews formed themselves into a common political unit through which they secured a sense of being one people occupying their own land, established a nation and, as members and citizens therein, set before men a new model of personal worth.

As do other creatures of nature, men feel a necessity to affirm territorial claims so that they can put down roots and flourish. Thus, Machiavelli wrote:

Love for a man's native land is caused by nature,[300]

and from revenge for violating it no tyrant can protect himself.[301]

Rome violently exploited the relation between men and the land in order to exalt its monopoly of power and in so doing destroyed creative power in the conquered nations and, ultimately, as Machiavelli himself recorded,[302] in itself. Organizers and administrators of the Christian community developed the belief that the Church in alliance with the Empire was the successor of both Israel and Rome and that through baptism one received his soul and through the sacrament of communion became a rightful heir in the new Israel.[303] The leaders of the religious and political organizations thereby exploited the membership until through the Renaissance and the Reformation the individual man began to be perceived as being, by nature and by God, endowed with individuality of ultimate worth to be secured through his instrument, the state, which he joined with others in organizing for that purpose.

That this claim of a rightful access to home-land cannot be denied is the message of Israel's millennia-long history and out of it has spread abroad the development in mankind of the sense of nationhood and the conviction that every man is equally and undeniably entitled to whatever sense of dignity any other man is realizing through it—even that, in our day, of the members in the atomic club to be achieved at whatever cost or in the struggle for it to bring all to nuclear annihilation.

The Florence of Machiavelli's childhood and youth was that of her greatest splendor. The twenty-year-old Lorenzo inherited the family's political and economic leadership in the same year as that of the birth of Machiavelli. G. F. Young has succinctly described the city's prosperity in the early years of Lorenzo's control:

> Florence's commerce immensely increased, her ships, built in her port of Pisa, trading to the Black Sea, Asia Minor, Africa, Spain, England, France, and Flanders. And with the spread of her commerce increased also her influence as the center of Art and Learning. The pride which Florentines took in all this is brought home to us when we find Giovanni Rucellai, in detailing in his memoirs a long list of personal benefits for which he desires to offer up thanks to the Almighty, amongst them thanking God that he "was a native of Florence, the greatest city in the world, and lived in the days of the magnificent Medici."[304]

And summarizing Lorenzo's achievements, Young wrote:

> He had in twenty-two years perfected that which his grandfather had begun, and created between Venice, Milan, the Pope, and Naples, a firm balance of power which so long as his influence watched over it would keep Italy at peace . . . Instead of the chronic enmity with her neighbors which had hitherto always been Florence's condition, Lorenzo—a master in conciliatory action—had in the course of twenty-two years gradually established friendly relations with Siena, Lucca, Bologna, Faenza, Ferrara, Rimini, Perugia, and Citta di Castello; thus encircling Florence with a ring of friendly states—a more lasting guarantee for her peace than even a general balance of power. These achievements had brought Italy to that condition referred to by Guicciardini as the most prosperous experienced for a thousand years, and had made Lorenzo recognized even beyond the Alps as the leading statesman of his age.[305]

Following the death of Lorenzo, the exile of the Medici, the immolation of Savonarola, Florence became a republic in which Machiavelli was invited to serve under the leadership of one whom Orestes Ferrara has termed:

> le plus honnête et le plus démocratique chef d'État florentins . . . Son gouvernement, personnel, quoique non exempt de fautes, fut par sa forme vraiment populaire et l'excellence de son administration, une oasis dans le désert.[306]

> the most honest and the most democratic head of a Florentine government . . . His government, and personnel, although not exempt from faults, was in its form truly popular and the excellence of his administration, an oasis in the desert.

Machiavelli's experience of service to this Florence, his city, in its return to republican government, and his own deep-rooted dedication to the common

good,[307] quickened that perception of the significance with which official participation enhances an individual's existence to which he repeatedly bore witness[308]
(above, pp. 56–57).

In the time of such nation-building kings as Ferdinand of Spain (1492–1516),
Louis XII of France (1498–1515), Henry VIII of England who became king in
1509 and Charles V who became Emperor in 1515, Machiavelli lamented the
degradation which the blindly ambitious fomenters of inter-city conflicts were
continuing to bring about in Italy. In the *Discourses* he wrote:

> He who is born . . . in Italy or in Greece . . . has reason to find fault with
> his own time and to praise others. For in the others there are many things
> that make them admirable; in these there is nothing to redeem them from
> every sort of extreme misery, bad repute and reproach; in these no care is
> given to religion, none to the laws, none to military affairs, but they are
> foul with every sort of filth. Moreover these vices are so much the more
> detestable the more they are found in those who sit in judgment seats, give
> orders to everybody and expect to be adored;[309]

> nothing good can be expected in regions that in our times are evidently
> corrupt, as is Italy above all.[310]

In *The History of Florence,* he had a respected and patriotic citizen of 1372 say:

> Truly in the cities of Italy all is collected that can be depraved and that
> can deprave any man; the young are lazy, the old licentious, and both
> sexes and every age abound in vile habits. Good laws, because they are
> ruined by bad customs, do not remedy this condition;[311]

and later he took up the theme again:

> peace it cannot be called in which princedoms are continually attacking
> one another with armies. Wars, however, they cannot be called in which
> men are not killed, cities are not sacked, princedoms are not destroyed,
> because those wars became so feeble that they were begun without fear,
> carried on without danger, and ended without damage. So the vigor that
> in other countries is usually destroyed by long peace was in Italy destroyed
> by the cowardice of those wars, as is made clear by what we shall relate
> from 1434 to 1494. The reader will see there that at last a new road was
> opened to the barbarians, and Italy put herself back into slavery to them;[312]

and in the *Prince*, when seeking to spur on the young Medicean prince to assume
leadership, he characterized the Italians as:

> more slave than the Hebrews, more servant than the Persians, more scattered

than the Athenians, without head, without order, beaten, despoiled, lacerated, devastated, subject to every sort of ruination.[313]

In "Tercets on Ambition," he set forth in specific detail the human suffering and anguish which the disorders persistently inflicted:

From Ambition come those wounds that have killed the Italian provinces.
Pass over Siena's fraternal contests; turn your eyes, Luigi, to this region, upon these people thunderstruck and bewildered, you will see how Ambition results in two kinds of action: one party robs and the other weeps for its wealth ravaged and scattered.
Let him turn his eyes here who wishes to behold the sorrows of others, and let him consider if ever before now the sun has looked upon such savagery.
A man is weeping for his father dead and a woman for her husband; another man, beaten and naked, you see driven in sadness from his own dwelling.
Oh how many times, when the father has held his son tight in his arms, a single thrust has pierced the breasts of them both!
Another is abandoning his ancestral home, as he accuses cruel and ungrateful gods, with his brood overcome with sorrow.
Oh, strange events such as never have happened before in the world! Every day many children are born through sword cuts in the womb. To her daughter, overcome with sorrow, the mother says: "For what an unhappy marriage, for what a cruel husband have I kept you!"
Foul with blood are the ditches and streams, full of heads, of legs, of arms, and other members gashed and severed.
Birds of prey, wild beasts, dogs are now their family tombs—Oh tombs repulsive, horrible and unnatural!
Always their faces are gloomy and dark, like those of a man terrified and numbed by new injuries or sudden fears.
Wherever you turn your eyes, you see the earth wet with tears and blood, and the air full of screams, of sobs, and sighs . . .
Alas! For while with another's affliction I am keeping my thought engaged and my speech, I am weighed down with greater fear. I see Ambition, with that swarm which Heaven at the world's beginning allotted her, flying over the Tuscan mountains; and already she has scattered so many sparks among those people swollen with envy that she will burn their towns and their farmsteads if grace or better government does not bring her to nought;[314]

His Carnival Song, "Hymn by the Blessed Spirits," was an appeal for relief through effective control by the newly-elected pontiff, Leo X, Giovanni de'Medici:

Blessed spirits are we, who from celestial benches come here to present

110

ourselves on earth, because we see the world in so many afflictions, and for slight causes such cruel war; we come to show him who errs that our Lord is greatly pleased when arms are laid down and continue unused. The pitiable and cruel affliction of miserable mortals, their long distress and suffering without remedy, their lament for countless ills that day and night make them complain, with sobs and distress, with loud voices and sorrowful outcry—each of these asks and beseeches compassion. This to God is not pleasing, and cannot be to one who of humanity has even a touch. Therefore he has sent us to show you how just is his wrath and his anger, since he sees his kingdom—his flock—disappearing little by little, if the new shepherd does not control it.[315]

The cause, he diagnosed in the *Prince* and in *The Art of War*:

it all results from the weakness of the heads: because those who are wise are not obeyed—and each one thinks he is wise—since up to now no one has risen so high, in both ability and Fortune, that to him the others yield;[316]

The common belief of our Italian princes, before they felt the blows of Transalpine war, was that a prince needed only to show quickness and cleverness in quotable sayings and replies, to know how to spin a fraud, to be adorned with gems and with gold, to sleep and eat with greater splendor than others, to be surrounded with wanton pleasures, to deal with subjects avariciously and proudly, to decay in laziness, to gain positions in the army by favor, to despise anybody who showed them any praiseworthy course, and to expect their words to be taken as the responses of oracles. It did not enter the minds of these wretches that they were preparing themselves to be the prey of whoever attacked them. From that came in 1494 great terrors, sudden flights, and astonishing losses; and thus three of the most powerful states in Italy have been many times spoiled and plundered. But what is worse is that those who are left continue in the same error and live by the same bad system, and do not consider that those who in antiquity wished to keep their states did and caused to be done all those things that I have discussed, and that their effort was to prepare the body for hardships and the mind not to fear perils.[317]

Such had become the condition of Italy that Machiavelli would seem to prescribe for it "a kingly hand" to lay foundations for a well-ordered state[318] (above, pp. 60–62); however for Tuscany, he concluded:

there is equality so great that a prudent man, understanding the ancient forms of society, could easily have introduced there well-regulated government. Yet to her great misfortune, up to these times she has found no man who has had the power or wisdom to do it.[319]

As for his own city, Florence, Machiavelli, in responding to the opening provided

111

by Pope Leo X for suggestions for "Remodeling the Government of Florence," proposed:

> because to form a princedom where a republic would go well is a difficult thing and, through being difficult, inhumane and unworthy of whoever hopes to be considered merciful and good, I shall pass over any further treatment of the princedom and speak of the republic, both because Florence is a subject very suitable for taking this form and because I know that Your Holiness is much inclined toward one; and I believe that you defer establishing it because you hope to find an arrangement by which your power in Florence may continue great and your friends may live in security.[320]

Indeed, in the long run and for many reasons, republican government, in Machiavelli's estimation, was superior to other forms. In *The History of Florence,* when recounting the growing alarm over indications that the Duke of Athens was moving to turn his control of the government of Florence into a tyranny, Machiavelli represented a member of the Signoria as warning:

> only authority freely given is durable,[321]

and in the "Discourse on the Remodeling of the Government of Florence," he wrote Pope Leo X,

> without satisfying the generality of the citizens, to set up a stable government is always impossible,[322]

and

> in order to give perfection to the republic after the lifetime of Your Holiness and of the Most Reverend Monsignor . . . There is no other way for escaping these ills than to give the city institutions that can by themselves stand firm. And they will always stand firm when everybody has a hand in them, and when everybody knows what he needs to do and in whom he can trust, and no class of citizens, either through fear for itself or through ambition, will need to desire revolution.[323]

In the *Discourses,* when considering "Where is the Guardianship of Liberty Most Securely Placed?" he gave an analysis of the body of citizens:

> in every republic there are rich men and men of the people . . . those should be put on guard over a thing who are least greedy to take possession of it. And without doubt, if one will look at the purpose of the nobles and of those who are not noble, there will be seen in the former great longing to rule, and in the latter merely longing not to be ruled, and as a consequence greater eagerness to live in freedom, since they can have less

hope of taking possession of it than the great can. Hence if the common people are set up to guard liberty, it is reasonable that they will care for it better, and since they cannot seize it themselves, they will not allow others to seize it.[324]

Moreover,

the cause of the bad and of the good fortune of men is the way in which their method of working fits the times . . . Thence it comes that a republic, being able to adapt itself, by means of the diversity among her body of citizens, to a diversity of temporal conditions better than a prince can, is of greater duration than a princedom and has good fortune longer. Because a man accustomed to acting in one way never changes, as I have said. So of necessity when the times as they change get out of harmony with that way of his, he falls;[325]

For a republic . . . the method of choosing allows not merely two able rulers in succession but countless numbers to follow one another. Such a succession of able rulers will always be present in every well-ordered republic;[326]

good organizers of republics ordain that when the highest offices of the city (where it would be dangerous to put inadequate men) are to be filled, if popular opinion seems directed toward an inadequate choice, every citizen has the right (and it is to be considered an honor) to announce in the public assembly the shortcomings of the candidate; then the people, not lacking knowledge of him, can decide better. . . In the choice of magistrates, then, the people judge men according to the indications they think most reliable; when they can be advised like princes, they err less than princes;[327]

every city ought to have methods with which the people can express their ambition, and especially those cities that intend to make use of the people in important affairs;[328]

it is not right for a republic to be so organized that a citizen can without any recourse be injured for promulgating a law in harmony with free government;[329]

nothing makes a republic so firm and solid as to give her such an organization that the laws provide a way for the discharge of the partisan hatreds that agitate her;[330]

The aspirations of free peoples are seldom harmful to liberty, because they result either from oppression or from fear that there is going to be oppression. And whenever their beliefs are mistaken, there is the remedy of assemblies, in which some man of influence gets up and makes a speech showing them how they are deceiving themselves. And, as Cicero says, the people, though they are ignorant, can grasp the truth, and yield easily when by a man worthy of trust they are told what is true;[331]

I say that a people is more prudent, more stable, and of better judgment than a prince. Nor is it without reason that the voice of the people is likened to that of God, because general opinion possesses marvelous power for prediction; indeed through some mysterious efficacy it appears to foresee its own happiness and misery;[332]

excellent men come in larger numbers from republics than from kingdoms, since republics usually honor wisdom and bravery; kingdoms fear them. Hence the first cultivate wise and brave men; the second destroy them;[333]

we see that cities where the people are in control grow enormously in a very short time, and much more than those that have always been under a prince, as Rome did after she expelled the kings and Athens after she freed herself from Pisistratus. This comes from nothing else than that governments by the people are better than those by princes . . . if we consider all the people's faults, all the faults of princes, all the people's glories and those of princes, the people will appear in goodness and in glory far superior. And if princes are superior to people in establishing laws, forming communities according to law, setting up statutes and new institutions, the people are so much superior in keeping up things already organized that without doubt they attain the same glory as those who organize them;[334]

It is easy to learn why this love for free government springs up in people, for experience shows that cities never have increased in dominion or in riches except where they have been at liberty . . . The reason is easy to understand, because not individual good but common good is what makes cities great. Yet without doubt this common good is thought important only in republics, because everything that advances it they act upon, and however much harm results to this or that private citizen, those benefitted by the said common good are so many that they are able to press it on against the inclinations of those few who are injured by its pursuit;[335]

the common benefit gained from a free community is recognized by nobody while he possesses it: namely, the power of enjoying freely his possessions without any anxiety, of feeling no fear for the honor of his women and his children, of not being afraid for himself, because no one will ever admit that he has any obligation to a government which does not harm him. Therefore, as I said above, the state that is free and that is newly established, comes to have partisan enemies and not partisan friends;[336]

114

A bad opinion about the people arises because everybody says bad things about them without fear and freely, even while they are in power. Of princes everybody speaks with a thousand fears and a thousand cautions.[337]

As a responsible official from 19 June 1498 to 7 November 1512, in a position of great sensitivity respecting affairs both domestic and foreign, Machiavelli experienced republican government in operation. Subsequently, his writings demonstrate, as indicated above, that he considered the republican form not only consonant with the traditional aspirations of the Florentine people as publicly interpreted, but generally: more flexible for responding to changing times; more useful both for channelling the rivalries of the ambitious and the broad-based participation of the people; more likely to be well-advised in the selection of officials and policies; more congenial to the development of a higher quality of human character in a larger number of people since the discovery and cultivation of individual potentialities depend upon opportunity for public service[338] (and the better the country, the higher the potentialities in the citizens);[339] more successful in increasing the prosperity and happiness of a growing population; more resourceful in self-renewals and, hence, more firmly based and enduring.

In successive centuries as states manifested new excellencies they incited in individuals new aspirations releasing new energies for realization. Although the political units tended to increase in size and cohesion, the description which Machiavelli gave of the politics and statecraft of the Italy and Europe of his time continued to characterize the states on through the nineteenth and twentieth centuries; however, wide-ranging scientific inquiry penetrated ever new areas of human affairs and at the same time knitted and strengthened human interrelationships struggling forward wherever denials of human aspirations persisted or recurred.

As barriers of time, space, cultural diversity dissolved, clearer and more comprehensive perspectives were able to bring to attention more distant and subtle consequences of social processes and reveal that certain traditionally-held assumptions of their effectiveness were plausible due only to veils of insensitivity and that re-appraisal is essential. Attendant upon increasing mobility, the ferment of rising expectations, the expansion of educational opportunity, the recognition that the authority of government derives only from the consent of the governed and that its continuing franchise springs from the quality of its public service, the termination of human slavery, the expansion of the suffrage, the mounting challenge to unequal treatment wherever encountered—all have been contributing to subject to radical testing the continuing validity of forms and practices long assumed as elemental principles of institutions. Machiavelli's relation to the process found clear recognition by Tommasini when he wrote:

Ora cotesta verità effetuale è forse un amaro solletico per chi la specula;

115

ma è dolore profondo pel vivo che in fatto la subisce. Il Machiavelli la supportò e come dolore e come solletico; e considerò insieme l'immaginazione della vita e i suoi fenomeni come una serrie d'illusioni che bastano a piegar i volontarî inconsci e i lscivi alle necessità di natura; delle quali illusioni dove una se ne manifesta e cade, un'altra ne sorge subito, e si sostituisce a quella che sparve. All'uomo conscio pertanto si rivela nella coscienza il suo Dio; e degli entra così nel numero di quei pochi che sono fra gli *exutontimoroumenoi*, vera aristocratia dell'umanità. I sensitivi accattano poi quella consolazione che possono dalle attrative estetiche.[340]

Now that effectual truth is perhaps a bitter pleasure for him who observes it; but it is a deep pain in the life of him who experiences it. Machiavelli confronted it both as pain and as pleasure; and considered together the imagination of life and its phenomena as a series of illusions which suffice to bend the unwary volunteers and the shallow to the necessities of nature. With regard to these illusions, where one manifests itself and falls, another suddenly rises up and substitutes itself for that which disappeared. To the man proceeding with awareness, his own God reveals himself in the conscience; and thus he enters the number of those few who are among the *exutontimoroumenoi*, the true aristocracy of humanity. The sensitive collect, then, such crumbs of comfort as they can from aesthetic attractions.

Yet notwithstanding Machiavelli's courageous forays to extend the knowledge of truth in the management of public affairs, there remained in his outlook assumptions which have come to be perceived, or suspected, to derive their appearance of validity only from the force used to buttress them—a force coming to be seen as: at least obsolete, presently illusory, increasingly inapplicable, unserviceable, and potentially destructive.

Among these assumptions are the following:

1. that in order to organize a new state it is necessary for one man to concentrate all power into his own hands and himself to ordain its method of operation (above, pp. 59–62)—

(The establishment of the United States of America through the process of a constitutional convention and subsequent ratification of the instrument of government which it formulated and its continuing survival is proof positive that the more broadly-based and less violent procedure is not only more practical but also far more prudent. Subsequently, many other states have owed their establishment to the process of constitutional convention and referendum);

2. that, on the one hand, the state should avail itself of religion as an instrument of policy, Machiavelli had no doubt (above, pp. 49–52); although, on the other hand, he deplored priests' use of it to make men subservient (above, 100–105)—

(Subsequently, Thomas Jefferson, James Madison and Benjamin Franklin successfully struggled for the separation of church and state in the United States and the Supreme Court has continued to give the principle firm support);

3. that one can be another's master has become an ever less tenable claim—

(Communication arts and jurisprudence still are engaged in the struggle to formulate adequate procedures for research into such impositions and the boundaries for the right of privacy, *Griswold v. Connecticut* [1965];

4. that it is natural conditions which dictate conflict between men and that in time of peace there is no place for every man (above, pp. 14–15)—

(The discovery of unsuspected natural resources and the developing technology have amply demonstrated that man-made exclusionary policies, not any law of nature, account for tension-creating maldistribution of economic goods);

5. that the common good is known and can be adequately defined by one man (above, pp. 59, 62–64)—

(On the contrary, adequate definition of the public- or common-good requires the members' effective participation in the whole decision-making process—from initiation throughout evaluation of the consequences. For this fact, the history of democracy, as well as the indications from the psychological and social sciences, provide a steadily growing body of evidence);

6. that the nature of human nature is predictably known and that there is valid basis for adjudging and executing judgment on others as "good" or "evil" and that human nature is basically "evil" (above, pp. 33–37)—

(Findings through the biological, behavioral, psychological sciences and explorations in ethics and religion indicate that the jury is still out on the nature of human nature);

7. that organization through membership defines one's essential self and that the collective (be it: city, country, nation, church, race, class) is an entity and relates to the membership as an organism to its parts and benefits through treatment analogous to that of medicine and surgery (above, pp. 18–20, 55–56, 60–61, 84, 92)—

117

(Evidence from experimental psychology is lacking for any "Over Soul" of a group or a "group mind"[341] [the dependence of the state upon resort to force, as well as that of the corporation as "an artificial person" created by and dependent upon the enforceability of the law of the state, provides further evidence of the fictional character of fictions as entities. When real people find their ostensibly public power employed to assure to the artificial persons—as natural and constitutionally-guaranteed "rights"—inherent advantages at their expense, their growing treatment of voting and political participation as an exercise in futility further indicate the collectives' fictional character]);

8. that a state is an entity which to be healthy requires an aggressive posture (above, pp. 80–81, 85–89)—

(Similarities in the behavior of states and that of a grievously injured organism, as demonstrated by Dr. Kurt Goldstein, prompts the suggestion that, instead of entities, they are but pathological reactions of parts of mankind suffering injury (above, pp. 9–10);

9. that public purpose can transmute into social benefits behavior which, if indulged in for private ends, would occasion injury and ruin (above, pp. 59–62, 99) and that *raison d'état* can confer validity upon acts of violence—

(The competence of power-holders to determine the rightful application of power has grown increasingly qualified, during subsequent centuries, by the necessity for accountability to those from whom the power is derived and over whom it is exercised);

10. that knowledge of cause and effect in human affairs is available due to uniformities and can serve as a basis for effective action (above, pp. 69–70, 89–92, 99)—

(However, John Dewey demonstrated that that which we designate as "cause and effect" is limited to observed statistical frequency);[342]

11. that human nature is predictable (above, pp. 69–72) is a claim so speculative that "behavioral sciences" are taking shape as systematic inquiries into such a possibility;

12. that force (above, pp. 51, 59–63, 77–89, 92) and fraud, (above, pp. 34, 49–50, 92) can be integrated successfully into, and be accepted as, reality is confronted by increasingly diversified, subtle, successful

techniques available for implementing the growing imperative for discovery and disclosure;

13. that a death-grip over others, a capacity to strike terror into them, evokes awe-inspired power, confers individual and/or civic greatness (above, pp. 51, 59–63, 92)—

(However, opposed to and confronted by personal dignity, it manifests itself as cowardice);

14. that history is a manual for effective use of force (above, pp. 71–72]—

(Granted that Machiavelli perceived and warned against historians' bias in favor of conquerors [above, pp. 73–74], he did not proceed to point out that such chronicles convey a distorted impression by exalting as successful the utility of force when the total human event is not presented in perspective; and that indulgence in apologies for guilty consciences does not serve as a reliable guide for human policy);

15. that wars can be beneficial and result in prosperous victors (above, pp. 80–82, 85–89, 93) as Machiavelli himself recorded (above, pp. 93–98), was already suspect—

(Twentieth century experiences have increasingly disproved that wars can be waged entirely at others' expense and to one's own profit. Applied science and technology in manufacturing, commerce and communications have so interknit human relationships that it grows ever more inescapably evident that disastrous consequences fall also on the "victors." Furthermore, the idea that the modern nation-state would content itself with a citizen militia and not prolong terms of command and enlistment, and that those who profit from war would not seek to make their business a continuous operation, and that the social health would not be corrupted by belligerent pride, likewise has proved illusory. Just as did Rome, the modern states have developed their professional armies and ambitious general staffs, against which Machiavelli cited the ruinous course of the Roman Empire [above, pp. 93–98].

Chapter Four

"BACK TO BEGINNINGS"

Leaving aside, now, the evaluation of the fictions encountered in Machiavelli's writings, a fresh attempt "to return to the beginnings" (above, p. 7) is in order. Through reconsideration of the preparation and formative experiences of the founder of modern political science, can clues relevant for the direction of political science effectual for today and the days ahead, be discerned?

Recorded traces of his own introspection indicate that he applied to himself personally the counsel which he attributed to Castruccio Castracani on his death-bed:

> It is in this world of great importance to know oneself, and to be able to measure the forces of one's spirit and of one's position.[1]

Describing to his friend Vettori the exhilaration he was finding in the studies and reflections which were giving rise to the composition of the *Prince,* Machiavelli wrote:

> On the coming of evening, I return to my house and enter my study; and at the door I take off the day's clothing, covered with mud and dust, and put on garments regal and courtly; and reclothed appropriately, I enter the ancient courts of ancient men, where, received by them with affection, I feed on that food which only is mine and which I was born for, where I am not ashamed to speak with them and to ask them the reasons for their actions; and they in their kindness answer me; and for four hours of time I do not feel boredom, I forget every trouble, I do not dread poverty, I am not frightened by death; entirely I give myself over to them.[2]

Eight months earlier, Machiavelli had written him:

Fortune has determined that . . . I must talk about the government; I must either make a vow of silence or discuss that.[3]

How central for him was this interest, as already observed (above, pp. 3–4), he recognized early and repeatedly in subsequent years.[4]

Self-perception sufficient for self-reliance in action is the criterion which unfailingly won Machiavelli's endorsement whether in himself, in other individuals, in generals, in princes, in republics. Herein is, in reality, the essence of "the power" without which "men cannot make themselves safe"[5] (above, p. 15). In the draft of his letter to the exiled former head of the government in which he had served, Machiavelli wrote:

each man should do what his spirit dictates to him, and with boldness.[6]

To his friend Francesco Vettori, he wrote:

I believe that it is at all times the duty of a prudent man to reflect on what may harm him, and to foresee things when they are at a distance, and to assist what is good and to resist evil in time.[7]

That he consciously and scrupulously cultivated his ability to observe and reason about public affairs has already been noted (above, pp. 3–4). In writing Guicciardini of his work on the *History,* he confided:

I . . . shall try to act in such a way that, since I tell the truth, nobody will be able to complain.[8]

Although he considered that working out boldly one's own promptings through participation with others-involved best clarifies one's perception of himself and his relationships, when official service was denied him, his passion for public service did not diminish (above, pp. 6–7). Within the new confinement it took the form of making his reading serve his purpose. In his letter to Vettori regarding the composition of "a little work *On Princedoms,*" he explained:

And because Dante says that it does not produce knowledge when we hear but do not remember, I have noted everything in their ["the ancient men's"] conversation which has profited me.[9]

By enriching mutually his experience-born insights and his study of the actions of men who had effected human history, he generated a resource of such general value that with confidence he offered it both to contemporary prospective leaders and to the young who might be attracted into public service. In his letter to Piero Soderini he wrote of reading and experiencing the actions of men and their methods of procedure.[10]

In his dedication of the *Prince* to the young newly-appointed Duke of Urbino,[11] he mentioned the same sources.[12]

Seeking to penetrate the neglect by the powerful Medici unresponsive to his offers of experienced service, he wrote Vettori, the Florentine ambassador to Pope Leo X,

well may anybody be glad to get the services of one who at the expense of others has become full of experience.[13]

In the dedication of the *Discourses,* he wrote:

I believe I have got away from the common custom of those who write, who always address their works to some prince and, blinded by ambition and avarice, praise him for all the worthy traits, when they ought to blame him for every quality that can be censured. So in order not to run into this error, I have chosen not those who are princes, but those who because of their countless good qualities deserve to be; not those able to load me with offices, honors, and riches, but those who, though unable, would like to do so.[14]

and, in the Preface, they are still the same personally available resources which, with excessive modesty, he mentioned:

my poor talents, my slight experience of present affairs, and my feeble knowledge of ancient ones.[15]

Not quite as explicitly—due perhaps to his recognition that

it is a rash thing to treat material with which one has not dealt professionally[16]

in the dedicatory preface to *The Art of War,* he referred to those same two sources:

judging from what I have seen and read.[17]

Especially essential, according to Machiavelli, is well-grounded self-evaluation for one undertaking to establish or maintain a state:

when they [innovators] depend on their own resources and are strong enough to compel, then they are seldom in danger;[18]

A wise prince . . . seeks advice continually, but when it suits him and not when it suits somebody else; moreover, he deprives everyone of courage to advise him on anything if he does not ask it. But nonetheless he is a big asker and then, on the things asked about, a patient listener to the truth. Further, if he learns that anybody for any reason does not tell him the truth, he is angry . . .

Because many judge that some princes who are reputed prudent are so considered not on account of their own natures but on account of the good advisers they have around them, I must explain that without doubt they are deceiving themselves. This is a general rule that never fails: a prince who is not wise himself cannot be advised well . . .Therefore it is to be concluded that good advice, from whomsoever it comes, must originate in the prince's discretion, and not the prince's discretion in the good advice;[19]

a wise prince takes care to base himself on what is his own, not on what is another's;[20]

those defenses alone are good, are certain, are durable, that depend on yourself and your own abilities;[21]

a general when he is obliged either to flee or to fight, almost always chooses to fight, since perhaps by this method, though it is very doubtful, he may be able to win; in the other, he must lose in any case;[22]

a prince who has an army assembled, and sees that for lack of money or of friends he cannot keep such an army a long time, is altogether mad if he does not tempt Fortune before his army begins to go to pieces, because if he waits, he certainly loses; if he makes the attempt, he may conquer;[23]

no military force can be employed that is more useful than one's own;[24]

no one can use as a foundation forces other than one's own;[25]

it is much better to tempt Fortune when she possibly will favor you than, not tempting her, to face certain ruin.[26]

As the passing years deepened the frustrating realization that he was finding no Medicean prince willing to accept his guidance, increasingly Machiavelli conceived for himself the role of mentor for coming generations of leaders. The first inkling he gave of thinking of himself as an educator, indicates a strong aversion to the idea. Exactly six months after the letter in which he mentioned his work *"On Princedoms,"* he wrote Vettori:

I shall continue, then, among my lousy doings, without finding a man who remembers my service or who believes that I can be good for anything.

124

But it is impossible that I can remain long in this way because I am using up my money, and if God does not show himself more favorable to me, I see that I shall one day be forced to leave home and hire out as a tutor or a secretary to a constable, since I can do nothing else, or fix myself in some desert land to teach reading to boys, leaving my family here. They could reckon that I am dead, and would get on much better because I am an expense to them, being used to spending and unable to get on without spending.[27]

In the *Discourses* he anticipated an attentive response by the young, since, as he wrote, he hoped thereby to

show the way to someone who, with more vigor, more prudence and judgment, can carry out this intention of mine;[28]

I shall be bold in saying clearly what I learn about Roman times and the present, in order that the minds of the young men who read these writings of mine may reject the present and be prepared to imitate the past, whenever Fortune gives them opportunity. For it is the duty of a good man to teach others anything of value that through the malice of the times and of Fortune you have been unable to put into effect, in order that since many will know of it, some of them more loved by Heaven may be prepared to put it into effect.[29]

In the *Prince* he had written:

[Fortune] is the friend of young men, because they are less cautious, more spirited, and with more boldness master her.[30]

In *The Art of War* he had his spokesman Fabrizio Colonna say:

this is the business for young men, I am persuaded that young men will be more fit to discuss it, as they are quicker to carry it out.[31]

Earlier, he had written:

I am willing that you, Cosimo, and these other young men should here question me, because I believe that your youth makes you more interested in military matters and readier to believe what I shall say. Men of another age, with their hair white and the blood in their bodies turned to ice, are commonly some of them enemies of war, some beyond correction, believing that the times and not bad customs force men to live thus.[32]

And he closed the treatise with a return to the appeal to youth:

I repine at Nature, who either should have made me such that I could not see this or should have given me the possibility for putting it into effect. Since I am an old man, I do not imagine today that I can have opportunity for it. Therefore I have been liberal of it with you who, being young and gifted, can at the right time, if the things I have said please you, aid and advise your princes to their advantage.[33]

The didactic purpose emerges again in the preface to *The History of Florence*:

If any reading is useful to citizens who govern republics, it is that which shows the causes of the hatreds and factional struggles within the city, in order that such citizens having grown wise through the sufferings of others, can keep themselves united. If the experiences of any republic are moving, those of a man's own city, when he reads about them, are much more moving and useful.[34]

The same conception of the educator's encouragement for the young and of the transference of hope to them, appears in one of his last letters, that to his "dearest son Guido:"

I have received your letter, which has been a great pleasure to me, especially since you write that you are completely cured, because I could not have better news. For if God grants life to you and to me, I believe I can make you a man of standing, if you wish to play your part as you should . . . But it is necessary for you to learn letters and music, since you see how much I am aided by the little skill I have. So, my son, if you wish to give pleasure to me and bring prosperity and honor to yourself, do well and learn, because if you help yourself, everybody will help you.[35]

In the *Discourses,* he had written:

It is very important that a boy of tender years hears praise or blame of a certain thing, because it will of necessity make an impression according to which he will govern his conduct in all periods of his life.[36]

As one's ultimate resource, Machiavelli recognized courage. A reminder in one of his last letters to Vettori is characteristic of his standpoint:

you can save yourselves if you do not give up your courage;[37]

and in the *Discourses*:

I assert, indeed, once more that it is very true, according to what we see in all the histories, that men are able to assist Fortune but not to thwart her. They can weave her designs but cannot destroy them. They ought,

126

then, never to give up as beaten, because, since they do not know her purpose and she goes through crooked and unknown roads, they can always hope, and hoping are not to give up, in whatever fortune and whatever affliction they may be;[38]

and again,

If, as soon as the purpose of your adversary is revealed, you prepare forces, even though they are inferior to his, he esteems you. You are also more esteemed by neighboring princes, and when you are under arms, some decide to aid you who, if you abandon yourself, never will aid you;[39]

in the *Prince*:

She [Fortune] shows her power where strength and wisdom do not prepare to resist her, and directs her fury where she knows that no dykes or embankments are ready to hold her;[40]

and in *The Art of War*:

nothing is so likely to succeed as what your enemy thinks you unable to attempt, because usually men are injured most where they fear least . . . the best remedy that can be used against a design of the enemy is to do willingly what he intends you shall do by force; by doing it willingly, you do it in order and to your advantage and his disadvantage. If you do it when you are forced to, it is your ruin;[41]

and again in the *Discourses*:

A Republic or a Prince Should Not Put Off Benefiting Men until Times of Necessity;[42]

A prince or a republic ought to appear to do through liberality any action compelled by necessity;[43]

He reported Cesare Borgia as saying:

"the favor that has to be done, a man had better do of himself and with good will rather than without."[44]

Impelled by his deep concern to serve the common good,[45] convinced that "it is well to reason about everything,"[46] setting as his aim to analyze the consequences of men's attempts in public affairs to "show a bold face to Fortune,"[47] to discover the underlying reasons for success or failure of such attempts,[48] and so to expound them as to provide a useful guide for those seriously engaged in such an endeavor,[49] Machiavelli was exploring and advocating an education for action effective in promoting in human relations the territorial basis essential for living together through intelligent will. Considering religious zeal exhausted,[50] revolted by the pervasive corruption and misrule under the guise of government (above, pp. 109–111), Machiavelli, as Plato in *The Republic*,[51] endeavored to summon up the will to escape from the life of a community of swine wallowing complacently in their own filth[52] and to secure order befitting men.

Chapter Five

FACTORS CONTRIBUTING TO MACHIAVELLI'S DEVELOPMENT

Whence came the new direction which Machiavelli expressed? Might the pursuit of such an inquiry reveal clues significant in guiding choice for a currently more constructive direction?

CONTRIBUTIONS FROM HIS FLORENTINE HERITAGE

The citizens of Renaissance Florence could draw from its vibrant history and contemporary pre-eminence, inspiration, encouragement, and a sense of responsibility for the utmost development and use of their talents. In it Machiavelli understood his very reason for existence.[1] During the twelfth, thirteenth, fourteenth and fifteenth centuries, Italian cities—Genoa, Pisa, Siena, and, latterly, Florence—had grown rich, enlarged their freedoms and advanced their culture through highly profitable financial, commercial and industrial relations with the less-developed suppliers of raw materials in the countries to the north and west. Gradually, in reaction, defensive measures and structures took shape. Already in Magna Charta (1215) English churchmen revolted against the papal practice of bestowing lucrative offices in the English church upon Italian favorites who continued to reside in Italy. In mid-thirteenth century, both popes and Holy Roman emperors employed Florentine firms as their bankers. Within the city, through their guilds, the people were gaining participation in public affairs to an unprecedented degree. By the fourteenth century, Florentine banking houses were so deeply involved in England that when Edward III, waging war on France, in 1339 defaulted on his debts and disenfranchised foreign bankers, such an economic depression befell the city that the banking and business community brought in the Duke of Athens and imposed on the city a tyrannical dictatorship.[2] Growing tension between the steadily concentrating power under the leadership of the Wool Guild and the masses of workers of little or no skills who were finding themselves frustrated by prospects of arrested opportunity and, after 1343,[3] were gaining increasing political power, culminated in the summer of 1378 in a briefly successful victory by the Ciompi—the industrial masses who termed themselves "the people of God" due to their having no other resources. Two waves of reaction—one at the end of that same summer and the other four years later—re-instated the pre-revolt framework but henceforth workers imported from abroad, but denied civil rights or prospects by the military power of the city, were kept in subjection to the production policies of the privileged guilds. With closely-knit financial, commercial, industrial resources, leading Florentine families, among which, in the early fifteenth century, the Medici gained pre-eminence, were establishing branches throughout Europe, while at home they exploited the dependent cities, the countryside and the poor.[4]

Although the tap-root of democracy in Florence had been severed and constitutionally the movement put to rest, protestation of support for Florentine liberty continued to flourish in official letters and rhetoric as never before. A favorite theme of the humanist heads of the Florentine chancery was praise of Florentine liberty.[5] During the war between Florence and Pope Gregory XI, Coluccio Salutati, in the words of the historian Ferdinand Schevill, interpreted

the struggle to the world as the insurrection of oppressed subjects against an overbearing master . . . [and] affirmed that the single issue involved was Liberty, for which his fellow-citizens were represented as unselfishly sacrificing themselves to the sole end that the brave little communities of central Italy might not perish under the heel of an inhuman tyrant.[6]

From 1427 to 1444, Leonardo Bruni, "its greatest living humanist,"[7] served as chancellor. Through his research he

destroyed the popular legend of Florence's foundation by Caesar and established as the time of its origin the republican Rome of Sulla[8]

and was

the first to see the political implications of the new theory on the Roman origins of Florence, according to which the city had been founded . . . before Rome had become subject to the power of one man.[9]

Still more basic and original for a Florentine, Machiavelli held to be his Tuscaninity. In the *Discourses,* he wrote:

That men, born in any region show in all times almost the same natures;[10]

That [method for increasing their size] followed by the ancient Tuscans

130

was a league of several republics in which none went beyond any other in authority or in rank. As they conquered, they made the new states their companions, as the Swiss do now and as the Achaeans and the Aetolians did in ancient times in Greece . . . In Italy, before the Roman empire, the Tuscans had great power on sea and on land [*Livy, 5.33*]; though there is no detailed history of their affairs, yet some little record and some signs of their greatness remain. We know that they sent to the shore of the upper sea a colony called Adria, which was so noble that it gave its name to the sea that the Latins still call the Adriatic. We also know that from the Tiber as far as the foot of the Alps that circle the mass of Italy, men submitted to their arms. Notwithstanding this, two hundred years before the Roman forces grew great, the Tuscans lost their authority over the region called Lombardy; that province was occupied by the French . . . The Tuscans, then, lived with that equality and proceeded in their expansion in the first manner mentioned above . . . The method of leagues earlier mentioned . . . is, after the Romans, the best. Though through it you cannot grow very great, two good things result: first, you do not easily draw wars down upon yourself; second, all you take, you keep easily.[11]

The special appeal which Bruni's discovery held for Machiavelli as one maintaining republican preferences in a Florence still struggling against the growing Medicean trend toward a princedom, becomes clear in Machiavelli's treatment of relations between ancient Tuscany and Veii as reported by Livy:

in the times when the Romans went to besiege Veii, Tuscany was free, and it so much enjoyed its liberty and so much hated the name of prince that when the Veientians for their protection had established a king in Veii and were asking aid from the Tuscans against the Romans, the Tuscans, after holding many consultations, determined not to give aid to the Veientians so long as they lived under a king, thinking it not too good to defend a country of those who had already submitted to another.[12]

In the records of ancient times, Machiavelli found a helpful analogy for much of the frustration and disillusionment he and his city had suffered during his own official service:

in ancient times . . . the Tuscans . . . oppressed by the Romans and many times put to flight and defeated by them, seeing that with their own forces they could not sustain the Roman attack, agreed to give the French who lived in Italy on this side of the Alps a sum of money, on their promise to unite their armies with the Tuscan armies and march against the Romans. What resulted was that the French, after getting the money, would then not take arms, saying that they accepted it with the condition not that they would fight the Tuscans' enemies but that they would abstain from plundering their territory. Thus the Tuscans through the avarice and treachery of the French, were deprived at once of their money and of the aid they hoped for [*Livy, 10.10*]. Thus it appears from this instance of the ancient Tuscans and from that of the Florentines that the French have always used the same methods. From this it easily can be inferred how much princes can trust them;[13]

Thus . . . Tuscany was once powerful, religious and vigorous, having her own customs and her native language. All this achievement, as I have mentioned, was wiped out by the Roman power, so that there remains only a record of the name.[14]

However, the tradition from ancient Tuscany provided him a source of hope and encouragement. He considered that even down to his own time there was evident some survival of the ancient spirit:[15]

if the imitation of the Romans seems difficult, that of the ancient Tuscans ought not to appear so, especially to the present Tuscans, because, if the former could not, for the reasons given, set up an empire like that of the Romans, they were able to gain in Italy the power that their manner of proceeding yielded them. This was for a long time secure with the utmost glory of authority and of arms, and with the highest reputation in manners and religion.[16]

The tradition also provided him with a basis for perceiving that, despite all of Rome's prestige, power and longevity, Rome had not so entirely eradicated the native love of liberty that there did not survive hope for its effective renewal—the cause to which Machiavelli was feeling himself dedicated. Rooted in his Tuscaninity, Machiavelli could see in the methods of Rome the destruction not only of the liberty and *virtù* of those whom it conquered, but, equally effectively, of its own.[17] Leo Strauss has commented:

precisely because he believed that the men who are born in a country preserve through all ages more or less the same nature, and as the nature of the Romans was different from that of the Tuscans, his [i.e., Machiavelli's] hope was also grounded on his recollection of Tuscan glory; the old Etrurians had made a decisive contribution to the religion of the Romans. He seems to have regarded himself as a restorer of Tuscan glory because he too contributed toward supplying Rome with a new religion or a new outlook on religion. Or perhaps he thought of Tarquinius Priscus who, coming from Etruria, strengthened the democratic element of the Roman polity.[18]

Moreover, as a descendant of landed nobility who had been pressured, as the condition of permission to return from exile following the Ghibelline victory in 1260, to become bourgeoisie in the city of tradesmen and manufacturers,[19] did he feel somewhat apart from, if not superior to, those who dominated the decision-making in the city and find deep congeniality in the role of critical observer?

In the institutions of Florence, as compared with those of Rome, Machiavelli detected a flaw which made the domestic discords of Florentine history injurious to her rather than that source of strength which he considered those of Rome to have been for her.[20] The cause, he held, reached back to the difference in the method of their origins. Rome, established by one man, had a firm and adequate foundation.[21] Florence, however, established and long governed as a colony, had never been rightly formed as a state:

> if it is difficult for cities of free origin, which like Rome have ruled themselves, to find laws which will keep them free, we cannot wonder that it is not merely difficult but impossible for cities of origin immediately servile to organize themselves in such a way that they can live in peace and according to law. This is evidently true of the city of Florence. Since at her origin she was subject to Roman authority and had always lived under the control of others, she remained for a time humble, without planning for herself. Then, when there came a chance for taking breath, she undertook to make her own laws; these, being mingled with old ones that were bad, could not be good. And so she has gone on governing herself for the two hundred years for which there are trustworthy records, without ever having had a government because of which she could truly be called a republic. Difficulties like hers have always existed for all those cities whose beginnings were like hers. And though many times, through free and public votes, full power to reform her has been given to a few citizens, nevertheless they have never organized her for the common benefit, but always for the advantage of their own party; this has caused not order but greater disorder in that city.[22]

Rubenstein has documented the prolonged and resourceful struggle to preserve Florentine liberty and equality in the face of the pressures of the powerful families, and ultimately the Medici, to gain control of the republic.[23] For outspoken opposition in official assembly to proposals favored by the oligarchs, despite prior promises of freedom of speech, an earlier Machiavelli, by name Girolami, "suffered torture, exile and finally death in imprisonment."[24]

Donald Weinstein has traced the development among Florentines through three centuries of a concept of special mission and destiny:

> [what we have been calling the myth was] . . . a conviction which persisted throughout the Republic's history and intimately connected with her life. The substance of what we have been calling the myth was the belief that Florence had a special destiny of leadership in the furtherance of certain high political, moral and religious principles, a destiny appointed by God who would reward her gloriously if she fulfilled His expectations. In form,

the myth consisted of two main themes, both of which can be found in its earliest appearance, in the thirteenth century, the theme of Florence as the daughter of Rome and the theme of Florentine rebirth . . . from early on aspirations for power were disciplined by a sense of responsibility for promoting justice and liberty, while the idea of rebirth was associated with a restoration of republican government as well as of a new spirituality . . . The struggle with the papacy, the Ciompi upheaval and Milanese aggression combined to force a rethinking not only of Florence's position *vis-a-vis* the other Italian states but also of the relationship between the individual and the city state. One product of this rethinking, as Hans Baron has shown, was civic humanism, with its ethos of individual freedom and civic responsibility to an idealized free republic. Another, and probably related, development was the new assertion of Florence's mystical destiny to religious and political supremacy, reflecting not only the break from papal tutelage and the successful defense of liberty, but also a new sense of the Florentine state as the source and guarantor of social justice and well being. The appearance of the New Jerusalem theme, which was a stronger version of the old theme of rebirth, expressed this new emphasis upon domestic harmony founded upon mutual responsibility as the prerequisite for world leadership. Weakened by private greed and selfish exploitation and beset by godless and tyrannical enemies, the Florentines would cleanse themselves, unite in a spirit of communal love and assert their dominance in a new age of spiritual perfection and peace. During Cosimo de'Medici's time it was a support for the consensus upon which his leadership was based. It also served the anti-Mediceans of the 1460's in their protest against tyranny. Later it provided suggestive themes for the poets and artists who spun a *mystique* around Florence and her ruler, Lorenzo the Magnficent. The discontent of the post-Laurentian 1490's expressed itself in deploring the plight of the "lovely lady" and foretelling her ultimate liberation, just as the woman clothed in the sun would be liberated from the attacks of the seven-headed beast. Savonarola also embraced the Florentine myth, finally, which helps explain why his movement attracted such a broad spectrum of support, not only from the populace, long since imbued with the radical millennian myth of the Fraticelli and the Ciompi, but also from the *literati* and the artists who had their own eclectic versions. The main new element in the Savonarola movement was the prophet's own personality; its literature was a combination of three centuries of Florentine mythology—Guelf republican, Ciompi millenarian, Roman imperialist and Laurentian mystical and Neo-platonic. All these themes survived Savonarola's downfall in 1498, and the Savonarolan episode was itself incorporated into later prophesies as another event long since predicted. Thus the myth absorbed Savonarola as it had absorbed other occurrences in Florence's history, treating each of them as a determined event, a milestone on the predestined path toward the realization of Florentine glory.[25]

Largely in reaction to the economic policies of the papacy and its allies in pursuing their financial, commercial and industrial interests, centers of power were emerging and giving leadership and force to the countries of France, England and Spain. By 1494 with the descent of the French army, under Charles VIII, into Italy began the series of shocks through which the realization grew, as if by repeated turns of a rack, that, regardless of the professions of aid to one city or another or to the papacy, the French, the Spaniards, the Emperor, and the Pope—all, despite their promises of assistance, only took from Italy and together left: her, poorer; the people, all further from freedom and independence; and the city states, no longer politically adequate for coping with the threats to freedom and security.[26]

CONTRIBUTIONS FROM HIS FAMILY

The family was of profound influence throughout Machiavelli's life. Their ancient lineage and distinguished services during the history of Florence was for him an undoubted source of strength, stability and inspiration. The Machiavellis claimed an ancestry of distinction reaching back to the former lords of Montespertoli. As a Guelf family exiled in 1260 but returning after reconciliation with the new government, they came to be numbered among the "middle class noted families."[27] Perhaps in Machiavelli's character there was still a trace of the ancestral assumption of noble superiority,[28] of Guelf privilege and independence even though long since formally renounced. Detectable in Machiavelli's writings is a continued appreciation of the mettle which the nobles had nourished.[29] To their own disadvantage, Machiavelli held, the people of Florence had pressed their victory against them too far. In *The History of Florence,* concerning domestic conflicts, he wrote:

the enmities that at the outset existed in Rome between the people and the nobles were ended by debating, those in Florence by fighting; those in Rome were terminated by law, those in Florence by the exile and death of many citizens; those in Rome always increased military power, those in Florence wholly destroyed it; those in Rome brought that city from an equality of citizens to a very great inequality; those in Florence brought her from inequality to a striking equality. It must be that this difference of effect was caused by the different purposes of these two peoples, for the people of Rome wished to enjoy supreme honors along with the nobles; the people of Florence fought to be alone in the government, without any participation by the nobles . . . the Florentine people's desire was harmful and unjust, so that the nobility with greater forces prepared to defend themselves, and therefore the result was blood and the exile of the citizens, and the laws then made were planned not for the common profit but altogether in favor of the conqueror . . . since the people won, the nobles continued to be deprived of high offices, and if they wished to get them again, they were forced in their conduct, their spirit, and their way of living not merely to be like the men of the people, but to seem so. From this came the changes in ensigns, the alteration in the titles of families that the nobles carried out in order to seem like the people. Hence the ability in arms and the boldness of spirit possessed by the nobility were destroyed, and these qualities could not be rekindled in the people, where they did not exist, so that Florence grew always weaker and more despicable[30] [above, p. 82].

May not Machiavelli's conviction that an inherent right to a sense for courageous action is reconcilable to the establishment of public order and essential for the promotion of the common good, have echoed his family's traditions from the nobility and his conception of the nobility's contributions in the Florentine as well as the Roman republic? May not his enthusiastic dedication to the creation and establishment of the citizen militia have had its roots in his pride as a descendant from the nobility and his determination to provide for his republic a citizen body worthy of it? Whatever the factors which contributed to it, that is a truly distinctive characteristic which Tommasini pointed out when writing:

Egli vede da presbite, discerne egregiamente il fondo estremo delle cose, ma o non vede, o non vuol vedere quello che gliene sta proprio sott'occhio. Forse, come già accennammo, è disdegno delle circostanze, o fiducia di poterle signoreggiare; ma il merito e la sventura del Machiavelli sta appunto nel disdegnar lui quasi sempre l'ambiente suo.[31]

He was farsighted; he discerned remarkably the ultimate ground of things; but he did not see, or did not wish to see, that which stood directly under his eyes. Perhaps, as we have already noted, he scorned the circumstances, or was confident in being able to master them; but the merit and misfortune of Machiavelli consists exactly in almost always scorning his circumstances.

After the return of the exiled Guelf families to the city (1267), during the next two centuries the Machiavellis gave distinguished services to the city: twelve as gonfaloniers and fifty-four as priors. One had attained sainthood in the Church and one, martyrdom in the cause of liberty. The records indicate a traditional inclination for identification with the defense of the people against the oligarchical tendencies of the great families.[32]

Although his own father was a doctor of laws and at some time had been treasurer in the Marches, the chief economic base for the family seems to have been revenue derived from land holdings in Val di Pesa[33] rather than from the practice of his profession. The sense of civic security appears to have been overcast by some imputation as yet undetermined—whether as to his father's legitimacy of his financial credit rating[34]—serious enough, in the opinion of

Niccolo's friends, to endanger his own eligibility for remaining in office.

Niccolo and his father were held together by feelings of, what Ridolfi characterizes as, "affectionate intimacy."[35] To the influence of his father, knowledgeable in both Greek and Latin,[36] may be accredited Machiavelli's life-long love of Latin literature and especially of Livy's *History* (above, p. 133).

Two older sisters and a younger brother completed the family in which he was raised.[37] He was already twenty-seven years of age before death struck the family when, in 1496, his mother died.[38] Four years later, death took his father,[39] and soon thereafter, his elder sister.[40]

In August 1501, Niccolo married Marietta Corsini.[41] Between 1502 and 1513 she bore him at least eight children[42] of whom four sons and a daughter lived to maturity.[43] Following the death of Machiavelli's elder sister, Machiavelli and his wife received into their home the young nephew, Giovanni Vernaccia, whom they raised as one of their own.[44] It was to him, more than to any other, after Giovanni's business career took him to distant Pera, that, during the times of deepest loneliness, Machiavelli bared his feelings.[45]

CONTRIBUTIONS FROM HIS ECONOMIC CIRCUMSTANCES

Inherited land ownership gave Machiavelli a sense of belonging, of independence, of stability, a refuge in adversity, a refreshment from fatigue and a spur to conservation of those material resources through distinctively personal application and exertion. A glimpse as to how his land served him, he gave in his celebrated letter to Vettori on 10 December 1513.[46] The title to the holdings, modest in amount, reached into the dim past.[47] Indeed, perhaps the earliest of the writings of Machiavelli which has come down to us is a letter written on behalf of all of the Machiavelli families in defense of certain land titles against claims asserted by the powerful Pazzi family.[48] The success achieved by this letter to Giovanni Lopez, cardinal of Perugia, reinforced as it had been by one from the Signoria, doubtlessly deeply impressed the young Machiavelli, then in his twenty-second year. Revenue from the rents continued to be a major source of family income,[49] although probably insufficient to prevent Machiavelli's father from being listed among debtors.[50] Bernardo's brother, Niccolo's uncle, Totto, left to Bernardo his share of the inheritance[51] as, a generation later, upon entering the priesthood did Niccolo's brother, Totto,[52] so that the family's estate in its entirety passed from Niccolo's grandfather to Niccolo's children.

As had his father,[53] Niccolo felt the need to supplement income from the rents with salary from public office and when that was cut off he expressed anxiety over the prospect of poverty befalling his family and himself. Despite his letters of response to the questions on great power politics posed for him by his friend, the Florentine ambassador to Pope Leo X, and notwithstanding

Machiavelli's report of the completion of the *Prince*, when no prospect for employment was appearing, he began to be haunted by the limitations of his resources for his wife, his growing family of four sons, a daughter and himself. In April 1514, he suggested to Vettori that he help him get an adjustment in taxes[54] and about two months later he expressed personal distress, deeper than at any other time, over his economic condition.[55]

Amid the tumultuous events toward the end of 1511, Machiavelli made his first will[56] in which he bequeathed all to the unrestricted care of Marietta, his wife—a provision unchanged in his second will. As Tommasini remarked:

> Il testamento di lui ci comprova la riverenza ch'egli conservò sempre per la sua compagna, e la fiducia in cui visse e morì, ch'ella sapesse non pure educar l'animo di quelli, ma amministrarne e proteggerne le sostanze. Lei sola lasciò tutrice e curatrice de'minori, sciolta dall'onere di rendere conto della tutela sua.[57]

> His will proves for us the esteem which he always kept for his companion, and the confidence, in which he lived and died, that she knew not only to guide the spirit of the children but to administer and protect their material goods. Her alone he left as guardian and trustee of the children, freed from the burden of rendering account of her guardianship.

Machiavelli's concept of poverty was for him a source not only of anxiety but also of pride and strength. Looking back on his early life, he viewed it as having been spent in somewhat straightened circumstances.[58] Even though, because of their landholdings, the Machiavellis were considered among the *popolani grassi* [rich commoners] of Florence,[59] Niccolo was born into a branch burdened with debt[60] and which, as was the custom, treated their land as an inviolable family trust.[61] The rapidly growing prosperity of the banking, commercial, industrial families placed under special strain those dependent upon income from the produce of their lands and the rewards from their professional training.[62]

Machiavelli's official correspondence on nearly all of his missions abroad—the first mission to France;[63] the mission to Caesar Borgia;[64] the first mission to Rome;[65] the legation to Julius II;[66] the third mission to France[67]—registers the personal hardships which expenditures beyond his salary occasioned him.

Machiavelli came to view the relative poverty of the land-holding poor as a prime source of the civic virtue of republican Rome as long as such poverty prevailed:

> We have argued elsewhere that the most useful thing a free state can bring about is to keep its citizens poor . . . experience reveals that four hundred years after Rome had been built, her people were still in the utmost poverty. I cannot believe that any conditions are stronger in producing this effect

than the knowledge that poverty did not close your road to whatever rank and whatever honor, and that men went to seek Ability whatever house she lived in.[68]

Repeatedly in the *Discourses* he affirmed:

well-ordered republics ought to keep their treasuries rich and their citizens poor;[69]

and later:

I could show with a long speech that poverty produces much better fruit than riches, and that one has honored the cities, the provinces, the religions, and that the other has overthrown them, if the writings of other men had not many times made the subject splendid.[70]

In response to the question, "What are these things you would like to introduce that are like the ancient ones?" he had his spokesman in *The Art of War* begin his response:

To honor and reward excellence, not to despise poverty.[71]

Poverty, as a personal prospect, however, presented itself not only as a spur to mastering his resources and putting them to the maximum use but also as a potential cause for anxiety. After revealing to Vettori that he had written *"On Princedoms,"* he closed his letter as follows:

The giving of it [to Giuliano de'Medici] is forced on me by the necessity that drives me, because I am using up my money, and I cannot remain as I am a long time without becoming despised through poverty . . . Of my honesty there should be no doubt, because having always preserved my honesty, I shall hardly now learn to break it; he who has been honest and good for forty-three years, as I have, cannot change his nature; and as a witness to my honesty and goodness I have my poverty.[72]

In other letters to Vettori he returned to the same theme.[73] To his nephew he revealed, even more deeply, anxiety due to economic insecurity.[74]

Before himself, however, Machiavelli kept in mind his concept of the "important citizens" of republican Rome:

[a] noteworthy thing is to observe the noble minds of those citizens. When they are put at the head of an army, the greatness of their spirits raised them above every prince; they took no account of kings or of republics; they were confused or terrified by nothing whatever; yet on returning to

private stations, they became economical, humble, careful of their little properties, obedient to the magistrates, respectful to their elders, so that it seems impossible that one and the same spirit could undergo such change.[75]

Perhaps he drew some personal consolation from the philosophic perspective which he occasionally expressed that

human wants are insatiable;[76]

and the remedy which he perceived:

men never do anything good except by necessity . . . Hence it is said that hunger and poverty make men industrious, and the laws make them good.[77]

CONTRIBUTIONS FROM HIS RELIGION

Biographers have related Machiavelli's ventures in poetry, his cultivation of a gift for writing, and perhaps his attention to religion, to the tradition that his mother was a composer of religious verses—none of which has come down to us.[78]

Indications of an intimate religious sentiment occur in a diversity of his writings: in his letter to his son Guido;[79] in the formula with which generally he closed his letters to his nephew:

May Christ watch over you[80]

and which is found also at the close of an especially personal letter to Lodovico Alamanni;[81] in deferential references to Saint Francis and Saint Dominic[82] (above, p. 101; in his letter of 17 May 1521 to Guicciardini[83] (above, p. 105); most deeply and fully expressed in "An Exhortation to Penitence,"[84] which, in the words of Ridolfi, is

rightly described as the climax of the author's Christian thought;[85]

and, finally, in his last hours:

When his friends had gone, he remained alone with his family, and quietly preparing himself for death, 'he allowed Fra Matteo to hear him confess his sins', and the latter stayed with him until his last breath.[86]

Machiavelli's remark

He who reads the Bible intelligently[87]

140

may reflect a critical interest quickened by Antonio Brucioli, one of the members of the company which gathered for conversations in the Rucellai Gardens, who was engaged in translating the Old Testament into Italian.[88] The powerful ferment created through the fusion of reform with the enhancement of the vernacular had been demonstrated, more than a century before Machiavelli's time, by John Wycliffe's translation of the Bible into English. This same insight was prompting Machiavelli to enrich the language of Dante, Petrarch and Boccaccio with his "Decennali," the *Prince, Discourses, The Art of War, The History of Florence* and "Discorso o Dialogo intorno alla Nostra Lingua,"[89] and Martin Luther to translate the Bible into German.[90]

Earlier religious contexts may have been the source of certain maxims which Machiavelli treated as basic in his thinking. Long before Machiavelli in his *Discourses* had asserted:

of mixed bodies, such as republics and religions, I say that those changes are to their advantage that take them back toward their beginnings,[91]

John Wycliffe in his *De demonio mevidiano* had written:

Medium autem sanandi hunc morbum in clericis foret, ad statum, quem Cristus instituit, ipsos reducere.[92]

However, the means of healing this sickness in the clergy would be to bring them back to the condition which Christ instituted.

The maxim that

A man must be alone if he is to organize a republic afresh or remodel her with complete annulment of her old laws,[93]

a churchman had already formulated as a criticism of the movement to reform the church by means of a council[94] (above, p. 59). The maxim that

all armed prophets win, and unarmed ones fall,[95]

in Tommasini's estimation,[96] had its derivation in the concern expressed by Petrarch, by way of Dante, regarding Fra Dolcino.

The concept of *virtù*, as employed by Machiavelli, had its origin in scriptural scholarship. Over a century and a half before Machiavelli entered public life, in 1447, Pope Nicholas V had brought Lorenzo Valla to Rome[97] and "appointed him Apostolic Writer." This "best of all classical scholars" of the time[98] applied philological criticism to the Biblical texts and was the first to study Latin texts of the Gospels critically in light of the Greek texts. In 1505 Erasmus published Valla's *Annotations on the New Testament*.[99] One potentially highly significant example of Valla's contributions was the recovery and re-establishment of the original meaning of this concept. Tommasini has pointed out:

> È il Valla alla parola *virtù* riconobbe nel Nuovo Testamento lo stesso significato di *dunamis,* col quale in seguito la usò il Machiavelli.[100]

> It is Valla who with respect to the word *virtù* recognized in the New Testament the very same meaning of *dunamis* with which subsequently Machiavelli used it.

John Knox in his exegetical comments on Romans 1:16 has written:

> Now Paul calls this gospel the *power of God.* The term is used throughout the *New Testament* to designate a miracle, a manifestation of God's omnipotence, a mighty work of God . . . But Paul does more than call the gospel a *proclamation* of the *dunamis,* it *is* the *dunamis.*[101]

Tommasini has shown that Valla's influence on Machiavelli's thinking was profound and diverse.[102] His perspective toward Moses and the Evangelists as historic rather than as sacred figures[103] foreshadowed Machiavelli's own.

A critical attitude toward the clerical sale of indulgences gives further indication of Machiavelli's affinity for religious renovation. Two references suggest that Machiavelli considered the sale of indulgences a pervasive means by which the deepest human relations were being corroded.[104]

Committing himself to observe men's behavior and by it to weigh their professions, to concern himself with "how men live" rather than "how they ought to live,"[105] Machiavelli found, as already noted (above, pp. 100–105), the Roman Church exasperating in policy and its local priests characteristically venal, callous and dull in conduct.

Through his profound study of Machiavelli and religious thought, Tommasini arrived at the considered judgment that

> Il risorgimento della fede adunque per via d'una riformazione religiosa, provocata e ottenuta in qualunque modo, fu certo tra le aspirazioni più vive e intime del Machiavelli.[106]

> The revival of faith, then, through a religous reform, aroused and obtained by any means whatever, was certainly one of Machiavelli's most lively and intimate aspirations.

That Machiavelli found the significance of religion to consist primarily in its usefulness as an instrument of public policy, his writings make abundantly clear. In one of his earliest letters, the one in which he summarized a sermon which he had heard Savonarola preach, he quoted him as having said: Prudence is straight thinking in practical matters.[107] From his study of the ancients he cited the examples of Moses, Numa, Lycurgus, Solon, as evidence of the importance of resort to the use of religion in the establishing and maintaining of states. In this role accorded to religion, as noted above (pp. 49–52), he found strong confirmation in Livy's *History* (above, pp. 49–51). Early in the *Discourses* Machiavelli devoted five chapters to the subject[108] and in the *Prince* he emphasized as pre-eminent the necessity for "a wise prince" to appear to be religious.[109]

However, the cultivation of religion, in itself, Machiavelli was convinced, was not sufficient. It was not enough even with the additional talents and achievements of a Savonarola

whose writings show his learning, his prudence, and his mental power.[110]

It is true that in his early letter Machiavelli manifested a critical, if not actually hostile, attitude toward Savonarola:

So, encouraging them [his adversaries in Florence] to share in the union that has begun . . . he [Savonarola] tries to set all of them against the Supreme Pontiff and, biting him, says of him what could be said of the wickedest man you can think of. Thus, according to my judgment, he keeps on working with the times and making his lies plausible.[111]

When the people lost faith in Savonarola—according to Machiavelli, in part due to his not applying against his own followers a law which he himself with great effort had had made[112]—there was manifested, in Machiavelli's opinion, a spirit of partisanship and the inadequacy of religion by itself in governmental processes:

In our times Fra Girolamo Savonarola was unarmed; hence he was destroyed amid his institutions when they were still new, as soon as the multitude ceased to believe him, because he had no way to keep those who had once believed or to make the unbelieveing believe.[113]

That the inherent truth or falsity of a religion should not be a matter of concern for the government, but, rather, only the continued, scrupulous performance of the customary rituals of the religion[114]—such was the considered judgment of the apostle of *la verità effettuale*[115] (the effectual truth) and observer of "how men live."[116] He appears never to have questioned that it is within the power of the government

to oblige citizens to love one another,[117]

or the capacity of an effective leader to coerce and manipulate the beliefs of the people for purposes of government.[118]

143

To the religion of the early Romans Machiavelli credited much of the nerve, fiber and vigor of the republican citizens.[119]

Once he advocated that Pope Leo X, "the new shepherd," lead a new crusade against the ruler of Turkey in the hope that Christendom would put aside its internal conflicts:

since in you [Christians] religious zeal is exhausted.[120]

The use of religion as a cloak by which bad men conceal their evil and often win for themselves credit, Machiavelli fully recognized.[121]

The most serious charge which he leveled against the religion of his time was, in his eyes, that

Our religion has glorified humble and contemplative men rather than active ones. It has, then, set up as the greatest good humility, abjectness and contempt for human things . . . Though our religion asks that you have fortitude within you, it prefers that you be adapted to suffering rather than to doing something vigorous.

This way of living, then, has made the world weak and turned it over as prey to wicked men, who can in security control it, since the generality of men, in order to go to heaven, think more about enduring their injuries than about avenging them.[122]

While on the legation to the court of Rome, Machiavelli wrote the Signoria:

you will consider well whether it is good not to be overcome by humility and ceremony, since power and fortune cannot walk with them.[123]

Although he held the Roman Church and the priests responsible

that we have become without religion and wicked,[124]

he judged as

still greater . . . the second reason for our ruin: this is that the Church has kept and still keeps the region divided.[125]

Recalling, then, Machiavelli's sense of total obligation to one's country and that it becomes

e tanto viene a esser maggiore in coloro che hanno sortito patria più nobile,[126]

as much greater in those whose country of origin is more noble, one can gain perspective for his declarations:

> One's country should be defended whether with disgrace or with glory; she is properly defended in any way whatsoever;[127]

> A good citizen for love of his native city will forget private injuries;[128]

> I love my native city more than my soul.[129]

Machiavelli based his opinion that there had been a misinterpetation of "our religion" by

> the worthlessness of men, who have interpreted our religion according to sloth and not according to vigor[130]

on the following ground:

> For if they would consider that it allows us the betterment and the defense of our country, they would see that it intends that we love and honor her and prepare ourselves to be such that we can defend her.[131]

Great liberties, taken through interpretation both of Christianity and of Machiavelli's standpoint, have resulted in a great diversity of opinion regarding Machiavelli's own relation to religion in general and Christianity in particular. In his own writings he made very clear that he held in reverent regard religious insights of David,[132] Jesus,[133] Peter,[134] Saint Francis,[135] and that it had been "the worthlessness of men"[136] which had turned Christianity away from

> the form in which its giver had founded it[137]

and

> interpreted our religion according to sloth and not according to vigor.[138]

Such a phrase as Machiavelli's

> He who reads the Bible intelligently[139]

suggests that he may not have been unaware of recent and contemporary advances in critical scholarship applied to the Bible (above, pp. 140–142).

Machiavelli's observation that a misinterpretation of Christianity had served to weaken men and make them vulnerable to exploitation,[140] has prompted some of his biographers and commentators to consider that, in seeking to awaken men to their potential dignity, he placed himself outside of the Christian religion, or, indeed, of any religion.

Friedrich Meinecke, in *Machiavellism, The Doctrine of Raison d'Etat and Its Place in Modern History,* wrote:

Machiavelli held firmly to the absolute validity of religion, morality and law;[141]

in the main the element of antiquity in him rose anew out of the tradition and hereditary feeling, which in Italy had never been entirely lost. In spite of his outward respect for the Church and for Christianity (frequently mingled with irony and criticism); and in spite of the undeniable influence which the Christian view had on him, Machiavelli was at heart a heathen, who levelled at Christianity the familiar and serious reproach (*Disc.,* II, 2) of having made men humble, unmanly and feeble;[142]

It was . . . a historical necessity that the man, with whom the history of the idea of *raison d'état* in the modern Western world begins and from whom Machiavellism takes its name, had to be a heathen; he had to be a man to whom the fear of hell was unknown, and who on the contrary could set about his life-work of analysing the essence of *raison d'état* with all the naivety of the ancient world. Niccolo Machiavelli was the first to do this.[143]

Leo Strauss, through his subtle analyses in *Thoughts on Machiavelli,* advanced a more unequivocal position:

In *Discourses* [II, 12] Machiavelli would seem to have inferred from the human, not heavenly, origin of Biblical religion to which he had alluded seven chapters earlier, that the dogmatic teaching of the Bible has the cognitive status of poetic fables;[144]

The first of the two examples which Machiavelli uses in that chapter [*Discourses* I, 26], entitled, "A new prince ought to make everything new in a city or province he conquers" is King David, according to the Gospels, the ancestor of Jesus. The measures that men like King David must employ at the beginning of their reign, i.e., in order to found or establish their states, are described by Machiavelli as "most cruel and inimical, not only to every Christian manner of living but to every humane manner of living as well." One measure of King David was to make the rich poor and the poor rich. In speaking of this measure Machiavelli quotes the following verse from the Magnificat: "He filled the hungry with good things, and sent the rich empty away." That is to say, he applies to the tyrant David an expression which the New Testament, or Mary, applies to God. Since he characterizes as tyrannical, a way of acting that the New Testament

146

ascribes to God, he leads us to the conclusion, nay, says in effect, that God is a tyrant. In his own strange way he accepts the traditional view according to which David was a godly king or walked in the ways of God. It is for the sake of making this extraordinary and shocking suggestion that he uses the only quotation from the New Testament which he ever uses in either the *The Prince* or the *Discourses*.[145]

an unbelief like Machiavelli's . . . takes seriously the claim to truth of revealed religion by regarding the question of its truth as all important and . . . therefore is not, at any rate, a lukewarm unbelief . . . Furthermore, if, as Machiavelli assumes, Biblical religion is not true, if it is of human and not of heavenly origin, if it consists of poetic fables, it becomes inevitable that one should attempt to understand it in merely human terms. At first glance, this attempt can be made in two different ways: one may try to understand Biblical religion by starting from the phenomena of human love or by starting from political pheonomena. The first approach was taken by Boccaccio in his *Decameron;* the second approach was taken by Machiavelli . . . "reading the Bible judiciously," Machiavelli discerns that the actions of Moses were not fundamentally different from those of Cyrus, Romulus, Theseus or Hiero of Syracuse: to "read the Bible judiciously" means to read it not in its own light but in the light of the fundamental political verities.[146]

Giuseppe Prezzolini has rendered a yet more absolute judgment:

Virtue, in Machiavelli's meaning, is merely human activity, the faculty of always meeting a fact squarely, seizing opportunity, acting swiftly and bringing to bear, in any given circumstance, one's utmost resources. This Machiavellic virtue is a concept unmistakably modern, devoid of all Christian content; it is a concept anti-Christian and anti-Catholic, because anti-passive. Virtue is the antithesis of goodness, without necessarily being evil: it is an activity superior both to good and ill;[147]

The kernel of Machiavelli's thought is that politics is a human activity incompatible with Christian morality. He advocated the ideal of the Roman state, the great political creation which he believed was weakened and destroyed by Christianity;[148]

Machiavelli's message is simply this: A stable social order among men cannot be maintained without resort to conduct which is condemned by Christian morality. In other words: From the point of view of Christianity, the statesman's art is always immoral, always anti-Christian;[149]

The country of one's birth and upbringing is the only divinity recognized by the atheist Machiavelli;[150]

one may suppose that there are still Christians who read St. Augustine and the anti-political apologists of the early Christian centuries down to the time of Tertullian. Machiavelli was not a Christian, but the Christianity of those days conceived of politics and the political order not very differently than he did. Early Christian thought, particularly as summed up in St. Augustine, was, to that extent, Machiavellian.[151]

And in *Machiavelli, the Florentine,* he wrote of

Machiavelli's atheism . . . so fundamental, so sincere, so all-informing, so absolute.[152]

Perhaps the most extreme position is that which Max Kemmerich expressed in his *Machiavelli*:

Wie wir schon wissen, war er aus politischen Gründen ein Feind nicht nur des Papstes, sondern auch des Christentums, da es Sanftmut über Kraft, Dulden über Handeln, Demut über den Willen zur Macht stelle, für Vaterlandsliebe und Kühnheit der Seele keinen Platz biete. Er war nicht Heide, denn er glaubte gar nichts und hielt zwar die Religion für eine Erfindung von schlauen Priestern und Staatsmännern, aber trotzdem für jedes Staatswesen aus praktischen Gründen für unentbehrlich. Denn was dem weltlichen Arme unerrichbar bleibe, das greife noch der geistliche.[153]

As we already know, he was an enemy, on political grounds not only of the Pope, but also of Christendom, in that it placed meekness above force, patience above action, humility above the will for power. For love of fatherland and boldness of spirit, it offered no place. He was not a heathen because he believed in nothing whatsoever and indeed considered religion to be an invention of cunning priests and politicians, but, nevertheless, essential for every state on practical grounds. For that which remains beyond the reach of secular arms, the religious seizes.

More recently, Harvey J. Mansfield, Jr. has concluded from his study of Machiavelli's major works, that Machiavelli was leading a "conspiracy against Christianity:"

When the reader understands the need for worldly honor in politics, he will join Machiavelli's conspiracy against Christianity; for Christianity clearly denies the desire for worldly honor. But the precise effects of this denial are unclear, since Christianity despite its intention cannot dispense with worldly honor;[154]

Christianity was from the first a religion of the people. Then princes found it necessary to adopt the Christian religion as a way out of "the so-great confusion existing then in the world" (*F.H.* 1:9);[155]

Why the ancient Roman system failed in modern Italy could be seen in the actions of the crucial factor in the system, the Pope. The Pope was head of a religion that, scorning worldly honors and political glory, appealed to the people rather than princes; according to the ancient Roman system, he was therefore in the equivocal position of the plebeian prince, ambitious above his rank yet hostile to all of noble rank . . . The Pope was a prince of the people, who because of the character of the "sect" that gave him office, could not be bribed or rewarded in the usual way with honors. He and the Church he heads have renounced both the use of arms and self-advancement, and so he can neither be offered nor can he accept worldly honors which require the use of arms in one's own advancement . . . As Pope, he cannot be a prince of any kind unless he is superior to the worldly, or the natural, princes. It is his very "spiritual power" that makes him faithless to his worldly engagements (*F.H.* 8:17);[156]

The foundation of the common good, according to Machiavelli, is the preference for one's own, as this preference makes it possible for orders naturally disparate to coexist if not to live in union. Nobles and people coexist when the city can expand to serve their needs and provide both glory and security. The common good, to speak plainly, is a good taken from foreigners that is common to one people and its princes (*F. H.* 4:3–7); it can subsist only so long as human beings are divided in political allegiances, and understood to be divided by their sects, into natives and foreigners (*F.H.* 5:11; 6:32). The Christian Church does not observe this distinction, but the factual truth of its internationalism is subservience to foreigners. If the common good is at the expense of foreigners in booty and glory, princes cannot operate for the common good with foreign arms; the foreigners, that is the mercenaries, will keep the spoils intended for their employers (*F. H.* 5:2);[157]

Parties in Florence had evil effects because they were used under the influence of the Christian religion, as instruments of private revenge. This transpolitical religion does not distinguish between domestic and foreign affairs; it keeps modern princes from seeing the distinction clearly, and its priests, so far as they can, prevent princes from acting on the distinction. But the distinction between domestic and foreign affairs, as we have seen, is necessary to the distinction between public and private affairs, for the public is based on the common good of two disparate orders of men who happen to inhabit a locality together. They will ally if they have enemies to oppose; and if they ally, they will sustain the public good against private interests within. There will be no natives if there are no foreigners, and no public good if there are no natives. The very universality of Christianity causes it to support private attachment to one's own against public control. When this universality is applied to the belief in absolute revenge, the result is violent excitement of a private passion.[158]

For a right perception of the value of Machiavelli for contemporary policy, it is important to recognize that for him the meaning of the Christian religion was not entirely identical with his evaluation of the pretensions of authority on the part of the religious institutions and their officials through their claims as representatives of the Founder and renewers of the Christian religion. That, in his writings, he perceived and acknowledged a distinction[159] has been noted above (pp. 100–104). His reaction is manifested throughout *Mandragola*, against the hypocrisy of the professed exponents of the Christian way and, throughout the *Discourses* and *The History of Florence*, against the impotence of the ecclesiastical leadership to accomplish anything but confusion in the attempt to gain the power and the glory, the rejection of which Jesus explicitly set as his own course and that for those who would be his followers.[160] This reaction is not rightly interpreted as constituting also a rejection of the core of the experiential record of the life and teaching of Jesus. Such a misinterpretation of Machiavelli's perspective obstructs an understanding of his indication of *wherein* man can adequately choose prudence.

In his article "Machiavelli" published in *Novissima Encyclopedia Monografica Illustrata*, Alfredo Oxilia affirmed:

D'altronde la povertà era il minore dei suoi mali, ed egli li sooportava tutti, si dica quel che si vuole, con profondo spirito religioso: "Io sto bene del corpo, scriveva al nipote nell'agosto del '13, ma di tutte l'altre cose male. E non mi resta altra speranza che Dio m'aiuti, e infino a qui non mi ha abbandonato affato". Dove la prima frase potrebbe essere convenzionale; ma la seconda, che nel momento della maggiore sfortuna riconosce l'aiuto di Dio, è indubbiament sincera. E perciò quando il Guicciardini, nel 1521, scrive al Nostro che l'onor suo "si oscurerebbe se in questa età *egli si desse* all'anima, perchè avendo sempre vivuto con contraria professione, sarebbe attribuito piuttosto al rimbambito che al buono", non possiamo dedurne altro che la superficialità della scrivente. A lui, in buona fede, il Machiavelli sembrava irreligioso, perchè certo non era assiduo alla messa come il Vettori e lui stesso e la grande maggioranza degli ingegnosi ma vanissimi loro contemporanei con a capo il loro degno papa, Leone X; mentre il Machiavelli era proprio la *rara avis* che in un'età atea e bacchettona si distaccava da tutti e nell'apparenza e nella sostanza; uomo integro e profondo, e, perciò, di tutti i tempi. Del resto già il Villari affermava che le sue lettere sono "davvero un monumento di grande importanza nella letteratura del sec. XVI, "poichè egli e ìl solo fra tutti che dimostri una piena coscienza di sè."[161]

On the other hand, poverty was the least of his ills, and he endured all, say what one will, with deep religious spirit: "I am well in body," he wrote to his nephew in August '13, "but in all other things sick. And there remains for me no other hope but for God to help me, and up to now he has not at all abandoned me." Where the first expression might be conventional; yet the second, that in the moment of greatest misfortune recognized the aid of God, is undoubtedly sincere. And for that reason, when Guicciardini, in 1521, wrote to Ours that his honor "would be sullied if at this time of life *he should give himself up* to spiritual life, since he had always shown an opposite attitude of mind, it would be attributed to his entering his second childhood rather than to goodness," we cannot draw other conclusion than that of the superficiality of the writer. To him, in truth, Machiavelli seemed irreligious, because certainly he was not regular in attendance at mass as Vettori and himself and the great majority of their contemporaries with, at their head, their worthy pope, Leo X; while Machiavelli was genuine, the *rare bird* who in an atheistic and ostensibly religious age detached himself from all both in appearance and in reality: a man just and deep, and, therefore, of all seasons. In other respects, Villari has already affirmed that his letters are in very truth a monument of great importance in the literature of the sixteenth century "because he is the only one among all who demonstrates a full consciousness of himself."

CONTRIBUTIONS FROM HIS OFFICIAL SERVICE

When, on 19 June 1498, Machiavelli was appointed First Secretary of the Signoria, he was in the beginning of his thirtieth year of age. Slightly over three months earlier he had drafted his letter to Ricciardo Bechi in Rome in which he reported having heard Savonarola predict that

Florence was going to prosper and master Italy.[162]

Subsequently the prophet had been hanged and his body burned; but the city was making a new beginning and providing Machiavelli an arena for exercising and developing his capacities. How favorable was the governmental ambience can be perceived from the evaluation by Orestes Ferraro who has written: Florence was

une ville qui respectait profondemént le souvenir de ses libertés médiévales, et qui fut la dernière à les perdre. Harmoniser le besoin d'institutions libres avec l'utilité d'un fonctionnement ordonné, tel fut le but des réformateurs. Et ce but, ils l'atteignirent, car, de l'avis général des grands politiques de l'époque, jamais Florence n'eut un meilleur gouvernement que celui qui dura de 1494 à 1512.[163]

a city which profoundly respected the memory of its medieval liberties, and which was the last to lose them. To harmonize the need for free institutions with the utility of a functioning establishment, such was the aim of the reformers. And this aim, they attained, because, in the general opinion of the great political leaders of the period, never did Florence have a better government than that which lasted from 1494 to 1512.

Pocock has succinctly described the elements of this republic during the period of Machiavelli's official service:

The crucial step taken after the flight of the Medici in 1494 was the adoption of what was generally described as the Venetian constitution (*il governo veneziano* or *alla veneziana*). This . . . consisted at Florence practically in a Consiglio Grande, a Signoria, and a Gonfaloniere, and ideally in a perfect harmony of the many, the few, and the one, such as Venice was supposed to have achieved. Yet in practice the perceived bias of the 1494 constitution was toward the many. It was universally agreed that its most essential institution was the Consiglio, in which an indefinitely large number (though by no means all) of the citizens had the right to participate, and that the existence of the Consiglio gave the regime the character of a *governo largo* . . . by refusing to confine citizenship to an exactly defined *(stretto)* group among the inhabitants, acknowledges that civic participation is a good, something that men aim at, that develops men toward goodness, that it is desirable to extend to as many men as possible. *Governo,* the word most closely corresponds to our "constitution," is in Florentine vocabulary almost interchangeable with *modo di vivere,* or simply *vivere;* and it is observable that it is always *governo largo,* not *stretto,* which is indicated by the phrase *vivere civile.*[164]

Of the influence of Savonarola upon Machiavelli personally, his writings afford no basis for clear judgment (above, p. 143): however, following the auto-da-fè of Savonarola, Machiavelli, as an official in the government of the republic, came to hold in high regard the Grand Council, the institution which Savonarola had introduced. Years later, when in 1520 at the request of Pope Leo X, Machiavelli formulated and submitted his recommendations for "Remodeling the Government of Florence," in his proposal he wrote:

the whole general body of citizens . . . will never be satisfied (and he who believes differently is not wise) if their power is not restored or if they do not have a promise that it will be restored. And because to restore it all at one time would not be for the security of your friends, nor for the upholding of the power of Your Holiness, it is necessary in part to restore it and in part to promise to restore it in such a way that they [i.e., the general body of citizens] will be altogether certain of having it again. And therefore I judge that you are under the necessity of reopening the Hall of the Council of One Thousand, or at least of the Six Hundred Citizens, who would allot, just as they formerly did, all the offices and magistracies except the aforementioned Sixty-Five, the Two Hundred, and the Eight of *Balìa* all of these during the life of Your Holiness and of the Cardinal you would appoint.[165]

Whitfield has found in the *Prince* ideas and phrases strongly reminiscent of Savonarola's *Del Reggimento e Governo delle Citta di Firenze.*[166] Machiavelli

152

agreed with Savonarola that it had been "our sins" which had brought about "the present ruin of Italy," but Machiavelli added,

they were not at all such as he supposed they were, but these I have mentioned; and because they were princes' sins, the princes have suffered punishment for them.[167]

The fall of Savonarola, Machiavelli attributed in the *Prince* to his having been unarmed.[168] In the *Discourses* he offered a slightly more detailed analysis:

the Frate could not overcome envy because he did not have power enough and because he was not well understood by his followers who did have power. Nevertheless this envy did not continue through his ignorance, for his sermons are full of accusations against "the wise men of the world," and of invectives against them; so he called those who envied him and opposed his measures.[169]

In his survey of Florence's turbulent decade, after the French invasion in 1494, which Machiavelli wrote in order to stir up popular support for re-instituting in Florence a citizen militia, he gave an evaluation of the Savonarolan interlude:

But that which to many was far more distressing and brought on disunion, was that sect under whose command your city lay. I speak of that great Savonarola who, inspired with heavenly vigor, kept you clearly bound with his words. But many feared to see their country ruined, little by little under his prophetic teaching;
hence no ground for your reunion could be discovered, unless his light divine continued to increase, or unless by a greater fire it was extinguished.[170]

Machiavelli's most weighty analysis of the support which Savonarola had enjoyed for a time appears in the *Discourses*:

The people of Florence do not consider themselves either ignorant or rude; nevertheless they were persuaded by Brother Girolamo Savonarola that he spoke with God. I do not intend to decide whether it was true or not, because so great a man ought to be spoken of with reverence, but I do say that countless numbers believed him without having seen anything extraordinary to make them believe him, because his life, his teaching, the affairs he dealt with were enough to make them lend him faith.[171]

Further on, Machiavelli attributed to a biased use of power a weakening of popular support (above, p. 143):

Among other enactments to give the citizens security, he got a law passed

153

permitting appeal to the people from the sentences of the Eight and the Signory in political cases. This law he urged a long time and gained with very great difficulty; but when, a short time after its confirmation, five citizens condemned to death by the Signory on behalf of the government attempted to appeal, they were not permitted to do so; thus the law was not observed. This took away more of the Frate's influence than any other event, because the right of appeal, if valuable, should have been observed; if it was not valuable, he should not have had it enacted. This happening was the more noticed inasmuch as the Frate, in all the sermons he delivered after this law was broken, never either condemned those who broke it or excused them; for he was unwilling to condemn their action, which was to his advantage, and excuse it he could not. This conduct, by revealing his ambitious and partisan spirit, took influence away from him and brought him much censure.[172]

With his last reference to Savonarola, in a letter of 17 May 1521 from Carpi to Guicciardini, in a light-hearted context, he wrote:

more crafty than Fra Girolamo[173]

and thus seems to have returned to the mood in which he wrote the early letter (above, p. 143).

The deepest influence which Savonarola had on Machiavelli may have been indirect in nature. By broadening the base of the republican government and increasing the power of the people in it, Savonarola had given new life to the popularly-based civil order. The most important institution which he had introduced continued after his death to be the most democratic element in the government in which Machiavelli was a responsible and sympathetic participant. From it he may have derived encouragement to view as realizable the formulation and establishment of government for the common good.

With a constant awareness of the danger of imminent death for its liberties, throughout the life of the republic, the government of the city was one so delicately balanced between internal factions externally related, that an awareness of the potential implications of all forms of human behavior was of vital and crucial importance for its security and survival.[174]

Machiavelli's position in the government, Ferrara has described as follows:

dans le domaine administratif il se borna au rôle d'instrument secondaire;[175]

in the administrative area he was limited to the role of a secondary instrument;

l'on peut presque affirmer que, dans l'obscurité des bureaux, le continuateur de la diplomatie florentine d'alors, ce fut lui.[176]

154

one can almost affirm that, in the obscurity of the bureaus, the preserver of the continuity of the Florentine diplomacy at that time, was he.

Although during his years of official service he was sent on more than thirty missions,[177] not once did he bear the title of "ambassador"; however, once, in June 1509 in Piombino during preliminary feelers with representatives from Pisa with a view toward negotiations for terminating the war, a member of the delegation from the Pisan countryside addressed him as "ambassador."[178]

In "The Advice to Raffaello Girolami When He Went as Ambassador to the Emperor," prepared in October 1522, he set forth in detail objectives and procedures repeatedly manifested in his own letters and reports relating to specific missions conducted earlier.[179]

Qualities characteristic of his services on missions won recognition early in his diplomatic career. In a letter to him while on the legation to Cesare Borgia, Niccolo Valori, a member of the Signoria, wrote, as translated by Ferrara:

Quoique je sache bien que vous êtes informé par la correspondance officielle que je suis d'accord avec elle (la mission), je ne puis cependant omettre de vous dire deux mots pour vous exprimer ma satisfaction. Votre raisonnement et les rapports que vous faites ne pourraient recevoir une approbation meilleure ne mieux nous apprendre ce que j'ai toujours reconnu chez vous: une façon de raconter nette, juste et sincère, en quoi l'on peut avoir une confiance absolue.[180]

Although I know well that you have been informed by the official correspondence that I am in agreement with it (the mission), I can not omit, however, saying to you two words to express my satisfaction. Your way of reasoning and the reports which you make could not receive higher approbation or better acquaint us with that which I have always recognized in you: a way of reporting which is clear, true and sincere, in which one is able to have absolute confidence.

Of the mission to the court of Pope Julius II, 25 August to 26 October 1506, Ferrara wrote:

Une fois de plus, la vraie mission de Machiavel consistait à ècouter, à scruter, à veiller et à faire son rapport.[181]

Once more, the true mission of Machiavelli consisted in listening, weighing, observing and making his report.

With respect to the same legation, Ridolfi commented:

When the matter was discussed, the opinion of the gonfalonier pre-

155

vailed . . . not to oppose the Pope's demand but to play for time as long as possible. The commission was therefore entrusted to Machiavelli, who was by now accustomed and resigned to temporizing missions.[182]

All the time he was growing in the understanding of the limits to the effective power of words and coming to appreciate the element of luck in those instances in which events seemed to crown words with success rather then disaster. While on the legation to Cesare Borgia, in one of his dispatches he wrote:

prudent men, as are Your Lordships, know it is not enough to do your duty, but that you need to have good luck.[183]

Above all, his missions provided him with the model which served through the rest of his life to kindle hope and evoke the exercise of his talents to advance the public good. Convinced that the conditions in Italy demanded the creation of a new state, he encountered and observed in Cesare Borgia a man so creating his moment of opportunity that the qualities of conduct and the measures he chose convinced Machiavelli that they were such as are essential for state-building and state-maintenance. Nearly twelve years had elapsed since their first meeting in June, 1502[184] and more than ten since those August days of 1503 when, with a fateful blow, fortune turned against his hero[185] and by December led to his ignominious fall[186] and nearly seven after the obscure death in 1507,[187] when Machiavelli wrote to Vettori his commendation of the methods of Cesare Borgia (above, p. 65) as those by which a new prince could gain and consolidate power. Machiavelli had been at the court of Cesare Borgia in Sinigaglia on 31 December 1502 at "the flashpoint of power" and had been favored by Cesare Borgia with a private conference within a few hours after the perpetration of the stunning coup. From the dispatches which Machiavelli wrote while on that mission can be gleaned specific attributes which were becoming components of his ideal founder-deliverer as they are to be encountered in his later writings. Thus:

Your Lordships . . . should remember that I am dealing with a prince who manages things for himself; and if one is not going to write phantasies and dreams, one must verify things, and verifying them takes time; and I am trying to spend it and not throw it away;[188]

Anybody who examines the qualities . . . recognizes this Lord as a man courageous, fortunate, and full of hope, favored by a pope and a king, and injured by the other side [i.e., *the Vitelli*, etc.] not merely in a state that he hoped to conquer, but in one that he had conquered;[189]

You must recall that nobody speaks with him except three or four of his ministers and some foreigners who have to deal with him about matters of importance, and he does not come out of an antechamber except at eleven or twelve at night or later; for this reason there is no opportunity to speak with him ever, except through an audience appointed; and when he knows that a man brings him nothing but words, he never gives him an audience;[190]

As I have many times written to Your Lordships, this Lord is very secretive, and I do not believe that what he is going to do is known to anybody but himself. And his chief secretaries have many times asserted to me that he does not tell anything except when he orders it, and he orders it when necessity compels and when it is to be done, and not otherwise. Hence I beg that Your Lordships will excuse me and not impute it to my negligence if I do not satisfy Your Lordships with information, because most of the time I do not satisfy even myself;[191]

I have nothing to write, save to report this anew, that if the words and proceedings point to an accord, the orders and preparations indicate war;[192]

events make peoples [sic.] brains spin;[193]

The Orsini and Vitelli [by considering the formation of an alliance with the other commanders in the Duke's service to advance themselves by curbing his power] have made a gesture that is enough to make him [the Duke] wise even if he were not, and have shown him that he needs to try to keep what he has conquered rather than to conquer more. And the way to keep it is to continue to be armed with his own arms, to gain his subjects' favor, and to make allies of his neighbors. That is his intention . . .;[194]

nearly two weeks later,

I have hastened to write this to Your Lordships, to let you see that . . . he who is armed well, and with his own arms, gets the same effects wherever he turns;[195]

and a month later,

Messer Remirro this morning was found in two pieces on the public square, where he still is; and all the people have been able to see him. Nobody feels sure of the cause of his death, except that so it has pleased the Prince, who shows that he can make and unmake men as he likes, according to their deserts.[196]

Machiavelli's missions impressed upon him the weakness of a policy based upon buying time and, from foreigners, protection. The expressed purpose of his legation to Cesare Borgia, as revealed in his dispatch of 15 October 1502,

157

from Imola, was to characterize his other major missions also:

> As to the postscript that Your Lordships write to me about temporizing, not committing you, and seeking to learn his purpose, I believe that up to now I have done the first two things, and on the third I have used my wits.[197]

While on his first mission to France, he wrote back:

> Your Excellencies should not imagine that good letters or good arguments are of any use, because they are not understood . . . all this is superfluous, because such matters are considered by them in quite another way and seen with a different eye from that of anyone unfamiliar with conditions here, because they are blinded by their own power and the thought of immediate advantage, and esteem only those who are well armed or those who are prepared to give money.[198]

Relative to the legation to Emperor Maximilian, Ridolfi commented:

> It was always hard to reach an agreement with the Florentine government over a question of money and this time the . . . task was rendered even more arduous by the immense distance, which often served the Ten to temporize and get out of a difficulty;[199]

> But once again events proved right those in Florence who took, as they said 'the advantage of time'. The Emperor was again thoroughly beaten by the Venetians . . . The invasion of Italy, the coronation in Rome, the punishment of the French, the restoration of Imperial authority, all again took on the inconsistency of dreams. Nor were the Florentines in the habit of taking shadows for reality, or paying for them more than they were worth.[200]

Machiavelli's third mission to France had the same purpose: namely, to temporize while making no commitments;[201] and, likewise, his fourth.[202]

Against counting on "the advantage of time," he was to warn, later, in the *Prince*:

> Nor did they [the Romans] ever approve what all day is in the mouths of the wise men of our age: to profit from the help of time; but they did profit from that of their own vigor and prudence.[203]

With respect to the deepening crisis of 1511, Ridolfi commented:

> the Florentines, hindered by their internal divisions, by their avarice and their passion for delay, did nothing.[204]

The subsequent disaster which befell the republic and in its fall carried Machiavelli down with it, utterly discredited in his eyes the bases of its foreign policy. Of France, the city's chief ally, he wrote:

La buona fortuna de'Franzesi ci tolse mezzo lo stato; la cattiva ci torrà la libertà.[205]

The good fortune of the French has taken away from us half the state; the bad will take away from us liberty.

As to his judgment regarding the impossibility of purchasing security with gold, in both the *Discourses* and *The Art of War* he left no doubt:

Riches, too, not merely do not defend you but get you robbed sooner. Nothing can be more false than that common maxim that says riches are the sinews of war . . . gold is not enough to find good soldiers, but good soldiers are quite enough to find gold . . . since [the Romans] made their wars with steel, they never suffered from scarcity of gold, because by those who feared them it was brought to them even in their camps . . . Again I repeat that riches are not, then, the sinews of war; but good soldiers are;[206]

Men, steel, money, and bread are the sinews of war; but of these four the most necessary are the first two, because men and steel find money and bread, but bread and money do not find men and steel. An unarmed rich man is the booty of a poor soldier.[207]

Personal involvement in the popularly-based government wholly dependent upon powerful allies and auxiliary and mercenary soldiers[208] as it waged its war for economic survival, with repeated and painful shocks forged Machiavelli's conviction that only a new instrument could sustain the cherished liberty. During his first ten years as Secretary of the Ten, he had a special responsibility to carry forward the achievement of his city's primary objective: the reconquest of its access to the sea. The series of disastrous frustrations which Florence suffered as the struggle dragged on, schooled him in the unreliability of outside forces and convinced him of the necessity to generate more deeply in the inhabitants and their leadership an allegiance adequate for the new scale of political affairs coming into being.

Awareness of the quality of strength derived only from independence (personal and public) becomes manifest repeatedly in his writings and his prescriptions for policy: in the draft of his letter to the ex-gonfalonier;[209] in the *Discourses*;[210] to which might well be added:

159

when [men] rely on these [their hopes] and do not make an estimate of themselves, they fall;[211]

and advices in the *Prince*.[212] A similar recommendation with respect to amorous affairs he gave in a light-hearted letter to Vettori:

I beg you to follow your star . . . and not let an iota go for the things of the world.[213]

From his own experience in public service, Machiavelli had come to know that it is through exerting oneself in public responsibilities that one grows in perceiving his true nature.[214] Moreover, he was convinced that

excellent men come in larger numbers from republics than from kingdoms.[215]

Representing his city abroad, especially conceiving and winning the official endorsement of a new system of defense for his city at home and organizing and administering it, nourished the conviction that one finds his worth through his service in making his country free. Deprivation of office was only to intensify this "hunger and thirst after" *virtù* (energy in state building and state maintenance). In his advice to the young ambassador, he wrote:

any difficult business, if one has the ear of the prince, becomes easy.[216]

Deeply aware of the direct relation of safety to power,[217] he strove to keep himself attuned in readiness and in evident availability to be called again into public service.

His personal self-reliance emerges as a discipline with distinctively moral overtones peculiar to it. Among its aspects are:

1. to reason about everything;[218]
2. to develop and maintain, regarding public affairs, judgment free from partisan bias;[219]
3. to concern himself, in regard to public affairs, with only the effectual truth of events;[220]
4. to make available, especially to the young, lessons learned from experience which they may be more fortunate in bringing to constructive application;[221]
5. to defend as praiseworthy only honorable deeds.[222]

As to his judgment of specific brands of immorality in politics, he left no doubt. In the *Prince* he noted the structure of the papacy as rendering it incapable of establishing firmly a state,[223] indisposed in mind and spirit to defend it properly,[224] and hence responsible for the introduction of mercenaries into Italy. In the *Discourses*, as worse than the examples of conduct set by the priests due to which

we have become without religion and wicked,

he considered

that the Church has kept and still keeps this region divided.[225]

Again, in *The History of Florence*, he indicated the incompatibility of the structure of the papacy and state establishment and maintenance,[226] the failure of the weapons at the disposal of the papacy, its resort to the introduction of foreign soldiers into the peninsula,[227] and the personal ambition and avarice of the popes.[228] In *The Art of War*, he delineated the corruption and weakness which characterized the Italian princes under these pressures.[229]

That a political community, also, must rely on its own resources if it is to achieve security was the conviction that Machiavelli had arrived at within his first eight years of office and which was to remain as a dominant concern in his writings and endeavor throughout the rest of his life. Already in 1502, reporting the conduct of Cesare Borgia faced by the mutiny of the leaders of his mercenary forces, Machiavelli commended to the Ten Cesare Borgia's intention thenceforth to provide himself with his own soldiers.[230]

After quoting the concluding lines of the "First Decennale,"[231] written in 1504, Tommasini summarized its message and purpose:

Riaprire il tempio a Marte, riordinare civilmente la guerra colle patrie milizie, sottrarre le sorti di Firenze all'arbitrio vile de'mercenari, de'condottieri cospiratori, pieni l'animo di duplicità e d'avarizia, ecco la mira che il segretario della repubblica insegna al popolo; ecco l'idea che semina in mezzo alla moltitudine, sperando che maturi e fruttifichi.[232]

Reopen the temple of Mars, put the war in good civic order again with the country's militia, take the fortunes of Florence away from the vile discretion of the mercenaries, of the conspiratorial condottieri, full of the spirit of duplicity and avarice, this is the aim which the secretary of the republic pointed out to the people, this is the idea which he sowed in the midst of the multitude, in the hope that it would mature and bear fruit.

On 30 December 1505, he was granted authority to recruit for the militia.[233] On 2 October 1506 was enacted the ordinance for the militia in the preamble of which he wrote:

161

Whereas it has been observed by the Magnificent and Exalted Signors that . . . your republic . . . lacks only to be well provided with arms . . . these signors judge it well that she should be armed with her own weapons and with her own men,[234]

and, on 6 December following, was established the Nine Officers of the Florentine Ordinance and Militia of which on 12 January 1507 he was elected secretary.[235] How enthusiastically he entered into the work of recruiting and training the militia is indicated, as Ridolfi reports, by the following:

On the 16th of April, having heard that the Ten wished him to go to Cascina where the commissioner Niccolo Capponi was looking after the rearguard services and the supplies for the whole army, he wrote: 'I know that being stationed there would be less arduous and dangerous, but if I had not wanted danger and hard work, I should not have left Florence. So may it please Your Lordships to leave me here in the field to work along with the commissioners on matters that arise, for here I can be of some use, but there I should not be doing any good and I would die of despair.'[236]

The formation, recruitment and training of the citizen infantry in all aspects of which he participated vigorously, its role in bringing the war with Pisa to a successful conclusion[237] (although ultimately the process was through peace by negotiation rather than by military action), the formation of the citizen cavalry in March, 1512, gave substance to his dream—which even the rout of the milita and the sack of Prato by the Medici-supporting Spanish army on 29 August 1512[238]—did not destroy. In *The Art of War* he had his spokesman Fabrizio Colonna say:

I do not at all mean by this that such an army cannot be beaten, because the Roman armies were beaten many times, and the army of Hannibal was beaten, so one can see that an army cannot be organized of which anybody can promise that it never will be defeated. Hence these wise men of yours ought not to measure the uselessness of this army by its having lost once but should believe that just as it loses, so it can conquer and remove the cause of the loss. And if they investigate this situation, they will find that it has not resulted from a defect in method, but from the organization's not having been made perfect. And as I have said, they ought to provide for it not by finding fault with the citizen army but by improving it. How this is to be done you will learn as we proceed.[239]

Indeed, his subsequent reflection transformed his dreams into the developing conception of the adequate leader and the endeavor to indentify and/or inspire one competent to fit himself for the role.

In office, personally involved in the republic's efforts by diplomacy and, failing that, by military power first through mercenaries and then through the citizen infantry to recover Pisa, Machiavelli came to view as of primary importance for the maintenance of a secure state: the initiating, organizing and sustaining of the citizen forces. When deprived of office and unsuccessful in his repeated attempts to regain opportunity for public service, he sought by writings to stimulate the young Medici and/or the young sons of leading Florentine families to understand the requirements and fit themselves adequately for the requisite leadership. In the *Prince*, he affirmed:

> The principal foundations of all states, the new as well as the old and the mixed, are good laws and good armies. And, because there cannot be good laws where armies are not good, and where there are good armies, there must be good laws [ed. note: *he is thinking . . . well-governed states are defended by their own citizens, who value the blessings secured for them by good and wise rulers*]. I shall omit talking of laws and shall speak of armies;[240]

> Wise princes, therefore, always reject these [mercenary and auxiliary] armies and turn to their own; they chose rather to lose with their own soldiers than to win with the others, judging that not a true victory which they gain with foreign armies;[241]

> I conclude, then, that without her own armies no princedom is secure; on the contrary, she is entirely dependent on Fortune, not having strength that in adversity loyally defends her. Wise men have always said and believed that "nothing is so weak or shaky as the reputation of a power that does not rely on its own strength" [Tacitus, *Annals* 13.19]. Armies of your own are those made up of your subjects or citizens of your state or of dependents.[242]

In the *Discourses* he declared that only armies of one's own countrymen can have the fellow-feeling and mutual regard[243] and be receptive of the kind of training and discipline essential for a good army.[244] Fighting for their own glory and under a leader for whom they feel affection, the native army excels in vigor.[245] In *The Art of War,* the citizen army emerges as the appropriate and effective expression of men's innate and militant love for the land of their birth[246] and hence arises the capacity in every land for those born in it to constitute good soldiers.[247] The energies of young men find in military exercises congenial outlets:

> The citizen army, whether large or small, makes no inconvenience because this method does not take men from any of their affairs and does not tie them up so that they cannot carry on their business, since they are required to assemble for training on holidays only. This does no harm either to the

country or to the men; on the contrary, it would please the young men, who on festival days now remain wretchedly idle in their usual resorts, because they would go with pleasure to these exercises, for since the managing of arms is a fine spectacle, young men enjoy it . . . Yet if such a levy would give to those who are enrolled in it some annoyance in times of peace (what they are I do not see), there are for recompense all the benefits that an ordered military force brings to a country, because without it nothing is secure.[248]

Machiavelli prefaced the whole work with the affirmation that a basic and indispensable harmony exists between the civilian life and the military life.[249] For a policy of enlistment or recruitment, Machiavelli recommended:

as to force . . . one ought to take a middle course, in which there would not be force alone nor free will alone.[250]

The rewards from the toil and effort required to form and train such an army he considered to consist in the availability of the most useful kind of military force,[251] in superiority over the neighbors and in legislative initiative and authority.[252]

That it was a practical program which he was proposing, Machiavelli clearly believed:

no activity today carried on by men can more easily be brought back to ancient methods than warfare, but it can be so brought only by men who are princes of such great states that they can assemble from their subjects at least fifteen or twenty thousand young men . . . In Italy, then, to know how to manage an army already formed is not enough; a general must first know how to form it and then know how to command it. Yet for this there must be princes who, having much territory and many subjects, have opportunity to do so.[253]

In *The History of Florence* his enthusiasm for the citizen army breathes vitality into his description of the government of Florence in the thirteenth century,[254] the people's defense of Florence against Castruccio Castrascani[255] and the Genoese people's defense of their freedom.[256]

Regarding Machiavelli's concern for the effective defense of the state, Ferrara has written:

Nous ne voyons Machiavel prendre une attitude quasi fanatique qu'à propos d'une seule chose: la guerre et tout ce qui la concerne. On dirait que c'est, en quelque sorte, le *leit-motiv* de son existence. Dans *le Prince,* comme dans les *Discours sur les Décades de Tite-Live,* dans *Castruccio Castracani,* comme dans les *Histoires,* partout dans son œuvre on sent s'élever son esprit et sa plume s'ennoblir quand il parle de la guerre, des milices et de la nécessité d'une action belliqueuse. La guerre, dans la conception machiavélienne, est la libération, la libération de l'étranger: misérable, exigeant, ingrat, et la libération aussi des *condottieri,* seigneurs servis par des hommes d'armes, prêtes à offrir leur bras au prix de continuelles demandes d'argent, mais également prêts à se battre le moins possible;[257]

We do not see Machiavelli take an attitude almost fanatical, except toward only one thing: war and all that concerns it. One would say that it is, in a certain sense, the *leit-motiv* of his existence. In the *Prince,* as in the *Discourses on the Ten Books of Titus-Livius,* in *Castruccio Castracani,* as in the *Histories,* throughout his work one feels his spirit rises and his pen is ennobled when he speaks of war, of the militias and of the necessity for a belligerant action. War, in the Machiavellian conception, is liberation, liberation from the foreigner: miserable, demanding, ungrateful, and liberation also from the *condottieri,* lords served by men-at-arms, ready to offer their arms at the price of continual demands for money, but equally ready to engage in the least fighting possible.

Si l'on cherche, chez Machiavel, la note dominante de sa pensée et de son action, c'est celle qu'il faut faire la guerre avec ses propres armes, ses sacrifices et sa gloire propre . . . Organiser des milices de citoyens capables de défendre, aux heures tragiques, le sol de la patrie, les biens matériels et l'honneur de la famille, telle est l'idée qui l'accompagne au cours de toute son existence. On peut suivre ce grand travail dans ses actes administratifs, dans ses livres et dans ses continuelles pérégrinations dans les camps, aux heures difficiles de sa chère Florence. Giuseppe Canestrini a réuni, dans un volume de près de quatre cents pages, tous les documents: ordres, proclamations, circulaires, lettres, etc., que Machiavel écrivit de 1502 à 1512; c'est-à-dire pendant la plus grande partie de sa charge, au temps de la République et de la cavalerie, outre un rapport sur la nomination de capitaine-général. Nous avons également vu l'intérêt qu'il prit à la guerre contre Pise. Sa correspondance privée est remplie de passages concernant ces questions. *Le Prince* et les *Discours sur les Décades de Tite-Live* contiennent des digressions continuelles où, abandonnant la politique, il parle du métier des armes. Dans ces deux livres, des chapitres entiers, l'un après l'autre, traitent des choses de la guerre du point de vue technique. Il consacra à cette étude tout un ouvrage: *l'Art de la guerre.* A la fin de sa vie, pendant les deux dernières années, nous le voyons parcourir le nord et le centre de l'Italie, au service du Pape de de Florence, aux côtés de son protecteur et ami Francesco Guicciardini, passionnément absorbé dans des plans d'organisation militaire ou de systeèmes de défense.[258]

If one seeks, with Machiavelli, the dominant note of his thought and his action, it is this: that it is necessary to make war with one's own arms, sacrifices and glory. To organize militias of citizens capable of defending, in tragic hours, the soil of the homeland, the material goods and honor of the family, such is the idea which accompanies him in the course of his whole existence.

One can follow this great labor in his administrative acts, in his books and in his continual journeys in the camps, in the difficult hours of his dear Florence. Giuseppe Canestrani has brought together, in a volume of nearly four-hundred pages, all of the documents: orders, proclamations, circulars, letters, etc., which Machiavelli wrote from 1502–1512; that is to say, during the greatest part of his charge in the time of the Republic. One knows that he composed the Ordinances of the infantry and of the cavalry, besides a report on the nomination of the captain-general. We have likewise seen the interest which he took in the war against Pisa. His private correspondence is full of passages concerning these questions. *The Prince* and the *Discourses on the Ten Books of Titus Livius* contain continual digressions where, abandoning politics, he speaks of the metier of arms. In these two books, entire chapters, one after the other, treat of matters of war from a technical point of view. He devoted to this study an entire work: *The Art of War*. At the end of his life, during the last two years, we see him traversing the north and center of Italy, in the service of the Pope and of Florence, by the side of his protector and friend Francesco Guicciardini, passionately absorbed in the plans of military organization or of systems of defense.

So distinguished was Machiavelli's contribution in these matters that Ridolfi has observed:

> The Florentine secretary was the first to make political theory of the national militia, the first to give it practical application with regular levies and stable ordinances under the control of a government official.[259]

Service in the government of Florence as a republic left Machiavelli with the deep and abiding conviction that a republican form best nurtures a people free and uncorrupted (above, pp. 111–115).

With creative initiative exercising powers of military administration and diplomacy for his city in time of war, Machiavelli developed a perspective which he struggled, despite fluctuating personal conditions, to maintain steadfast. Furthermore, he was observing in Italy the final paroxysms of the Middle Ages without the birth of the new order for itself while it was reduced to serve as the field of battle in which others in striving against each other were achieving their new form. Thus, of the League of Cambrai in which in the spring of 1509 the King of France, the Emperor Maximilian, Pope Julius II and the King of Aragon joined in waging war against Venice,[260] Tommasini commented:

> Così l'armi spirituali e le temporali insieme dolosamente s'adoperavano a fiaccarla [Venezia]; così, dopo oppressa Genova nel Mediterraneo, coll'oppressione di Venezia sull'Adriatico tendevasi a compiere il fatale annien-

tamento d'Italia. Restava Firenze in piedi, Firenze che tanta parte aveva avuta e tanta gioia nella caduta delle repubbliche rivali, e a cui le male arti non dovevano fruttare nè libertà, nè potenza. Ma la lotta che s'iniziava in questa nostra penisola non era tale da lasciare fidanza di salvezza ad alcun membro della nazione. Questa non sentiva sè stessa ed era suo destino che la civiltà del rinascimento in lei iniziatasi, in lei prima morisse; che la sua morte fosse primo principio di rigenerezione ai popoli scesi a combattere sopra i campi d'Italia la lotta della loro novella vita.[261]

Thus the spiritual and the temporal arms together craftily exerted themselves to break her [Venice]; thus, after it oppressed Genoa on the Mediterranean, with the oppression of Venice on the Adriatic, the intention was to complete the fatal annihilation of Italy. Florence remained last, Florence which had had so great a part and taken so much joy in the fall of her rival republics, and for whom the evil arts were not to bear fruits either of liberty or of power. But the struggle which had its beginning in this our peninsula was not such as to leave confidence in salvation to any member of the nation. It did not perceive its own self and it was its destiny that the civilization of the Renaissance initiated in it, in it dies first; but its death was the very beginning of the regeneration of the people who descended to fight out on the fields of Italy the struggle of their new life.

Ferrara has observed perceptively the nature of the influence upon Machiavelli due to the quality of the administration in which he served:

Machiavel fut grandement aidé dans les *Discours* par le fait qu'il appartenait au gouvernement de la dernière cité italienne qui ait maintenu, au moins formellement, une constitution républicaine à quoi tous les citoyens s'intéressaient. Ce milieu de riches bourgeois—les Medici eux-mêmes n'étaient pas autre chose—qui vaquaient chaque jour à leurs affaires commerciales et qui étudiaient et réglaient celles de l'État, dut influer sur lui de telle sorte que, lorsqu'il en écrivit, il ne put parler de la chose publique comme d'un sujet qui dépendît de causes surnaturelles (influence divine sur le souverain, intervention du cier peut-être), mais comme d'une conséquence de l'harmonie de tout l'ensemble social. On a dit, avec beaucoup d'exactitude, que l'Italie fut le laboratoire où furent expérimentées toutes les institutions. Avec ce critère nous pouvons affirmer que Florence, industrielle et commerciale, expérimenta souvent des institutions qui provenaient d'un esprit très pareil à celui qui a crée et maintenu les grandes démocraties modernes.[262]

Machiavelli was greatly helped in the *Discourses* by the fact that he belonged to the government of the last Italian city which had maintained, at least formally, a republican constitution in which all of the citizens interested themselves. This environment of rich bourgeoisie—the Medici themselves were not anything else—who occupied each day with their commercial affairs and who studied and directed those of the state, exerted an influence upon him of such a sort that, when he wrote of it, he could not speak of public affairs as of a subject which depended on supernatural causes (divine influence on the sovereign, perhaps intervention of heaven), but as of a consequence of the harmony of the entire social ensemble. It has been said, with a great deal of exactitude, that Italy was the laboratory where all of the institutions were experimented. With this criterion, we are able to affirm that Florence, industrial and commercial, often experimented with the institutions which progressed with a spirit like to that which has created and maintained the great modern democracies.

His tireless industry and scrupulous honesty comported with the tone of the administration in which he served and throughout his writings he castigated those who betrayed the trust of their city by using office for private advantage. In *The Horizon Book of the Renaissance,* Garret Mattingly has written:

among his contemporaries surely Niccolo Machiavelli was one of the least Machiavellian . . . One inappropriate virtue is particularly surprising. It even surprised Machiavelli himself. The man who wrote that men are moved so predominantly by self-interests that princes need take account of no other motives, that "a man will resent the loss of his patrimony more than the murder of his father," was himself the devoted, unselfish servant of his ungrateful state. He lived in an age when the use of public office for private gain was perfectly customary. He had during most of his fourteen years as a servant of the Florentine republic unrivaled opportunities to enrich himself at the expense of the condottieri and other contractors with whom as secretary of the Ten of War he had to deal. Yet he quitted Florentine service as poor as the day he had entered it.[263]

Thirteen months after the loss of office, he wrote to Vettori regarding the presentation of his work *"On Princedoms"* to the Medici in the hope of obtaining employment and, as noted above (p. 139), referred to his perennial poverty as evidence of his honesty.[264]

When at last a Medici, Cardinal Giulio (later to become Pope Clement VII), did arrange employment for Machiavelli as the writer of the history of his city, shortly thereafter an offer came from his former patron, the ex-gonfalonier-for-life, Piero Soderini, that he accept the secretaryship for the republic of Ragusa. Undisconcerted by Machiavelli's choice to continue to work on the history, on 13 April 1521 Soderini was able to transmit to him from Prospero Colonna, the celebrated Roman condottiere, the offer of service as his secretary. Fabrizio Colonna whom Machiavelli had chosen to represent him as the chief spokesman in *The Art of War* was a cousin of Prospero's. Besides the Orsini with whom both Lorenzo the Magnificent and his son Piero had been joined in marriage, the Colonna had, through recent centuries,[265] been Rome's other leading family.

The salary being offered Machiavelli was five times that which he was to receive under the contract for the history and more than double that received by the first secretary of Florence. As Ridolfi has recorded,

> [Soderini] urged him to accept this great opportunity, considering it 'much better than staying there writing history for *fiorini di sugello*'. . . .
> To accept would have meant leaving an honorable public office to serve at the court of a foreign master. He would have more pleasure from a florin enjoyed in liberty in Florence than from five received as a courtier.[266]

Consequently, doubtlessly with renewed spirit and inner contentment, he continued, as later he was to express it,

> to write what has been done at home and abroad by the Florentine people.[267]

CONTRIBUTIONS FROM PATRONS AND FRIENDS

Machiavelli's capacity to attract others as friends and to involve them in collaboration for promoting his perceptions of the common good was a cardinal factor in his development.

MARCELLO ADRIANI

Before the veil of obscurity had lifted sufficiently for events in his life to be clearly established, perhaps as a student in classes at the university in Florence, Machiavelli had so impressed Marcello Adriani who, on 13 February 1498, was made the first secretary of the republic, head of the First Chancery, that it may have been he who sponsored the appointment of Machiavelli as secretary of the Second Chancery;[268] however, the fact that Adriani stood godfather to Machiavelli's first child cannot be taken as proof that their relationship deepened into friendship.[269]

From the beginning of Machiavelli's years of service, both in his bureau and on his missions abroad, he became surrounded with friends attracted at once by his high spirits and lively intelligence.

FRANCESCO AND PIERO SODERINI

With the power of the French-supported Cesare Borgia growing ever more threatening,[270] the Florentines determined to strengthen the power of the executive in their government.[271] As the Gonfalonier of Justice, Piero Soderini,[272] rose to the new post of supreme executive,[273] he recognized in Machiavelli a reliability in observation, a congeniality in dedication to the common good and a clarity and freshness of reporting which could be of great service to the republic. In the words of the historian Ferdinand Schevill,

> So satisfactorily did he [Machiavelli] perform these [initial] services that, on Soderini's express orders, he was sent repeatedly to Louis XII and Emperor Maximilian, and at least once to every Italian ruler, great or small, who in any way affected the Florentine destiny.[274]

It was, however, with those who collaborated with Machiavelli on missions abroad and who became acquainted with the qualities of his mind and spirit as he worked under stress that relations of friendship developed which endured through subsequent years. So it was with the Gonfalonier's brother, Bishop Francesco Soderini. In June, 1502, at the Gonfalonier's instigation, Machiavelli was sent to accompany the Bishop to Urbino to parry Cesare Borgia's prospective request for a military commission and to report on his actions and intentions.[275] Previously, the Gonfalonier had been one of three Florentine ambassadors who had negotiated with him.[276] As Machiavelli studied and sought to identify the elements contributing to the Duke's aggrandizement, his ability to raise and form an effective army out of the young men of the tumultuous region over which he had gained control held for Machiavelli increasing fascination. Perhaps it was during this mission that he heard Bishop Soderini remark:

> that among the reasons for praise permitting anyone to call the Pope and the Duke *great* was this: they are men who recognize the right time and know how to use it very well;[277]

and Machiavelli added:

> This opinion is confirmed by our experience of the things they have carried through when they had an opportunity.[278]

Thus, Machiavelli's attention was called to the importance of timely action, a quality of statesmanship which subsequently he repeatedly emphasized.

Meanwhile the influence of the Bishop and his brother was growing steadily and, with it, that of the young secretary. When Piero Soderini was elected Gonfalonier for life, it had been Machiavelli who reported the news to him in Arezzo.[279] In the spring of 1503 while the Bishop was serving as Florentine ambassador to France, Pope Alexander VI made him a cardinal.[280] In the rising fortunes of Cardinal della Rovere culminating in his election and taking the name of Julius II and on the consequent unremitting crumbling of Cesare Borgia's influence and personal security, Machiavelli, on legation to the papal court, consulted constantly with Cardinal Soderini and reported to the Ten. Of their relations during this time, Ridolfi has written:

He [Machiavelli] is often at the house of Cardinal Soderini with whom he has renewed his old friendship . . . he continually sings the Cardinal's praises in his letters to the Ten[281] and the Cardinal is equally assiduous in writing to Florence in praise of Machiavelli; so much so that there are some among the Signoria who are not pleased with this friendship . . . The Cardinal too had stood godfather to Machiavelli's little boy [born while Machiavelli was in Rome][282] and it was he who encouraged the envoy to resist the first recall of the Ten. When at last Machiavelli decided to obey, Soderini wrote the Ten regretting that Machiavelli had been taken away from him, and begging them to take good care of him because of his quite extraordinary prudence and diligence.[283]

Alarmed by the mortal danger to the republican liberties of Florence which the startling abilities and boundless ambition of Pope Alexander VI and his son, Cesare Borgia, the Duke of Valentinois, were posing, and privileged to witness together the portentous rise and the seemingly almost miraculous collapse of the threat, Machiavelli and the Cardinal considered measures which might be taken to protect their beloved city from any such hazard in the future. In the course of their deliberations, there began to take shape the concept that out of the citizenry could be formed a militia which could serve the city as effectively and loyally as Cesare Borgia's Romagnan conscripts had supported him.[284] That the Cardinal gave encouraging support for the idea is indicated in the letter which he wrote Machiavelli on 24 May 1504:

> The argument against the militia is invalid *in re tam necessaria et salubri;* and suspicion is not justified *de vi, quae non paretur ad commodum privatum sed publicum.* Do not desist in your efforts, for perhaps one day you shall have the glory of it, if nothing else.[285]

The Cardinal became godfather, again, for still another son born just nine months after the return from Rome.[286]

Machiavelli worked mightily to strengthen interest in the project for the militia not only on the part of the Cardinal and the Gonfalonier but also on that of the broader public. In order to alert the citizenry to the dangers ahead and the need for the city to look to its own defense, he dashed off the "First Decennale," the closing lines of which are:

> Therefore my spirit is all aflame; now with hope, now with fear, it is overwhelmed, so much that it wastes to nothing bit by bit; because it seeks to know where your ship can sail, weighted with such heavy weights, or into what harbor, with these winds. Yet we trust in the skilful steersman, in the oars, in the sails, in the cordage; but the voyage would be easy and short if you would reopen the temple of Mars.[287]

He dedicated the "Decennale" to Alamano Salviati, the leader of the Gonfalonier's opposition.[288] Aided by events further discrediting the mercenaries in the city's employment, Machiavelli persuaded the Gonfalonier to steer the initial phases of the necessary legislation through the Signoria and the Council of Eighty.[289] Now Machiavelli began recruiting troops and he won approval for his request that the city hire as drillmaster for the incipient militia "the notorious" one whom Cesare Borgia had employed in that capacity.[290] On February 1506, during carnival, he presented the Florentines with a memorable parade.[291] On the 6th of the following December was created the ordinance which he himself had drawn up, as Ridolfi reports it:

> the *Nove ufficiali dell'ordinanza e milizia fiorentina* (the nine officers of the Florentine ordinance and militia), then the first magistrature to be set up to govern permanently the military affairs of the state . . . The new office of the Nine required a Secretary, and this could only be Machiavelli, while he remained of course chancellor of the Second Chancery and secretary of the Ten.[292]

In recognition, Cardinal Soderini wrote him, as quoted by Ridolfi,

> 'We do not believe that in Florence anything as worthy and well-founded as this has been done for some long time' in defense of its new freedom, a divine gift not a product of men.[293]

Some time after the restoration of the Medici rule in Florence in 1512, Pope Leo welcomed to his court in Rome both the ex-Gonfalonier and the Cardinal. The relation between the three of them, however, was considered by Machiavelli's friend at court, the Florentine ambassador Francesco Vettori, too fragile and delicate for him to follow through on Machiavelli's suggestion that it be tested as an avenue for courting papal favor for Machiavelli.[294] Years later, between Cardinal Soderini and Cardinal Giulio de'Medici (later Pope Clement VII), developed rivalry for election to the papacy and the latter brought about Cardinal Soderini's imprisonment in the Castle Sant'Angelo.[295]

BIAGIO BUONACCORSI

Between Machiavelli and his assistants in the office of the Second Chancery flourished a relationship which generated support and strength. Ridolfi recounts:

> Of that Second Chancery, which had come to be so much part of his life and soul, he was the very life and soul. As we gather from the letters of his assistants and from this last letter of Vespucci, the absences of their chief were felt almost physically; they missed his conversation, his amusing sallies and jokes, which gave fresh inspiration to the clerks.[296]

Perhaps to the period between his appointment in July, 1498 and his marriage in August, 1501[297] should be ascribed some of his Carnival Songs[298] as well as his "Articles for a Pleasure Company."[299]

When abroad on legations and missions, Machiavelli had the assurance that the routine responsibilities of the office were receiving competent attention especially subject to the dedicated concern of Biagio Buonaccorsi, his chief assistant in the Second Chancery throughout the fourteen years of Machiavelli's secretaryship. Tommasini described him:

> coadiutore suo, cieco d'ammirazione per l'alto intelletto dell'amico, geloso della sua benevolenza e di soli tre anni più giovane di Niccolò. Dotato d'un cuore squisito e d'un ingegno mediocre, non mancava ad alcun gentile officio della vita, e, borbottando, dapertutto accorreva colla sua buona voglia. Un piccolo segno di premura bastava a consolarlo; una pretensioncina affettuosa non soddisfatta bastava a metterlo di malumore.[300]

> his co-worker, blind with admiration for the high intellect of his friend, jealous for his good wishes, was but three years younger than Niccolo. Endowed with a highly sensitive heart and a mediocre talent, he was not lacking in any kind service for life, and, muttering, was on hand everywhere with his good will. A small indication of solicitude was sufficient to give him comfort; a slight affectionate pretension not satisfied was sufficient to put him in bad humor.

From time to time, Buonaccorsi informed him of the mood occasioned by his reports to the government,[301] of the happenings within the bureau,[302] of intrigues on the part of any seeming about to take advantage of Machiavelli's absence in the hope of displacing him in his office,[303] of rumors of proposed changes in the salary scale or employment policies.[304] Buonaccorsi sent him news about his wife and family.[305] He substantiated and reinforced words of praise he heard spoken about his chief[306] and to the Gonfalonier he spoke effectively of Machiavelli's need for adequate salary.[307] It was to Buonaccorsi that Machiavelli, when on the mission to Cesare Borgia, wrote for a copy of Plutarch's *Lives*.[308] Buonaccorsi's letters breathed an affectionate encouragement which came most clearly to expression in a letter—sent while Machiavelli was on that same mission—in which he prayed

God bless you and bring you greatness.[309]

Loyal to the last, with the restoration of the Medici, Buonaccorsi shared with his chief the loss of office.[310] Along with Cardinal Soderini and Marcello Virgilio Adriani, the First Chancellor of the republic, Buonaccorsi had been chosen to serve as godfather for his eldest son, Bernardo.[311] In helping throughout

173

the fourteen years to carry on the work of the office and maintain it as a firm basis of operations, Buonaccorsi and his colleagues had released Machiavelli to attend and to observe deeply the widely divergent political processes not only of the leaders of the small city states of Tuscany but also those of the nation state in its struggle for identity and unity.

NICCOLO VALORI

The tendency for Machiavelli's associates on embassies abroad to become helpful and enduring friends had manifested itself more than a year before he accompanied Bishop Soderini on the mission to Cesare Borgia in Urbino.[312] On one of the several missions in 1501 to the strife-torn city of Pistoia, Machiavelli, accompanied by Niccolo Valori, had the charge to rid the city of factions and to inflict such punishments as the two legates considered necessary to bring the unruly under control.[313] A year later, Valori sent him the words of encouragement quoted above (p. 105).[314] Twelve days later, Valori wrote him:

Would to God that every man would do as you do, they would make fewer mistakes;[315]

and then, revealing the depth of his feelings for Machiavelli, he wrote on October 31:

As I have no brothers, I propose to regard you as a brother and that you do the same to me; and you may take this in lieu of a bond.[316]

In January, 1504, Machiavelli was sent to join him who was then serving as Florentine ambassador to France.[317] In the following March, Machiavelli left to return to Florence but months later when Valori requested the Gonfalonier to grant him leave to return to Florence, he urged (though in vain) that Machiavelli be chosen as his replacement.[318] During that year Valori stood as godfather to Machiavelli's second son, Lodovico.[319]

After the fall of the government and the restoration of the Medici, Valori was one of the two with whom the anti-Medicean conspirators consulted regarding their plans. Although Valori had coldly rebuffed any suggestion of participation, his name, along with that of Machiavelli and about a score of others, was included in the list the conspirators had made of possible sympathizers. The list, accidentally found on 18 February 1513, was turned over to the Eight, who had all arrested and tortured.[320] Following the trial, on 7 March, Valori was sentenced to two years imprisonment.[321] With the election of Cardinal Giovanni de'Medici as pope on 11 March, Florence exploded in a general jubilation bringing not only permission for the re-admission of the Soderini to the city but the release of Machiavelli from his prison cell.[322] Regarding Valori, Machiavelli's biographers offer no further word.

FRANCESCO VETTORI

The most significant, lasting, celebrated and productive of these friendships was that with Francesco Vettori.

As Maximilian, "King of the Romans,"[323] persistently declared his intention of going to Rome to receive the imperial crown and demanded of Florence, along with other cities, tribute to defray his expenses, Gonfalonier Soderini proposed that Machiavelli be sent to the German court to report on developments. Counteracting the Gonfalonier's unswerving support of the policy of reliance on France, the aristocratic opposition, including those working for the return of the Medici, looked to the "Emperor" as a potential ally.[324] They were influential enough to succeed in defeating the Gonfalonier's nominee and in having Francesco Vettori, five years younger than Machiavelli,[325] sent in his stead on 27 June 1507.[326] The Gonfalonier's persistence, however, along with the increasingly threatening turbulence occasioned by uncertainty over Maximilian's intentions, resulted in Machiavelli's being dispatched on 17 December to join Vettori. The preceding events would hardly appear as a propitious preparation for congenial relations between the two.

They met on 11 January 1508 at Bolzano.[327] The Ten gave Vettori reassurance that no lack of confidence in him had prompted the sending of Machiavelli.[328] Tommasini has traced the tactful process through which the delicate situation became the beginning of the life-long friendship. The long journey from Florence had exhausted Machiavelli's resources. As Tommasini described the situation:

> . . . nel poscritto della sua prima lettera da Bolzano, à il buon tatto d'aggiungere: "quando per alcuna ragione vostre signorie volessino mi fermassi qui qualche dì, *il che io non credo,* o mi mandino danari, o scrivino a Francesco me ne dia sopra di loro; benchè Francesco infino a qui non mi abbi mai negato cosa veruna, ma sopra di me".—Per parte loro i Dieci si rivolgono destramente al Vettori: "Niccolò scrive che desiderebbe tornarsene, avendo satisfatto alle commissioni sue; e noi non sappiendo se ti accade servirtene di costà , non li aviamo dato licenzia; però scriverrai quello te ne occorre, e *facendo conclusione in questo mezzo,* se ne potrà allora tornare con tale conclusione per via sicura". Questo era un dir chiaro, che Niccolò doveva restare sino alla fine de'negoziati; di soprappiù al Vettori si racommandava "di provvederlo ancora di qualche somma di danari" e s'aggiungeva: "per altra nostra gli scriverreno quello che abbi ad fare".—Francesco non intese a sordo: "al Machiavello, in mentre arò denari per me, no ne mancherà ancora al lui: *né giudico, per cosa del mondo, fussi bene lo richiamassi; ma prego Vostre Signorie che sieno contente ci stia tanto che le cose sieno composte; lo stare suo è necessario;* nondimeno quando accadessi cosa che importasse il venir suo e il cammino non sia molto pericoloso, son certo che lui non recuserà ogni fatica e pericolo per amore della città."[329]

175

. . . in the postscript of his first letter from Bolzano, he [Machiavelli] had the good taste to add: "if for any reason Your Signors might wish that I stop here several days, *which I do not think,* either would they send me money or write Francesco that he give me some on their own account; although Francesco up to the present has never denied me anything, yet on my own account." On their part, the Ten skillfully addressed Vettori: "Niccolo writes that he desires to return, having completed his commissions; and we not knowing whether you agree that this serves your purpose have not given him permission; therefore would you write that which occurs to you regarding it, and, *if you so conclude,* that he be able to return with such conclusions by a safe route." That was to say clearly that Niccolo ought to remain until the end of the negotiations; besides, they recommended to Vettori, "to provide him again with a sum of money" and they added: "however they will write him that which he is to do."—Francesco was quick to understand: "as to Machiavelli, as long as I have money enough for myself, Machiavelli will not lack anything; *nor do I think that for anything in the world it would be well that he be recalled; but I beg Your Signors that they be content that he be kept here until matters are settled; his stay is necessary;* nevertheless if something should happen that would require his return, I am sure that he will not refuse any fatigue or danger for love of the city."

Summarizing the hardships being encountered by Maximilian as well as the two legates, Ridolfi has written:

the unfortunate Maximilian was bearing the burden of these unhappy political conditions, unable to collect even a part of the money and troops promised by the Diet. Our two Florentines were also in some difficulties, caught between the parsimony of the Republic and the Emperor who was "at sea with few provisions", between the vague instructions of the Ten and the even greater uncertainties of the Emperor . . . The Florentine who was used to French loquacity was further disconcerted by the almost ridiculous secrecy with which everything there [at the Emperor's court] was surrounded. All these secrets added to the vast size of the country and the difficulty of communicating with Florence made Machiavelli and Vettori feel "as though they were on some lost island."[330]

In February, when Vettori took sick, instead of going to observe the Diet which the Emperor had summoned to meet in Ulm, Machiavelli remained by the side of his friend.[331] It was mid-June before he returned to Florence.[332] (Early in 1510, Vettori, also, became godfather to one of Machiavelli's infants.)[333] More than two years later, when seeking permission to return to Florence from his third mission to France, Machiavelli received word from Vettori that Robert Acciaiuoli, the new ambassador to France, was on his way and Vettori added:

I have asked Roberto to send you back soon, so that while losing him we will at least have you back . . . Filippo [Casavecchia] and I long for you every day.[334]

At that fateful hour on the night of 30 August 1512, when Francesco Vettori's brother, Paolo, along with three companions, all of leading families, burst into the Gonfalonier's quarters and rudely confronted him with the demand for his abdication, the Gonfalonier sent Machiavelli for Francesco who personally conducted him to the safety of Vettori's house and then on to Siena.[335]

Two days after Machiavelli's release from prison[336] and again after five more days,[337] Machiavelli wrote Francesco and expressed thanks to him and his brother for their assistance in bringing about his freedom:

I can say that all of life that is left me I consider that I owe to the Magnficent Giuliano de'Medici and your Pagolo.[338]

Vettori replied that events, however, had outstripped his efforts on Machiavelli's behalf.[339] These letters, together with those of 9 April[340] and 16 April[341] reveal the difficulty which Machiavelli was having in coming to accept his friend's reluctance in approaching the Medici on his behalf.

Machiavelli wrote to Vettori of missing the privilege of discussing with him world affairs; in communicating local gossip, he found no adequate substitute. By mid-April, Vettori began to open the way for serious correspondence. He posed for discussion policy questions of practical importance and thereby provided nourishment which encouraged Machiavelli in the development of his judgment derived from experience and enriched by continuous study. The letter of 29 April[342] is the first in the remarkable series which continued through that summer. In July, Vettori wrote that Pope Leo was considering the formation of new states—one for his brother, Guiliano and one for his nephew, Lorenzo.[343] Vettori's younger brother, Paolo, and Giuliano de'Medici (who was nine years younger than Machiavelli and therefore four years younger than Francesco) were close friends.[344] The news from the Ambassador fired Machiavelli's imagination. Here appeared an opportunity to put all his experience, observation and reflection to practical use in the service of young Giuliano who, as newly-appointed Gonfalonier of the Church,[345] might lead forces for the "redemption of Italy." By December, Machiavelli wrote Vettori:

[I] have composed a little work *On Princedoms*, where I go as deeply as I can into considerations on this subject, debating what a princedom is, of what kinds they are, how they are gained, how they are kept, why they are lost. If ever you can find any of my fancies pleasing, this one should not displease you; and by a prince, and especially by a new prince, it ought to be welcomed. Hence I am dedicating it to his Magnificence Giuliano.[346]

177

On 31 January 1515, he confidently communicated to Vettori his recommendations of policy for Giuliano.[347] The following letter to Giuliano from the papal secretary, Piero Ardinghelli, however, brought to an abrupt end any prospect for a fruitful development:

> Cardinal de'Medici questioned me yesterday very closely if I knew whether Your Excellency had taken into his service Niccolo Machiavelli, and as I replied that I knew nothing of it nor believed it, His Lordship said to me these words: "I do not believe it either, but as there has been word of it from Florence, I would remind him that it is not to his profit nor to ours. This must be an invention of Paolo Vettori; . . . write to him on my behalf that I advise him not to have anything to do with Niccolo."[348]

Soon thereafter, however, Giuliano contracted a long illness and died in March, 1516.[349]

Meanwhile, Francesco Vettori, on 15 May 1515,[350] had returned to Florence which by then was under the control of the Pope's young nephew, Lorenzo,[351] with whom Vettori had a close friendship.[352] In that same month, in the words of Ridolfi,

> Lorenzo had himself elected captain general of the Florentines . . . Leo had him march on Urbino, which he took in the course of a few days during June 1516, and on the 8th of October he became Duke of Urbino by papal investiture.[353]

As early as August, 1513, Machiavelli had written to Vettori a letter full of praise for Lorenzo's character and way of life in Florence.[354] In the view of many, and not only in that of his very ambitious mother, Alfonsina Orsini de'Medici, Lorenzo seemed destined to achieve success where Cesare Borgia had failed.[355] Machiavelli saw in him the potentialities for becoming the leader who would drive the foreigners out of Italy and bring security and peace to the peninsula. Consequently, sometime between September, 1515 and September, 1516, he dedicated to him the *Prince*.[356] Whether or not the "little work" was ever presented to Lorenzo is not known with certainty.[357]

Both Machiavelli and Vettori felt at ease with each other in expressing to each other the gamut of interests and experiences. Whenever Machiavelli sensed a danger lest reference to his needs, his misfortunes, or his expectations might place a burden upon his friend's disposition, he swiftly shifted the tenor of the communication to others of their shared interests. In his letter of 18 March 1513, written within a week after his release from, as Ridolfi described it, "twenty-two days of manacles and shackles,"[358] after taking notice of, but with a deft reference trying to treat lightly, his troubles, he turned first to gossip about mutual acquaintances and then added:

178

Every day we are in the house of some girls to recover our strength; only yesterday we were in the house of Sandra di Pero to see the procession pass; and so we go on spending our time on these rejoicings [over the election of Cardinal de'Medici to the papacy as Leo X] getting pleasure from what is left of life, so that I feel as though I were dreaming.[359]

The weighty correspondence carried on through the spring and summer of 1513, nourished by Machiavelli's recurrent hopes for renewed recognition and employment, was succeeded by letters of levity during the winter of fading expectations. But, in April, 1514, Machiavelli wrote:

Will it be, then, after a thousand years, a reprehensible thing to write something else than stories? I believe not. And therefore I have decided, leaving aside every irrational hesitation, to beg you to straighten out for me a confusion in my head.[360]

The tension inherent in the dialogue between Machiavelli and Vettori received the sharpest expression in the letter of 31 January 1515.[361] Beginning by entering into his friend's mood for giving free rein to the passion of love, Machiavelli abruptly improvised a justification for returning to their other chief mutual interest:

Anybody who saw our letters, honored friend, and saw their diversity, would wonder greatly, because he would suppose now that we were grave men, wholly concerned with important matters, and that into our breasts no thought could fall that did not have in itself honor and greatness. But then, turning the page, he would judge that we, the very same persons, were light-minded, inconstant, lascivious, concerned with empty things. And this way of proceeding, if to some it may appear censurable, to me seems praiseworthy, because we are imitating Nature, who is variable; and he who imitates her cannot be rebuked. And though we have been accustomed to give this variety in a number of letters, I wish to give it this time in one, as you will see, if you read the other page. Now spit.[362]

And he continued by sketching for Vettori the ideas of policy which might prove useful for Giuliano de'Medici in becoming a new prince.[363] In Vettori's letter of July, 1513 upon which Machiavelli modeled his most famous letter, that of 10 December 1513, Vettori, in his detailed description of his way of life had written:

Si vous me demandiez: "Avez-vous une maîtresse?" je vous répondrais: "Oui, les premiers temps de mon séjour; mais, après, par peur de la saison d'été, je me suis abstenu. Néanmoins, j'ai une dame très bien élevée qui vient d'elle-même souvent, sans que je la demande: sa beauté est raisonnable et ses manieères aimables. J'ai aussi, dans le quartier, une voisine à qui je ne déplais pas."[364]

179

If you should ask me: "Have you a mistress?" I would reply: "Yes, at the beginning of my stay; but after, for fear of the season of summer, I have abstained. Nevertheless, I have a 'dame' very well raised who comes of herself often without my asking her; she is fairly good-looking, and her manners are agreeable. I have also, in the quarter, a neighbor to whom I am not displeasing."

Lorenzo's rising fortunes were not accompanied by a strengthening of his character. In the words of Ridolfi,

There was no hope now of winning over the affections and the favors of those Medici princes, least of all of the degenerate Lorenzo. Vettori was in France, and would return from France with Lorenzo, becoming more of a courtier as his master became less of a citizen.[365]

The result was to weaken, and indeed to terminate, the relationship with Vettori as a source, as Machiavelli had written, of "that food which only is mine and which I was born for."[366]

However, it must never be forgotten that, in the time of Machiavelli's deepest crisis, it had been Francesco Vettori who, with a friendship steady and strong, had been available with an understanding heart and with a mind which provided a continuing link which opened the way for Machiavelli, the man of action, to become transformed into the man of reflection and, while becoming disappointed in his struggle to serve as a political mentor for the young Medicean princes, in seeking to discern and express the effectual truth in politics, to become the political scientist for the new era.

Years later, scarcely three months before his death, Machiavelli, again on a mission abroad for his city, was corresponding with his old friend Francesco Vettori in Florence, on the weightiest matters of war and peace.[367]

THE RUCELLAI CIRCLE

To whom the credit belongs for providing Machiavelli with access to the company accustomed to frequent the spirited gatherings of friends in the gardens of Rucellai, we have not learned. According to Sydney Anglo,

We know that at some point, certainly after 1514, and probably a good deal earlier, Machiavelli drifted into the circle of upper-class intellectuals who used to meet in the Orti Oricellari.[368]

Cosimo [Rucellai] who used to preside over informal discussions . . . was one of the dedicatees of the *Discourses;* while *The Art of War* was largely dedicated to his memory. And amongst the many friends who participated in these meetings were Zanobi Buondelmonti, the other dedicatee of the *Discourses,* Battista della Palla; Luigi Alamanni, the poet; and Jacopo Nardi and Filippo dei Nerli, the historians.[369]

Included among additional participants, according to Tommasini, was Francesco Vettori.[370] Could it have been he who facilitated the introduction to the company?

Disaffected by the democratic policies of Piero Soderini, the Rucellai were among the aristocratic patrician families which formed a nucleus of supporters of the exiled Medici.[371] In 1507–1508, they had encouraged Cardinal de'Medici to arrange the marriage between Clarice, the daughter of Florence's former ruler Piero de'Medici, and the young Filippo of the powerful Strozzi family.[372] In order to bring him to punishment for this breach of the official policy, the Gonfalonier had charges brought against the young man.[373] It was believed that it was Machiavelli who drew up the document of accusation.[374] Later, Filippo refused to take part in a plot against the life of the Gonfalonier and indeed arranged for it to become known and foiled.[375] The invalid Cosimo Rucellai surrounded himself with a literary company of such brilliance that some have considered it the continuation of the Florentine Platonic Academy.[376]

Perhaps as early as 1515, but probably by 1516–1517,[377] Machiavelli was a much appreciated member and may have been conducting commentaries on Livy's *History* and discourses on the art of war. Acquaintances made there became his permanent friends: Zanobi Buondelmonti, Lorenzo and Filippo Strozzi, and Luigi Alamanni.[378] At the instigation of his auditors, Machiavelli collected his reflections on Livy's *History* into a book.[379] In the dedication of it to Buondelmonti, Machiavelli showed that he had come to ground his hopes more in the civic consciences of private citizens than to fix his faith on an appeal to the possibility of stirring princes, seemingly favored by Fortune, to strive for honor and glory.[380]

The death of Cosimo in 1519 was the first of the shocks which would abruptly end the creative sessions of

the 'friends of the cool shade', as the habitués of the Orti used to describe themselves.[381]

In that same year, following the death of Lorenzo de'Medici, the Duke of Urbino, Cardinal Giulio de'Medici returned to Florence from Rome,[382] in order himself to take the reins of the government. Around 10 March 1520, Lorenzo Strozzi, together with some other members of the Orti circle, introduced Machiavelli to the Cardinal. Ridolfi recounts:

When he heard of that visit, Filippo Strozzi wrote to his brother: 'I am very glad that you took Machiavelli to see the Medici, for if he can get the masters' confidence, he is a man who must rise.'[383]

181

To Lorenzo Strozzi, Machiavelli dedicated *The Art of War* for which he had chosen as interlocutors members of the Rucellai "circle"[384] who had frequented the gardens in 1516.[385] It was one of those who was to open the way for Cardinal de'Medici to begin to take an active interest in Machiavelli. As Ridolfi explains:

> On the 25th of April his friend and close companion at the Orti, Battista della Palla, who is on very good terms at court because of his long record of allegiance and a gift he had made of extremely valuable sables, sends him from Rome a whole budget of good news. He has told the Pope, who is very fond of such things, about their meetings in the Orti, and how much they all value Machiavelli's intellect. He had spoken warmly of the *Mandragola* which was ready to be acted in His Holiness's presence. Leo was the sort of man who might more easily be won by a coarse comedy than by *The Prince:* he would have enjoyed the jokes and rejected what was bitter. Having thus first got him in a good mood, the clever courtier induced the Pope to give him a message for Cardinal de'Medici telling him to give effect to his good will towards Machiavelli with a 'commission to write, or something similar.'[386]

Sent on a mission to Lucca, Machiavelli with great industry improved his time and demonstrated his ability for historical narrative[387] by his *Life of Castruccio Castracani* which he wrote in the heroic manner of Plutarch,[388] finished by the end of August, dedicated to Zanobi Buondelmonti and Luigi Alamanni and submitted to members of the circle for reading and review.[389] Buondelmonti encouraged him to give serious thought to undertaking the writing of the history of Florence.[390] Upon his return to Florence by November 8th, he was, in the words of Ridolfi:

> employed by the Florentine Studio, of which Cardinal de'Medici was head and Machiavelli's brother-in-law, Francesco del Nero, administrator.[391]

During the following year, preoccupation with the preparation of the *History* was interrupted by the brief mission to Carpi. In August came the printing of *The Art of War*.[392] On December 1st, Pope Leo died.[393] Cardinal Giulio de'Medici, after frustrating Cardinal Soderini's maneuvers to secure for himself the papacy, returned to Florence and gave his attention to plans for reforming the government of the city.[394] Meanwhile the Soderini were gathering forces to bring about a more drastic change.[395] Within the Orti circle, passion for change took the form of a conspiracy aimed at the assassination of Cardinal de'Medici on June 19th, Corpus Christi day.[396] Machiavelli's closest friends, Zanobi Buondelmonti and Luigi Alamanni, were the leaders of the conspiracy; Battista della Palla was among the conspirators.[397] Warned in time of the discovery of the plot, Buondelmonti and Alamanni succeeded in fleeing the city but two others were seized, confessed, and on June 6th were beheaded.[398] Upon that same day,

Machiavelli's brother Totto died. Machiavelli, himself, appears not to have been implicated in the conspiracy and escaped suspicion.[399] The work on the *History* continued.

When, at length, in 1527, following the sack of Rome and the imprisonment, by the invading imperial forces, of Giulio de'Medici who was by then Pope Clement VII,[400] the Medici were again overthrown in Florence and a republic re-established, Zanobi Buondelmonti and Luigi Alamanni were on hand supporting the idea that Machiavelli be chosen once more as secretary of the republic;[401] but, unlike the Medici who when taking over the government in 1512 had refused to retain Machiavelli as secretary of the republic, in 1527 the new republican government decided to retain the Medici-appointed secretary and disregard the presentation in Machiavelli's favor.[402] Eleven days later, Machiavelli was dead.[403]

FRANCESCO GUICCIARDINI

Early in 1512, counter to Gonfalonier Soderini's objective of strengthening the French alliance, the Council of Eighty voted to send an emissary to the King of Spain. The choice fell upon a young doctor of laws, by age ineligible to hold public office, Francesco Guicciardini. He may have chafed under the instructions written and handed him by the Secretary of the Republic, Niccolo Machiavelli.[404] The following year he returned to Florence again under the control of the Medici and to a steadily more distinguished career as governor in states of the Church.[405] Meanwhile, Machiavelli, deprived of office, exiled, imprisoned, tortured, would be spending long years seeking ways to win the favor of the Medici and return to public service. Although denied active participation, he continued faithfully to develop his talents for political analysis. When at last his friends succeeded in stirring in Pope Leo and Cardinal de'Medici sufficient response to give him the commission to write *The History of Florence* and give him additional minor assignments, he was ready to respond to the smallest opportunity for serving in a representative capacity. Years earlier, he had written Vettori:

> there is my wish that our present Medici lords will make use of me, even if they begin by making me roll a stone; because then if I could not gain their favor, I should complain of myself.[406]

One of the first of these missions, that to the monks of Carpi—11 to 19 May 1521—required him to pass through Modena of which Guicciardini was governor.[407] On the way to Carpi, Machiavelli stopped briefly there.[408] Shortly afterwards, Guicciardini wrote him of the incongruity of the assignment for a man of Machiavelli's experience and abilities.[409] Machiavelli suggested that they use the occasion for enacting together a living comedy at the expense of the monks' credulity—a game which they both entered into with relish and which gave rise to an exchange of brilliant letters until Machiavelli brought it to a timely end.[410] Machiavelli returned to Florence and, following the alliance between Leo X and Charles V against France, Guicciardini was made commissioner general of the papal forces.[411]

Machiavelli was beginning to receive recognition for the results of his labors and genius in various fields. *The Art of War* was being eagerly read.[412] *Mandragola* was performed with great success at Monteloro toward the end of 1521 or beginning of 1522[413] and in Venice during the carnival season of 1522.[414]

Meanwhile, Machiavelli was carrying forward his work on the *History*. In August, 1524 he wrote Guicciardini of feeling the need to guard against subjective bias and distortion in treating the more recent events.[415] On 13 January 1525, the performance of *Clizia* in Florence added greatly to his fame.[416]

By then, Machiavelli had finished revising the first eight books of the *History* and expressed to Vettori his desire to go to Rome and in person to present it to the Pope. In March, Vettori counselled him against interpreting the Pope's interest as auguring well for such a visit; but, following a later report of further encouraging words from the Pope, by May, Machiavelli did make the presentation personally[417] and received a gift of 120 gold ducats from the Pope's private treasury.[418]

Machiavelli, however, was a man of letters and a historian by default of opportunity to prove himself a man of action. Before he had left Rome, he had stirred the Pope and his advisers[419] with the idea of strengthening the papal forces by recruiting the young Romagnans and forming them into a militia. Machiavelli left Rome on a special mission to his friend Guicciardini, at that time President of Romagna.[420] Now, in the words of Orestes Ferrara,

Guicciardini was, perhaps, as Villari says, the coolest and the most practical head in Italy at that moment.[421]

Through his agents, Guicciardini had called to the Pope's attention the practical difficulties and the possible dangers involved in espousing the plan

which [as Guicciardini wrote] if it could be brought to the desired fruition, there is no doubt that it would be one of the most useful and praiseworthy things which His Holiness could do.[422]

Time passed with no decision forthcoming.[423] Machiavelli waited in Faenza from June 20th[424] to July 26th.[425] During their weeks together, as their subsequent correspondence manifests, their friendship deepened. Ridolfi quotes an exchange of letters just after Machiavelli's return to Florence.

After your departure Maliscotta [a 'respectable courtesan'] spoke most honorably of you and praised very much your manners and your conversation. I am delighted with this, for I desire your every pleasure.[426]

To which Machiavelli replied:

I received your letter, in which you tell me how much I am favored by Maliscotta; and I am prouder of this than of anything I have in the world.[427]

At Guicciardini's request, Machiavelli inspected some property which Guicciardini had bought by proxy and other property which he was considering for purchase.[428] He entered deeply into his friend's concern for making suitable matches for his friend's four[429] daughters.[430] Guicciardini encouraged the prospect for the production of *Mandragola* in Faenza during the following carnival season,[431] but increasingly the complexities of foreign policy displaced all other considerations in Machiavelli's letters.

In August, at last, in Florence "the magistrates charged with forming a government" included his name among those from whom officers of the city might be chosen.[432]

Adverse events were disconcerting the strongest minds and stoutest hearts by the end of 1525. On December 19, he wrote his friend:

Of the things of the world I have nothing to tell you, since everybody cooled down on the Duke of Pescara's death, because before his death they talked of new restrictions and similar things; but now that he is dead, each man is a little reassured, and since he seems to have time, he gives time to his enemy. I conclude at last that on this side there is no possibility for doing, ever, anything honorable or vigorous about living or dying with justice, so much fear I observe in our citizens, and so unwilling they are to oppose him who is getting ready to swallow them up, nor do I see any exception to this, so that he who is to act after consulting with them will not do anything other than has been done up to now;[433]

and on the 26th Guicciardini wrote him that *de rebus publicis* he had lost his compass:

che se accadesse qualche sinistro, non potrem dire che ci sia stata tolta la signoria, ma che ci sia vergognosamente sfuggita dalle mani.[434]

but if some disaster should happen, we would not be able to say that the Signoria had been taken away from us, but that it had slipped shamefully from our hands.

A bright moment came with the news that during carnival time again in Venice *Mandragola* had scored a major triumph.[435]

By the following March, however, Machiavelli was recommending to Guicciardini another version of his plan for strengthening the papal forces. Giovanni de'Medici, "delle Bande Nere"—son of the redoubtable Caterina Sforza and, in descent by the younger line from Bicci de'Medici (founder of the family power), of the same generation as Clement VII—was demonstrating the most promising qualities of leadership and military genius.[436] Even in his early twenties he had been included in the supreme war planning council of the Pope[437] who, however, manifested a reluctance to promote his influence.[438] In the letter of March 15th, Machiavelli recommended to Guicciardini that the Pope secretly finance Giovanni delle Bande Nere for forming an army under Guicciardini's direction in order to rid Italy of the foreigners.[439] Not winning papal favor, this suggestion proved fruitless.

Guicciardini had been acquainting the Pope with the contents of Machiavelli's letters in which he set forth his perception of the developments and prospects of great power politics. His analyses of events and of the necessity to reinforce the defenses of Florence, in view of the inevitability of war, led the Pope, in accordance with Guicciardini's recommendation,[440] to order Guicciardini to request Machiavelli's participation in drawing up the plan for strengthening the fortifications.[441] Ridolfi has summarized the proceeding by which Machiavelli was at last called back not only into the official service of his city but this time as a responsible policy maker in its military defense!

War was inevitable . . . it was necessary to think of defense and attack. As for defense, the first thing the Florentine Pope and his Florentine minister [Guicciardini] thought of was Florence, which was so vulnerable on the Oltrarno side. Count Pietro Novarra, a famous military engineer, had been sent there to see to the defenses, but it was decided to set beside this Spanish refugee, Machiavelli, a theoretician of the art of war and a Florentine.

Machiavelli was always prompt and ready, and when Guicciardini had written him by order of the Pope on the 4th of April, he consulted the same evening with the Cardinal of Cortona and the next day he was up on the walls discussing with Novarra a bold design. This was sent to Rome with a report written by Machiavelli, which has been praised in recent times by historians of military art.

First it must have been praised by Clement VII and his counsellors, as its author was at once called to Rome where he succeeded in firing the Pope's enthusiasm and even Guicciardini's. He left again on the 26th or 27th of April with the order for the provisions to be made and his head 'full of ramparts'. During that time the new magistrature of the Curators of the Walls (Procuratori delle mura) was formed at the instigation of Machiavelli during his discussions in Rome; and he was elected secretary and quartermaster with his son Bernardo as assistant.[442]

From sometime before July 13th[443] to around October 30th,[444] again November 30th[445] to December 5th,[446] from the following February 3rd[447] to around April 22nd,[448] Machiavelli was on official missions to Guicciardini with the troops in the field for the purpose of keeping the home government informed of developments there and of being of assistance to Guicciardini. He was with the allied armies during the siege of Milan and probably in the capacity of papal commissioner.[449] When Guicciardini followed the army on the road towards Rome, Machiavelli seems to have accompanied him.[450] As the two shared the ordeal of months of camp life amid the frustrations of crumbling power, their mutual respect and friendship deepened. When Guicciardini had sent Machiavelli to observe conditions attending the siege of Cremona and exercise his judgment on the best procedure, he had written of him as "a man of great competence."[451] On April 16th, from Forli, Machiavelli wrote Vettori in Rome:

> With this north wind we too must sail and, if we decide on war, we must cut off all the affairs of peace, and in such a way that the allies will come on without any hesitation, because now we cannot hobble any more but must go like mad; often desperation finds remedies that choice has been unable to find . . . I love Messer Francesco Guicciardini; I love my native city more than my soul; and I tell you this through the experience which sixty years have given me, namely, that I do not believe that ever more difficult articles than these were struggled with, where peace is necessary and war cannot be abandoned; and we have on our hands a prince who scarcely is able to deal with peace alone or with war alone.[452]

Early on May 6th, Rome was taken by the Imperial forces and the pillage began. The Pope was held prisoner in Castle Sant'Angelo.[453] Having reached Orvietto, Guicciardini seems to have sent Machiavelli to Civitavecchia where he would find Andrea Doria in charge of the ships. Machiavelli's last letter to Guicciardini, that of 27 April 1527, reported his conversation with the Admiral.[454] Exactly one month later, Machiavelli was dead.[455]

Friendship with Guicciardini refreshed Machiavelli's spirit with appreciative companionship in his social conduct, encouragement of his achievements as dramatist and historian and, most importantly, provision of a way for him as a man of action to return to the arena of political affairs in the military and diplomatic defense of his beloved city.

CARDINAL INNOCENZA CIBO

While serving his city and attracting influential friends, to the very end he sought thereby to open ways for encouraging his sons to cultivate their talents in preparation for future opportunities. When, through Guicciardini's and Pope Clement's support, he became secretary of the Curators of the Walls, he took his eldest son, Bernardo, as his assistant.[456] The same concern appears in the letter of 2 April 1527, in which he wrote to his youngest son, Guido,[457]

I have made a new friendship with Cardinal Cibo (it is so great that I myself wonder at it), which will be of service to you.[458]

Cardinal Innocenza Cibo, papal legate in Bologna and cousin of Pope Clement, made the month which Machiavelli spent there during the winter of 1527 while on the mission to Guicciardini a period of personal recuperation and refreshment.[459] The letter to Guido was perhaps the last to his family.

THE MEDICI

The field of force in which Machiavelli functioned and, to the best of his abilities, strove to apply and cultivate his talents, was dominated during his entire life by the Medici. No understanding of his life and thought can be achieved without a consideration of the influence which they had upon his development.

Throughout Machiavelli's youth, Lorenzo the Magnificent was fascinating Florence by not only championing the arts and letters and personally achieving distinction in the latter but also by dazzling Italy with the successes of his diplomacy. Machiavelli was scarcely one month old when the twenty-year-old Lorenzo was married to Clarice Orsini whose family for 300 years had been one of the most powerful in Rome.[460] Six months later, Lorenzo, upon the death of his father, became head of the Medici family and its vast network of commercial enterprises.[461] Florence continued in form a republic; but in power and prestige Lorenzo, as had his father and grandfather, exceeded all other citizens. Machiavelli was nearing his ninth birthday when in the cathedral during high mass a son of the chief rival family, the Pazzi, with the connivance of the Archbishop, attacked Lorenzo and murdered his brother. The consequent lynching of the Archbishop and the involvement of the Pope in the attempt to break the power of the Medici led to war between Florence and the Papacy joined by Naples.[462] After nearly two years of bitter conflict, by boldly going to Naples to negotiate with the king, Lorenzo returned to Florence with a peace in which the Florentines rejoiced.[463] When, later in the year, the Turks, by capturing Otranto, gained a foothold in Italy, the Pope found it expedient to effect a reconciliation with the government of Florence and the prestige of Lorenzo grew throughout Italy.[464] Meanwhile, Lorenzo was availing himself of the opportunity to supplement the republican structure with instrumentalities of his own which ensured the continuance of that covert power which had been accumulating in the hands of the Medici for three generations and especially since 1434 when Cosimo had been recalled after a year of banishment.[465] Indeed, the Medici had been prominent in the city's affairs as early as 1304.[466] According to Schevill, writing of Salvestro de'Medici in 1378,

He belonged to a family which, beginning with the thirteenth century, had been steadily coming to the front by the usual avenue of trade and which by the fourteenth century had gained a secure position among the popolo grasso by its merchant enterprise coupled with its strict adherence to Guelph principles. While there were many Florentine families both richer and more prominent, the Medici by Salvestro's time were already an "old" clan in the sense that for several generations their representatives had been admitted to all the offices of the republic.[467]

During the turbulent months of the Ciompi revolt in 1378 and the recovery in 1382, Salvestro de'Medici had associated himself with the democratic cause and, although he was no immediate ancestor of what became the ruling branch of the family, his reputation did lend an aura of popular approbation to the very name of Medici of which Giovanni de Bicci de'Medici became the beneficiary.[468]

By 1489, so great had Lorenzo's influence become that he succeeded in getting Pope Innocent VIII to make his fourteen-year-old-son, Giovanni (later, Pope Leo X), a cardinal (the act to become effective—because of Giovanni's extreme youth—only after three years).[469] Tommasini has quoted a remark made by Messer Niccolo Giugni to Lorenzo which summarizes the progress of the family:

"L'avolo tuo superò i nobili e i potenti; tuo padre e' provvidi et sapienti; tu hai vinti i Pazzi: ora hai a fare con gli arrabbiati."[470]

Your grandfather overcame the nobles and the powerful; your father, the provident and the wise; you have conquered the Pazzi: now you have to deal with the enraged ones.

Machiavelli's own father held a post in the government under Lorenzo.[471] At the time of Lorenzo's death, Machiavelli was within a month of his twenty-third birthday.[472]

With Lorenzo's death collapsed his policy of balance of power which had helped protect the peninsula from invasion. Machiavelli was twenty-five when Charles VIII with his army stormed into Italy with the result that the Medici were expelled from Florence; Savonarola gained the leadership; and Florence lost control of the commercially strategic seaport, Pisa.

Machiavelli had just passed his twenty-ninth birthday when, four weeks after the hanging and burning of Savonarola,[473] the Council of Eighty selected him as Secretary of the Signoria, first Secretary of the Second Chancery and, shortly afterwards, Chancellor of the Ten.[474] Official missions took Machiavelli to France and Rome at times during which the young Medici were also present at those courts. His discreet aloofness probably generated attitudes which were later to block his advance.[475] In 1512, following the flight of the head of the republican government, the "Gonfalonier-for-life" Piero Soderini,[476] and the restoration in Florence of the power of the Medici, on the chance that he might demonstrate his possible usefulness as a servant of the state rather than be treated as a partisan of a discredited regime, Machiavelli sent a detailed account of the events marking the change of government to a certain lady,[477] a friend of the Medici, perhaps but improbably, to Alfonsina Orsini de'Medici herself, the widow of Lorenzo's eldest son, Piero, who had lost power fifteen years before and had died in exile. To Cardinal Giulio de'Medici, Machiavelli recommended a policy of generosity throughout the transition and, to the supporters of the Medici, a policy of forbearance.[478] All in vain.

On 7 November, 1512, Machiavelli was stripped of his office[479] and three days later confined to Florentine territory and required to post bond in the amount of 1000 gold florins[480] A week later he was banned from entering the Palazzo for a year.[481] On the 18th of the following February was found a listing of possible supporters of an attack upon the new government. The name of Niccolo Machiavelli had been included.[482] The leaders of the conspiracy were captured and confessed their intention. Machiavelli was arrested, tortured with "six turns of the rope," and held in prison.[483] Two sonnets which, while there, he composed and, possibly through his friend Paolo Vettori (the brother of Francesco, at that time Florentine ambassador at Rome), may have sent to Giuliano de'Medici, called attention to his condition and may have helped win for him some modification of the sentence.[484] Following the death of Pope Julius II, the death of Pope Adrian VI, and the election of Cardinal Giovanni de'Medici as Pope Leo X, the freeing of prisoners as part of Florence's general celebration included release for Machiavelli.[485] On March 18th in his letter to Francesco Vettori, he attributed to "the Magnficent Giuliano" a share in having brought about the recovery of his freedom.[486] His "Hymn of the Blessed Spirits" was his psalm of gratitude and his expression of hope that the reign of the new pope would be characterized by peace within Christendom.[487]

Now Machiavelli turned to his close friend, the ambassador:

Keep me, if it is possible, in the Signor Giuliano's memory, so that, if it is possible, he or his family may employ me in something or other, because I believe I would bring honor to him and profit to myself.[488]

From March, 1513 through December, 1514, Machiavelli sought through his friend to find some way to win from the Medici opportunity to manifest his capacity for public service.[489] With a gift of thrushes snared on his farm and accompanied with another sonnet in which he urged Giuliano to test for himself the quality of his (Machiavelli's) service and not be misled by others' opinions, he again sought to gain Giuliano's attention.[490] Neither this device nor varied appeals to his friend brought the desired offer of employment.

Vettori did, however, as already noted (above, pp. 177–180) by his letters provide opportunity for Machiavelli to make comprehensive and penetrating analyses of the kaleidoscopic turbulence of great power relationship.[491]

Now Pope Leo wished to carve out a principality for his brother, Giuliano, who, at thirty-five, was three years younger than himself. Attempts to fulfil such ambitions for members of one's immediate family had become a well-established tradition with popes. In his *History,* Machiavelli attributed to Nicholas III, of the house of Orsini, the beginning of the subordination of the papacy to family advancement.[492] In July, 1513, Vettori wrote Machiavelli a letter which in historical perspective proved to be of utmost significance. As Vignal reports it:

Vettori fait part à Machiavel de l'intention de Léon X de donner des États à son frère Julien et à son neveu Laurent, "Dès qu'il est devenu pape, sa première pensée a été de ravoir Parme et Plaisance, dont son preédécesseur Jules II, s'était emparé sans aucun juste titre, et qui avaient été reprises par le duc de Milan pendant la vacance du Saint-Siège." Ce qui porte l'ambassadeur "à croire que Léon X a le désir de donner des États à ses parents "c'est l'exemple donné par ses preédecésseurs, les papes Calixte, Pie, Sixte, Innocent, Alexandre VI et Jules II, et si quelques-uns n'ont pas agi de même, c'est qu'ils ne l'ont pas pu. D'ailleurs, on voit que les siens s'occupent peu de Florence; ce qui montre qu'ils ont en vue des États tout établis, et où ils n'aient pas sans cesse à gagner les habitants." Mais on ne sait pas encore "sur quel état on a jeté les yeux." Nous verrons plus tard que c'est cette nouvelle qui determinera Machiavel à écrire son traité du *Prince,* compose en effet pendant l'été 1513.[493]

Vettori informed Machiavelli of the intention of Leo X to give states to his brother Giuliano and to his nephew Lorenzo. "From the time that he became pope, his first thought has been to recover Parma and Plaisance of which his predecessor Julius II had taken possession without any just title and which had then been retaken by the Duke of Milan during the vacancy of the Holy See." That which led the ambassador to believe that Leo had the desire to give states to his relatives "is the example set by his predecessors, the popes Calixtus, Pius, Innocent, Alexander VI and Julius II, and if some had not acted in the same manner, it is that they were not able to. However, one sees that his relatives concern themselves little with Florence; a fact which shows that they have in view states already established, and where they do not have constantly to win over the inhabitants." But it is not yet known "on what state he has cast his eyes." We will see later that it is this news which determined Machiavelli to write his treatise concerning the *Prince,* composed in fact during the summer 1513.

Tommasini has brought out the close linkage being drawn—especially by young Lorenzo's mother, Alfonsina Orsini de'Medici, but also by others—between the exploits achieved by Cesare Borgia and the prospects for the Pope's brother and his younger nephew.[494] Of Machiavelli's response to Vettori's news, Ridolfi commented:

By virtue of his age, nation, family, and class he [Machiavelli] always inclined with all his heart to the popular state, and this inclination he long nourished on the deeds of republican Rome, the only Rome he loved. But against this inclination, his farsighted intellect told him that Italy was moving into the age of princes; therefore, he must write on principalities. In those very days, as his *Discourses* on Livy reached the chapter where it is shown that 'a corrupt people attaining freedom has the greatest difficulty in maintaining its liberty', turning his eyes from ancient Rome to the Italian cities of his own time, he considered 'that all those members were corrupt'. Now 'it is necessary to resort to extraordinary means such as violent action and force of arms, and above all to become prince of the state'. Only 'a new prince' could revive those rotting limbs; only in such a prince could Lazarus in the end find 'his redeemer'. Ten years before, Borgia had nearly succeeded with the help of good fortune and a Pope; and after the disappearance of the Borgias, Julius II again showed what the Church might do in Italy. Now the Church was led by a Florentine, who united the power of the Florentine state with his ecclesiastical power; he had a younger brother and a young nephew, both seeking to rule, and he himself was also marvelously 'favored by heaven and by fortune'.[495]

Through the good offices of Francesco Vettori's brother, Paolo, a close companion of Giuliano, it appeared for a time that Machiavelli might have a share in Giuliano's prospectively rising fortunes; but Cardinal Giulio de'Medici blasted any such possibility (above, p. 178). Machiavelli appears to have sensed that he had no friend in the papal secretary. A little over a year earlier in his letter of 10 December 1513, he had written Francesco:

I have talked with Filippo [Casavecchia] about this little work of mine [*"On Princedoms"*] that I have spoken of, whether it is good to give it or not give it, whether it would be good to take it myself or whether I should send it there [to Giuliano in Rome]. Not giving it would make me fear that at least Giuliano will not read it and that this rascal Ardinghelli will get himself honor from this latest work of mine.[496]

The Pope's plans for assisting his younger brother to develop for himself a princedom had sparked Machiavelli's composition of the *Prince*; however, Giuliano died in March, 1516.[497]

Meanwhile, the Pope entertained perhaps even greater ambitions for his twenty-four-year-old nephew to whom he had turned over the government of Florence. Young Lorenzo became captain general of the Florentine forces in May, 1515 and Duke of Urbino in October, 1516.[498] In 1518, the Pope secured as a bride for him a relative of the king of France.[499] While at work on the *Prince,* Machiavelli had written Vettori the letter in which he praised Lorenzo's conduct in Florence and suggested that Vettori acquaint the Pope with Machiavelli's favorable impression:

The management of his house is so arranged that, though we see there much splendor and liberality, nonetheless he does not abandon the life of a citizen. Thus in all his movements, outside and inside, nothing is seen that offends anybody or is to be censured; at which everybody appears to be much pleased. And although I know that from many you can learn this same thing, I have chosen to describe it, so that from my account of it you can get such pleasure as comes to all the rest of us who continually experience it; and you can when you have opportunity, give assurance of it to His Holiness, our ruler.[500]

Eventually, it was to Lorenzo that Machiavelli dedicated the *Prince*.[501] It was through Lorenzo's daughter, born four days before the death of her mother[502] and within the first month of her life bereft also of her father[503] and known to history as Catherine de'Medici, Queen of France, that "this little work" was to be treated by her enemies as the major source of the negative implications characterized as "machiavellian."[504] In the words of Tommasini:

Caterina de'Medici provoca, senza sua intenzione, come vedemmo [I, 11–13] l'odio contro il libro del *Principe,* l'avversione contro al Machiavelli, l'origine del machiavellismo.[505]

Catherine de'Medici, without any intention on her part, provoked, as we saw, the hatred against the book, the *Prince,* aversion against Machiavelli, the origin of Machiavellism.

Since early in 1515, the Pope had put Lorenzo in charge of the government of Florence,[506] instructed him in techniques of extending and consolidating his hold over the city,[507] invested him with the title of Duke of Urbino[508] and secured for him a French princess as his wife.[509] The death of Lorenzo, on 4 May 1519,[510] required the Pope to give attention again to the government of Florence which he did through Cardinal Giulio who took up residence there.[511]

Early in his reign, Pope Leo had not only appointed his cousin Giulio a cardinal but also of each of his three married sisters one son: Innocenzo Cibo, Giovanni Salviati, and Niccolo Ridolfi.[512] Giulio de'Medici had been born out of wedlock during the year after his father, Giuliano, brother of Lorenzo the Magnificent, had been murdered during mass in the cathedral.[513] Lorenzo the Magnificent had raised his nephew in his own family.[514] According to Young:

Leo's creating Giulio a cardinal was entirely illegal, the latter being barred by the canons of the Church on account of the illegitimacy of his birth.

The historian of Leo's life says:—"The Pope got over the difficulty by simply declaring him legitimate."[515]

Around 10 March 1520, Lorenzo Strozzi, brother-in-law of the Pope's niece[516]— and some others of the company accustomed to participate in Machiavelli's conversations in the Rucellai Gardens—took Machiavelli to meet Cardinal Giulio who received him graciously.[517] Machiavelli began to become beneficiary of the Medici patronage. The *Mandragola* may have been read in the Rucellai Gardens and Ridolfi risks the conjecture:

> that a performance was given during the great celebration which took place on the return of Lorenzo with his French bride (7 September 1518), provided it were admitted that at that date the play was already finished and the actors had learned their parts.[518]

(However, since, in the play, the young native Florentine, Callimaco Guadagni, leaves Paris in order to find out what truth there might be in the rumor of the unparalleled beauty and virtue of a certain Florentine lady, might there not have been a touch of offended patriotic pride which would have seemed in poor taste as part of the celebrations of welcome for the French princess as the bride of the resident head of Florence's most prominent family?) In any case, the play was scheduled to be given in the Pope's presence and the Pope himself sent word to Cardinal Giulio to give Machiavelli a "commission to write, or something similar."[519]

Again there were missions abroad—not, however, concerned with affairs of state; yet, with matters of great financial import affecting relatives of the Pope.[520] It was while in Lucca on such a mission that Machiavelli wrote his "Life of Castruccio Castracani."[521] Upon his return he accepted the commission for writing the *The History of Florence*.[522] Ridolfi has described the arrangements:

> The exact conditions were yet to be determined, and the future historian himself drafted them in his own hand to del Nero:
>
>> 'The substance of the commission should be as follows: that he be employed for . . . years, at an annual salary of . . . , his duties to be to write the annals or the history of the things that have been done by the state and city of Florence from the date that seems most appropriate to him, and either in Latin or Tuscan whichever he pleases.'

But the terms of employment were in fact established as follows: by the decision of the officials of the University on the 8th of November, Niccolo Machiavelli was commissioned to serve their institution for two years beginning on the 1st of November, one year definitely and the second subject to re-election, in whatever way they should think necessary, *et*

194

inter alia ad componendum annalia et cronacas florentinas, et alia facien-dum, [and, among other things, for composing the Florentine annals and chronicles and performing other services] with a salary of 100 *fiorini di studio.*[523]

It was soon thereafter that Machiavelli, among others, was invited to offer suggestions regarding the government of the city.[524] According to Ridolfi, the Cardinal

asked him to write a *Discourse on Florentine affairs after the death of Lorenzo,* to be presented to the Pope who was seeking advice on the way to organize the State of Florence now controlled by two ecclesiastics, himself and the Cardinal, without legitimate heirs.[525]

As Tommasini described the circumstances:

Niccolò riceve invito, non può ben affermarsi se da parte del cardinale soltanto o coll'intesa preventiva anche del papa, a formulare uno schema di nuova costituzione per la città e lo stato. È certo che il disegno ch'ei ne tracciò, è indirizzato al pontefice; ch'egli giudicò l'invito come uno di quei fortunatissimi momenti della vita degli uomini e delle città, in cui queste posson ricevere da un solo la forma di governo che risponde alle necessità proprie; e quelli dare norme che bastino ad assicurare la lunga felicità della patria. Illusioni![526]

Niccolo received the invitation, not able for sure to confirm whether on the part of the Cardinal solely or with the anticipated intention of the Pope also, to formulate a plan for a new constitution for the city and the state. It is certain that the draft which he drew up is directed to the pontiff; that he judged the invitation as one of those most fortunate moments in the life of men and of cities in which they would be able to receive from one man alone the form of government which corresponds to the special needs; and to give norms which would serve to assure the long term happiness of the country. Illusions!

Machiavelli's response was his "Discourse on Remodeling the Government of Florence," dedicated to Pope Leo X.[527] In his recommendation, Machiavelli applied his formula already expressed in the ninth chapter of Book I of the *Discourses* (above, p. 64). Although in his proposal Machiavelli recommended the re-establishment of the city's traditional free institutions in form, he suggested that they not become so operative in fact during the lifetime of either the Pope or the Cardinal who, by the covert devices which he suggested, could conduct the city as a principality.[528]

195

Pope Leo died on 1 December 1521.[529] Of his impact upon the development of Machiavelli, Ridolfi concluded:

> perhaps Pope Leo, the benefactor of so many mediocre poets and literary men, without knowing it himself and without anyone else then noticing it, had really benefited the great Florentine Secretary: firstly by arousing his illusions and his great imagination with his changing ambitions, and secondly by leaving him to despairing and fruitful idleness. So literature which owed so much to the Medici family for its assistance, owes a great deal more to Leo because he did not assist Machiavelli.[530]

The death of Pope Leo left the government entirely in the hands of the Cardinal. Again, this time for himself, the Cardinal invited suggestions on the proper government of the city. According to Ridolfi,

> It was a clever way of investigating people's thoughts and discovering what ambitions were fermenting in certain Florentine minds.[531]

Machiavelli, in response to the invitations extended to him, proposed substantially the same structure and procedures which he had submitted to Pope Leo but this time he put them in the form of a proclamation.[532]

Conspiracy aborted whatever prospect there might have been for reform.[533] Machiavelli's closest friends were implicated;[534] he himself was clearly not involved.

Frustrated in his aspirations to succeed his cousin as Pope, Cardinal de'Medici threw the election to Cardinal Adrian Dedel of Utrecht—who had been Emperor Charles V's tutor—and, upon his death after but twenty months,[535] succeeding in becoming elected, took the name of Clement VII on 18 November 1524.[536]

Early in 1525, the Pope vetoed the suggestion, made by his cousin-in-law, the father of Cardinal Salviati, that Machiavelli be sent as secretary to his son as papal legate to the court of Spain which had become "the hub of European politics."[537] (It was to Cardinal Salviati that Machiavelli had sent, in 1521, the first printed copy of *The Art of War* to reach Rome.[538]) Shortly thereafter, as noted above (p. 184), Machiavelli presented to Pope Clement the completed eight books of the *History* and aroused his interest in the proposal that a papal militia be created in Romagna[539] (above, p. 184). In September 1525, Machiavelli was notified that the Pope had directed that his salary for writing the *History* be doubled.[540]

The increasingly serious military situation prompted the Pope, as recounted above (p. 186) on Guicciardini's recommendation, to open the way for Machiavelli's long-sought official participation in developing strategy for the military defense of the city and other papal holdings. Of this period, Ridolfi has written:

> as the ice was broken and he was now in moderate favor with the Pope and those who ruled Florence for him, Machiavelli would now have plenty of those modest employments involving a lot of inconvenience and little gain in the way of money or honor. He needed both, yet he went on being satisfied with what he was given. He will never again return to the tragedy of the *Histories*, being entirely absorbed by the real life tragedy now nearing its climax. In this he went on playing minor parts.[541]

For Florence, the conspiracy against the life of Cardinal de'Medici had had as consequence a tightening of the Medicean control of the city which he continued to exercise personally even after his election to the papacy. As Ridolfi summarized it:

> ill advised by his own sympathies or by the ambitions of his followers, or irritated by the hatred of his adversaries, he turned his plans to the aggrandisement of two Medici bastards: Ippolito, the son of Giuliano, and Allesandro, who was thought to be the Cardinal's own child, although at that time he passed as the son of Lorenzo Duke of Urbino.[542]

Growing discontent with the Pope's surrogate rule in the spring of 1527 reached the verge of insurrection[543] so that when the Imperial forces stormed and sacked Rome and took the Pope captive, Medici rule again came to an end in Florence.[544]

What significance for Machiavelli had the new expulsion of the Medici and the revival of republican government in Florence? According to Busini, as quoted by Ridolfi,

> Messer Piero Carnesecchi, who came with him [Machiavelli] from Rome with one of his sisters, says he heard him sigh many times, when he heard that the city was free. I think he was regretting his conduct, because in fact he greatly loved liberty; but he regretted having involved himself with Pope Clement.[545]

Despite the efforts of his friends on his behalf that he be returned to office in the restored republic, no place was found for his talents.[546] Within ten days after the office of secretary for the republic was filled, Machiavelli was dead.[547]

What record did Machiavelli leave of his own opinion of the Medici? Commissioned by Cardinal Giulio de'Medici to undertake the writing of the history of their turbulent city in which for over two centuries[548] the members of the Medici family had shared in or exercised leadership, desirous to provide "reading . . . useful to citizens who govern republics"[549] and to "kindle such [free spirits] to avoid and get rid of present abuses,"[550] Machiavelli confessed in a letter to Guicciardini,

> having come to certain particulars I need to learn from you if I give too much offense either by raising up or lowering these things.[551]

In dedicating the *History* to his patron who, during its composition, had become Pope Clement VII, he set forth a gracious ambience for his perspective.

> And because Your Blessed Holiness especially charged and required me to write in such a way of the things done by your ancestors that I should be far from all flattery (because however much it pleases you to hear men's true praises, to the same extent fictitious praises and those described with special favor displease you), I greatly fear lest, as I describe the probity of Giovanni, the wisdom of Cosimo, the kindness of Piero, and the high-mindedness and prudence of Lorenzo, I may seem to Your Holiness to be disobeying your orders. Of that transgression I clear myself before you and before anybody whom such descriptions displease as inaccurate, because finding how full of their praises were the accounts of those who at various times have written of them, I was obliged either to write of them just what I found or, as hostile, to be silent about them. And if underneath their excellent works was concealed any ambition which, as some say, was opposed to the common good, I who do not recognize it in them am not obliged to write of it; indeed in all my narratives I have never permitted a dishonorable deed to be defended with an honorable reason nor a praiseworthy deed, as though done for an opposite purpose, to be blackened . . . I have then striven, Most Holy and Blessed Father, in these writings of mine, without defacing the truth, to satisfy everybody; and perhaps I have not satisfied anybody, and if this should be so, I shall not be astonished by it, because I judge it impossible, without angering many, to write on the affairs of their own times. Nevertheless, I come cheerfully into the field, hoping that, as by the kindness of Your Holiness I am honored and supported, so by the armed legions of your most sacred judgment I shall be aided and protected; and with the same spirit and confidence in which I have written up to now, I am going to continue my undertaking, if life does not desert me and Your Holiness does not forsake me.[552]

Perhaps Machiavelli felt himself somewhat less inhibited when, according to his friend Donato Gianotti, he confided:

> I cannot write this history from the time when Cosimo took over the government up to the death of Lorenzo just as I would write it if I were free from all reasons for caution. The actions will be true, and I shall not omit anything; merely I shall leave out discussing the universal causes of

the events. For instance, I shall relate the events and the circumstances that came about when Cosimo took over the government; I shall leave untouched any discussion of the way and of the means and tricks with which one attains such power; and if anyone nevertheless wants to understand Cosimo, let him observe well what I shall have his opponents say, because what I am not willing to say as coming from myself, I shall have his opponents say.[553]

And, following this suggestion of indirect testimony, Allen Gilbert, in his foreword to his translation of the *History,* continued:

Yet even in such speeches, Machiavelli sometimes substituted for his first draft softer second thoughts: for example, a speech by Rinaldo degli Albizzi is changed from direct to indirect discourse, and the following is bolder than the final form:

> Union and prosperity are impossible while Cosimo de'Medici lives in this city, because his way of living surpasses what is proper for a citizen; his excessive wealth makes him bold; with it he has bribed all the heads of the common people and many other citizens, in such a way that in all the councils and magistracies of the city he can do what he wants to; our soldiers are like his partisans, because he employs whom he likes, whom he likes he gets rid of . . . he lacks nothing of being prince but the title. It is the duty therefore of a good citizen to find a remedy for this, to call the people to the Public Square, and to take over the government, in order to restore to the republic her liberty. [Cf. bk. 4, chap. 28]

> That even a weakened form of this stood in the manuscript put in the hands of Giulio de'Medici, Pope Clement VII, is astonishing enough, a tribute to Machiavelli's desire to write a history that would inspire all lovers of the common good of man in whatever age or nation.[554]

Machiavelli, as already observed (above, p. 169) interpreted the charge in his commission to be

to write out what has been done at home and abroad by the Florentine people,[555]

with emphasis upon service to the common good.[556]

Of the founder of the Medici dynasty, Cosimo, the Pope's great-grandfather, Machiavelli gave a tempered, factual appraisal. He was able to avoid giving an evaluation of his own of Cosimo by attributing to "public decree" the inscription on Cosimo's monument, "Father of his Country."[557] If the remarks which Gianotti recorded are authentic, may Machiavelli have taken opportunity for expressing his own judgment when he spoke of Cosimo's enemies as slandering him, as a man who loved himself more than his city and this world more than the other?[558]

Machiavelli concluded the chapter on the character of Cosimo with the subtly ambiguous observation:

> If when writing of the things done by Cosimo, I have imitated those who write the lives of princes, not those who write general histories, nobody should be astonished; since he was a man rare in our city, I have been obliged with an unusual method to praise him.[559]

May not one detect even here a criticism of one who sets the course for subverting the government of his city from that of a republic to that of a princedom? In "A Discourse on Remodeling the Government of Florence," he characterized Cosimo's government as

> tending more toward the princedom than toward the republic[560]

and later on he affirmed

> to form a princedom where a republic would go well is a difficult thing and, through being difficult, inhumane and unworthy of whoever hopes to be considered merciful and good.[561]

It should not be overlooked that in recounting the struggle leading to Cosimo's dominance, Machiavelli recorded that a Machiavelli, in the cause of the defense of the city's freedom, suffered martyrdom, from responsibility for the infliction of which Machiavelli carefully shielded Cosimo's reputation.[562] In "A Discourse on Remodeling the Government . . . ," he gave a concise and perceptive appraisal of Cosimo's rule:

> If yet it lasted longer . . . the cause lay in two things: one, that it was established with the people's aid; the other, that it was controlled by the prudence of two such men as Cosimo and Lorenzo his grandson.[563]

His verdict on Lorenzo is found in the concluding chapter of the *History*:

> His reputation, because of his prudence, daily increased, since in discussing affairs he was eloquent and penetrating, in settling them wise, in carrying them out prompt and courageous. Nor can any vices be brought up against him that soiled his great virtues.[564]

Lorenzo's eldest son, Piero, two years younger than Machiavelli, directed the government for only two years before, during the disturbances occasioned by Charles VIII's invasion of the peninsula, the Medici were driven out. He died in exile.[565]

By the time Machiavelli composed the "First Decennale," six years of official life had given him ample opportunity to perceive the near fatal consequences of the Medici rule. In this poem Machiavelli wrote:

> discordant Italy opened into herself a passage for the Gauls and suffered barbarian peoples to trample her down.
> And because to comply with them your city was not prepared, he who held her reins was scourged by their violence.
> So all Tuscany was in confusion; so you lost Pisa and those states the Medici family gave to the French.
> Thus you could not rejoice as you should have done at being taken from under the yoke that for sixty years had been crushing you.[566]

Lorenzo's second son, Giovanni, six years younger than Machiavelli, was he who through Lorenzo's influence had been designated a Cardinal long before reaching the age required[567] and became Pope Leo X.[568]

Giuliano, Lorenzo's third son, nine years younger than Machiavelli, appointed by Leo as "Gonfalonier of the Papal forces," took up his residence in Rome.[569] It was to him that Machiavelli, while in prison, had written the two sonnets in an attempt to show light-hearted humor despite the pain of physical torture and the distressingly grim surroundings.[570] It was Giuliano with whom Machiavelli hoped that his friend Francesco Vettori would intercede on his behalf and win for him employment.[571] It was Giuliano for whom the Pope was planning to create a princedom[572] and whom, consequently, Machiavelli originally had in mind when writing "*On Princedoms*" as a guide for a "new prince."[573]

With Giuliano's death in March, 1515,[574] it was to Piero's son Lorenzo whose way of life in Florence had won Machiavelli's praise[575] that Machiavelli, as well as the Pope, looked for fulfilment of their hopes for Florence and for Italy. It was of him that Machiavelli wrote in his "Pastoral: The Ideal Ruler"[576] and to whom, in the end, he did dedicate the *Prince*[577] but death soon removed both Lorenzo and Pope Leo.

Following the brief reign as pope of Adrian VI and his death,[578] the election of Cardinal Giulio de'Medici as pope, though it removed from Florence one who was proving himself a capable governor of the city,[579] provided a new center of power and, for Machiavelli, nourishment of hope. As Cardinal de'Medici in Florence, he had given Machiavelli employment at the University and sent him on private missions.

At this time, in the junior branch of the Medici family, with meteoric rise was appearing a young military genius. The great-grandson of Cosimo's younger brother Lorenzo, Giovanni "delle Bande Nere" seemed to Machiavelli to be fully endowed to become the protector of Florence and the deliverer of Italy. In a letter to Guicciardini, Machiavelli wrote:

A few days ago it was said throughout Florence that the Lord Giovanni de'Medici was raising the flag of a soldier of fortune to make war where he had the best opportunity. This rumor stirred up my spirit to imagine that the people were saying what ought to be done. I believe anyone who believes that among the Italians there is no leader whom the soldiers would more gladly follow and whom the Spanish more fear and more respect; everybody also thinks that Lord Giovanni is bold, prompt, has great ideas, is a maker of great plans. We could, then, secretly making him strong, have him raise this flag, putting under him as many cavalry and as many infantry as we can . . . It could make the King [of France] change his opinion . . . since he would see that he has to do with people who are alive and, in addition to arguments, show him deeds. If we cannot use this method and yet are to make war, I don't know what we can do, and nothing else occurs to me.[580]

Papal unresponsiveness blasted this hope even before death soon removed Giovanni himself.[581]

Only once did Machiavelli give Clement VII unqualified praise. In the words of Tommasini,

L'allusione al figlio naturale lasciato da Giuliano, "ripieno di quella virtù e fortuna che in questi presenti tempi tutti il mondo conosce" [M., Ist., viii, 9. Ibid. 36] è il solo complimento, no destituito d'ironia, che Niccolò indirizza a Clemente VII pontefice.[582]

The reference to the natural son left by Giuliano, 'full of that virtue and fortune which in these present times all the world knows,' is the sole compliment devoid of irony, which Machiavelli directed at Clement VII, pontiff.

However, the passage cited continued with Machiavelli promising

when we come to present affairs, if God gives us life, we shall set them forth at length.[583]

But that time for Machiavelli was never to come.

In the gathering gloom of the powerful Medici, there remained in the main line of descent only Clement VII. Machiavelli's letters provide significant clues to his estimate of the Pope's inadequacy for meeting the demands of the times. With most probable reference to the Pope, he wrote Guicciardini on 19 December 1525, each man is a little reassured, but since he seems to have time, he gives time to his enemy.[584]

In the following August the Pope unilaterally disarmed himself and within a month was a prisoner of the Colonna faction in Rome.[585] Early in November, Machiavelli wrote:

> We could have won the war and have not known how; the Pope has trusted more in one pen full of ink than in a thousand infantrymen, who would have been enough to guard him.[586]

Later in the same month, he analyzed for Bartolomeo (Cavalcanti?) the situation with special emphasis upon the recent military mistakes made by the Pope:

> we might have deferred but not lost the campaign, if our bad arrangements had not been added. These . . . have been two: the first is that the Pope has not raised money in times when he could with reputation have done so, and in the ways used by other popes. The other is that he remained in Rome in such a condition that he could be captured like a baby—something that has snarled this skein in such a way that Christ could not straighten it out; because the Pope has taken his soldiers from the field.[587]

When the situation became yet more difficult, he confided to Guicciardini his judgment of the Pope's incompetence for managing either peace or war.[588]

Three weeks later, on 6 May 1527, Rome fell before the onslaught of the Imperial forces composed of Spanish and German soldiers and was sacked.[589] For the second time within eight months the Pope found himself a prisoner.[590] Ten days later the Medici rule in Florence collapsed and with it the official authority which at long last with his tireless and resourceful labors Machiavelli had achieved.[591] Just five weeks later, Machiavelli was dead.[592]

But death itself failed to stay the course of the mingled fortunes and fates of Machiavelli and the Medici. The "little work" which, if seen, had almost certainly not been read by him to whom it had been dedicated, became, in the hands of his daughter, a powerful influence and a tool with which her enemies deeply discredited both her, it and its author. According to Friedrich Meinecke:

> In 1576 the Hugenot, Innocent Gentillet, published anonymously the book: *Discours sur les moyens de bien gouverner et maintenir en bonne paix un Royaume ou autre Principaute, divisiez en trois parties: a savoir, du Conseil, de la Religion et Police que doit tenir un Prince. Contre Nicolas Michiavel Florentine.* He dedicated it to the Duke Francois d'Alencon, the youngest of the four sons of Henry II and Catherine de'Medici . . . Gentillet hoped and wished that this man, who was heir to the throne at the time, would put an end to the recent foreign tyranny which had existed in

France for more than fifteen years, and would restore the good old French way of ruling. By foreign tyranny, however, he meant the rule in France of Italians and Italianized Frenchmen, hence Catherine de'Medici and her court and the new vicious doctrines of Machiavelli, which they had applied and circulated and which were completely corrupting the healthy French nation. It was only after the death of Henry II in 1559 that Machiavelli's name and renown had become known in France, and it was only since then that the business of government was carried on here *a la Italienne* or *a la Florentine*. It was notorious that the books of Machiavelli had been as frequently in the hands of the courtiers, as a breviary is in those of a village priest. The author of the Latin translation of Gentillet's work, which appeared in 1577, directly accused Queen Catherine of being the devil's chosen instrument for spreading the poison of Machiavelli in France . . . It was not merely the pious Hugenot in him [Gentillet] that took offense; it was first and foremost the Frenchman in him, chivalrous in thought and deed, who suddenly realized that his whole world and way of life were threatened, that morality, honour, the interests of his class, and all peaceful and secure enjoyments of the old rights and privileges were no longer safe if the State was to be ruled by the diabolically cold calculation of princely advantage.[593]

So, henceforth, during the next four centuries, the name and work of Machiavelli became embroiled in the turbulence—as in the name of faith and patriotism the institutions of religion and nationality struggled kaleidoscopically in developing their modern forms.

Chapter Six

PRIVATE CITIZEN AS RESPONSIBLE OFFICIAL

Addiction to poetry, study and writing, Machiavelli perceived as a dangerously debilitating fascination against which, with his continual endeavor to think out and express his experience usefully, he strove to be on guard and protect himself. In *The History of Florence* when beginning to treat of Cosimo de'Medici's assumption of power, Machiavelli wrote:

> the virtue of military courage cannot be corrupted with a more honorable laziness than that of letters; nor with a greater and more dangerous deception can this laziness enter into well-regulated cities.[1]

At this point, may Machiavelli have had in mind Cosimo's encouragement of the study of Greek and the establishment of the celebrated "Platonic Academy?"[2] In the preface to the first book of the *Discourses,* he challenged the prevailing attitude of readers of histories in

> that the most worthy activities which histories show us . . . are sooner admired than imitated . . . so that as we read we do not draw from them that sense or taste that flavor which they really have. From this it comes that great numbers who read take pleasure in hearing of the various events they contain, without thinking at all of imitating them;[3]

and by way of justifying his own literary labors he sought to present them as a summons to the imitation of virtuous deeds:

> Wishing, then, to get away from this error, I have decided . . . it is necessary that I write what, according to my knowledge of ancient and modern

affairs, I judge necessary for a better understanding of them, in order that those who read these explanations of mine may more easily get from them that profit for which they should seek acquaintance with books.[4]

A clue as to how to read with profit, he gave in his description for Vettori of his work in progress.[5] In Lugurio's distrust of Messer Nicia's common sense, Machiavelli, in *Mendragola,* shows the final result of thoughtless reading:

So I hope you won't spoil everything by talking, because a man in your station, who sits all day in his study, understands just books, and can't manage practical affairs. *(aside)* This fellow is so stupid I'm afraid he'll spoil everything.[6]

In the *History,* Machiavelli showed that Stefano Porcari's hope, inspired by Petrarch's poetry taken as prophecy, together with a passion to rebuke "the evil habits of the prelates" and provide leadership for "the discontent of the barons and the people of Rome," proved no substitute for practical judgment; and consequently his laudable intention resulted only in the "almost always inevitable ruin."[7]

Nevertheless, a deep and enduring sense of obligation impelled Machiavelli to persist privately as a responsible official (despite deprivation of public recognition), through his reading and writing, to make a way for expressing, both for his own times and for those immediately ahead, the truth which he was distilling from his own experience and studies. During the brief interval between his own loss of office and his imprisonment and torture, Machiavelli wrote in his letter of response to the exiled ex-gonfalonier:

the reason why different ways of working are sometimes equally effective and equally damaging I do not know, but I should much like to know.[8]

Early in his exile from the city, he wrote Vettori:

If you are sick of discussing public affairs, after seeing many things turn out contrary to the notions and concepts you form, you are right; the like has happened to me. Yet if I could speak with you, I couldn't help filling your head with castles in Spain, because Fortune has determined that since I don't know how to talk about the silk business or the wool business or about profits and losses, I must talk about the government; I must either make a vow of silence or discuss that.[9]

Finding that his work *"On Princedoms"* lifted his spirits, replenished his strength[10] and clarified his values,[11] he proffered the fruits of his labor in a bid for active service[12] (above, pp. 8, 123). Through the *Discourses* he sought to attract and

206

instruct the youth to champion the common good.[13] Throughout, he emphasized the practical nature of his purpose. *The Art of War* indicates a similarly practical aim:

> judging from what I have seen and read . . . it is not impossible to bring military practice back to ancient methods and to restore some of the forms of earlier excellence . . . I have determined to write out what I have learned about the art of war;[14]

and further on,

> I shall never depart, in giving examples of anything, from my Romans. If we consider their life and the organization of their republic, we shall see there many things not impossible for introduction into any state in which there is still left something good . . . He who accomplishes such a thing plants trees beneath the shade of which mankind lives more prosperously and more happily than beneath this shade.[15]

Summarizing succinctly his purpose in writing the treatise, he explained:

> I have not been attempting to show you exactly what an ancient army was but rather how in these times an army can be organized that will be more effective than ours are;[16] (see above, p. 72)

and he closed *The Art of War* with his re-affirmation of the validity of his prescriptions and his reliance upon ready understanding on the part of "the young and gifted" to "aid and advise your princes to their advantage."[17] Also in *The History of Florence* appear explicit statements of his practical, didactic purpose[18] (above, pp. 70–72).

It was a serious truth, even though in a context of jest, which Machiavelli expressed when he wrote Guicciardini:

> because I never failed that city [Florence] by not benefiting her when I could—if not with deeds, with words, if not with words, with gestures—I do not intend to fail her this time either. It is true that I know I am opposed, as in many other things, to the opinion of the citizens there.[19]

May one not understand by "deeds" his years of official service; by "words," his years of study and the writing of the great trilogy of the *Prince*, the *Discourses*, *The Art of War* followed by the *History;* by "gestures," his endeavor to convey his message through the theater, especially his mirror to moral decadence, his play, *Mandragola?*

Profoundly rooted in Machiavelli's personal motivation and system of values was *virtù*. The new life which the term had received through the scholarly studies by Lorenzo Valla, found congenial stimulus in Machiavelli's way of thinking[20] (above, pp. 141–142). According to Allan Gilbert,

> Strength *and* wisdom *render the single word* virtù *which is not equivalent to the English* virtue, *as now generally understood. Commonly Machiavelli uses the word as did his contemporaries and predecessors as far back as Dante. If he is in any way exceptional, it is that now and then he gives it more suggestion of moral excellence then was usual. For the most part, the word has little ethical suggestion, or none at all.*[21]

In defining the term, Pocock writes of

> its Machiavellian meaning of the skill and courage by which men are enabled to dominate events and fortune.[22]

Virtù, Valla had identified as that power manifested in the "mighty works" of Jesus and his disciples.[23] According to John, Jesus said to the disciples:

> In the world you will have trouble. But courage! The victory is mine. I have conquered the world;[24]

and in I John it is written,

> every child of God is victor over the godless world.[25]

The antithesis here is between *virtù* manifested in the name of the dynamic spirit of God and the mechanical drift of "the world." Machiavelli perceived *virtù* as challenger to Fortune. That power is a function of effective service to the common good, is a theme which runs through much of his writing. The search for clarity in perspective and the perception of *la verità effettuale della cosa*[26] led him to confront and attempt to take the measure of the strength of Fortune. Thus in "Tercets on Fortune:"

> By many this goddess is called omnipotent, because whoever comes into this life either late or early feels her power. She often keeps the good beneath her feet; the wicked she raises up; and if ever she promises you anything, never does she keep her promise;[27]

in "Tercets on Ambition,"

> in the world most men let themselves be mastered by Fortune.[28]

Holding, in the *Prince*, that Fortune leaves to the free will of men half, or slightly less than half, of a chance to give direction and achieve management,[29] and, in "Tercets on Fortune," that

208

Her natural power for all men is too strong and her reign is always violent
if prowess still greater than hers does not vanquish her,[30]

he arrived at the conclusion that Fortune's power is inverse to a man's ability[31]
(above, pp. 90–91).

How important to Machiavelli personally was the endeavor to prevail over
"Fortune" can be glimpsed from his letter to Vettori written just a week after
his release from twenty-two days in prison and torture on the rack.[32]

As to turning my face to resist Fortune, I want you to get this pleasure
from my distresses, namely, that I have borne them so bravely that I love
myself for it and feel that I am stronger than you believed.[33]

It was this capacity of men to show "Fortune a bold face"[34] which intrigued
Machiavelli to explore, observe, study, try to understand, explain and make
available for use. From time to time he dropped hints of the solitary and lonely
way which such exploration involves, as when he wrote in the preface to the
Discourses,

I have determined to enter upon a path not yet trodden by anyone; though
it may bring me trouble and difficulty.[35]

and in a letter to Guicciardini with reference to his work on the *History,*

I shall keep on taking counsel with myself.[36]

That his conviction that *virtù* is effective energy in public service and that
a man derives and discovers his own worth through it, was profound and constant,
excerpts from works written under different circumstances of his life demonstrate.[37] That a man owes it to himself through responsible public service
to strive for the betterment of his country, Machiavelli perceived, since he
considered that one's obligation to honor his country grows in proportion to the
greater nobility of his country. In responsible service in his state, therefore, a
man grows in perceiving and understanding truth in himself, in his relations with
others and with his land—and ground of his being.

In writing of ways, helpful and harmful, by which citizens gain reputation
in a city, he stated:

a reputation gained by unselfish conduct benefits the republic, since it is
not gained with partisanship, being founded on the common good, not on
private favor.[38]

The pernicious consequences of actions in disregard of the common good, he
set forth most dramatically in *The History of Florence* in an address which he

attributed to a spokesman for "many citizens, moved by love for their country," in a meeting with the Signoria[39] and, a second time, in the beginning of Book 7.[40] Tommasini has pointed out,

> Poi che Niccolò, ogni volta che gli occorre parlare di chi non merita l'ammirazione universale, di chi non vince con grandezza certa l'adulazione e l'infidia partigianesca; in una parola, degl'idoli di una fazione; ricorre a certe scappatoie rettoriche, a certi equivoci artificiosi dietro a cui a un tempo stesso rifugia il vero e mette sè al coperto, non irritando passioni, illudendo gl'illusi e provocando e soddisfacendo l'acume del giudizio ne'men confidenti e negli scettici.[41]

> Then Niccolo, every time that it occurs to him to speak of one who does not merit universal admiration, who does not win with certain grandeur the admiration and partisan envy; in a word, of the idols of a faction; he resorts to certain rhetorical pretexts, and certain artificial equivocations (providing at the same time refuge for the truth and cover for himself) not stirring up passions, baffling the deluded ones and both arousing and satisfying the keenness of judgment in the less confident and in the skeptics.

Identifying the common good with the safety and advancement of one's native city or country,[42] for its sake Machiavelli condoned whatever course of action its safety and the defense of its liberty might require[43] (above, pp. 19–20). Indeed, Cicero, as Tommasini pointed out, had already declared:

> 'Iupiter ipse sanxit, ut omnia quae republicae salutaria essent, legitima et iusta haberentur.'[44]

> 'Jupiter himself sanctioned it, in order that all things which might be salutary for a republic should be considered lawful and just.'

Although Machiavelli held that, with respect to *individuals*

> To believe that new benefits make men of high rank forget old injuries is to deceive oneself,[45]

and

> every ruler can be reminded that never have new benefits erased old injuries; and so much the less in so far as the new benefit is less than the injury,[46]

yet he did maintain that subsequent *public* benefits can obliterate private cruelties to individuals[47] and that, after power has been secured, its use for public service can eventually win not only men's but even God's favor.[48] Although he praised

210

founders of states who, before their death, so provided for the distribution of accumulated power that the government became that of a republic,[49] he considered it excusable that one would not do so at the risk of losing his own princedom.[50] Holding that

not individual good but common good is what makes cities great[51]

and that the acquisition of power

for the common good and not for his own ambition[52]

transcends every scruple,[53] Machiavelli found in himself a deep responsive endorsement to the exhortation, in 1420 by Gino Capponi (who was credited with the first capture of Pisa[54])

che [Dieci della balìa uomini pratichi] amino il Commune più che il loro proprio bene e che l'anima[55]

That the Ten administrators of authority [Dieci della balia uomini pratichi] loved the City more than their own goods and their own soul.

Repeatedly he praised those who proved that they valued civic service more highly than they did personal salvation.[56]

A sense of something of the meaning for Machiavelli of being a Florentine is communicated by Garrett Mattingly in his essay on Machiavelli in *The Horizon Book of the Renaissance*:

He was a Florentine of the Florentines, and the citizens of his city were the quintessence of the new spirit that was then stirring in Italy. Not at first, of course; in the years after the great Guelph victory, after the popes had broken the power of the Empire in Italy forever, Florence was only one of the vigorous, turbulent city republics with which northern and central Italy swarmed . . . At first most of these new states were republics. Then, as the bigger fish devoured the smaller, not only were there fewer independent cities, but fewer of the survivors were republics.
Presently came the anxious moment when on the Italian mainland only one republic was left or only one that mattered . . . Only Florence still held out.[57]

Recognizing himself as dedicated to serving the common good,[58] considering that the founder of a well-ordered government, as he characterized him in the *Discourses*, is

211

a prudent organizer of a republic and one whose intention is to advance not his own interests but the general good, not his own posterity but the common fatherland,[59]

that

Without satisfying the generality of the citizens, to set up a stable government is always impossible,[60]

that

only authority freely given is durable,[61]

and, again in his proposal for remodeling the government of Florence that:

There is no other way for escaping these ills than to give the city institutions that can by themselves stand firm. And they will always stand firm when everybody has a hand in them, and when everybody knows what he needs to do and in whom he can trust, and no class of citizen, either through fear for itself or through ambition, will need to desire revolution,[62]

accordingly, that citizens should be given special inducements and rewards through seeking recognition by such "public methods" as

advising well and acting better, for the common good,[63]

it was with respect to one pursuing such an aim that Machiavelli wrote:

Nor will a prudent intellect ever censure anyone for any unlawful action used in organizing a kingdom or setting up a republic. It is at any rate fitting that though the deed accuses him the result should excuse him; and when it is good, like that of Romulus, it will always excuse him, because he who is violent to destroy, not he who is violent to restore, ought to be censured.[64]

Machiavelli assumed an element in the state which transcended any conventional ethical criterion. When he wrote:

truly no region is ever united or happy if all of it is not under the sway of one republic or one prince,[65]

he adjudged it a lesser offense that

through the bad examples of that court [i.e., the Roman Church] this land [Italy] has lost all piety and all religion

212

GENEALOGICAL TABLE OF THE MEDICI

Giovanni di Averardo de' Medici (gen. Bicci) (1360-1429) m. Piccarda Bueri

Cosimo il Vecchio, Pater Patriae (1389-1464) m. Contessina de' Bardi

Lorenzo (1395-1440) m. Ginevra Cavalcanti

Piero Francesco (1430-1467) m. Laudomia Acciaiuoli

Piero il Gottoso (1416-1469) m. Lucrezia Tornabuoni

Giovanni (1421-1463)

Lorenzo il Magnifico (1449-1492) m. Clarissa Orsini

Giuliano (1453-1478)

Lorenzo (1463-1503) m. Semiramis d'Appiano

Piero Francesco (1486-1525) m. Maria Soderini

G. ovanni (1467-1498) m. Caterina Sforza

Giovanni delle Bande Nere (1498-1526); Condottiere m. Maria Salviati

Cosimo I. (1519-1574) Duke of Florence (1537) Grand-duke of Tuscany (1570) m. Eleanor of Toledo

Piero lo Sfortunato (1472-1503) m. Alfonsina Orsini

Giovanni (1475-1521) Pope Leo X

Giuliano (1479-1516) Duke of Nemour m. Filiberta of Savoy

Lorenzo (1492-1519) Duke of Urbino m. Madeleine de la Tour d'Auvergne

Piero Strozzi

Caterina (1519-1589) m. Henry II., King of France

Giulio (1478-1534) Illegitimate; Pope Clement VII

Ippolito (1511-1535) Illegitimate; Cardinal

Clarissa (1493-1528) m. Filippo Strozzi

Lorenzino (1514-1548)

Giuliano (1520-1588)

Laudomia m. Piero Strozzi

Alessandro (1511-1537) Illegitimate; Duke of Florence m. Margherita v. Austria-Parma Daughter of Emperor Charles V.

Francesco (1541-1587) Grand-duke of Tuscany m. 1 Joanna of Austria m. 2 Bianca Cappello

Isabella m. Paolo Orsini

Ferdinando I. (1549-1609) Cardinal (1563) Grand-duke of Tuscany m. Christine of Lorraine

Pietro (1554-1604) m. Eleanor of Toledo, the Younger

Maria (1573-1642) m. Henry IV., King of France

Cosimo II. (1590-1621) Grand-duke of Tuscany m. Maria Magdalena Archduchess of Austria

Ferdinando II. (1610-1671) Grand-duke of Tuscany m. Vittoria della Rovere

Cosimo III. (1642-1720) Grand-duke of Tuscany m. Margarite of Orleans

Anna Maria Ludovica (1667-1743) m. Johann Wilhelm Elector of Pfalz-Neuburg

Gian Gastone (1671-1737) Grand-duke of Tuscany m. Anna von Sachsen-Lauenburg

than

that the Church has kept and still keeps this region divided . . . she is the cause why the land has been unable to unite under one head.[66]

In light of his view that good and evil are defined within the framework of a secured order to maintain which is the function of religion, one can understand the basis upon which he considered that the papacy's interference with the development of the region's unity under a single power was a more serious moral offense than the immoral examples set by the faithless prelates[67] and one can perceive the deeper dedication he felt for strengthening the possibilities for realizing the common good through Florentine leadership.

An affirmation of the reality of the individual free man, a challenge to that of the group, an exaltation of the individual soul rather than the corporate church was an element in the Renaissance and in the Reformation carried furthest subsequently, perhaps, in the Quakers; yet Machiavelli's view that the value of a man derives from the use which his city, prince, king, republic, country makes of him[68] approximates the traditional ecclesiastical position that it is through baptism into the church that one is re-born into eternal life and that outside the church there is no salvation. According to Machiavelli, all men are whirled around on the wheels of Fortune and one's fame depends upon his being found in active service in the common good at the moment that death overtakes him.[69]

Absence of *virtù* Machiavelli portrayed most graphically. Of the mercenary captains entrapped for their disloyalty by Cesare Borgia, he wrote:

And when night came on and the disturbance had been stopped, the Duke decided to have Vitellozzo and Liverotto killed; and taking them into a place together, he had them strangled. At that time neither of them used words worthy of their past lives; Vitellozzo begged that the Pope be petitioned to give him plenary indulgence for his sins; Liverotto, weeping, put on Vitellozzo all the blame for the injuries done the Duke;[70]

and despite the high regard in which, both before and after, he held Cesare Borgia's statecraft, in Cesare Borgia himself, when abandoned by Fortune, Machiavelli depicted a man without *virtù* . Letters from the official mission to the Papal Court trace the developing realization:

It is not known whether he [the Duke] is going to leave or to stay . . . Others say he is not intending to leave Rome but to wait for the coronation of the Pope [Julius II] who will make him Gonfalonier of Holy Church, according to the promises; with the reputation gained from that he can get back his territory. Others, not less prudent,think that this Pontiff, having for his election had need of the Duke, to whom he made big promises, can do

214

nothing else than keep him expectant in this way; yet they fear that, if the Duke does not adopt some other plan than remaining in Rome, that he will be deceived, because they know the natural hatred which His Holiness has always had for him; the Pope cannot so soon have forgotten the exile in which he spent ten years. Yet the Duke lets himself be carried away by that rash confidence of his, and believes that the words of another man are going to be surer than his own have been.[71]

[the Duke] said that you [the Florentine Signoria] had always been his enemies . . . that he will try to make you the first to repent of it . . . He believes you soon will see your state ruined, and he is going to laugh over it . . . And here he went on at length with words full of poison and anger . . . as skillfully as I could I got away from him—which seemed to take a thousand years;[72]

We see that this Pope is dealing with him *a ferri puliti* [ed. note. *Apparently proverbial. With polished tools, deftly and vigorously*] . . . We see that his sins have little by little brought him to penitence.[73]

So it seems that this Duke little by little is slipping into his grave.[74]

Again, in *Mandragola,* the stupid judge, Messer Nicia, exemplifies the man without *virtù:*

> Everybody knows how happy he is
> who is born stupid and believes everything.
> Ambition does not disturb him,
> fear does not upset him—
> these two that ever are the seeds
> of pain and discontent.[75]

And in the eighth chapter of "The (Golden) Ass," confronting the form and conversation of

> that hog [that] raised his snout all smeared with turd and mud such that to look at him made me sick,[76]

Machiavelli manifested his profound disgust for those who, though endowed with human form, turned away from striving after *virtù.*

The only valid power is function. The truth of the matter is endowed with that quality of behavior which arouses, attracts, organizes others' support through proving mutually, creatively refreshing. Heroic leadership as the means for making manifest the enlarged political unit so that it would gain acceptance as reality, was Machiavelli's prescription. Power privately consumed, unless it provokes mutually-destructive reaction, wastes away through corruption. Professional hypocrisy, through which principles were being exploited for personal and family profit and advancement in ecclesiastical, political, military affairs, Machiavelli pereceived to be a long-standing corroding factor. "Principles" as conventionally being experienced had long since lost effectiveness. He concluded that only through drastic, extraordinary measures could regard and service for the common good be made a way of life among people who either had not experienced it or had let it wither away. Machiavelli issued a clear summons and challenge for mastery through effective will (i.e., *virtù*) as the way for liberation for his city and country. However, although Machiavelli considered that effective initiative for establishing or reforming a state could be expected in the undertaking by one man alone,[77] it required more than the one man to conceive the action for the common good, in order to bring it about and to establish the institutions for its endurance.[78]

As Machiavelli saw it, the deed or line of action of the one-man-founder-or-reformer of a state had to have in it that which reached down and through to, and found kinship with and echo in, energetic responsiveness of the inhabitants. Their awareness of such a rightful title to the land that fear of death will not move them to accept surrender of it, keeps alive that

> ability in arms and boldness of spirit

without which a people grows

> always weaker and more despicable.[79]

Therefore,

> never did anybody establish a republic or kingdom who did not suppose that the same persons who inhabited it would need with their weapons to defend it.[80]

As Kemmerich observed:

> nicht was sein soll, interessiert ihn, sondern was ist und was man auf Grund der bestehenden, Verhältnisse organisch daraus mit Klugheit, Erfahrung und Tüchtigkeit machen kann. Im Gegensatz zum Individualismus and skrupellosen Egoismus seiner Zeit ordnet er die Persönlichkeit bedingungslos dem Staate und dessen Zwecken unter. Diese sind rein politischer und miliätärischer Natur und unterscheiden sich auch hierin wesentlich von denen des Aristoteles mit seinen grossen kulturellen Zielen. Hatte sich dieser von der Spekulation zur Methode der Beobachtung und Erfahrung, zur Sachlichkeit, durchgerungen, eine ungeheure Geistestat, so geht Machiavelli auf diesem richtigen Wege noch einen grossen Schritt weiter,

indem er stets aus den Erscheinungen auf die Ursachen schliesst, diese sozusagen rein herausdestilliert und nunmehr jeweils praktisch verwendet. Für eine irgendwie beschaffene Spekulation bietet sein System keinerlei Raum mehr.[81]

It was not what ought to be that interested him, but what is and what can be produced organically through prudence, experience and ability. In contrast to the individualism and unscrupulous egoism of his time, he unconditionally subordinated the personality to the state and its aims. These are purely political and military in nature and differentiate themselves essentially also from those of Aristotle with his great cultural goals. As the latter pressed beyond speculation to the method of observation, experience and objectivity, a phenomenal achievement of the mind, so Machiavelli continued a great step further on this true course, in that he steadfastly inferred the causes on the basis of the phenomena, as it were, distilled out purely and utilized practically each time. His system offered no room for speculation however produced.

The thread of continuity throughout Machiavelli's life has been clearly identified by Tommasini:

Puù scrivere, ma il suo pensiero è all'azione, il suo scritto è un tentativo per riguadagnare la via e la carriera sua.[82]

He is able to write, but his thought is for action, his writing is an attempt to get back on the track and his career.

Only insofar as one is sharing in power does the possibility exist for rightly understanding truth in human behavior and hence of perceiving the nature both of the stimuli and of the potential for response essential for state-forming and -preserving. This realization found expression, as one of several elements in his persistent and, at times, near desperate appeals—unconditional, seemingly humiliating and unworthy—for re-employment in public service or, at least, by the masters of the city. Another element was his concern that the liberties of his region be recovered and be more firmly based. Changing events revealing his country's need made him restive in the face of his impotence for having a more active share in helping shape them. And, furthermore, always as head of a household, with that concern and regard for his wife manifested in his personal wills,[83] father of two daughters (the first of whom died in infancy)[84] and four sons[85] and entrusted by inheritance with an estate which he as a citizen and householder had determined not to let be impaired under his management, he was keenly aware of the threat to his personal self-respect which continued unemployment posed.[86] In these circumstances, his hunger and thirst for knowledge and understanding of the workings of will and decision-making in human

217

relations and his determination to show that he "had not slept or been playing"[87] was to bear fruit as political science.

Machiavelli sensed that one's own direct experience was the kernel of validity, that one grows in inner dignity and integrity through responsible service in social enterprise[88] rooted in the shared relationship of people and homeland, and he esteemed human beings as being sufficiently potentially responsive to this outlook for him to exert himself to the utmost in order to work it out and, in practical terms, to set it before those hopefully prudent princes whom he saw as available candidates for leadership and those young men conceivably maintainers or securers of freedom and liberty as citizens in a republic. Under necessity, in Machiavelli *virtù* became his writings.

Realistically, however, in light of the imprisonment and torture which he had suffered under the administration of the Medici, a question arises as to how seriously he could have expected employment at their hands. In the *Discourses* he had entitled a chapter:

A Man Should Not Be Injured and Then Assigned to Important Administration and Control.[89]

Useful innovation derived from experience was the criterion which he advanced for achievement in a profession.[90] To this standard he held himself accountable.[91] Machiavelli zealously sought to proclaim the good news that through establishing a healthy, aggressive state[92] and participating in it, citizens acquire their personal dignity and nobility and become human beings at their best—unless their "excellence . . . was turned into pride"[93] so that they come to require a prince or renewal through the arising of a self-restrained law-giver-reformer;[94] however, rarely, if ever, has such a benefactor appeared.[95]

At the height of his official career, Machiavelli served in an advisory capacity rather than as one exercising decision-making authority. As a top-level bureaucrat, however, he had excellent opportunity for observing significant factors in events and for developing and maintaining his influence through scrupulously prudent suggestions for policy. The description given by Ferrara of Machiavelli's role during his mission to the court of Pope Julius II[96] is applicable to the whole of his official career.

The "First Decennale" is his diagnosis, as a responsible official, of foreign affairs and relations, with the aim of stirring popular support for his prescription for a new military policy.[97] The "Second Decennale," composed after his loss of office,[98] continued the chronicle of the deepening insecurity which was spreading and engulfing Genoa, Pisa and Venice.

Personal correspondence with his friend, Francesco Vettori, the Florentine ambassador at the court of Rome, provided essential nourishment which engendered suggestions of policy hopefully intended for the attention of the Pope and his advisers.[99] Frustrated in his hopes for renewed employment, Machiavelli worked over his memories of his own experience in the light of continual reading of history.

An indication of the two sources which he recognizes in his major works appeared first in his letter of January 1512–(1513) to Piero Soderini.[100] To the same sources he referred in his dedication of the *Prince*,[101] the preface to the first book of the *Discourses*,[102] and in the preface to *The Art of War*.[103]

In the *Prince* he delineated for a prospective new prince the qualities of initiative needed for consolidating a new state and for providing sound foundations for stable order and concluded with an appeal to recognize the present moment and available resources as most favorable for the leadership of liberation. Writing of his work to his friend, the Florentine ambassador at the papal court at the time during which the Medicean pope was giving active consideration to carving out new states in order to promote princely careers for both his younger brother and a still younger nephew, Machiavelli suggested that

> by a prince, and especially by a new prince it ought to be welcomed. Hence I am dedicating it to His Magnificence Giuliano.[104]

Subsequent scholarly studies arrive at varied evaluations of the work. Thus, the estimate by Benoist:

> le caractère véritable du *Livre du Prince,* qui n'est ni une apologie, ni un pamphlet, mais une espèce de 'manuel de géométrie politique,' vide de toute morale, ou plotôt décharge de tout élément moral.[105]

> the true character of the book, of the *Prince,* which is neither an apology, nor a pamphlet, but a kind of 'manual of political geometry,' empty of all morality, or rather discharged of every moral element.

According to Allan Gilbert, writing on "The Nature of the Prince,"

> Machiavelli's perfect prince is to be found only in the realm of the imagination . . . Niccolo's delivering ruler is the poet's dream of a monarch who masters the world's harsh realities. Had he remained a more practical man, Machiavelli would have looked with despair on Italian ills as beyond cure. But from exact yet imaginative observing of good and bad, he gained material for a poet's vision.
> Whatever else the *Prince* may be, it is first of all a poem of trust that human goodness, strength and wisdom, personified in an ideal ruler, can afford men such measure of happiness as follows from good government.[106]

In the judgment of Leo Strauss:

Is it not possible to understand the patriotic conclusion of the *Prince* as a respectable coloring of the designs of a self-seeking Italian prince? There can be no doubt regarding the answer; the immoral policies recommended throughout the *Prince* are not justified on grounds of the common good, but exclusively on grounds of the self-interest of the prince, of his selfish concern with his own well-being, security and glory. [For the author's defense of this interpretation see his n.53, pp. 309–10]. The final appeal to patriotism supplies Machiavelli with an excuse for having recommended immoral courses of action . . . These observations are not to deny that Machiavelli was an Italian patriot . . . We merely deny that his love for his fatherland, or his fatherland itself, was his most precious possession. The core of his being was his thought about man, about the condition of man and about human affairs. By raising the fundamental questions he of necessity transcended the limitations and limits of Italy, and he thus was enabled to use the patriotic sentiments of his readers, as well as his own, for a higher purpose, for an ulterior purpose. One must also consider an ambiguity characteristic of Machiavelli's patriotism . . . we become aware of a tension between his Italian patriotism and his Florentine patriotism. Or should one not rather speak of a tension between his Roman patriotism and his Tuscan patriotism? There exists a close connection between the trans-patriotic core of his thought and his love for Italy. Italy is the soil out of which sprang the glory that was ancient Rome. Machiavelli believed that the men who are born in a country preserve through all ages more or less the same nature. If the greatest political achievement which the world has ever known was the fruit of the Italian soil there is ground for hope that the political rejuvenation of the world will make its first appearance in Italy: the sons of Italy are the most gifted individuals; all modern writers referred to in either the *Prince* or the *Discourses* are Italians. Since that political rejuvenation is bound up with a radical change in thought, the hope from Italy and for Italy is not primarily political in the narrow sense. The liberation of Italy which Machiavelli has primarily in mind is not the political liberation of Italy from the barbarians but the intellectual liberation of an Italian elite from a bad tradition. But precisely because he believed that the men who are born in a country preserve through all ages more or less the same nature, and as the nature of the Romans was different from that of the Tuscans, his hope was also grounded on his recollection of Tuscan glory [supporting evidence in author's note 55, p. 310].[107]

J.H. Whitfield has emphasized the very practical significance of the *Prince* as a reminder to the Medici of Machiavelli's availability as one competent and peculiarly fitted to serve as secretary to the redeemer of Italy.[108]

In the *Prince* Machiavelli, as no other elsewhere, delineated the Renaissance drive for power over others; however, when one views the final chapter in the context of the concern for the common good which he repeatedly affirmed in his writings, an idea of responsible public service for the common good is found to be intrinsic in that which he recognized as power.

In looking to Livy for guidance in deliverance from contemporary corruption[109] and using as a handbook Livy's recorded remembrance of the glory of ancient Tuscany and the *virtù* of republican Rome, Machiavelli could not consider himself to be violating the wide-spread and profound sense of civic pride prevalent among Italian cities. Felix Gilbert has pointed out:

> men were inclined to reject the entire idea that one government might be or ought to be patterned after another. Each city was thought to be a unique formation; each city had its own patron saint . . . It was assumed that the patron saint held his protecting hand over the fate of the city. The institutions which had been created in earliest times when the city had acquired its patron saint were believed to be sacred.[110]

Now it was through the study of Livy that Machiavelli felt one could come to understand the institutions through which the citizens of republican Rome, the founder of Florence, had for centuries promoted and preserved their liberty. In reading Livy, Machiavelli was impressed that when Ancus Martius sought to make reforms,

> he determined to go back to the earliest source and conduct the state offices of religion as they had been organized by Numa.[111]

Thorough consideration of the necessity for this strategem constitutes the first chapter of the third book of the *Discourses*.[112] Consequently, for Machiavelli, as a citizen of the republic of Florence, going back to its beginnings led him to Livy's *History*.

Much of the spirit of Machiavelli's relation to Livy's *History* is similar to that attributed by Tommasini to believers' use of sacred texts:

> un'intima e generale tendenza, indizio d'un'intima legge che governa le istituzioni religiose fondate su libri o scritture sacre . . . è nella continua comparazione,che s'istituisce tra l'indirizzo che pare si determini da quelle scritture e l'andamento delle istituzioni umane che procedendo accennano a dipartirsene. Ond'è che l'eresie sorgono tutte col preconcetto di rifarsi ai principî, di riandare alle origini, d'interpretare autorevolmente o correttamente i testi inviolabili, di non deviare dalle tracce iniziali. E il metodo storico per queste contingenze piglia così il sopravvento a macerare e sconvolgere l'edificio dogmatico, quando la coscienza sociale e storica è per svengliarsi.[113]

> an intimate and general tendency, indicative of an intimate law which governs religious institutions founded on books or sacred scriptures . . . consists in the continual comparison which establishes itself between the direction which seems to be pointed out by that scripture and the course of the human institutions which in their process seem to depart

from it. Hence it is that all heresies arise with the preconception of beginning again at the beginning, of returning to the origins, of interpreting authoritatively or correctly the inviolable texts, of not deviating from the initial track. And the historical method through this contingency thus takes advantage of flailing and throwing into confusion the dogmatic structure, when the social and historic conscience is for waking it up.

In fact, Leo Strauss has written:

> He did not read Livy as we are wont to read Livy. For Machiavelli, Livy's work was authoritative, as it were, his Bible. His way of reading Livy was nearer to the way in which all theologians of the past read the Bible than to our way of reading either Livy or the Bible.[114]

It may have been that in Machiavelli's home there was no copy of the Bible to challenge the primacy of Livy. In the *Libro di Ricordi di Bernardo Machiavelli* (kept from 30 September 1471 to 19 August 1487) the appearance of "the Bible" in the list of borrowed books has prompted Ridolfi to raise the question:

> Could it be that there was no Bible among all those books in the Machiavelli household?[115]

Such a seemingly surprising omission could, perhaps, become more understandable in light of the fact that there had been wide-spread ecclesiastical obstructions to the circulation of editions (especially in a country's vernacular) of the Bible among the laity.[116]

In his *Discourses* it was the ancient religion of civic dedication in republican Rome which Machiavelli exalted and through it provided example and rationale for the spirit of modern nationalism.

Various precepts fundamental in Machiavelli's thought find emphasis in Livy's *History* also.

The study of history as a source for political wisdom and imitation, Livy commended in his preface:

> There is this exceptionally beneficial and fruitful advantage to be derived from the study of the past, that you see, set in the clear light of historical truth, examples of every possible type. From these you may select for yourself and your country what to imitate, and also what, as being mischievous in its inception and disastrous in its issues, you are to avoid.[117]

Skepticism regarding the validity of claims of divine intervention in human affairs but, nevertheless, recognition of the repeated resort to the use of such claims as an important part of political strategy, Livy expressed in the "Preface" and, subsequently, especially in Book 1, "The Earliest Legends."

The traditions of what happened prior to the foundation of the City or whilst it was being built, are more fitted to adorn the creations of the poet than the authentic records of the historian, and I have no intention of establishing either their truth or their falsehood. This much license is conceded to the ancients, that by intermingling human actions with divine they may confer a more august dignity on the origins of states. Now, if any nation ought to be allowed to claim a sacred origin and point back to a divine paternity that nation is Rome. For such is her renown in war that she chooses to represent Mars as her own and her founder's father, the nations of the world accept the statement with the same equanimity with which they accept her dominion.[118]

The claim of a "return to first principles" as a device for justifying and strengthening "reforms"[119] has already been mentioned (above, pp. 55, 141).

For the maxim that one who succeeds in concentrating power and founding or reforming a state should not leave the power concentrated and susceptible to abuse by a successor, Machiavelli cited, as precedent, Romulus's creation of the Senate.[120] Machiavelli might have recognized as parallel Servius Tullius' abandonment (upon the discovery of the conspiracy against him) of the intention to institute a reform of government[121] and Cardinal Giulio de'Medici's termination of consideration of all proposals for reform which included Machiavelli's proposal for an eventual broadening of the base of the government of the city.[122]

In Livy's *History*, Machiavelli found, also,[123] confirmation of both the Florentine republic's bitter experience from 1494 to 1512 and his own conclusion:

if Florence had not been forced by necessity or conquered by passion, and had read or learned the ancient habits of the barbarians [i.e., the French and the Emperor], she would not have been deceived by them at this and many other times, for they have always been of one sort and have under all conditions and with everybody shown the same habits . . . From this it easily can be inferred how much princes can trust them.[124]

In the preface to his *History,* Livy described his aim as that of

writing a complete history of the Roman people.[125]

When Machiavelli, in the preface to his *History* expressed, as his purpose

to write of the things done at home and abroad by the Florentine people,[126]

may he have been responding to a prompting by Livy?

The very form itself of the *Discourses* had such originality that it holds a distinguished place in the history of literature. Tommasini has pointed out:

223

Lo stesso titolo di *Discorsi* ch'egli pose alle sue considerazioni, atteso il tema che tratta e la breve e tagliente dell'opera, à in sè qualcosa di nuovo, destinato a svegliare imitatori in Italia e fuori. I *Discorsi* colla loro disinvoltura valgono gli *Essais* del Montaigne e di lord Bacon, e furono forse prototipo del genere.[127]

The very title of *Discourses* which he gave to his considerations, with attention to the theme with which it deals and the brief and piquant form of the work, have in themselves something novel. The *Discourses* with their detachment are worthy of the *Essays* of Montaigne and of Lord Bacon, and were perhaps the prototype of the genre.

"A Discourse on Remodeling the Government of Florence"[128] provided a structure and process whereby Pope Leo X and/or Cardinal Giulio de'Medici during their lives could exercise "monarchical" powers but with the death of both would leave Florentines their traditional republican institutions through which they would be able to enjoy their liberties fully restored in accordance with the pattern which he advocated in the *Discourses*.[129] In the opinion of Allan Gilbert:

This work is valuable chiefly as showing the flexibility and yet the firmness of Machiavelli's conception. On the one hand he realizes, as the *Prince* had already indicated, that conditions exist in which absolutism cannot be avoided; on the other, he is sure that for Florence the best form of government is the republican. Even his belief in such a possibility—sometimes called an illusion—is not doctrinaire; Florence can be prepared for it by a process of education that admits the fallibility of human material. Though Machiavelli abhorred Medici tyranny, he could accept it when no better possibility was offered; though he estimated Savonarola as dangerously ambitious and as inadequate in practical affairs, yet he could accept part of his theory, notably the approval of a Great Council, as fundamental to Florentine government.[130]

Tommasini observed:

Quello che bensì predomina nel pensiero di Niccolò è il problema immediato che la sua città è tratta prossimamente a risolvere, in un modo o nell'altro; il problema della sua costituzione politica. Ed egli non lascia sfuggire occasione di metterne i termini netti.[131]

However, that which predominated in the thought of Machiavelli is the immediate problem which the city was drawn to resolve very soon, in one way or another; the problem of its political constitution. And he did not let escape the opportunity to put it in clear terms.

After eight and one half years of official service, Machiavelli wrote "A Provision for Infantry" which became law 6 December 1506. He had the satisfaction of preparing the measures for the Florentine militia—both infantry and, later, cavalry—and seeing them adopted into law, of enlisting and training recruits, exhibiting the new forces in parade, exulting in their contribution to the recovery for Florence of its seaport, Pisa, but then, also, the humiliation of the disastrous rout at Prato. Yet he did not lose faith in the idea[132] and *The Art of War* presents fully developed his conception of the elements essential for making a state powerful for its own protection and that of the common good. If, as Vignal has pointed out,[133] the three works are to be considered a trilogy in the treatment of statecraft (with the *Prince* concerned with the creation of a new state and the *Discourses* with its governance), *The Art of War* is concerned with provision for its strength. In considering Machiavelli's contribution to military science, Ridolfi wrote:

> Military science was for him only an aspect of political science, and he was convinced that the beginning of Italy's troubles lay in having separated military from civil life . . . Villari's masterly judgment is still valid, that Machiavelli was the first to lay the foundations of modern tactics "and did so with an intellectual boldness no less than that with which he embarked on the founding of political science."[134]

Machiavelli's desperate efforts for re-employment contributed the *Prince* and much of the correspondence with Francesco Vettori. His dedication to the mission of Florence for promoting liberty for him and his fellow citizens bore fruit as the *Discourses,* "Dialogue on Language," "Discourse on Remodeling the Government of Florence," *The Art of War,* and, to a degree, *The History of Florence.* Central for the *Prince*, the *Discourses* and *The Art of War* was that drive for observing and understanding the relation between men's behavior and the consequences—out of which political science has developed. To his struggle against discouragement, melancholy and the threat of despair, posterity is indebted for some of his correspondence with Vettori, much of that with his nephew, Giovanni Vernaccia, "The (Golden) Ass" and *Mandragola.*

Although "The (Golden) Ass" begins with braying, kicking and biting against adversities which befall men, the experience of refreshing love enables the prudent one to realize that whatever the insecurity and restlessness attendant upon man's condition, it is infinitely to be preferred to the indolent self-calming complacency of one who, like a swine, contentedly indulges himself in the state of nature. May the "woman of utmost beauty, but breezy and brash"[135] be the "lovely lady" of the myth of Florence? (above, p. 134)

Machiavelli's play *Mandragola* has been termed

the comedy of a society of which the *Prince* is the tragedy.[136]

Written at the time that Lorenzo de'Medici, the Duke of Urbino and head of the government of Florence, had contracted marriage with a French princess, the play began with a debate on the timely topic of the comparative beauty and virtue of French and Italian women. The chief character, a young Florentine who for twenty years had been living in Paris, decided to return to his native city in order to find out for himself whether or not Madam Lucretia, the young wife of the old judge, Messer Nicia, really matched her incomparable reputation as

a beautiful wife, virtuous, courteous, and fit to rule a kingdom.[137]

Could it have been without significance that for this paragon of virtue Machiavelli chose the name of her whose violation occasioned purging Rome of the Tarquins and the establishment of the virtuous Roman republic?[138] In Machiavelli's opinion, decadence and moral corruption characterized his contemporary Florentines. His Carnival Song, "By the Devils Driven out from Heaven" began

Once we were—but now no longer are—blessed spirits; because of our pride we all were driven from Heaven;
and in this city of yours [Florence] we have seized the rule, because here we find confusion and sorrow greater than in Hell.[139]

Did he have in mind with his play—as did a later playwright—"to catch the conscience"[140] of his sovereign (in Machiavelli's case, his city) by showing how complacent bourgeoisie, how conventionally ceremonial and venal clergy, and how unsophisticated innocents were adjusting themselves in the institutions which they were continually corrupting by turning the best maxims to base purposes? Was he holding up a mirror to contrast the patriotic Roman action of vengeance to uphold Lucretia's virtue with supine Florentines' guilty snickers of amusement at the modern Lucretia's reconciliation with the enjoyment of adulterous self-indulgence after being snared in the hoodwinking of her husband made blindly credulous by their mutual desire to have children? Throughout the play, Machiavelli showed the survival of Christian principles and practices as still available but effective only in the form of a means of deception and exploitation of the weak and the simple. Of the play, Kemmerich has written:

Sehr lustig, aber eine Lustigkeit, hinter der die Tränen lauern, die fast mehr die Seele aufrührt als die Tragik des blutigen "Principe", eine Gesellschaftssatire von erschütternder Realistik.[141]

Very amusing, but an amusement behind which tears lurk, which disturbs the soul almost more than the tragedy of the bloody *Prince,* a social satire of shattering realism.

Ridolfi concluded:

If, however, there were a purpose behind it, one could hardly say that this was to make people laugh when the comedy has far more the effect of making people think. It is easier to recognize in it, both for its thought and its poetic and human insight, the writer of the *Prince* than the author of the *Discourses,* even if Fra Timoteo with his cynical arguments and his 'face of a great rogue' may seem the artistic representation of the concepts theorized over in chapter 12 of book 1 of the *Discourses:* 'On the importance of respect for religion, and how Italy has come to ruin because that respect has failed on account of the Roman Church.'[142]

With two trenchant excerpts from the play, Adolfo Oxilia has perceptively indicated Machiavelli's own attitude toward his undertakings and their probable effect:

Quell'accento machiavelliano inconfondibile, colto che sia una volta, si ritrova qui nel prologo: *nessuno s'affatica alle opere generose, che il vento dissipa e la nebbia ricopre;* e l'autore sembra irridere a sè quando pone in bocca a Callimaco, pel suo sciocchissimo amore, le parole stesse che uscivano dal suo cuore sanguinante: "A me bisogna tentare qualche cosa, sia grande, sia pericolosa, sia dannosa, sia infame: meglio è morire che vivere così!"[143]

That unmistakable Machiavellian accent, once caught, is found again here in the prologue: *no one wears himself out for noble works which the wind scatters and the fog covers;* and the author seems to laugh at himself when he places in the mouth of Callimacho, for his most silly love, the very same words which he used of his own bleeding heart: "I must attempt something, be it great, be it dangerous, be it harmful, be it infamous: it is better to die than to live in this condition!"

Tommasini viewed at length critics' appraisal of the play[144] and Ferrara concluded as follows:

Dans cette relativité "[sic] que constitue le théâtre italien, *la Mandragore* est une des œuvres les plus importantes. Macaulay l'estime supérieure aux meilleures comédies de Goldoni, et Vittorio Osimo, dans la préface à une édition de cet ouvrage, datée de 1927, allant plus loin encore, la définit: "Une comédie tragique, la seule tragédie des années quinzecents, le *capolavoro* de la littérature dramatique italienne." Par contre, beaucoup d'auteurs l'ont méprisée; mais, d'accord avec Macaulay et Osimo, ii faut compter parmi ses fervents admirateurs des hommes tels que les Italiens: DeSanctis, Gioda, Amico; et Voltaire, Klein, Hildebrand parmi les étran-

227

gers. Villari, le grand biographe de Machiavel, fait des réserves; mais Oreste Tommasini, non moins important comme biographe et plus attentif encore, soutient l'opinion que *la Mandragore* est un chef-d'œuvre.[145]

In this relativity 'which constitutes the Italian theater,' *The Mandragola* is one of the most important works. Macaulay esteemed it superior to the better comedies of Goldoni, and Vittorio Osimo, in the preface to an edition of this work, dated 1927, going still further, terms it: "A tragic-comedy, the only tragedy of the fifteen-hundreds, the *capolavoro* of Italian dramatic literature." On the contrary, many others have disparaged it; but, in accord with Macaulay and Osimo, one must count among its warm admirers such men as the Italians: DeSanctis, Gioda, Amico; and Voltaire, Klein, Hildebrand among the foreigners. Villari, the great biographer of Machiavelli, held reservations; but Oreste Tommasini, no less important as a biographer and still more observant, supported the opinion that *Mandragola* is a *chef d'œuvre*.

With his *History of Florence,* Machiavelli far transcended the chronicles of events recorded by earlier humanist Florentine chancellors upon whose works, as sources, he drew heavily. Indeed, a comparison of his own draft of the terms for his commission[146] (above, pp. 194–195) with the expression of his purpose as indicated in his dedication of the *History*[147] (above, p. 169) shows that his perspective seems to have deepened in the process of study and composition.

Writing the *History* in the common language, he broke with the humanist tradition and he broadened the horizon by relating the city's internal processes to those affecting its foreign policies.[148] A secular system of values took the place of the ecclesiastical which, with the chroniclers, had held the monopoly for centuries[149] and a more republican standpoint replaced the aristocratic and plutocratic biases manifested by the earlier humanists.[150]

Because of his endeavors to identify and trace deep and far-reaching connections in historical events, Machiavelli has been widely acclaimed as the originator of the philosophy of history.[151] In explaining the migration of peoples as the natural consequence of overpopulation and the emergence of new secular states formulating their respectively appropriate laws and finding their security in the discipline of their own citizens,[152] he was treating human history as the record of beings of the earth struggling with each other in working out their wills and fortunes, and, as already noted, according to Burckhardt, his city as an organism developed out of natural processes[153] (above, p. 57). In a similar vein, as cited by Tommasini, A. Schmidt observed:

Seine Betrachtungsweise des Staates ist nicht juristich, sondern, wenn mann man so will, naturwissenschaftlich.[154]

His way of looking at the state is not juridical but, as it were, that of a natural scientist.

Later, Tommasini further interpreted Schmidt's observation:

lo Schmidt rileva come, pel rispetto metodologico, il Machiavelli sia tale che traccia a dirittura la via; com'ei sia e si senta proprio, come dicono i tedeschi *bahnbrecher;* com'egli vada animosamente verso l'avvenire, perchè esamina prima completamente il passato d'ogni cosa; inaugura cioè il metodo storico, il quale è il solo che si colleghi e confaccia coll'indirizzo naturalistico, nel quale non reca angustie di criterî soggettivi o professionali.[155]

Schmidt continues how, with respect to methodology, Machiavelli was of the kind who blaze the trail completely, who was and felt himself to be, as the Germans say, a *bahnbrecher,* who made his way courageously toward the future, because first he examined fully the past of everything: that is, he inaugurated the historical method which is the only one which can be connected to and is consistent with the naturalistic trend into which it does not bring the limitations of subjective and professional criteria.

In his *Des Revolutions d'Italie,* as quoted by Tommasini,[156] Quinet observed:

il [Machiavel] a ouvert la voie à l'auteur de *l'Histoire Universelle*

Machiavelli has opened the way for the author of the *Universal History*

and Tommasini concluded:

signoreggia con la sua sintesi la storia non solo di Firenze, ma d'Italia e d'Europa.[157]

he dominated with his syntheses the history not only of Florence, but of Italy and of Europe.

Allan Gilbert noted:

Machiavelli's desire to write a history that would inspire all lovers of the common good of man in whatever age or nation.[158]

Machiavelli, at the dawning of nationalism in language and government, found that that which he was himself too advanced to achieve in formal government he was able to achieve fully in language. After detailing Machiavelli's indebtedness to the humanists, in indicating Machiavelli's transcendance of their limitations, Tommasini wrote:

chè il presente per Niccolò dichiara e riscalda il passato, non questo basta colle sue forme morte a irrigidire e confondere la vita viva; e Italia è oramai tutta l'Italia, tutta una patria.[159]

229

Because the present for Machiavelli explains and warms up the past, it does not with its dead forms rigidify and confuse the life of the living; and Italy is thenceforth all Italy, all one country.

Of distinctive, but varied, significance are brief works, the matured fruits of impressions deeply implanted by experiences on missions abroad. Most famous of these is "A Description of the Method Used by Duke Valentino in Killing Vitellozzo Vitelli, Oliverotto Da Fermo and Others."[160] As in the brief works "On the Method of Dealing with the Rebellious Peoples of the Valdichiana,"[161] "de rebus pistoriensibus," "Cosi di Francia, a di Lamagna," Tommasini perceived an identical objective:

> E il Segretario, nella cui mente s'andavano man mano sviluppando nuove idee politiche, nuovi precetti in opposizione a quelli vigenti, cercava di poterli recare innanzi agli occhi di chi governava, appoggiati all'esperienza, confortati dall'opportunità . . . cercava menare la mente de'magistrati a principî, che poi troviamo incorporati nelle dottrine politiche di lui.[162]

And the Secretary in whose mind new political ideas were developing step by step, new precepts in opposition to those which were current, sought to be able to place them under the eyes of him who governed, supported by experience, encouraged by opportunity . . . he sought to turn the minds of the magistrates to principles which then we find incorporated in his political doctrines.

"The Life of Castruccio Castracani of Lucca," written during the mission to that city on which he had been sent "by private interests and private citizens,"[163] although composed for the practical purpose of demonstrating qualification for being granted the rumored opportunity to write the history of Florence,[164] according to Tommasini,

> parrà chiaro che il Machiavelli con questa sua *Vita di Castruccio* non intese ad altro che a dare esempio d'una mitografia vera e propria, secondo il concetto antico; che è quanto dire risuscitò l'antico genere di biografie peripatetiche, e fu il precursore di quella specie di romanzo moderno, che forse ignora la genesi sua remota, in cui si suole spacciar come realtà storica un'idelità d'assetto politico e sociale che a chi scrive può sembrare desiderabile si sperimenti in fatto, a che intanto si figura come cosa già esistita, cognita, certa.[165]

it will appear clear that Machiavelli with this *Life of Castruccio* intended nothing other than to give an example of real and genuine fiction, according to the ancient conception; that is, so to speak, he revived the ancient kind of Peripatetic biography, and was the precursor of that species of modern novel, which perhaps is ignorant of its own remote origin, in which one is accustomed to give forth as historic reality the idealization of a political and social utopia which to him who writes may seem desirable if tried out in fact and which meanwhile is set forth by him as already existent, known, certain.

Concerning the "Ritratto di Cose di Francia" and "Ritratto delle Cose della Magna,"[166] an excerpt from Machiavelli's "Advice to Rafaello Girolami When He Went as Ambassador to the Emperor" may throw light upon the process of their composition:

I have seen also men prudent and experienced in embassies using this method: they put, at least once very two months, before the eyes of him who sends them the exact condition and situation of the city or the kingdom where they are representatives. When well handled, this device brings great honor to the writers and is of great value to the man receiving their letters, because he can more easily make plans when understanding matters in detail than when not understanding them.[167]

Machiavelli developed a capacity for comprehensive characterization of countries which he observed, the significance of future consequences of which Kemmerich has pointed out:

gilt es aber festzsustellen, welche natürlichen Hilfsquellen ein Land besitzt, wie dessen politische und militärische Institutionen sind, welche Wirkung die Persönlichkeiten auf die Zeitereignisse ausüben, so wrude darin Machiavelli von niemandem erreicht, geschweige denn übertroffen. Hier bewährt sich seine ganze eminente Begabung . . . Machiavelli ist nach Villaris kompetentem Urteile der erste, der das ganze Material in seinem Geiste zu ordnen verstand. Dadurch wird er zum Vater der künftigen politischen Wissenschaft, bzw. der Nationalökonomie. Allerdings verfolgte er ganz bestimmte Ideale, die er bisweilen in die Dinge hineintrug.[168]

however, it is worth confirming what natural resources a country possesses, what kind of political and military institutions it has, what effect personalities exert on events; in this respect Machiavelli had no equal, much less any superior. Here he proved his entirely distinguished talent . . . Machiavelli is, according to Villari's competent judgment, the first who understood to arrange the entire material in his mind. Thereby he was to become the father of the future political science or, that is to say of the national economy. Indeed, he completely followed up certain ideas which occasionally he actualized.

So, when deprived of office and with his name dropped from the list of those who could be chosen to fill public responsibilities, he remained dedicatedly responsible as private citizen. He did not succumb to that laziness from which, as he observed (above, p. 205), spreads civic corruption. Instead, he reworked out of his reflections upon his recent experiences in public affairs and his continuous reading of ancient ones, a discipline of instrumental prudence to be made available to those daring to exercise power.

Chapter Seven

RECOGNITION OF TRUTH THROUGH ANALYSIS OF ACTS OF WILL FOR THE COMMON GOOD

Deeds of contemporary men—especially in the public affairs of Spain, France, England, Germany, with reverberations in the Italian peninsula—were so arresting attention that Machiavelli responded with persistent endeavor to search out in them any relationships which would provide Florentine leadership ever greater effectiveness. Capacity for effective action as being indicated by leaders emerging through forming, out of the people of their respective lands, disciplined forces, was contrasting starkly with rhetorical claims of transforming power by ecclesiastical interpreters of intellectualized dogmas, performers of mechanical rituals. As Machiavelli observed in the *Prince*:

> there is such a difference between how men live and how they ought to live that he who abandons what is done for what ought to be done learns his destruction rather than his preservation, because any man who under all conditions insists on making it his business to be good will surely be destroyed among so many who are not good. Hence a prince, in order to hold his position, must acquire the power to be not good, and understand when to use it and when not to use it, in accord with necessity.[1]

In his sketch for a letter of January, 1512–(1513) to the former gonfalonier, Machiavelli analyzed the power of Fortune over men:

> since men in the first place are shortsighted and in the second place cannot command their natures, it follows that Fortune varies and commands men and holds them under her yoke.[2]

Of the extent of Fortune's power, he gave the following estimate in the *Prince*:

> I judge it true that Fortune may be mistress of one half our actions but that even she leaves the other half, or almost, under our control.[3]

The cultivation of foresight and discretion and thereby the reduction of the power of Fortune in human affairs became the focus of his attention. In that same letter to Piero Soderini, he wrote of his desire to understand underlying factors which give rise to seemingly contradictory outcomes of political behavior.[4] His faith in the value of applying experience-derived intelligence to the direction of public affairs kindled his mind and motivated unflagging exertions throughout his life. He deeply felt, as he wrote in the *Discourses,*

> About courage in important matters no one without experience can promise himself certainty.[5]

Central in Machiavelli's search, the concept "prudent" has been significantly interpreted by Allen Gilbert:

> *For the word* prudent, *as for* wise . . . *there is no equivalent in the Italian; Machiavelli uses the verb* debbe. *If this be rendered* ought *or* must *the implication is* if he hopes to succeed as conqueror or prince. Dovere (debbe) *is used with the sense (recognized by dictionary-makers) of logical necessity. The full meaning is,* The *prince is wise; therefore he must act as Machiavelli says.*[6]

Machiavelli's thought has proved to be truly seminal in implications the significance and worth of which have become clearer only as subsequent conditions became congenial for their articulation and enunciation. Friedrich Meinecke has pointed out:

> For posterity, however, what he presented with this kind of generalizing and didactic intention, very often takes on all the fascination of a genuinely historical view which fuses together inseparably and intuitively both the individual and typical elements. Altogether then the remarkable power of attraction which Machiavelli exerts on thinking men today rests on the fact that his thoughts often contain some concealed driving-force which leads on beyond themselves, in such a way that he frequently offers more than he is directly intending to offer.[7]

A contemporary political scientist has written:

> Most of the political institutions of his [Machiavelli's] day have long since disappeared but he is very much with us.[8]

Much the same can be said of much of Machiavelli's writings as has been said of The Revelation of St. John:

> particular situations were treated so profoundly that principles emerge which are applicable in every situation.[9]

In seeking out "the effectual truth" for promoting the common good and with startling pungency presenting his judgments, Machiavelli left an imprint which, even after nearly five hundred years, remains indelible on political thought. Religious reformation, political revolutions, development of military and industrial technology and scientific method have all taken their toll from his work and yet a powerful leaven remains working toward more rational human governance. Even if, as Federico Chabod has pointed out,[10] when Machiavelli exalts the citizen militia it is from the thirteenth century free communes that he drew his confidence and when he prefers the people and republican institutions to princes and princedoms it is from pre-Imperial Rome that he drew his inspiration, in the face of the frustration personally experienced and the disintegration everywhere prevailing in secular and religious concepts and practices, Machiavelli continually projected new hope expressed not only in writing but also in personal endeavors which, in centuries to come, were to catch the attention of those shaping the forms and practices of the new political institutions and speculation. Such was Machiavelli's venture to apply his energy and skill for securing the liberties of his fellow citizens and the liberation from foreign exploitation that men in subsequent generations have invested him with their own aspirations toward securer freedom through membership in a more inclusive yet realistic political order. In his essay on Machiavelli, Lord Morley wrote:

> [Machiavelli] was assuredly a moralist, though of a peculiar sort and this is what makes him, as he has been called, a contemporary of every age and a citizen of all countries.[11]

Machiavelli emphasized change as a constant and, in this respect also regarding everything and all times as being the same,[12] sought for clues and trends which could be recognized as significant for human organization and direction.

What were those insights of his which have present significance for the emerging political order?

First, and most fundamentally, responsible action focused through personal dedication to the more inclusive yet practical service of public- or common-good was the experiential and personal genesis in Machiavelli of political science.

A vivid sensitivity to the more inclusive political relationship coming into being, made clear to him the necessity for a deeper commitment to the common good and a more disciplined release and engagement between human energies (physical, emotional, intellectual) and the natural resources. This perception worked in him with such energy that, acting on it as a fact endowed with a validity superior to the conventional behavior of his fellow men, he so affirmed the anticipated whole as present reality that he stands out as the exponent of force. Indeed, he was convinced that a negative element is inherent in human affairs:

hate is incurred as much by means of good deeds as of bad.[13]

He had his spokesman in *The Art of War,* Fabrizio Colonna, exclaim:

I do not believe you believe that in time of peace everyone has his place.[14]

Accordingly, there emerges his psychology of political organization, as set forth early in the *Discourses,* the kernel of which is

men never do anything good except by necessity[15] (above, p. 6).

Light on the irrelevance, in Machiavelli's view, of value judgments in political matters, therefore, perhaps appears in the attitude which he attributed to "one of the older and wiser" Lucchese patriots striving to strengthen the will for defense of his city under siege by the Florentines:

You must always have heard that when things are done through necessity, neither praise nor blame is or can be deserved.[16]

Machiavelli, during subsequent centuries, has been cited and employed as authority for the view that force is necessary and effective in statecraft and that the executive must have available means for *raison d'état* to act beyond the bounds of law and even in conflict with conventionally accepted law. It is of the nature of power that its truth expresses itself only in deeds. It is elemental personal force in effective change which confirms human beings in their conviction when living transcends in validity any convention or institution and displaces the old with the new. Understanding deeply the perception that "Liberty is the luxury of self-discipline," as formulated later by a wise Frenchman, Machiavelli conceived of it as prudent will in action. Regardless of changes of personal fortune, he held fast to and expressed repeatedly the conviction that only through recognition of, discipline of, and reliance upon one's own forces can security be achieved and established (above, pp. 121–127). Whatever one has at hand are his best resources with which his best can be accomplished and one should never give up the endeavor to make the best of them.[17] To observe and to make understandable "necessity" which goes beyond and makes use of "good" and "not good" for the sake of holding and using power,[18] is the objective of

Machiavelli's study and writing. The capacity for effective will in the arena of responsible action is the condition for verification in being alive, and, as the very source of understanding and right valuation, it cannot be subject to or conditioned by preconceived claimants to knowledge or ethics.

Other elements which he deemed essential in behavior characteristic of effective state-building, Machiavelli set forth clearly. That pre-eminent among these is the ability to use timely force, the bringing together of his relevant reflections makes clear.

> when they [innovators] depend on their own resources and are strong enough to compel, then they are seldom in danger. This is the reason why all armed prophets win, and unarmed ones fall. Because, in addition to what has been said, the people are by nature variable; to convince them of a thing is easy; to hold them to that conviction is hard. Therefore a prophet must be ready, when they no longer believe, to make them believe by force;[19]

> When a man of that sort [a very strong man, devoted to his father and his native city and very respectful to his superiors], comes to commanding rank, he reckons on finding all men like himself, and his strong spirit makes him command strong things; that same spirit, after they are commanded, expects them to be carried out. It is a true rule that when you give harsh orders, you must be harsh in having them carried out; otherwise your expectation will be deceived. This teaches that if you expect to be obeyed, you must know how to command. Men who know that compare their capacities with those of the men who are to obey. When they see that such capacities correspond, then they give commands; when they see lack of that correspondence, they refrain from it. Therefore a prudent man was wont to say that if a state is to be held with force, he who uses force must correspond in strength with him who is subject to it. When such correspondence exists, we can believe that such use of force can continue; but when he who is subject to force is stronger than he who is using force, we must fear that any day such use of force will end . . . a man who commands hard things must be hard, and he who is hard and commands hard things cannot let them be carried out with gentleness. He who lacks this hardness of spirit should guard himself from giving extraordinary orders, and in ordinary ones he can use kindness; for ordinary punishments are not charged to the prince but to the laws and the regulations.[20]

> Force and necessity . . . not writings and obligations, make princes keep their agreements;[21]

> A wise prince, then, has no other object and no other interest and takes as his profession nothing else than war and its laws and disciplines; that is the only profession fitting one who commands, and it is of such effec-

tiveness that it not merely maintains in their rank men who are born princes but many times enables men born in a private station to rise to princely stations;[22]

But they [arms and force] ought to be reserved for the last place, where and when other methods do not suffice.[23]

Effective will requires constant attention directed to the magnetizing and energizing aim:

a wise prince takes care to devise methods that force his citizens, always and in every sort of weather, to need the government and himself; and always they will be loyal.[24]

Reforming the government of a people who had become "corrupt" (i.e., deficient in dedication to the common good), requires drastic measures.[25]

Although Machiavelli's proposal for remodeling the government of Florence indicated that he considered necessary for the city a princely or "monarchical" rule during the lives of Pope Leo X and Cardinal Giulio de'Medici, but that they so manage the government that the people could thereafter receive and maintain true republican institutions, he considered the corruption throughout Italy to have penetrated so deep that the leadership of a kingly nature would be essential for its liberation.[26] Meinecke has written:

Amid all the rottenness of the public spirit, which he saw around him, Machiavelli never lost his reforming zeal. The idea of the regeneration of a fallen people was the fundamental thought that moved him; and to carry out this idea, he did not recoil even from the most frightful methods, which were put at his disposal by a demoralized age. On the one hand, he was in this respect entirely a product of his time, without any moral feeling in the choice of his methods; but on the other hand, as regards his final aims, he was a moralist in the highest sense of the word . . . the vigorous radicalism of Machiavelli . . . in spite of all the wickedness of his methods, had nevertheless concealed a strong power of belief.[27]

The use of force he considered essential for a leader not only when founding or restoring a kingdom or a republic but also continually available as a necessary instrument in its maintenance (above, pp. 80–81).[28] Felix Gilbert has referred to

Machiavelli's stress on power and on the struggle for greater power as the one and only significant factor in politics.[29]

Dominance or submission seemed to Machiavelli the only alternatives available to men. "Words to be Spoken on the Law for Appropriating Money" provides a clear exposition of his position:

> All the cities that ever at any time have been ruled by an absolute prince, by aristocrats or by the people as is this one [Florence], have had for their protection force combined with prudence, because the latter is not enough alone, and the first either does not produce things or, when they are produced, does not maintain them. Force and prudence, then, are the might of all governments that ever have been or will be in the world . . . without force cities are not preserved but come to an end. That end is either destruction or servitude . . . every city, every state ought to consider as enemies all those who can hope to take possession of her territory and against whom she cannot defend herself . . . men cannot be, and ought not to be, faithful servants of that master by whom they cannot be either defended or punished . . . You cannot call them your subjects, but rather those of the first who attacks them . . . these princes will be your friends when they cannot attack you; and again I say it to you, because among private men laws, writings and agreements make them keep their word; but among princes, nothing but arms make them keep it.[30]

Observant courage is indispensable especially for effective public life. That which Machiavelli wrote with respect to the command of armies, in view of the central role in government which he gave to war, may be considered to have more general application:

> Indeed though all branches of knowledge require experience if they are to be perfectly understood, this one [the command of armies] demands experience to the utmost.[31]

Sydney Anglo has convincingly demonstrated that in breaking away from the traditional perspective of writers on government, Machiavelli

> was not alone in asserting the need for practicality in political thinking, and in his rejection of purely imaginary projections. Realism was in the air: words like *reason* and *necessity* dominated the day-to-day administration of the Italian city states. Systematic thinkers and historians, too, apart from Machiavelli, assumed the priority of *ad hoc* solutions to political problems, over general rules of universal applicability from which one was supposed to deduce justification for political action.[32]

Important and effective as Machiavelli considered force to be (above, pp.

77–81), its power he held to be contingent upon its continued, undiminished maintenance:

> alliances between rulers are maintained with arms, and those alone are what keep them in force;[33]

> it is not disgraceful not to keep promises that you are forced to make. Forced promises in public matters, when the force is removed, will always be broken, without disgrace for him who breaks them.[34]

Fraud, however, appeared to Machiavelli more generally useful in state-building and -maintenance:

> it is plain how much folly and how little prudence there is in asking a thing and saying first: I wish to do such an evil with it. One should not show one's mind but try to get one's wish just the same, because it is enough to ask a man for his weapons without saying: I wish to kill you with them. For when you have the weapons in your hands you can satisfy your desire;[35]

> I believe it very true that rarely or never do men of humble fortune come to high rank without force and without fraud . . . Nor do I believe that force alone will ever be enough, but fraud alone certainly will be enough . . . it [fraud] has always been necessary for those to use who from little beginnings wish to climb to high places—something which is the less to be censured the more it is concealed.[36]

In human nature he considered he found fertile ground for fraud to flourish. The prevalence of the simple-minded and those hard pressed by necessities, together with those impelled by their ill-considered hopes provide a would-be deceiver with a constant abundance of people ready, if not eager, to see in his proposals the promise of fulfilment of their desires:

> the generality of men feed themselves as much on what seems to be as on what is; still more, many times they are moved more by the things that seem than by the things that are;[37]

> they [men] do not know how to put limits to their hopes. And when they rely on these and do not make an estimate of themselves, they fall;[38]

> experience in our time shows that those princes have done great things who have valued their promises little, and who have understood how to addle the brains of men with trickery; and in the end they have vanquished those who have stood upon their honesty.
> You need to know, then, that there are two ways of fighting: one according to the laws, the other with force. The first is suited to man, the second to

the animals; but because the first is often not sufficient, a prince must resort to the second. Therefore he needs to know well how to put to use the traits of animal and of man . . . for one without the other does not secure him permanence.

Since, then, a prince is necessitated to play the animal well, he chooses among the beasts the fox and the lion, because the lion does not protect himself from traps; the fox does not protect himself from the wolves. Those who rely on the lion alone are not perceptive. By no means can a prudent ruler keep his word—and he does not—when to keep it works against himself and when the reasons that made him promise are annulled. If all men were good, this maxim would not be good, but because they are bad and do not keep their promises to you, you likewise do not have to keep yours to them. Never has a shrewd prince lacked justifying reasons to make his promise-breaking appear honorable. Of this I can give countless modern examples, showing how many treaties of peace and how many promises have been made null and empty through the dishonesty of princes. The one who knows best how to play the fox comes out best, but he must understand well how to disguise the animal's nature and must be a great simulator and dissimulator. So simple-minded are men and so controlled by immediate necessities that a prince who deceives always finds men who let themselves be deceived . . . in general men judge more with their eyes than with their hands, since everybody can see but few can perceive. Everybody sees what you appear to be; few perceive what you are, and those few dare not contradict the belief of the many, who have the majesty of the government to support them. As to the actions of all men and especially those of princes, against whom charge cannot be brought in court, everybody looks at their result. So if a prince succeeds in conquering and holding his state, his means are always judged honorable and everywhere praised, because the mob is always fascinated by appearances and by the outcome of an affair; and in the world the mob is everything; the few find no room there when the many crowd together.[39]

However, deceit and fraud receive from Machiavelli no indiscriminate approval. In "Tercets on Ambition," Deceit is listed along with Envy, Sloth, Hatred, Cruelty and Pride as

companions which with their pestilence . . . fill the world;[40]

and in "Tercets on Fortune,"

Usury and Fraud enjoy themselves with their crew, powerful and rich.[41]

In Book Five of *The History of Florence,* he wrote:

And if in describing the things that happened in this corrupt world, I do not tell of the bravery of soldiers or the efficiency of generals or the love of citizens for their country, I do show with what deceptions, with what tricks and schemes, the princes, the soldiers, the heads of the republics, in order to keep that reputation which they did not deserve, carried on their affairs.[42]

Earlier, he had represented the spokesman for a group of patriotic citizens as having addressed the Signoria in 1372 as follows:

And because religion and the fear of God have been extinguished in all men, an oath and a pledge are valuable as far as they are profitable, for men employ them not with the purpose of observing them, but to use them as a means for deceiving more easily. And the more easily and securely the deception succeeds, the more glory and honor it gains. Hence pernicious men are praised for their ingenuity, and good men are blamed as foolish.[43]

For rousing "the poorest of the people" to insurrection in 1378, to "one of the most fiery and of greatest experience"[44] were given the words:

If you will observe the way in which men act, you will see that all those who attain great riches and great power have attained them by means of either force or fraud; those things, then, that they have snatched with trickery or with violence, in order to conceal the ugliness of their acquisition, under the false title of profit they make honorable . . . none come out of servitude except the unfaithful and the bold, and out of poverty except the rapacious and fraudulent. God and Nature have put all men's fortunes in their midst, and these fortunes are more open to stealing than to labor, and to bad rather than good arts. From this it comes that men devour one another; and they who are weakest always come off worst.[45]

In describing Count Francesco Sforza's methods in building up his power, Machiavelli wrote:

he was not restrained by the fear or the shame of breaking his word, because great men call it shame to lose, not to gain by trickery.[46]

The value judgment which he applied with respect to deception and fraud, Machiavelli set forth clearly in the *Discourses*:

Although to use fraud in all one's actions is detestable, nevertheless in carrying on war it is praiseworthy and brings fame; he who conquers the enemy by fraud is praised as much as he who conquers them by force. This appears from the judgment given on it by those who write the lives of great men . . . I do not believe that fraud deserves fame when it makes you break promises you have given and pacts you have made, because such fraud, though it sometimes wins for you position and kingly power, as was explained above [*Discourses*, 2:13; the *Prince*, chap. 8], will never give you glory. I am speaking of fraud used against an enemy who does not trust you, such as appears especially in the conduct of war.[47]

Besides promotion of the public good (above, p. 235) and deeds which through force (above, pp. 237–240) or fraud (above, pp. 240–243) effect change, a broader and deeper involvement of the inhabitants of the land characterized the emerging political order. Men with a potential for shared feeling for and commitment to their native land were, in Machiavelli's estimation, a prime requisite for an effective state. Something of almost an organic relation between a people and their land, although not explicitly so stated yet approximated in his "Discorso . . . Lingua . . . Florentine,"[48] had fundamental significance in Machiavelli's perspective. Successful migrations of peoples, he noted, are followed by the establishment of their own laws and institutions and the fixing of a national character.[49] People of the country, unlike those of cities, have not been tainted by "corruption"[50] and are potentially receptive to the discipline requisite for state formation.[51] In the example of Moses, Machiavelli found Biblical sanction for the use of force in the imposition of the essential discipline and in the acquisition and defense of the country claimed as the rightful homeland.[52]

In the ancient world ever since the third century B.C. with the Cynics, the Stoics and the Epicureans, provincial attachment had been discredited in favor of cosmopolitanism. In the Empire of Augustus and afterwards, the prized membership was that of being a Roman citizen. Begun under the Roman republic and continued during the Empire, military service was rewarded with grants of land on the frontiers of conquest. Following the fall of the Empire, through feudalism came a new affirmation of the relation to the land which grew stronger as the rising monarchies found allies in the workers of the land for breaking the power of the nobles. Although the Christian religion had arisen out of the land-prizing Jewish culture's protest against the de-nationalizing challenge of Rome, traditionally the members of the Christian communities considered themselves pilgrims and aliens in this world. But by the sixteenth century, the overwhelmingly agricultural peoples of Europe were deeply rooted in the good earth as their homelands and it was out of this sense that Machiavelli affirmed the religious sanction for patriotism and thus reaffirmed the ancient Jewish claim of a homeland in the name of religion. In Machiavelli's eyes, the saving grace of the Christian religion seems to have been

it allows the betterment and the defense of our country . . . it intends that we love and honor her and prepare ourselves to be such that we can defend her.[53]

Conquest by foreigners, he held, entailed the destruction of the indigenous *virtù*.[54] It was, therefore, in the authentic spirit of the ancient Jewish Zealots that Machiavelli looked upon the foreign powers and their agents in Italy as "barbarians" to extirpate whom was a divinely-sanctioned mission.[55] In his letter of 17 May 1526 to Guicciardini he referred to them in extreme terms:

> Free Italy from long anxiety; root out these frightful beasts which beyond the appearance and the voice have nothing human.[56]

"Italy?" What realistic expectation did the name "Italy" stir in Machiavelli when he spoke of it? Despite the closing chapter of the *Prince* with its passionate appeal for a leader who would dedicate himself to uniting Italy[57] and the letter *de profundis* to Guicciardini,[58] in his calmer moments he could write Vettori:

> As to this union of the Italians, you make me laugh, first, because there will never be union here to do anything good. Even though the leaders should unite, they are not sufficient, because there are no armies here worth a farthing except the Spanish, who, because they are few, are not enough. Second, because the tails are not united with the heads. The people of this generation will compete in submitting to the Swiss before they will move a step to use any opportunity that arises;[59]

> Do not trust at all in those armies which you say will one day produce some fruit in Italy, because that is impossible. First, with respect to them, there would be many leaders and those disunited, and I cannot see that a leader can be found who will keep them united. Second, with respect to the Swiss. For you need to understand this: the best armies are those of armed peoples; and they cannot be restricted except by armies similar to themselves . . . So do not, therefore, rely on Italian armies, if they are not either uniform like Swiss armies, or, being mixed, if they do not form one body like theirs.[60]

Some have held that "Italy" signified to Machiavelli nothing less than the whole country united.[61] In *The Art of War,* Machiavelli wrote:

> And I assert to you that, of those who today have states in Italy, he, rather than any one else, will be lord of this country who first sets out on this road [of instituting and employing a citizen army][62]

and Machiavelli then cited the example of Philip of Macedonia who went on to conquer all of Greece and lay the foundation for his son, Alexander, to make "himself the ruler of the world."

When, however, the unification of Italy and the progress of freedom became identified in Machiavelli's mind with dedication to the dominance of Florence and its ruling family, the scientist's objectivity of perspective and of truth-seeking detachment loses validity in the endeavor to impose on Pisa, Milan, Rome, Naples, Venice, a fiction which they would resist as intolerable. Of Machiavelli's position, Arnoldo Mondadori has interpreted Chabod's conclusion as follows:

> La sua analisi delimita l'ideale italico del Machiavelli a contenuti lontani dalle interpretazioni del Risorgimento. Il Machiavelli vedeva uno stato regionale, non nazionale, sufficientemente forte per catalizzare i principati minori e respingere lo straniero, troppo debole (purtroppo) per svolgere un'azione interna egemonica. La realizzazione di simile stato gli appariva comunque subordinata a leggi genetiche valide universalmente, e da lui, primo, messe in luce.[63]

> His analysis defines the Italian ideal of Machiavelli as in content far removed from the interpretation by the Risorgimento. Machiavelli envisioned a regional state, not national, sufficiently strong to serve as a catalyst for the lesser powers and to repulse the foreigner, but too weak (by far) to develop internally the requisite leadership action. The realization of such a state appeared, however, as subject to genetic laws universally valid and by him first brought to light.

Regarding the scope of Machiavelli's patriotism, Ridolfi has observed:

> Beyond the love for his own small city state and its liberties, which has been recognized in him since his own times, there is no one today who does not see in him more clearly than in any other Italian of his age the glimmerings of a loyalty to a wider nation.[64]

Throughout *The Art of War* and the *Discourses,* Machiavelli developed the theme of the citizen as soldier. He affirmed that love of one's country is implanted by nature[65] and that it is ineradicable by any tyrant.[66] Native-born inhabitants are potentially dedicated defenders of their homeland[67] and are amenable to the requisite training and discipline.[68] Among men born and raised together there generates the *esprit de corps* of confident, victorious armies.[69]

Warfare, Machiavelli perceived as effective public expression in realizing the adequate way of operation. Warfare, according to him, is properly a monopoly belonging to public authority.[70] The purpose, or aim, in going to war, he stated clearly. In both the *Prince*[71] and the *Discourses*[72] he quoted from Livy[73] with slight variations:

> A war is just for those to whom it is necessary, and arms are sacred to those who save in arms have no hope.

And in *The History of Florence,* without specific reference to Livy, he represented the leader of the Florentine exiles, in soliciting the assistance of the Duke of Milan, as saying:

> Only those wars are just that are necessary; and arms are holy when there is no hope apart from them.[74]

His most detailed statement of war aims appears in the *History*.[75]

To be successful in war, one must wage it with a citizen militia.[76] For a war to be effective, it must be big, swift, short and decisive.[77] The victor must be able to exact the full cost from the defeated enemy and enrich the public treasury;[78] keep the treasury rich, the individual poor.[79] As a consequence of a successful war, the citizens are to be able, and will desire, to return to their farms, crafts and professions to carry forward their constructive activities on a higher level because of their enhanced commonwealth.[80] A war which results in higher taxes (overt, or hidden as inflation) for the citizens is one which has missed its aim. When, following the war of 1422–1427, the movement for tax reform raised the prospect of a system under which the incidence of taxes would be proportionate to capacity to pay and, as reported in the *History*

> that there be a review of times past, in order to learn how far . . . the powerful had fallen short in payments; they [proponents of reform] intended that the rich should be made to pay enough to equalize them with those who, in order to pay more than was right, had sold their possessions. This demand, more than the *catasto*, terrified the rich.[81]

Moreover, wars which lead to prolongation of emergency powers[82] and to resort to auxiliary, mercenary and/or professional soldiers disrupt that essential unity between civil and military life (which he prized)[83] so that the citizens cease to understand and willingly to generate the discipline which the continued availability of the public services they demand requires.[84] As a specialized military element develops in the population, there grows a special interest committed to perpetuating warfare, to strengthening a faction enriched thereby, and to increasing the number of people for whom peace has no place and who are ever more available for and dependent upon the military leaders for their livelihood with the result that there develop armed forces with private rather than public loyalties.[85]

Machiavelli held the mistaken illusion that republican Rome had been able to shift the costs of its wars from itself to those whom it conquered.[86] He did not relate the deepening social crisis to the cumulating domestic costs but attributed to ambitious leaders and the imperial guard the growing corruption and drift toward professional armies.[87] He did not sufficiently consistently charge the war policy with the exhaustion of the native manpower and the resort to recruiting alien peoples for the army and then rewarding them with landed estates on the frontiers.[88] He recognized that the Roman conquest of other cultures destroyed the human talents and the *virtù* that had been generated in them,[89] that the Empire itself fell prey to pride, corruption and weakness[90] and that never had subsequent recovery taken place.[91] He found himself tempted to lay the blame for this failure upon "false interpretations" of "our religion;"[92] but, upon reflection, checking himself, he granted it to be the result of the imperial course of military action.[93]

Machiavelli did not establish the relationship between the cultural aggression of Rome at its height and the cultural affirmation of the Jewish legal and prophetic tradition into a new galvanization of personality into a reorientation of aim through the examples and teaching of Jesus, Peter, Paul and John so that, driven by apocalyptic expectations, there became manifest a way of living and of human interrelationships with which the institutions and attitudes upon which Rome operated were unable to cope and which brought the disintegration of the previously established structures of authority.

Driven from official service and required to rely upon words as his means for action, Machiavelli sensed the validity of the saying

Good words must always face the bad facts or they become false and sentimental.[94]

Despite his emphasis on critical reason and his striving for the perception and expression of "the effectual truth," he concluded that truth itself bows before and serves power.[95] In order to win acceptability for force, the transformation of poetic myth into fiction introduced into reality as authoritatively sanctioned and force-supported "fact," found many precedents in Livy's *History* and, indeed, was the special function which Machiavelli described as that of religion during the period of republican Rome. Faith was a quality to be especially cultivated in the people.[96] Although officials of the religious institutions should not adapt their "revelations" to the purpose of the powerful—at least not in ways detectable by the people—the authorities themselves, in emergencies, were recorded as successfully managing the oracles and the auspices so as to secure evident sanction for their deeds or intentions.[97] The state, conceived as constructed and maintained for the "common good," having a purpose which outweighs private scruples,[98] as presented by Machiavelli, transcends the value of one's individual soul spent in its service.[99] In order to achieve unity adequate to promote human dignity and to make it secure, resort to pious frauds and cruel measures, according to Machiavelli, are necessary and therefore justified. As a means by which to bring together a divided people, he held that a foreign war could be rightly undertaken: thus, in his "Song of the Blessed Spirits," while at the same time showing the depths of his compassionate response to human misery and suffering which had been inflicted by the violent policies of Julius II, he urged on the new pope, Leo X, the launching of a crusade against the Turks as a way for healing for self-inflicted wounds of Christendom.[100]

For the "deliverance" and "redemption" of Italy, he saw the need for "a kingly hand."[101] In darkest colors he portrayed the condition of Italy.[102] He saw Italy divided[103] and without any prospect of union.[104] He saw the leaders and armies in Italy unreliable.[105]

For the remedy, already in the "First Decennale" Machiavelli proclaimed:

> the voyage would be easy and short if you would reopen the temple of Mars;[106]

in "Tercets on Ambition,"

> And when someone blames Nature if in Italy, so much afflicted and worn, men are not born so vigorous and hardy, I say that this does not excuse and justify our lack of worth, for discipline can make up where Nature is lacking;[107]

and in *The Art of War,*

> [in Italy] it has been necessary to turn to discipline, which is of such great power that it has enabled the few to overcome the spirit and the natural persistence of the many;[108]

> And do not ever believe that reputation will come to Italian arms except through the means I have shown and by the work of those who have great states in Italy, because this form can be impressed on simple men, rough and native, not on the malicious, the badly governed, and the foreign.[109]

In enunciating and embodying the fusion of disciplined energy (both civilian and military), Machiavelli lived forth the life of the new Italian and manifested the deeper and more inclusive loyalty requisite for the nation state, and even beyond.

When the user of words, himself, takes his words as effective power, does a confusing blindness becloud him and transform his influence from that of intelligence and reason lighting the way of creation to that of fiction and deception, kindling the violence of destruction? Is this the form which, to the user of words, that temptation takes which, for generals, Machiavelli warned against when he wrote:

> often the desire for victory so blinds one's perceptions that they see nothing except what appears to their advantage?[110]

248

Some examples of the length to which the temptation can lead are offered by Tommasini:

l'Orrafi, abate olivetano e teologo del principe Rinaldo cardinal d'Este, il quale ebbe coraggio di scrivere: "Chi non si ingannare non sa essere uomo. Coll'arte si perfeziona la natura, coll'inganno l'uomo. L'inganno è in terra come Mercurio in cielo. Tutti, o in bene o in male, ingannano; ma in un principe è più necessario ciò che in altri è utile;"[111]

Oraffi, Olivetan abbot and theologian of the prince Rinaldo, Cardinal d'Este, had the temerity to write: 'Who does not know how to deceive does not know how to be a man. With art, nature is perfected; with deception, men. Deception is on earth as Mercury is in the heavens. All, whether in good or evil, deceive; but in a prince it is far more necessary than it is useful in others;'

also, a satirical epigram from the humanist writing *Epistolae obscurorum virorum:*

quod non est mendacium quando aliquis dicit aliquid pro fide catholica.[112]

that is not a lie when someone says something on behalf of the catholic faith.

Of Machiavelli, in this regard, Tommasini adjudged:

Ma il Machiavelli era tutt'altro qui che un freddo calcolatore; era un patriota caldissimo, che s'illudeva e sperava d'illudere. Il sentimento patrio non incomincia a vivere che d'illusioni.[113]

But Machiavelli was here something entirely other than a cold calculator; he was a very warm patriot who beguiled himself and hoped to beguile. The patriotic sentiment does not commence to live except on illusions.

In the lightest vein, Machiavelli himself treated the subject in the letter in which he suggested to Guicciardini that they engage in a farce of prestige at the expense of the monks of Carpi:

Your Lordship knows that these friars say that when one is confirmed in grace, the Devil has no more power to tempt him. So I have no more fear that these friars will make me a hypocrite, because I believe I am very well confirmed. As to the lies of the Carpigiani, I should like a contest in that matter with all of them, because quite a while ago I trained myself in such a way that I do not need Francesco Martelli for a servant, because for a long time I have not said what I believed, nor do I ever believe what

I say, and if indeed sometimes I do happen to tell the truth, I hide it among so many lies that it is hard to find.[114]

The borderline at which confidence in the adequacy and effectiveness of available evidence gives way to appeal to faith and manipulation of others' trust, Machiavelli well expressed in his discussion, in the *Discourses,* of the use of religion by Numa as a means for winning the approval of the people of Rome for his new regulations.[115]

Symbolically, in his "Life of Castruccio Castracani," he represented Castruccio as having outgrown and put aside interest in becoming a priest and enthusiastically having entered upon training for the profession of a soldier.[116]

Occasionally, Machiavelli expressed doubts that such a human being as his wise man can be expected to appear.[117] Nevertheless, to bring order out of chaotic violence, to fix attention upon a transcendent common- or public-good, to attract support of others whom he considered did not see as clearly or as deeply or as far as he did, to achieve and maintain a unity through which the members may feel an enhanced dignity, to provide courage and confidence for engaging in a course of action dispelling oppressive fear with a collective mission—so necessary was the concept of the heroic leader for Machiavelli's predilection, that he invested his treatment of selected figures in history and a series of contemporaries with the qualities of his desired redeemer for his city, region (Tuscany), country (Italy). Significantly, then, he expressed his confidence in the great effectiveness of fraud.[118]

Does, then, Machiavelli, the detached observer seeking the effective truth of the matter[119] and trying

always to keep my judgment firm, especially in these things, and not let it be corrupted by a vain contest, as do many others,[120]

give way before Machiavelli, the patriot advocating force, fraud and fiction for the promotion of the special interest of his city's or country's cause; or herein did Machiavelli manifest himself as poet[121] or prophet?[122]

In their interrelations with each other and their environment, people in their sense of need reach out and strike out for help and, through fear-instilling and hope-supporting responses, some draw power to themselves from others who come to expect assistance in meeting their needs. While this expectation is being served, or at least nourished, the reciprocity continues. Force, fraud, laws and simple-mindedness constitute this reciprocity, in Machiavelli's judgment, although without mutually equivalent power.[123] Moreover, in the view of Machiavelli, unless the founder or renewer of control prove able to transform his violently seized power into a lawful one voluntarily supported by those over whom he had been exercising rule, he would have failed to leave the state established.[124]

250

To be secure, a state requires, in Machiavelli's judgment, both "good arms" and "good laws."[125] Since he was convinced that arms to be "good" had to be one's own,[126] i.e., a citizen army, there was implicit the assumption of a widespread sense of civic responsibility which ensured, in his view, that when there are good armies, there must be good laws.[127] Machiavelli expressed his perspective most succinctly in his dedication of *The Art of War*.[128] His confidence lay in his belief in the possibility that a public-spirited leader would be able to convert his firm hand (even though it be a fist) or control sanctioned through religion into structures guided by maxims of wisdom and rules of law which would stir in the citizens with reverential sensibilities and disciplined bodies a recognition of their own will and a mutual endeavor in carrying forward government in freedom. Such leadership, Machiavelli perceived, required men ready to subordinate their own personalities[129] to a leader wholly dedicated to his country[130] and together with him to let their energies implement the wider and deeper emerging purpose of making liberty more secure.[131]

Machiavelli manifested personal responsibility to himself and his conception of the common good in his present moment. Tommasini has observed:

> di rado incontra uno scrittore che offra, come lui, tanta costanza di sistema in ogni sua manifestazione filosofica e letteraria; e pochi come lui volsero ogni sussidio d'arte a restauro del'educazione civile.[132]

> rarely does one encounter a writer who offers, as does he, such great constancy of system in all of his manifestations—philosophic and literary; and few as he turn every resource of art to the restoration of civil education.

As a deeply loyal and responsibly experienced citizen of the city comparable only with Athens in its infatuation with its liberty, he recognized that the continued survival of a free republic requires continual and permanent creativity.[133] Personally, he tried to do his part in contributing to this creative service through developing and exercising to their highest capacity his powers of observation, reflection and reporting.[134]

Leo Strauss has called attention to levels of validity which Machiavelli accorded his data.[135] The highest validity, he gave to that which was subject to his own perception and that of his contemporaries through personal experience.[136] He gave weight to belief in the *vera memoria* ("trustworthy records")[137] of historians as they recorded events back to a certain date; and less credence to *memorie delle antiche istorie* ("records of ancient history").[138] Occasionally a general distrust of historians brusts forth.[139]

In two dispatches written while on the legation to Duke Valentino, Machiavelli gave clues as to his methods:

> Your Lordships . . . should remember that I am dealing with a prince who

manages things for himself; and if one is not going to write phantasies and dreams, one must verify things, and verifying them takes time; and I am trying to spend it and not to throw it away;[140]

It is well to learn everything and then separate them according to their effects.[141]

to his friend Vettori, he wrote, referring to the King of Spain:

When I see a man making a mistake, I suppose he will make a thousand of them; and I do not believe that under this decision he has now made there is anything else than what is seen, because I don't drink the label on the bottle, [Ed. Note: Literally, I do not drink districts, that is, I am not so impressed by the name of the region where a wine is produced that I forget to observe its quality.] and in these matters I do not intend that any authority should move me without reason. Hence I hold to the conclusion that Spain may have made a mistake and understood badly and concluded worse.[142]

In a similar vein,

I do not know what Aristotle says about states made up of detached pieces, but I do consider what reasonably can be, what is, and what has been.[143]

Machiavelli made a practice of attempting to examine human behavior in its totality. An example is the eloquent speech he gave to a leader of the mass of the Florentine poor in 1378.[144] In it, despite Machiavelli's expressed disapproval of doctrinaire equality,[145] he set forth their grievances and objectives in the most plausible manner, denigrated values which he customarily affirmed, and exalted those which, elsewhere, he identified with corruption.

His own perspective and purpose in the interpretations composing the *History*, he confided to Guicciardini, as already noted (above, pp. 122, 154, 198):

I shall keep on taking counsel with myself and shall try to act in such a way that, since I tell the truth, nobody will be able to complain.[146]

That present exercise of power conditions the degree of validity of perspective, was an insight which kept Machiavelli mindful of limitations inherent in the competence of the observer and adviser with respect to the decision-making authority. His "Advice to Raffaello Girolami when he went as Ambassador to the Emperor" described Machiavelli's own methods, when on missions abroad, of gathering, weighing and reporting information to his official superiors.[147] Repeatedly, in his official dispatches, he deferred his depiction and interpretation of situations to the judgment to be exercised by those in authority; thus:

> I know it is a presumption to make a judgment of events, and especially of those which change every hour; nonetheless it appears to me never to err in writing to Your Lordships what opinions the wise men have of events here, so that you can with the usual prudence always make a better judgment. [148]

Especially in letters from his mission to Cesare Borgia, which occurred early in his career, he evidenced a need to affirm his recognition of the superior quality of the judgment available to those in executive authority:

> Now Your Lordships, knowing what is said here, can decide about it best, as much more prudent and of greater experience. I think it good to write you all I hear. [149]

In the last analysis, it is only the power-exerciser who can judge the truth of the matter and is responsible for its official interpretation. [150]

A natural consequence of the view that the power-holding, decision-making authority is the center of valid perspective is that the adviser should always heed the limitations of his position and not trespass upon the role of one with superior authority by immoderate advocacy of a recommendation. Out of ripe experience Machiavelli wrote

> of those dangers which citizens, or a prince's advisers, undergo in taking the lead in a serious and important decision, when all the advice on the matter will be charged to them. Such advising is dangerous because, since men judge things by their results, all the evil produced by an undertaking is charged to the man who advised it; if good results, he is indeed commended; but by a great deal the reward does not weigh as much as the harm . . . It is, then, something very certain that those who advise a republic and those who advise a prince are put in the following straits: if they do not, without reservation, advise things that they believe useful, either for the city or for the prince, they fail in their duty; if they do advise them, they put themselves in danger of life and position, since all men blindly judge good and bad advice by its outcome. After considering how they can avoid both this reproach and this danger, I see no other way than for an adviser to be moderate and not to seize upon any of the plans brought forward as his own undertaking, and to speak his opinion without passion, and without passion modestly to defend it, so that the city or the prince who follows it does so voluntarily, and does not seem to enter upon it as pushed by your urgency. When you act thus, it is not reasonable that a prince or a people should wish you ill because of your advice, since they have adopted it without opposing the wishes of many other advisers. The

danger arises whenever many oppose you, for if your plan results badly, they unite to ruin you. And if by such moderation you miss the glory gained by being alone against many in urging something that results happily, your course still has two advantages. One is that it lacks danger. The other is that if you advise a thing modestly, and through opposition your advice is not taken, yet from other people's advice some calamity results, you obtain the utmost glory. And though you cannot enjoy glory resulting from the distress either of your city or your prince, nevertheless it has some value for you.[151]

Hazardous as are the risks run by advisers to the powerful, high are the rewards to be gained. As Machiavelli indicated to Rafaello Girolami:

any difficult business, if one has the ear of the prince, becomes easy.[152]

Truth can be known only through sufficient understanding of events for their mastery and in its deepest meaning can be sought in the experience of responsible civic participation in the self-governing community. The ancient Greek philosopher Heraclitus observed:

Among those who sleep, each one lives in his own world; only those who are awake have a world in common.[153]

Inherently, the search into truth has to be social in process—a fact which Machiavelli understood clearly. Thus, he wrote to Soderini:

. . . I should like to know. So in order to get your opinion I shall be so presuming as to give mine;[154]

and to Girolami:

A man who wants others to tell him what they know must tell them what he knows, because the best means for getting information is to give it . . . because men who see that they can get something are eager to tell him what they know.[155]

In his essay entitled "The Prince and the State," J. H. Plumb has written:

Sensitive, thoughtful men [of the Renaissance] realized that this was a world like to none other . . . The key to their problems they knew to be rooted in the lives and actions of men, not in universal mysteries or the attributes of God. Consequently, there is an astonishing freshness about the historians and the political philosophers of the Renaissance, and, as with the painters and sculptors, the greatest by far were the Florentines, and the greatest of the Florentines was Niccolo Machiavelli, whose speculations about the nature of men's political actions were as remote from the thinkers of the Middle Ages as Leonardo da Vinci's drawings are from the illuminations of the missals;[156]

and in "The Dawn of the Renaissance,"

Some of the most original minds . . . particularly Machiavelli and Leonardo da Vinci, sought truth not in argument but in observation. Machiavelli brooded on men and events, on the effects of political action and on the consequences of chance . . . the men of the Renaissance, by the range of their inquiries, by the freshness of their skepticism, and by the sharpness of their observation, gave impetus to, and helped to acquire intellectual acceptance for, the search for truth on earth instead of in heaven.[157]

Dante's love of his native city had led him in exile to the harmonies of mediaeval Heaven: Machiavelli's sensitized him to intimations of truth to be perceived in dynamic human relations—to the effectual truth, implicit in deeds of prudent will by men manifesting the ability to understand how to shape their natures and their times so that they master the turns of Fortune.

Unsparingly, Machiavelli gave to his city of his physical strength, his devotion, his intelligence and creative initiative since he recognized in his native city the medium through which there was hope for freedom and enlightenment not only in civic but, indeed, in very personal terms.[158] For the survival of freedom in the framework of the city, he had lived through experience, both in and out of official participation in government, to see that not concentration of power for life in the hands of Piero Soderini—faithful to the laws and dedicated to the freedom of the citizens[159]—nor his own unstinting services of mind, heart, physical strength, diplomatic skill and patriotic fervor in developing a citizen militia and cavalry, sufficed. Under the popes was bursting forth in Italy that impulse to larger political allegiances which had already prevailed in England, France, Spain and which Machiavelli himself was seeking to utilize by way of the Florentine Medicean popes and princes. As student of records of human behavior, as responsible public official—be it as secretary in the ministry at home or abroad; be it as innovator, organizer and director of the militia to meet the perceived needs of the city more adequately than by the traditional means of foreign mercenaries; be it as poet to gain public understanding and brace its nerve for coping with the impending dangers and to win official support for the new direction which he perceived as essential; be it as technical analyst seeking to counsel either those in power or young men who might be fired to promote more worthy goals for the city; be it through long preparation as dramatist to give lurid and brilliant portrayal of the corrosive practices eroding the institutions, private and religious; be it as chronicler and diagnostician-historian of his city; be it as close and sharp observer and piquant articulator determined to mirror the effective truth through which men can make and keep themselves free; and throughout all, as husband and father sufficiently caring and loving to hold together a family and leave his wife as sole executrix of the estate, a son who died in the defense of the city, another an officer in the Tuscan navy, and another as a distinguished churchman[160]—so worthily did Machiavelli prove himself. Doing whatever he could to help his city, country and mankind—for both the living and those who were to come after—he kept his mind and judgment clear for seeking out the truth about effectiveness in political affairs and felt the pull of the possibility of objective understanding as a guide for decision-making.

The branch of the government in which Machiavelli served the republic was one which demanded sensitive, efficient services to the government of the day and at the same time the maintenance of continuity throughout times of change.[161] Insulation from hazards of change, however, could be won only at the cost of alienation from really centrally responsible participation in the determination and execution of policy. The perspective of the minister and adviser, thus, inherently lacked the true focus found in executive authority. Perhaps, as a measure of compensation, the secretaryships and chanceries developed for themselves a glory of their own. The Florentine Chancery was a department in which the Humanist tradition had long been firmly established. J. H. Plumb has recorded:

> Humanists were prized additions to every court and carefully nurtured their reputation as the only men qualified to fill the posts of secretaries and orators. They flourished in Rome under the patronage of such popes as Nicholas V, Sixtus IV, and even Alexander VI, as well as in the literary salons of rich and worldly cardinals. Under Julius II and Leo X, however, they gradually became less erudite and assumed a new elegance and stylistic sophistication . . . But the greatest change lay in the fusion of pagan and Christian ideals in Rome. There no longer seemed to be any conflict between the two.[162]

In Florence, it was a tradition for the Humanist chancellor to combine the duties of the office with chronicling the history of the city.[163] Their professional status provided the basis for a somewhat detached standpoint.

Perhaps in Machiavelli's character still another factor which contributed to a certain detachment in attitude can be found in traces of the assumption of ancestral noble privilege and independence even though long since formally renounced[164] (above, pp. 135–136). In any case, in a time of factional change, Machiavelli manifested a certain non-partisan detachment in his observation, analysis, exposition and articulation of political developments in which we can detect glimmerings of a dawning professional civil service and of a publicly-oriented political wisdom.

Having struggled for centuries to achieve and maintain its freedom by playing pope against emperor and seeking protection in the French alliance, in 1512 the republic of Florence found itself unsupported by France and confronted by the Pope, the Emperor and the rising power of Spain in alliance. When, under pressure, the government fell, Machiavelli served responsibly the fleeing Gonfalonier by helping provide safe conduct for his departure into exile. Machiavelli continued to attend to the duties of his offices during the dissolution of his authority. He attempted to interpret the change in a way which would conserve the institutions of the self-governing republic. The purpose of his "Letter to a Lady" (Alfonsina Orsini de'Medici?)[165] may have been to bring to the attention of the new masters his qualities of articulate objectivity which they might find useful in their government of the city. Despite the acts exiling him and excluding him from entering the main government building, Machiavelli returned whenever the regime sought his assistance regarding details.[166] He gave friendly recognition to the ex-Gonfalonier, at personal risk, by responding to his letter.[167] He maintained friendly relations with some of those involved in bringing about the fall of the Gonfalonier. Deprived of access to the instrumentalities of government, he utilized creatively in the service of human freedom that which he still had at hand and could command: i.e., his memories, the records of the great deeds of the ancients and his own finely-honed powers of analysis and inference. He gave life to the classical records as, in his not-to-be-denied will for remaining fully alive, he merged them with perceptions derived from his varied official service and accumulated, formulated and communicated maxims and principles which signalized a new method by which men could confront and endeavor to cope with fortune and could hope more effectively to engage their experience deliberately in the service of their chosen aims. As one who derived his central values from the popularly-based government which his city had cherished, Machiavelli retained a background of political conscience which brought into stark relief the pragmatic behavior of the leaders when he affirmed it even though not in accord with the current preferences of those from whom he hoped to obtain resumption of employment.

Were the Medici alienated by his role in ensuring safe conduct for the Gonfalonier in leaving office, the palace and the city?[168] In his "Letter to a Lady," did his implicit recommendation that the republican institutions be kept in force cause offense?[169] Were the Medici affronted by his letter to Cardinal Giulio in which he counseled against the setting up of a commission to track down holders of property formerly belonging to the Medici and to recover it for them?[170] Was it known that he had received a letter from the ex-Gonfalonier and perhaps responded to it? Did his repeatedly expressed belief that corruption in Florence and Tuscany had not gone so far but that a wise lawgiver could yet save the city and the region, keep him suspect in the eyes of the Medici?[171] He had been implicated but not convicted—though tortured and imprisoned—in connection with the conspiracy of 1513.[172] In 1515 Cardinal Giulio sent from

Rome advice to his cousin, the Pope's brother, Giuliano de'Medici,

not to have anything to do with Niccolo.[173]

Although Machiavelli himself was not involved in the conspiracy of 1522 and was concentrating his attention in writing the *History* on commission by the Cardinal, two close friends of Machiavelli's and members of the Rucellai circle were the leaders of the conspiracy.[174] Consequently, throughout the years, from 1512–13 until 6 September 1525, his name was listed among those ineligible for public office.[175]

In seeking to serve Florence despite the Medicis' seizure of control, and continuing to try to deal with them as if they were intending to prove themselves primarily citizens of the republic, Machiavelli developed the standpoint foreshadowing that of objective, professional civil servants. In trying to serve human freedom through patriotic Florentine republicanism, he generated objective analysis of experience in public affairs as the reliable guide for policy decisions.

Was it not his abiding loyalty to the common good as identified with republican liberty which the ambitious Medici sensed and which continued to warn them against embracing him as a reliable member among their adherents? Their direction and his own could not but diverge—however resourcefully he might try to bridge the chasm. Regardless of his eloquent pleas for them to prove themselves leaders according to his ideal—his dedication and concluding peroration of the *Prince*,[176] the close reasoning of the "Discourse on the Reform of the Government of Florence," and the stirring appeal of its final paragraphs,[177] the call in "The Hymn of the Blessed Spirits" for a unifying crusade,[178] the hopes lyrically expressed in "A Pastoral: the Ideal Ruler,"[179] his project for the formation of a papal militia under Giovanni delle Bande Nere[180]—his was a call alien to their ears.

The unstinting dedication which characterized Machiavelli's citizenship—expressed in his secretaryships, his embassies, his labors for reviving a citizen militia and cavalry, his proposals for governmental reform, his dialogues, plays, history of his city, work on its fortifications—enhanced his writings with a quality and impact such that people cannot forget him or avoid, generation after generation, having to try to come to terms with him. As with respect to politics in the *Prince* so with respect to social institutions in his play *Mandragola*, he manipulated ethical and moral sentiments and phrases, inverting and perverting them in seemingly most unsuitable situations as if to find out what if any intrinsic strength survived the severest and subtlest testing. Through, and beyond, acknowledging, giving literary expression to and, so to speak, enculturing the force state, Machiavelli manifested awareness of the human potentiality for intelligent observation of political behavior as the guide adequate for promoting human security in freedom and so encouraged and presaged the yet-to-appear political science.[181]

A clear summons to the recognition of the salutary power to be found in guidance through analysis and reflection upon political experience, Machiavelli issued in his "Second Decennale:"

> if you turned your prudence to learning the ill and finding its remedy, such great power from heaven would be taken.[182]

His city, however, was not to be the beneficiary of his prescription. The alliance between Pope Clement VII and Emperor Charles V, sealed in the betrothal of the Emperor's illegitimate daughter to Alessandro de'Medici,[183]

> thought to be the Cardinal's [i.e., the later Pope Clement's] own child, although at that time he passed as the son of Lorenzo, Duke of Urbino,[184]

together with the abandonment of Florence by France and Venice,[185] presaged the end of the independence of Florence as a republic. Alessandro, who, as Duke of Florence, entered the city on 5 July 1531,[186] was murdered on 5 January 1537 by his distant cousin, Lorenzino de'Medici, next in line of succession. Lorenzino's flight from the city opened the way for his third cousin, the seventeen-year-old son of the celebrated soldier, Giovanni de'Medici "delle Bande Nere," to establish his claim to the succession. With great skill and ruthless determination he, during the next thirty-seven years, expanded and consolidated his control into the Grand Duchy of Tuscany which continued under his heirs until 1737,[187] and afterwards as an Austrian dependency until Napoleonic times. Never to be finished was the great Fortezza de Basso being built for the security of Duke Alessandro and his heirs which more than symbolically was in reality the tomb of republican opposition and insurgency and the model for the secular forces of reaction and repression in Rome, Turin, Antwerp.[188] Consequently, the myth of order and security through violence appeared triumphant over guidance through cooperative participant observation.

Out of the Florentine passion for liberty, however, Machiavelli had distilled a ferment which would continue to work for enlarging the order of human freedom through the growing perception of effective will for living in truth. Affronted by the chaos wrought by the prostituting of the highest universal sanctities to the narrowest private interests, responsive to service for a more inclusive public as the effectual political unit, Machiavelli held that no conventional sanctity should be let distract from that action which could establish that larger unit—first through individual manifestation subsequently carried on through to its distributive achievement as the establishment of a republic based on first principles. Vignal has observed:

selon l'importance accordée par les temps et par les lieux à la loi morale (puisqu'il y a toujours une loi morale), on fera à Machiavel une place plus ou moins grande. Faut-il ajouter que le problème moral dépend lui-même de la valeur qu'on accorde à la vie humain? Quand les conditions religieuses enlèvent de son prix à la vie de l'homme, le problème moral s'éteint, et il ne reste plus, pour mettre un frein aux violences naturelles, que la crainte des autres hommes ou la pitié qui sans doute elle-même, quoiqu'on en ait dit, n'est qu'une extériorisation de l'instinct de conservation.[189]

according to the importance given by the times and the places to the moral law (since there is always a moral law), one grants Machiavelli a place more or less great. Need it be added that the moral problem itself depends upon the value accorded to human life? When the religious conditions remove any price on human life, the moral problem disappears and nothing else remains for putting a curb on natural violence but the fear of other men or pity which, without doubt, itself, whatever one might say about it, is nothing but an externalization of the instinct of conservation.

Was the situation such that, although Machiavelli recognized that there is goodness in human nature,[190] relative to the manifestation of evil it seemed to play so small a role[191] that he came to consider it the part of realism to treat it as if it were non-existent?[192] Boldly taking his position,

Omitting, then, those things about a prince that are fancied, and discussing those that are true,[193]

Machiavelli sought to confront political reality in all its manifestations and through reason[194] to find or construct a pattern of sufficient coherence and strength to give meaning in and through its undistorted reflections. Commenting on Machiavelli's discussion of conspiracies, Benoist observed:

Il est, en tout cas, remarquable, que, pas une fois, l'auteur ne pose la question de la "moralité" des conjurations, mais disserte seulement de leur utilité et de leur difficulté, avec balance de leurs chances et de leurs risques. C'est preécisément la marque, le sceau du "machiavélisme."[195]

It is, in any case, remarkable, that, not a single time, does the author raise the question of the "morality" of conspiracies, but treats only of their utility and of their difficulty, as balanced against their chances and their risks. This is precisely the mark, the seal of "Machiavellism."

Was not his consideration of trickery, deception, fraud and the uses of cruelty but an aspect of his discovery and feeling out the uses of the mind and reason in human affairs? Certainly, the evidence is clear that he felt reservations about the use of cruelty and fraud;[196] however, in his desire to explore truth in power for the innovator in the search,[197] the focus was not yet sufficiently developed to provide clear perspective and fully reliable discrimination. From his tale "Belfagor, the Devil Who Married"[198] and his play *Mandragola*,[199] one may infer that he held the opinion that there was a chance that a man can prove himself shrewder than the devil and hence, that, despite the story of the Garden of Eden, the eating of the fruit of the tree of knowledge is good provided that a man combines courage with his intelligent, patriotic initiative.

Chapter Eight

ELEMENTS, IN MACHIAVELLI'S WRITINGS, WORKING TOWARD A SCIENCE OF POLITICS

Is it well-founded to identify Machiavelli's thought with the science of politics and is the essence of his thought rightly perceived as a demonstration of the effectiveness of fraud; and, if so, thereby to give political science not merely the characteristic of endorsing the employment of force and fraud as constructive instruments but to arrive at the conclusion that their use is its essential stamp and dye? Is there consistency and unity in his thought; and, even if not, are there elements which have contributed to the science of politics?

The first requisite for the coming into being, the maintenance, or the reform of a state, Machiavelli perceived to be a clear and firm understanding of human nature: i.e., in Machiavelli's judgment:

that all men are evil.[1]

Indispensible in the beginning is a supernal and forceful innovative leader[2] (above, pp. 59–62). An essential factor in achieving and maintaining such predominant authority, according to Machiavelli, is the manifestation of self-confidence in action demonstrated by dramatically either destroying the past's value-freighted relics which might prove obstructive, or converting them into an instrument serving the new direction. Thus through "sacrifices" on a great scale the new way is revealed and momentum instituted for going ahead on it under awe-inspired—or at least awe-inspiring—leadership. This theme emerges throughout the *Discourses*.[3] The concluding chapter of the *Discourses,* entitled, "A Republic, if She Is To Be Kept Free, Requires New Acts of Foresight Every Day; and for What Good Qualities Quintus Fabius Was Called Maximus," is devoted to "heroic" acts.[4]

263

That Machiavelli himself suspected that his hoped-for leader had no oper-
ational counterpart in fact, has been previously demonstrated (above, pp. 66–69,
74–75).

A third element consists of a people, uncorrupted, responsive to the "common good":

> Let no one oppose this belief of mine with that well-known proverb: "He
> who builds on the people builds on mud"; it is indeed true when a private
> citizen lays his foundation on the people and allows himself to suppose
> that they will free him when he is beset by his enemies or by public
> officials. In this case he often finds himself deceived, as in Rome the
> Gracchi, and in Florence Messer Giorgio Scali. But when he who builds
> on them is a prince who can command, is a stout-hearted man who does
> not waver in adverse times, does not lack other preparations, and through
> his courage and his management keeps up the spirit of the masses, he is
> never deceived by them, but receives assurance that he has made his
> foundations strong;[5]

> As to those who have prudently set up a republic, one of the most necessary
> things they have arranged has been to set up a guardian for liberty, and
> according as they have placed him well, that free government is more or
> less lasting . . . if the common people are set up to guard liberty, it is
> reasonable that they will care for it better [than the rich or the nobles],
> and since they cannot seize it themselves, they will not allow others to
> seize it;[6]

> [the people] wish two things: one, to avenge themselves on those who are
> the cause of their being slaves; the second to get their liberty again . . . a
> small part of them wishes to be free in order to rule; but all the others,
> who are countless, wish freedom in order to live in security. For in all
> republics, in whatever way organized, positions of authority cannot be
> reached by even forty or fifty citizens. And because this is a small number,
> it is an easy thing to secure oneself against them, either by getting rid of
> them or by bestowing on them so many honors that according to their
> stations they are for the most part contented. Those others, for whom it
> is enough to live secure, are easily satisfied by the making of ordinances
> and laws which provide for the general security and at the same time for
> the prince's own power[7] (above, p. 114).

The youth of the land is seen as Machiavelli's ultimate sanguine surmise
for a people uncorrupted, suitable material on which the emerging innovative
and prudent ruler would be able to stamp the form requisite to

> bring him glory and her [their country's] people general happiness;[8]

> by the work of those who have great states in Italy . . . this form can be

impressed on simple men, rough and native, not on the malicious, the badly governed, and the foreign. A good sculptor will never think he can make an excellent statue from a piece of marble badly blocked out, but he can from one still in the rough.[9]

To valuation of one's native land, patriotism, Machiavelli made a signal contribution. In this, he was cooperating with a major dynamic in history. Every being's claim throughout his life to a rightful place of his own on the earth he inhabits, is the eternal progenitor of history—the evidence of the prime mover at work in him. To reconcile this drive with social acceptability continues to be the anguish of history. While continuity of the Jewish cultural experience in confrontation with the dominance and decline of the power of ancient Egypt, the rise and fall of Babylonia, Assyria, Chaldea, the Alexandrine empire, Rome, the Moslems, the Crusades, the British and the French empires, deepened the sense of the inevitability of the collapse of empires, there persisted the belief that the Jewish people on their "promised land" were destined to be the instruments for manifesting the essence of eternal rule and dominion.[10] Pessimistic toward the perspective of non-Jewish political order, they have been and continue to be optimistic with respect to their own spirit of nationhood. From the point of view of mankind, the pretension of a part, or of one cultural group, to be competent or adequate for directing the whole, or others, has proved provocative and given rise to counteracting anti-bodies conducive to violence and mutual destruction.

Affirming the power which is awareness of one's birthright and sensing that such awareness was potential among the youthful inhabitants of the land and that, aroused, organized and properly directed, it would prove impregnable, Machiavelli, through the love for the freedom nourished in his city, was conceiving a new political force and for its articulation he strove with whatever resources he could muster. Leo Strauss has perceptively indicated Machiavelli's outlook:

The first book of the *Discourses,* which almost opens with a praise of the most ancient antiquity, literally ends with a praise of the many Romans "who triumphed in their earliest youth." Machiavelli addresses his passionate and muted call to the young—to men whose prudence has not enfeebled their youthful vigor of mind, impetuosity, and audacity. Reason and youth and modernity rise up against authority, old age, and antiquity. In studying the *Discourses* we become the witnesses, and we cannot help becoming the moved witnesses of the greatest of all youth movements: modern philosophy.[11]

In the creation of the citizen militia and cavalry he had worked with the rough youth of Florence's outlying districts (Mugello, Casentino, the Chiusi district)[12] and in them invested his hopes for the defense of the city. Later, throughout his writings, it is to youthful leaders and raw forces such as these that he looks for his convictions to bear fruit. In the *Prince,* he gave the reason for his hopes:

always . . . she [Fortune] is the friend of young men, because they are less cautious, more spirited, and with more boldness master her.[13]

Repeatedly he explicitly directed his appeal to youth: thus, in the *Discourses*:

I shall be bold in saying what I learn about Roman times and the present, in order that the minds of young men who read these writings of mine may reject the present and be prepared to imitate the past, whenever Fortune gives them opportunity . . . some of them more loved by Heaven may be prepared to put it into effect;[14]

and in *The Art of War,* he had his spokesman, Fabrizio Colonna, say:

I am very willing that you, Cosimo, and these other young men should here question me, because I believe that your youth makes you more interested in military matters and readier to believe what I shall say. Men of another age, with their hair white and the blood in their veins turned to ice, are commonly some of them enemies of war, some beyond correction, believing that the times and not bad customs force men to live thus. So ask questions of me, all of you, with assurance and without hesitation . . . I shall be glad not to leave in your minds any uncertainty;[15]

I should like to have us follow the Venetian custom, namely, that the youngest speak first, because, since this is business for young men, I am persuaded that young men will be more fit to discuss it, as they are quicker to carry it out;[16]

the citizen army . . . would please the young men, who on festival days now remain wretchedly idle in their usual resorts, because they would go with pleasure to these exercises, for since the managing of arms is a fine spectacle, young men enjoy it;[17]

and in the concluding paragraph,

Since I am an old man, I do not imagine today that I can have opportunity for ["putting these ideas into effect"]. Therefore I have been liberal of it with you who, being young and gifted, can at the right time, if the things I have said please you, aid and advise your princes to their advantage.[18]

How deeply-rooted in one's native land Machiavelli considered a man to be, stands out clearly throughout Machiavelli's writings. The bond, generated by nature,[19] inspires and whets mutual assurance of the most powerful kind.[20] Against it no tyrant can secure himself.[21] Its preservation and strengthening should be given precedence over any other consideration.[22] Indeed, it is through

266

serving and promoting it that a man wins his worth[23] (above, pp. 13–20, 56–57). Those who violate it, forfeit trust:

> It is dangerous to believe banished men . . . vain are the pledges and promises of those who are excluded from their native city. For as to their loyalty, it must be reckoned that whenever through other means than yours they can enter again into their native city, they will leave you and ally themselves with others, notwithstanding any promises they have made. And as to vain promises and hopes, so violent is their desire to return home that they naturally believe many things that are false, and to these they artfully join many others. Hence, between what they believe and what they tell you they believe, they fill you with such hope that, if you rely on it, you either enter into useless expense or go into an enterprise in which you are ruined.[24]

In *The History of Florence* he singled out for praise those who subordinated every private consideration to the common defense:

> It was noteworthy that citizens who a little before had fought for the exiles' return when, unarmed, they prayed to be restored to their native city, on seeing those exiles armed and trying by force to get control of her, took arms against them (so much higher these citizens esteemed the common good than they did their private friendship) and, uniting with the people, drove the invaders back with force to the place whence they had come.[25]

As a fourth element, a well-disciplined citizen army, as already demonstrated, Machiavelli considered to be indispensable. Machiavelli's official service occurred just as the European reaction against the financial-commercial-industrial exploitation by the papal alliance with the Italian city states finally began to assail the peninsula itself with devastating and bewildering impact. As early as Magna Carta (1215) English churchmen had successfully challenged papal patronage in favoring Italians and, a century and a quarter later, after gaining a monopoly over the export of English raw wool, through trying to keep up with the demands of Edward I and Edward III for loans for the wars in France, major Florentine banking firms collapsed[26] with the result that foreigners were officially banned from conducting banking in England. Through the next century and a half, papal craft and the ingenuity of, especially, Florentine businessmen generated ever-increasing wealth and the appearance of power which culminated in the personal diplomacy of Lorenzo the Magnificent. Two years after his death, the meteoric invasion by Charles VIII of France set in train the fateful and ever-more-violent entanglements from which none of the city states of the peninsula proved able to extricate itself with freedom and prosperity. Accustomed to win their wars profitably at a distance, Florentines began to find that declining resources bought from mercenaries and auxiliary forces less satisfactory defense in conflicts threatening their own borders.

As Secretary of the Second Chancery and of the Ten,[27] then of the Nine of the Florentine Ordinance and Militia,[28] during the war to recover its access to the sea,[29] Machiavelli was in direct contact with the inadequately motivated, corrupt and apparently treacherous mercenary and auxiliary soldiers upon whom the city was relying as it struggled to restore its prosperity and protect its independence and freedom. He may have personally participated in the decision to execute the celebrated commander Paolo Vitelli on the charge of treachery in the prosecution of the campaign against Pisa.[30] Although Florence had to depend on France as its chief ally, there was evidently no identity of interest.[31] When the forces which the French supplied proved mutinous, it was Machiavelli who bore the news from the field to the city and, subsequently, as its representative to France, was able to gain for his frustrated and embarrassed city no adequate recompense.[32] Nine months later, during his mission to Duke Valentino, he was profoundly impressed with the increase of power occasioned by the Duke's daring replacement of mercenary forces with the army which he developed out of recruits drawn from the region which he had conquered.[33]

Machiavelli sensed the need to make the citizens of Florence directly and actively involved, and personally aware physically of the costs of enjoying the benefits of membership in Florence as a free republic. He not only began to agitate for the formation of a citizen militia[34] but organized a pilot demonstration[35] and, for the city, wrote the statute the preamble of which succinctly sets forth the rationale for the citizen militia.[36] He personally recruited and trained the young men from the region and supervised the day-by-day flow of supplies.[37] In his "First Decennale," published while he was recruiting men for the militia,[38] he paid his respects to the new citizen militia:

And you [Florence] did not keep your valor hidden but with stronger weapons equipped yourself, so you could better oppose all outrage.[39]

He closed his patriotic manifesto with his exhortation for the city to "reopen the temple of Mars."[40]

As Ridolfi has indicated, evidently he felt himself the forger of the instrument which he hoped would give his city leadership in the saving of Italy.[41] Exhilarated by the part played by the militia in the victory over Pisa[42] and undaunted by their disastrous rout when encountering veteran Spanish forces,[43] when driven from office, in his major written works—the *Prince*, the *Discourses*, especially in *The Art of War, The History of Florence*, and in private letters—he still plead the cause of the citizen militia as the only sound basis for political power:

the armies with which a prince defends his state are either his own, or they are mercenary or auxiliary or mixed . . . I shall never hesitate to use as an example Caesar Borgia and his actions . . . never was he esteemed high until everybody saw that he was sole master of his own troops;[44]

268

I conclude, then, that without her own armies no princedom is secure; on the contrary she is entirely dependent on Fortune, not having strength that in adversity loyally defends her;[43]

no one can use as a foundation forces other than one's own, and . . . one's own forces can be organized in no other way than in a citizen army, nor in other ways can regulations for armies be introduced into any place, nor is there any other method for establishing a military system.[46]

In the face of the gathering storm of the imminent Imperial invasion, in the spring of 1526 Machiavelli was urging the Pope and Guicciardini, as governor of Romagna, to raise and equip a citizen army in that papal state as a bulwark against the advancing horde; but in vain.[47] Just how central in the life and work of Machiavelli was the idea of the citizen militia and his concern for its establishment, Ferrara has clearly indicated.[48]

A fifth element, which was subsequently to be formulated as "the consent of the governed," he closely approached when he wrote,

only authority freely given is durable;[49]

and, concerning Florence,

Without satisfying the generality of the citizens, to set up a stable government is always impossible.[50]

In the same vein are judgments scattered throughout his works[51] (above, pp. 112–115). Machiavelli described *The History of Florence* as an account

of the things done at home and abroad by the Florentine people.[52]

It should be emphasized, however, as appears clearly indicated in his chapter, entitled "A Republic or a Prince Should Not Put Off Benefitting Men until Times of Necessity,"[53] that concern for the people is as an instrument of policy on behalf of the ruling individual or group, not that the strength of the state lies in the people's recognition that the very existence of the state is by virtue of their own political awareness and organization.

A sixth element, essential according to Machiavelli's judgment, is an aggressive posture.[54]

A seventh element is the administration of justice. In "A Provision for Infantry," Machiavelli wrote:

your republic is well founded on good and holy laws, and organized for the administration of justice.[55]

In commenting upon this section, Allan Gilbert observed,

Though justice is the foundation of Machiavellian theory, he seldom, as here, speaks directly on it.[56]

Doubtless he implied the inclusion of the administration of justice in "good laws" and "good government" to which he made repeated reference.[57] The meting out of justice must be prudent but signal.[58]

An eighth element consists in a form of government appropriate to the conditions of the people subject to it. The republican form, he considered, provides advantages with respect to security, stability and freedom.[59] These advantages he attributed to such factors as: (1) the people's greater desire to be free from oppression than to be rulers over others;[60] (2) the broad-based participation by the people with their great diversity of talents (above, pp. 112–113) and (3) the responsiveness of the people to guidance through the truth (above, pp. 113–114). A kingly government befits the setting up of a new state or the reforming of a corrupt one:

Men gladly change their ruler, believing that they will better themselves. This belief makes them take up arms against him, but in doing so they deceive themselves, for later they learn through experience that they have become worse off. This situation results from another natural and normal necessity, namely that a new prince is always obliged to damage his recently gained subjects with soldiers and to oppress them in countless ways necessitated by his recent conquest. Hence you have as enemies all those you have damaged in taking possession of that princedom, and you cannot retain as friends those who put you there, since you cannot give them such satisfaction as they looked forward to, and since you cannot use strong medicines against them because you are indebted to them. Always, even though a new prince is very strong in armies, he must have the inhabitants' favor when moving into a new province;[61]

where the matter is so corrupt that the laws are not restraint enough, along with them some greater force must of necessity be established, namely, a kingly hand that with absolute and surpassing power puts a check on the over-great ambition and corruption of the powerful;[62]

From all the things explained above comes the difficulty or the impossibility of maintaining a government in a corrupt city or of setting up a new government there. Indeed when in such a city one is to be set up or maintained, necessity demands that it be inclined more toward kingly rule than toward popular rule, in order that those men who, on account of their arrogance, cannot be controlled by law may in some fashion be restrained by a power almost kingly. To try to make them become good in other ways would be either a most cruel undertaking or altogether impossible, as I said above on what Cleomenes did.[63]

270

Practically, of the best kind of government, Machiavelli indicated his opinion:

so favorable to her [Rome] was Fortune that even though she passed from the government of the king and the aristocrats to that of the people, through the same steps and for the same reasons that are discussed above, yet never, in order to give authority to the aristocrats, did she take all authority away from the kingly element, nor did she entirely remove the authority of the aristocrats to give it to the people, but continuing her mixed government, she was a perfect state. To this perfection she came through the discord between the people and the Senate, as will be shown at length in the next two chapters.[64]

A ninth element, that of sovereignty, received one clear expression:

When a prince or a republic is willing to undergo toil and put effort into these methods and this training, always it is true that in his country there are good soldiers. Such princes are superior to their neighbors; they give laws and do not take them from other men.[65]

A tenth, and universal, essential in Machiavelli's conception of the state, is self-renewal:

because in everything, as we have said elsewhere,[66] is hidden some evil of its own that brings forth new emergencies, there must be new laws to provide against such evil;[67]

those [republics and religions] are best organized and have longest life that through their institutions can often renew themselves or that by some accident outside their organization come to such renewal. And it is clearer than light that if these bodies are not renewed they do not last. The way to renew them, as I have said, is to carry them back to their beginnings, because all the beginnings of religions and of republics and of kingdoms must possess some goodness by means of which they gain their first reputation and their first growth;[68]

from one such enforcement of the law to the next, there should be a lapse of not more than ten years, because, when that time has gone by, men change their habits and break the laws; and if something does not happen to bring the penalty back to their memories and renew fear in their minds, so many offenders quickly join together that they cannot be punished without danger;[69]

If a state were fortunate enough, as we said above, to have frequently a leader who with his example would renovate its laws, and would not merely stop it from running to ruin but would pull it backward, it would be everlasting.[70]

271

In attitude, Machiavelli was personally conservative. That he did not conceive of himself as a conspirator or a revolutionist is evident when one considers his relation to the conspiracy of 1512,[71] that of 1522,[72] his advices on conspiracies—

> private persons do not enter into any undertaking more dangerous and rash than a conspiracy, for in all its stages it is difficult and very dangerous. For this reason, many are attempted and very few have the outcome desired. In order, then, that princes may learn how to guard themselves against these dangers, and that private persons may be more cautious about entering into them—or rather that they may learn to be content to live under whatever rule Chance provides—I shall deal with conspiracies at length, not omitting anything important for the instruction of either sort of person. And certainly Cornelius Tacitus' axiom is golden, in which he says that men must honor past things and obey present things; they should wish for good princes, but should endure those of any sort. Certainly he who does otherwise generally ruins himself and his native city[73]—

and, further evidence he provided by his account of the labor troubles and the Ciompi uprising of the summer of 1378.[74]

At the close of the sixth book of *The Art of War,* in considering the factors in a general's strength, Machiavelli brought together very succinctly as elements of power: prudence, force, organization, discipline and ability.[75]

Machiavelli's attitude which prompted his exploration toward a science of politics was a faith in human capacity, a refusal to excuse failure as Fate or to rely on Fortune for success: thus, although

> in the world most men let themselves be mastered by Fortune;[76]

and

> We have seen and see every day . . . frequently after long prosperity a man who finally loses does not in any way blame himself but accuses the heavens and the actions of the Fates;[77]

he believed that

> Where men have little ability, Fortune shows her power much;[78]

> I well believe that . . . Fortune, wishing to show the world that she—and not Prudence—makes men great, first shows her forces at a time when Prudence can have no share in the matter, but rather that everything must be recognized as coming from herself;[79]

weak men . . . grow vain and are made drunk with good fortune, assigning all their prosperity to an ability which they have not displayed at any time. As a result, they become unbearable and hateful to all around them. From this situation, then, issues some sudden change in their lot, and when they look that in the face, they fall at once into the other defect and become despicable and abject;[80]

those [princes in Italy] who still hold them [their states] do not know how to use any remedy and have no wish to, because they hope without any trouble to keep going through Fortune and not through their own strength; they see, since there is little vigor here, that Fortune rules everything, and they are willing to have her rule them and do not hope to rule her;[81]

since Fortune wants to do everything, she wishes us to let her do it, to be quiet, and not to give her trouble, and to wait for a time when she will allow something to be done by men;[82]

men who commonly live amid great troubles or successes deserve less praise and less blame, because most of the time we see that they have been pushed into a destructive or elevated action by some great advantage that the Heavens have bestowed on them, giving them opportunity—or taking it from them—to work effectively. Skilfully Fortune does this, since she chooses a man, when she plans to bring to pass great things, who is of so much perception and so much ability that he recognizes the opportunities she puts before him. So in the same way when she intends to bring to pass great failures, she puts there men to promote such failure. And if anybody there is able to oppose her, she either kills him or deprives him of all means for doing anything good . . . I assert, indeed, once more that it is very true, according to what we see in all the histories, that men are able to assist Fortune but not to thwart her. They can weave her designs but cannot destroy them;[83]

a man succeeds in erring less and in having prosperous fortune if time fits his ways, for you always act as Nature inclines you;[84]

greatly displeasing to Fortune is he who does well.[85]

Very rarely Machiavelli himself verged upon the temptation to indulge himself in the kind of excuse which he disparaged. Thus, in letters to his nephew, he lamented:

As to myself, I have become useless to myself, to my relatives, and to my friends, because such has been the decision of my sad fate;[86]

273

As in many of my letters I have said to you, Chance, since you left, has done the worst for me that she can, so that I am brought down to a condition enabling me to do little good to myself and less to others.[87]

In "The (Golden) Ass," he had his guide, the gracious lady, console the hero with the words:

"Among modern peoples and among ancient . . . never has anyone borne more ingratitude or greater toil.
Through your own fault this did not overtake you, as it happens to some, but because Chance was opposed to your good conduct. Chance closed upon you the gates of pity above all when she led you into this place so savage and strong.
But because weeping has always been shameful to a man, he should turn to the blows of Fortune a face unstained with tears;"[88]

and in the concluding paragraph of *The Art of War* he had his spokesman say:

And I repine at Nature, who either should have made me such that I could not see this or should have given me the possibility for putting it into effect.[89]

However, there is always the possibility, according to Machiavelli, that the power of Fortune is more limited than it appears at the moment to be:

in order not to annul our free will, I judge it true that Fortune may be mistress of one half our actions but that even she leaves the other half, or almost, under our control . . . She shows her power where strength and wisdom do not prepare to resist her, and directs her fury where she knows that no dykes or embankments are ready to hold her;[90]

They [men] ought, then, never to give up as beaten, because, since they do not know her [Fortune's] purposes and she goes through crooked and unknown roads, they can always hope, and hoping are not to give up, in whatever fortune and whatever affliction they may be.[91]

Through preparation for challenging Fortune's rule, according to Machiavelli, by courageous action when opportunity opens and through study and communication when opportunity for overt action is denied, men discover and show their ability:

he who depends least on Fortune sustains himself longest;[92]

prudence makes use of men according to the times;[93]

"Fortune's malice can be overcome with prudence, if you check the ambi-

274

tion of the men I have mentioned, annul the laws that breed factions, and adopt those suitable for a truly free and law-abiding government;"[94]

great men are always in every sort of fortune just the same; if that varies, now raising them, now putting them down, they do not vary, but always keep their courage firm and so closely united with their way of life that we easily see that Fortune does not have power over a single one of them;[95]

where men have little ability, Fortune shows her power much, and because she is variable, republics and states often vary, and vary they always will until some one arises who is so great a lover of antiquity that he will rule Fortune in such a way that she will not have cause to show in every revolution of the sun how much she can do;[96]

I believe . . . that a prince succeeds who adapts his way of proceeding to the nature of the times;[97]

As for me, I believe this: it is better to be impetuous than cautious.[98]

Occasionally Machiavelli offered a glimpse into the attitude which he cherished for himself. In his second letter to Francisco Vettori after release from prison and torture, he wrote:

As to turning my face to resist Fortune, I want you to get this pleasure from my distresses, namely, that I have borne them so bravely that I love myself for it and feel that I am stronger than you believed;[99]

and in "The (Golden) Ass" he responded to the wise advice of his compassionate guide:

I do not accuse the Heavens or any other, nor do I intend to lament so ill a lot, because to evil more than to good I am wonted,
but if I must pass through the gates of Hell to that good you have spoken of, I am willing—much more through those ways by which you have taken me.
Fortune, then, may make of my life all that she must and all that she chooses, for well I know that for me she never will grieve.[100]

When denied the privilege of official service, he found a way by which to combat significantly the "malice of Fortune"[101] through exploring the possibility of signal consequences of intelligent courage and recording his reflections on his

lengthy experience with recent matters and continual reading on ancient ones.[102]

275

That it was Machiavelli's clear intention to engage in a study of the state in order to promote an objective understanding of it, is Ferrara's considered conclusion:

> Machiavel écrivit les *Décades* ou les *Discours* comme il avait écrit *le Prince*, dans le même but objectif d'examiner la vie de l'État, avec l'aide de ses expériences, en se servant des faits historiques pour confirmer ses thèses préconçues . . . Tout nous force à penser que les deux ouvrages, ainsi que nous l'avons longuement établi au chapitre précédent, sont complémentaires et traitent objectivement de l'État dans le temps et dans l'espace, c'est-à-dire en dehors de tout intérêt pratique. Nous avons insisté sur ce point, parce que nous le croyons d'importance capitale pour juger Machiavel et ses œuvres;[103]

> Machiavelli wrote the *Decades* or the *Discourses* as he had written the *Prince,* with the same objective purpose of examining the life of the state, aided by his experience, making use of historical facts in order to confirm his preconceived theories. Everything forces us to think that the two works, even as we have established at length in the preceding chapter, are complementary and treat the state objectively in time and space, that is to say apart from every practical concern. We have insisted on this point because we believe it to be of capital importance for judging Machiavelli and his works;

and later regarding two of the letters written to Vettori on 20 December 1514, Ferrara commented:

> il demeure fidèle à sa méthode d'examiner tous les extrêmes, toutes les solutions, toutes les hypothèses, sans mettre, sinon dans le raisonnement, rien de personnel, rien de sentimental, rien qui soit l'expression d'un désire éprouvé ou d'une opinion préconçue.[104]

> he remains faithful to his method of examining all of the extremes, all of the solutions, all of the hypotheses, without introducing, unless reasonably, anything personal, anything sentimental, anything which might be the expression of a cherished desire or of a preconceived opinion.

Therein Ferrara found also an affinity with *Mandragola*:

> Pour nous, *la Mandragore* est, dans le domaine de la littérature, ce que les *Discours* et *le Prince* sont dans celui de la politique . . . Machiavel s'y montre humoriste, antireligieux, averti des mœurs du temps. C'est l'analyste qui, dans l'examen d'un cas, n'apporte aucune idée préconçue. Dans *la Mandragore,* comme dans les *Discours* et *le Prince,* il étudie ce qui arrive et non pas ce qu'il souhaite, la réalité et non pas le rêve. De

temps en temps, une remarque pathétique, qui jaillit du plus profond; mais ce n'est qu'un instant, comme toujours chez les ecrivains qui ne révèlent qu'involontairement leurs états d'âme. Quand on étudie cette piece, on ne sait qui est bon et qui est mauvais, tant les personnages en sont humains.[105]

In our opinion, *Mandragola* is, in the domain of literature, that which the *Discourses* and the *Prince* are in that of politics . . . Machiavelli shows himself humorist, anti-religious, opposed to the customs of the times. He is the analyst who, in the examination of a situation, does not inject any preconceived ideas. In *Mandragola,* as in the *Discourses* and the *Prince* he studies that which happens and not that which he hopes, the reality and not the dream. From time to time a touching remark which leaps up from the greatest depths; but it is but a moment, as always with the writers who only involuntarily reveal their spiritual states. When one studies this piece, one does not know who is good and who is bad, to so great a degree are the characters human.

Experiences in Italy formed somber contrasts with impressions gained on missions to France and Germany and with news of events in Spain. Although Machiavelli saw an Italy deeply corrupted (above, pp. 109–111, 248) yet persistent hope spurred him on to passionate endeavors. In *The Art of War* he wrote:

By Italy's condition I do not wish you to be dismayed or terrified, because this land seems born to raise up dead things, as she has in poetry, in painting, and in sculpture.[106]

He closed the *Prince* with the following exhortation:

Let your glorious family, then, undertake this charge with that spirit and that hope with which men undertake just labors, in order that beneath her ensign this native land of ours may be ennobled and, with her guidance, we may realize the truth of Petrach's words:

Valor against wild rage
Will take up arms, and the combat will be short,
Because ancestral courage
In our Italian hearts is not yet dead.[107]

When "the glorious family" failed to respond, Machiavelli's continuing purpose found expression explicitly in his chief writings[108] (above, pp. 70–72).

His "Portraits of the Affairs of France,"[109] and his "Portraits of the Affairs of Germany,"[110] occasioned by his missions abroad and his organizing of his observations and reflections upon their institutions, customs, economic life and military systems, contributed to the study of government new dimensions and a more comprehensive approach.

To the theory of the state, Machiavelli contributed, according to L. G. Pelissier, as quoted by Tommasini, three tenets:

"nationalité de l'état, unité de l'état, objectivité de l'état, ces trois nécessités de l'état moderne."[111]

"the nationality of the state, the unity of the state, the objectivity of the state, these three necessities of the modern state."

The nature and role of the individual in Machiavelli's perspective emerges, generally, as a function of one's political community. Most clearly delineated as an individual is the heroic and rarely-if-ever-to-be-encountered founder[112] or reformer[113] of the state. Machiavelli counselled that private persons

learn to be content to live under whatever rule Chance provides;[114]

however,

a republic without citizens of reputation cannot last and cannot in any way be governed well;[115]

and

Men become excellent and show their ability only as they are employed and brought forward by their prince or republic or king as it may be.[116]

Therefore channels for gaining reputation should be established and regulated:[117]

a republic ought to have among its laws this: that the citizens are to be watched so that they cannot under cover of good do evil and so that they gain only such popularity as advances and does not harm liberty.[118]

An energy innate in individuals, Machiavelli considered, is set free through dedicated service to the land of one's birth.[119] More than any others, the native-born can be counted upon to give their country their utmost in support.[120] It has been said,

The Renaissance established the dignity of man.[121]

In this respect, Machiavelli is *par excellence* a man of the Renaissance. Scattered throughout his writings are observations and judgments demonstrating that Machiavelli recognized human individuality as an ultimate core of strength. This core is found to be composed of diverse elements: some positive, some negative.

First, is free will. In the *Prince*, once[122] he ascribed to Fortune this gift to men but in the following, and closing chapter, he wrote:

God does not do everything, so as not to take from us free will and part of the glory that pertains to us.[123]

A second core element found, is a necessitous drive for power.[124]
Third, a center of decision-making inheres in each individual:

Ciascuno secondo la sua fantasia si governa; . . . Non consigliar persona, ne pigliar consiglio da persona, eccetto che un consiglio generale: che ognuno faccia quello che gli getta l'animo, e con audacia.[125]

Each one governs himself according to his own fancy . . . I do not give advice to anyone, nor take advice from anyone, except this general advice: that each man do what his spirit dictates to him, and with boldness.

A wise prince . . . seeks advice continually, but when it suits him and not when it suits somebody else . . . he is a big asker and then, on the things asked about, a patient listener to the truth . . . it is to be concluded that good advice, from whomsoever it comes, must originate in the prince's discretion, and not the prince's discretion in the good advice.[126]

A fourth is the potentiality for keeping the initiative—i.e., courage.[127]
A fifth, an unpredictably ingenious self-defense reaction—a negative element, an ineradicable reaction against disregard and oppression. Of Machiavelli's relevant observations and judgments quoted (above, pp. 11–12) and/or cited (pp. 68–89) the following two are representative:

If a man is greatly injured either by the state or by a single person and is not avenged to his satisfaction, if he lives in a republic, he seeks, even with its ruin, to get his revenge. If he lives under a prince and has any nobility in himself, he is never quiet until in some way he has avenged himself on him, even though he sees therein his own injury;[128]

Still another cause—a very great one—makes men conspire against a prince: this is the desire for liberating their native land which he has conquered . . . From this passion no tyrant can protect himself except by laying down his tyranny. But because no one will do that, there are few tyrants who do not come to a bad end.[129]

A sixth element is conscience. Machiavelli's most direct and explicit treatment of conscience can be found in his "Exhortation to Penitence:"

279

Those who are ungrateful to God—it is impossible that they are not un-friendly to their neighbors. Those are unfriendly to their neighbors who are without charity. This, my Fathers and Brothers, is the only thing that takes our souls to Heaven; this is the only thing that has more worth than all the other virtues of men; this is that of which the Church says at such length that he who does not have charity does not have anything.[130]

Its negative aspect expresses itself in a kind of fear which Machiavelli described in his treatment of conspiracies in the *Discourses*[131] and in *The History of Florence*[132] (above, pp. 52–53). Later, Kant was to perceive that

since each man has within him a conscience, you must treat him as a center of dignity.[133]

In considering as tyrannical methods used by David and by Philip of Macedonia in setting up their new states, Machiavelli manifested a sensitivity to the concept of mankind as a whole. In *Discourses* he wrote:

These methods are very cruel, and enemies to all government not merely Christian but human, and any man ought to avoid them and prefer to live a private life rather than to be a king who brings such ruin on men. Notwithstanding, a ruler who does not wish to take that first good way of lawful government, if he wishes to maintain himself, must enter upon this evil one.[134]

In declaring

I love my native city more than my soul,[135]

Machiavelli was affirming as of supreme validity the active, personally respon-sible, constructive, public participation. For him, with his continual striving tempered by repeated frustrations, such participation had become the feeling, the search for, and the exposition of the effectual truth available to men in the direction of public affairs. Tommasini concluded:

quel civile rispetto alla coscienza de'singoli . . . fu principale idealità proclamata dal Machiavelli.[136]

that civil regard for the conscience of individuals . . . was the principal ideal condition proclaimed by Machiavelli.

The relation between conscience and Machiavelli's quest for truth, Tommasini explored with great insight, as already noted (above, pp. 115–116).[137]

A seventh element is love of country. When on the legation to Caesar Borgia, in a letter to the Ten, Machiavelli made reference to a natural affection that every man ought to have for his country.[138]

An eighth element, present as a potentiality, is imperturbability:

> great men are always in every sort of fortune just the same; if that [i.e., fortune] varies, now raising them, now putting them down, they do not vary, but always keep their courage firm and so closely united with their way of life that we easily see that Fortune does not have power over a single one of them.[139]

As a ninth element, suited accordingly to men's nature, is responsiveness to freedom in social communciation. Describing conditions under which it seemed to him that men have best flourished, Machiavelli wrote of

> golden days, in which every man can hold and defend what opinions he wishes . . . in short, the world rejoicing, the prince satisfied with respect and glory, the people with love and security.[140]

Machiavelli conceived of no solitary, atomistically individual virtue, however great the attributes and potentialities of individuals. It was always a "common good" to be served. Hence, a tenth requisite and potentiality which he counted upon in the individual, was a capacity for resilience—the realization that the deepening corruption, weakness, misery was not an inescapable fate. The awareness of the disease, he saw as a shock essential to stir and discipline youthful energies for restoring *virtù* as a working order. He reminded his readers:

> Then [in ancient times] men overcome in war either were killed or kept in perpetual slavery, so that they passed their lives wretchedly; conquered cities were either laid waste or the inhabitants driven out, their goods taken from them and they themselves sent wandering through the world. Hence those conquered in war suffered the utmost of every misery. Terrorized by this dread, men kept military training alive and honored those who were excellent in it.[141]

Holding that

> the foundation of all states is good military organization, and that where this does not exist there cannot be good laws or anything else good,[142]

he was convinced that for there to be a system of laws which ensures justice and liberty, the citizenry needed to be stirred to *virtù* through having brought home to them the continual sense of the presence of death and the value of life which the instituting of the citizen militia would, in his judgment, accomplish.[143]

As Machiavelli realized that authentic Christianity requires sincerely operative personal fellow service,[144] he considered that the modern state requires a personally operative disciplined patriotism. Since the former seemed, although desirable, inadequately practicable and too unobtainable, he devoted himself to bringing about the latter.[145] As Aristotle in *The Politics*[146] perceived that with power-driven tools men would have no technical need for masters or slaves and could enjoy abundance in a classless society, but, rejecting the idea as impractical, directed men's thoughts toward a violently competitive struggle as the way for political- and economic-man, so Machiavelli perceived that by objective study of human endeavor to establish the order of freedom men could find adequate guidance if the insights were followed through with intelligent will, but, looking for that capacity only in terms of an elite operating through his city and rejecting as impractical reliance upon a quality of goodness in human nature, he directed men's thoughts toward violent competitive struggle as the way for political man.

That in the Italians, especially the Florentines as Tuscans,[147] the processes of corruption had not penetrated so deeply as to make totally impossible the recovery of *virtù*, was a conviction which Machiavelli repeatedly affirmed. Awakened by witnessing Cesare Borgia's success in forming a loyal army by conscripting young men in Romagna which he had conquered,[148] Machiavelli, through his own experience in getting established a civic militia in Florence, through his efforts to get Pope Clement VII to raise a papal militia under Guicciardini, and his subsequent proposal to Guicciardini for encouraging the formation of one under the command of Giovanni de'Medici, delle Bande Nere, tried his utmost to substantiate his hope. In the *Prince*, he declared:

> In Italy there is no lack of matter on which to impose any form; there is a great power in the limbs, if only it were not wanting in the heads.[149]

In his "Discourse on Remodeling . . . Florence," he recommended to Pope Leo X, and later to Cardinal De'Medici:

> I shall pass over any further treatment of princedom and speak of the republic, both because Florence is a subject very suitable for taking this form and because I know that Your Holiness is much inclined toward one; and I believe that you defer establishing it because you hope to find an arrangement by which your power in Florence may continue great and your friends may live in security. Since I believe I have discovered one, I hope Your Highness will give attention to my discovery, so that if there is anything good in it, you can make use of it and also learn from it how great is my wish to serve you.[150]

Later, in *The History of Florence,* he wrote:

> Florence has come to such a condition that easily a wise lawgiver could reorganize her with almost any form of government.[151]

282

His ardent hope found repeated expression in *The Art of War* and in *The History of Florence*.[152]

Yet an eleventh endowment which Machiavelli came to expect and to rely upon was a capacity for men to feel themselves essential members of an earthy and realistic relationship more comprehensive than that in and for which they had been brought up and to which they had an organic affinity. In writing *The History of Florence*, as Jacob Burckhardt observed,[153] Machiavelli had come to sense his city as a living being. Some of this perspective carried over into the more inclusive conception—that of regional or national unity—of which, as Ridolfi has pointed out,[154] Machiavelli was beginning to envision the necessity. Furthermore, the methods of choosing leadership which will guarantee the combination of valor and prudence, Machiavelli considered to be those characteristic of a well-ordered republic rather than of a hereditary monarchy.[155]

What are the implications of Machiavelli's conviction that a republic successful in enjoying its liberties must be dynamically expansive?[156] Does this conclusion indicate that our political structures, far from being areas of stable relations or verifiable units, are "states" only in name but in reality are but violent projections of fictional aspirations? Does the inherency of force and violence in the processes of founding and maintaining "states," as Machiavelli conceived them and as they presently manifest themselves, indicate that these forms as currently conceived and promoted are in conflict with the very nature of men and human relations? May it be that only all of mankind as a whole can be the basis for stable policy and that, as such it requires its own systems-approach? Unless Mankind develops and begins to employ methods appropriate to its government in terms universal, is it inevitable that "states" as presently conceived and constituted will intensify the forcible exploration toward it and culminate either in a world tyranny or in a nuclear holocaust and the annihilation of human life on earth? Meanwhile, are the endeavors in research and development, not only in the physical but also in the social, psychological and biological sciences, destined to implement and accelerate policies of violence productive of counteraction and retrogression?

Although Machiavelli indicated that a wise ruler could increase his reputation and influence through being lavish with other people's resources,[157] that wars can be waged for public profit,[158] and cited ancient, but especially Roman, history as proof,[159] as early as the first quarter of the fifteenth century, rich Florentine citizens were beginning to come to the realization that the city could not fight a war without their having themselves to pay much of its cost in higher taxes;[160] and now in the twentieth century to an increasing extent sectors of the business community recognize that the demands of the military establishment weigh upon them as a suffocating incubus depressing productivity and that inexorably the costs of war fall also on the "victors" even though in the "victor" states the rich and powerful still seek to devise and employ tax systems which would leave intact for them their anticipated gains. The growing power of labor, and with it social democracy, together with the emergent economic power of raw-material-producing countries and an increasingly critical religious and humanistic body of opinion, all manifest that the old exploitive procedures can no longer be taken for granted as either economic or glorious. "Modernization," capital accumulation, computerization and high technology unaccompanied by shared decision-making and equitable access to the enjoyment of the fruits and benefits of cost efficiencies may but increase social unrest, unemployment and technological vulernability. "Advances" in atomic weaponry together with unresolved problems in the control of the waste products and proliferation of the capacity for nuclear weapons production generate widespread withdrawal of active citizen confidence in "self-governing" processes through the established political structures.

Chapter Nine

HISTORICAL AFFIRMATION OF DIRECT PERSONAL ACCESS TO CREATIVE POWER

As Machiavelli freed historiography from the religious shackles which had restricted the chroniclers,[1] is there to be detected in his confidence in the possibilities for reasoning in terms of critically observed human experience the emergence of political science as systematic treatment of essential prudence freed from nationalistic shackles?

May a re-examination of the origins reveal, as available resources, elements in Machiavelli's thinking which, heretofore without the conditions suited for their practically constructive use, have become presently at hand for the realization of undreamed-of general good?

The Roman socio-political dynamics of internal conflict and external expansion to which Machiavelli accredited the military *virtù,* boldness of spirit and excellence of citizens,[2] culminated in a weakening pride disqualifying for self-government and blighting throughout succeeding centuries that very same *virtù* not only in all those over whom it extended and exercised its control, but also in its own people.[3] Although indicating that he would prefer to place the blame for the decline upon the influence of the precepts of the Christian religion interpreted as averse to war,[4] Machiavelli granted that deeper analysis found the deteriorization inherent in the military process.[5]

Was it that the Scriptures were too generally unavailable, unknown and ignored[6] and the papal policies[7] and the practices of the prelates too perverse[8] for Machiavelli to seek seriously in the religious tradition for remedies through returning to the origins of Christianity? Derived though it was from the movement for church reform[9] and recognized by Machiavelli as essential for the life of political as well as religious institutions, renewal through return to the beginnings concerned Machiavelli only in matters political[10] and military.[11] True, he took note of an intrinsic authenticity in the religion of the founder of the religion of

285

Christendom[12] and the renovations by Saint Francis and Saint Dominic,[13] but he evaluated such efforts at renewal as but leading to deeper enslavement of the people to the irresponsible exploitation by hypocritical self-serving prelates.[14] Instead, he undertook to demonstrate that living experience, observed and evaluated in the perspective of classical civic *virtù* could provide an adequate guide for progress toward human security and liberty.

However, even as the ancient Romans,[15] Machiavelli felt the necessity, in his own way, to have recourse to God.[16]

Violent promotion of sanctified conceit as esoteric wisdom did not meet with ready acknowledgement on the part of all of those in Rome's way. In violently overriding others' identification with the land of their birth and in flaunting pridefully its own authority and accepting in its citizenship people uprooted from all lands, Rome provoked Jewish nationalism, ancient messianic hope and a sense of imminent apocalypse which prompted the affirmation of essential personal relationship to the creator of the earth and its resources and the mutuality of all people as rightful managers in the common interest of all of the resources created and owned by none but graciously entrusted for the well-being of all. A very different concept of God emerged with Jesus and his immediate followers. As presented by Lynn Harold Hough in his comment on the message of the author of Revelations:

> The belief that the world is ruled by a God who is righteousness alive is the most important conviction which can be held in the mind of man. The belief that the God who is living righteousness is also the God of suffering love has in it the power to make all things new. These two beliefs were the precious inheritance of [John] the man of Patmos.[17]

With Jesus' baptism came the conception of the possibility of a new mind and spirit employing human form. There followed self-preparation, according to the tradition of the temptations, during which he required that he eradicate from himself any dedication to economic achievement,[18] to mastery of natural forces,[19] or to political power and prestige.[20] Developmental preparation continued through his affirmation of that which was more sincerely and generously fundamental than conventional rituals, presumption of obedience to parents[21] and regard: for family ties,[22] for pride of nationality,[23] for his followers' expectations concerning the nature of his leadership,[24] for his own sense of purpose by keeping in abeyance his own will in order to let be fully manifested the Creator's purposes,[25] for the proffer of physical assistance as support from members of his group of followers,[26] even for his own understanding of the meaning of it all,[27] through his words of his final gift.[28] Thus voluntarily letting be severed the psychologic umbilical cord of individual personality, he entered into that which was and is intrinsically his own, beyond *com*-prehension, yet

286

which continues to light up all relationships with a penetrating power which at once reveals their inadequacy and transciency in their conventional manifestations but also vivifies and nourishes the seed of potentiality which is the essence of their meaning and strength. It has been said:

> The originality of Jesus is that he made the fatherhood of God the central doctrine of the Christian faith. He transformed the doctrine into a spiritual experience which gave new meaning and value to the whole of life.[29]

Jesus manifested that each individual aware of his relationship to the source of creative power has authority over conventional limitations pressed upon him as "reality." Hence the understanding and appropriating for the perception of oneself of the indications for meaning in living, given in the life and teaching of Jesus, leads not to a denial of living in this world and a morale inferior to that of the Roman citizen, but to the encountering of practical affairs and facing through conventional fictions with a questing tolerance, a critical discrimination, a stouter courage, a compassionate love which contributes a firmer basis for a broader freedom. Jesus himself said,

> I have come that men may have life, and may have it in all its fullness.[30]

A pregnant term both in the Gospels and the writings of Paul is *dunamis* which, with the fresh insight into its original meaning which Lorenzo Valla had recovered,[31] Machiavelli was to employ[32] for political renewal. He regarded God as the forgiver of men such as King David and Peter who had repented sins of action[33] rather than God as the rescuer of "Brother Lazarus" and the condemner of Uguccione della Faggiuola.[34]

Jesus struggled in himself confronting alternatives, finding out those which he renounced and the way to keep taking soundings and sightings to keep in the main channel of the Creator's will and to avoid getting off course.

To be effective as an instrument for one's own constructive moral development requires non-violent direct social action and a continuing detection and purging of any element of masochism, self-hate or insincerity; because the presence of such factors transforms the energy spent into the calling into being and the nourishment of violent adversaries. Action impregnated with authority is based upon, flows out of, is, the expression of sincere recognition that in and by oneself one does not adequately, inclusively, perceive the inner inter-relatedness of oneself, that only in most responsible action in coming to grips with and accepting full accountability to-and-with the unpleasant and violent manifesta-

287

tions of others does one catch the reflection of aspects of himself, have the possibility of seeing how to grow in the knowledge of his own true self and develop his corresponding being. Such is the nature of living power. As in sincerity each comes to his own ground in himself known through his involvement with his fellow-men, he reduces his need to draw on others for his sense of being and meaning. So does he lose impulse both for committing violence at others' expense, and for looking to others (instead of to himself in his relation to them) as a source of that truth and wisdom which is revealed in courageous, direct, mutual experiencing of mutuality assuming those forms functional for it.

Jesus kept working himself free from letting develop inner contradictions;[35] because such inner weaknesses, as a means of avoiding notice, project themselves into one's perception of others, blind one to one's own and the other's nature, and provoke in the others self-defensive reaction.[36]

When non-violent direct action proceeds out of self-mastery and sincerity, its purpose can be objective and consequently have as an impact the arousing of tensions in others' habitual reactions which result in the stirring and growth of mutually shared conscience active in service.

The Deuteronomist reported Moses as saying in his great address to "the Chosen People,"

> Out of all nations you were his chosen people as you are this day. So now you must circumcise the foreskin of your hearts and not be stubborn any more, for the Lord your God is God of gods and Lord of lords, the great, mighty, and terrible God. He is no respecter of persons and is not to be bribed; he secures justice for widows and orphans, and loves the alien who lives among you, giving him food and clothing. You too must love the alien, for you once lived as aliens in Egypt.[37]

As the rite of circumcision served those sharing in creation to remind them of their Creator so earnest repentence opens the way to compassionate love. The relationship is manifested in the interdependence of the two great commandments,[38] the illustration of the second with the parable of the good Samaritan[39] and in the Lord's prayer the conditioning of the quality of forgiveness one can receive upon the quality of forgiveness which he practices.[40]

Jesus' first sermon, as reported by Luke,[41] began with a reading from Isaiah 61:1–2 which has been paraphrased as follows:

> The Lord has anointed me to bring good news to poor people, to proclaim release to captives and sight to the blind, to send the crushed on their way with their troubles left behind them, and to announce that God's time for doing all this has arrived.[42]

Fear-driven, atomized, lonely, individualized humanity, buffeted in a mean-

288

ingless chaos of chance, ground down under imperial tyranny, began, through Jesus' living and speaking, to hear the word that through the initiative of the inexhaustible and unlimited love of God for each one, they could begin to win status and self-awareness as belonging and having a purpose which each, through living responsibly, comes to recognize as the fulfilment of his innermost and instinctive desires released in friendly working relationship with his fellowmen. Jesus revealed a perception of God as willing that his children be living fully in the joy of their strength, availing themselves of regenerating forgiveness and repentence and, not cringing fearfully burdened and submissive for exploitation by manipulators of the sense of guilt and dependence, but going forward in the creative communion of mutual revelation through questing endeavor. Theretofore, as guides, there had been the law and the prophets, but

> Ever since the coming of John the Baptist the kingdom of Heaven has been forcing its way forward, and men of force are seizing it.[43]

By "men of force," may "men of decisive action" be meant? Very perceptively, Paul W. Hoon has observed:

> Action, more than thought or emotion, vitally apprehends and consolidates meaning as personal possession.[44]

Jesus made it clear that experience of the kingdom of Heaven is a personal event.[45] It has been pointed out that

> C'est surtout avec le Christianisme que la foi est declarée volontaire[46]

> It is above all with Christianity that faith is declared voluntary

and that awareness of the fatherhood of God comes, and is available only, through acts of love manifesting sincere forgiveness of others for their "trespasses."[47]

Justice Oliver Wendell Holmes observed (as quoted in a television broadcast):

> The life of the law has not been logic; it has been experience.

Likewise, Jesus emphasized action:

> Do not suppose that I have come to abolish the Law and the prophets: I did not come to abolish, but to complete.[48]

In his exposition on I Corinthians, John Short has commented:

> the deeper meaning of power is effectiveness in achieving our pur-

289

poses . . . We have seen what the inspired writers of the Bible conceive to be the purpose of God. Paul has put it into clear focus for us. It is to achieve "a commonwealth of God" . . . in which every single soul, the man with one talent as well as he with ten, can have a part.[49]

Herein appears a notable contrast with the standpoint given by Machiavelli to his spokesman in *The Art of War* when he had him affirm:

I do not believe you believe that in time of peace everyone has his place.[50]

Creative love secures survival; denial of a rightful place engenders fear-driven rivalry and conflict. Jesus drew the contrast:

You know that in the world, rulers lord it over their subjects, and their great men make them feel the weight of authority; but it shall not be so with you. Among you, whoever wants to be great must be your servant, and whoever would be first must be the willing slave of all—like the Son of Man; he did not come to be served, but to serve, and to surrender his life as a ransom for many.[51]

The announcement of "the good news" of the birth of Jesus begins with

Do not be afraid; I have good news for you; there is great joy coming to the whole people.[52]

Later, to his disciples, Jesus said:

Have no fear, little flock; for your Father has chosen to give you the Kingdom . . . Be ready for action;[53]

and still later,

Set your troubled hearts at rest, and banish your fears . . . the Prince of this world approaches. He has no rights over me; but the world must be shown that I love the Father, and do exactly as he commands; so up, let us go forward![54]

The first letter of John records:

There is no room for fear in love; perfect love banishes fear. For fear brings with it the pains of judgement, and anyone who is afraid has not attained to love in its perfection. We love because he loved us first. But if a man says, 'I love God,' while hating his brother, he is a liar. If he does not love his brother whom he has seen, it cannot be that he loves

290

God whom he has not seen. And indeed this command comes to us from Christ himself, that he who loves God must also love his brother.[55]

The all-inclusiveness of the message is repeatedly affirmed:

Then he said to them: 'Go forth to every part of the world, and proclaim the Good News to the whole creation. Those who believe it and receive baptism will find salvation';[56]

[the Gospel] is the saving power of God for everyone who has faith;[57]

[Jesus] is also able to save absolutely those who approach God through him; he is always living to plead on their behalf;[58]

Come forward, you who are thirsty; accept the water of life, a free gift to all who desire it.[59]

In ancient Israel, men were considered to belong to the tribe and through it to the nation. In both ancient Greece and ancient Rome, the value of a man was considered to be the quality of his citizenship. Subsequently, ecclesiastical theory held that through baptism into the Church one received his soul.

Machiavelli sought to know and make known "the effectual truth"[60] by means of reasoning about everything.[61] It was by means of knowing through loving service given to each one to the uttermost that Jesus sought to know and make known the effectual truth. As Machiavelli examined prospects for maintaining or restoring free government in "corrupt cities," so Jesus carried into relations with "sinners," those rejected by institutions and conventions, the regenerating proof of their acceptability to "the Father."

Jesus' reliance on that which was his own as prompted by seeking openness to God's will and purposes[62] has its correspondence in Machiavelli's prescription

a wise prince takes care to base himself on what is his own, not on what is another's.[63]

Jesus' summons to freedom and peace was a call to action. Affirming that

Ever since the coming of John the Baptist the kingdom of Heaven has been forcing its way forward and men of force are seizing it,[64]

he called his disciples to

Be alert, be wakeful;[65]

Be ready for action, with belts fastened and lamps alight . . . Hold your-

291

selves ready, then, because the Son of Man is coming at a time you least expect him . . . I have come to set fire to the earth, and how I wish it were already kindled;[66]

Keep a watch on yourselves . . . Be on the alert, praying at all times for strength to pass safely through all these imminent troubles and to stand in the presence of the Son of Man.[67]

Throughout his teaching he emphasized action as essential. There was: the initially reluctant son who changed his mind and finally did as his father wished;[68] the condemnation of "the doctors of the law and the Pharisees" insofar as

They say one thing and do another. They make up heavy packs and pile these on men's shoulders, but will not raise a finger to lift the load themselves;[69]

and the story of the good Samaritan which concludes with the command:

Go and do as he did.[70]

With a portrayal of the final judgment as a clarification of his teaching, he said:

Then the king will say to those on his right hand, "You have my Father's blessing; come, enter and possess the kingdom that has been ready for you since the world was made. For when I was hungry, you gave me food; when thirsty, you gave me drink; when I was a stranger you took me into your home, when naked you clothed me; when I was ill you came to my help, when in prison you visited me." Then the righteous will reply, "Lord, when was it that we saw you hungry and fed you, or thirsty and gave you drink, a stranger and took you home, or naked and clothed you? When did we see you ill or in prison and come to visit you?" And the king will answer, "I tell you this: anything you did for one of my brothers here, however humble, you did for me."[71]

The heart of the prayer which he taught his disciples as a means for renewing their strength is a petition for assistance in endeavoring to bring the will of God into manifest *earthly reality*:

Thy kingdom come, Thy will be done, On *earth* as in heaven. Give us *today our daily bread* [author's emphasis]. Forgive us the wrong we have done, As we have forgiven those who have wronged us.[72]

The specific action prescribed is the extension of forgiveness to others because

292

it is this act which re-conditions one so that further growth becomes possible for him.[73] He charged his followers to be the good news in action:

> You, like the lamp, must shed light among your fellows, so that, when they see the good you do, they may give praise to your Father in heaven;[74]

> Always treat others as you would like them to treat you; that is the Law and the prophets.[75]

According to Matthew, Jesus closed his great sermon with these words:

> What then of the man who hears these words of mine and acts upon them? He is like the man who had the sense to build his house on rock. The rains came down, the floods rose, the wind blew, and beat upon that house; but it did not fall, because the foundations were on rock. But what of the man who hears these words of mine and does not act upon them? He is like a man who was foolish enough to build his house on sand. The rain came down, the floods rose, the wind blew, and beat upon that house; down it fell with a great crash.[76]

The Gospels are accounts of Jesus' living in action and through deeds of affirmation and confrontation proceeding on to the cross. John closed his account with the words:

> There is much else that Jesus did. If it were all to be recorded in detail, I suppose the whole world would not hold the books that would be written.[77]

Thus, not through ritual practices, legalistic prescriptions or quietistic withdrawal, but through "minding the Light" sensed in acts of love for another, each discovers himself whole in the order of creation.

The economy of inclusive, personal love brings into being one's awareness of those, as infinitely valuable, whom one has been accustomed to overlook, disregard and treat as nothing and, through the shock of a kind of obverse after-image, enables one to get a glimpse of them as victims of one's own obtuseness and blindness and, through remorse of conscience, to purify his own heart so that he comes to be able more nearly to see more deeply into his fellow-man as he really is, to "see God"[78] and "in him . . . live and move, in him . . . exist"[79] and come to understand how to serve acceptably and be able to do so. Citizenship in "the kingdom," the "commonwealth of God," is conscience discovering oneself in the affirmation of creative love. The political economy of the Gospels proceeds through creative cooperation among men open, as are men of science, to the cosmos-creating will. According to Paul,

> 'knowledge' breeds conceit; it is love that builds.[80]

293

It is not given to the individual to *know* the TRUTH or the GOOD or CAUSE AND EFFECT. One has to feel his way through ambiguities and if he attributes to himself the certainty of knowledge, he thereby indulges himself in false pride and gives offense in denigrating others whose elements essential for real understanding he thereby is ignoring. Such self-idolatry generates mutually destructive rivalry. On the whole, as John Knox has suggested:

> As a matter of fact, it might be argued that we can really see goodness only in others (it turns into evil when we observe it in ourselves) and that we can really see evil (in all its range and depth) only in ourselves.[81]

The action which Jesus practiced and encouraged was:

> Love your enemies and pray for your persecutors; only so can you be children of your heavenly Father, who makes his sun rise on good and bad alike, and sends the rain on the honest and dishonest . . . You must therefore be all goodness, just as your heavenly Father is all good.[82]

Resort to violence as an act of personal loyalty, he specifically rebuked[83] as he did also the invocation of divine intervention to avenge a nationalistic affront.[84]

Luke recounted the *acts* of the apostles in the book which bears that title. Paul catalogued a diversity of hardships endured in the course of his ministry[85] and still ahead for him was imprisonment, trial and martyrdom. Repeatedly he wrote in terms of the most intense forms of action: of an athlete of the spirit engaged in a race,[86] or in a boxing contest,[87] or as a soldier of the spirit preparing for or engaged in battle.[88] In his letter, James wrote:

> Only be sure that you act on the message and do not merely listen; for that would be to mislead yourselves;[89]

> If [faith] does not lead to action, it is in itself a lifeless thing.[90]

Certainly, as Machiavelli wrote, it was a misinterpretation of Christianity as founded to consider and practice it as a religion of passivity and withdrawal.[91] Yet the Gospels provide no explicit foundation for that specific activity which Machiavelli attributed to it as its saving grace: namely, "the defense of our country"[92] if in that is to be included military action, or an exclusive allegiance or loyalty. Although Machiavelli includes much besides, the whole tenor of his life and writings places special emphasis upon defense as meaning aggressive war. The historical fact is that during the first two centuries of the Christian era, according to Roland H. Bainton,

> From the end of the New Testament period to the decade A.D. 170–80

there is no evidence whatever of Christians in the army. The subject of military service obviously was not at that time controverted. The reason may have been either that participation was assumed or that abstention was taken for granted. The latter is more probable. The expansion of Christianity had taken place chiefly among civilians in urban centers. Few as yet were converted while in the army. Converts not already in the ranks had many reasons against volunteering, and they were not subject to conscription. As slaves or freedmen many were ineligible. The danger of idolatry in the army was greater than in civilian life. And to these considerations the rigorism of the Church which throughout the second century would not admit to communion penitents guilty of apostasy, adultery, or bloodshed, and the likelihood appears greater that the Church withheld its members from military service than that they were permitted to serve without a single reproach or penalty.[93]

The attitude of ecclesiastical writers toward military service on the part of Christians during the same period shows a correlation with the data on actual practice. The period in which we have no evidence of Christians in the ranks is also the period in which there is no specific prohibition of such service . . . The period from A.D. 180 until the time of Constantine exhibits both in the East and the West a number of more or less explicit condemnations of military service. In the East we have already observed the witness of Celsus and Origen to total abstinence for the period up to A.D. 250 . . . In the West, Tertullian was the most unambiguous when he said that "Christ in disarming Peter ungirt every soldier."[94]

With the consolidation of church organization and the increase of its wealth and influence, its official position became increasingly one of compromise with the state.

The bishops were happy to accept Constantine's patronage and willing, in return, to follow his directives. They would also use their influence in the service of the state—with the fourth century begins their condemnation of Christians who refuse to perform military service.[95]

Machiavelli seems to have considered that he was contrasting his perspective with that of Jesus when he wrote:

there is such a difference between how men live and how they ought to live that he who abandons what is done for what ought to be done learns his destruction rather than his preservation, because any man who under all conditions insists on making it his business to be good will surely be destroyed among so many who are not good.[96]

To this statement, Allan Gilbert has appended the explanatory footnote:

That is, he who abandons a teacher who can instruct him in what is done (the world as it is) for one who teaches only what the teacher thinks is right to do (mere theory) will gain learning which, if he acts on it, will ruin him. Machiavelli is interested in "what ought to be done" in the complex world of affairs rather than in the simpler one of dogma.[97]

Both Jesus and Machiavelli recognize that through the most responsible involvement with their fellowmen men become able to discern action appropriate to the dynamic potentiality of what is being done; but whereas Machiavelli was accepting as effective the power of individual human will, Jesus was seeking and indicating meaning in terms of a will at once more intrinsic and more comprehensive.

For Jesus, the covenant between God and his people was not merely an historic tradition, nor was it a professional monopoly to be exploited for status and wealth by the priesthood, the lawyers, the statesmen and the bureaucrats. The law and the prophets derived their validity only insofar as those who claimed tradition as their profession continued through their actions to demonstrate consistency with it. The land, the temple, the ceremonies, held significance only insofar as they continued effectively serving it through bearing witness to its essential practicality. In accordance with the witness of the Deuteronomist,[98] Jeremiah,[99] Ezekiel,[100] Isaiah[101] and stirred by John the Baptist's testimony and the extremity of foreign oppression, Jesus realized in the Covenant a living personal reality to be acknowledged and put into action. Walter Russell Bowie has written that Jesus

never thought of himself in isolation. He identified himself in utter symphathy with his nation's need.[102]

Jesus saw himself as engaged in the work of preservation and fulfilment.[103]

Now among the ancient prophets had been those who had predicted that the time would come when the Covenant would be opened to include the Gentiles.[104] Responding to the Roman centurion's faith, Jesus made the initial act in full recognition of the precedent he was setting.[105] S. MacLean Gilmour has presented in detail the evidence that

Luke was eager to stress the fact that Christianity was a world religion that recognized no racial limitations. Luke's version of Jesus' genealogy traced Jesus' ancestry to Adam, the primal man, rather than to Abraham, the father of the Jewish people . . . The Gospel of Luke anticipates the declaration of the apostle Paul with which the book of Acts comes to an end. "Let it be known to you then that this salvation of God has been sent to the Gentiles; they will listen."[106]

In the *Acts of the Apostles*, Luke recorded Philip's baptism of the Ethiopian,[107]

Peter's baptism of the centurion, Cornelius, and his household in Caeserea,[108] Paul's and Barnabas's, in light of the ancient prophecies, turning to the Gentiles;[109] and Peter's declaration to Cornelius and those assembled with his household:

> I now see how true it is that God has no favourites, but that in every nation the man who is godfearing and does what is right is acceptable to him.[110]

Jesus and Machiavelli were in accord in advocating and taking direct action in the name of the common good which: for Jesus, was perceived as full commitment to doing the will of the Creator; for Machiavelli, was perceived as determined by the prudent will of the founder or reformer prone to cloak his actions in the claim of divine authority and guidance.[111] At the cost of accepting crucifixion, Jesus spent his life demonstrating the way by which one creates meaning among men. Machiavelli, loving his native city more than his own soul,[112] opened the way for so relating to public affairs that through critical attention to lessons derived from observant participation men may curb the violent sport of Fortune. Each, out of his own courage, was building and bequeathing a system of meaning through valuing most highly those who were affirming in accomplished fact their respective perceptions of the common good. Through his way of living among people, Jesus was practicing and making evident a new order of truth.

Machiavelli struggled throughout for opportunity for official service for his city and, when denied this, for keeping his mind informed and his attitude attuned by considering events factually,[113] in the light of reason,[114] objectively and without bias.[115] Both made it clear that one knows on the level of one's responsible participation.

The Hebraic (Israelitic) valuation of the "Chosen People," the Land, the Book, the Law and the Roman valuation of the family and the public good, were proved, in the arising of Jesus' witness, to be inadequate for the order and development of mankind. Hence, as Harnack pointed out,

> Das Christentum hat die politischen Religion entwurzelt.[116]
> Christianity has uprooted political religion.

Yet it was not to a life of renunciation and deprivation that Jesus invited men but, rather, that men

> may have it in all its fullness.[117]

Perceiving that in themselves none of the earthly "goods" give men a sense of security and relief from anxiety, and that at best they are but symbols of each one's need for awareness of the presence of loving care, he was communicating that men are members of a creative order in accordance with which action in love generates a response, as the writer of Ephesians expressed it, from

> him who is able to do immeasurably more than all we can ask or conceive.[118]

As to family and land, Mark reported Jesus as saying:

> I tell you this: there is no one who has given up home, brothers or sisters, mother, father or children, or land, for my sake and for the Gospel, who will not receive in this age a hundred times as much—houses, brothers and sisters, mothers and children, and land—and persecution besides, and in the age to come eternal life.[119]

As to the fruits of the earth, Matthew quotes Jesus:

> Therefore I bid you put away anxious thoughts about food and drink to keep you alive, and clothes to cover your body. Surely life is more than food, the body more than clothes . . . All these are things for the heathen to run after, not for you, because your heavenly Father knows that you need them all. Set your mind on God's kingdom and his justice before everything else, and all the rest will come to you as well.[120]

As to the great tradition of the law and the prophets, according to Matthew, Jesus gave assurance of its complete fulfilment.[121] Jesus affirmed the presence of the immediacy of value in human experience which had been foreshadowed in Jewish tradition, and especially by major prophets, during earlier centuries.[122] Then Jesus communicated awareness of God as father[123] and people's relation with each other:

> But you must not be called "rabbi"; for you have one Rabbi, and you are all brothers. Do not call any man on earth "father"; for you have one Father, and he is in heaven. Nor must you be called "teacher"; you have one Teacher, the Messiah. The greatest among you must be your servant. For whoever exalts himself will be humbled; and whoever humbles himself will be exalted.[124]

During subsequent centuries, authorities, through institutions of state and church, had claimed ownership of the land, alienated the people from a sense of property in it, used religion to relate their emotions to institutional support and personal "otherworldliness," accepted imperial assistance for suppression and attempts at eradication of "heretics,"[125] as a means for promoting unity within. Christendom turned the *pax dei* (peace of God) into the *bellum romanum* (Roman war) of the First Crusade for the "recovery" of Jerusalem,[126] and under Pope Innocent III turned the weapon of the crusade into wars against "heretics" in Italy, France and the Rhone, Meuse and Rhine valleys.[127] A climax came when Pope Boniface VIII launched a crusade against the Colonna, the great Roman family rival to his own, the Orsini.[128]

Machiavelli, through his support for the common good and self-government, perceived the necessity to restore and implement the personal emotional valuation of the relation to one's native land.[129] Machiavelli's affirmation found physical expression in the formation of the citizen militia, the precursor of conscript national armies, and intellectual expression in the pioneering of the way toward political science. Contemporaneously, the impulse for disciplined personal activism within the institutional framework of the church took the form of the Society of Jesus of Ignatius Loyola.[130]

In the true scientific spirit, Jesus valued the exception as indication of the direction for inquiry toward deeper and more comprehensive understanding. The parable of the good shepherd searching until recovery of the one lost sheep,[131] of that of the woman rejoicing over finding the lost coin,[132] of the father forgiving the son (who, after wandering in distraction, had come back to himself) and celebrating the return,[133] of the suspended judgment illustrated in the parables of the wheat and the tares[134] and of the net full of good and bad fishes,[135] the injunction

> Love your enemies and pray for your persecutors; only so can you be children of your heavenly Father, who makes his sun rise on good and bad alike, and sends the rain on the honest and dishonest—[136]

all have worked to enhance regard for the worth to be explored and found in everyone else as the medium through which one can come to perceive and appreciate more truly the nature of the reality of which one is oneself a part and consists. The fundamental explanation which John gave is:

> God is love . . . We love because he loved us first.[137]

Here there is no room for the adage "the exception proves the rule" or that the real whole is saved through the sacrifice of any of its parts or members. In science, only that is considered to be known as a law when there can be formulated a generalization which includes all of the relevant phenomena in their diversity: beyond toleration and justification as data, comes transfiguration—a manifesting of the whole in a new form. As a part of his last discourse with his disciples, according to John, Jesus promised, on leaving, to

> send you from the Father—the Spirit of truth that issues from the Father—he will bear witness to me.[138]

According to Amos N. Wilder,

'truth' in the Johannine vocabulary has the sense of shared reality rather than correct knowledge.[139]

And in Mark's account of the interrogation before the High Priest, Jesus is recorded as saying,

you will see the Son of Man seated on the right hand of the Power.[140]

To the Pharisees, in response to their question, "When will the kingdom of God come?"[141] he responded,

in fact the kingdom of God is among [or, "within"] you.[142]

Consequently, the spirit manifested in Jesus' living witness of the covenant of love between God and mankind throughout the human condition, is, according to the Gospels, destined to prove to be the effective instrument in establishing ultimate authority—the living universally fulfilling order. Since each human being is composed of and compacted by his experience of being noticed, recognized, accepted, loved and, in response, of establishing his own form in existence—and cannot, therefore, reconcile himself to accept as reality impressions veiled as hostile—only that which invites his voluntary cooperation with his own betterment in view, can elicit his own adherence and support. Hence, order derives from consent illumined through the unobstructed openness to, search for and living toward truth; and power, derived from consent by a society jealous for its freedom of communication, serves to protect the life, liberty and that which pertains to each one: i.e., the equal right to the full development of his potentialities without the shadow of inferiority. So living love through truth constitutes freedom, as a natural right.

Joy in living, releases energy and courage for deepening and expanding human relationship which instigates the forming of institutions as a means of sustained service. But if the flow is mechanical, there is, also, the mechanical ebb. Unless the joy is of sufficient strength, innovative creativity and endurance to keep awake the discipline for the new energy to nourish the new growth, the new form draws sustenance from the heritage of the no-longer-living progenitors whose deadhand diminishes its capacity to cope with its on-going relationships, tends to reduce the spontaneity, creativity and personal touch in them and to resort to the mechanicality of rigidifying habits. There grows a deadening within, despite the outward appearance of continuing life. The deadened tend to treat others as nothing more than subordinate objects manipulated by outward events and available to be manipulated for the promotion of one's own partial and exclusive programs.

Was the Christian Church to which Paul referred as the body of Christ[143] and as "a colony of Heaven,"[144] immune to the infection of that process? Was Tommasini correct when he wrote:

> Ora il cristianesimo, entrando in relazione ed attrito col mondo antico, senza pregiudizio dell'intima natura sua, maravigliosamente secondò l'opera d'assimilazione necessaria, inoculandosi germi che fermentarono a vantaggio della sua diffusione, senza offesa d'alcuno dei principî informativi, che costituiscono la sua propria essenza?[145]

> Now Christianity, entering into relation and friction with the ancient world, without prejudice to its special nature, marvelously pursued the work of necessary assimilation, inoculating itself with the germs which agitated for the benefit of its own diffusion, *without harm to any of its formative principles which constitute its own essence?* (author's emphasis)

Basic to the Roman state was its civic religion[146] with its demand for total commitment on the part of the citizens, its holocausts, as Machiavelli termed it,

> the magnificence of their sacrifices . . . there was the deed of sacrifice, full of blood and ferocity in the slaughter of a multitude of animals; this terrible sight made the men resemble it,[147]

its demand for unity.[148] In the Athenian state the worth of a man was measured by his achievement as a citizen. Out of the tension between the sense of justice, mercy, loving kindness attributed to God's relation to man, as interpretation by the prophets developed while Jewish culture was struggling for survival despite the assaults and dominance of a succession of ancient imperial powers, there emerged religion as an interior, individualized, personal, universally available faith.[149] Following through the internalization and personalization of religion by Elijah, Jeremiah and Ezekiel and the prospect of its inclusiveness proclaimed by Isaiah, Jeremiah, Hosea and Malachi; as noted above (pp. 296–297), Jesus, Philip, Peter, Paul and Luke liberated men from the exclusivity of the descendants of Abraham as "the Chosen People." Paul, born a Roman citizen as well as a Jew,[150] raised and educated as a Pharisee,[151] before his conversion himself a persecutor of the new faith,[152] sought in Roman authority protection against the conservative reactionary efforts in the name of traditional religion to suppress and eradicate the new way.[153] Through his appeal to Caesar,[154] he found in the violently powerful imperial authority a temporary shield under the protection of which the new faith was able to continue to spread. Jesus had called men directly to full consciousness and immediate action as citizens in "the kingdom of God." He had emphasized conduct as evidence of one's citizenship in it. Therewith a new dynamic began a new history. In his exposition on I Timothy 3:9, Morgan P. Noyes quoted the American philosopher Josiah Royce:

faith is the soul's insight or discovery of some reality that enables a man
to stand anything that can happen to him in the universe

to which Morgan added,

Such faith is the source of power.[155]

But another aspect of the new religion began to compete for at least equal
recognition. Tommasini appended to his statement

Certo, dal sermone della montagna al credo di Nicea, s'era corso già un
tratto non breve, rispetto alla semplicità della fede

Certainly, from the sermon on the mount to the creed of Nicea had already
been traversed a distance not short with respect to the simplicity of the faith,

the following quotation from Hatch, *The influence of Greek ideas and usages
upon the Christian Church*:

The change in the centre of gravity from conduct to belief is coincident
with the transference of Christianity from a semitic to a greek soil.[156]

Besides winning converts to the new faith, a major concern of Paul's was the
organizing of believers into local churches and knitting the churches into a
comprehensive body. Subsequently, growth in numbers, expansion of services,
accretions of land and wealth, problems of administration, tensions with the state
over refusal to perform emperor worship,[157] periodic persecution, heightened
the role of the organization and of its officers. Modifications in attitudes and
practices became apparent. Bainton has noted:

The Thundering Legion, which contained Christian soldiers in A.D. 173,
was recruited in the province of Melitene in southern Armenia. In that
same district, early in the fourth century when a persecuting emperor
attempted to enforce idolatry, the Armenian Christians took up arms and
defeated him. In Syria, Abgar IX, the king of Edessa (A.D. 179–216) was
converted to Christianity in 202 and for the remainder of his reign made
this religion the official cult of Osrhoene.[158]

With Constantine came the most dramatic change. In the words of *The Columbia
History of the World*:

While Christianity had been uncommon and the empire prosperous, the
Christians' refusal to worship the pagans' gods had been generally ignored.
But now Christians were everywhere, and the disasters of the empire proved

that the gods were angry, presumably at the Christians' "atheism." In 249 the emperor Decius decided to stamp out Christianity. But next year he was killed trying to stop an invasion of the Goths. This ended the persecution and probably persuaded many that the Christians were right—"the deaths of the persecutors" became a favorite theme of their propaganda. The next two reigns were equally brief and disastrous. Then Valerian renewed the persecution in 257 and was captured, with much of his army by the Persians in 259. His son Gallienus called off the persecution and officially permitted the practice of Christianity . . . in 303 Gallienus' edict was rescinded and persecution renewed. By this time Christians were so numerous that the decision to persecute involved a great economic sacrifice and administrative effort. This probably influenced Constantine, when he seized power in the west in 306, to let persecution there lapse. His mother Helene's devotion to Christianity, his own belief that he was under the protection of the Christians' god, and the strength of Christianity in Italy and the east, which he hoped to conquer, also shaped his decision. After his conquest of Italy in 312 he arranged with his co-emperor for the toleration of all religions, but immediately began in his own domain to patronize Christianity. After eliminating his co-emperor in 324 he seized the treasuries and estates of most pagan temples . . . but he gave vast sums to the Christians, especially for building . . . The bishops' powers were increased by the increase of the funds they controlled . . . [Christianity] was an *organized* cult, as none of the pagan cults had been. It was also an *intolerant* cult, not only intolerant of those who worshipped other gods without the state's permission (this paganism had often been), but intolerant, by inheritance from Deuteronomy, of anyone who worshipped any other god at all, and thence, by theological extension, of anyone who practiced Christianity "incorrectly" . . . There was no empire-wide church government . . . However, the members of the church thought of it as a unity.[159]

Saint Cyprian, bishop of Carthage, martyred in 258 A.D.,[160] proclaimed:

Chi scinde la Chiesa, distrugge la fede, conturba la pace, dissipa la carità, profana i sacramenti.[161]

Who divides the Church, destroys the faith, disturbs the peace, dissipates charity, profanes the sacraments.

The term "heresy" had been used customarily as a term of praise

L'*haeresis* era, per così dire, indizio di intellettuale nobiltà e d'educazione privilegiata; perchè di siffatte opinioni e norme morali si fermavano per lo più nelle scuole filosofiche. Ve n'ebbe peraltro anche fuori, e tra'giudei in particolare formicolarono.[162]

Heresy was, so to speak, an indication of intellectual nobility and of privileged education; because such opinions and moral norms became established for the most part in the philosophic schools. However there was some outside, and among the Jews in particular they flourished.

At first, but one of many "heresies"—yet considering its own as the only true faith—the Church combatted others' beliefs as heresies.

E le chiese assunsero così forma accentratrice, pur rimanendo autonome, pur rimanendo le chiese; ma si convinsero che essenzialmente nell'unità estrinseca fosse l'espressione caratteristica della intrinseca verità delle fede. Mantenere l'unità, combattere l'eresia, parve così principale compito; e sovente ogni varietà sembrò eresia.[163]

And the churches assumed a centralized form, although remaining autonomous, although remaining the churches; but they convinced themselves that essentially in external unity was the expression characteristic of the intrinsic truth of the faith. To maintain unity, to combat heresy, this seemed the principal task; and often every variation seemed heresy.

"The first instance of judicial capital punishment for heresy," according to H. Ch. Lea, occurred in 385.[164] With the carefully fostered belief that apart from the Church there was no salvation, an institutional relationship between the human being and the collective similar to that between the Roman or Athenian citizen and his city was being reaffirmed.

By 1095, Pope Urban II, at the Council of Clermont, sought to reduce domestic violence in Christendom by summoning all to become unified through undertaking together a war for protecting access to the holy shrines held by the Saracens.[165] So the Crusades began.

The thirteenth century Church was able to command unprecedented political, economic, administrative and intellectual resources; however, in parts of Europe which were experiencing economic and political renewal,[166] began to burst forth protests against glaring contradictions between official policies and practices in the name of the Christian religion and its precepts. Innovative religious experiments sprang up only to encounter violent hostility in the form of official Church crusades, now directed within Christendom,[167] and the establishment of the papal inquisition.[168] During the fourteenth century the Church itself was subjected to captivity, schism and the beginning of the systematic re-examination and translation into the vernacular of the Scriptures themselves; the gospel message itself began to be broadcast by lay preachers among the common people.[169] Among the members of the church the realization began to grow that their religion had provided for them a role different from that of being an exploitable resource for the power, wealth and glory of the institution and its officers.

The overbearing exploitive policies and programs of the Church gave rise not only to dissident religious experiments but constituted a major factor in the emergence of the nation states. The first official appearance of the adjective "English" occurs in the Magna Carta's provision terminating papal patronage in the offices of the church in England. A century later, for the French king, Philip IV, in his contest against the imperious claims of Pope Boniface VIII, John of Paris, "A Dominican but . . . also a Frenchman," in his important defense of the king's position, *De potestate regia et papali* (1302–1303) was

perfectly definite in asserting the independence of France.[170]

The emerging nation states, just as ancient Rome, sought to exploit the idea of God and the practices of religion in order to sanctify secular policy and control; however, individualism, conscience and the scientific method in pursuit of understanding and truth continued to draw nourishment through the tap root affirmed by Jesus in the direct relation to the Creator as personally available.

305

Chapter Ten

POWER AS PARTICIPATORY EXPLORATION TOWARD TRUTH: JESUS, MACHIAVELLI AND CHRISTIANITY

Does the analytical study of the affirmation by Jesus that ours is a moral universe and that of Machiavelli, in the tradition of Anaxagoras,[1] that ours is a mind-ordered universe, give a basis for the endeavor to distill from human experience a political ethics general for mankind?

E. Troeltsch, in his *Politische Ethik und Christentum,* concluded:

Es in Wahrheit eine unmittelbar und wesentlich aus den christlichen Ideen abgeleitete politische Ethik nicht gibt;[2]

In fact there is no immediate and fundamental ethic which is derived from Christian ideas;

and Tommasini observed:

a'tempi nostri ogni dì più si conferma e propaga l'opinione che il campo della fede sia di sua natura universale ed ecceda ogni limite di circoscrizioni politiche, d'affinità o diversità etniche; che, se anche essa può influire nella vita interna dello Stato, non è atta ne a costituire propriamente un'etica civile, nè a svilupparne il sentimento negl'individui. Questo può solo essere effetto dell'opera sociale, può solo trovar fondamento nella pubblica coscienza, educata alla severa e sincera considerazione di ragguagli storici. Ricostituire però accanto alla coscienza religiosa la coscienza storica e civile fu istintivo, spontaneo, costante sforzo del Machiavelli; e a questo fine andò incessantemente per virtù d'ingegno e d'intuito, col metodo delle sue considerazioni, coll'esempio suo di scrittore.[3]

In our times every day the opinion is confirmed and propagated that the field of faith is by its nature universal and transcends every limit of political boundaries, of ethnic affinity or diversity; that even if it is able to exert influence in the internal life of the state it is not suited either to constitute a civil ethic of its own, or to develop the sentiment in the individual. This is able to be achieved only through the work of the society, it is able to find its basis only in the public conscience trained in accordance with the ruthless and sincere considerations of the judgments of history. Therefore, to re-establish, alongside of the religious conscience, the historical and civil, was the instinctive, spontaneous, constant thrust of Machiavelli; and toward this goal he proceeded ceaselessly by virtue of his talent and intuition, with the method of his reflections, with his own example as writer.

In the judgment of Friedrich Meinecke,

> The most serious discrepancy in his [Machiavelli's] system of thought—a discrepancy which he never succeeded in eliminating and which he never tried to eliminate—lay between the newly discovered ethical sphere of *virtù*, and of the State animated by *virtù*, on the one hand, and the old sphere of religion and morality on the other. This *virtù* of Machiavelli was originally a natural and dynamic idea, which (not altogether unhappily) contained a certain quality of barbarity (*ferocia*); he now considered that it ought not to remain a mere unregulated natural force (which would have been in accordance with the spirit of the Renaissance) but that it ought to be raised into a *virtù ordinata,* into a rationally and purposively directed code of values for rulers and citizens. The *virtù ordinata* naturally set a high value on religion and morality, on account of the influence they exerted towards maintaining the State. In particular, Machiavelli spoke out very forcibly on the subject of the indispensability of religion (*Disc.,* 1, 11 and 12); at any rate he was strongly in favour of a religion which would make men courageous and proud. He once named 'religion, laws, military affairs' together in one breath, as the three fundamental pillars of the State. But, in the process, religion and morality fell from the status of intrinsic values, and became nothing more than means toward the goal of a State animated by *virtù*. It was this that led him on to make the double-edged recommendation, which resounded so fearsomely down the centuries to come, inciting statesmen to an irreligious and at the same time dishonest skepticism: the advice that even a religion tinged with error and deception ought to be supported, and the wiser one was, the more one would do it.[4]

The Scriptures indicate a profound aversion of prophetic to political leadership. When "the elders of Israel" petitioned the judge Samuel:

> appoint us a king to govern us, like other nations . . . to lead us out to war and fight our battles,[5]

and Samuel presented their request to "the Lord," he received as a response the advice that the people must be permitted to learn the lesson from their mistake in turning from "the Lord's" to human military leadership.[6] Again, centuries later, the prophet Jeremiah predicted that the law would be so internalized that there would be no need for institutions of education or government.[7] Centuries still later, Jesus announced the advent of the order of loving service.[8] Sherman Johnson has observed:

> Jesus never deals directly with the responsibilities of free citizens in a democratic state. His teaching of course has political implications, but how it should be applied is one of the most difficult problems of Christian social ethics.[9]

The *Epistle to Diognetus* asserted:

> Christians inhabit their own lands but as sojourners. They share in all things outwardly as citizens, and endure all things as strangers. Every foreign land is theirs, and every land is foreign.[10]

The Christian concept, as presented in Revelations, is that the individual's acts have eternal significance in that—involved in the ultimate and complete victory of good, light, truth over wickedness, darkness, falsehood and deception—they are building character. Hence it is not consistent with such assumptions as those which Machiavelli inferred that all things remain the same[11] or that a cyclical pattern pervades history.[12] The prophet Ezekiel had proclaimed:

> Have I any desire, says the Lord God, for the death of a wicked man? Would I not rather that he should mend his ways and live?[13]

At the conclusion of the parable of the finding of the lost sheep, Jesus spoke of the

joy in heaven over one sinner who repents.[14]

From the perspective that God, the creator of beings, is love,[15] and that

in him we live and move; in him we exist . . ."We are also his offspring,"[16]

guided by "the spirit of truth,"[17] a "political ethics" extracted from partisan historiography accepting fictions as axioms and partisanly chronicling the violent conflicts for dominance over others for exploitation of the land and the people thereon, is a case in which pathology tends to obliterate the remembrance of the possibility of health and the methods for achieving it.

The fusion of temporal and spiritual claims climaxed in the ecclesiastical imperialism fully developed as a theory in the *De ecclesiastica potestate* by Egidius Colonna and in the papal bull *Unam sanctam* issued in 1302 by Pope

309

Boniface VIII.[18] As a summarizing conclusion Egidius Colonna wrote:

> It follows therefore that you ought to admit that you have your inheritance, and all your property, and all your possessions, rather from the Church and through the Church and because you are a son of the Church, than from your father after the flesh and through him and because you are his son.[19]

It was against supporters of such papal claims that John of Paris wrote his treatise *De potestate regia et papali*.[20] In it he helped lay the foundation for the defense of a political ethic as distinct from the ecclesiastical. According to Sabine:

> He argues in his opening chapters that the church requires universality but that political authority does not. Civil society arises by a natural instinct and men are diverse in their inclinations and interests . . . The self-sufficing community which he adopts from Aristotle is for him the kingdom, and he sees no difficulty in admitting as many such autonomous units as there actually are . . . He adopts from Aristotle, as St. Thomas had done, the view that civil government is necessary in itself to a good life and is therefore justified by its ethical benefits even apart from its sanction by Christianity.[21]

Thus was opening the conflict between the emerging states, the Church, and, with the Reformation, the diversifying religious sects which was to lead to the affirmation of the individual as endowed with rights of autonomous conscience, reason, private property and, through the separation of church and state, the freedom of association with others for the promotion of the common good.

Meanwhile there continued those who had not forgotten that Jesus had affirmed a political ethic in his prophecy to the High Priest:

> You will see the Son of Man seated at the right hand of the Power[22]

and who kept before themselves the goal that their wills become instruments for transforming human relations into more mutually beneficial processes. The essential dynamics in Christian terms has been expressed by R. H. Strachan in his comment upon the observation by A. E. Taylor in *The Faith of a Moralist*:

> We appreciate a great forgiveness only because we credit the forgiver with a true estimate of the gravity of the act he loves us well enough to forgive;[23]

and Strachan explained,

> Only thus do the children of God gain the courage and persistence to keep alive in themselves and in the world of men that tension between life as it is and life as it ought to be;[24]

or, as more basically expressed by John,

We love because he loved us first.[25]

May we have reached the stage in mankind's culture in which a political ethic for mankind incorporating the Christian insights not only can be formulated but must be implemented if we are not to drift blindly headlong into atomic holocaust?

Characteristic elements for such a political ethic are:

1. Power (*virtù, dunamis*) is the "eternal" breaking into the "temporal."

2. Love in action, is communication between "the children" in awareness of their creator.

3. Each is unalienably endowed with rightful claim to dignity and equality of opportunity for the discovery and development of his talents, to security in his respect for his roots in the land, to acceptance as a reciprocally concerned, new being, living forth uniquely, unencumbered by negative imagination or by past "sins."

4. Reconciliation through forgiveness of others, enlightens one's self-understanding, his perception of others as they are, and blazes the trail into enhanced experience.

5. The "Spirit of Truth"[26] is the advocate for each and the regulator in public interest. One's deepest exploration, highest privilege, most immediate duty to each other, is right treatment of human nature. Functioning growth in communion and conscience enhances power.

6. An expression of creative love, each belongs to nothing less than an all-including community experienced as increasing truth, goodness, beauty, as understanding of the meaning of sincerity in the search deepens through implementation.

Despite the deflection, by Machiavelli's time, of the conventional and institutional practices in the name of the religion which claimed Jesus as its founder, and fully recognizing Machiavelli's expressed aversion to such practices, closer acquaintance with his life and writings reveals him as no "anti-Christ," as affirmed by Giuseppe Prezzolini in the title of his biography of Machiavelli published in Italy in 1954, nor an "atheist," as characterized by him in "The Christian Roots of Machiavelli's Moral Pessimism,"[27] nor a "heathen," as judged by Friedrich Meinecke.[28] Moreover, the often-drawn antitheses between power and conscience, will and love, the state and the individual, force and science, should not be let obscure or obliterate indications in Machiavelli's thought of relationships to Christianity which, recognized as intrinsic elements and restored as operating factors in the science which he initiated, may still contribute to further constructive developments for mankind.

No such imperative for a personal resort to and confrontation with the Scriptures as impelled Jesus, a Wycliffe, a Huss, a Luther, a Calvin, or even a Lorenzo Valla, stirred Machiavelli, but it was out of the ferment among the believers[29] that he received and made his own the principle of seeking remedies for institutional ills by returning to the beginnings[30] and therefrom drawing renewed strength for advancing freedom through the renewed study of the republican form of government of Rome at the time of its founding of Florence.[31]

For serving vitally a more inclusive kinship than the traditional children of Abraham, namely, the brotherhood of mankind, Jesus kindled a new sense of more immediate obligation in personal conduct. Machiavelli was concerned for the development of a political *virtù* and vigor adequate for a community more effective than the current city states—one which must be conceived of as being ever more expanding and inclusive and strengthened through the involvement of the young citizens in the militia. Both Jesus and Machiavelli felt personally anguished by the fateful prospect which each envisaged for his respective homeland. After recounting the hypocricies of the religious and civic leaders who gained authority through external observances and then used the power thus gained for extortion of personal privileges and for exploitation of those under their control, Jesus exclaimed:

> You snakes, you vipers' brood, how can you escape being condemned to hell? . . . Believe me, this generation will bear the guilt of it all.
> O Jerusalem, Jerusalem, the city that murders the prophets and stones the messenger sent to her! How often have I longed to gather your children, as a hen gathers her brood under her wings; but you would not let me. Look, look! there is your temple, forsaken by God;[32]

and again,

> When he came in sight of the city, he wept over it and said, 'If only you had known, on this great day, the way that leads to peace! But no; it is hidden from your sight.'[33]

In August 1513, Machiavelli wrote Vettori:

> I do believe that they [the Swiss] can become masters of Italy, by reason of their nearness and our disorders and vile conditions. And because this

frightens me, I wish to remedy it, and if France does not suffice, I see no other resource; and I am now ready to weep with you over our ruin and servitude, which, if it does not come today or tomorrow, will come in our time.[34]

Toward the end of his life he wrote Guicciardini whom the Pope had placed in charge of his forces to combat the Emperor,[35]

now God has brought things back to such a state that the Pope is in time to hold him [the Emperor], if this time is not let go. You know how many opportunities have been lost; do not lose this one or trust any more in standing still, turning yourself over to Fortune and to Time, because with Time there do not always come the same things and Fortune is not always the same. I would speak further, if I were not talking with a man who did not know secrets and did not understand the world.[36]

In each, however, a profound assurance challenged the conventional drift toward ruin. Jesus, affirming that the time for action had arrived,[37] lead his disciples in living responsibly (above, pp. 291–294).

Action, purposive for the more inclusive value, and of such an intensity as to be qualified by suffering, is the tap root through which the new moral order sends forth its young shoots and flourishes as individual character naturalized in the citizenship of the emerging power being thereby revealed. The religious aspect receives an explanation in James W. Clarke's exposition on II Thessalonians 1:5–10:

This is a moral universe . . . In the Incarnation he is the God who came down, who could not stand apart from the pain and suffering of the family he created, and who must in his Son encourage, heal, and save it. In the Incarnation he identifies himself with humanity, becomes bone of its bone, flesh of its flesh, and heart of its heart, and so enters with it into similarity of experience. In the Cross we see God taking to himself man's sin, weariness, and sorrow; the eternal conscience being wounded for our transgressions, the eternal innocence being bruised for our iniquities, and the eternal holiness gathering the chastisement of our indifference to himself. But we see yet more, for in it man receives forgiveness, redemption, sympathy, strength, inspiration, and constant incitement to fresh moral striving. Man's experience from the beginning is that God is his helper . . . The Christian believes with Jesus and Paul that it [suffering] can be used. He is not exempt from it, but when it comes he can employ it to fertilize his character . . . When Paul thought of the pains inflicted upon himself—accusations of hypocricy, cowardliness, greediness, usurpation, lying, beatings, stonings, imprisonment, and shipwreck—he said that they had taught him serenity and had actually furthered the gospel.[38]

313

In office, stung by the city's disastrous reliance upon auxiliary and mercenary forces, Machiavelli conceived of tapping the loyalty and energies of native-born youth and undertook to win official endorsement for instituting a civic militia and then personally participated in the recruiting and then the training of the men enlisted. Undaunted by the fall of the government, his dismissal from his post and his exile from the city to his farm, by writing the *Prince* he sought to inspire the young Medicean princes and, by the *Discourses* and *The Art of War*, to arouse prominent young Florentines to emulate the mind and spirit of men of republican Rome. Through direct conversations with Pope Clement VII, he won serious consideration for his proposal that a militia be created in Romagna[39] and, when given opportunity, he entered with total dedication into creating for his city a more adequate system of defensive walls[40] and giving such other services as Guicciardini, his friend and the commander of the papal forces, requested.[41] Through it all, he was coming to perceive, demonstrate and advocate the observation and analysis of human behavior as the most reliable guide for policy formation.

For both Jesus and Machiavelli, a sense of relation to a more inclusive whole was so imminently pressing for recognition in expression that it provided the fearless impulse and the energy conducive to disciplined preparation essential for timely and effective action in the midst of the undetermined potentialities for "good" or "bad," "*virtù*" or "Fortune," "law" or "accident," and led to deeds of an authenticity such that they have become fundamental elements with which those who came after could carry forward toward realization of that of which each had had intimation.

How open-ended was the common good which Machiavelli aspired to serve has been clearly indicated by Harvey C. Mansfield, Jr.:

> But if the Romans are to be imitated, they must be imitable; they must have acquired their empire by virtue, not by fortune or accident (II 1). Since—or if—all "accidents" are planned, an empire so acquired will grow as large and remain as durable as nature allows. The limit on human virtue is revealed to be nature, not fortune, and Machiavelli must look at the Romans not merely in competition with their neighbors or other regimes, but also among sects that have ruled a "part of the world" (II 5) for long, though precisely defined, periods of time. Can the limit of nature on human virtue be overcome, so as to fulfill Machiavelli's promise to benefit "each one," not merely in Florence, Italy, or the modern West, not merely of any particular sect, but (as we suppose) of the "human generation?" To do so would require that the Romans be imitated up to this limit and then surpassed. Machiavelli admires Rome and holds it up for admiration in a beautified and rationalized image to the fainthearted who fear that nothing great can be attempted, yet from the height of his ambition he also criticizes Rome, more quietly but unmistakeably, for the attention of the strong-hearted. They are to know that it is not enough to imitate Rome, as the others are to know it is not too much.[42]

Both Jesus and Machiavelli understood for themselves the nature of fear and its consequences for others. Luke begins the public announcement of the message with angels proclaiming:

Do not be afraid; I have good news for you: there is great joy coming to the whole people.[43]

Jesus in his last discsourse with his disciples impressed upon them:

Have no fear, little flock; for your Father has chosen to give you the Kingdom . . . Be ready for action.[44]

In one of Machiavelli's last letters to his friend Francesco Vettori, distressed at the mounting dangers from the advancing imperial forces, he sought to strengthen him with the words:

you can save yourselves if you do not give up your courage.[45]

In *The Art of War* he wrote:

Never lead your soldiers to battle if you have not first made yourself sure of their courage and established that they are without fear and in order. Never make a trial of them except when you see that they expect to win.[46]

He observed that it is through managing men's fears that a prince builds and maintains his power, and a republic its security:

since men love at their own choice and fear at the prince's choice, a wise prince takes care to base himself on what is his own, not on what is another's;[47]

A Republic If She Is To Be Kept Free, Requires New Acts of Foresight Every Day;[48]

and a people filled with fear are wholly vulnerable.[49]

Even if official actions were providing ineffective direction in public affairs, Machiavelli manifested in the following statements no hidden uncertainty or lack of confidence that reliable guidance can be found:

it is well to reason about everything;[50]

I believe it is at all times the duty of a prudent man to reflect on what may harm him, and to foresee things when they are at a distance, and to assist what is good and to resist evil in time;[51]

315

Oh proud men, ever you have arrogant faces, you who hold the scepters and the crowns, and of the future do not know a single truth! So blinded are you by your present greed which over your eyes holds a thick veil that things remote you cannot see . . . If you turned your prudence to learning the ill and finding its remedy, such great power from heaven would be taken.[52]

As the antidote to fear, Jesus prescribed:

Set your mind on God's kingdom and his justice before everything else, and all the rest will come to you as well;[53]

Do not be afraid, only show faith.[54]

May not the psycho-dynamics of the prayer which he taught his disciples to pray consist in: first, in directing one's attention, through remembrance of the loving creator of the universe, to one's real I—the core of one's being as derived from, consisting in, and secure in the love which characterizes the universe (As there dawns this knowledge, one's obsessive fears begin to lose their grip, vanish, give place to perspective for right action.) and as participant in the creative will; then, in petitioning for the continuance of that nourishment of spirit which enlightens and strengthens one even to courage for extending to others that quality of forgiveness which conditions one for the ability to receive in oneself the regenerative refreshment and releases communion bearing fruit in the building together of new order. There follows recognition of the need for continuing help and guidance if one is to keep adequately alert and aim-directed. The prayer concludes with a return to the affirmation of faith in the eternal reality of the power.

The author of Hebrews formulated this description of faith:

Faith gives assurance to our hopes, and makes us certain of realities we do not see.[55]

Recently, it has been defined as

whole-hearted belief on the basis of evidence, but not wholly conclusive evidence, and of interpretation which is reasonable, but which falls short of absolute proof.[56]

However, James explains and warns:

faith; if it does not lead to action, it is itself a lifeless thing . . . faith divorced from deeds is barren.[57]

Both Jesus and Machiavelli perceived a reality from which each derived a fearless confidence, the source of courage: for Jesus, it was that the universe is the expression of a loving Father; for Machiavelli that the social order is characterized by prudence.[58] Peter, even as Jesus and Paul, conveyed the conviction that, in the words of Alfred E. Barnett,

> the universe is moral not mechanistic . . . God of righteousness, not blind fate, determines the course of history[59]

and, as Elmer G. Homrighausen expressed it, this conviction inspired an

> unflagging attitude of expectant confidence . . . immediately embodying the righteousness of *the new heaven and . . . new earth* of Christian expectation.[60]

Likewise, an "unflagging attitude of expectant confidence" embodying the empirical reasonableness of the more inclusive allegiance and the nobler quality of its citizenry, repeatedly found personal expression, (as noted above, p. 249) in Machiavelli.

Through becoming finely attuned to people's deeply-felt but scarcely intimated needs and aspirations, precursors of a new order convey to other individuals a solidity and specificity in their relation to being alive on the good earth and induce an awareness of rights essentially characteristic as roots of very being. At best it is the role of the would-be official to convey to the incipient parts—feverishly, clamorously, threateningly demanding priority for their own "needs"—the creatively comprehending, strengthening, compassionate, refreshening, healing, renewing, regenerating relationship to be found through such recognition and reaffirmation of the whole in terms of which there comes about a change in the attitudes. The *present* realization that this power, felt received in participation, is not given for personal appropriation but rather for sensitive application in mutual service, distinguishes, as Machiavelli perceived, the prudent and high-minded founders.[61] In Jesus, a sense of love of the common creator as the deepest attribute of personal character provided a spirit of forgiveness and confidence in mutual endeavor for good, right through willingness to accept crucifixion. Machiavelli, although considering as ineradicable in human personality the desire for revenge for past injuries suffered, even to the extent of ruining one's own country and bringing harm to oneself in the process of getting it,[62] in himself cherished for his city a love which dispelled any sense of personal grievance.[63] Both prescribed for those who would enter into and become members of the new order the cultivation of a similar disposition. Thus Jesus:

317

If anyone wishes to be a follower of mine, he must leave self behind; day after day he must take up his cross, and come with me;[64]

and Machiavelli:

A Good Citizen for Love of His Native City Will Forget Private Injuries.[65]

He held that one should learn to will, and do graciously in time, that which is necessary.[66]

Both perceived that it is in service that power is generated and that individuality is compounded through active dedication to a mission. The element of truth implicit in and promoting the formation of heroes through mythmaking, arises out of the shock given to the tendency to accept as reality limitations upon one's own capacity to undertake that which one ought, with the confidence of effective application. In order for one to get in touch with his inner unique creativity and to relate to that creative initiative in others, he must come to perceive the specific density and nature of the gravitational pulls of the habitually-regarded "objects" and interests around him as psychological constructs the substance of which is identical with his own habitual inclinations and desires and discriminate these from that creative initiating energy which is "I AM" in himself and able to be encountered and cooperated with "THAT" in another and, with each other (others), thereby to form instruments through which action can flow effectively so long as there is unimpeded interplay between the energy expended and the awareness of the purposing to which it is being directed. Thus, speaking of the price in conventional values which one would have to pay if one would enter on the new way which Jesus was pioneering, he said:

If anyone comes to me and does not hate [John Knox, "Exposition," Luke 14:26, I.B., 8, 259: *The Abingdon Bible Commentary* says that it goes back in root to an Aramaic word meaning to "love less,"][67] his father and mother, wife and children, brothers and sisters, even his own life, he cannot be a disciple of mine. No one who does not carry his cross and come with me can be a disciple of mine—So also none of you can be a disciple of mine without taking leave of all his possessions.[68]

Both Jesus and Machiavelli signally articulated human relationship transcending their cultural traditions. Jesus was criticized as

a friend of tax-gatherers and sinners.[69]

He was shocking men to "think differently" (the original meaning of "repent"— *metanoein)* by breaking conventional rituals in order to direct attention back to the original values conventionally ignored, obscured, forgotten, but essentially

318

valid. Machiavelli, by recording affairs of state as, with studied detachment, he observed them, enlarged awareness of human behavior and in doing so affronted hypocritical professions of superior goodness and pretenses of achievement of good government and so, charged with attacking and destroying the reputations of the "good" his name, as "Old Nick," came to be identified with that of the devil. And yet, in his endeavor to see and show as practical "the effectual truth,"[70] he was enabling men to become less pretentious but more perceptive regarding themselves and others and, hence, less blindly, reactively, mechanically violent. He bespoke human nature as at once more energetic, tragic, hopeful and more broadly interrelated than customarily assumed. He sensed the need for a more wholistic view of past events than that taken customarily by historians[71] and occasionally revealed a glimmer of obligation to mankind as a whole as when he wrote:

> These methods are very cruel, and enemies to all government not merely Christian but human, and any man ought to avoid them and prefer to live a private life rather than to be a king who brings such ruin on men.[72]

Insofar as Jesus' dynamic protest against habit-blindness had been transformed into contemplative otherworldiness,[73] entangled with papal ambition[74] and clerical corruption (illustrated by the character of Frate Timoteo in *Mandragola*),[75] Machiavelli turned to the fierce territorially aggressive policy of republican Rome for vindication of that political nativism which, in reaction against papal imperialism and the secular claims of the Holy Roman Empire, had given rise to the new princes of England, France and Spain and out of which he anticipated a power for Italy. Concerned for the development of adequate *virtù* and vigor, he deduced from the Roman example that it required commitment to a program of continuous military expansion[76] but either he did not consider sufficiently seriously that the destruction of the *virtù* and vigor which he recognized and attributed to the latter days of the republic—and especially to the Empire[77]—was an inherent consequence of the destructive misuse of human and material resources, or he accounted for the decline as but a proof of an over-ruling cyclical process in human affairs.[78]

Ultimately, however, Machiavelli did not reconcile himself to such fatalistic mechanicality. He found that in

observing the truth of the matter as facts show it,[79]

purposing

to write something useful to him who comprehends it,[80]

turning

319

prudence to learning the ill and finding the remedy, such great power from heaven would be taken.[81]

He seems not to have fully perceived that, through the centuries-long ordeal of imperial attacks, defeats and oppression (Assyrian, Egyptian, Chaldean, Babylonian, Persian, Alexandrian, Roman), in Judaea there had come to active human expression justice as love-through-truth firmly rooted in the personal present. Compromised and enshackled though it had become subsequently, persistently it found means of expression more inclusive, comprehending and adequate for the expanding order of free men—and of such Machiavelli was himself a signal exponent in the great tradition.

Jesus in word and deed recognized each as having his (her) own place through the congeniality of the creator characterized as omniscient and caring.

Are not sparrows five for twopence? And yet not one of them is overlooked by God. More than that, even the hairs of your head have all been counted. Have no fear; you are worth more than any number of sparrows.[82]

He presented God as a loving Father so concerned about each as to search until he finds anyone lost[83] and those who would qualify for citizenship in the kingdom of heaven as those who had ministered to whomever was in need[84] and that upon coming to the realization that such is one's own nature, one becomes a new man.[85] Jesus affirms that individual well-being consists in awareness of loving, life-giving relatedness which is the source for joy in the active dispelling of fear-filled alienation. In the words of the epistle to the Ephesians,

You must be made new in mind and spirit, and put on the new nature of God's creating, which shows itself in the just and devout life called for by the truth;[86]

and of Paul,

now you yourselves must lay aside all anger, passion, malice, cursing, filthy talk—have done with them! Stop lying to one another, now that you have discarded the old nature with its deeds and have put on the new nature, which is being constantly renewed in the image of its Creator and brought to know God;[87]

the only thing that counts is new creation.[88]

Insight into the psychological dynamics has been contributed by Robert H. Wicks in his "Exposition" on Philippians 2:1–5:

Any moment when we are prompted to love, we know something is moving us (an "incentive") which is not like the force of our will, yet when the

320

incentive moves us to act, it is our will that has to perform the act. This mixture of motive powers can never be analyzed and divided distinctly into its differing parts, because our spirit was created on purpose to be possessed by God's Spirit. The Spirit "bloweth where it listeth," and where it blows from is not always plain, because its sources may be in memories of those who long ago captured our imagination by the spirit which possessed them.[89]

In word and deed, Machiavelli, also, recognized a natural individuality—perhaps only a potentiality—in need of regeneration. The gift of "an individual disposition" and "an individual imagination," in writing to Soderini, he attributed to Nature.[90] Opportunity for its expression, he ascribed in the *Prince* once to Fortune:

in order not to annul our free will, I judge it true that Fortune may be mistress of one half our actions but that even she leaves the other half, or almost, under our control;[91]

and once to God:

God does not do everything, so as not to take from us free will and part of the glory that pertains to us.[92]

In *The Art of War*, however, with the rejection of the assumption

that in time of peace everyone has his place,[93]

there is ultimately only necessity-born impulse[94] which incites one to make his own place for himself.[95] Fear-born aggression, individualized, is the ground of human reality as Machiavelli generally presents it. It is for one to affirm spiritedly the guidance prompted by his own nature:

ognuno faccia quello che gli detta l'animo, e con audacia;[96]

each man should so what his spirit dictates to him, and with boldness;

it is better to be impetuous than cautious;[97]

I believe, have believed, and will always believe that it is true, as Boccaccio said, that it is better to act and repent than not to act and repent;[98]

I beg you to follow your star . . . and not let an iota go for the things of this world;[99]

No man without inventiveness was ever great in his profession;[100]

men cannot make themselves safe except with power;[101]

it is much better to tempt Fortune when she possibly will favor you than, not tempting her, to face certain ruin;[102]

often when a man is doing something, plans reveal themselves to him which, if he stood still, would forever hide themselves;[103]

They [men] ought, then, never to give up as beaten, because since they do not know her [Fortune's] purpose and she goes through crooked and unknown roads, they can always hope, and hoping are not to give up, in whatever fortune and whatever affliction they may be;[104]

you can save yourselves if you do not give up your courage;[105]

if you help yourself, everybody will help you;[106]

those defenses alone are good, are certain, are durable, that depend on yourself and your own abilities;[107]

no one can use as a foundation forces other than one's own.[108]

An irreducible core of unpredictable reaction characterized the individual, as Machiavelli described him. Disregard of it is at the cost of security itself (above, pp. 11–12).

Individuality, however, is not impervious to the working of conscience.[109] The regeneration through which men gain a fighting chance to secure the possibility for development and liberty, Machiavelli perceived in the disciplined solidarity of men native to the same land.[110] As Jesus prescribed rebirth in the spirit of living in love and truth, Machiavelli prescribed it in disciplined patriotism for the citizens and the experience-distilled prudence for the rulers.

As for himself, as Machiavelli wrote Francesco Vettori:

if Fortune had wished that the Medici, either in affairs in Florence or abroad, or in their private business or in that of the public, had only once employed me, I should be satisfied. Nevertheless, I do not mistrust myself in reality. And when this happens and I do not know how to sustain myself, you may grieve for me; but that which has to be, let it be;[111]

and in his dedicated service to his city he perceived his worth.[112]

Jesus' valuation of individuality emphasized: fearless security in awareness of one's own being as derived from a loving power;[113] growing enlightenment through mutual forgiveness;[114] abstention from passing judgment upon others;[115] treatment of others as one would like to be treated;[116] service to others in need;[117]

and direct action without violence. Jesus proceeded serenely, graciously self-aware, responding to their hearts' content to others feeling need. Thus he nullified the strategems of terror by which institutional exploiters of fear habitually and conventionally in the name of God and the law acquired and sustained their prestige and power.

As time went on, however, at length even Jesus' name was used to alienate people further from security in land, in person and in hope for improvement in their living conditions in this life, while at the same time to aggrandize the wealth and power of claimants of eternal as well as temporal authority,[118] and promote their personal irresponsibility and self-indulgence.[119] Machiavelli perceived that there had been a misinterpretation of Christianity.[120] He sought to revive in the human nature of the Italians that sense of dignity which Livy had described as the vigor of the Roman citizens in the early days of the republic. Since the records of the life of Jesus were not currently available to people, conventional Christianity was not subject to critical correction in light of them and no longer symbolized the active, personally responsible involvement which had distinguished its founder. As Tommasini has made abundantly clear, in no sense was Machiavelli, as recorder of observed phenomena, either a-moral or atheistic.[121] He was endeavoring to revivify in human personality a confidence in the availability of a fighting chance for doing something honorable or vigorous about living or dying with justice.[122] Machiavelli launched, also, a challenge against exploiters of fear. His valuation of individuality ultimately involved a call for the application of prudence distilled from observation gained through responsible participation.[123]

Both Jesus and Machiavelli used shock to bring their compatriots to awareness of inadequately regarded perils. Repeatedly, Jesus signalled:

Keep awake then; for you never know the day or the hour;[124]

Be alert, be wakeful. You do not know when the moment comes . . . And what I say to you, I say to everyone: Keep awake;[125]

Be ready for action, with belts fastened and lamps aldight;[126]

If you have ears, then hear.[127]

In his own terms, Machiavelli warned:

I do not believe you believe that in time of peace everyone has his place;[128]

To believe that without effort on your part God fights for you, while you are idle and on your knees, has ruined many kingdoms and states.
There is assuredly need for prayers . . .
But there should be no one with so small a brain that he will believe, if

his house if falling, that God will save it without any other prop, because he will die beneath that ruin;[129]

men cannot make themselves safe except with power;[130]

a prince . . . cannot plunder a man so completely as not to leave him a dagger for revenging himself; a man cannot be so dishonored as not to retain a spirit determined on revenge;[131]

and, on the other hand, he emphasized the energy released in one when implementing self-interest:

One can observe . . . how much difference there is between an army that is satisfied and fights for its own glory and an army that is ill disposed and fights for its leader's ambition;[132]

not individual good but common good is what makes cities great. Yet without doubt this common good is thought important only in republics.[133]

In *The History of Florence,* he represented a member of the Signoria as warning the imported head of the government, the Duke of Athens, who was obviously moving toward attempting a tyranny over the city,

Have you considered how important and how strong in a city like this [Florence] is the name of liberty, which no force crushes, no time wears away, and no gain counterbalances?[134]

Contrasting assumptions regarding the individual's place in nature and the universe led Jesus and Machiavelli to contrasting perceptions regarding the nature and source of power and that which it effects. Jesus loved each as endowed with inestimable value—a beloved son of a Father-creator;[135] Machiavelli, considering that in time of peace there is no place for everyone,[136] that the wise prince forms his young men into his army,[137] held that men achieve their worth through service to the state,[138] that the Roman method of expansion makes a state "always richer and more powerful"[139] and that the individual is able to become more noble in the nobler kind of country.[140] Rather than draw out others' energies and exploit them for his own indulgence and satisfaction as he pictured worldly leaders doing,[141] Jesus stirs in those responsive to him the discovery and recognition of the inner effective strength native to them: as in the case of the Syro-Phoenician woman[142] and of the Samaritan leper[143] and on an additional occasion when he explained: "Your faith has made you whole."[144] Both Jesus and Machiavelli called attention to there-to-fore overlooked resources of power which each proclaimed as of utmost importance: Jesus, the individual's resource in his faith; Machiavelli, the native born's feeling for his native land and compatriots.[145]

The former (faith) affirms the Creator's purpose in and for one's own being (existence), the latter (patriotism), aroused and disciplined by the leader of the state, serves and promotes "its" purposes. Each affirmation became the ground which subsequently bore fruit in the form of an institution: faith, the church; patriotism, the militant nation-state. But both Jesus and Machiavelli acclaimed the ennoblement of the individual[146] through responsible service growing in understanding truth.[147]

Chapter Eleven

CULTURAL CHANGES REQUIRING
RE-EVALUATION OF POLITICAL
PERCEPTIONS AND PROCESSES

Even as in Aristotle's time, and again in Machiavelli's, in the twentieth century, cultural change—especially, in technology—has outstripped the capacity of the traditional governmental institutions and their guidelines to manage, or even to channel, the dynamic turbulent processes at large. Herein may be perceived an imperative for a quantum leap in political science comparable to that which Aristotle and Machiavelli each made in his respective period. Orestes Ferrara has observed:

On a dit, avec beaucoup d'exactitude, que l'Italie fut le laboratoire où furent expérimentées toutes les institutions. Avec ce critère nous pouvons affirmer que Florence, industrielle et commerciale, experimenta souvent des institutions qui provenaient d'un esprit très pareil à celui qui a crée et maintenu les grandes démocraties modernes. C'est pour cela, certainement, que lord Acton affirme que Machiavel vit encore parmi nous et lord Morley, reprenant cette pensée, qu'il représent une force vive chez les modernes. Les *Discours* de Machiavel, insistons-nous, sont un livre moderne comme le sont, même sans les a ccepter dans leur ensemble, les principes d'Aristote, car les institutions qui sont à la base des écrits de ces deux hommes et qui furent celles de leur époque respective sont de la même nature que les nôtres.[1]

It has been said, with a great deal of accuracy, that Italy was the laboratory where all the institutions were tried out. In accordance with this judgment we can affirm that Florence, industrially and commercially, often tried out institutions which derived from a spirit very similar to that which has created and maintained the great modern democracies. It is for this reason, certainly, that Lord Acton held that Machiavelli still lives among us and

Lord Morley, taking up again this thought, that he represents a living force among people. The *Discourses* of Machiavelli, we insist, are a modern book as are, even without accepting them in their entirety, the principles of Aristotle, for the institutions which are at the base of the writings of these two men and which were those of their respective epoch are of the same nature as ours.

May the similarity extend to the necessity for the projection of a new initiative along the line of the development which each, in his respective time, indicated for mankind?

From the thirteenth century, at an accelerating rate, economic, political, religious factors and rationalizations intermingled, dissolving old allegiances, precipitating new structures, and engendering more serious attitudes toward one's relation to the world in which he was living. By early fourteenth century, family-owned financial-commercial firms were becoming European in scale, breaking through city, and even national confines. By late fourteenth century, the Florentine Woolen Guild was initiating features of modern industrialism and was attracting masses of foreign workers but was withholding from them access to economic and political power enjoyed by native residents of the city. Meanwhile, in England, suspecting that tithes exacted from English communicants were finding their way through the Avignon-based Popes to aid French kings in their wars against England, John Wycliffe began that research into the Church practices and papal claims which led him to the translation of the Bible into English, to the denial of scriptural basis for some of the alleged sacraments and certain traditions of papal authority, and to his theory of condominium: i.e., that, since only God is the creator, each person who would carry on the way of Jesus should administer whatever resources come under his control in such a way that every person among his contemporaries will come to realize himself as a co-worker with his Loving Father in the work of creation.

Increasingly, the arena of political concern shifted from cities to nations claiming absolute sovereign power and from connections by rivers and seas to those over oceans. The ideas and symbols of nationality elicited responses diverse in intensity and period of time among individuals and peoples as they sorted out and grouped geographically into territorial units and were coming to awareness of the importance of their relationship to the land and the uses and distribution of its resources. Sometimes the Scriptures were used as the basis for the denial of any rightful claim to private property;[2] sometimes supporters of ecclesiastical power claimed for the Pope through the Church the sole authority for vesting property rights;[3] similar claims were made on behalf of kings, beginning with John of Paris at the beginning of the fourteenth century.[4]

The new printing presses were enabling pamphleteers to turn ideas into social forces. Followers of Wycliffe, Luther and Calvin were spreading among the people the reading of the Bible itself.

Commercial enterprises, encouraged by governments, competed in offering land (taken from aborigines by force and/or trickery) and releases from religious and political restraints to whomever would demonstrate a capacity for organization sufficiently responsible to make the venture into the newly-discovered lands and to turn them into sources of profit for their investors and of additional power for the governments. In individuals—regardless of country of origin, family status or religious belief—throughout the West, the hope grew ever stronger for achieving a full and guaranteed right to access to land and protection while working out one's own life style so long as he respected others working out theirs. The Old Testament provided ample precedent for religious sanction for violently clearing the land of its native inhabitants in order to establish "the Wilderness Zion" of Governor Bradford, John Cotton and Thomas Hooker in "the New World." The New Testament, together with the payment of debts owed by the royal family to his father, gave William Penn the encouragement to institute "The Holy Experiment" of Pennsylvania and offer to religious pacifists a secure refuge on fertile lands under their own ownership. Those responsive to the hope for freedom brought with them a sense that *they* were indeed "the chosen people" entering into "the land of promise." The first book printed in America was *The Bay Psalm Book* published in 1640.[5] In North America was developing a society characterized by an unprecedented mixture of peoples. The authors of *The Growth of the American Republic* record:

> Pennsylvania was a portent of America to be; the first large community in modern history where different races and religions lived under the same government on terms of equality.[6]

Voluntarism, and a sense of security in "rights" accompanied, however, importation of Blacks as slaves and the uprooting, deportation and/or genocide of the native peoples.

From time to time individuals have enunciated signals for the further direction of mankind. Thus the Dutch physicist, astronomer, mathematician, Christian Huyghens (1622–1695) affirmed:

> The world is my country and science is my religion

and the United States of America was born with the declaration that

> All men are created equal. Governments derive their just powers from the consent of the governed and are instituted to protect life, liberty and the pursuit of happiness.

The perception for the evaluation of institutions was being shifted from subjects' acceptance of claims of authority to citizens' assertion of critical judgment of its performance as an instrument for serving the general welfare. Bills of rights became part of basic law and representative government became increasingly answerable to the people through the electoral process. A significantly responsible participant in both the American and the French revolutions, Thomas Paine, hearing Franklin remark: "Where liberty is, there is my country," has been credited (perhaps apocryphally but, even if so, significantly) with the response, "Where liberty is not, there is mine."[7]

The winning of the American Revolutionary War, the survival of the government of the Confederation, the Constitutional Convention drawing up the constitution of the federal republic, its endurance during the subsequent two centuries, the growth of individual enterprise in agruculture, commerce, finance, industry, the introduction of power-driven machinery for producing consumers' goods, the expansion of free public education, advances in the technology of communication through the development of newspapers and magazines, the telegraph, radio, television satellite transmission, the expansion of the suffrage, the encouragement of massive immigration to develop the resources of the territory of continental extent, the expansion of participation in the processes of decision-making through the formation and re-formation of political parties and the electoral procedures, the egalitarian advances whereby women and racial and cultural minorities are being assisted in becoming full participants in policy-formation and -execution, the efforts to curb the influence of money in elections and legislation, the growing concern for the environmental impact of policies, the world-wide immediacy of popular reactions to events, the universally rising expectations for equality of opportunity for security in dignity and in the right to freer development of individual potentialities, the computer revolution enabling the significant processing of more complex data—all make even less endurable the continuance of traditional disparaging presumptions.

In ancient Greece, both Plato (*The Republic)* and Aristotle (*The Politics)* considered unequal treatment a necessity if some were to be sufficiently liberated to cultivate and manifest "the good life;" that only by a system of "law" based on force within and war abroad could the "necessary" class structure be maintained. In his *Politics,* however, Aristotle observed that if means of production could be operated by mechanical power there would be no longer an excuse for the maintenance of the division of human beings into "masters" and "slaves."[8] Jesus repudiated the distinction on theological, ethical and personal grounds. Masses of people are awakening to the fact that it is only in the culture-lag of traditional institutions violently preserved in the service of exploitive privilege that the frustrating obstructions continue.

Confidence in the prospect that an enhanced quality of life was to become universally assured was exploded with the outburst of the world wars, the collapse of the League of Nations, the dropping of the atom bomb, the paralysis of the United Nations through the policies of "the leading powers"—the super-states, the arms race out of control consuming irreplaceable natural resources and eroding the standard of living of people throughout the world while smothering hopes with the growing fear of the future as promising only apocalypse followed by prolonged gray, noxious winter. Symptomatic also of the inadequacy of the current political practice and outlook is the phenomenon of the fractured states and the chronic tensions such as those between Israel and the uprooted Palestinians, the inhabitants of Namibia and the invasions from South Africa, the strained relations between India and Pakistan. Neither the United States of America nor the Soviet Union, despite unparallelled natural resources under their respective control, can maintain economic or political health through a policy of self-sufficiency. No nation "is an island unto itself." In trying to make itself secure by supplementing its deficiencies through trying to acquire control over the resources of others, a great power destabilizes them and thereby contributes to generating deeper rivalries and tensions. The break-up of the nineteenth century empires and the proliferation of the nation states which, in accordance with the principle of the self-determination of peoples, the twentieth century has witnessed, may have, for the moment, heightened somewhat the sense of personal dignity in those peoples formerly under colonial rule but most peoples remain far from the enjoyment of equality of status with that of citizens of states members of the atomic club and these latter, themselves, find decreasing sense of security as the "military-industrial complex" projects ever more devastating and expensive programs to which it secures commitment by governments in mutual rivalry. OPEC made all deeply aware of world-wide interdependence for energy resources. Monetary policies of the United States impact heavily on the economic health of all other countries. Industrial production programs of Japan, Germany and the United States reflect in each other's unemployment statistics. Demographic trends proceed with little relation to food production policies. Industrial pollution respects no national boundaries in generating acid rain, which destroys the life of forests, rivers, lakes and their dependent wildlife. As Max Kemmerich has written:

die Völker und Staaten sind auf diesem Planeten auf ein Zusammenleben angewiesen. So haben sich die Verhältnisse in einem wesentlichen Punkte geändert gegenüber den Zeiten Machiavellis, als nur absolute und sterbliche Fürsten auf der Bühne agierten. Dieses kann man durch Mord endgültig beseitigen, ein ganzes Volk aber nicht![9]

The peoples and states on this planet are allotted a common life. But the relationships have changed in an essential way in contrast to the times of Machiavelli when only absolute and mortal princes acted on the stage. These could be eliminated illegally through murder, but not a whole people!

The long period of openness of the new world to immigration regardless

331

of religion, nationality, economic status or skill, the availability as a matter of personal choice of citizenship, and, as a matter of personal industry, of economic advancement, the relaxation or abandonment of many social constraints in the process of family formation, the separation of church and state, the expansion of free public education, contributed to the liberation of personality while at the same time focusing upon it responsibility for choice of direction and achievement of significant goals promoted by a nexus of public relations at once accommodating and resilient. Innovations in statecraft (such as the confederated republics becoming the United States of America, the British Commonwealth of Nations, the League of Nations, the United Nations), buttressed and implemented by advances in technology rendered obsolete historically accepted limitations of area, size of population, number of components considered feasible for human organization,[10] and of temporal survival.[11]

As with the French invasion of Italy in 1494 began the series of shocks through which gradually dawned the realization that city states were no longer politically adequate for coping with threats to freedom and security, so the two world wars, the use of the atom bomb, the development of nuclear energy, the hydrogen bomb, the neutron bomb and anti-satellite laser beam have initiated consequences challenging the political adequacy of any political system based upon the assumption of national sovereignty. By Aristotle's criterion of self-sufficiency as an essential for statehood, under conditions brought about by modern technology, it becomes increasingly evident that only through organization as world community can self-sufficiency be approximated.

While technological innovation was bringing the ocean depths, space, the moon, the planets at the farthest limits of our solar system, within the reach of man or his guided instruments and for the first time making as a rational possibility the abolition of poverty, the generalization of material abundance, together with leisure for all to explore the good life, emotional attachment to institutions which had long served as means for liberation continued to draw upon man's loyalties and energies even though their use for institutional aggrandizement was proving to be increasingly at the cost of restricting their members' freedom, reducing their standards of living, increasing domestic and international tensions and deepening the sense of fear. As the institutional organization used religion to exploit Christendom prior to the social revolt known as the Reformation, so the military-industrial-commercial-financial nation state is using patriotism for exploiting the inhabitants of the land. Nationally-based multi-national corporations creating more lucrative instruments as, at greater social risk, they reach for oil, minerals, metals, other raw materials and cheap labor, make their profits under guise of their country's cause; and demand their defense as the patriot's duty while either defeating entirely the creation of, or paralyzing any institution or procedure which might bring them to, effective public accountability.

332

How can the good news make way: that it is not physical nature that is failing mankind and condemning all to a bleak future of frustrated hopes but, rather, that it is rectifiable human policy determination?

The nations most vehemently posing as defenders of democracy and free institutions are, at the same time, the very ones which are officially pursuing "power" through increasing their own armaments, on an expanding scale merchandizing throughout the world weapons of destruction, and utilizing not only diplomatic and commercial but also religious, scientific, academic and every form of communications as vehicles for an ever-expanding network of espionage, covert operations in wars of nerves against both domestic and foreign targets. During nearly seventy years, those seeking to submit others to willful, arbitrary and exploitive rule have been able to advance their control by exciting and manipulating fears on both sides of the capitalist-communist crusade, and each, respectively, thereby excused its failures to realize for its adherents progress toward the goals promised as the reward for the solicited or exacted support.

"Every nation is a wild beast on leash. Give it a little play and it will be at another's throat." So, around 1926 on a visit to Chicago, responded Dr. Fritjof Nansen, the League of Nations' High Commissioner on Refugees and former Arctic explorer, when, answering affirmatively the question posed by the author as to whether, many years previously when ice-bound for months, he had arrived at any fundamental perspective which he had subsequently found to remain valid.

Mechanical, violent, unique reaction has been found characteristic of injured organisms in proportion to the depth of the injury (above, p. 9). Intensification of violence has appeared at times when men have been treated as significant merely in terms of the part of the earth which they happened to inhabit or in terms of special ideological values with which they were associated.

Arrogation, to such parts, of the attributes which can pertain only to a whole, brings into operation a fiction working for its establishment at the cost of human inter-group conflict, terror, warfare and intra-group violation of human rights in the name of "law and order."

Periods of transcendence of former cultural restrictions have, at times, involved a shattering of old identifications in all of their "sanctities" and the appearance of a heightened sensitivity to the feasibility of a deeper and more inclusive relationship among human beings: thus, Ikhnaton, growing up in the expanded Egypt of Amenhotep III; Solomon, likewise, in David's Israel; Socrates, in Periclean Athens; Jesus in Augustus's empire; Machiavelli, in Lorenzo's Florence; Bacon and Shakespeare in Elizabeth's England; Newton, Locke, George Fox, William Penn, in mid-seventeenth century England; Washington, Franklin, Jefferson, James Madison, Paine, in the American colonies winning independence—all ventured forth in the light of new, deeper, more effectual truth.

Observation of the pathological behavior of fragmented sectors of a wounded organism, each acting as if it were an absolutely competent whole, results in many misleading inferences and falls short of—or, more accurately, digresses from—arriving at reliable understanding of the real whole when operating in its healthful coordination. Friedrich Meinecke has trenchantly treated Machiavelli's confrontation of the problem:

the initial application of the new scientific method, and its effect on historical life, were frightful and shattering. A prince must also learn how not to be good—this was the requirement of *necessità,* by which all human life was governed and constrained. But it was quite another matter to decide whether, on the one hand, the moral law should be broken only in the practice of politics, or whether, on the other hand, it was permissible to justify (as from now on became possible, and in fact more and more tended to happen) such an infringement by the plea of unavoidable 'necessity'. In the first instance, the moral law itself had, in its sanctity as a supra-empirical necessity, remained entirely unimpaired. But now this supra-empirical necessity was broken down by an empirical necessity; the force of evil was fighting for a place alongside of good, and was making out that it was, if not an actual power of good, then at least an indispensable means for obtaining a certain kind of goodness. The forces of sin, which had been basically subdued by the Christian ethic, now won what was fundamentally a partial victory; the devil forced his way into the kingdom of God. There now began that dualism under which modern culture has to suffer; that opposition between supra-empirical and empirical, between absolute and relative standards of value. It was now possible for the modern State, following its own inmost vital impulse, to free itself from all the spiritual fetters that had constrained it; it was possible for it, as an independent power acknowledging no authority outside this world, to effect the admirable accomplishments of rational organization, which would have been unthinkable in the Middle Ages, but were now to increase from century to century. But it already contained the poison of an inner contradiction, from the very moment it began its ascent. On the one hand religion, morality and law were all absolutely indispensable to it as a foundation for its existence; on the other hand, it started off with the definite intention of injuring these whenever the need of national self-preservation would require it. But surely (it will be asked) Machiavelli must have felt this contradiction, and the serious consequences it was bound to have.
He was not able to feel it, for the reason that his cast-iron theory of *necessità* concealed it from him, or because (as he believed, at least) the theory of *necessità* resolved the contradiction. The same force which impelled princes to refrain from being good under certain circumstances, also impelled men to behave morally; for it is only from necessity that men perform good actions (*Principe,* ch. 23). Necessity was therefore the spear which at the same time both wounded and healed. It was the causal mechanism which, provided that *virtù* existed in the State, saw to it that the necessary morality and religion were present, and that any failing in

334

that regard were made good. Thus the theory of the struggle between *virtù* and *fortune,* and the theory of *necessità,* worked together very closely to justify the prince in the use of underhand measures, and to prevent this from being harmful in his opinion. For all the time Machiavelli held firmly to the absolute validity of religion, morality and law. Even in the most evil and notorious chapter of the *Principe,* chapter 18, which justifies breach of contract, and declares that a prince (and especially a new prince), for the purpose of maintaining the State, 'is often obliged (*Necessitato*) to act without loyalty, without mercy, without humanity, and without religion'—even in this chapter he still emphasizes that a prince, when he *can,* should not leave the path of morality, but only that he should, in case of necessity (when *necessitato*), also know how to tread the path of evil . . . It was in the spirit of the time to delight in tracing precise and rectilinear paths; and in opposition to the straight path of Christian morality Machiavelli laid down another path, just as straight in its own way, a path which was directed exclusively toward the goal of what was useful for the State. He then proceeded, with a pleasure which was characteristic of him, to draw from it the most extreme consequences.[12]

However, the "religion" convenient for Machiavelli's theory of the State was not the religion of the founder of Christianity. Although Machiavelli acknowledged that misinterpretation of Christianity had become identified with it as commonly considered and practiced—not least of which was undervaluation of one's relationship to his country[13]—he appears oblivious of the emphasis on the immediate, earthly and current relevance to personal and social behavior which characterized Jesus's own actions and teachings and that the new order which he was exemplifying pertained neither to some indefinite future on earth nor to some other-worldly state but, since the coming of John the Baptist, that

the kingdom of Heaven is upon you.[14]

Moreover, to the founder of the religion, material needs and concerns were not matters of irrelevance. Jesus sought to convey to his hearers a sense of security in the knowledge that their creator had established a reciprocity between the environing resources, their fellow men and the fulfillment of their needs. When he said

Your Father knows what your needs are before you ask him,[15]

he was making more intimate and personal the ancient insight:

To the Lord your God belong heaven itself, the highest heaven, the earth and everything in it.[16]

335

In the reciprocity, the human factor takes the form of personal action generously kindled by forgiveness of others:

> If you forgive others the wrongs they have done, your heavenly Father will also forgive you;[17]

> Pass no judgment, and you will not be judged. For as you judge others, so you will yourselves be judged . . .First take the plank out of your own eye, and then you will see clearly to take the speck out of your brother's,[18]

perceiving and helping meet the other's need:[19]

> Always treat others as you would like them to treat you: that is the Law and the prophets.[20]

So, as the completion of Jesus' presentation of the reciprocity in operation, he said:

> I bid you put away anxious thoughts about food and drink to keep you alive, and clothes to cover your body . . . your heavenly Father knows that you need them all. Set your mind on God's kingdom and his justice before everything else, and all the rest will come to you as well.[21]

Moreover, the scale of Jesus's perspective is that of the whole world rather than that of a particular segment as "God's country" defining its self-preservation and security as necessitating a dominance over unwilling subjects within its sphere of influence, and a policy threatening aggression against potential foreign challengers.

Are not the hostilities between nations indications that the adequate relationship is in reality only between people of the earth and the world as a whole, and that the attempt to establish and enforce authority in terms of any less inclusive grouping results in violent propagation of fictions? Are we becoming confronted by the fact that there is a *practical worldly necessity* for a universally human public responsibility required for policy-determining on all scales and levels—individual, group, institutional—if any are to avoid incineration in a thermonuclear holocaust?

That Machiavelli recognized in his time the human necessity for institutions which would draw more deeply than theretofore on men's understanding, foresight, prudent will, love for country and energies, is apparent in the models which he constructed or held up as examples for imitation as founders of states and in his untiring labors to awaken leaders and fellow citizens to the need for broad-based involvement symbolized in his prescription of a citizen militia. Moreover, he brought out into the light for rational observation and constructive consideration the obverse and dark side of those who were giving vent to their energies in attempting to impose their "services" imperiously and press forward their prescriptions ruthlessly.

Now, again, indications of the sense that traditional institutional forms inadequately channel contemporary human energies are widespread, numerous and diverse: the arms race, frequent resort to terror, kidnapping and assassination of leaders, mounting incidence of violent crime, the spread of "the drug culture," mushrooming experiments in "life styles," varied attempts at "consciousness-raising." From a religious standpoint, Nicholas Berdayev has written:

> There is no longer any room in the world for a merely external form of Christianity based upon custom . . . The world is entering upon a period of catastrophe and crisis when we are being forced to take sides in which a higher and more intense kind of spiritual life will be demanded from Christians.[22]

Likewise, do the emerging times demand of citizens, if they are to operate in a free society, a renewing and deepening of civic virtue? Is the inadequate and destructive nature of the objectives for which appeals are being made—domestically, in the name of "law and order;" in foreign relations, in the name of "national security"—becoming sufficiently manifest to bring attention to the necessity for a truer kind of call for support in terms of a more sincerely constructive political endeavor: more open, more directly participatory, more sensitively responsive and accountable? The idea of "getting the state off our backs" may obscure and distract from the recognition of need for perception of the requirements of membership in a more inclusive and adequate order.

For present-day mankind struggling to curb the destructive inclinations of rival "sovereign" states and to give form and content to processes identifying and fortifying the more inclusive common good, has Machiavelli a significant message? The name, ideas, prestige of Niccolo Machiavelli is still so regarded in political thought, policy making, political action and even the vernacular, that recovery of that in his life and work which is germinal and perennially salutary is important for a political science which is to prove itself relevant and serviceable.

Many are those who have written to praise Machiavelli in times both past and present; many have written to damn him. Monumental studies have undertaken to present, if not to explain, his thought in terms of his life and times. His writings have been flailed, threshed and distilled—sometimes for the writer's self-justification in terms of antitheses to his maxims, sometimes for confirmation in terms of supplementary illustrations of their continuing validity. Each generation reinterprets him in its newly-developing context. In ours, what message for the common good has he for securing the order for free men when the atomic clock ticks away, ever-more-threateningly to strike doom while in the meantime mankind is murderously wasting its opportunity for achieving well-being, and is using up its irreplaceably physical and social resources and energies in grasping for dominance and ignoring that it is of the essence of men that they cannot accept dominance, by one over another?[23] What, if any, of the values fundamental in Machiavelli's perspective have relevance for the future as it is emerging?

Is there to be found in people today that which in Machiavelli's thought and action enabled him to will the work that was his own: i.e., to challenge human will for rational confrontation? Did he thereby exemplify and raise as a standard that which continues to be the very essence of citizenship in the order of human freedom, whatever the form and scale which its expression requires?

A major condition of Machiavelli's constructive political thought is his underlying assumption that in experience can be found meaning which can be apprehended with sufficient coherence to be understood and so utilized as to effectuate clearly chosen and willed aims and that the pursuit of such prudence is of supreme importance. Did this assumption have its root in the Florentine's passion for human freedom and his confidence in the possiblity of devising a citizen-supported form adequate for its effective promotion? The conclusion of his "Oration: 'Words To Be Spoken on the Law for Appropriating Money . . .' " bespeaks the depth of his dedication to freedom:

> I tell you that Fortune does not change her decision when there is no change in procedure; and the heavens do not wish or are not able to support a city that is determined to fall in any case. Such a fall I cannot believe in, when I see that you are Florentines and that in your hands rests your liberty. For that liberty I believe you will have such regard as they always have had who are born free and hope to live free.[24]

As leaders of the Protestant Reformation were influencing Christians, as responsible stewards, to divert their resources from indulgence in games of chance and to foster constructive, productive enterprises,* Machiavelli was issuing a summons to challenge Fortune with prudence and to curb the destructive violence which Fortune's rule entails.[25]

A contributing factor in Machiavelli's drive for arousing and promoting civic conscience is alluded to in the "Discorso . . . intorno alla Nostra lingua . . . " when he wrote that the duty to honor and serve one's country comes to be as much greater in those as their country of origin is more noble.[26] Thus Machiavelli proclaimed the opportunity and responsibility of citizens to make a fruitful investment on behalf of their descendents of the heritage of freedom for which their

---

*At his course (given in 1925–26) at the University of Geneva on The Industrial Revolution, Dr. William E. Rappard, then an official of the League of Nations, attributed the greater prosperity of the Protestant cantons of Switzerland to the fact that their legislation had prohibited the divergence of money into games of chance, whereas such games had flourished under the auspices of religion in the Catholic cantons.

ancestors had gloriously struggled in order to bequeath it to them. In terms of religion, Henry J. Cadbury explained Jesus' teaching of "the principle of proportionate duty:"

> In proportion to their advantages the rich (as Jesus often sees them) have acted as to deserve no blessing, while the poor have often deserved better than might have been expected of them . . . What this would mean when applied to modern nations like our own is rarely recognized. Our moral condemnation of other peoples too often assumes that they are to be judged by identical standards and if we are more decent than they, all is well with us. But if we should begin with Jesus' principle of proportionate responsibility, we would recognize that it requires of a more highly favored people not a slight moral superiority, but a really great difference. Our geographical remoteness from the friction centers of Europe and Asia, our great natural resources, our abundant Lebensraum, our educational standards, our long political experience with democratic institutions and our knowledge, if not our practice, of Christian ethical standards, put on us the duty of corresponding generosity, chivalry, understanding.[27]

Unlike Jesus or Gandhi, Machiavelli served in public office, exercised it innovatively in a highly sensitive post in time of a war vitally significant for his city and, when deprived of office, exerted himself to the utmost to continue prepared and ready, should his endeavors to secure return to public service prove fruitful.

Furthermore, he held that there must be generated and communicated a sense of necessity:

> men never do anything good except by necessity;[28]

> He then who wishes that a city be stubbornly defended, or that an army in the field should contend stubbornly, ought above everything to impose such necessity on the hearts of those who are going to fight.[29]

For a people to become a self-governing community, the individuals have to be working toward perception of their respective unique potentialities; and in recognition of the fact that each, in a self-governing community, is an official, they have to articulate responsibly and affirm by participation their distinctive contributions. Each one's role involves living forth a new reality in political ethics. Rejected, must be the temptation to project or support an imagined entity which provides, as a cover to excuse, justify, or even sanctify, resort to attitudes and acts which he would not openly acknowledge as his own. Affirmed, must be manifestation of constructive energy in entering upon ventures for the common good which without confidence in others' rallying to support would be utterly unachievable.

In stating it as his aim to discover the effectual truth and describe how men behave rather than how they ought,[30] Machiavelli formulated a goal for the science of politics which serves as a challenge and a guide. As Herbert Butterfield has pointed out, Machiavelli's contributions are not without strong personal coloration.[31] He disparaged the statecraft which he observed as practiced by his contemporaries in contrast with that which he formulated as practiced by pre-Imperial republican Rome and which he judged to be persistently relevant in light of his theory that human nature does not change[32] and that history consists of recurrent cycles.[33] His perception of uniformities in human behavior and his assumption of an underlying consistency gave him confidence for the development of an attitude of objectivity essential for founding a science of politics. As the impulse for operation on a broader scale manifested itself in the leadership of Caesar and Augustus for the management of which the ways of republican citizenship were inadequate, so the Renaissance renewal of republicanism, even though instructed by Roman experience as reported by Livy and interpreted by Machiavelli, proved inadequate for the management of the Medici or the rising monarchies of the nation states. However, in Machiavelli's dedication to the perception of the effectual truth and its direct expression, he was manifesting and exercising a quality of presence which was independent and not committed to, but was a more reliable guide for, the essence of patriotic citizenship—that which would continue and project into the land of the living the creative heritage of which his own existence was a witness and to which it was due.

May it not be that Machiavelli should be considered a prophet who cultivated political science as a seed which, nourished by the endeavors of those committed to *novus ordo saeclorum* ("new order of the ages"—the inscription on the Great Seal of the United States as reproduced on its paper money), will relate method to will so that living can proceed toward living in truth? In his writings there is a glimmer of perception that with the progress toward self-government the influence of political prudence will increase.[34] Moreover, in his perception of the wisdom of redistribution of power after its concentration had been used and had effected its purpose,[35] may there not be the germ of the idea developed in the nineteenth and twentieth centuries as "the disappearance of the state?" Sherman E. Johnson has written:

The rabbis said that in the messianic age the great sea monster Leviathan would be salted and given to the people as food (as in Psalms 74:14).[36]

May it be that, ultimately, the authority raised through the state to the level of human awareness, through political science as "the salt," will become the property of the people in their freedom?

Wherein is Machiavelli relevant or needed in a world of atomic missiles, laser-beams, neutron bombs, inter-planetary space platforms?

340

It is, and will still continue to be, important:

1. to exert courageous will, rather than to give way to temporizing inde cision.[37] Through the drive for expansion the adequately comprehensive unit is found out and achieved;[38]

2. to participate in public service which reveals and enhances one's worth;[39]

3. to recognize the ultimate worth of each individual—in derivation both positive[40] and negative;[41]

4. to believe that experience has meaning;[42]

5. to dedicate oneself to serving the common good;[43]

6. to examine and reason about everything;[44]

7. to search out and express effectual truth;[45]

8. to love one's native land so that one gives to it and requires for it the most honest, skilled service of body, heart and mind;[46]

9. to discern and emphasize the interrelationship between preservation of the order of freedom and the systematic, disciplined involvement of the citizens (evidenced in Machiavelli's work for the creation, establishment of the citizen militia and his advocacy of its further employment);

10. to observe and evaluate the consequences of attempting to deflect the demand for social justice and displace it with aggressive foreign policy, glory and pride;[47]

11. to seek out and express uniformities in human nature utilizable for its direction toward assuring greater freedom;[48]

12. to be open to and give recognition to the processes of change—espe cially those substantiating more inclusive relationships.[49]

(One of Machiavelli's perceptive realizations was that the traditional city state unit, however well in the past it had served the cause of human freedom and well-being, was no longer adequate. A larger, more inclusive unit—no less, but

341

rather more, personally to be cherished—was becoming necessary and essential. When he came to writing the history of his city, he realized that the city was no self-sufficient entity able to be interpreted as in independent isolation but that events in the whole peninsula and the factional processes within the city involved each other reciprocally so that the history of the city demonstrated that Italy was more like a living—even though suffering—organism. His endeavor to perceive and present the effectual truth drew him into the service of the more inclusive relationship and the evaluation of habitual conventions as corrosive destroyers. Therein he recognized a love for his native city greater than for his "own soul."[50] To struggle against the obsolescent traditions and conventions which he was perceiving as increasingly injurious, he realized that new energies must be recognized, mobilized and appropriately disciplined. Most important among these was prudence: mature emotional and intellectual involvement fused with even-tempered observation freed from the customary psychological barriers. In various ways his *History* bears the stamp of this perspective. In writing it, he made use of the vernacular; and in evaluating elements for strength and validity, he highlighted deeds of patriots and misdeeds of those who resorted to mercenary and auxiliary forces for defense. Also, writing the *History* from a secular standpoint, he freed writing of history from the grip of ecclesiastical and humanistic conventions[51] and, taking new soundings, traced strong undercurrents relating events significantly and contributing to better understanding of human behavior. As an example, he treated population pressure as a cause for migration of peoples.)[52]

13. to hold oneself responsible to give more significant service in light of one's greater privileges and advantages.[53]

(Machiavelli's concern with and penetrating treatment of the interrelation between the individual and the state is, as Vignal has well pointed out, a basic reason for the perennial interest in him and his work.)

L'oeuvre de Machiavel soulève donc les problèmes qui naissent de l'éternel conflit entre l'intérêt public et le droit individuel;[54]

The work of Machiavelli raises . . . the problems which are born of the eternal conflict between public interest and individual right;

Dans quelle mesure l'intérêt public est-il compatible avec la liberté individuelle? C'est parce que cette mesure n'a pas encore été trouvée et qu'elle ne le sera vraisemblablement jamais, que l'oeuvre de Machiavel demeure toujours en étroit rapport avec l'actualité politique.[55]

In what measure is public interest compatible with individual liberty? It is because this measure has not yet been found and that probably it never will be that the work of Machiavelli always continues in close relation with political actuality.

A broadly-based government, Machiavelli recognized as a safeguard against tyranny.[56] Moreover, the dedication to the public interest and purpose must be demonstrated as a living influence continually manifested innovatively:

> a republic without citizens of reputation cannot last and cannot in any way be governed well . . .A well-ordered republic, therefore, opens the ways, as has been said, to those who seek support [i.e., reputation from popularity] by public ways, and closes them to those who seek it by private ways, as Rome did;[57]

> general reputation can be gained through some extraordinary and noteworthy action, even though private, that has ended honorably . . . since its origin and basis are fact and your deeds, [this method] gives you as it originates such a great name that afterwards you must actually do many things contradicting it before you annul it. Men born in a republic should, then, follow this formula, and early in life strive to become prominent, through some unusual action. Many Romans in their youth did this either by proposing a law for the common benefit, or by bringing a charge against some powerful citizen as a transgressor of the laws, or by doing something else noteworthy and strange which would make them talked about.
> Not merely are such actions necessary as a start in giving a man a reputation but they are also essential for preserving and increasing it. To do so he must produce new wonders, as through his whole life Titus Manlius did . . . Any citizen who wishes popular support should gain it early, with some noteworthy action, as did Titus Manlius;[58]

> A republic, if she is to be kept free, requires new acts of foresight every day.[59]

Thus, only if, and so long as, throughout those constituting the broad base, there permeates a sensitiveness to and a swift responsiveness to meeting the needs which lead people to join together to protect themselves against oppression, the threat of it,[60] or unequal treatment in their endeavors to achieve their potentialities, can freedom be secure.

Deeply related to fostering courage, Machiavelli found to be regard for the religion of one's native country.[61] Indeed, it was through attributing to Christianity endorsement of defense of one's native land that he championed it against it "misinterpreters."[62] If one substitutes the value of patriotism for that of religion in Gerald R. Cragg's analysis of men's basic need, one finds a striking similarity with Machiavelli's outlook:

the qualities which we actually need. What is necessary is zeal guided by the true knowledge which is a result of genuine religious insight . . . First, we need spiritual insight—the perception which is able to distinguish between the true and the false. We must be able to see religious values as they really are without confusing them with specious substitutes . . . Second, true knowledge . . . is the appropriation of all the insights that we have gained, and their use in fashioning an interpretation of life that will be adequate to all our needs. Third, knowledge of this kind provides . . . [zeal] with a reasonable foundation, a comprehensive outlook, a firm grasp of the relevant facts, and the secret of unflagging endurance.[63]

In his endeavor to curb the power of Fortune and increase that of prudence, Machiavelli was seeking to reduce violence in human affairs,[64] to expand the reach of stable relations. He concluded that only heroic leadership could win acceptance as reality for the enlarged political unit. The action affirming and illuminating the public relationship deepens and enlarges it and at the same time reveals, evokes and/or creates in other individuals, new potentialities and enhances the sense of one's worth in his own eyes as well as in the estimation of others.[65]

In considering that one derives his worth from the use the state makes of one, Machiavelli was reaffirming the long familiar subordination of the individual to the collective. Pericles, Plato, Aristotle interpreted the meaning of a man's life as consisting in the quality of his citizenship. The Jewish view that the way toward justification lay through living according to the Torah as the expressed will of God, and the ecclesiastical that it lies through living membership in the Church as the body of Christ, affirms a similar relationship. Paul exemplified the endeavor to reconcile the Greco-Roman tenet that good citizenship is the condition and source of virtue with the Christian way. He wrote:

Every person must submit to the supreme authorities. There is no authority but by act of God, and the existing authorities are instituted by him; consequently anyone who rebels against authority is resisting a divine institution, and those who so resist have themselves to thank for the punishment they will receive. For government, a terror to crime, has no terrors for good behavior. You wish to have no fear of the authorities? Then continue to do right and you will have their approval, for they are God's agents working for your good. But if you are doing wrong, then you will have cause to fear them; it is not for nothing that they hold the power of the sword, for they are God's agents of punishment, for retribution on the offender. That is why you are obliged to submit. It is an obligation imposed not merely by fear of retribution but by conscience. That is also why you pay taxes. The authorities are in God's service and to those duties they devote their energies.[66]

Moreover, not only by word but by example, Paul endorsed regard for the forceful state as an indispensable protector. When threatened, it was his Roman citizenship to which he called attention as protection against flogging by the local authorities.[67] It was under protection by the military that he eluded the conspirators determined to take his life.[68] And, finally, in his "appeal to Caesar," he recognized and sought justice through the court of Rome,[69] only eventually to be martyred at the Emperor's command.

Machiavelli, however, was emphasizing not only the value and obligation of citizenship but was also giving powerful endorsement to the Renaissance emphasis upon the freedom of the will.[70] In the course of the Reformation this tenet was to progress radically in theology to the elimination of all intermediaries between the individual and the encouraging, creative source of love, truth and strength and to the sanction of an open way for intercourse between the individual and his Creator, the freedom of religion and the separation of church and state.

The collective began to be looked upon not as in itself an ultimate entity to be served but rather as an instrument for serving the well-being of the human beings availing themselves of its services. The collective serves as a shell protecting from the impact of outside influences and conserving essential nourishment for the growing individual until the individual has gained its own strength and sufficient maturity to break forth into its own creative expression when it is finding the shell becoming a constricting barrier. The collective, to change the analogy, is but a scaffolding to aid in the process of building. When the building has been completed, it has to be eliminated in order for it not, by continuing, to prove itself a distorting obstruction. If it were to be left and treated as part of the building itself, as part to be incorporated in the end product, it would weaken and deface the intended form. With the fiction overcome, the individual can not only endure, but indeed be vitalized and refreshed, in the light of a new and more liberating sense for truth.

The inherent conflict between the valuation of the collective as the creative source and of the individual as the energetic initiator is already clearly apparent in Machiavelli's writing when, for example, he concluded that the founding of a state requires the assumption that "all men are evil,"[71] and that only under necessity do they prove good.[72] He was probably giving expression to a position more characteristic of his general standpoint when he quoted:

that when things are done through necessity, neither praise nor blame is or can be deserved.[73]

Yet through his own personal experience and observation of others, Machiavelli perceived that men can turn their faces to resist Fortune,[74] exercise their abilities in the public interest,[75] can discern how to assist Fortune,[76] and even curb her power[77] which is always violent.[78] Herein is manifested the *virtù* achievable by men in Machiavelli's eyes.

The sovereign remedy, the indication of which Machiavelli detected in initial operation and which he enthusiastically prescribed—i.e., the autocratic founder[79] or reformer,[80] or leader in crises[81] served by the patriotically inspired citizen army,[82] eventuated in the nation states of the following centuries. Be it through the leaders' prudence, or due to democratically undeniable popular demand, subsequent decentralization and dispersal of power which he recommended[83] has been formally recognized in philosophy as a matter of "natural right," sanctioned in radical theology such as that of the Quakers, guaranteed in legal prescriptions, and increasingly explored in use.

At the same time, the explosion of knowledge through scientific inquiry and its application in ever more diverse fields of human activity has made even more imperative the reduction of the violent power of Chance or Fortune in change.

So profound was his probing in his quest, that clues for further guidance still emanate from his work and thought. Regarding the conditions essential for effective innovation in statecraft, he wrote:

> that city is in a somewhat unhappy position which, not having chanced upon a prudent founder, is obliged to reorganize itself . . . Those . . . that, if they do not have a perfect constitution, have made a beginning that is good and adapted for getting better, can through the meeting of unexpected circumstances become perfect. But it will certainly be true that they will never put themselves in order without peril, because enough men will never agree to a new law that looks to a new order in the city, if some necessity does not show them that they need to do it. And since this necessity cannot arise without danger, it is an easy thing for such a state to crash before its organization is made perfect.[84]

Machiavelli placed reliance upon the foresight of a leader's exercising effectively forceful will through attachment to his native land. That the prospect for the appearance of such a leader was more a hypothetical ideal than a matter of historical record, Machiavelli evidently suspected.[85]

Has the sense of inherent individual worth, the right of individual choice of political allegiance, the acceptance of the instrumental function of government, the liberating potentiality experienced in the application of scientific research, the anarchy of multi-national corporations, the unbridled military technology, the increasingly evident self-defeating impact of resort to force in human relations—have these factors, taken together, yet prepared adequately for effectuating the deeper insight of Machiavelli: i.e., that in the distilling of wisdom perceived in the process of participation in public service can be found guidance for human progress in freedom and the reduction of violence? The model of the heroic, charismatic leader successfully implementing his will for his country with the patriotic energies of the citizen army pitted against the forces of "evil" and chaos incorporated in foreign masses, has proved itself too obviously fictional and costly to continue to attract, galvanize and maintain the progress of mankind toward freedom. In accordance with "the principle of proportionate duty," as heirs of the fruitful labors of the new scholarship making evident in the records of original Christianity that

> the Word became flesh; he came to dwell among us . . . full of grace and truth,[86]

the achievements of providers of new technology, the expanders of horizons, the refiners of human sensibilities, it would seem that with new courage men can generate ways of more generous liberation.

Of what nature is the needed courage? Is it that of personally confronting and admitting openly enough psychological inadequacies so that, finding mutuality, people together can discover themselves, respectively, and work out cooperatively liberating expression in programs of action and forms of relationships able to transcend the exploitive fear-motivating factions? In light of participatory democracy and of the social and psychological sciences, can there be tapped a zest in being, a communion in conscience, a quest for truth evoking a sense of dignity in responsible human solidarity more fundamental than that experienced in religious or political membership—each of which has lent itself to serve as an instrument of fratricidal conflict? As the bursting of worn out—even corrupted, prostituted, brutalized—symbols finds shocking expression in deeds of "alienation," "terrorism," "criminality," can they be met by falling back on the convenient, conventional identification of "right" with the availability of force, or rather, must they be confronted by letting the signal of distress reach within to the theretofore unacknowledged sense of mutual human need? That inner echo in response to the overt protest against disregard of human dignity, is indeed more worthy of awe and respect than any representative of past-generated institutionalized authority, because the essence, the development-tension, the potentiality of the species is the tympanum which is responding. A listening awareness generates a sense of possibility for constructive understanding which persists through the dissolving or shattering of egos and enhances with a new and memorable quality the self-experience of each and becomes a shared reality for future reference.

Machiavelli perceived that in the process of striving to establish a new order

> it is an easy thing for such a state to crash before the organization is made perfect.[87]

At first, only one, or a few, foresees the need for change;[88] then, when more see it, used to living in one way, they do not like to change, and so much the more when they do not look the evil in the face but need to have it indicated to them through reasoning.[89]

Moreover, purposive, intelligent courage, in seeking for continued support, has to contend against the vulnerability to the fear of insecurity enflamed by the force-buttressed structures of fictions as through evasions they delay for time to build up means for defending themselves with all their forces. If the process of reform should include among its means its own resort to force, as Machiavelli considered it necessary to do,[90] it would infect itself with the same radical malady which worked for the destruction of the old and the replacement of which is the sole justification for the costly expenditure of energy for reform.

In terms of metaphysical sanction, religion undertakes to motivate people to let come forth and to make the best of themselves and each other individually and in groups. Patriotism motivates people together to be aware and, together and individually, to make the most of their land as a land of privilege. As Machiavelli observed, religion is vulnerable to fading away into fantastic other-worldiness;[91] patriotism, to spending itself in prideful violence.[92]

Can the harsh and deceptive methods which characterize the covert "intelligence" policies and practices of states in their international relations, and the entrapments and conventional discriminatory, legalized domestic usages in the name of "property" and "corporations" be superseded without such a threat of impairment of conventionally perceived personal identity that all one's vital energy will become available only for resistance to proposals or prospects for change? Can loyalty and truth with reference to mankind and sincerity with reference to oneself, adequately temper and make up interpersonal relations so as to substantiate transnational citizenship?

That such an order is a possibility for people has been foreseen and promised in religious terms by Jeremiah[93] and by Jesus.[94] In this regard, Thomas Jefferson bridged the perspectives of religion and government. In a letter to Dupont de Nemours, he wrote:

I believe . . .that there exists a right independent of force;[95]

and in a letter to James Cabell:

I do believe that if the Almighty has not decreed that man shall never be free (and it is a blasphemy to believe it) that the secret will be found in the making of himself the depository of the powers respecting himself, so far as he is competent to them, and delegating only what is beyond his competence by a synthetical process, to higher and higher orders of functionaries, so as to trust fewer and fewer powers in proportion as the trustees become more and more oligarchical;[96]

348

and in a letter written from Paris, 2 July 1787:

I have no fear, but that the result of our experiment will be that men may be trusted to govern themselves without a master. Could the contrary of this be proved, I should conclude, either that there is no God, or that he is a malevolent being.[97]

Ralph Waldo Emerson perceived a continuing but limited function for the state:

The antidote to the abuses of formal government is the growth of influence of private character, the growth of the individual . . . To educate the wise man, the state exists, and with the appearance of the wise man the state expires.[98]

Somewhat similarly, Henry David Thoreau, in his *Essay on Civil Disobedience,* compared the relation between the state and the accomplished individual to that between a tree and the fruit which it releases when matured.[99] The former dean of the Graduate Faculties of Political Science, Philosophy and Pure Science of Columbia University, Dr. Frederick James Eugene Woodbridge (1867–1940), affirmed:

Men will look for miracles, no doubt, but when they had ceased to expect them from nature or education or government, they may look for them where they are possible—in their own souls. No miracle seems ever to happen there until the search for it elsewhere is abandoned.[100]

John Dewey made the appraisal:

We have advanced far enough to say that democracy is a way of life. We have yet to realize that it is a way of personal life and one which provides a moral standard for personal conduct.[101]

The person carrying on and effectuating his own work in self-mastery, feels, and has, neither need nor place for "leaders" and hierarchies. He is not seeking out others on whom he can project demands for fulfilment of those desires and expectations for which in himself he is unwilling to pay the price and so he does not fall victim to the "leaders' " self-defensive violent coercion through which they seek to prevent his coming to discover that their use of his energies is not directed to meet his expectations but rather to serve their own.

How achieve the wish, the more comprehending sensitivity, the conduct, the discriminating evaluation requisite for functioning constructively generating the new order?

The prudence which Machiavelli prescribed in terms of a prince who is bringing into being a new state, is as relevant for the individual as citizen of the greater liberation who is seeking to administer his energies for making his living significant therein for himself and for others. As a beginning, Machiavelli observed:

a wise prince takes care to base himself on what is his own, not on what is another's.[102]

And how is one to discover and discern what is one's "own?" According to Machiavelli, by repeated initiatives, by expressions of intelligent will in public service:

About courage in important matters, no one without experience can promise himself certainty;[103]

no one can use as a foundation forces other than one's own;[104]

Men become excellent and show their ability only as they are employed and brought forward by their prince or republic or king as it may be;[105]

An army . . . becomes confident when well armed and organized and when each man knows the others; such confidence and organization cannot appear except in soldiers who are born and live together. The general must be so esteemed that the men trust his prudence; and they always will trust it if they see him prepared, attentive, and courageous, maintaining well and reputably the dignity of his rank. And he always will maintain his dignity if he punishes offenses and does not make the soldiers labor without result, keeps his promises to them, presents them with an easy road to victory, and conceals or makes light of things that at a distance appear dangerous. These things, well carried out, give an army strong reasons for trusting him, and trusting, to conquer;[106]

When a prince or a republic is willing to undergo toil and put effort into these methods and this training, always it is true that in his country there are good soldiers. Such princes are superior to their neighbors; they give laws and do not take them from other men;[107]

They [men] ought, then, never to give up as beaten, because since they do not know her [Fortune's] purpose and she goes through crooked and unknown roads, they can always hope, and hoping are not to give up, in whatever fortune and whatever affliction they may be;[108]

often when a man is doing something, plans reveal themselves to him which, if he stood still, would forever hide themselves;[109]

Necessity comes when you see that if you do not fight you must surely lose, that, for instance, you lack money and therefore your army is certain to go to pieces; or that hunger is going to attack you; or that your enemy is expecting to increase his army with new men. In these instances you should always fight, even if you are at a disadvantage, because it is much better to tempt Fortune when she possibly will favor you than, not tempting her, to face certain ruin;[110]

a general when he is obliged either to flee or to fight, almost always chooses to fight, since perhaps by this method, though it is very doubtful, he may be able to win; in the other, he must lose in any case;[111]

a prince who has an army assembled, and sees that for lack of money or of friends he cannot keep such an army a long time, is altogether mad if he does not tempt Fortune before his army begins to go to pieces, because if he waits, he certainly loses; if he makes the attempt, he may conquer;[112] (above, pp. 321–322).

Qualifying for *transnational* citizenship proceeds through:

(1) trying out and developing one's own capacity to make choices and bring about and achieve results and thereby come to understand and anticipate the costs of one's desires and intentions rather than seeking for others who will promise and serve one, or placing faith in their promises proffered, and then blaming or trying to punish them for not fulfilling one's inadequately thought out or estimated anticipations which were inherently realizable only through one's own successful endeavors;

(2) assuming more self-responsibility for participating in the making of decisions which will affect oneself;

(3) using and strengthening one's own sense of security in status by encouraging others in their own respective awareness of "I Am" and recognizing that comparisons between people are inherently without basis in fact and that presumptions of superiority become boomerangs which return to inflict injury on the unsuspecting user;

(4) demonstrating and establishing that: it is by overcoming, not renouncing, that living proceeds; power is acquired through achievement of right; and freedom is experienced and happiness is known in enjoyment of endowments engaged in serving the public good;

(5) understanding human behavior through the perception that others' acts are their best possible expression of their entire aggregate of the gifts which they have received of food, shelter, clothing, encouragement, recognition, acceptance, perception of potentiality, confidence, hope and conscience and that, so treated, they open the way for mutual understanding and cooperation;

(6) strengthening capacity to unlock injuries remembered and thus release one's

inner energies for celebration of mutual kinship—substantiated in mutually-valued transcending service.

Thus, citizenship now requires a new morality of interpersonal loyalty and openness for the intimations of more shattering, yet deeply more encompassing, beckonings toward truth in reference to human nature expressing itself specifically in those who make up mankind. The political economy of the Gospels which proceeds from the self-aware individual creatively cooperating under the common creating "will of God," has formerly been identified with the church, the nation, the organized means of production (be it individual or collective). None of these is proving itself sufficient. As through the centuries during which the ancient empires, and then the Church, seemed to have a monopoly on defining and enforcing their respective value system, individuals who kept their own vision clear bore in themselves the potentiality for mankind's further development, so now, when the society—as a religious-political-industrial-technological complex (be it capitalistic or Marxist)—comes with totalitarian claims, one needs to see, feel and be clear in living forth in integrity with his fellows.

The health of the order (whether just emerging or long-established) requires that the goal be such that awareness of it keeps people continually, cooperatively contributing their best in the joint endeavor. Machiavelli recognized the importance of cultivating in people such a sense of need:

a wise prince takes care to devise methods that force his citizens, always and in every sort of weather, to need the government and himself, and always then they will be loyal;[113]

A Republic, if She is to be Kept Free, Requires New Acts of Foresight Every Day;[114]

He then who wishes that a city be stubbornly defended, or that an army in the field should contend stubbornly, ought above everything to impose such necessity on the hearts of those who are going to fight;[115]

We can learn from the words Livy gives [Valerius Corvinus] what a general must be if his army is to trust him. He spoke thus: "Then also you should consider under whose leadership and control the battle is to be entered, whether you are to listen to him merely as a splendid spellbinder, ardent only in words, ignorant of military affairs, or whether he knows how to handle weapons, to march ahead of the standards, and to show activity in the thickest press of battle. My deeds, not my words, soldiers, I wish you to follow; to ask from me not merely instruction but even example . . ." (Livy 7.32). These words, well considered, teach everybody how he should act if he is to hold the rank of general.[116]

352

The new order builds, however, not through deeds and words evoking fear, rendering people vulnerable to others' control, but through deeds and words manifestly creative and thereby releasing and encouraging others' creative participation. Jesus transmuted awe into love. Machiavelli perceived authority as autonomous will informed by participation for public good. Adam Smith presented wealth as the conversion of lonely uniqueness into public utility. The new citizen is the self who, having internalized institutionalized discipline, is living creatively in interpersonal relations exploring toward truth.

What is the kind of tempering requisite for raising to its highest potential errant human nature endowed with freedom of will? Under the thrall of empire- and state-building, leaders have tried to build up the force of their states sufficiently to exceed that of the force which might be brought against them, and for doing so have won great support from the respective inhabitants. The release of much of human energy seems to be triggered through the perception of an adversary. It is the real or imaginary threat from some others on the other side of some religious, political, economic, demographic, ideological line which raises the elan, galvanizes the cohesion. Many define their values in terms of those whom they exclude and seem to fear being weakened through too great inclusion of the different.

However, force in the form of violence in human relations, itself is an indication of illness and therefore in itself lacks strength. Underlying its manifestation is the sense that, lacking the possibility of objectifying an adversary, one would be driven to look within for that which is impelling one toward or into aggressive behavior and to risk discovering that that which, as the source of his very strength, he is proclaiming as his innate light of truth—the true faith worth defending at the cost of others' lives and, in extremity, possibly even of one's own—is in reality in itself but a dark uncertain fiction impelled by an unfaced inner fear. Fiction uses up its energies in forcefully trying to close off and shut out other vibrant possibilities, and works to its own nullification. Machiavelli wrote:

he who gains dominion and not at the same time strength, must fall. He cannot gain strength who grows poor in wars even though he is victorious, because he lays out more than he gets from his conquests.[117]

In proportion to the health of the order, violent force dissipates and vanishes and its dissolution or dissipation facilitates the release of appreciative understanding and cooperation. With true insight Pogo pronounced:

We have met the enemy and it is us.

The processes of understanding through love and of science through hypothesis and experiment are open-ended and give the impulse for further search. A distinguished educator has well said:

> I have long ago learned that all of us are much smarter than any of us.[118]

Consonant with the teaching of Jesus is the perception of power and rank diametrically opposed to the *real politik* of conventional statecraft. Jesus delineated the contrast starkly:

> You know that in the world, rulers lord it over their subjects, and their great men make them feel the weight of authority; but it shall not be so with you. Among you, whoever wants to be great must be your servant, and whoever would be first must be the willing slave of all.[119]

Helpful service to one's fellow men as the way of qualifying for membership in "the kingdom" is a salient part of the message of the parable of "the good Samaritan"[120] and an emphasis to which Jesus returned repeatedly.[121]

On the other hand, the appropriation, aggrandizement, consolidation of energies inwardly released in the presence of others' mis-adventures, confusion, poverty, weakness, vulnerability, forms the hard core of conventional states and aspirants to power therein. According to Machiavelli, men's wants are never satisfied.[122] Since a "natural instinct" incites each to gain at each others' expense and is controlled only by laws or greater force which provides opportunity for wisdom and goodness,[123] statemakers assume that men are evil.[124] The state subsists through keeping its inhabitants necessitous[125] and grows great through instigating and using for its purposes their sense of necessity:

> that kingdom which is pushed on to action by energy or by necessity will always go upward.[126]

However, the possession of authority generally corrupts those who possess it.[127]

The alternative is to be found in the right use of the intelligence and the feelings (the "mind" and the "heart"): i.e., attention alert to the implications which messages from the senses may convey regarding the integrity, well-being, exercise and expression of the truth in one's being. Development, through interpersonal relations, of the objective perception of oneself—avoiding both susceptibility to that hypnotic subordination to another which makes one a tool for his plans, and the domination by one's own aggressive arrogance toward another which would make use of another for one's own plans—helps to avoid the traps which would entangle one's energies in impulses of hostility and to keep one free for deeds appropriate to his own nature. So he grows in ability to take toward himself as his guide that point of view designated by George Herbert

354

Mead as "the generalized other"[128] and become master of himself. Exodus 25:20, through the symbolism of the cherubim, indicates that through looking together face to face, inward and toward "the mercy seat," voluntarily sacrificing individuality while poised for upward soaring toward the mystery of Truth, can be understood God as working in oneself together with others. Jesus brought "forgiveness of sins" from "God in Heaven" to the interrelation between men on earth.[129] Likewise is needed affirmation of individual worth through bringing the strengthening of the significance of one's being from "leader" in "organization," "group," or "corporate body," to self-aware participant. Structures of mutual aid are instrumentalities through participation in which individuals develop toward their self-knowledge in proportion to the level of responsibility of their self-observing, attentive participation and the magnitude of the organization in which they participate. Through feeling one's need and personally experiencing the struggle for effectuating the utilization of resources for responding to the needs of each, one grows in his sense of need for, and appreciation of, his fellow citizens. Only participants in value-defining can secure understanding pertinent to the nature and power of the obstacles and processes for carrying through the responsibilities.

In his characterization of the first century apostles, Tommasini has given indication of qualities needed for bringing into being the transnational order also:

l'opera degli apostoli di Galilea fu più che scuola; fu sitituzione umanamente universale, che insegnò soccorrendo; che invase, occupò, provocò tutto l'uomo a ricercare in sè stesso l'intimo vincolo che lo collega alla convivenza infinita;[130]

the work of the apostles of Galilee was more than a school; it was a humanly universal institution which taught through helping; which invaded, occupied, stirred up the whole man to search out in himself the very most intimate bond which connects him with the infinity of beings living together;

il Cristo era venuto a mettere discordia tra figlio e padre, tra madre e figlia, tra i membri della stessa famiglia, tra l'anima dell'uomo e l'uomo [Matteo X, 34–36]. Tale è veramente il portato della coscienza fedele, che sciolta d'ogni altro riguardo, invasata del dovere e del diritto della sua fede, secondo quella dirittura opera, fa del pensiero e dell'azione una necessaria concordanza logica e non à pace finchè questa non le sia assicurata da ogni oppressione, da ogni violenza esteriore. Tale è il cristianesimo forte, che ringagliardendo l'anima la fa ad un tempo padrona e serva di sè stessa; e collettivamente aspira a tanta libertà e grandezza, che nessuna altra scuola o civiltà ne conseguì mai simile. E questa mirabile energia diffusa ampiamente pel mondo, lo alterò vivificando anche precedenti dottrine, stendendosi, come per calorico repente, anche laddove i primi apostoli della fede direttamente per certo non la recarono.[131]

Christ had come to bring discord between son and father, between mother and daughter, between the members of the same family, between the spirit of the man and the man [Matthew 10:34–36]. Such is truly the result of the faithful conscience, which freed from every other regard, obsessed by the duty and the right of its own faith, according to that direct labor, makes of the thought and the action a necessary logical concordance and has no peace until it has secured it from any oppression, from any exterior violence. Such is the Christian forte (strength), which, inspiriting again the soul, made it at the same time master and servant of itself; and collectively sought after such liberty and greatness, that no other school and culture ever won comparison. And this wonderful energy poured forth abundantly for the world, changed it bringing life even to teachings which preceded, and spreading itself, as by a sudden burst of heat, even there where the first apostles of the faith for certain did not take it.

In the republican Rome which Machiavelli presented as a pattern for emulation, domestic civil peace and the cooperation of the nobles and the people within institutionalized aggression as "legal order," was won through militarization and degradation of the people at home and expanding warfare abroad. Government which in operation is the organized thrust for maintenance and increase of privileges for which payment is exacted from others, divides people into the violently overbearing and the fearful, embittered, united together only in foreign conquest. The attention of neither is focused on perceiving the unique quality of each citizen's own experience, the constructive validity through it, and the diagnosis and solution together of the problems of those in need. However, the Christian perception of service as a criterion of worth had grown so pervasive that, for Machiavelli, the public or common good was the touchstone by which the true value of an action was to be judged. The advancement of "the general good," he considered as the intention proper for "a prudent organizer of a republic"[132] and for one careful about preserving his reputation. Many passages such as the following in Machiavelli's writings lend credence to the view that, although at the time he was writing he had in mind Florentine citizens and their political traditions, his observations may be considered to be more generally applicable:

Without satisfying the generality of the citizens, to set up a stable government is always impossible;[133]

it is not right for a republic to be so organized that a citizen can without any recourse be injured for promulgating a law in harmony with free government;[134]

not individual good but common good is what makes cities great. Yet without doubt this common good is thought important only in republics,

356

because everything that advances it they act upon, and however much harm results to this or that private citizen, those benefited by the said common good are so many that they are able to press it on against the inclination of those few who are injured by its pursuit;[135]

the common benefit gained from a free community . . .: namely, the power of enjoying freely his possessions without any anxiety, of feeling no fear for the honor of his women and his children, of not being afraid for himself.[136]

The settlement of North America, the experiences in the American colonies, the emergence of the United States of America, greatly strengthened religious, political, economic, social voluntarism and political democracy. The relationship between people and government underwent profound changes. A basic characteristic throughout was the acknowledgement of irreducible pluralism. America came to symbolize, and for millions to provide, a land-based haven for individuals from all backgrounds to found institutions of which the reason for existence has been, and continues to be, to implement their joint endeavors to promote the life, liberty and equality of opportunity for each to realize his full potentiality without the shadow of inferiority, and together to affirm human rights seeking to formulate, experiment with, and experience participation in the direction of human affairs adequate for human freedom.

In diverse forms the Protestant Reformation affirmed the validity of the individual experience. As a variety of religiously-based communities established, in their respective ways, their social and political experiments in "the New World," pluralistic individualism grew into acceptability, if not appreciation. At last, this individual, endowed as he had been by the Judaeo-Christian tradition, enlightened by the humanistic, civic reasoning of the Greeks and the Romans, had an open field for social ventures.

When the physician John Locke turned his diagnostic reasoning upon the examination of human nature in politics, he found that, in and for each individual, experience writes the record and for that true expression of the record, both for individual and social well-being, freedom of education, of speech, of association, of enterprise, and of policy formation through freely elected representatives, are essential.

Building on traditions developed from Thomas Hooker, Roger Williams, William Penn (whom he termed the world's greatest law-giver) and John Wise, Thomas Jefferson accented the pursuit of happiness as the supreme object which led people to pool some of their energies and form government. In Francis Hirst's *Life and Letters of Thomas Jefferson,* the following sentence from Lord Kames' *The History of Property* is "reputed to be a major source of Thomas Jefferson's ideas on natural right and individual liberty:"

The perfection of human society consists in just that degree of union among the individuals, which to each reserves freedom and independence as far as is consistent with peace and good order.[137]

According to Jefferson, it was "the pursuit of happiness" which pertained to, or belonged to each one (*proprius*—from which the word "property" is derived).

Examined psychologically, one's zest and direction of living is found to be the integrating of the sparks of understanding, welcome, affection which burst in upon one and give him substance and impulse to work out and generate his value, his self-awareness. In further enhancement of this possibility, people find that their talent of organization is effectively employed. Here was a new factor. One searches the New Testament in vain for endorsement, or even consideration, of participation in governmental organization, public service and public administration. It was left for human beings, especially under American conditions, to work out the procedures and behavior appropriate for free men together. Thus was being elaborated for the first time governmental institutions formed by individuals aware and jealous for their unalienable rights yet, for the purposes of states, delegating powers adequate for promoting greater freedom, holding them accountable therefor as their instruments, and providing for such further adaptations as would be found desirable.

In his introduction to his *Thoughts on Machiavelli,* Leo Strauss has written:

The United States of America may be said to be the only country in the world which was founded in explicit opposition to Machiavellian principles. According to Machiavelli, the founder of the most renowned commonwealth of the world was a fratricide; the foundation of political greatness is necessarily laid in crime. If we can believe Thomas Paine, all governments of the Old World have an origin of this description; their origin was conquest and tyranny. But "the Independence of America [was] accompanied by a Revolution in the principles and practice of Governments"; the foundation of the United States was laid in freedom and justice. "Government founded on a moral theory, on a system of universal peace, on the indefeasible hereditary Rights of Man, is now revolving from west to east by a stronger impulse than the Government of the sword revolved from east to west" [*Rights of Man,* Part the second, Introduction]. This judgment is far from being obsolete. While freedom is no longer a preserve of the United States, the United States is now the bulwark of freedom. And contemporary tyranny has its roots in Machiavelli's thought, in the Machiavellian principle that the good end justifies every means. At least to the extent that the American reality is inseparable from the American aspiration, one cannot understand Americanism without understanding Machiavellianism which is its opposite. But we cannot conceal from ourselves that the problem is more complex than it appears in the presentation by Paine and his followers. Machiavelli would argue that America owes her greatness not only to her

358

habitual adherence to the principles of freedom and justice, but also to her occasional deviation from them. He would not hesitate to suggest a mischievous interpretation of the Louisiana Purchase and of the fate of the Red Indians. He would conclude that facts like these are an additional proof for his contention that there cannot be a great and glorious society without the equivalent of the murder of Remus by his brother Romulus.[138]

Despite Machiavelli's deeply-held view that a new or reformed government must be the work of one man who employs whatever means necessary to concentrate all power in his own hands,[139] the independence of America was considered, decided upon, and declared by a congress and achieved by victory in the Revolutionary War; the government of the several states and of the federal republics was established by means of legslative assemblies or constitutional conventions and acts of ratification. Justice Oliver Wendell Holmes observed:

A constitution is made for people of fundamentally different opinions.[140]

Many innovations or major developments have, during the past two centuries given opportunity for practical experience on an unprecedented scale in responsible popular government. Among these as institutionalized patterns or programs in process are: separation of church and state; governments deriving their just powers from the consent of the governed; the instrumental, limited character of government; written constitutions implemented through the judiciary; constitutionally-based bills of human rights; the independent judiciary; the federal structure of government; Congressional power over military appropriations and the declaration of war; openness to people throughout the world who are seeking escape from oppression; universal free public education; broad expansion of the suffrage; election of policy-determining officials; democratization of the process of nomination of candidates for office; equalization of voting districts; curbing of political impact of private funds; opening of governmental processes to public observation and inspection; equality under the law of officials and private citizens.

By his years of official service, made painfully sensitive to the vulnerability of the people of Italy in whatever political entity their lot was cast, late in life once more vested with weighty public responsibilities, while personally engaged in strengthening the walls of his city, Machiavelli appealed to his friend Francesco Guicciardini, the lieutenant of the papal forces, to arouse and summon emotional drive essential for deliverance,[141] even as, years earlier, he had appealed to the young Medicean princes to assume leadership.[142] "Barbarians" was his term for the foreigners whose mercenaries fought in Italy for them[143] and/or who themselves invaded the peninsula.[144] As early as 1504 in his "First Decennale," he applied the term to "the Gauls" (the French of 1494 under Charles VIII).[145] In his letter to the Ten, 2 September 1510, he reported Julius II's declared intention of delivering Italy from servitude and out of the hands of the French;[146]

but when the Pope raised his banner with the charge *Fuori i Barbari* (Out with the Barbarians!), only Venice found it expedient to give substantial cooperation.[147] Although his own government, under Soderini, stood side by side with France, the objective of national liberation continued, through the years, to work deeply as an enzyme in the development of Machiavelli's motivation. It was foreign exploitation to which Machiavelli attributed the addiction of Italian princes and republics to that reliance on mercenary forces[148] which continually laid waste the land, kept the states weak and the people enslaved. To win, among Florentines, acknowledgment of the power innate in themselves as free citizens, to organize, discipline, consolidate and affirm it, possibly as Italians, became Machiavelli's personal venture for securing the heritage of freedom.

What are the current barbarians which lay waste the land, enslave the people, check initiatives toward more inclusive relations?

Cultivating and purveying fears, "leaders" (political, financial, commercial, industrial) draw to themselves people's attention, win recognition and influence for the production, in mounting quantities, of ever more destructive weaponry. Pretences of adherence to and the employment of the processes of self-government and free enterprise economy, are devoted to distracting individuals from exploration of their own talents for advancing their own well-being and that of mankind and, instead, to rendering the inhabitants into a supply of manpower useful for the political and economic organizations.

Insinuating themselves into privileged access to public authority, multi-national corporations, operating in the rarified controls of the political stratosphere through manipulating and bribing public authorities, acquire, extract and process raw materials with minimal return to the laborers throughout the world who are kept in ignorance and poverty while their venal governments are kept servilly dependent for outlets for the natural resources as their primary source for funds.

Open-ended and universal as religion and scientific method may be in their tenets, they too become enmeshed and distorted in serving the programs and special interests of the political and corporate structures.

Everywhere, popular support for violent nationalism is nourished in the name of "history"—all too frequently significant only as an arrangement of past events interpreted through the glorification and partisan justification of the deeds of users of overwhelming force against human adversaries. Since history, as generally composed in the past,[149] has served as an apology (as the author has termed it) for the guilty consciences of those who have pursued their subjective aims through violence inflicted upon their fellow men and have found and rewarded ingenious interpreters and eloquent defenders of their deeds, the effort to distill from recorded history a secular conscience inevitably results in the reationalization known as *raison d'état*.[150]

Training for commitment and sensitivity to serving the job market provided by finance, commerce, industry and, to a less degree, by the professions, supplants or distracts from education in self-discovery and the liberation of unique perceptions and skills into broader service.

The model of the atomistic, "self-sufficient," yet, however inconsistent, aggressively competitive individual realizing "self" in terms of winning "superiority" over others, provides organization with people as agents preconditioned for "management" and "advancement" through the programs of political structures and economic corporations. With attention diverted from perception of the source and nature of his unique constructive potentialities, the individual undertakes to present himself as endowed with utility for others' purposes until he, in turn, can acquire the power to subject others to his.

Can the liberation of the creative, autonomous potentialities in individuals resist, transcend, master and employ as instruments for further development, forces bent on exploiting and reducing other human beings to serve purposes alien to them?

Chapter Twelve

CREATIVE CONTRIBUTION OF PARTICIPATION-DERIVED REASON TO POLICY FORMATION AND POLITICAL PRACTICE

As "a voice crying in the wilderness" and presaging deliverance with unification of Italy through application of reason derived from the more objective study of political experience and prudent application of the findings, in Machiavelli is perceived renewed significance on the part of those looking for yet further liberation through progress toward world community. As he saw the need to utilize reason in the formation of policy for freeing Italy "from the barbarians," so now those forming policies leading toward human freedom and security need to utilize a political and social science which is purified of violent fiction and proceeds through analyses and interpretations of consequential relationships in patterns more inclusive, objective and freer than the nationalistic models. Only a history which reflects total social experience—including the perspective of the victims valued equally with that of the "victors," the oppressed and the violated as well as the oppressors and the violent,[1] "the quiet of the land" as well as the mythologized "leaders"—can now provide a source from which reliable guidance can be derived.

Machiavelli seems to have sensed the need for the emergence and development of the trans-municipal or national citizen-militant. There is now need for the emergence and development of the trans-national or world-conscious citizen in active service. If the coming of atomic technology is not to prove devastatingly unmanageable, men will find themselves compelled to relate together in accordance with the rule of essential equity and achieve reduction of nuclear power to a serviceable instrument. Military hardware provides no firm ground for constructive action. Gifts and loans of military hardware cannot buy the elements conducive to fruitful cooperation.

How may be identified the nature and developed the strength of the public spirit adequate for the building and maintenance of the transnational state of mankind as the Greek and Roman Stoics did for the Roman Republic (which, however, missed the mark in becoming the Roman Empire) and as Jesus did (whose followers, however, got off the track in forming the Church)? Can that step be taken which Lynn Harold Hough sensed as lacking when he wrote:

> Even such a book as Martin Buber's *Paths in Utopia* in many ways a searching study of the difference between a utopia based on coercion and a utopia making room for freedom, never faced the problem of the making of individual man capable of living in utopia?[2]

In the generating of the human character essential for the larger unit—a subject treated by Machiavelli in terms of the application of reason to public affairs[3] and the creation of the citizen militia[4]—the Greek heritage of reason, the Hebraic of election, the Christian of love, the mediaeval Scholastic churchman Wycliffe's doctrine of condominium, the eighteenth century patriot Jefferson's declaration of "the right to life, liberty and the pursuit of happiness" (which he perceptively sublimated from "property"—later to be included with the other two as constitutionally guaranteed), and Paine's dedication to cooperating with those struggling for freedom yet to be won, are not to be diminished but enhanced through the new affirmation which translates history according to new elements and laws of power, gives to the present a new perspective and to the future a new potentiality.

Citizenship in a self-governing society implies one's employing responsible participation as a process of education into more realistic self-consciousness and proceeding through more sincere and compassionate service.

In the "Fear not!" with which the "Good News" in the Gospel according to Luke begins, lies a profound injunction. If one loses sight of the creativity within and loses courage for the joyful quest pursuing it, and begins identifying himself with impulses of doubt and fear, more and more he interjects his old habit-bound self by indulging in attitudes and actions which divert him from his aim. Considering the need for holding direction in an undertaking, Machiavelli cited Livy's warning:

> as soon as each man gets to thinking about his personal danger, he becomes worthless and weak.[5]

"Privacy" may be, as Justice Brandeis is reported to have said, "the right most valued by civilized man," but, from a religious perspective, John Short has cautioned, there is a limit to the loneliness man can bear, and the ultimate loneliness is that of the soul bereft of God.[6]

Disestablished by fear, at an accelerating rate one lets himself find as shelter another or others who offer protection in return for his support through obedience to their rigid regulations serving their purposes. So a part of him in the name of himself as the "whole" tries to adapt himself to pretense, intolerance of difference, commitment, blind obedience to the fear-nourishing "leadership" by another who insistently demands, "Trust me!," and who may be inclined to misuse even—or perhaps, rather, especially—the concept of mystical unity with "God" as a device by which to open the way for claiming an objective basis for authority over another or others.

The adequate leader is one's own goal clearly perceived, and it is through responsible participation in the largest available relevant group that the perception becomes clarified. Many of the qualities which Machiavelli perceived as essential for the prince in attaining and maintaining a state, are the same which are essential for each person for bringing under his own mastery his own effective will in the formulation and execution of his own creative purposes. The apostle Paul conceived "law" to be educative in function,[7] an instrument through which men become acquainted with standards of justice and the good, a means for jabbing awake our consciences.[8] The leader and the state serve to call attention to responsibilities in the struggling to fulfill which men come to the realization of their need for "grace." If, however, the law, the leader or the state is served as being the ultimate purpose and good in itself, rather than as the awakener of one to awareness of the unique, ultimate, creatively individual striving to be one's best in and through relationship with others, one misses the mark. Jesus' rejection of the temptation to commit himself to the seeking of power[9] and his non-identifying himself with the patriotic Zealots' cause against the Roman political control, gave the ultimate negative evaluation to Samuel's concession to the people's clamor that a kingship be instituted;[10] so men have now reached the moment of ultimate evaluation of *raison d'état*. Men are creatures of the earth and as such they are impelled to know themselves as rightfully rooted not only as members of countries, but also of continents, of oceans, of solar systems, of galaxies, of the not-yet-named, of the Unnameable(?). An ultimate right of everyone is security in the enjoyment of equal respect accorded to his roots in the good earth and its resources created and bestowed by a loving creator. Jesus communicated reassurance against resignation to deprivation of material necessities[11] and Paul cautioned against letting material considerations become a barrier between people.[12]

Experiencing renewal through participation in the government of his city, Machiavelli attributed the deepest significance to his relation to it.[13] In collaboration between men in the public service of their common territorial unit, he identified the solid foundation for human character.[14]

Although recognizing that statecraft had always assumed that men are by nature evil,[15] in his passion to "bring benefit common to everybody,"[16] and in his advocacy of using observation of experience and applying inferences based thereon as the way to effectual truth, he manifested a belief that men are capable of right discrimination and, under its direction, prudent behavior.[17] Taking men as firmly rooted in the earth, imperturbably considering their conduct, and regarding it as essential "to reason about everything"—especially about public affairs—[18] Machiavelli did not restrict himself to the traditional and conventional bias and prejudice against human nature, but rather initiated a process for the discovery of its nature as it reveals itself in the unprejudiced participant.

Participating personally in the political process, one has opportunity to gain insight into oneself and his relationship with others if he perceives his experience reflectively. In affirming a living right to access to essential resources despite restrictive conventions, moments of "being on the spot" when one is called inescapably to accountability, provide self-revelation, the opportunity to weigh the cost of sincerity, to understand the meaning of honesty and to become adept in it. One can become aware of a social framework available for the process of coming to his own equilibrium and of becoming sufficiently strong in it to stand forth more firmly and independently. One can become alert to the vivifying benefits to be derived from reaching out and up to living in more inclusive relationships which at once conserve sensitivity to the old and call forth responsiveness to others previously unknown.

Resources for liberation which Machiavelli recognized included:

(1) concern with public affairs which he had grown to know as that food which only is mine and which I was born for;[19]
(2) personal development through participation in public service;[20]
(3) realization that one's best resources are one's own at hand;[21]
(4) exercised;[22]
(5) trained;[23]
(6) applied spiritedly;[24]
(7) directed through intelligent will enlightened by reason derived from observed responsible participation;[25]
(8) aided by inventiveness;[26]
(9) by the development of a body of collaborators,[27] and
(10) by periodic renewal through reconsideration of origins.[28]

How can men begin to perceive themselves as citizens of the living order taking form and being served by emerging science?

Eternal values continue to work themselves out into temporal manifestation. The impulse for human action has grown to the degree of atomically armed super-powers sending forth explorers into outer space. The ancient Jewish claim to land, love of it and cultivation of it into fruitfulness, has become generalized as manifested in the spread of national patriotism into the over 150 members of the not-even-yet-universal United Nations. The insights of the great religions have continued to permeate and inter-knit mankind despite the fracturing of religious institutions. The Renaissance's exaltation of the individual as of ultimate value, the Protestant Reformation's affirmation of the freedom of man as having direct access to the Creator through the soul and the Inner Light, the democratic perception of organization as an agency for implementing the general will while protecting the civil rights of each against erosion in the name and on behalf of some "collective," the application of scientific method to the development of means for responding to and stimulating human needs and desires—all have continued through enhancing the worth and dignity of the individual to modify the social environment.

Long ago, in times comparatively much more constricted, the Psalmist declared[29] and later the apostle Paul repeated

The earth is the Lord's and the fulness thereof.[30]

Jesus gave living recognition that no human beings are either aliens or exiles. Migrant workers are most manifest emissaries of the all-caring Creator evoking response in His service.

The realistic recognition of the right of every person, including the other, to be aware of and to enjoy his dignity to the full degree that one finds consistently desirable for one's self, requires one to face and divest himself of every privilege at the expense of another and to assist the other in consciousness of his own security. In clarifying the aim sustaining the uniqueness of one's own life, it becomes his magnetizing attention, releasing his energy in appropriate behavior. Each affirms himself as endowed with ultimate potentialities: whether in religious terms such as the Quakers' belief that "there is That of God in every man;" or in such secular terms as Machiavelli's recognition that a prince, despite all his concentration of power, cannot nullify or annihilate a living man's reaction.[31]

Truth in social order is approached through living the way of understanding being related all together. Constituted by the *de facto* preponderantly favorable impact of external and internal influences, one may feel himself limited by and constricted in their terms and yet impelled to transcend them. Such may be the source both of the sense of human bondage and of the sense of the existence of a greater power of utterly different quality which is essential for the realization that there can be and is an exit from such bondage.

367

According to Machiavelli, escape from the life of swine[32] requires that, limited as one is in understanding,[33] one must be deliberately audacious,[34] beyond all inner security,[35] daring even inner Hell,[36] intentionally accepting in and for himself the costs[37] while accrediting to the political authority of the common good, the profits.[38]

Did an error develop in traditional statecraft: in that it was assumed that in trying to put in operation a public policy one could keep intact one's conception, thus avoid inner confusion and the hell attendant upon action involving others, by violently exacting sacrifice from them as their obligation to submit to his program in the name of the well-being of the country or of the common good? The claim of a knowledge of a process or of a power relevant to but outside of every one's experience may tempt one to claim a superior and more general knowledge of it than that available to another and on the basis of that claim to use it as a fiction for establishing a control expansible into ecclesiastical, political, economic, technological or similar hierarchies. Since the power affirmed is outside experience, it cannot be tested as to whether or not the claimant's assertion of superior knowledge of it is in truth superior for another for whom it is being prescribed as the way for promoting his best interests. Fear of letting oneself be seen just as he is leads one to seek refuge in the "objectivity" of symbols (words, programs, structures) bereft of the essence of truth and projected both to inspire respect (awe) and to distract from the discovery of the hidden insecurity.

In accordance with one's recognition, awareness, articulate manifestation of his being, he neither fearfully feigns weakness by investing his strength in others hopefully to serve as a crutch but eventually experienced as a rack, nor does he grasp ignorantly and violently for that which is not proffered thorugh others' prudent good will. Only as one exercises the courage of being with others in terms of his search for awareness of the nature of his own being can there be communication in truth. This is a baptismal process. The rite of baptism is to symbolize that the going through of such a risking of "security" is the way not of annihilation but of becoming more truly alive; and so the rite provides a shock to serve as a reminder in future crises for voluntarily confronting and facing through temptations of panic, for summoning courage for paying attention to one's essential relationship. In *Gold of the Gods,* Erich van Däniken has quoted D. L. Pieper:

> Panic fear of a mistake is death to any form of progress. Love of truth is its letter of safe conduct.[39]

Experiences of acceptance, welcome and appreciation of one in light of his diversity and uniqueness, shock him into deeper and more inclusive vitality and release efficient energy toward the level of his highest potential, the autonomy of "I Am." Friendship is the medium in which such an acceleration or quantum leap of growth occurs. Thus Jesus termed his companions, "friends."[40] A self-governing society both implies and helps develop members aspiring toward personal autonomy with openness and sincerity in mutual relations. Therein, the idea of leadership—except in the most pluralistic and specifically functionally responsible sense—is a patent fiction. A self-governing society can exist and proceed only to the extent that its members are striving as individuals and together for individual self-mastery. Cooperation in self-responsibility for mutually chosen and expressly defined purposes continuously monitored to stay on course, has to be ever on guard against claims of leadership which would sway its powers and deflect its direction. Only through such achievement in process is there a functioning democracy. Situations which one views as so "corrupt" that "right action" would require violence[41] and provoke hatred, indicate that one's perspective with regard to them is not yet sufficiently true and valid to indicate the line for policy or action which would prove effective or constructive. The continuous intermixture and flux of "good" and "evil" was noted by Machiavelli when he wrote:

> As we have said elsewhere, in the actions of men—besides the other difficulties in trying to bring something to perfection—in connection with good there seems always to be something bad, which so easily grows up along with the good that to avoid bad while striving for good seems impossible. This is apparent in everything men do;[42]

and by Jesus in two parables: that of the wheat and the tares[43] and that of the net full of edible and inedible fishes.[44] Although, according to Machiavelli, intervention by Fortune may favor one,[45] such a gift confers no security:[46] from it develops nothing of consequence since the chances are that subsequent changes will as likely sweep away the illusory stability. The above two parables of Jesus indicate the inadequacy of human discrimination for achieving just judgment. Matthew 7:1–5 and Luke 6:37 record Jesus as enjoining human judgment of one's fellows as inherently hypocritical. Paul[47] and James[48] add full concurrence. And, remembering the ancient Deuteronomist,[49] Paul wrote:

> My dear friends, do not seek revenge, but leave a place for divine retribution; for there is a text which reads, 'Justice is mine, says the Lord, I will repay.'[50]

Machiavelli placed his hope in intervention by courageous, prudent forceful will in service of the common good; but that the hope had historical validity, he was not certain; however, to give reality to it as a matter of faith in action, he adjudged worth one's soul.[51]

Giving his example of conduct for the common good in the moment of

369

supreme crisis, Jesus refused both to proceed on merely his own will and, also, even to let his cause be supported or defended by the force of violence. Early in his ministry he had declared:

> It is meat and drink for me to do the will of him who sent me until I have finished his work.[52]

In his farewell prayer, he said:

> Father, the hour has come . . . I have glorified thee on earth by completing the work which thou gavest me to do . . . I have made thy name known to the men whom thou didst give me out of the world. They were thine, thou gavest them to me, and they have obeyed thy command.[53]

in the Garden of Gethsemane, he prayed:

> My Father, if it is possible, let this cup pass me by. Yet not as I will, but as thou wilt.[54]

Later, when as a gesture of support for Jesus' defense one drew and used a sword, Jesus said to him:

> Put up your sword. All who take the sword die by the sword;[55]

or, as John recorded it:

> Jesus said to Peter, 'Sheathe your sword. This is the cup my Father has given me; shall I not drink it?'[56]

One's own initiative does not open to him direct contact with another. Initially one uses stereotypes and categories which he has received by chance from his particular background. Recognizing their inherent irrelevance and his own diverse variability, one can train oneself to hold them back and oneself in reserve so that whenever there is opportunity for direct contact with another one can try to be present with the other person, openly attentive to him as he is, and not let any predetermined category intervene. As a Quaker once witnessed in a meeting for worship:

> We need to look beyond categories to faces.

An act of awareness, involving as it does appreciation and respect for the individuality and personality of the other as well as oneself, in itself, for all involved, is an opening out from loneliness and bondage and it does not necessarily carry with it a prescription for the other's "salvation" through his becoming conformed

370

to one's own way. The potential understanding is an unknown whole the authority of which the predetermined particular can displace only by means of a compassionless fiction violating the reality. The tissue of fiction contrasts with that liberating congeniality which, proceeding out of one's unique fear-confronting-and-fear-dispelling integrity, relates to that sought and encountered in another. Development to self-mastery proceeds through cooperating in joint undertakings planned and carried on mutually.

Sensitive to the necessity to tap deeper levels of energy if the movement toward political liberation was to be sustained, Machiavelli looked to the formation of the patriotic citizen army. Machiavelli sensed that men born in the same country and raised together,[57] "simple men, rough and native,"[58] tillers of the soil and craftsmen,[59] were untapped reservoirs of emotional energy capable of being disciplined and trained as a citizen army into an effective instrument for the will of a new prince[60] and that

> men who are princes of such great states that they can assemble from their subjects fifteen or twenty thousand young men[61]

could reinstitute the "ancient methods" of warfare. In the *Discourses* he wrote:

> Those who fight for their own glory are good and faithful soldiers.[62]

This need for evoking a new quality of civic energy continued to be a major consideration throughout Machiavelli's life and writings.[63]

What latent, or new, resource in the human spirit can serve mankind as a common bond adequate for today's more inclusive relationship and prove immune to the internecine rivalries to which religions and nationalisms of the world have fallen prey? Can disciplined non-violent action guided by thinking differently but in accord with the evidence from one's own experience, temper participants to endure hardships of patience while working for mutual understanding? Can it generate morale even transcending that of the partisan soldier—out of which the nations states took form? Can the way of reconciliation, through which, in mutual recognition of mutual needs, traditionally hostile peoples undertake an endeavor for mutual benefit and control it accordingly, provide a flexibility which makes possible availability for creative innovative initiative resulting in security and enrichment in both spiritual and material goods?

Is there not herein to be found the meaning of Paul's observation:

> Christ ends the law and brings righteousness for every one who has faith?[64]

Although members of each side in an adversary relationship may have experienced elements of the evidence, not until it has been considered together can there be participation with certainty in an act of judgment. Shared sensitivity to mutually

recognized inclusive source of strength and validity enhances the sense of freedom. Pretensions of righteousness, claims of privilege, fear-born temptation to
violent persecution under the guise of religion and patriotism, incite group conflict. Fred D. Gealy has written:

> the exercise of power is Christian only when fully joined with love and
> these two with self control.[65]

"Faithful and True," the name of the rider on the apocalyptic white horse who,
according to the Revelation of St. John[66] is to execute just judgment, combines
the virtue of faithfulness which is commonly recognized as essential in politics
with a substitution of Truth for falsehood, treachery, deception, cunning which
is as generally considered essential for the acquisition and maintenance of political
power. Paul affirmed that living faith through the spirit as revealed in Christ
nullifies or extirpates the defects and shortcomings which have been the occasion
for law and constitutes sufficient sustenance for human society.[67]

It would be an abuse of non-violence for it to be used merely as a strategy.
In fundamental matters such as science, religion and politics as well, the true
perspective requires inclusion and not exclusion. In science, knowledge of the
law of the phenomena is not affirmed until all the relevant data is comprehended
in the formula or statement: the exception does *not* prove the rule. In religion,
the recognition that "there is That of God in every man," in government, the
recognition that "governments derive their just powers from the consent of the
governed" (with the corollary that powers not derived from consent are not just),
implies an attitude of mutual listening out of which comes formulation of any
methods and structures pertinent to the promotion of the constructive development
of each and all involved.

The Genesis story accounts for the creation of man through the will of
higher influence without a woman, and woman as brought forth out of man.[68]
The Matthew[69] and Luke[70] stories account for the incarnation of the divine nature
through the will of higher influence without man, and the man-child brought
forth out of woman. Together they bring to attention that the new being does
not belong to either, nor, indeed, to both, of the physical human parents as their
creature and heir but in essence is of a higher order to full consciousness in
which by its help along with one's own cooperation one can arrive.[71] The ministry
of Jesus shows the way of using one's personality responsibly thereto[72] so that
one comes to the "end" as oneself perceiving "death" as the voluntary severing
of the psychological umbilical cord of personality and thereby releasing the self
to serve as a seed for living fruitfully beyond its limitations. Since men are so
constituted that they cannot reconcile themselves to unequal treatment, if one's
"advantages" and "privileges" are not to become magnets drawing disasters to
them, they must be perceived and used not as "rights" to be claimed, defended

and enjoyed but, instead, to be recognized as in reality providing a limited and brief time for achieving effective service in relieving others' contrasting "necessity" and thereby gaining in oneself illumination of one's otherwise ignored "dark side." Thus "time" is a function of "privilege" and if eternity is a right, it is created through the responsible use of time and in proportion to the quality of that use. Man is given the potentiality for full awareness in creative communion, attainable through the discipline of living in mutual love, coming to glimpse the direction in which truth may be sought and the more reliable order be established. A man's inner motivation is what he can give in love and together with others aspire toward as aim. As applied science, refining the environing physical resources, results in technology which renders material poverty and "necessity" evermore potentially obsolete, sharing of resources to meet human needs becomes psychologically imperative as the alternative to the hell of all-consuming fear materialized in locks and bolts and lethal weaponry. Real security is found not in built-in obsolescence as a way to wealth and shrewd gamesmanship as a way to power, but in the permanence of that quality which is service in love. Awareness of being is realized as mutual reciprocity in seeking—despite the deceptive and illusory hope which incites grasping for security and certainty.

The quest for truth knows no boundaries of privilege. Privilege is always generated by unfounded claims of knowledge and buttressed by violence. As long ago as the writing of the ancient poem known as Hannah's prayer, men have been put on notice:

Cease your proud boasting, let no word of arrogance pass your lips; for the Lord is a god of all knowledge; he governs all that men do. [73]

The living exploration toward truth defines valid relationship—an on-going inventive inquiry not characterized by absolute comprehension. One's medium for work is reason based on observation of one's shared responsible experience as shared with whomever else is concerned. Paul indicated a limitation upon the individual's understanding when he asked:

Among men, who knows what a man is but the man's own spirit within him? [74]

Yet Paul observed that self-knowledge itself is not a possession but a struggle, for which one's own resources are not sufficient:

The good which I want to do, I fail to do; but what I do is the wrong which is against my will; and if what I do is against my will, clearly it is no longer I who am the agent, but sin that has its lodging in me.
I discover this principle, then: that when I want to do the right, only the

wrong is within my reach. In my inmost self I delight in the law of God, but I perceive that there is in my bodily members a different law, fighting against the law that my reason approves and making me a prisoner under the law that is in my members, the law of sin. Miserable creature that I am, who is there to rescue me out of this body doomed to death? God alone, through Jesus Christ our Lord![75]

And Jesus prescribed as remedy for the inner turmoil and confusion:

If you forgive others the wrongs they have done, your heavenly Father will also forgive you; but if you do not forgive others, then the wrongs you have done will not be forgiven by your Father.[76]

he also said,

Blessed are the meek, for they shall inherit the earth.[77]

Considering that the early English usage of the term, "meek," signified "temper," as in the tempering of steel, whereby, through hammering with the alternating shocks of heat and cold water, the metal is pounded clear of impurities, given durability and the possibility of receiving a keener edge; it becomes understandable that one who, in a crisis situation can keep his temper, maintain his "cool," becomes able to perceive more possibilities in the situation, means for bridging differences or ways for creative innovation which transcends the conflict. He becomes an instrument through which the area of stable relations (i.e., the state) manifests sovereignty (the supreme dispute-settling authority) and thus comes to "inherit the earth."

Consensual process becomes an opening toward a larger whole in which one gains more clarity regarding himself, is granted a glimpse into a uniquely other person, and realizes a more reliable perception of the common ground of mutual concern. This return to first principles brings the realization that claims to knowledge are but pretensions for securing recognition, power, glory and that they are intrinsically without foundation. However, one who comes forward to offer not an assertion but a query and an opportunity for shared exploration, in the face of violently proposed and defended "magnificencies" seems, indeed, a foolish, weak robber subverting the "necessary order" and worthy only of being cast forth and extirpated. Both psychologically within himself and socially in relation with others he promotes reduction to the primaeval insecurity. Yet, in itself, this endeavor to perceive truly at the cost of sacrifice of every habitual prop of certainty, this reliance entirely on tested reason as the source of validity affirmed without force of authority[78] or fraud, the faithfulness implied by giving cultural expression to one's affirmations—non-violent, immediate, and direct— manifests a power which certainly characterized the original essence of that which subsequently had been misdirected into the imposing deceit which Machiavelli perceived as commonly practiced "Christianity"—a misinterpretation which had emasculated the impulse to *virtù* (power, *dunumis*)[79] and had sanctioned only weakness, degradation and corruption.[80] The intrinsic reality, however, was the undaunted living uniqueness of the incomparable individual-in-responsible-relationship, guided by "a still small voice," "a low murmuring sound,"[81] letting go the accidental alien attachments,[82] manifesting "I AM; that is who I am."[83] NOW is the point of the contact but it means nothing unless the qualifying current is turned on and is flowing through. Order apart from value is but mechanical force. Order through value is creative love. That *virtù* *(dunamis)* of primitive Christianity, nourished by reason distilled from responsible public participation for the common good, Machiavelli perceived as the motive power of the invincible patriotic army.

It is an intrinsic and essential characteristic of political truth that striving for it generates power, yet attaining it never eventuates; because there are other personalities always also central to be considered in every situation old or new. Moreover, our inferences of anticipated consequences have as their basis only observed frequencies of past performances and although intentional experiment provides especially persuasive evidence for probability, the human variables constitute factors too unique for any one's conclusive reliability. Effectiveness in the political process requires, as has been said of a prophet, the manifestation of the combination of deep love, powerful dissent and unwavering hope. Facing up to necessity releases men's most constructive energies. Working with others toward the fulfillment of needs, the answer to questions, the consolation of loneliness, one discovers and confirms his own being and kinship with others and develops immunity to that misuse of relationship which generates the leadership-follower nexus with its miasma of myth.

For his time, Machiavelli recognized the possibility and the necessity for a more efficacious employment of human experience. Considering that persistent uniformities in human behavior made it always available for understanding,[84] either by alert observation on the part of those engaged in the process of responsible participation for promoting the common good[85] or by the serious study of records of ancient times,[86] he sought to stimulate and bring into operation the new quality of attention requisite for promoting a higher degree of security and freedom in human affairs. The opportunity for enlightenment which attends strategic involvement, he observed, risks impairment by a blinding intensity of the desire to succeed.[87] If profit is to be derived from the opportunity for enlightenment offered by the records, a special sensitivity must be cultivated and utilized in reviewing biblical[88] as well as secular[89] sources. Moreover, one must be on guard against the omissions,[90] the subjective biases[91] and, especially,

the malice of historians who follow Fortune; usually they are satisfied to honor the conquerors.[92]

Thus Machiavelli pointed the way toward more objective observation and more reasoned consideration of political events and decision-making.

Although the aim and many of the guidelines which he prescribed have but grown in strength and relevance during the four succeeding centuries, the history of the emergence of such revolutions in technology as those of printing, power-driven machinery, biological and health sciences, in government such as the English, American, French, Russian and Chinese revolutions and the dissolution of empires, bring to mind the words of Paul:

> to shame the wise, God has chosen what the world counts folly, and to shame what is strong, God has chosen what the world counts weakness. He has chosen things low and contemptible, mere nothings, to overthrow the existing order. And so there is no place for human pride in the presence of God.[93]

Radio, television and satellite communication may give a temporary advantage to the image-makers of charismatic "leaders," but improved world-wide, instantaneous communications, combined with more wide-spread mass education arouses and builds up the governing element in each individual together with association with others. Furthermore, the historians' span of attention broadens to take account of more basic consequences in the lives of more of the people rather than, primarily, to exalt the glory of military sacrifices engineered by the heroic "leader."

In the period of transition from the city-state to the larger political unit of the nation-state, Machiavelli's thought provided clues for the political science of the succeeding period. His perception that security and freedom demand of men self-realization through creative citizenship[94] in a more-inclusive self-governing whole,[95] that the dignity of each roots in unencumbered title to land freed from "barbarians"[96] and in the responsible exercise of his own intelligent will in the service of the common good,[97] that

> it is well to reason about everything[98]

and

> I do not judge and I shall never judge it a sin to defend any opinion with arguments, without trying to use either authority or force;[99]

> I do consider what reasonably can be, what is, and what has been;[100]

not only guided men toward the more ample freedom of citizens of nation-states but continues to impel them toward the deeper commitment of compassionate will to master the advanced technology for the service of all mankind.

When Machiavelli affirmed that he loved his native city more than his soul,[101] when he wrote approvingly of those who bore similar testimony regarding themselves,[102] and when he declared that the potential quality of men improves with the nobility of one's country,[103] was he, with reference to the sense of obligation in human relations, affirming that there are principles which are deeper and higher than one's own there-to-fore sense of individuality and that one has to let go of his sense of self-importance in order to fulfill his greater potentiality? When he said that the prudent restorer of a state would establish institutions for the survival of which no single individual would be indispensable but which the people would be able to operate as a republic,[104] was he but indicating the necessity to achieve detachment so that the structure of the order would be a manifestation of the principles themselves? If the founder or the restorer had not achieved such detachment from his own personality in his relationship to his new order and if the state was still commingled with the personality of the leader, it would be vulnerable to the fiction-based attempt at appropriation by the next chance personality and a new cycle of disorder would have to be gone through before the deliverance of the state in its objective form would have been achieved. Such capacity to perceive and to cherish the as-yet-unrealized, more inclusive relationships so deeply as to subordinate in their service values long held sacred and at the same time to relinquish personal attachment for the results in the process, are characteristics essential in the builders of a transcendent order.

Discriminating judgment must be maintained in seeking from Machiavelli guidance into the future. He recognized the danger of blindness due to excess of zeal.[105] Was there evidence of just such blindness in loving his city more than his soul[106] in tending to believe that the common good could be served by the elimination of obstructive individuals[107]—notwithstanding his recognition of the unpredictable resourcefulness of individuals in their self-defense[108] and the difficulty of obliterating the psychological consequences provoked by the use of violence[109]—or in accepting, as useful, sacred deceptions[110] notwithstanding his recognition that

Time . . . is the father of every Truth?[111]

Did Moses, in his zeal to consolidate wayward "followers," verge on such blindness[112] and Paul, in his anguish over not being able to convince more of his fellow countrymen to become believers in the Christian message?[113] Yet Jesus said,

What does a man gain by winning the whole world at the cost of his true self?[114]

and he perceived the understanding of the law as arrived at through the integrity of the living soul.[115] "Soul," "city," "country," "Law" are together rooted in veritable reality and are not rightly conceived so long as they are thought to be, or are treated as, in conflict with each other.

No longer in any of the land-based, sovereignty-asserting, competitive nation-states can the inhabitants find resources sufficient for providing the good life. The effort to make up for the lack by building up military power is steadily driving down the standard of living, restricting civil liberties and poisoning the minds with fear verging on panic. Despite the ancient perception of Moses,[116] of the Deuteronomist,[117] of the Psalmist,[118] of Paul,[119] and Jesus' affirmation of the ultimate value of every person,[120] with the continuing illusion that wars can be won, these states are devoting increasing shares of their limited resources to instruments of terror, are diminishing resources for renewal of strength which the meeting of human needs would achieve, and are leaving ever-increasing numbers of people without a place in time of peace.[121] So unrealistic is *Real-Politik:* so illusory, its foundation! The glimmering of the fact that war[122] and violent revolution[123] are beyond the realm of rational management, Machiavelli already recorded, but notwithstanding his fascination with the importance of reasoning[124] and his concern for recording "the truth of the matter as facts show it" ("the effectual truth"),[125] he did not reach through to the conclusion that warfare is intrinsically impolitic. Twentieth century experience has pounded home hard, this lesson. It has likewise become clearer that a science of human behavior cannot be based on the presumption that one can by violence establish[126] or reform[127] a state, or that its health can be maintained through the pursuance of a policy of military aggression.[128] With the strengthening of the revolutionary idea that the state is established as an instrument to serve the well-being of the citizens ("deriving its just powers from the consent of the governed," as stated in the American Declaration of Independence, and, in the Constitution of the United States, "to promote the general welfare,") there develops a check on such policies as those requiring that the people be kept poor[129] and necessitous,[130] a curb on those whose ambition blinds them,[131] a realization that the economic costs of wars are inescapable,[132] and that inherently and inevitably wars generate a self-nourishing military factor which tends to grow out of any control.[133]

Spreading through mankind, finding expression in a diversity of relationships of mutuality and self-government, is the realization that the state is not an achievement which can be realized by some for others and delivered to them. Each one, as he struggles to exercise a more perceptive, effectively responsible role in the directing of himself and of the groups and organizations of which he is a member, is constructing the authentic state which pertains to him and is determining his, as well as its, character. Immediate and alert personal involvement is the intrinsic element in the political process which sensitizes one's perspective sufficiently for wisdom in action. Experiencing in oneself and encountering in others the potentiality for both uniquely undefeasable self-defense[134] and as uniquely creative cooperation, generates an open-ended attitude for surveying, projecting and pioneering along the way toward the order of freedom. Seeking forth, toward fairness and truth, drains away the emotional energy which motivates the impulse to make use of the authority of the group (on any level) as justification for turning its general power against some, or any, of its members. Out of consideration, grows a deference sensitive to power as an influence working for the common good insofar as the power is conceived of and respected as contributed to and distributed among all, but as corrupting and corroding the social fabric when laid hold of and exploited by any for its private advantage. In terms of religion: God as a guide for man's endeavors is the antithesis of "God" conceived of and treated as an instrument of man's will.

Being present in human relations as observing participant open to the new, the different, the potential, can provide for a future more reliably aware in truth. The Greek word, "*metanoein*" (usually translated as "to repent"), means, literally, "to think differently." Consequently, John the Baptist and Jesus were saying:

Think differently, for the kingdom of heaven is upon you.[135]

Scrupulous attention to the whole of respective phenomena as their consequences unfold, may yet validate Machiavelli's confidence that intelligent, serious observation of human experience can provide guidance adequate for the direction of human affairs away from the violent rule of Chance[136] and toward the establishment of security and liberty. Machiavelli's ultimate integrity expressed itself in that quality of his attention to human behavior in public affairs which makes him an unarmed prophet, but not one among those whom he considered destined to fall[137] but, rather, as pioneer in political science, eternally an official counsellor in the republic of mankind.[138]

The science of politics, just as every other science, can have no other aim, concern, or allegiance than that of the search for "the truth, the whole truth, and nothing but the truth." In this period of recognition of the violently apparent inadequacy of the current political units for protecting and fostering the full and free development of the human spirit, political science cannot, without self-betrayal, serve as an apologist, instrument or patriotic lackey of the "sovereign state," the corporation (be it national, multi-national, religious, class), or any ideology other than that, if it be so designated, inherent in the process of exploring the nature of influence and power among human beings.

In order that thinking about political processes might become a science of politics, previously accepted fictions have to be identified and discarded. If there has been something about the state, as it has been conceived and represented, which has entailed graft, deception, and violence, may more discriminating examination reveal whether or not it is an intrinsic characteristic or is but an accidental association to be eradicated?

As the Christian community of service became institutionalized as a church, entered into an administrative partnership with the declining Roman Empire, developed a network of specialized professionalisms giving increasing priority to concern for material wealth and security of power in the name of the institution, Jesus' original imperative for interpersonal, non-violent, courageous mutual service became obscured. Characteristic of the Renaissance was human energy in search of meaning. Primarily from his reading of Livy's account of pre-Imperial republican Rome, Machiavelli formulated a merger of civic and military discipline which appealed to many in varied lands as the conception of the political process which corresponds most closely to political affairs as observed in operation. Dedicated to the promotion of the common good, testing in the light of reason experiences of things modern and study of things ancient, Machiavelli made advances in method which, however, did not fully immunize him from acceptance of certain currently prevalent attitudes which continue to encumber political thinking and preclude its becoming a science.

For thinking to qualify as a serious and consistent search for the truth of the matter—to qualify, in fact, as a scientific inquiry—the first requirement is that full recognition be accorded to all of the data with any claim to relevance. As a means of solving problems in human relations, any prescription which involves the killing of any of the persons concerned, involves both the attempted destruction of a part of human experience the unobstructed testimony of which is relevant for the understanding of the whole situation and the implausible presumption that the psychological, and social nexus among human beings is so weak and tenuous that a member can be eliminated without incalculable and inevitable consequences. While recording as fact that initiators of wars[139] and of violent revolutions[140] cannot control their termination and results, Machiavelli—despite reservations regarding the historicity[141]—or even the possibility[142]—still endorsed the hope that heroic violence could establish, restore, promote public good.[143] Then, furthermore, he viewed the cultivation and heightening of domestic tension—due to leaving unreconciled the grievances between the rich and the poor[144]—and the systematic attempt at the conversion of that tension into the policy of continual aggressive warfare waged by republican Rome, as the generator of that mixture of civic and military discipline[145] which he admired as *virtù* and the conditions for which he specified when, in *The Art of War*, in response to the question:

What are these things you would like to introduce that are like the ancient ones?

he represented Fabrizio Colonna as responding:

To honor and reward excellence, not to despise poverty, to esteem the methods and regulations of military discipline, to oblige the citizens to love one another, to live without factions, to esteem private less than public good, and other like things that could easily fit in with our times.[146]

However, in deploring the lengthening of military commissions,[147] the professionalization of the armies,[148] the destruction of talent and *virtù* in countries conquered,[149] and the exhaustion of *virtù* at home,[150] he did not acknowledge the whole process as an inevitable consequence of the unremedied inequities left to fester and to corrode the human relations.

Powerful factors insulated Machiavelli, along with people of his time, generally, from direct contact with the records of the life and teaching of Jesus. Institutional religion had too deeply offended those confident in finding validity and authenticity in being alive—and especially the Italians having the papacy in their midst with its policies for keeping them politically divided and those prelates whose way of life, instead of exemplifying standards for emulation, permeated the society with corruption.[151] Among the people, the Bible circulated scarcely, if at all.[152] Practices and policies of churchmen attracted attention chiefly as examples of hypocricy on the part of those in power and of exploitation of the ignorant and the weak. Under such conditions, the records of the origin of the religion held little attraction for those seeking improvement in governmental policies. Consequently, in his study of human affairs, Machiavelli did not concern himself with the basis of Jesus' rejection of the Pharisaic and Roman authority as well as of the appeal of Zealots' program of protest, nor did Machiavelli explore the implications of the resolution of conflict and the making of decision implicit in Jesus' teaching through taking into account the deeper, subtler, more indirect consequences of human conduct and their relation to the common good.

Now that application of the methods of physical science have produced weaponry of such a magnitude that the politically most powerful governments threaten each other with nuclear-charged missiles, now that the social and psychological sciences elaborate techniques to enhance the influence which "leaders" exert by means of television and other media, and now that an ever-increasing proportion of the gross national production of industrial nations is dedicated to serve fiction-fed fears—in order to achieve mastery and direct mankind out of and away from headlong, suicidal drift, a rigorously scientific method applied to the observation and analysis of political experience must take into account the totality of each political phenomenon under consideration, eradicate the ancient but still widespread delusion that the good of the whole can be defined and served by the killing of some and the violating of the human rights of others, and cultivate the realization, clearly and constantly, that only insofar as the well-being of all is sought, assured and served can any one perceive and promote his own.

Any innovation involves some procedure which gives to "[airy nothings] a local habitation and a name."[153] To intensify the experience of intimations of aid to the liberation of man's spirit, Plato fashioned myths. To clarify the way by

381

which men might "think differently" and become fearlessly courageous living forth truth, Jesus communicated through parables. Along with the emergence of scientific inquiry came the formulation and testing of hypotheses. Already in Machiavelli's writings occur such harbingers of the coming dawn, of a science of politics, as:

it is well to reason about everything[154]

and

I do not judge and I never shall judge it a sin to defend any opinion with arguments, without trying to use either authority or force.[155]

Although the conviction attendant upon the perception of new truth may fire one with energy and determine one's course of future conduct, as recorded in the accounts of the baptism of Jesus and of Paul's vision on the road to Damascus, bringing into existence the mode appropriate for its communication requires creative pioneering. Inexorably the pursuit of science disciplines the explorer to evaluate with more discrimination that which he takes for granted and to exercise more meticulous precision in all relevant procedures. When, in the name of any self-justifying enthusiasm, one's strength of conviction so carries one away that he disregards the medium essential for the working out of the insight into realization, that which began as a potentially fruitful hypothesis becomes transformed into an increasingly explosive fiction destined to involve its own self-annihilation in its destructive consequences.

In calling attention to the vital contribution made by the civic innovator for the common good, Machiavelli did not establish it as an inseparable corollary

that all men are evil and that they are always going to act according to the wickedness of their spirits whenever they have free scope[156]

and that states are established and maintained only by leaders who resort to the use of violence.[157]

As Florence from the early thirteenth century on, so great nation-states of the West in the twentieth century have had to face the fact that those who, as producers of raw materials and as the victims of unequal treatment, had been coerced into building up that power, were, with increasing effectiveness, terminating the exploitive relationships and struggling to redress the balance, or even themselves to become the exploiters. Now, as then, mechanically rising tensions threaten to form a devastating vortex drawing into its mindless dance toward the apocalyptic black hole the unprecedented energies and wealth accumulated, released and put to work by human culture. The history of political progress has recorded the tapping in human beings of deeper emotional resources adequate for bringing into existence more inclusive processes able to harness hitherto wild energies in the management of enterprises on a grander scale. Presumptive claims of present *knowledge* of "good" and "evil" but feed appetites for violence in promotion of the fictions. Both in the incipient "leaders," as founders or reformers, and in the available "followers," the rightness of aspirations and impulses are so mixed with blinding stereotypes and arbitrarinesses that any hope for escape from disaster requires not only the newly-generated temper of the scientist dedicated to the quest for the perception of the truth of the matter but also the awareness of a personal conviction that one's own development is realizable and can be pursued only through the service of the common good—"the common good" as defined only through the full and free participation of all those affected by the decision being made.

Instead of violently buttressed myths and *mystiques* of charismatic "leadership," heightened awareness of one's own subjective demands, together with more restraint in projecting them at others' expense, and with greater sensitivity to the dispositions of others, makes available energies for human interaction in more objective and mutually constructive terms and constitutes the growing point of society. The fruits of good temper are: sense of humor, keenness, resourcefulness and patience. The accumulation and administration of power in the service of meeting needs is a process of openness to critical scrutiny, to continuous mutual planning and review. In the struggle, the "leader's" initiative becomes clarified into the enlightenment of disciplined self-knowledge and release into kindred service, and the "follower's" fearful timidity becomes transformed into the enlightenment of disciplined self-respect and release into meaningful participation. In this way, individuals' experience-generated data become reconciled in the open-ended, social-scientific-executive-political searching to define, and cooperating to achieve, an end result which strengthens and refreshes all. Yet, as has been observed: "In the army of the Lord, all are wounded." Any predetermined or immature concept of the whole to be served as worthy of violence-demanding allegiance, entails distortion and misinterpretation of the data, even untrue manipulation of it or the, ultimately vain, effort to destroy it.

The political process can bear its potential fruit as applied science only insofar as it puts in practice the essential way of science. Understanding literally the term "science," one perceives it as the act of knowing and, therefore, as involving an open-ended seeking, so long as, and to the degree that, proof of certainty has not been established. Whenever in human relationships force, "fortune," or "accident" are proposed as an effective factor, there science finds a challenge to work itself out. In the arena when, in full panoply of armor, claimants proclaim authority, when science enters and functions, it is as a probing ray which displaces the violent fictional "cover-ups" with the formulation and projection of hypotheses still to be posed and researched before a sound judgment in knowledge can be affirmed. Thus, knowing is seeking for becoming. Science confronts secretive, aggressive, privilege-demanding, exploitive repression, with openness to the turmoil of clamorous needs through which voluntary association generates authority through service. The action of working together, clarifying and articulating needs and ministries, awakens participants to insights into themselves and to similarities with others and opens the way for expressions marked by higher degrees of integrity, sincerity and compassion which elevate above the social horizon new concepts of a greater whole worthy of struggle for its realization. In thereby redefining himself and his relationships, each finds less inclination blindly to project hostile reactions at others' expense than alertly to assay the current condition for options available for achieving the common good. In and through service to it one gets glimpses into his own and its potentialities, and exerts himself for their achievement. Less firmly bound by prior stereotypes, habit patterns, and conventional value assumptions, with open-ended sensitivity to all intimations of pertinence, one's labors become an effective and responsible instrument through which the new is given factual recognition.

Coping with the requirements for a more inclusive and generous order and one of higher dimension, calls upon and releases new qualities in human nature. Thus Machiavelli came to sense the emerging need that citizens cultivate a deeper-rooted, more disciplined public loyalty and he strove to institute the citizen militia through which could develop better men in a better sort of country. For his citizen-soldiers he hoped for an education which would generate a new character, because

wherever there are good soldiers there must be good government;[158]

if for every other order of men in cities and kingdoms every diligence should be used to keep them faithful, peaceful, and full of fear of God, in the army it should be redoubled. Because from what man ought his native land to expect greater fidelity than from that one who has to promise to die for her? In whom ought there to be more love of peace than in him who can get nothing but injury from war? In whom ought there to be more fear of God than in a man who every day, being exposed to countless perils, has great need for his aid? This necessity, well considered both by those who give laws to empires and by those who are put in charge of military training, would bring it about that the life of soldiers would be praised by other men and with great zeal followed and imitated;[159]

and since one is indebted to his country for his being and for

all of the good which fortune and nature have granted . . . as much greater it comes to be in those whose country of origin is more noble,[160]

he concluded that:

excellent men come in larger numbers from republics than from kingdoms, since republics usually honor wisdom and bravery; kingdoms fear them. Hence the first cultivate wise and brave men; the second destroy them.[161]

Readiness for effective action is the intrinsic significance to be understood in Machiavelli's emphasis upon rulers' reliance upon their own "good armies"[162] and the effectiveness of the action requires that it embody or substantiate the goal, thus: in the leader's cultivation of prudence,

A wise prince . . . seeks advice continually, but when it suits him and not when it suits somebody else; moreover, he deprives everyone of courage to advise him on anything if he does not ask it. But nonetheless he is a big asker and then, on the things asked about, a patient listener to the truth. Further, if he learns that anybody for any reason does not tell him the truth, he is angry;[163]

in the development of courage in the people,

every city ought to have methods with which the people can express their ambition, and especially those cities that intend to make use of the people in important affairs;[164]

in the presentation of programs and policies as demanded by necessity,[165]

how slow men are in things in which they think they have time, and how rapid they are when necessity drives them.[166]

And herein is a defect in the conventional political "wisdom" when tested in the light of Machiavelli's own foretaste of a science of politics. That concept of human nature in politics which he held to be demonstrated by all interpreters of statecraft does not accord with or correspond to that capacity for rational consideration which he held due it and which he sought to accord it. A radical contradiction infected it. On the one hand, for purposes of statecraft, he quoted with seeming approval the propositions that:

all men are evil;[167]

and, from the point of view of religion:

That tongue made to glorify God blasphemes him; that mouth, through which he must be fed, he makes into a sewer and a way for satisfying the appetite and the belly with luxurious and excessive food: those thoughts about God he changes into thoughts about the world; that desire to preserve the human species turns into lust and many other dissipations. Thus with

385

these brutish deeds man changes himself from a rational animal into a brute animal. Man changes, therefore, by practicing this ingratitude to God, from angel to devil, from master to servant, from man to beast.

Those who are ungrateful to God—it is impossible that they are not unfriendly to their neighbors. Those are unfriendly to their neighbors who are without charity . . . Whoever, then, lacks it must necessarily be unfriendly to his neighbor: he does not aid him, he does not endure his faults, he does not console him in tribulation, he does not teach the ignorant, he does not advise him who errs, he does not help the good, he does not punish the evil. These offenses against one's neighbor are grave: ingratitude against God is very grave;[168]

that the recourse to force and fraud are indispensable means for achieving greatness;[169] yet, also, that there is in any man an irreducible core of self-defense;[170] and that

Promises Made Under Compulsion Should Not Be Kept.[171]

On the other hand, Machiavelli recognized that in men is a capacity for foresight and the obligation to make the most of it[172] and that neglect of it by rulers incurred the hazards of Fortune.[173] His observation of the continual availability of an abundant supply of men susceptible to deception[174] and his idea of God as lover of the strong and active[175] may be interpreted to tempt seekers after power to maximize the force under their command at the risk, even in the name of God, of the annihilation of the species itself without the possibility of taking into account the consequences; however, a criterion of *science* is the enrichment of life *(crescat scientia vita excolatur,* as knowledge increases, life is enriched—the motto of the University of Chicago) and it is distinctive of even life itself that it bears within it the seeds of its own construction.

Machiavelli alerted us to the possibility of a way of thinking salutary to our time, not subject to some of the accidental limitations upon his. As in religion the Old Testament accepted mankind as burdened with a sense of guilt for "original sin" from the necessity for which in the New Testament Jesus by his courageously-lived search liberated mankind to the extent that, according to Paul and John, individuals lay hold of that potentiality through living love for one another,[176] so the old politics of partiality burdens mankind with a sense of need for leadership through violence. Both Jesus and Machiavelli shared the deeply-felt realization that the human individual is incapable alone to define the public order. In the prayer which he taught his disciples to pray, Jesus addressed *"our* Father" and then indicated the name unspeakable. And Machiavelli, despite his emphasis upon the necessity that one man alone be the founder[177] or reformer of a state[178] acknowledged that rarely, if ever, such a man had appeared or will ever appear.[179] Moreover, he held that the outcome of revolutions[180] and of wars[181] do not prove subject to the will of their initiators. Machiavelli and Jesus, each, despite traditionally powerful inhibitions or restraints, pioneered in awakening in individuals an initiative and a vitalizing competence: Jesus, in summoning one to forgive other's trespasses against oneself[182] and thus by-passing the priestly claims as professional mediators for God in having power to forgive sins;[183] and Machiavelli, in transferring defense from professionals to patriotic citizen militias and emphasizing self-reliance as the source of power in dealing with others and as the foundation of understanding.[184]

Process without fiction requires development of a capacity, while experiencing a sense of indeterminancy, to engage in a double-headed inquiry: internally, perceiving and defining the elements of the need or objective; externally, perceiving the differences in the relations which others have to the concern, the possibilities for constructive cooperation; then, through patient, mutual inner reconstruction until the achievement of a moment for common action, to sense consensus for giving reality to the anticipated common good. In the process one comes to see and remove the "plank" in his own eye and may see that there is but a "speck" in his brother's eye which the latter may be already in the process of removing.[185] It has been well said,

> Whenever groups or individuals try to live and work together, the forgiving and tolerant attitude becomes possible only as all parties recognize that nobody can possibly be totally right. New truth appears where partial views meet.[186]

The meeting of others' "trespasses" with grace and compassion enlightens one as to his own shortcomings and releases mutual help and strength for their transcendancy. A private, courageous dedication to the pursuit of the truth of the matter and adherence to it, a public openness to scrutiny and judgment and a readiness to re-evaluate one's own behavior and its outcome, to recognize the errors and mistakes as they become manifest to oneself, keeping alert to all of the evidence—especially as it is expressed in the unpleasant manifestations of others and thereby is borne in upon one as also within oneself—such conduct brings into being an action team competent for operating effectively on a level of deeper influences, a higher level of responsibilities, as the transmitter of a higher charge for greater potentialities, and the enunciation of insight and wisdom unbiased by impulses of fear or of quests for power—save fear of deviation from reflecting light from the direction of distant truth and fear of deviation from the favor of the grace of the living Creator as the seat of real power, authority, and value. Robert Wicks has written:

> we were created to prove that more which is true and good can become real for all of us. We are born self-centered creatures with a capacity to

be transformed into creators who can prove in new situations what is the inexhaustible will of the Creator—a will that is partly known in what has happened, and mostly concealed by the unknown future.[187]

In his poem "Safety," Rupert Brooke wrote:

> . . . Safe shall be my going.
> Secretly armed against all death's endeavor.
> Safe though all safety's lost; safe where men are falling;
> And if these poor limbs die, safest of all.[188]

In his television serial *Ascent of Man,* Jacob Bronowski has said:

Science is at the brink of the known feeling forward into what can be hoped.

The apostle Paul perceived love as the source of knowledge and judgment. Of his prayer for them, he wrote the Philippians:

that your love may grow ever richer and richer in knowledge and insight of every kind, and may thus bring you the gift of true discrimination.[189]

When one individual claims a knowledge for himself *and* others, more valid and beyond the purview of those others' experience, he opens the way for basing upon it a claim of authority superior to that of the others and for constructing upon it a hierarchy for control unaccountable to those over whom it is exercised and from whom it exacts support. To avoid such fiction-generated and force-but-tressed eruptions: members of the Religious Society of Friends have eschewed "the leadership principle;" scientists require the replicability of experiments; and free societies require fully limited and responsible governments.

Many folk sayings related to a great diversity of human activity testify to the fact that moments arrive in which if appropriate action is not taken the occasion for achievement is lost. Among such sayings are: "strike while the iron is hot;" ". . . when it comes to a boil;" "when it spins a thread;" "the moment of critical mass;" "catch opportunity by the forelock; it is bald behind." Significant evidence that interpersonal and group relations can take place with scrupulous regard for the presence of all concerned *and* with timely effectiveness has been provided, since the late seventeenth century, repeatedly through the procedures, skills and achievements, not only in fields of science but also in the experience of members of the Religious Society of Friends (Quakers). Grounded in the conviction that "there is That of God in every person," it has been characteristic of Quakers at their best to endeavor to achieve reconciliation in conflict situations. Assembled in the atmosphere of silent, "holy expectancy" of the meeting for worship or meeting for business, whenever there emerges between participants a struggle for power, a recall to the silence together provides occasion for egoism and partisan feelings to subside and for theretofore unanticipated options to be brought to light. Since as

The wind blows where it wills; . . . So with . . . spirit,[190]

whoever feels the need can initiate the call for a special meeting full participation in which becomes available to all who consider themselves concerned or involved in the matter at issue. Of Carl Jung it has been said,

Religion was for him nothing if not obedience to awareness.[191]

Likewise, Lord John Pentland observed in the presence of the author:

The miracle of Christ is consciousness.

The lack of power-driven technology which, according to Aristotle,[192] necessitated and justified the institutions of slavery and war, is no longer a condition providing a valid argument for their continuance. Indeed, the application of science to improvements in the means of production make human poverty, class conflict and war but anachronisms and culture-lags. The growth of constitutional democracy, implemented with freedom of religion, press, association, universal education and enterprise (in truth not distorted by governmentally-created corporations), demonstrate that power is that which derives "from the consent of the governed" and serves "to promote life, liberty, the pursuit of happiness" (i.e., equality of opportunity for each and all without a shadow of inferiority). Consequently, Machiavelli's assumption that evil in human nature[193] requires the harsh intervention by leaders violent and treacherous (above, pp. 59–62) has grown less convincing. Indeed, there is a dawning intimation that it is not in personal "leadership" nor in organizations or projected systems, but that it is in the apperceptive interrelationships experienced in venturing forth through loving-will-energy that one approximates living in truth. The effective breadth of discretion respecting ends and means is determined by, is a function of, understanding through love active in service. Personal, individual awareness of power as it becomes distributively assimilated,[194] becomes a new attribute operative within oneself and, there-through, pervasive of relationships among human beings. Machiavelli wrote:

a man has no greater duty in life than that [to honor and serve his country], being dependent on it, first, for his being, and, then, for all of the good which fortune and nature have granted him, and as much greater it comes to be in those whose country of origin is more noble.[195]

389

For citizens in the democracy of mankind guided by the autonomously questing science of power, the measure of a man becomes the effect of his choices upon the realization of his potentialities as manifested by the character and grace revealed in the highest conceivable example, the person of Jesus.[196]

Although in the life of his city, during the years immediately following his death, Machiavelli's faith in guidance through cooperative participant observation seemed utterly vanquished as assassination gave way to despotism and the never-finished Forteza da Basso demonstrated the insecurity attendant upon reliance upon violence rather than the will for self-government and liberty,[197] out of his passion for liberty, Machiavelli, in projecting rational consideration of political behavior, had initiated a ferment which would work for enlarging the order of human freedom through the growing perception of effectual will for living in truth and establishing the order of free men.

Mankind's experience of rebirth in making living meaningful through voyages of discovery, translations of ancient manuscripts, the use of less costly means for the dissemination of ideas and the processing of materials for stimulating and responding to people's wants, the instituting of procedures for detecting, arousing, assembling, organizing, implementing, administering, and keeping accountable power in human relations by way of: the spread of public health services, the development of representative constitutional government, universal education, newspapers, radio, television, satellite communication, universal suffrage and the facilitation of its operation, computerized polling and canvassing techniques, removal of fiscal and procedural restraints used for subjecting some to the exploitive manipulation by others, the increase in the capacity of organizational structures (not only in the political arena) to serve vastly greater numbers of people, the encouragement of the perception of the inherent relationship between living personally meaningfully and participating responsibly in decision-making processes for the common good, the placing of limitations on official secrecy and authority for "covert actions," the laws protecting the public's right to know—all indicate the kind of changes which bring pressure on policy makers to proceed through more authentically conceived consensus in terms of more openly validated data. Significant in this regard is Machiavelli's judgment respecting the people's influence in government.[198]

Chapter Thirteen

POST-MACHIAVELLIAN CHANGES REINFORCING DIRECTION GIVEN BY HIM

In the light of changes since his time, Machiavelli's political wisdom still points a true direction ahead.

Developing search for the effectual truth of the matter,[1] as indicated through personal[2] and governmental[3] dedication to promoting the common good and maturing experience with scientific method keeps, as its highest priority, its openness to redefinition.[4]

The deep relation which he recorded between the experience of liberty and opportunity for growth in character[5] has become increasingly manifest and is leading to the understanding that only goals defined by and for the benefit of *all* the earth's inhabitants can prove tolerable. "Freedom" sought in terms of the privilege of a part exacted at the expense of others entails an unprofitable, violent, suicidal course—another demonstration of the inescapably organismic character of earth-born and earth-responsible human society which reacts mechanically and violently when experiencing injury.

While pursuing the inclination "to try to govern others"[6] reliance upon "one's own resources" realistically appraised, was one of Machiavelli's chief emphases.[7] For self-governing societies, the advice which Machiavelli offered to princes, founders of states, generals, becomes relevant to the individual in his becoming aware of his civic potentialities, organizing and effectively employing them. Serving the common good provides one with opportunity to be discovering who one is: the more responsibly one is serving the more inclusive loyalty, the more intelligently emotional one's relationship and perception of the nature of the availability in the present moment for appropriate service as witness, the clearer grows one's recognition of who one is potentially;[8] why one is; what is one's obligation; and how love, truth, and ordered significance converge.

Until every last member of a currently deprived category—and, also, those lost without a category—can feel himself on the road to meaningful freedom, until each can enter on a way knowing for himself and making friends with the dark parts in his own personality and, as a more integrated personality, can communicate with and appreciate others, no one's loyalty is clear in definition, either for himself or among others, or secure in practice. Ultimately, there is no citizenship except in that democracy of the world in which each and all are free both within themselves and in association with others.

Mobility of individuals, families, whole peoples, opportunities for individual choice in giving up citizenship in the country of one's birth and in acquiring that in the country of one's choice, has not obliterated shared experience of needs as a source of strength for common action. Machiavelli perceived in "soldiers who are born and live together" the indispensable source for the confidence and organization essential for a victorious army.[9] The modern counterpart to the compatriots to whom Machiavelli made reference may be considered to be such people as feel themselves stirred by the same "necessity" to identify themselves with each other.

The Florentine experience, especially as interpreted by Machiavelli, proved to be a rewarding source of inspiration, encouragement and enlightment for seventeenth and eighteenth century thinkers seeking to develop institutions more firmly bound to the detection and promotion of the common good. Orestes Ferrara has called attention to the sudden revival, late in the eighteenth century, of interest in the writings of Machiavelli.

> Dans l'aube encore brumeuse de l'époque moderne, après deux siècles d'ostracisme légal, *le Prince* revit le jour. En 1768, on publia une édition á Paris, l'année suivante une autre à Venise, une troisième à Londres en 1772.
> L'apothéose eut lieu à Florence. Il y eut une édition officielle in 1782. Et, in 1787, on inaugurait le monument avec l'épigraphe: *Tanto nomini nullum par elogium.*[10]

> In the still foggy dawn of the modern epoch, after two centuries of legal ostracism, the *Prince* saw again the light of day. In 1768, an edition was published in Paris, the following year another in Venice, a third in London in 1772. The glorification took place in Florence. There was an official edition in 1782. And, in 1787, there was dedicated the monument with the inscription: *Tanto nomini nullum per elogium* (for such a name, nothing by way of eulogy).

In 1775 in London was published the Ellis Farnesworth edition of *The Works of Nicholas Machiavel*, in four volumes. Martin Fleischer has pointed out:

In the seventeenth century Machiavelli enjoyed his greatest influence among thinkers of republican persuasion like Harrington, Spinoza, Neville, and Sidney. They praised him for his insights into the dynamics of political life and for his celebration of civic culture; and since they were generally men who advocated change, perhaps they praised him above all for his political activism—for his idea, that is, that a people who have not been corrupted beyond the point of no return, can revitalize their political existence and regain control of their fate through acts of political intelligence and energy inspired by bold leadership.[11]

To the above list of thinkers, Neal Wood adds Milton and Marvel, with the comment regarding them all:

And, of course, they were devoted pupils of Machiavelli, finding in the *Discourses* a rare fount of political wisdom;[12]

Although Sidney cites Machiavelli fewer times in his monumental *Discourses Concerning Government* (1698) a work much longer than Harrington's *Commonwealth of Oceana* (1656) and in language less adulatory, he seems closer to the spirit of the Florentine than does Harrington.[13]

Pocock and Fleischer trace the development into the eighteenth century:

the Aristotelian, Machiavellian, and now Harringtonian "science of virtue," or sociology of civic ethics, had to be restated with paradigmatic force and comprehensiveness for the eighteenth-century West at large. Montesquieu, seen from this angle, is the greatest practitioner of that science, and this is the period during which Machiavelli's reputation as the chief of civic moralists stood at its highest and blanketed most references to his moral ambiguity. But the price to be paid was that every treatise on politics which could not transcend the limitations of this style was likely to end, not only in moral exhortation, but in the suggestion that virtue as a quality of the personality was the only agency likely to cure corruption. Machiavelli had taken this line, while conceding that individual *virtu* in a corrupt society faced a task so difficult that merely human actors would almost certainly be defeated by it; only the heroic, the quasi-divine or truly inspired might succeed;[14]

It was Montesquieu, who, having absorbed Machiavelli and Sidney, took to heart both what he read and observed of English party conflict, of the commercial hustle and bustle, and of the struggles for liberty in the sombre city of the Thames;[15]

The very themes of Machiavelli that are emphasized by Sidney are those Montesquieu makes his own: the passionate advocacy of liberty, the hatred of despotism, the belief that absolutism is rooted in corruption, the prescription of a mixed constitution, a paradigmatic description of the behavior of a free people, the call for a return to first principles, and the necessity of domestic conflict;[16]

Machiavelli and his contemporaries, Florentine history and the image of Venetian practice, left an important paradigmatic legacy: concepts of balanced government, dynamic *virtu,* and the role of arms and property in shaping the civic personality;[17]

the end product of the Florentine experience was an impressive sociology of liberty, transmitted to the European Englightenment and the English and American revolutions, which arose in reply to the challenge posed by the republic's commitment to existence in secular history;[18]

It was in the Aristotelian and civic humanist channel that the stream of republican tradition was to flow, and Machiavelli as a historical figure, to whom theorists like Harrington and Adams referred, was to swim quite successfully in that channel.[19]

Machiavelli was no stranger to the interests and purposes of the authors of the Declaration of Independence of America and the framers of the Constitution of the United States.

Benjamin Franklin's (1706–1798) acquaintance with Machiavelli may well have begun with his access to James Logan's "remarkable library" which included works of Machiavelli and Guicciardini.[20] Pace observed,

of the great Italian literary figures whom Franklin cited, Machiavelli left the most appreciative imprint. Among the works of the Florentine Secretary, Franklin seems to have known the *Discourses* on Livy, as well as the *Prince;*[21]

Franklin cited Petrarch in Italian. As for Dante, Ariosto, and Machiavelli, there is no way of knowing whether he read them in the original or in translation.[22]

John Adams (1735–1826), Clinton Rossiter has referred to as "one of the few colonists who dared or cared to use Machiavelli."[23] An entry in his diary for 8 December 1760 noted, "Began Machiavelli;"[24] later, "1770, August 19, Sunday," he recorded:

Mr. Royal Tyler began to pick chat with me—Mr. Adams, have you ever read . . . Machiavelli and Caesar Borgia . . . [Mandeville] The Author of the Fable of the Bees understood Human Nature and Mankind, better than any Man that ever lived. I can follow him as he goes along. Every Man in public Life ought to read that Book, to make him jealous and suspicious.[25]

Adams referred to Machiavelli as one

> to whom the world is so much indebted for the revival of reason in matters
> of government;[26]

and preceded his extensive resume of the commentary upon *The History of Florence* with the following words of caution:

> As Machiavelli is the most favorable to a popular government, and is even
> suspected of sometimes disguising the truth to conceal or mollify its defects,
> the substance of this sketch will be taken from him, referring at the same
> time to other authors; so that those young Americans who wish to be
> masters of the subject, may be at no loss for information.[27]

At the conclusion of "this sketch" (in length, over 175 pages), in his evaluation of the quality of popular participation throughout the history of the government of Florence, Adams wrote:

> Let the reader now run over again in his own mind this whole story of
> Florence, and see himself whether it does not appear like a satire, written
> with the purpose and only purpose of exposing to contempt, ridicule, and
> indignation, the idea of "a government in one centre," and "the right
> constitution of a commonwealth?" . . . From the beginning to the end, it
> is one continued struggle between monarchy and aristocracy; a continued
> succession of combinations of two or three parties of nobles, rich, or
> conspicuous families, to depress the people on the one hand, and prevent
> an oligarchy or a monarchy from arising up among themselves on the
> other. Neither the first family, nor any of the others their rivals, made any
> account of the people, excepting now and then for a moment, for the
> purpose of violence, sedition, and rebellion.
> Instead of devising any regular method for calling the people together with
> a reasonable notification before hand of the time, place, and subject of
> deliberation, a little junto of principal citizens concert a plan in secret
> among themselves, give notice previously to such as they please, their
> own defendants and partisans, order the bells to be rung, and a little flock
> of their own creatures assemble in the piazza. There the junto nominate a
> dozen or a score of persons for a balia, to reform the state at their pleasure;
> no reasonable method of voting for them, no instructions given them; the
> people huzza and all is over.[28]

Of Machiavelli's own proposal for the reform of the government of Florence, Adams concluded:

> Machiavel, from his long experience of the miseries of Florence in his
> own times, and his knowledge of their history, perceived many of the
> defects in every plan of a constitution they had ever attempted. His sagacity,

too, perceived the necessity of three powers; but he did not see any equal necessity for the separation of the executive power from the legislative. The following project contains excellent observations, but would not have remedied the evils.[29]

In considering that which he designated as "the great question," i.e.,

what combination of powers in society, or what form of government, will compel the formation, impartial execution and faithful interpretation of good and equal laws, so that the citizens may constantly enjoy the benefit of them, and may be sure of their continuance?,[30]

Adams quoted Machiavelli's observation regarding the necessity that the statemaker presume radical evil as characteristic of human nature and continued:

Machiavelli's translator remarks that although this seems a harsh supposition, does not every Christian daily justify the truth of it, by confessing it before God and the World? and are we not expressly told the same in several passages of the Holy Scriptures, and in all systems of human philosophy?[31]

A little further on, Adams wrote:

Machiavel is right when he says: "Men are never good except through necessity. On the contrary, when good and evil are left to their choice, and they can practice the latter with impunity, they will not fail to throw everything into disorder and confusion;"

to which Adams added the footnote,

So great is the depravity of the human heart, that ministers, who only can know it, are in charity to mankind bound to keep it a secret.[32]

In *Novanglus,* Adams expressed agreement with Machiavelli's tolerance for popular commotions:

It is a saying of Machiavel no wise man ever contradicted, which has been verified in this province that "while the mass of the people is not corrupted, tumults do no hurt." By which he means, that they leave no lasting ill effects behind.[33]

However, he dissociated himself from Machiavelli's conclusion that there is a fundamental incompatability between the continued sufferance in the community of rich men and the preservation of a free commonwealth:

396

Machiavel, not perceiving that if a commonwealth is galled by the gentry, it is by their overbalance, speaks of the gentry as hostile to popular governments, and of popular governments as hostile to the gentry . . . But the balance, as I have laid it down, though unseen by Machiavel is that which interprets him, when he concludes, "The he who will go about to make a commonwealth when there be many gentlemen, unless he first destroys them, undertakes an impossibility;"[34]

Wherefore, as in this place I agree with Machiavel, that a nobility or gentry overbalancing a popular government, is the utter bane and destruction of it, I shall show in another, that a nobility or gentry, in a popular government, not overbalancing it, is the very life and soul of it.[35]

In 1764, Thomas Jefferson (1743–1826) placed with the *Virginia Gazette* an order for books which included the two volumes *Opere di Niccolo Machiavelli* and the two–volume *Della Istoria d'Italia* by Francesco Guicciardini.[36]

James Madison (1751–1836), in his "Commonplace Book, 1759–1773," made his first reference to Machiavelli in the course of noting from the *Memoirs of the Cardinal de Retz* the opinion:

One of the greatest misfortunes which the despotic Power of the Ministers of the last Age has brought upon the State, is the Custom which their private (but mistaken) Interest has introduced, ever to support the superiour against the Inferiour. That Maxim is one of Machiavelli's, whom most of his readers do not understand, and whom others take to be a great Politician for no other reason but for having ever been Wicked.[37]

Pursuant to his resolution adopted by the Congress of the Confederation on 21 November 1782, Madison reported on 23 January 1783, "a list of books to be imported for the use of the United States in Congress assembled." In the list of 505 titles of 1300 volumes were the four volumes of the Farnesworth edition of Machiavelli's *Works*.[38]

In his *Alexander Hamilton and the Constitution,* Clinton Rossiter has recorded:

as a young man Hamilton [1757–1804] did the reading required of prospective Founding Fathers in such heroes of all true Whigs as Locke, Aristotle, Cicero, Coke, and Montesquieu, and he also ran, with an eye out for useful insights as well as wicked doctrines, through such anti-heroes as Hobbes and Machiavelli and such "sophists" as Spinoza and Rousseau. To no one of these famous philosophers, not even to Locke, did he pay much homage by way of quotation or salutation in his public or private writings. He was not a man, except when cast as lawyer, to appeal to authority for support of his eloquence and logic. Like Hobbes he seems to have chosen to be remembered as a wise man who used his brains rather than his book-shelves.[39]

What is possibly Hamilton's earliest reference to Machiavelli appeared in the *Danish-American Gazette* of 10 April 1771, in the article "Rules for Statesmen" attributed to him. As Broadus Mitchell has noted:

> From "some years gleaning from Machiavel, Puffendorf, &c" he would endeavor to advise "by what means a Premier may act most to the honour of his Prince, and the enlargement of his own power."[40]

While an undergraduate at King's College, in *A Full Vindication of the Measures of Congress from the Calumnies of their Enemies, in Answer to a Letter under a signature of A. W. Farmer and The Farmer Refuted: or a more comprehensive and impartial view of the Disputes between Great Britain and the Colonies,* in the words of John C. Miller, "the young student of Machiavelli" wrote:

> The promises of princes and statesmen . . . are of little weight. They never bind them longer than till a strong temptation offers to break them; and they are frequently made with a sinister design.[41]

Miller concluded:

> Hamilton held the "great man" view of history. He tended to glorify the hero, the great state builders, the daring and farsighted who had brought order out of chaos and raised nations to the pinnacle of power. He did not think that the people had leadership, political wisdom and initiative in themselves—leadership came from the exceptional individuals, the "natural aristocrats" and the rich and educated . . . In the writings of Plutarch and Machiavelli he found a wealth of examples of leaders who, dedicating themselves to a great cause, had triumphed over adversity. Hamilton, too, had found his cause—the creation of a nation—and he was sustained by the conviction that all the obstacles to its realization could be overcome by the exercise of wisdom and resolution on the part of a determined man;[42]

> Hamilton's credo was audacity and yet more audacity. Where others temporized, calculated the risks and paused in indecision, Hamilton acted; he was above all a man of action, not a philosopher seeking some elusive abstract truth. Whether consciously or not, he based his life upon a maxim of Machiavelli: "I certainly think that it is better to be impetuous than cautious."[43]

In the opinion of Clinton Rossiter,

> It is a common practice among intellectual historians to bracket Hamilton's

name with that of one of the giants of political theory . . . and there seems to be a disposition among learned men who have a visceral as well as intellectual preference for Jefferson to put Hamilton in his place by labelling him "the American Hobbes" or, somewhat less often, "the American Machiavelli."

This is, I think, to treat him both carelessly and arrogantly. While he, like all political thinkers of sense and courage, made grateful use of many of the insights of those two brilliant teachers, he was a man who simply could not have written either *The Prince* or *Leviathan*. Even in his toughest moments he was too old-fashioned a moralist to be called a Machiavellian;[44]

He was first and last a stout believer in morality, both public and private, as the foundation of free government;[45]

As further evidence of Hamilton's moral approach to the problem of power, it should be noted that he often used "political science" and "moral science"—even "ethics" and "politics"—as interchangeable terms;[46]

As a final touch in this quick portrait of Hamilton as Whig, we should note that he put abundant trust in "reason" and "experience" as the chief guides to personal conduct, social decision, and moral progress . . . For Hamilton, as for all the men of his generation, experience was the test of reason and reason the interpreter of experience, and both together were the highest source of political wisdom. His constant search was for "solid conclusions, drawn from the natural and necessary progress of human affairs."[47]

Machiavelli had written in the *Discourses*:

in order that the minds of the young men who read these writings of mine may reject the present and be prepared to imitate the past, whenever Fortune gives them opportunity;[48]

and it was young men in the American colonies of Massachusetts, New York, Pennsylvania, Virginia who were being stirred, enlightened and encouraged to build new institutions to secure liberty and promote the common good. The twelve years from the time of the battle of Lexington and Concord to that of the Constitutional Convention were the years in the life of: Alexander Hamilton, from 18 to 30; James Madison, from 24 to 36; Thomas Jefferson, from 32 to 44; John Adams, from 40 to 52. Then there was Benjamin Franklin, from 69 to 81, in mind and spirit as young as any.

During the century and three quarters between the first English settlements along the Atlantic coast of North America and the establishment of the government of the United States, the colonists had coped ingeniously with unprecedented physical and social challenges. The undeveloped territories offered escape and haven for experiments by a diversity of religious and political dissenters during the convulsive changes of seventeenth century England. In New England town meetings, and in Virginia, Pennsylvania and several of the other colonies, elected representative colonial assemblies were accustoming a greater proportion of the people to considering public matters and even to participation in the making of decisions regarding taxation: thus, the Virginia House of Burgesses was established in 1619; the West Jersey Concessions and Agreements of 3 March 1676, written in part by William Penn, provided for an electorate made up of all resident proprietors, freeholders, and inhabitants voting by secret ballot, an elected general assembly, and that

> They [the Commissioners of the Province] are not to impose any Tax, Custom, or Subsidy Tollage, Assessment, or any other Duty whatsoever . . . upon the Said Province and Inhabitants thereof, without their own consent first had.

The freedom of conscience and worship given recognition had already precedents in the colonial settlements, Providence (1636), Rhode Island (1643) and New Amsterdam (1647). That the recognition and legal protection for human rights and the institution of democratic processes which William Penn, as proprietor, promoted, had continued as a pervasive influence is the considered judgment of twentieth century historians: thus Morrison, Commager and Leuchtenburg, in *The Growth of the American Republic* have written:

> Penn, unlike the Puritans, believed in the essential goodness of human nature . . . Herein the note later stressed in American history by Jefferson and Emerson is first boldly struck;[49]

and Malone and Rauch, in their *Empire for Liberty, The Genesis and Growth of the United States of America*:

> No colony was more directly responsible than Penn's for the character of later American life and institutions.[50]

From the native American (Indian) peoples, by way of French philosophers and Thomas Jefferson, came the phrase "consent of the governed" as the legitimization for governmental authority.[51] From native American peoples came, also, apparently essential contributions to that which many have considered to be the principle achievement of the Constitutional Convention: i.e., the federal form of government. Although the "official date" for the founding of the League of the People of the Longhouse ("The Iroquois Confederacy") is 1390, Paul A. W. Wallace favored the date c. 1450—in either case well before contact through Columbus with European culture and traditions.[52] Benjamin Franklin was a member of the conference held in Lancaster, Pennsylvania in 1744 "between the representatives of the Five Nations and the colonies of Maryland, Virginia and Pennsylvania to settle some land disputes and agree on defensive measures against French invasions from Canada" at which Canassatego, of the Onondagas,

> urged the delegates to unite, on their own initiative, according to the model of the League which had flourished for at least two hundred years. He quoted extensively from the words of Degandawidah (*sic*) with the eloquent phrase, "We the Mohawk, the Seneca, the Oneida and the Cayuga people, set up this tree of government."[53]

In 1751, as quoted by Max Savelle, Benjamin Franklin wrote to Archibald Kennedy:

> It would be a very strange Thing if six Nations of ignorant Savages should be capable of forming a Scheme for such an Union, and be able to execute it in such a Manner as that it has subsisted Ages and appears indissoluble; and yet that a like Union should be impracticable for ten or a Dozen *English* Colonies to whom it is more necessary and must be more advantageous, and who cannot be supposed to want an equal Understanding of their Interests.[54]

In his *League of the Ho-de-No-San-Nee or Iroquois,* the anthropologist Lewis H. Morgan wrote:

> Franklin's plan of union which was the beginning of our Federal Republic was directly inspired by the wisdom, durability and inherent strength which he had observed in the Iroquois constitution.[55]

On 25 July 1775 when the Second Continental Congress declared their jurisdiction over Indian tribes, the Congress appointed as the three directors of Indian affairs: Benjamin Franklin, Patrick Henry and James Wilson. In 1787, Benjamin Franklin was the oldest member of the Constitutional Convention which formed the federal system of government. Lewis Morgan wrote:

> When the Colonies became the United States, the Iroquois recognized the similarity of the League and gave to the new nation the name of The Thirteen Fires.[56]

Through the great diversity of opening and expanding opportunities which characterized the long, turbulent period from the founding of Jamestown in 1607 to the assembling of the Constitutional Convention in 1787, ideas of equality sprang up, flourished and matured. Foremost in articulating them was the thought and leadership of Thomas Jefferson. Garry Wills, in *Inventing America, Jeffer-*

son's Declaration of Independence, has pointed out:

> The only two references to equality in Jefferson's pre-Declaration writings are to equality of ability and equality of property. In his draft instruction for the Virginia delegation to 1774's Continental Congress (*A Summary View*), Jefferson wrote: "Can any one reason be assigned why 160,000 electors in the island of Great Britain should give law to four million in the states of America, every individual of whom is equal to every individual of whom in virtue of understanding, and in bodily strength" (*Papers, I, 126*) . . . The only other reference to equality is a paraphrase from his reading of Montesquieu: "In a democracy, equality and frugality should be promoted by the laws, as they nourish the amor patriae. To do this, a census is advisable, discriminating the people according to their possessions; after which, particular laws may equalize them in some degree by laying burthens on the richer classes, and encouraging the poorer ones."[57]

Jefferson's efforts to have included in the Declaration of Independence a condemnation of the slave trade, his leadership in Virginia for the abolition of entail and primogeniture, his concern for the development of a system of public education, and, along with James Madison, for the termination of religious establishment and for effecting the separation of church and state, demonstrate his practical applications of his belief.

The records do not reveal the processes of thought which prompted Jefferson to modify Locke's trilogy of natural rights—i.e., life, liberty, property—and for "property" to substitute "pursuit of happiness." Hawke has pointed out:

> "property" slipped from sight with the same calculation that brought forth "pursuit of happiness." Mason had said that among men's rights was that of "pursuing and obtaining happiness." Jefferson revealed realism as well as precision of thought in his revision of Mason's phrase. Man does, said Jefferson, have a right to pursue it. Jefferson was wise, too, in shunning a definition of happiness, though it would permit his phrase to be wildly misused.[58]

Certainly he perceived the consent of the governed as working through government for the equalization of opportunity and the dissipation of the suffocating miasma of prejudice and affliction of imputed inferiority—so that each might seek to come to awareness of that which pertained to or belonged to him, his essential property, and, therein, his "happiness."

The relation of the ideas of the Declaration of Independence to the thought of the time has received clear delineation in Carl Lotus Becker's *The Declaration of Independence, A Study in the History of Ideas:*

> In writing to Lee in 1825, Jefferson said again that he only attempted to

express the ideas of the Whigs, who all thought alike on the subject. The essential thing was

> Not to find out new principles, or new arguments, never before thought of, not merely to say things which had never been said before; but to place before mankind the common sense of the subject, in terms so plain and firm as to command their assent . . . All its [the Declaration's] authority rests on the harmonizing sentiments of the day, whether expressed in conversation, in letters, printed essays, or the elementary books of public right, as Aristotle, Cicero, Locke, Sidney, etc.

> . . . one may say that the premises of this philosophy, the underlying preconceptions from which it is derived, were commonly taken for granted. That there is a 'natural order' of things in the world, cleverly and expertly designed by God for the guidance of mankind; that the 'laws' of this natural order may be discovered by human reason; that these laws so discovered furnish a reliable and immutable standard for testing the ideas, the conduct, and the institutions of men—these were the accepted premises, the preconceptions of most eighteenth century thinking, not merely in America but also in England and France.[59]

As the Declaration of Independence did for succeeding generations, it continues to serve both as a goad and a magnet for peoples everywhere throughout the world to achieve the realization of and the entrance into the exercise of their birthright.

Among the American colonies, diversities had had opportunity to emerge, flourish and become entrenched; but, also, the conviction of the necessity to organize together for mutual survival had been ratified by a successful war for independence. Despite Machiavelli's judgment that a state is best founded by one man alone and that, because of their diverse opinions, a large number are unfit to organize a government,[60] the fifty-five men who participated in the constitutional Convention of 1787, through a process of multiple compromises, developed a frame of government and embodied it in a written constitution which for two centuries has served as a guide for the republic which in many respects still symbolizes in the minds and hearts of men the prospect for freedom through law. With great perspicuity, Benjamin R. Barber has pointed out the virtue in what he has termed "the compromised republic":

> To insist on discovering public goods was only to generate faction and occlude those private interests that alone, pitted against each other, promised the semblance of consensus. In short, the system turned necessity into a virtue and placed public purposelessness at the very core of the value structure. This was the meaning of proceduralism, of the adversary method, of pluralism, and of the agreement to disagree . . . The republic worked because it never tried to contrive a center; and thus, by eliciting the assent

of the citizenry to this value default, acquired a center after all—in the acquiescence of the people to purposelessness.[61]

That there be provision for a republic's expansion, Machiavelli had held to be indispensable.[62] As second only to the Roman method,[63] Machiavelli recommended as an example for imitation

> That followed by the ancient Tuscans . . . a league of several republics in which none went beyond any other in authority or in rank. As they conquered they made the new states their companions.[64]

In 1787, the Congress of the Confederation adopted "An Ordinance for the Government of the Territory of the United States Northwest of the River Ohio," Article 5 of which provided (in part):

> There shall be formed in the said territory not less than three nor more than five states . . . such state shall be admitted by its delegates into the Congress of the United States, on an equal footing with the original states, in all respects whatever; and shall be at liberty to form a permanent constitution and state government; *Provided,* The constitution and government so to be formed, shall be republican, and in conformity to the principles contained in these articles.

Thus was established the precedent for Article IV, of the Constitution of the United States and the subsequent practice thereunder. According to Machiavelli, however, such a league of republics had inherent limitations:

> Experience makes plain that this method of procedure has a fixed limit, for we have no example to show that it can be exceeded. A league may attain twelve or fourteen communities, and then not try to go any further, because when it reaches such strength as to believe it can defend itself from anybody, it does not strive for more dominion, both because necessity does not force it to gain more power and because it sees no profit in conquests, for the reasons given above;[65]

> The reason why it is impossible to grow greater is that you have a republic disunited and placed in various seats; this makes it hard for the parts to consult and decide. It also causes them not to be eager to rule, because the many communities participating in that rule do not value such an acquisition so high as does a single republic that hopes to be able to enjoy the whole. Besides this, disunited republics are governed by a council, and it is necessary that they be slower in every decision than those who live within one and the same wall.[66]

That Machiavelli identified three powers to be distinguished in government, John Adams noted in his comment upon Machiavelli's proposal for the reformation of the government of Florence.[67] Stanley Pargellis has succinctly traced the theory of balanced government:

> Though most of this vast literature in praise of balance was English, the origins of the theory were purely classical. First formulated by Aristotle's disciples, elaborated by the Stoics, woven into a philosophy of history by Polybius, and by him carried to Rome where Cicero embraced it, it thus had, in Addison's phrase, the authority of "the greatest philosopher, the most impartial historian, and the most consummate statesman of all antiquity" [Joseph Addison, *The Freeholder, or Political Essays*, No. 51 (1716)] . . . This was the theory advanced by Machiavelli to support the glorification of Rome.[68]

Subsequent to Machiavelli, Harrington, Locke, Blackstone and, especially Montesquieu refined the theory of mixed government with special emphasis upon the importance of the separation of powers and provision for mutual checks and balances. In evaluating Machiavelli's proposal for the remodeling of the government of Florence, Adams judged it inadequate because although Machiavelli's

> sagacity . . . perceived the necessity of three powers . . . he did not see any equal necessity for the separation of the executive power from the legislative.[69]

Opposition to the establishment of a standing army in time of peace was expressed in the Constitutional Convention in terms reminiscent of Machiavelli[70] (above, pp. 94–95). On 18 August, Elbridge Gerry

> Took notice that there was no check here against standing armies in time of peace . . . The people were jealous on this head . . . He thought an army dangerous in time of peace, and could never consent to a power to keep up an indefinite number;[71]

and on 23 August, James Madison declared:

> As the greatest danger is that of disunion of the states, it is necessary to guard against it by sufficient powers to the common government; and as the greatest danger to liberty is from large standing armies, it is best to prevent them by an effectual provision for a good militia.[72]

When, after the establishment of the government, Madison was able to steer through Congress the submission to the states of the proposals which became the first ten amendments, there was included as the second:

> A well regulated Militia, being necessary to the security of a free State, the right of the people to keep and bear Arms, shall not be infringed.

Pocock has commented:

> The Second Amendment to the Constitution, apparently drafted to reassure men's minds against the fact that the federal government would maintain something in the nature of a professional army, affirms the relation between a popular militia and popular freedom in language directly descended from that of Machiavelli, which remains a potent ritual utterance in the United States to this day. The new republic feared corruption by a professional army, even while—like England a century before—it saw no alternative to establishing one; and the implications of the rhetoric employed in this context were to be fully worked out in the debates and journalism of the first great conflict between American parties.[73]

The provision of Article II, Section 1 (5) that

> No person except a natural born Citizen, or a Citizen of the United States, at the time of the Adoption of this Constitution, shall be eligible to the Office of President

may remind one that Machiavelli considered that native born princes in countries governed with laws have not, historically nor currently, been those who

> have broken that bridle intended to restrain them.[74]

Likewise, Machiavelli would have approved Section 2 (1) of the Constitution:

> The President shall be Commander in Chief of the Army and Navy of the United States, and of the Militia of the several states, when called into the actual service of the United States,

in light of his observation:

> the kingdoms that have good laws do not give absolute command to their kings except in their armies; in this place alone sudden decision is necessary, so in it there must be one and only one authority. In other things he cannot do anything without consultation, and they are obliged to fear—those who give him advice—that he will have somebody near him who in time of peace will desire war, being unable to get his living without it.[75]

In contrast with the instrumental theory of government expressed in the Declaration of Independence in the phrases

> to secure these rights [Life, Liberty and the pursuit of Happiness] Govern-

406

ments are instituted among men, deriving their just powers from the consent of the governed,

also in the preamble of the Constitution and implicit in the Bill of Rights (the first ten amendments of the Constitution), certain tenets repeatedly affirmed by Machiavelli indicate affinity with the view that the citizen belongs to the state and derives his worth from it.[76] Already noted have been his frequently suggested comparisons of political problems with bodily illnesses.[77]

On the other hand, there may be found, also, in Machiavelli's thought some support for the position that the state is an association established for the purpose of promoting specific aims:

not individual good but common good is what makes cities great . . . without doubt this common good is thought important only in republics.[78]

The reason which Machiavelli presents on account of which "a prudent organizer of a republic . . . ought to strive to have authority all to himself'' is that he is

one whose intention is to advance not his own interest but the general good, not his own posterity but the common fatherland.[79]

The enlistment of the people's support, Machiavelli held to be indispensable for the state builder.[80] Is not the idea of government, not as a corporation to which people belong, but as an association deliberately set up as a means[81] for achieving specific purposes and limited to the pursuit of those ends,[82] to be found in these thoughts of Machiavelli?

When the framers of the Constitution entrusted to Congress the sole power to declare war (I.8) and to the more popular branch the initiative for the raising of revenue (I.7), is there not to be recognized more than an echo of Machiavelli's concern that a government be so structured as to place the guardianship of liberty in the hands of those most inclined to preserve and protect it:

as a consequence of [the people's] greater eagerness to live in free-dom . . . if the common people are set up to guard liberty, it is reasonable that they will care for it better, and since they cannot seize it themselves, they will not allow others to seize it?[83]

In 1780, Massachusetts, providing for a specially elected body for the expressed purpose, had drawn up a written constitution and included in it a procedure for its future amendment. Thus they set an example which the members of the Constitutional Convention of 1787 followed. Machiavelli had observed:

those are best organized and have longest life that through their institutions can often renew themselves.[84]

The combination of written constitution, implemented as the supreme law of the land for the observance of which all officials (local, state and federal) are individually bound by oath, the inclusion of a process available for amendment, and the subsequent development of judicial review, demonstrate the institutionalization of the means for continual renewal. Pocock has perceived that

> Machiavelli's *ridurre* [to return to first principles] ensured in the provision that the power of constitutional revision was always in the people and its exercise always potentially imminent.[85]

Continuing processes in American society and structure have been adding definition and substance to the concept of the rightful aspirations of human personality. Among these have been: (1) individual access to the ownership of land—culminating in the Homestead Act of 1862, the family-sized farm, the Full Employment Act of 1946, the Social Security system and the anti-poverty program; (2) the use of government as essentially instrumental and limited in character; (3) the formation and ratification of political institutions by constitutional conventions and referenda and enactment of legislation through initiative, referendum and recall; (4) the construction and practical use of written constitutions including bills of "unalienable" rights guaranteed to individuals and upheld and implemented by the courts and the executive; (5) the acknowledgement of irreducible pluralism: independent judiciary, separation of powers, separation of church and state; (6) the checks on the war power: deep reservations regarding a professional army, Congressional control over military appropriations and over the declaration of wars; (7) the expansion of the suffrage; (8) the periodic reapportionment of the elected representative bodies; (9) the emergence of the system of political parties with the development of standards of fairness in party structures and procedures and limitations on private financing; (10) the expansion of free public education making more broadly available the recognition and fostering of individual talents, child care centers, kindergartens, elementary-, secondary-, higher-, graduate- and professional-education; (11) the strengthening of official accountability through: "sunshine laws," "sunset laws," "right-to-know laws," conflict of interest laws, the making of governmental processes open to public observation, institutionalizing of ombundsmen and public advocates, provision of legal aid for the poor; and, in and through it all, (12) the elevation of the recognition of, regard for, and implementation of the people. Seventeenth- and eighteenth-century political thought, the Levellers, Penn, Sidney, Locke, American colonists—especially through their experiences in their colonial legislatures and the repeated opportunity of founding new political communities—encouraged participation in decision-making so that, in the twentieth-century polity of the United States, it was coming to be perceived as a personal imperative.

(The early phases of the elevation of the awareness of the idea and role of the people have been made apparent in the works of Pocock and of Wood. In the words of Pocock:

Wood traces, through the rich complexity of the utterances of this period [late eighteenth century America]—all articulate Americans seem to have been versed in the vocabulary of the sociology of liberty—the emergence of a new paradigm of democratic politics, designed by the masters of Federalist theory to overcome the crisis caused by the failure of natural aristocracy—though whether they intended to replace the last-named, or restore it, is not entirely clear. The crucial revision was that of the concept of the people. Instead of being differentiated into diversely qualified and functioning groups, the people was left in so monistic condition that it mattered little what characteristics it was thought of as possessing; and the various agencies of government—still essentially the legislature, judiciary, and executive separation theory—were thought of as exercised not immediately by social groups possessing the relevant capacities, but immediately, by individuals whose title to authority was that they acted as representing the people. All power was entrusted to representatives, and every mode of exercising power was a mode of representing the people;[86]

Wood's "end of classical politics" is at bottom predicated upon an abandonment of the closely related paradigms of deference and virtue. Because natural aristocracy failed the Americans in the moment of classical *rinnovazione,* they had to abandon any theory of the people as qualitatively differentiated, and therefore either virtuous in the classical sense or participant in government in ways directly related to personality, and at the heart of the Federalist thought arose something akin to the paradoxes of Rousseau—all government was the people's, and yet the people never directly governed. This price, once paid, the advantages of the great restatement of paradigms which accompanied the conservative revolution of 1787–89 were enormous. It permitted the overcoming of the widely accepted limitation which enjoined republics to be of finite size if they would escape corruption; the new federation could be both republic and empire, continental in its initial dimensions and capable of further expansion by means of simple extensions of the federative principle, greatly surpassing the semimilitary complex of colonies and provinces which had extended the Roman hegemony. It permitted the growth of new modes of association in pursuit of particular ends—political parties which, it has been argued by Chambers, were modern in precisely the sense that they were not based on a deference, and which mobilized participant energies on a scale undreamed of in ancient republics;[87]

If Americans had been compelled to abandon a theory of constitutional humanism which related the personality to government directly and according to its diversities, they had not thereby given up the pursuit of a form of political society in which the individual might be free and know himself in relation to society. The insistent claim that the American is a natural man and America founded on the principles of nature is enough to demonstrate that, and the pursuit of nature and its disappointments can readily be expressed in the rhetoric of virtue and corruption; for this is the rhetoric of citizenship, and a cardinal assertion of Western thought has been that man is naturally a citizen—*kata phusin zoon politikon* [according to nature, a political animal]. In this book we have been concerned with another tradition reducible to the sequence of Aristotle's thesis that human nature is civic and Machiavelli's thesis that, in the world of secular time where alone the polis can exist, the nature of man may never be more than partially and contradictorily realized. Virtue can develop only in time, but it is always threatened by corruption by time. In the special form taken when time and change were identified with commerce, this tradition has been found to have been operative over wide areas of thought in the eighteenth century, and to have provided a powerful impulse to the American Revolution.[88])

(13) The opening of the American land and society to an unprecedented and voluntary immigration of peoples from other lands and cultures demonstrated that regardless of racial, religious, economic, political conditions of origin, human individuals proved their capacity to respond constructively when stirred by the prospect of enjoying in freedom the fruits of their endeavors.

The evidence of this latent capacity manifested by people transplanted, gave strength to (14) the concept of self-determination as a right of people everywhere and to ever-spreading drives for making it an institutional reality. Pocock has called attention to Henry Nash Smith's

phrase "the fee-simple empire," as emblematic of the geo-political and millenialist rhetoric of the farming West which was rife in nineteenth-century America; and, with its echoes of what Webster had to say in 1787, the phrase may explain for us why a purely agrarian republic had to be a commonwealth for expansion.[89]

Encouragement of individual enterprise, accommodation for processes of competition, limitations upon hereditary, ecclesiastical, ideological inclinations to legitimize and justify privileged status, broadening freedom of association, expanding general education, sustained and helped keep open the arena for private action and invigorated resourceful, responsive and responsible individual personalities. Accompanying the nourishment of creative individuality, in political thought has grown a perception of available processes for mitigating the traditionally conventional presumption of radical evil in human nature and the necessity for fear-derived, force-based structures for security. Into opportunities through which the power-hungry could receive recognition were injected guidelines and limitations as the practical implications of the requirements of real self-government became better understood.

In directing men's attention to making the most of their opportunities through the use of their own resources at hand by showing to "Fortune a bold face,"[90]

Machiavelli was in the main stream of the acts and teachings of the founders of the Christian religion. Jesus and Paul called man to liberation from "elemental spirit":

> Next the devil led him up and showed him in a flash all the kingdoms of the world. 'All this dominion will I give to you,' he said, 'and the glory that goes with it; for it has been put in my hands and I can give it to anyone I choose. You have only to do homage to me and it shall all be yours.' Jesus answered him, 'Scripture says, "You shall do homage to the Lord your God and worship him alone;" '[91]

> Formerly, when you did not acknowledge God, you were the slaves of beings which in their nature are no gods. But now that you do acknowledge God—or rather, now that he has acknowledged you—how can you turn back to the mean and beggarly spirits of the elements? Why do you propose to enter their service all over again?[92]

> Be on your guard; do not let your minds be captured by hollow and delusive speculations, based on traditions of man-made teaching and centered on the elemental spirits of the universe and not on Christ.[93]

Machiavelli held up before men their responsibility to make best use of their fighting chance.[94]

For neither Jesus nor Machiavelli, was the course of effective action one primarily of introspection. Jesus had affirmed an intrinsic relationship between love of God and love of one's fellow human beings[95] and indelibly emphasized it with the parable of "the good Samaritan."[96] The criterion for final judgment, he declared, would be the record of service in helpfulness in meeting other's needs[97] and he said:

> If anyone wishes to be a follower of mine, he must leave self behind; he must take up his cross and come with me. Whoever cares for his own safety is lost; but if a man will let himself be lost for my sake, he will find his true self. What will a man gain by winning the whole world, at the cost of his true self? Or what can he give that will buy that self back?[98]

and to his accusers in the Council, he declared:

> from now on, the Son of Man will be seated at the right hand of the Power of God.[99]

Martin Fleischer has well epitomized Machiavelli's position in this regard:

411

In brief, for Machiavelli, the human soul is not capable of finding or realizing its own peace or harmony. It has no inner principle of integrity or unity. Both its restrictions and its goals lie outside itself—in the public arena and its relations to others. Like life itself the characteristic movement of the soul is growth understood as self-aggrandizement. Since this aggrandizement is both public and related to others it must be political in nature. It follows that true knowledge, Machiavelli's *vera cognizione,* cannot be found by turning inward in an examination of the self. The true reflection of the world of men is not to be found in the soul but in the political experience of peoples. This is the source of political knowledge, for Machiavelli the highest form of human consciousness.[100]

The implication for the relation between politics and ethics has been clearly drawn by Martin Diamond:

When ethics is thus understood as being concerned with the formation and perfection of human character, we may more readily understand not only why ethics and politics have a universal relationship proper to man as man, but also why a unique relationship between ethics and politics is necessarily formed within each particular political order.[101]

That the traditional institutions were no longer adequate for coping with the political issues, Machiavelli was deeply aware. As Count Carlo Sforza has written:

Machiavelli alone understood that it was necessary to rebuild from the ground up. As the first modern Italian who rejected all outmoded form, he understood that the Church and Empire were no longer living political forces . . . Another myth which seemed to be alive to many of Machiavelli's contemporaries, along with the Church and Empire, was the sovereign city-state. Machiavelli loved his native Florence almost as much as he loved Italy . . . But he knew well enough that the free Italian city-states— here you have his own words, "where all is for the good of all"—were but a memory cherished by the heart; he knew that their republican power had crumbled almost everywhere into the hands and estates of a few influential families who later were to become sovereigns.[102]

Whitfield has noted

the adjectives *piu sicure e piu fermo* . . . attest that we are on the Machiavellian quest.[103]

Deploring the distracted condition of Italy, in the *Discourses* Machiavelli wrote:

truly no region is ever united or happy if all of it is not under the sway of one republic or one prince, as happened to France and to Spain.[104]

412

According to Sforza,

> His state is the nation . . . He is the first European to state the need of
> nations for an independent life, a bulwark against the anarchy of feudal
> society and—for Italy—against the covetousness of the *condottieri* and the
> intrigues of the popes.[105]

Throughout, as Whitfield has demonstrated with penetrating analysis of the use
of the language in the *Prince*, the *Discourses*, "A Discourse on Remodeling
the Government of Florence," "The Life of Castruccio Castracani of Lucca,"
and *The History of Florence*,[106] Machiavelli advocated and sought the establishment of

> the *ordini* which are conducive to the maintenance of a *vivere civile e
> libro*.[107]

Never did he advocate resort to tyranny as a part of the process. As Whitfield
has concluded:

> Machiavelli never dreamt of giving other counsel to a tyrant than the wise
> one, to lay down his tyranny;[108]

> not only is he not concerned with having a tyrant, but he is concerned (in
> view of the Medici record in the past) with not having a tyrant. To be so
> concerned was to follow the compulsion of his instincts, and the lead of
> Savonarola. That is why he takes such trouble in the pages of the *Prince*
> to prevent the scions of the house of Medici from being warped to follow
> Piero de'Medici, or even Lorenzo the Magnificent in his more harmful
> tendencies. And if one lets oneself look for the statements, Machiavelli
> was clear enough, and cautious enough, in showing that he was dealing
> with consitutional states, and was not interested in despotic ones . . .
> The problem of the *Prince* is then obstinately that of meeting aggression,
> and the book is dictated by the fact that from the nature of things there
> neither was nor could be, any republic in Italy which could meet it . . .it
> is perfectly plain from the correspondence in the language between
> Machiavelli and Savonarola [*Del Reggimento e Governo della Città di
> Firenze*] that the author of the *Prince* was anxious, not only to seize the
> opportunity created by Leo's election to the papacy, but equally to dissuade
> his Medici candidate for the redemption of Italy from becoming at the
> same time merely the Medici tyrant on the pattern of pre-1494;[109]

> The ideal prototypes for Machiavelli's Prince are Moses (Dante's law-giver,
> *legista e obbediente*), Romulus (the *riordinatore* of a *vivere civile*), Cyrus
> (the affable) and Theseus (the slayer of monsters);[110]

Chapters 7 and 17 of the *Prince* with the subsequent remark on his 'inten-

413

zione alta,' makes it plain that Machiavelli does not propose Caesar Borgia as the pattern for a tyrant, but in the mold of Romulus. As with Romulus, the facts accuse, the effect excuses. But if it were not good it could not then excuse.[111]

Greatly as Machiavelli admired the methods employed by the Roman republic,[112] he considered that the example of the ancient Tuscan League was more practically available "for the present Tuscans"[113] and through the use of the vernacular in verse (the "Decennali") and treatises (the *Prince, Discourses, The Art of War, The History of Florence*), he developed instrumentalities of communication which would broaden and deepen the exchange of ideas and the forms of action among his contemporaries. It was a service analogous to that later performed by Thomas Paine at the beginning of the American Revolution, as described by Gordon Wood:

> Part of the remarkable effect created by Thomas Paine's *Common Sense* . . . resulted from its obvious deepening of the layers of audience to whom it was directed.[114]

In *The History of Florence,* after recounting how, through a policy of patience and peaceful alliances Florence eventually regained the control which had seemed lost when the subject towns had revolted, Machiavelli observed:

> Thus many times things are gained more quickly and with fewer dangers and expense by running away from them than by striving with all one's force and determination to overtake them.[115]

Commenting upon this passage, Whitfield has written:

> In these last words there is perhaps the most brilliant definition (is it not Machiavelli's own?) of *virtù*; and with them there is his certificate that *virtù*—whether it is that of Gualtieri or Castruccio, or of any other *eroe politico*—is a brittle weapon. For the Machiavelli of this mood, and he is the true author of the *Discorsi*, the *Istoria Fiorentine* and the *Vita di Castruccio*, the gentlest gamester is the surest winner. It is perhaps not extraordinary, in view of the fascination that the doctrine of strength and unscrupulousness read into the *Prince* has always exercised on Machiavelli's readers, that the plain, the eloquent, moral of Castruccio's dying speech, couched as it is in typically Machiavellian language, has not been heeded, or the affinities been seen with such passages as those quoted above—and they are no exceptions—from his maturest works. But in a world which is notoriously quicker in beating its ploughshares into swords than its swords into ploughshares, this advice from one who has been taken to know his humanity may be neither unwholesome, unwelcome, nor untopical.[116]

Thus both Jesus and Machiavelli affirmed commitment manifested in dedicated active service. Jesus, aware that each, despite one's own unawareness, has a rightful heritage and endowment, committed himself through realistic love, both universal and individual, to the release into effective present manifestation of the creative individuality of each one willing to live by the great commandment.[117] Machiavelli, perceiving each—even though uprooted, disunited and scattered—as distinguishing himself through fear-engendered repulsion of threatened aggression,[118] committed himself through observation and prudent courage to the release through the discipline of the common good into effective present manifestation of each one's essential *virtù*, his creative citizenship. Holding each as of ultimate value, Jesus' enlightening discipline is the guiltless, unjudgmental, non-condemnatory, compassionate, impulsive cooperation in mutually defining the course of action for mutual general benefit. Holding each as endowed with virtues respective to the land of one's birth, Machiavelli's encouraging discipline is the necessity-engendered comraderie fostered through facing up to alien aggression. The dynamics in Machiavelli's perspective inheres in the challenge of foreign enmity which prompts the sense of community and sustains the formation of the civic militia in which one comes to perceive and bring to maturity his essential being. For the citizens to be virtuous, the state must be healthy[119] and for the state to be healthy the people must be sparked and nourished by the sense of present danger of foreign attack which must be invented, if necessary, or provoked.

> Within her [Fortune's] palace, as many wheels are turning as there are varied ways of climbing to those things which every living man strives to attain . . .
> And those wheels are ever turning, day and night, because Heaven commands (and she is not to be resisted) that Laziness and Necessity whirl them around.
> The latter puts the world in order again, and the first lays it waste;[120]

> A prudent general lays every necessity for fighting on his own soldiers and takes it away from those of the enemy;[121]

> his soldiers, being in another ruler's country, necessarily fight and such necessity gives them vigor, as we have seen many times;[122]

> Some have forced their men to fight through necessity, taking from them every hope of saving themselves except by winning. This is the most spirited device and the best that can be used, if the soldier is to be made determined. His determination is increased by confidence in his general and his native land, and love for them. Confidence is caused by arms, discipline, recent victories, and the general's reputation. Love for a man's native land is caused by nature; that for his general, more by ability than by any kindness. Necessities may be many, but strongest is that which forces you to conquer or die.[123]

415

The dynamics of Jesus' perspective inhere also in facing up to that which appears as alien aggression but is perceived in conscience as related to an inadequacy in oneself[124] which, when faced up to, makes possible the shared compassion of forgiveness with another and the deep inner invigoration religiously expressed as God's forgiveness of one's own trespasses.[125] Machiavelli wrote, as referring to a condition contrary to fact:

> if men were content to live on their own resources and were not inclined to try to govern others . . .

and concluded

> men cannot make themselves safe except with power.[126]

May not this inclination "to try to govern others" be the form of expression taken by the sense of inner defect which one, taking for granted himself as an omnicompetent ego or individual, seeks to hide through crusading against "faults" in others? As Machiavelli conceived as "the most spirited device and the best that can be used"[127] for soldiers to find themselves "in another ruler's country,"[128] deprived of "every hope of saving themselves except by winning,"[129] so Jesus sparked with apocalyptic urgency the challenge with which understanding, expressed in loving service intolerant of prideful discriminations and with recognition of full worth in the oppressed, confronts the conventional inhumanities which express themselves as anger, torture and crucifixion. Jesus' call to reliance on one's own resources as those of a being who is living among others each of whom is rightfully-endowed heir of a loving creator, stirs one to the discovery of previously unnoticed sources of strength for personal creative affirmation with immunity to "leaders" exploitation of one's strength, emotions, mind. The assumption that some can be alienated from their land-based birth-right and that others can become powerful through appropriating and being "liberal" with others' lands and goods,[130] generates the fiction of "leaders" and the force-based state with violence and terror exacting "loyalty."

Jesus, manifesting the integrity potential in personality,[131] in exemplifying the individual's responsibility to live forth in action his unique and special creative witness, manifested the courage to face through the curse of "original sin" and affirm human nature as free to proceed guiltless in its full strength. Making his way among the guilt-ridden, exploited ones, he welcomed as friends and companions those who, perceiving, responding likewise in casting off whatever of the past was crippling, forgiving others' trespasses against them, acted forth their own integrity being discovered in loving association. Jesus' activism was impregnated with a comprehension and immediate compassion which eschewed violence against another. While summoning men, as children of a universal and impartial Father, to

416

Love your enemies and pray for your persecutors,[132]

he observed,

All who take the sword die by the sword.[133]

He pointed out the inherent limitations which invalidate the judgment which one attempts to pass upon others[134] and render any revenge morally inadequate.[135] He pointed out that through forgiving others the wrongs they have done, one finds forgiveness for wrongs he has done[136] and in treating "others as you would like them to treat you" the requirements for the good order are fulfilled.[137] Jesus' contact energized men leaving them freed from "sin"[138] and called to action[139] and, indeed, to action during this life on this earth.[140] It was the dynamic, active element in the Gospels which received recognition by Lorenzo Valla when he translated the Greek word *dunamis* with the Italian word *virtù*[141] and by Jesus himself in his reply to the High Priest:

From now on, you will see the Son of Man seated at the right hand of the Power.[142]

Jesus' objectivity in proving himself the conscious instrument of universal love[143] enabled him not only to surmount any fear of anything that any man might try to do to him but to make manifest that same Power seen as generally available.

Was it because Jesus himself was, and he was showing and teaching others how to be, no longer fearfully responsive to those accustomed to control through implanting and exploiting a sense of fear based on the dogma of "original sin," that he had to face crucifixion as a transgressor among transgressors due to the complicity of those who defended their action as for "the people" and the preservation of "the nation?"[144] Was it because Machiavelli's fusion of civilian, disciplined energy and the search for effectual truth as dynamic elements reciprocally indispensable has confronted, as a challenge, those greedy for power for themselves and their posterity—not only the Medici of his own time but also their counterparts during subsequent centuries—that the endeavor to work out, understand and make constructive use of the implications of his thought has had to contend with the poison injected into his very name? Is herein to be appraised the cost to him of "getting the master's confidence," as the condition of manifesting himself as "a man who must rise," to use the words of Filipo Strozzi when writing to his brother about the introduction of Machiavelli to Cardinal Giulio de'Medici?[145]

In his *Machiavelli and the Nature of Political Thought*, Martin Fleischer states clearly a major emphasis of Machiavelli:

as *animo* or spirit it [the soul] has *virtù* when it is fully itself and it is most

417

fully itself when performing politico-military deeds . . . The question thus becomes: if someone is not much good as a man, can he be a good man? While Machiavelli may not be prepared to abandon certain criteria of what is good, virtuous, or human even if these cannot be completely derived from his root concepts of *animo, virtù, grandezza, gloria,* etc., it is equally true that the measure of *umanità* can never be less than these. This is crucial to the understanding of the concept of *animo:* the soul is properly dominated by the quality of spiritedness, courage, action . . .Thus the *virtù* of *animo* that Machiavelli celebrates is magnanimity, not equanimity—greatness (with its reference to an external standard), not balance (with its reference to some inner criterion);[146]

Involved is the concept of the best education for the man and the citizen—for a republican the two cannot be separated. Such an education must have military training as its basis since it is the discipline that properly conditions the *animo* . . . what it [the *animo*] desires or values most is the ability to command any desire or bestow any value it wishes. Viewed from this perspective value is entirely a subjective matter. But the actual ability to command value is a function of social circumstances as well as of desire. This is the objective moment in the realization of value: the command of objects of desire that constitutes the supreme value—*the power to designate and appropriate values*—is the function of the social, more particularly the political order. (For Machiavelli, political power, not money, is the primary source of such command.) And the successes and failures of such orders can be observed and judged. Of course, in the last analysis, what the *animo* craves is the recognition of this greatness. Once again, the only fit arena for it is to display itself in politics, for all other forms of greatness (artistic, philosophical, etc.) are ultimately determined by political greatness;[147]

Machiavelli holds that desire is ultimately insatiable. The fact that man cannot acquire everything that he desires, especially glory, is the source of both human discontent and ambition. The human condition, then, is one of: 1) discontent; 2) desire for the means to satisfy desires; 3) domination of *animo* by these powerful desires and not by reason; 4) competition or conflict with others for these means; 5) scarcity and not abundance by virtue of the nature of human desire;[148]

It takes the highest prudence and *virtù* to be able to change one's ways to fit them to the requirements of new situations. There is no question that for Machiavelli this represents the consummation of the art of the statesman.[149]

That Machiavelli was a source of a current of profound influence in giving direction to the American political outlook, Joseph Cropsey has indicated in his essay, "The United States as Regime and the Sources of the American Way of Life":

> The formula "life, liberty, and the pursuit of happiness" grew out of the great act of self-emancipation on the part of European mankind that was the opening of the modern age. Machiavelli called on men to take their earthly existence seriously, and thus to win release for themselves from the worst of their cares. He breathed high-heartedness on men by politicizing minds that had been fixed on eternity. He naturalized man in the world, restoring him to nature, so to speak, while presupposing innovations in the meaning of nature that it would be impossible to take up here, but that entered into Hobbes formulations of natural rights and the state of nature. Inseparable from these formulations is Hobbes reservation to men of the right to preserve life, and their natural freedom to seek the means thereto, as well as the large measure of private discretion that belongs to men as they deliberate on the ends of their actions and seek their satisfaction, if not their contentment, in life.[150]

How Machiavelli brought into focus the nature of the citizen and his role in the militant nation-state, Pocock has skilfully traced.

> Applying an Aristotelian teleology to Roman ideas of *virtus*, it could be held that in acting upon his world through war and statecraft the practitioner of civic virtue was acting on himself; he was performing his proper business as a citizen and was making himself through action what Aristotle had said man was and should be by nature: a political animal. In this context the relation of *virtus* to *fortuna* became as the relation of form to matter. Civic action carried out by *virtus*—the quality of being a man (*vir*)—seized upon the unshaped circumstance thrown up by fortune and shaped it, it shaped Fortune herself, into the completed form of what human life should be: citizenship and the city it was lived in. *Virtus* might be thought of as the formative principle that shaped the end, or as the very end itself;[151]

> It looks, then, as if Machiavelli was in search of social means whereby men's natures might be transformed to the point where they became capable of citizenship. The combination of Romulus and Numa suggested ways in which the legislator might be freed from the necessity of acting merely as the "armed prophet" of *Il Principe,* who must coerce men the instant they ceased to believe in him; but this freed him at the same time from the need to be the superhuman demiurge we met in the same chapter, who needed only *occasione* to speak the word that transformed the unshaped matter. The legislator-prophet is an even rarer figure in the *Discorsi* than in the *Principe,* because the legislator's *virtù* is becoming less significant than the social and educational processes he sets in motion, and he can thus afford to live in time and be a lesser figure than Lycurgus or Moses. But

in diminishing the role of the legislator, Machiavelli has diminished his need of the Savonarolan doctrine that the establishment of the republic—the *prima forma*—must be the work of grace. If men do not need the superhuman in order to become citizens, but achieve citizenship in the world of time and fortune, the earthly and heavenly cities have ceased once again to be identical; and this again may be an ethical as well as a historical distinction. We are moving back to the point at which it is seen that "states are not governed by paternosters," and civic ends—including the virtue of citizenship—are divorced from the ends of redemption. This is the most subversive suggestion contained in the *Discorsi*—more so, it may well be argued—than any to be found in *Il Principe;*[152]

In Roman virtue [Machiavelli] has discovered a new form of active *virtù* which is peculiar to the many, and exists only in dynamic warrior states which are the people and give them civil rights; and his debt to the militia tradition in Florentine theory, plus his experience under Soderini in actually organizing a militia, leads him to ground citizenship upon military virtue to the point where the former becomes the outgrowth of the latter. The plebeian as Roman citizen is less a man performing a certain role in the decision-making system than a man trained by civic religion and military discipline to devote himself to the *patria* and carry the spirit over into civic affairs, so that he conforms to the dual model of the Machiavellian innovator displaying *virtù* and the Aristotelian citizen attentive to the common good. The Roman plebs displayed *virtù* in demanding their rights, virtue in being satisfied when their demands were granted. The analysis of the *Arte* defines both the moral and the economic characteristics of the citizen warrior. In order to have a proper regard for the public good, he must have a home and occupation of his own, other than the camp. The criterion is identical with that applied to the Aristotelian citizen, who must have a household of his own to govern so that he may not be another man's servant, so that he may be capable of attaining good in his own person and so that he may apprehend the relation between his own good and that of the polis;[153]

By basing the popular republic on the *virtù* of the armed citizen, Machiavelli had transformed the problem of popular participation from one of knowledge to one of will . . . The strength of Rome was that it could mobilize the maxims of *virtù* for purposes both military and civic, and continue doing so for centuries. But in the last analysis all depended on *virtù* as a quality of the individual personality, a devotion to the *respublica* which rested on political, moral, and economic autonomy. If the citizen in arms had all these things, and *buone educazione* besides, he would display Roman *virtù*, though higher than that he could not rise;[154]

The militarization of citizenship makes the *Discorsi* in an important sense more morally subversive than *Il Principe* . . . the republic can be morally and civilly virtuous in itself only if it is lion and fox, man and beast, in its relation with other peoples . . . Recognition of this duality, relatively easy for Polybius who had a less developed concept of a God who might be directing his universe on principles of justice, was for Machiavelli directly linked with his implicit refusal to treat the republic as a creature of grace. Its justice was spatially and temporally finite; toward other republics it could display only a *virtù militare*, and its ability to do this was determinative of its ability to maintain civic virtue internally. Virtuous republics were at war with one another. For this reason the Christian virtues and the civic could never coincide.[155]

Social conflict as an inherent and constructive factor in the development of virtue was affirmed both by Jesus and Machiavelli. According to the gospel of Matthew, Jesus said:

You must not think that I have come to bring peace to the earth; I have not come to bring peace, but a sword. I have come to set a man against his father, a daughter against her mother, a young wife against her mother-in-law; and a man will find his enemies under his own roof.
No man is worthy of me who cares more for father or mother than for me; no man is worthy of me who cares more for son or daughter; no man is worthy of me who does not take up his cross and walk in my footsteps. By gaining his life a man will lose it; by losing his life for my sake he will gain it.[156]

The place of social conflict in the thought of Machiavelli, Neal Wood has set forth:

The idea that the conflict [the countless quarrels and tumults between the classes] was beneficial to Rome originated with Machiavelli and not with Livy;[157]

Classical thinkers condemned social conflict, and in varying degrees accepted social competition. Machiavelli not only accepted social competition, but also believed that domestic conflict short of widespread violence, was beneficial. His notion was a radical break with past thought, and a herald of future theory;[158]

His concept of domestic conflict, with all its assumptions and implications, is one of the most novel and neglected of his outlook. His acceptance of social conflict as a positive good is clearly related to elements of his thoughts that break with the classical purview, or lower classical standards. In the first place, although Machiavelli refers to the common good as the end of the state, he has in mind not so much a moral end as the survival, security, and happiness of the citizenry, in a word, the public utility. Moreover, he never places the state in a cosmological hierarchy or universal moral order;[159]

Ever an ardent republican Machiavelli is one of the first modern devotees of liberty, and his libertarianism is related directly to his recognition of the beneficial effects of conflict. Finally, his fundamental emphasis upon politics as a means, as a series of techniques, his distinct preference for firm, swift, deft, and vigorous action, in a word, action typified by *virtù*, his condemnation of inaction, of procrastination, and indecisiveness, and his fear of social tranquility as a seedbed of enervation, indolence and civic corruption, all place him in the modern tradition. His implication that truth is the consequence of action rather than contemplation and that the wise man is an activist rather than a quietist is at variance with part of the classical position;[160]

Machiavelli, therefore, makes a number of rather radical suggestions of significance for future social and political theory:
1. The liberty of the citizen depends upon domestic conflict and opposition, and not on harmonious competition.
2. An important measure of the vigor of a state is the level of domestic conflict.
3. A much more vital and dedicated form of civic cooperation will emerge from conflict and opposition than from a situation of competition in which conformity and orthodoxy are stressed.
4. Politics is a kind of dialectical process characterized by a clash of opposites, their temporary reconciliation in a rather tenuous social balance, and then the need to readjust the equilibrium because of new causes of conflict.
5. Beneficial conflict in a "healthy" state like Rome must be distinguished from the factionalism and instability of corrupt states like Rome after the Gracchi and Florence in Machiavelli's day. In such states there is a breakdown of community, a loss of all sense of civic obligation and cooperation, a universal pursuit of narrow self-interest.
6. A well-ordered state will provide a variety of institutional outlets for conflict.[161]

The continued relevance for pluralistic societies of a high positive valuation placed upon social conflict is obvious. Such a perspective was to prove congenial and useful especially to James Madison when, as in *The Federalist* No. 10, he was demonstrating how, through implementing the diversity of conflicting interests, the new republic would grow in strength. As Robert H. Horwitz has written:

To judge from the overall character of *The Federalist*, it is evident that what Madison was pointing at here was the creation of a large commercial republic, one within which the widest possible range of interests would be fostered. No attempt would be made to restrain what Machiavelli bluntly described as "man's natural desire to acquire." On the contrary, acquisitiveness would be encouraged, and the citizenry given free scope in developing the abundant resources of a new country. Every form of agricultural, manufacturing, and commercial enterprise would be encouraged. The guiding and energizing principle of the community would be the vigorous pursuit of individual self-interest.[162]

However strong the emphasis which Machiavelli placed upon conflict as a constructive factor, the definite limits to it in operation which he perceived become highly significant when considered together and related to his central purpose of distilling from observed experience a means for reliable guidance and the reduction of the frustrating violence characteristic of the rule of Fortune.

Basically, in human individuality he recognized a threshold transgressions of which incur consequences which are unpredictable (above, pp. 11–12). An unsuccessful conspiracy against one may give rise within him to a trauma of insecurity (above, pp. 52–53). Furthermore, word given under duress does not bear trust (above, pp. 34, 98). The expectation that by means of war the initial aims claimed as reasons for entering upon it will be achieved, Machiavelli recognized to be a delusion (above, pp. 93–97):

Wars are begun at will but not ended at will.[163]

The economic costs of war and the institutional changes, eventually and inevitably inflict upon "victors" as well, profoundly degenerative transformations of character and situation:[164]

the people . . . intended that the rich should be made to pay enough to equalize them with those who, in order to pay more than was right, had sold their possessions. This demand . . . terrified the rich. So, to defend themselves, they did not cease to condemn the tax, declaring that it was very unjust . . . To this they added that those who, in order to govern the state, leave their businesses ought to be less burdened by taxation, since it is enough that they labor in person, and it is not just that the city should enjoy both their effects and their labor, but only the money of others . . . But the trouble consisted in something they did not speak of, because it pained them that they could not start a war without damaging themselves, having to share in its expenses like the others; if this method of taxation had been devised before, there never would have been war with King Ladislas, nor would there now be war with Duke Filippo, for these wars were undertaken to enrich the citizens, and not from necessity.[165]

"Success" incurs expanding involvement and changes in governmental structure and the temperament of the people, citizens and leaders:

"when power and territory increase, enmity and envy likewise increase;

from these things result war and loss."[166]

These words, which Machiavelli represented a Florentine emissary as speaking when addressing the Venetian Senate, epitomize the consequences of ancient Rome's policy as traced and interpreted by Machiavelli[167] (above, pp. 93–97). As a further limitation upon conflict, Machiavelli perceived that a victory may be pressed too far (above, p. 98):

> It is necessary, above everything that has been mentioned, to be careful not to bring the enemy into utter despair. About this Caesar was careful when fighting the Germans; he opened a road for them seeing that since they could not run away necessity was making them bold; he preferred labor in pursuing them when they were fleeing to danger in defeating them when they were defending themselves;[168]

Revolutions likewise, Machiavelli considered unmanageable.[169]

As for the heroic founder or reformer, Machiavelli had his doubts about the very possibility that such a leader had ever been nearer to historic reality than a Romulus or a Moses shrouded in legend. (above, pp. 65–69) In his own time, Machiavelli had witnessed the fate of Savonarola, the unarmed prophet;[170] the exemplary Caesar Borgia, victim of fortune;[171] and the, in his opinion, over-scrupulous Gonfalonier Piero Soderini, thwarted by immobility and inner rigidity.[172]

Perceiving the necessity for periodic renewal in human institutions such as republics and religions,[173] Machiavelli came up against the perhaps insurmountable obstacle of inflexibility in individual character.[174]

In *The History of Florence,* Machiavelli noted "and it seldom does come about" that a citizen arises able to achieve the needed renewal.[175] In the *Discourses,* he had written,

> it can easily be that no man of that sort will ever appear in a city[176]

but in composing the history commissioned by—and which he was to give to—Giulio de'Medici who, meanwhile, had become Pope Clement VII, did Machiavelli venture a note of positive hope with the possibility in mind that the Pope might yet adopt for Florence the policy outlined in the "Discourse on Remodeling the Government of Florence" which Machiavelli, at his request, had presented him several years earlier? Perhaps Machiavelli had seen in Cardinal Giulio de'Medici, when personally directing the affairs of the city, the potentiality of a constructive reformer[177] and, in view of the great enhancement of the leading citizen's powers through becoming pope also, was prompted to write in the *History:*

> I allow that when it comes about (and it seldom does come about) that by

a city's good fortune a wise, good and powerful citizen gains power, who establishes laws that repress strife between the nobles and the people or so restrain these parties that they cannot do evil, at such a time a city can be called free and her government can be considered firm and solid; being founded on good laws and good institutions, it does not need as do other governments, the strength and wisdom of one man to maintain it.[178]

In the *Discourses,* depicting and analyzing the psychological dilemma involved in the problem of affecting basic institutional reform led Machiavelli to call attention to

the difficulty or impossibility of maintaining a government in a corrupt city or of setting up a new government there.[179]

The general human tendency toward evil,[180] he held, is accelerated by increase of power.[181] In fact, only the fortune of a timely death accounts for the reputation of success.[182]

So, tenaciously sifting through the records of history and the observations of experience for clues, Machiavelli sought to advance human capacity "to turn a bold face to Fortune" and wrest a broader realm for human freedom.

Warfare has undergone more radical changes since Machiavelli's time than probably any other institution. The magnitude and diversity of continuing technological innovation makes us no more competent for evaluating the consequences and achieving the avowed purposes than Machiavelli proved himself to have been in his comments upon the introduction of artillery in battle strategy.[183] Already, Machiavelli perceived that, as a means for accomplishing objectives, war was not, in general, to be relied upon[184] and should be entered into only as the last resort.[185] The aims of war, as he identified them for republics as well as princes, were:

1) to confront necessity;[186]

2) to increase territory, wealth and glory;[187]

3) to transform men into citizen-soldiers through bringing them to identify themselves with their fellow-workers of the land of birth not only of themselves but of their ancestors and with their fatherland as the source of security for their future,[188] in the name of defense against alien hordes.

This last motivation found expression in Machiavelli's own passionate appeal in the conclusion of the *Prince* for Lorenzo to take leadership for Italy:

By no means, then, should this opportunity be neglected, in order that Italy, after so long a time, may see her redeemer come. I cannot express with what love he will be received in all the provinces that have suffered

425

from these alien floods, with what thirst for vengeance, with what firm loyalty, with what gratitude, with what tears! . . . What Italian will refuse him homage? For everyone this barbarian tyranny stinks;[189]

and a decade later when, in the midst of planning the fortifications of Florence on commission by the Pope, he wrote in a letter to his friend Francesco Guicciardini, President of Romagna, who was in Rome on the verge of being appointed lieutenant-general of the Pope's forces:[190]

You know how many opportunities have been lost; do not lose this one or trust any more in standing still, turning yourself over to Fortune and Time, because with Time there do not come always the same things, and Fortune is not always the same. I would speak further, if I were talking with a man who did not know secrets and did not understand the world. Free Italy from long anxiety; root out these frightful beasts, which beyond the appearance and the voice have nothing human.[191]

The breakthroughs in navigation, communication, fire-power, already spectacular in the fifteenth and early sixteenth centuries, continued with revolutionary momentum and implemented the emergence of conflicting empires which clashed with shattering consequences in the two World Wars of the twentieth century. Meanwhile, in its process of growth, the United States, as a magnate, continued to stir in individuals in all lands the possibility of escape from traditional religious, political and economic constraints and of the beginning of a new life in "the new world" by renouncing their old citizenship and voluntarily acquiring a new one. With the fragmenting of most of the former great empires, the enthusiasm for self-determination of peoples inspired the scores of "succession states." At the same time, under the leadership of the surviving great empire which had been most deeply wounded in the wars, was being forged in the name of the theretofore exploited masses, the program, by means of totalitarianly disciplined collectivism, to use the state as a temporary instrumentality aimed at achieving security, progressively improving productivity and promoting universal peace. However, more numerous than ever had grown the centers of more stridently patriotic nationalisms in confrontation with the all-overbearing struggle between corporate capitalism claiming prerogatives in the language of eighteenth-century liberal individualism and corporate collectivism claiming prerogatives in the language of nineteenth- and twentieth-century humanistic socialism with elements of first-century Christianity. Unbridled drive for "security" conceived by "great powers" as unchallengeable dominance, aggressively stimulated the escalation and spread of destructive power, nullified the attempt by treaty to "outlaw war," scuttled the League of Nations and is eroding the "great powers" mutual pledge through the United Nations to renounce war as an instrument of policy. Mobilizing unprecedented resources, each side is attracting into its respective programs

426

many of those most highly skilled in the physical, social and psychological sciences willing to sell the fruits of their scientific education and experimentation to the officials for the purpose of carrying forward the, from the point of view of mankind, partisan programs. The impetus for feeding the insatiable demand for weapons-systems is ever-accelerating even though the means for the complete annihilation of the human species has long since been passed. Moreover, the introduction and proliferation of land-, sea-, and air-borne weapons fully charged for thermo-nuclear devastation presents the prospect of the possibility that another war would escalate so that the fate of any unlikely survivors would be that of victims desperately ill, lacking available medical services, trying to eke out existence on poison-impregnated land. In the current feverish competition for devising more cost-efficient and more lethal implements—already of neutron and laser beam magnitude—and always "for defense," reduction in civil programs for public health, environmental protection, education, industrial safety are, in many countries, reversing the upward trend in the long struggle for improvement in the quality of life while the mounting governmental debts promise to deprive coming generations of economic resources to prevent continued decline. Young people are being programmed to project to distances half the world away devices for releasing death-dealing energy against populations inherently indispensable for the continued meaningful existence of these very same young people if they themselves are to have the possibility of well-being. Furthermore, as the skill grows for making the devices more simple, and the knowledge spreads, the fear grows that it may become available to be seized and used by groups and individuals even less restrained by a sense of social accountability.

Already, by the first quarter of the fifteenth century, as Machiavelli recorded nearly a century later, the commercial leaders of Florence had begun to have to face the fact that the economic costs of war boomeranged inescapably upon them.[192] In his *The Economic Consequences of the Peace*[193] John Maynard Keynes documented the same fact for World War I which was later underscored by the market collapse of 1929, the Great Depression, World War II as a means to combat it, and the subsequent endemic economic malaise.

Chapter Fourteen

FOR REPLACING VIOLENCE WITH PRUDENCE PROMOTING THE ORDER OF FREEDOM, CHANGE OF SCALE FROM PARTIAL TO GLOBAL-SYSTEM APPROACH

The necessity to rid itself of the plague of debilitating warfare of which Machiavelli sought to convince the Italians, now confronts mankind for the world as a whole; but the remedy which he proposed, i.e., that of prosecuting a war through which sufficient unity would be forged to drive the foreigners out, is in no way relevant or sufficient when it is realized that mankind in its entirety has to be served if policy is sound and the earth as a whole has to be left uncontaminated as the rightful heritage for the future generations.

Machiavelli was more of a realist than to be absolutely convinced of the effectiveness of the force which he observed and which he seemed to wish able to serve as the means for securing the order which he never fully clearly envisioned despite the professions of confidence in it by many of his nominal "followers" in subsequent centuries.

The problem of replacing violence with prudence promoting the order of freedom has become global and, indeed, is reaching toward inter-planetary dimensions.

Tension between conventional political rule and a different standard for greatness existed at least from the inception of Christianity and, indeed, roots back into the messages of some of the Hebrew prophets: notably, Isaiah and Daniel:

In days to come the mountain of the Lord's house shall be set over all other mountains, lifted high above the hills. All the nations shall come streaming to it . . . For instruction issues from Zion, and out of Jerusalem comes the word of the Lord; he will be judge between nations, arbiter among many peoples. They shall beat their swords into mattocks and their spears into pruning-knives; nation shall not lift up sword against nation nor ever again be trained for war;[1]

On that day the Lord will punish the host of heaven in heaven, and on earth the kings of the earth, herded together, close packed like prisoners in a dungeon; shut up in goal, after a long time they shall be punished . . . for the Lord of Hosts has become king on Mount Zion in Jerusalem;[2]

In the period of those kings God of heaven will establish a kingdom which shall never be destroyed; that kingdom shall never pass to another people; it shall shatter and make an end of all these kingdoms, while itself shall endure forever.[3]

In the Wilderness, Jesus had faced and rejected the temptation of political power.[4] Later, he explained true greatness as that won through self-perception[5] in meeting the needs of other individuals.[6] And again, in the Garden of Gethsemane, when being seized by the mob, Jesus rejected and rebuked the use of force for his defense:

At that moment one of those with Jesus reached for his sword and drew it and he struck at the High Priest's servant and cut off his ear. But Jesus said to him, 'Put up your sword. All who take the sword die by the sword;'[7]

and John recorded Jesus as saying:

My kingdom does not belong to this world. If it did my followers would be fighting to save me from arrest by the Jews.[8]

However, in the prayer which he gave as a pattern, Jesus included:

thy kingdom come, thy will be done, *on earth* [author's emphasis] as in heaven.[9]

The relations between the standard proposed by Machiavelli and those professed in the name of the Christian tradition have been the subject of a great body of literature through the centuries. In his *Discourses on Machiavelli*, J. H. Whitfield has written:

the sense of a contrast between morality and politics cannot be in any way a novelty in Machiavelli, even if it is part of Machiavelli . . . In fact, when Pius II, at the end of his *History of Bohemia*, remarks, 'Nobis persuasum est, armis acquiri regna non legibus' [We are persuaded, rule is acquired by arms and not by laws], the way is already open toward the observation of Vettori or of Guicciardini on the ultimate basis of all states in violence.[10]

Not unrelated are some of Machiavelli's recommendations for basic economic policy[11] and, again, for measures by which a state might attain greatness.[12]

In a penetrating analysis of eighteenth century expansion of Machiavelli's reasoning, Pocock has pointed out:

Like Machiavelli he [Montesquieu] knew that the Christian ethos made demands to which the civic ethos might refuse to give way, and that the latter might flourish best in periods close to barbarism, when there was no need to accord the rights of humanity to those who were not of one's city. But he also makes it clear that it was because the ethos of the ancient cities was essentially a warrior ethos, and commerce and even agriculture were despised, that Plato and Aristotle believed the personality could and must be entirely reshaped by music . . . Machiavelli, defining civic values as ultimately incompatible with Christian, had employed the concept of arms to express both the citizen's total devotion to his republic and the notion of a world too harsh in its treatment of noncitizens to profess any universal humanity. Montesquieu had added to this the concept of commerce, and had restored the conclusion, hinted at by Fletcher and Davenant, that commerce and culture were incompatible with virtue and liberty. Commerce brought with its pleasures more lively, perceptions more refined, and values more universal than those of the primeval Spartan, Roman, or Gothic citizen-warrior; but because it represented a principle more universal, and of another order, than that of the finite polis, it was ultimately incompatible with virtue in the sense of *vertu politique,* and though laws, education and manners might be devised that would check the growth of luxury, it could never be less than equally true that luxury corrupted laws, education, and manners. In the intermediate perspective, commerce and the arts could be seen as contributing to sociability and even to liberty and virtue, just as it was possible to establish a positive relationship between passion and reason; but the ultimate incompatibility remained. Commerce had taken the place of fortune; the republic could not control its own history forever or resist its own corruption; the particular and the universal remained at war;[13]

since land and commerce were already opposed as principles of conservation and growth, a movement of history from land toward commerce was enlarged, in the thinking of theoretical sociologists or "conjectural historians," into a scheme of social development which passed from hunters to

431

shepherds, farmers, and traders, with manufacturers beginning to make their appearance toward the end of the sequence . . . They (the Scottish and French conjectural historians) came, by the time of Adam Smith, to see the division and specialization of labor, and the resulting intensification of exchange, as the driving force which had moved society from each phase of its economic history towards the next; and this is not accidentally related to the circumstance that the whole Anglo-Scottish inquiry into the role of commerce in society and history had begun as a protest against the growth of a professionalized army—against what the classical and civic tradition had presented as the crucial and disastrous instance of specialization of social funciton. The citizen who allowed another to be paid to fight for him had parted with a vital element of his *virtus,* in every sense of that word; and the priest, the lawyer, and the rentier had been grouped with the soldier as paradigmatic instances of individuals whose specializations made them servants of others who became servants to them in their turn. Specialization, in short, was a prime cause of corruption; only the citizen as amateur, propertied, independent, and willing to perform in his own person all functions essential to the polis, could be said to practice virtue or live in a city where justice was truly distributed. There was no *arte* that he must not be willing to make his own. But if the arts proved to have been built up through a process of specialization, the culture itself was in contradiction with the ethos of the *zoon politikon;* and if it were further argued—as it clearly could be—that only specialization, commerce, and culture set men free enough to attend to the goods of others as well as their own, then it would follow that the polis was built up by the very forces that must destroy it.[14]

How persistent is the economic pattern of the military-commercially oriented state is illustrated in a *New York Times* editorial concerned with the social policy of the Reagan administration—one bent on an unprecedented growth and expansion of the armed services and, secondarily, the governmental fostering of commerce and industry:

> There is only one way in which Mr. Reagan's poverty program has provided for the poor. It is the way prescribed by Reaganaut theoreticians, notably George Gilder in "Wealth and Poverty," the book widely circulated in the Administration earlier this year. "In order to succeed," he wrote, "the poor need most of all the spur of their poverty."[15]

The affinity with Machiavelli's thinking is striking in light of his repeated conclusion:

> The most useful thing a free state can bring about is to keep the citizens poor.[16]

Implication for foreign policy appear in I. de Sola Poole's judgment:

> In the Congo, in Vietnam, in the Dominican Republic, it is clear that order depends on *somehow compelling* newly mobilized states to return to a measure of passivity and defeatism from which they have recently been aroused by the process of modernization.[17]

Certain of the qualities for citizenship which Machiavelli recognized as essential for the more inclusive order of freedom in his time are manifestly as indispensable for the builders and maintainers of the still more inclusive order currently taking shape.

Human individuality, Machiavelli perceived as basic; subsequently, legal guarantees of human rights have been incorporated, on the national level, in constitutions as bills of rights and, on the international level, in the United Nations' Universal Declaration of Human Rights and in the Helsinki Accords. The expansion of educational opportunity has contributed to specific implementation.

Repeatedly in his writings Machiavelli stressed the importance of giving full weight to the natural fact of human diversity.[18] He held that the ultimate reality inherent in another individual cannot be disregarded with impunity.[19] Intrinsically, as corollary, it follows that most reliable and serviceable are the means which one develops out of his own resources.[20] In *The Art of War,* he wrote:

> no man without inventiveness was ever great in his profession;[21]

and he counseled his youngest son:

> if you help yourself, everybody will help you.[22]

A second quality, also, like the first, rooted in "Nature," Machiavelli considered to be love of the country of one's birth and love of one's fellow countrymen.[23] The steady development of wider-ranging technology, the accelerating growth of the world's population, evidences of pollution of land, air, the waters of the rivers and oceans, but especially the increasing death-dealing potentiality of implements of war and the arms race out of control, together with revolutionary advances in the means of communication overcoming barriers of time, space, differences in cultures, have raised concern for the health of the earth's bio-systems and consciousness of dangers to our planet's prospect as a viable home for its people. Whereas Machiavelli perceived that nothing less than an ardent and resolute dedication in the service of the common good of the nation was essential in his day for securing the order of freedom, on the verge of the twenty-first century it grows ever more apparent that decision-making and the way of life must have the common good of all mankind on the earth as a whole for the frame of reference in order to ensure the survival of any.

Constructive participation in public affairs, Machiavelli recognized as an essential attribute of citizenship.[24] Very perceptively, Robert R. Wicks has written:

> There is no escape from social responsibility in the endless battle to change the outside order so that the inside worth of every man may have a better chance. We were created, for better or worse, to be together, and to take the consequences of each other's lives.[25]

The quality of a regime, according to Machiavelli, has its correlate in the quality of the individuals who compose it and in whom it is grounded. The better the country, the greater the potentiality for the character of the inhabitants. This perception by Machiavelli impels toward ever higher endeavor both within oneself and in responsible cooperation with others and the direct exploration of the kind of feeling and behavior, the form of person and of citizen, befitting the republic of mankind. Whitfield has noted the comparison which Toffanin made between Machiavelli and Guicciardini:

> He [Guicciardini] is the genuine pessimist about humanity, as Machiavelli, without realizing it, is the optimist.[26]

Of Machiavelli, it can be said, as Halford E. Luccock wrote of Jesus:

> He addressed the hero in the soul.[27]

Cultivation of prudent management, accountability and stewardship are the values fostered by the frugality which Machiavelli commended when advocating that the people be kept in poverty in comparison with the state but endowed with sufficient property for their interest, industry, skill and inventiveness to be enlisted[28] and to ensure a foundation for personal and social stability.[29] For both Livy and Machiavelli, Cincinnatus served as a model of citizenship in that from his small farm which he himself worked he was called to serve Rome as dictator in a military crisis and, upon the resolution of the crisis, returned to work his farm.[30] In *The Art of War,* Machiavelli returned to the same theme of the civilian-amateur-soldier.[31] Machiavelli took for granted that the wise ruler would see to it that civil responsibilities, professions and occupations would be sufficiently available to provide a place for those when peace made service in the army unnecessary;[32] yet the basic insecurity assumed by Machiavelli[33] required of each the alertness of the soldier-civilian.

That the well-being and freedom of all men are bound up with that of each has been recognized and affirmed throughout the ages not by religious leaders only but also by poets, pamphleteers and responsible officials. Jesus declared:

> anything you did for one of my brothers here, however humble, you did for me . . . anything you did not do for one of these, however humble, you did not do for me.[34]

Sixteen centuries later, the English poet and clergyman, John Donne, wrote:

> No man is an Iland, intire of itselfe; every man is a peece of the Continent, a part of the maine; if a Clod bee washed away by the Sea, Europe is the less . . . any man's death diminishes me, because I am involved in Mankinde; And therefore never send to know for whom the bell tolls; it tolls for thee.[35]

A century and a half later, Thomas Paine identified himself with whoever might not yet be free.[36] Carved in stone on the base of the Statue of Liberty looking out to the "old world" the words of Emma Lazarus send forth the message:

> Give me your tired, your poor,
> Your huddled masses yearning to breathe free,
> The wretched refuse of your teeming shore.
> Send these, the homeless, the tempest-tossed to me,
> I lift my lamp beside the golden door.[37]

And on 26 June 1963, President John F. Kennedy, addressing the throng in West Berlin, proclaimed:

> Freedom is indivisible, and when one man is enslaved, all are not free.[38]

"Vision plus valor" (i.e., "faith")[39] admits of no scarcity-affirming, privilege-seeking presumption, spreading contagion of paralyzing fear, but rather perceives the overflowing abundance realizable when loving concern and mutual understanding distribute the resources released through creative technology.

Studying the recorded past and, as a deeply involved and responsible participant, observing the current human behavior in public affairs, Machiavelli perceived in men a potentiality for *virtù*—an attitude and deeds of arresting quality attractive of followers and conducive to structures and institutions capable of renewals. As he reflected upon the twenty years which included the fourteen of his official experience, Machiavelli envisioned a quality of human foresight competent to curb the meaningless violence of Fortune's wheel and advance freedom through human prudence.[40] Martin Fleischer has noted:

Machiavelli does not have a concept of moral reason; there is no room in his world for natural law. What he does recognize is the human power to discern and devise the most effective means for accomplishing one's ends. The terms he most frequently uses to designate this power are *ingegno, prudenza, inganno*. These connote natural wit, ingenuity, intelligence, cunning, and similar notions.[41]

In his aim to serve the common good[42] and his aspiration to secure *uno vivere civile*[43] (a civil way of life) as the condition in which men can come to know themselves and to be their best,[44] Machiavelli perceived that the pursuit of the effectual truth[45] is the guide and guarantor of the way to it; and thus he achieved an insight of undiminished significance for the future. Recognizing the inherent individuality of each person[46] and unalienable capacity for vengeance,[47] man's possibility for innovation[48] and obligation for courageous action,[49] the importance of reasoning about everything,[50] and, then, concerning himself

with the truth of the matter as facts show it rather than with any fanciful notion,[51]

Machiavelli called attention to and manifested elements basic for confidence in the underlying lawfulness in experience which can be perceived and cooperated with by man.

However, as recent students of Machiavelli have pointed out, it is lawfulness found in unanticipated guise. Robert Orr has observed:

On Machiavelli's concrete moral recommendations the literature is not scarce and his views on what is hypothetically and circumstantially desirable are in general not obscure. But there are as well unmistakable indications of a view of what morality means for the temporal creature we know man to be. It is a life that implies recognition of its own contingency, that does not attempt to slip out of the time scale we know into some other rooted in eternity or in some foreordained schedule of events. The estimable character lives in the future, accepts responsibility for it—anticipating, preparing, confronting, making provision. The contemptible human being is one who evades the future, who, as he himself usually puts it, 'lives in the present.' To live in the present is an impossibility in a life in which what is conveniently called the present discloses either an immediate past or an immediate future. To attempt to live in an illusory present is to try to escape the life we know without effectively achieving the life we don't know, i.e., eternity. The virtues of "abnegation, humility, and contempt for mundane things" are only virtues in a life of which the end is paradise, and this is not a life that consists of trying to turn events right side up (*Discourses*, 2, 2). Those whose only anticipation is of heaven are attempting to have eternity in time; their morality is that of men who accept themselves as failures but who are unwilling to surrender life. It is suitable for no one else.[52]

Statecraft is not for those whose virtues do not exceed those of their fellows, in whom is not uncommonly the gift of *long* foresight, readiness for the unexpected turn of events, and ability to recreate these events as well as to recognize history in them. To display these qualities in the conduct of public affairs is to secure a fame which will outlast your own life—the only immortality available to creatures of time.[53]

Further clarification is provided by Pocock:

The air of Florence was heavy with apocalyptic, and Machiavelli could not have been as impervious to it as he may have liked to pretend. Innovations at the highest level, the creation of a just and stable society, had been attempted under the protection of the greatest concepts in Christian thought—nature, grace, prophecy, and renovation; and the attempt had failed, so that it must have been falsely conceived. It was a momentous and authentically terrifying question to inquire what came next. The myth of Venice provided one possible answer, more Platonic and Polybian than Christian, but *esprits forts* would be needed if any sort of virtue was to be set in the room of grace;[54]

In this setting, Machiavelli's *Il Principe,* written for the most part in 1512–1513, takes on a new aspect, that of the greatest of all theoretical explorations of the politics of innovation. Machiavelli's lack of optimate status—he belonged to the second of Alamanni's three classes [those who "desired only to be the recipients of honors and offices"][55]—set him free from optimate concerns; he could never be either a senator or a courtier and his mind was liberated to explore the absorbing topic of the new prince's relations with his environment. It is this which gives *Il Principe* the standing of any act of intellectual revolution; a breakthrough into new fields of theoretical relevance;[56]

What Machiavelli is doing in the most notorious passages of *Il Principe,* is reverting to the formal implementation of the Roman definition and asking whether there is any *virtù* by which the innovator, self-isolated from moral society, can impose form upon his *fortune,* and whether there will be any moral quality in such a *virtù* or in the political consequences which can be imagined as flowing from its exercise. Since the problem only exists as the result of innovation, which is a political act, its exploration must be conducted in terms of further political action.[57]

Machiavelli's dedication to the common good pioneered the projection toward a science of politics through his responsible participation in carrying forward the confident hope for advancing human freedom. In perceiving and enunciating the need for policies transcending regions and serving nations, he gave a precedent for conceiving and elaborating innovation whenever human needs require more comprehensive institutions for constructive service. Thus, he initiated, struggled to organize and make an objective reality of, and developed the theoretical basis for, the civil mililtia, the patriotic national army as a replacement for auxiliary, mercenary, and professional forces, and he cautioned against letting the supreme power fall into the hands of other than the native-born.[58] And through it all, he affirmed and fashioned a way of practical reasoning appropriate for direction in political affairs, as noted by Whitfield[59] and Count Carlo Sforza.[60]

That a new organization of a state or its effective reform requires the institution of a "new method," Machiavelli held to be even more basic than the introduction of new laws.[61] When the innovation entails the working out of a new order of power, innovation of method has to correspond with the innovation of form. The change in objective from that of service of the common good in terms of the "sovereign" nation-state to that of the common good of mankind as a whole, inevitably necessitates a corresponding change in method.

For the founding or reform of a city, republic or a kingdom, Machiavelli held:

> it is necessary that one man alone give the method and that from his mind proceed all such organization.[62]

Yet fifty-five men in a constitutional convention (presided over, it is true, by General George Washington dressed in full military uniform) with its work ratified by specially elected conventions in each of the thirteen states[63] set up the government of the United States of America and there developed the practice of setting up state governments by means of specially elected constitutional conventions with amendments to be enacted by popular referenda. The establishing of an order transcending nation-states will require a yet broader and deeper participation.

When in shock from the harrowing experiences of World War I, those who survived as "leaders" sensed the need for men to live within an order of laws sufficiently to set up the League of Nations; but they did not sense the need sufficiently to sacrifice the pride and rivalry embedded in the idea of "national sovereignty" to avoid the effort of "the Allies" to exact perpetual advantage at the expense of the defeated peoples (on the fictional charge of their "sole responsibility" for the war) and to avoid "the Allies' " rivalry among themselves for naval and military superiority over each other.

Similarly, in the wake of World War II, the sense of mutual need prompted the establishment of the United Nations; but the "Great Powers" could not bring themselves to sacrifice self-definition of national self-interest and the availability of the veto in the Security Council and to accept an over-riding accountability to the general common good. What kind of a shock is mankind waiting for which will be sufficient to arouse an *abiding* conviction that the survival of mankind is more to be fostered than pride in national superiority? If World War I and World War II could not bear the fruits of freedom through law, is there any reason to think that World War III, now being prepared, would leave mankind competent to effectuate such a high resolve? In the process of prosecuting the war do not the "leaders" and citizens of the participating countries, in fact, passionately and deliberatly *unfit* themselves for understanding and working with those who differ from them in thought and conduct? Is not, then, an essentially different method from that of world war as the kind of shock to bring the necessary quality of awareness to be explored and applied?

Both Jesus[64] and Machiavelli[65] described as an arena of turmoil and conflict that in which new order is being constructed. Machiavelli distinguished between conflicts which are domestic and those which are foreign. Domestic conflicts, carried on non-violently and able to be terminated by law, led to a sharing of *virtù* among the nobles and the people and an enhancement of force for conquering foreign foes.[66] May there not be found herein a clue indicative of the method appropriate for the order transcending the nation-state—now that all conflicts have become domestic with relation to mankind as a whole: in full recognition of diversity and rightful co-existence, non-violent engagement in seeking for and working out the common good? The threat of thermonuclear extinction constitutes a foreign enemy which challenges mankind as a whole with the necessity for founding a new order with the method essential for and appropriate to it.

Machiavelli was convinced that one good man cannot accomplish the new order through lawful means.[67] However, of the one man, Mohandas K. Gandhi, employing non-violence and "soul force," it has been written:

It is possible for a single individual to defy the whole might of an unjust empire and to save his honor, his religion, his soul and lay the foundation for that empire's fall or its regeneration.[68]

Moreover, what a good man cannot accomplish through lawful means, it may be that many may be able to through non-violent "civil obedience"—as Petra Kelley, Green Party member of the West German Parliament, has termed peace-making direct action.[69]

The intimation which Machiavelli glimpsed and the direction toward which he set out, by the mid-twentieth century had brought a major goal so clearly in view that, as reported by C. Mike Yarrow in *Quaker Experiences in International Conciliation*:

a group of social scientists of various disciplines who had been working on problems of conflict in different universities . . . produced a joint state-ment of principles on war and peace under the general heading "As the Social Scientist Sees It"

which affirmed:

439

We believe that if basic principles of social sciences are applied to national and international relations war can be eliminated.[70]

The correspondence between Dr. Nansen's insight into behavior characteristic of nation-states (above, p. 333) and Dr. Kurt Goldstein's clinical observation of the behavior of human organisms affected by injury (above, p. 9) suggests as a plausible inference that the appropriate and valid perspective from which to observe and interpret human behavior is that each one is to be understood as functioning as an integral part of, at least, the whole of mankind (if not of organic life or, even, all being) and that only when treated in accordance with its witness to such reflected light can its intrinsic energies flow forth contructively.

Does mankind constitute a planetary, organismic whole? From that perspective, can the violence-prone disorder—the reliance on fraud and fiction as "intelligence"—attendant upon the pretensions to national sovereignty, become understood with a more valid insight? May it be that the murderous violence attendant upon the rivalry of "National Interests," "National Security," and "National Honor" only provide evidence that it is not in accordance with basic reality to assume that states in origin and maintenance arise out of the necessities occasioned by an inherently evil human nature; rather, that it indicates that international affairs are but a manifestation of the deeply injured organism of organic nature proceeding in its blind course of action as, in prospect of growth, parts, convinced of their own inadequacy and consequent scarcity, and in reaction greedy for advantage, lash out against each other? The intimation, since ancient times, has been given expression in religious terms by the Psalmist,[71] by the Deuteronomist,[72] by Jesus,[73] by Paul,[74] but is still pressing for realization and articulation in institutional form and action.

On an inherent and direct relationship between the improvement of the quality of the state and the character of men serving it, Machiavelli was clearly convinced.[75]

That the treatment of any particular "national interest" or "good" as the ultimate, or as identical with that of mankind, is unsound procedure and not conducive to not only its well-being but even its very survival, grows ever more apparent as human interrelations become ever more complex and the growing magnitude of the traffic in destructive weaponry demonstrates. Moreover, the "virtue" romantically traditionally attributed to training for and participation in the wars of republican Rome or medieval feudalism, or even of citizen militias, is no longer relevant in a period in which wars are waged by means of professional national armies utilizing machinery which deals destruction indiscriminately to countless numbers far beyond not only visual but, indeed, comprehensive contact with such devastating consequences that the assertion that there are, or might be, "victors" can be based only upon the disregard and distraction from any initial or previous standards of the measure of values, and upon the post-hoc fabrication of superficially self-serving, but in reality suicidal, rationalizations as substitutions. In this technologically shrinking world, the responsibility for coping with the consequences of violence and rapacity press more immediately and penetrate more deeply then ever before. As Barber has noted in "The Compromised Republic,"

All political thinking today is conditioned by the seeming inevitability of a limited-growth economy, by circumscribed American power, by the compulsory interdependence of an increasingly transnational world, by the emergence of national (and even international) norms as the result of a national (international) technology, economy, and communications network, and by the failure of privatism and material success to answer non-material private needs or serve non-private life goals.[76]

Problems unable to be solved within the framework of nation states and relations between them, multiply and grow more crucial. Still present, but in aggravated form and on a greater scale, are many of the problems with which Machiavelli wrestled and upon which he reflected in a way which released for men during the intervening centuries, courage, insight and hope. As thirteenth-to fifteenth-century finance, commerce, navigation, had made imperative that exploration toward post-civic citizenship manifested in Machiavelli, so subsequent developments in communications, economic exchange, business orgainization, military technology, make imperative explorations towards transnational, global citizenship. Pocock has indicated the penetrating impact within citizens themselves:

In embracing the civic ideal . . . the humanist staked his future as a moral person on the political health of his city. He must in a totally non-cynical sense accept the adage that one should love one's country more than one's own soul; there was a sense in which the future of his soul depended on it, for once the justice which was part of Christian virtue was identified with the distributive justice of the polis, salvation became in some degree social, in some degree dependent upon others.[77]

After suffering the heaviest casualties in World War I and the loss, in World War II, of twenty million of its citizens, Russia, as the Soviet Union, has sought to transform itself into a force able to disintegrate any future external attack and has launched a crusade for communizing the world; and in the process of World War II, the United States, by dropping the atom bombs, introduced a new dimension of insecurities, terror and the arms race toward nuclear annihilation. Indulgence in planning for "limited nuclear war" which would bring death instantaneously to an estimated minimum of twenty million, not to mention the disease-generating environment with which other millions of "survivors" would be condemned to try to cope, indicate the necessity for mankind to alter the direction currently being charted by the official decision-makers.

"Setting up a new government" among a "corrupt" people, Machiavelli held

demands . . . a power almost kingly.[78]

With the tendency of the United States in its foreign policy to support conservative dictatorships in "developing countries" and to the Soviet Union to export "democratic centralism," what prospect is there for a transnational process which will enhance, or even maintain, regard for human rights and truly democratic procedures? The peculiar relevance of Machiavelli's way of thinking to contemporary society, Brayton Polka has pointed out:

> for all Machiavelli's discussion of politics in his major works, his genius lies in his tentative but precise discernment of the ethical dilemma which is the hallmark of the modern condition: the division between public and private, between subject and object, between different concepts of the good which cannot be related one to the other hierarchically but only existentially. When Machiavelli asks us to look to the end, he is really asking that we be aware of the peculiarly delicate relationship of means and ends: their relationship is not hierarchical or static, but, rather, dynamic, for our choice of ends will affect the means we employ, and the means we choose will affect the end we have in mind. So far as I am aware, Machiavelli is the first thinker in the West to posit, philosophically, the collision of aims, each good in itself.[79]

As to give thought to, and to work to bring into effective operation, the post-civic individual and citizen, became for Machiavelli a dominant concern, so now arises the necessity to consider the nature of the post-national individual and citizen. What kind of citizenry is requisite for bringing into being and maintaining the global polity? Quite rightly, Machiavelli held that the examination of political affairs must include a treatment of the nature of human nature. At this point he claimed general historical support for the pessimistic characterization which he ostensibly accepted.[80] A special example illustrating his generalization that

> in the actions of man . . . in connection with good there seems always to be something bad, which so easily grows up along with the good that to avoid bad while striving for good seems impossible. This is apparent in everything men do,[81]

is that

the more authority they [men] have, the worse they use it and the more overbearing they become.[82]

Perhaps herein lies, at least in part, the superior valuation which he placed upon the people when contrasted with princes:[83] in that the former is more amenable to counsel and correction.[84] Due to men's failure to consider experience seriously and to apply its teaching, in general they remain the same throughout time.[85]

However, in his view, the records of the past provide instances, unreliable (above, pp. 72–74) even though indispensable (above, pp. 70–72), as a source for prudence on the part of decision-makers and for his own constructive thinking.[86]

While recognizing that a realistic understanding of human nature is essential for the understanding of public affairs and for effective participation in them, did not Machiavelli with insufficient reservation commit himself to a conclusion with respect to which the subsequent development of the social and psychological sciences have demonstrated the necessity for withholding judgment and continuing basic research? He himself pointed out that oppression and the use of force could not prove so effective that it could annihilate the reaction of revenge.[87] Also, he cast doubt upon there ever having been in reality such a man as he postulated for the one-man founder or reformer of a state.[88] In *The History of Florence,* he pointed out that the financial and commercial magnates of the city were beginning to realize that even in "victory" they could not escape the taxes imposed to defray the financial costs of war.[89] He admitted conflict between war and policy[90] but did not carry this insight through to nullify his support for a policy of expansion which he had long commended as the means of preserving and enjoying republican liberties[91] despite the evidence which he presented of their destruction through the course of expansion as exemplified in the Roman empire.[92]

Must not any scientific exploration of human affairs entail an ongoing process of inquiry into the nature of personhood and interpersonal relations and include the perceptions experienced in one's feeling one's way along with those of others? May not clues for effective procedure be found in Paul's description of Jesus' course of action:

he did not think to snatch at equality with God, but made himself nothing, assuming the nature of a slave. Bearing the human likeness, revealed in human beings, he humbled himself, and in obedience accepted even death— death on a cross;[93]

or in Thomas Paine's identifying his own citizenship with that of men anywhere not yet free, or Gandhi living in the way toward liberation, rather than indulging himself in the claim of its attainment? The procedure of the scientist is not to

443

declare conclusions as laws but to employ hypotheses as a means for reaching a higher degree of reliability. The process has been well described by Robert R. Wicks:

New truth appears where partial views meet.[94]

From remote antiquity, as the way for beginning understanding, has come down the instruction: "Know thyself." Relatedness characterizes being. While one is of the locality, he is also of the state, of the nation, of the world, of the solar system and of the galaxy. Each level is at once an instrument and a responsibility. One cannot find well-being or security through running away from, or denying existence to, one part of himself and blindly exalting another. In trying to do so, he only builds up tensions which will later tend to break forth into self-destructive violence. Experience is a process of approximating a dynamic equilibrium. Acquaintanceship with oneself in distinction from others is a mutual undertaking. The process involves becoming aware not only of one's own diversity of "selves" and of how each, from time to time, presumptuously claims being as "I AM," but also of how different from one's own preconceptions is everyone else with whom one approaches understanding and how fictional are short-cut judgments of "good" and "bad," of "right" and "wrong," and that the way toward perception of social reality involves an endless and painful process in self-discovery and -education. Blindly and ignorantly, aggressions and inconsideratenesses happen. Recognition of one's own diversity and inconsistency, ignorance and blindness, may enable him to approach the other with compassion and thereby win from the encounter enhanced understanding, perhaps even of oneself. The working through, the deliberate sacrifice of, accidental attachments and coming through to a positive and reliable sense of "I am," constitutes the coming of age of a man (*vir*), the living forth of virtue. Perceptively, Pocock has written:

A term which was originally, and largely remained, part of the ethos of a political and military ruling class, *virtus* became assimilated to the Greek word *arete* and shared its conceptual development . . . *Arete* and *virtus* alike came to mean, first, the power by which an individual or group acted effectively in a civic context; next, the essential property which made a personality or element what it was; third, the moral goodness which made a man, in city or cosmos, what he ought to be;[95]

once Machiavelli begins to speak of it (*virtù*) as a means of the prince's rise to power, *virtù* becomes part of the act of innovation that exposes the prince to *fortuna* and renders itself necessary. In short, what had happened is this, Machiavelli's development of the theme of innovation has caused him, first, to employ the concept *virtù* in its purely formal sense of that

444

by which order is imposed upon *fortuna,* and, second, to do so in a way that separates it from the Christian and Aristotelian, moral and political contexts in which it ordinarily functioned. His decision to use the word in this way was his act of creative genius; we are looking at a genuine case of breakthrough in the employment of a paradigm.[96]

Relevant is Robert Orr's comment in his essay "The Time Motif in Machiavelli":

> Machiavelli has his own version of the doctrine that virtue is knowledge. It is *foreknowledge* that earns merit and brings such success as is deserved.[97]

Long before, early in the first book of his *Politics,* Aristotle had declared:

> He who can foresee with his mind is by nature intended to be lord and master.[98]

As Orr has indicated:

> The *virtù* of the Roman Republic was her constitution, her military organization, the qualities of her outstanding men, and the love of liberty of her citizens. *Virtù* is the intelligent precautions men can take to mitigate and soften the impact of events. Fortuna's powers are only magnified "where men have little *virtù*."[99]

Machiavelli attributed to Castruccio Castracani the saying:

> it is in this world of great importance to know oneself, and to be able to measure the forces of one's spirit and of one's position.[100]

To "know oneself" is to be able. Knowing that which one can count upon in oneself in specific circumstances improves his capacity for undertakings in accordance with his competencies. The very fact of being alive vests each one, biologically, with a right of unique worth. Jesus enhanced this right from nature with the message that each is the cherished[101] collaborator[102] of a loving and mindful creator[103] whose is the earth,[104] affirmed by Paul,[105] and with the demonstration that the creative response to love[106] manifests that each, as a creature of love, can find security only insofar as he is an instrument of love.[107] Machiavelli noted the individual's unalienable energy for reaction to injury[108] and the band of compatriots as the factor most effective for social organization.[109] Central in the dynamics through which order can become a practical reality, according to Jesus, however, is:

> For if you forgive others the wrongs they have done, your heavenly Father

will also forgive you; but if you do not forgive others, then the wrong you have done will not be forgiven by your Father.[110]

Jesus called attention to a two-fold effect: not only is the present interpersonal relationship clarified and rectified in the process of forgiveness, but the experience of the consequent release of tension and the joy of increased understanding so strengthens confidence in the availability and effectiveness of the process and the basic lawfulness and integrity of existence that it spreads innerly and begins to mollify past scars and replace locked-in fears with hopeful impulses for further reconciliations. Paul wrote to the Colossians:

> Be forbearing with one another, and forgiving, where any of you has cause for complaint: you must forgive as the Lord forgave you. To crown all, there must be love, to bind all together and complete the whole. Let Christ's peace be arbiter in your hearts.[111]

The sense of the need for forgiveness indicates an awareness that one has reached a personality boundary to be defined through the working out of mutual understanding. Forgiveness of one another is an opening for self-perception which relaxes inner fears and enables a new feeling of self to arise. Through this process one gradually gains the perception of *proprius* (that which in reality pertains to and belongs to him—i.e., his essential property) and of the nature of social structure which constitutes its support. Herein is the authority for which, as Pocock apparently indicates, Ireton and Hobbes sought in vain by and through formal institution:

> Ireton, backed by Cromwell, insisted that there must be engagements which no inner conviction entitled men to break, and that there must be structures of positive law, against which the "law of nature" was not a sufficient plea. His chief reason for saying this, he declared, was that the law of nature might decree that each man should have his own, but could not determine what was to be each man's. Property, an affair of particulars— Harrington was to call it "the goods of fortune"—must be distributed by human decisions, not by universal principles.
>
>> The Law of God doth not give me property, nor the Law of Nature, but property is of human constitution. I have a property and this I shall enjoy. Constitution founds property.
>
> The individual—Ireton was declaring—must be defined by human society if the latter was to exist; law and property must give him his social rights and personality if law and property were to have any security at all—and without them, what would he be;[112]
>
> Hobbes had laid it down that the observation of covenants—to be exact, the establishment of a law of nature that covenants must be observed—was

the only cure for the insecurity produced by the fears and fantasies of men, but had left it uncertain just how fearful and fantastic man arrived at the discovery of this law.[113]

Is not one's "property" and its cognate "pursuit of happiness"—the opportunity to develop one's potentialities without a shadow of inferiority—clarified through the process of one's forgiving another's trespasses and thereby one's becoming competent to accept within himself forgiveness of his own trespasses against others including the traditional imputation of "original sin?"

When the time of betrayal, trial and crucifixion was approaching, Jesus could say to the little band—each member of which was trying to prepare against the shock of discovering, in the course of the crisis, deeply hidden inner weaknesses and instabilities—

the Prince of this world approaches. He has no rights over me.[114]

Wilbert F. Howard has quoted as a paraphrase:

"there is no traitor within the citadel of my soul," or to change the figure to one suggested by the Hebrew phrase behind the Greek, "he has no claim against me."[115]

Free in himself from self-indulgent insincerities and scars covering up grudges held against others for past treatment of him, he, in his love for his friends, could be sensitive to their respective breaking points, understand and, in advance, give that peculiar strength of understanding encouragement which each would need for his subsequent recovery into yet greater power with his heart untroubled and the ability to go forward subsequently amid tribulations but with the strength of the inner peace which he confirmed in each.

May it not be that the supreme dispute-settling authority (i.e., sovereignty) inheres in the mutual understanding and the consequent reconstituting of personality which sincere forgiveness generates between and among individuals? Is not herein found to be the true basis for contract under law as ratified by mutually inner conviction? The principle of relationship liberating for and into a more humane and enlightening endeavor, refreshing for all participating, is set forth in the Declaration of Independence:

We hold these truths to be self-evident, that all men are created equal, that they are endowed by their Creator with certain unalienable Rights, that among these are Life, Liberty and the pursuit of Happiness. That to secure these rights, Governments are instituted among Men, deriving their just powers from the consent of the governed. That whenever any Form of Government becomes destructive of these ends, it is the Right of the People to alter or to abolish it, and to institute new Government, laying its foun-

447

dations on such principles and organizing its powers in such form, as to them shall seem most likely to effect their Safety and Happiness.

Creativity requires the unimpeded, cooperative attention of all the parts of an organism, experiencing the liberation, proceeding in love, exploring toward truth, abashed or disconcerted by no entrenched "mystery" protected against non-violent inquiry. As, in the religious tradition, confession precedes communion, so preparatory to the creative work itself is the educative process of divestment of the accidental accretions which would distract and cause one to miss that mark which is uniquely and properly his. It has been presumed by some that the rejection of human inequality automatically implies affirmation of the assumption of uniformity. Thus Pocock has written:

> This critique of *égalité des conditions* is basically Aristotelian; it is pointed out in the *Politics* that when men are treated as all alike, we fail to take account of them in those respects in which they are not alike; and it could have been pointed out further that a society in which every man is subservient to every other man, because dependent on him for any means of judging his own existence, is corrupt within the accepted meaning of the word, in a very special way and to a very high degree.[116]

The concept of "equality" belongs in a series which includes as other terms, "superiority" and "inferiority." Related also is "subservience." The series implies a qualitatively valid standard for measurement which, with respect to the intrinsic worth of a man, has not been objectified short of "the mind of God." The undeniable fact of human difference and individual uniqueness carries with it the corresponding diversity of respectively valid goals;[117] with respect to which The foregoing series is entirely irrelevant. The former may be represented as a hierarchy—

superior
equal (but *with respect to what?*)
inferior—

"equal" may be represented by another series: "a" differs from "b" from "c" et cetera . . . to the *nth* diversity.

Approach to moments of understanding of another is only through entirely unstructured, unprejudiced receptivity to the signals which that one intentionally directs. To presume an ability to make use of or exploit another is—as Hamlet protested to Guildenstern:

> 'Sblood, do you think that I am easier to be played on than a pipe? Call me what instrument you will, though you can fret me you cannot play upon me—[118]

448

or, in other words, to attempt to treat another person as worthy of less regard than that to be paid to a recorder [musical instrument]

Social participation is as much a continuous inquiry as a sustained expression. To attune one's will to the intelligent service of love or duty is to grow in the perception of the power of truth. Thus Machiavelli, stunned and frustrated by the recurrent experiences of the varied indications of the inadequacy of the traditional unit of government, yet, at the same time, as he wrote of himself,

> driven by the natural eagerness I have always felt for doing without any hesitation the things that I believe will bring benefit common to everybody;[119]

through his courageously resourceful daring for "the common good," generated and transmitted a body of systematic prudence as a legacy which continues to serve as a living challenge to man for self-awareness of the enhancement of personal worth through publicly responsible participation.

The search for more effective and adequate decision-making, quite as Machiavelli perceived with regard to governmental and religious institutions, needs to derive renewal and strength from reconsideration of the origins.[120]

Now, that, again, growing confusion and intensifying distractions insistently propound dilemmas and crises which the traditional institutions and processes leave unresolved, the remedy indicated is, as in Machiavelli's time, for innovation, but for innovation no longer on the scale of merely particular regions or national units,[121] but now on the scale required for the good of all mankind more sensitively interrelated as inhabitants of a little planet of which the trends in governments threaten all organic life with suicidal annihilation. Though the earth's maps no longer designate any area as *"terra incognita,"* men need not poison themselves and each other with a claustrophobia or seek in outer space for *Lebensraum*. Richer and more satisfying than fourteenth-century dreams of Cathay or sixteenth-century, of El Dorado, and more immediately personal, are the resources and rewards awaiting the explorers of inner space presently available to be pioneered through one's sincere forgiveness of others, reconciliation, understanding and love-in-action. Mutual understanding and enlightenment through sincere inter-personal forgiveness replaces inner tensions and ancient scars with releases of fresh energy and dispels crippling fixations and cribbed outlook with panoramic vision of theretofore hidden treasures within the reach of joint endeavor.

As aids for this enterprise of renovation, unprecedented resources are available for people (1) to "read the Bible *sensamente,"*[122] (with a feeling for its intrinsic meaning) due to twentieth-century scholarship and new translations, and, (2) through the new editions and translations of Machiavelli's works, to discover fresh insights and to reconsider his perceptions in the light of: their impact during four centuries, the sociological dimensions of modern historiog-

449

raphy, and the perspectives available through the social sciences.

Repeatedly, today, one finds in Machiavelli's writings profound affinity with cultural currents of his own time shaping the future. Thus, his whole exploration of recorded history and his clear-eyed observations of personal experience in seeking clues for more prudent decision-making exemplify the Renaissance "conversation" described by Pocock:

> The Renaissance was at its most Platonic in exalting the living relationship of the soul with the universal paradigm or value above the intellect's abstract contemplation of it; history could be praised more above philosophy on the grounds that the latter inspired the intellect with the idea of truth, but the former the whole spirit with concrete examples of it. Truth itself became less a system of propositions than a system of relationships to which the inquiring spirit became party by its inquiry. In consequence, participation in the humanist conversation, in one or other of its forms, became in itself the mode of relation to the universal, and the universal could be known and experienced by perpetual engagement in the conversation with particulars. The question was what form the conversation should take, what manner of conversation most fully realized the universal.[123]

To the question this posed, Machiavelli, as indicated in his discourse on the language,[124] would probably have found the following statement by Sheldon Wolin a relevant observation:

> The cultivation of political understanding means that one becomes sensitized to the enormous complexities and drama of saying that the political order is the most comprehensive association and is ultimately responsible like no other grouping, for sustaining the physical, material, cultural, and moral life of its members.[125]

In his zeal for the common good,[126] Machiavelli revealed a "revolutionary" temperament not unlike that which in religious terms has been attributed to "The Calvinist or classical Puritan individual":

> Walzer's *The Revolution of the Saints* presents the Calvinist or classical Puritan individual as the type of the first revolutionary, the first radically alienated man in modern Europe, filled with a sense of his loneliness— loneliness before God—associating with others on the basis of their common responsibility to values which are not those of society, and possessing a program of action whereby these values are to become the foundation of a reformation of the world.[127]

Again, in his conception of the individual as radically beholden to his native, traditional heritage,[128] he was reaffirming his conception of radical Christianity.[129] In this connection it is useful to consider a profound but little noted aspect of Paul's interpretation of the life and teaching of Jesus which has been given emphasis by Francis W. Beare:

> In Christian thinking, as this epistle [Colossians] makes clear, man is not saved *from,* but *with* the material creation; there is no fundamental dualism, but all, physical and spiritual alike, comes from God through Christ and returns to God through Christ. The redemption and reconciliation of man becomes the key to the redemption and reconciliation of the cosmos [cf. Romans 8:20 ff.]; where "the creation itself" is depicted as sharing the same bondage and grief, and awaiting the same liberation as "the children of God."[130]

From this perspective, for men to so cultivate any part of their environment that it achieves the potential of atomic or hydrogen power and then to use it for the destruction of fellow intelligencies constitutes radical cosmic treason. Pocock has traced that which may be understood as a congenial outworking of the above insight of Paul—the process by which in England and thence also in America

> the function of free proprietorship became the liberation of arms [from vassalage to freehold], and consequently of the personality, for free public action and civic virtue. The politicization of the human person had now attained full expression in the language of English political thought; God's Englishman was now *zoon politikon* in virtue of his sword and his freehold.
> If the basis of political personality was not to be property, in the real or (less probably) in the moveable sense, it was anchored in something more concretely material than the Aristotelian *oikos* [household], and Harrington showed himself inclined to discount Machiavelli's emphasis on a strictly moral corruption, as actual disintegration of the civic personality, as a main cause of decay of governments. When a government became "corrupt," he thought, it was less because the citizens had ceased to display the virtue appropriate to it than because the distribution of political authority was no longer properly related to the distribution of property that should determine it.[131]

Furthermore, as William Carey McWilliams has pointed out in his essay, "On Equality as the Moral Foundation for Community," Machiavelli envisioned a more exalted station as attainable by man:

> Rejecting the notion of a nature that includes and governs human kind, modern thought has also drawn a radical distinction between humans and beasts. Following the new routes opened up by the subtle Machiavelli, which were then clearly charted for all to see by such thinkers as Hobbes and Bacon, modern thought has directed men to master nature itself. Denying the distinction between God and man, it derives equality from the

451

distinction between human and nature. We are all equal because we are all destined to be masters, but it is mastery and not equality that is the goal.[132]

As a refuge for exiles and "outsiders" (religious, political, economic), the "new world" signified hope for opportunity to become one's creative self, i.e., achieve mastery, in part through the establishing and carrying on of more representative and accountable forms of public enterprise. Acquaintance through working together proceeded to erode ignorance-born barriers of culture, religion, race, and to replace them with appreciation for the enriching diversity.

Occasionally, in past ages, prophets and sages have glimpsed and proclaimed as a goal for which men have the potentiality to strive and ultimately to enter into, an order befitting their best development.[133] Jesus taught men to pray:

Thy will be done *on earth* [author's emphasis] as in heaven;[134]

In response when

The Pharisees asked him, 'When will the kingdom of God come?' He said, 'You cannot tell by observation when the kingdom of God comes. There will be no saying, "Look, here it is!" or "there it is!"; for in fact the kingdom of God is among you.'[135]

In Romans 11, Paul explained the expansion of the new order as to include all mankind. This same perception can be recognized in the observation by Pocock:

the tradition handed down from Joachim of Fiore through the Spiritual Franciscans, which declared that after an Age of the Father in which God had ruled through the covenant with Israel and an Age of the Son in which Christ ruled through his mystical body the church, there would come an Age of the Spirit in which God would be manifest in all men so chosen, as now he was incarnate in Christ alone—[136]

a position which can find a measure of support in Romans 8. Secular expression of an ultimate order of freedom in terms of government, philosophy and education has already been indicated (above pp. 343–349). Especially articulate was Thoreau:

There never will be a really free and enlightened State until the State comes to recognize the individual as a higher and independent power, from which all its own power and authority are derived, and treat him accordingly. I please myself imagining a State at last which can afford to be just to all men, and to treat the individual with respect as a neighbor; which even would not think it inconsistent with its own repose if a few were to live aloof from it, not meddling with it, nor embraced by it, who fulfilled all the duties of neighbors and fellow-men. A State which bore this kind of fruit, and suffered it to drop off as fast as it ripened, would prepare the way for a still more perfect and glorious State, which also I have imagined, but not yet anywhere seen.[137]

In *State and Revolution* Nicolai Lenin undertook to delineate the disappearance of the state through and following the dictatorship of the proletariat.

What signal does "the principle of proportionate duty" (above, p. 339) require of us in our time unless it be that of pioneering, maintaining, substantiating, advancing the thought-, institutional-forms and personal practice effectuating human rights and liberty?

The deepening and renewal of civic virtue requires an assurance of psychological and moral space transcending that provided in the anarchical rivalry of nation states. Deeds manifesting a new relationship among human beings need provide a channel for reconciliation among ancient peoples and also for manifesting between individuals grace adequately abundant to transform violence into disciplined energy sufficient for constructive cooperation.

Power is the energy released by the congruence of intentional effort and the perceived direction of relevant affairs. If this movement corresponds to the effort exerted, it is claimed as evidence of power: if the movement in affairs appears as but coincidental, it is characterized as "fortune" or "luck." Since the intention or aim is generated within the individual person, one's experience in the process of striving for it modifies and qualifies the appraisal of the consequences, and the adequacy of the fulfilment can be evaluated only in terms of one's own relevant experience. Others may offer, in exchange for one's endorsement and support, to accomplish his goal for him; they may try to discredit in his own eyes his own competence to effect his aspirations; they may play upon his fears of the consequences of his not entering into *their* plans for the use of his energies; they may offer themselves to serve as his representatives in order to win for him a victory through turning the problem into an adversary process; but as Yarrow has pointed out,

the adversary relationship cuts off constructive communication;[138]

consequently, whatever the others' accomplishments and however magnified and glorified, they fail to ring true when tested by the original intent itself remembered. Therefore, for example, power is a concern too personally vital to be entrusted to even elected officials. The devices of deception, distraction, evasion which characterize campaigns for election, result in slight, if any, relevance of the eventual "mandate" to any informed public judgment and, on the contrary, generate in the victor a sense of power invested, or entrusted, but unencumbered by responsible accountability—in fact, a sense of release to violence-prone responsibility related only to undefined abstraction.

Such practices have, as Whitfield has shown, grafted onto the term "politics"—objectively, the accumulation and use of power—a negative connotation foreign to its original meaning as well as to its employment by Machiavelli:

> there is a strong presumption that it [the word *politics*] will mean something questionable, far removed from the blameless sense it had when it was first minted as *politique* by Brunetto Latini, and translated as *politica* by Bono Giamboni. This from the *Tresor* is the *point de depart* for the history of the word in modern Europe, and the first reference given by the *Vocobolaria della Crusca;*[139]

> there is no word at all from this root [*polit-*] in *The Prince,* the *Arte d'ella Guerra* or the *Istorie Fiorentine.* But there is an isolated case in both the *Discorso sopra il reformare lo stato di Firenze* and the *Legations,* and there are eight examples in the *Discorsi sopra la prima deca.* That may seem a moderate abundance, but even so two of these instances are missing from the Giunta edition of the *Discorsi* of 1531, though quite clearly one of these two cases is merely an error in the text. Nine of these ten instances [see footnote] show *politico* as an adjective, and, except in one case, always as an adjective to the same noun, *vivere;* it is a *vivere politico.* In the tenth case, Machiavelli ventured one step further, and has made his adjective an adverb, *politicamente.* But it is an adverb modifying *vivere,* and the subject is *una città.* Such is the brief, and uniform, history of Machiavelli's use of the root *polit-*;[140]

and, in summary,

> It will be the upshot of this examination of Machiavelli's usage to show that he has no knowledge of any pejorative use for *policy.* What may be more surprising may be the proof that he knew no noun equivalent to this, either for *politics,* or for *politician.*[141]

Jesus spoke of "the Son of Man" as "seated at the right hand of the Power"[142] and "power" as accompanying the coming of "the Son of Man"[143] and the coming of "the kingdom of God."[144] Courageous integrity in service knows endowment of power.

Power need not let itself leak or be frittered away and dissipated into exploitation of induced fearfulness. Partial truths may provide ground for venture on more adequate possibilities and, in this process, as Yarrow observed,

> a trusted third party can present the . . . ideas and have them considered rather than immediately rejected.[145]

Yarrow's study of Quaker work for resolution of conflicts has called attention to elements suggestive for general application:

David C. McClelland, a social scientist called in as a consultant by the Ford Foundation, wrote almost entirely of the Quaker international affairs representatives in his report on centers. He described their objectives and methods of work in terms of conflict resolution: "The basic assumption is that, especially when tensions were high, people tend to believe about their opponents what fear leads them to believe, especially when their fear and anger prevents them from finding out the *facts* about what their opponents are thinking." Thus, he said, the Quaker intermediary worked to bring more reality perception to each side.[146]

The first necessity for a third party entering into conciliation is the establishment of confidence, and the basic qualities needed to establish and maintain credibility, according to Oran Young, are impartiality and independence . . .
Impartiality, however, implies an aloofness or indifference that does not adequately describe the Quaker approach. A more accurate though paradoxical description might be "balanced partiality"; that is, they listen sympathetically to each side, trying to put themselves in the other party's place. The evidence is clear that they were perceived as sympathetic listeners on both sides;[147]

Improving communication is perhaps the most pervasive third-party function, since it is required to clear up initial misunderstanding, to make accurate diagnosis possible, to explore alternative means, goals, and areas of commonality, and so on. Thus it is essential at all stages of the process, and is basic to the success of other functions;[148]

From the mission's [Quaker mission to Germany] journal we can separate the types of conciliatory activity that were carried on into four inexact though convenient categories: listening and asking questions; message carrying; understanding and assessment; and making proposals;[149]

Because of the fundamental belief of that of God in every man [the conciliators] treat the people with whom they are talking . . . with respect and attention. They really listen to them and I mean by that that they still the noise and confusion of their own thoughts and emotions and open themselves up completely to what the other person is trying to say, or perhaps feeling without expressing. This kind of listening . . . has a very real effect on the person being listened to. He becomes calmer, himself more receptive and open to ideas;[150]

The Quaker representative did not require any deference to this religious dimension in his discussion partner, but he sought it for himself. Under the best of circumstances it made him more courageous, more perceptive of his own internal conflicts and those of the other person, more aware of his own limitations and failings;[151]

A typical quotation used in the [group's] worship is one from Isaac Pennington, early Quaker writer:

Give over thine own willing, give over thine own running, give over thine own desiring to know or be anything and sink down to the seed which God sows in thy heart, and let that be in thee and grow in thee and breathe in thee and act in thee;[152]

Rather than believe that one of the participants is the aggressor and the other the victim, [a conciliator] should discipline himself to concentrate his sympathies on all those who are suffering as a result of the conflict . . . From this standpoint it is irrelevant to think of who is right and who is wrong; it is war that is wrong as a means of settling human disputes;[153]

If we appeal to our own basic values in trying to persuade our adversary of the truth of the proposal, he may be unconvinced, because those values are not his. But if we appeal to his values, we may appear to him or to ourselves to be deceptive, insincere, or opportunistic. The difficulty can be overcome by full and frank recognition of the situation and by building upon shared goals and upon diverging but compatible vital interests;[154]

Truth and love were the guidelines: courage to tell the truth and the spiritual resources to do it with love;[155]

Looking back on his interview experience, Roland Warren identified guidelines to the approach which were based both on psychological insight and on religious discernment:

1. "To acknowledge the truth—and there was at least a kernel of truth—in the point which the conversation-partner mentioned"
2. To avoid explosive issues where "his relationship to his conversation-partner was not sufficiently strong to bear the weight"
3. To avoid self-righteousness by respect for the other person
4. To understand the role of an official: "I made it quite clear to him that we feel our contribution lies in speaking our minds frankly, as Friends, but with a full realization that we do not bear decision-making responsibilities and also we do not have to weigh in all the factors which officials do and that we are undoubtedly unaware of some of these. We appreciate their listening to our point of view"
5. To avoid fear through the sense of "nothing to hide" in one's activities between the two Germanies and no ulterior motives of personal gain or organizational gain. "Fear is perhaps the greatest hindrance to Christian love;"[156]

456

important from the beginning was the effort to get representatives of the parties together to talk directly about the issues;[157]

A prime tenet of Quaker conciliation was to abstain from bringing political pressure to bear and to make the most of their lack of political power. As we have seen, the credibility of the Quaker conciliation was based on its non-political nature, its inability to call down sanctions of any kind. This enabled the team workers to be accepted and listened to as human beings of integrity by both sides. The lack of political power by the Quakers, who are a very small sect with little influence and less resources, was made into a general principle of "private diplomacy" by Adam Curle in his book *Making Peace*. "What is intrinsic to private diplomacy is its absolute separation from political interest and hence its potentiality to permit an open and relaxed relationship between human beings;"[158]

An important element was the Quakers were able to keep their conciliatory efforts out of the limelight;[159]

The Quaker participants were firmly convinced of the importance of more than one person on each errand of conciliation;[160]

As one reviews the activity of listening, message carrying, assessing, and proposing, one is impressed by the perseverance and ingenuity of the Quaker go-betweens, who kept up hope in a situation that was almost completely blocked . . . Most important, they helped to change the perception of the opposing leaders by demonstrating to each side that their counterparts were also reasonable and well-meaning people, motivated by similar ideas and pressures.[161]

The qualities identified as essential in effective conciliators are the same as those which, in interpersonal relations, condition one in coming to forgiveness of another. Now, confronted with physical scientists employed in releasing subatomic energy diverted into an arms race out of control; with biological scientists engaged in patenting new life forms through genetic engineering of recombinations of DNA; with communications scientists reaching to break through the barrier between pre-programmed and the anticipated autonomously-thinking computer—men find horizons expanding at revolutionary rates.

Striking, indeed, are the analogies at the close of the twentieth century with the cultural climate in which Machiavelli flourished. Taking counsel from courage, experience-enlightened prudence and foresight manifested by men of the past and his contemporaries, challenged

by reason of the great variation in affairs that we have seen in the past and now see every day beyond all human prediction,[162]

and judging

457

it to be true that Fortune may be mistress of one half our actions but that even she leaves the other half, or almost, under our control;[163]

by holding

it is well to reason about everything,[164]

and having determined to concern himself

with the truth of the matter as facts show it,[165]

Machiavelli explored in what way men might bring public affairs under their control in pursuance of

the natural eagerness I have always felt for doing without any hesitation the thing that I believe will bring benefit common to everybody.[166]

Although, to the fearful, the revolutionary changes may seem pregnant with apocalyptic terrors, more realistically they may be perceived as constructive achievements and, potentially, as means for the enhancement of the quality of life for all mankind. They incite new motivations energizing innovative social and technological experiments with the higher potentialities perceived in the natural resources and thereby encouraging responses to new criteria for virtuous endeavor. Two thousand years ago, Jesus proclaimed:

I have come that men may have life and have it in all its fullness;[167]

and

I am the way; I am the truth; and I am life.[168]

Apparently still present is the potentiality for abundance if men live in truth through diversity and confront and face down fear-nourishing fictions of hierarchical ranking asserted through "conspicuous waste."

Whether viewed as threat or as promise of benefit, however, the current changes stir mankind as a whole, to an unprecedented degree of interrelatedness of concern. The threat of nuclear holocaust, the continuance of no-longer-necessary poverty, generate increasing pressure within and among peoples for liberation. It was in the will for liberation that Machiavelli found one of man's deepest motives for action.[169] In his time he considered that the will for liberation required for its fulfilment the unity of a region or a nation.[170] Now the current changes require a will for liberation on a planetary scale and with a planetary response.

The quality of one's country bears a direct relationship to the potential character of its citizens, according to Machiavelli,[171] and their opportunity for development consists in their being engaged in official service.[172] In the opinion of Pocock,

> It looks . . . as if Machiavelli was in search of social means whereby men's natures might be transformed to the point where they became capable of citizenship.[173]

In response to the peoples' demand that the innovative release of energies in natural resources be employed to serve better, and more abundantly, peoples' needs and desires, constructive imagination is challenged to experiment with new social combinations for management and distribution.

Collaboration in new forms evokes new attitudes, goals, guidelines and behavior. Robert R. Wicks has noted:

> people develop their capacities neither by being helped nor by being paid, but through sharing common effort in interesting work on which their very existence depends.[174]

A diversity of shocks awakening them both to the dangers inherent in continuing with no longer adequate or relevant responses and to the possible advantages in exploring new directions, stirs them to the necessity for thinking differently and, as individuals, for helping to ensure that the new forms be so devised that they not frustrate but, rather, promote the participants' articulate integrity. Pocock has perceptively observed:

> Citizens are not engaged in knowing (and so creating) the universe and themselves, so much as in managing the relationships between one another's minds, wills, and purposes, and the appropriate quality of mind for this enterprise is not a Platonic *gnosis* as much as an Aristotelian *philia* or Christian *agape*.[175]

Inner development is a process of organismic integration through being sensitive to the diminished obstructions to total responsiveness to the more central direction. Discovery of mutuality of interests and kinship, experiences of the clarifying release through resolutions of conflicts and through understanding and forgiving—if not valuing—one another's differences, and the refreshing exhilaration of finding in the different a signal for appreciation and love, makes thinking differently a way of liberation. As men work their way through into new truth and come to understand its potential impact and spreading influences, they find themselves impelled

to institute new Government, laying its foundations on such principles and

459

organizing its powers in such form, as to them shall seem most likely to effect their Safety and Happiness,[176]

to take possession, in the name of the living, of the resources being made manifest. To the degree that one conceives and shapes his action so that its foreseeable consequences will serve to strengthen the association as an instrument of benefit for the others, as well, who are affected by those consequences, he proves himself at once an individual self,[177] manifests citizenship, and substantiates the state.[178]

Raymond T. Stamm has described the standard for Christian conduct in terms which demonstrate an identity of direction for that of citizenship in the order of freedom:

> No Christian may say to another, "I am the head; therefore you are subject to my commands," but only this: "We are equal in the sight of God; both of us are dependent on his grace, being nothing, having nothing that we have not received; therefore let us work together in his service, each using for the other's advantage whatever gifts God has given us."[179]

Security, unity, liberty were the values which Machiavelli identified as indicative of the effective unit of government and it was the inability of his contemporary Italian city states to provide these which prompted his exploration and reflections. The quest for security epitomized his whole endeavor. To all of his political and historical works might be applied his statement of his theme and purpose in the *Prince*:

> the things written above, carried out prudently, make a new prince seem an old one, and make him quickly safer and firmer in his position than if he were in it by right of descent. Because the actions of a new prince are more closely watched than are those of a hereditary prince; and when these reveal strength and wisdom, they lay hold on men and bind them to him more firmly than does ancient blood. Because men are more affected by present things than by past ones; and if in present conditions they prosper, they rejoice and ask nothing more; in fact, they will in every way defend a new prince, if in other things he does not fail himself. Thus he will gain double glory, for he will both begin a new princedom and will enoble and strengthen it with good laws, good arms, and good examples;[180]

> And those defenses alone are good, are certain, are durable, that depend on yourself and your own abilities;[181]

> never did anybody establish a republic or a kingdom who did not suppose that the same persons who inhabited it would need with their weapons to defend it.[182]

460

Unity under one republic or prince he considered indispensable to the happiness of the inhabitants of any region.[183] Liberty, he considered essential if a country is to achieve greatness.[184]

The emotional grounding for the state he found in the awareness of kinship through the citizens' identification with the land of their birth[185] and with *native* leadership[186] in the service of the common good.[187] According to Pocock,

> Machiavelli's contributions to republican theory were extraordinarily original, but were based on and limited to his decision that military dynamics was to be preferred before the search for stability. It was this decision that led him to investigate the military and social bases of political action and personality.[188]

"The military dynamism" which Machiavelli promoted for the security of the nation is far different from that generated attendant upon the development of modern military technology which has become counter-productive for the security, unity, liberty, and common good of mankind throughout the world. Given the diversity of weapon-systems and of geo-political positions, "parity" among powers as a goal provides unlimited justifications for programs of increase of specific means for combat. Only as decision-makers guide their policies with respect to their impact on people throughout the world can the human rights of any become more secure.

In Machiavelli's time, his plan for a citizen militia was a means whereby more of the citizens might be brought to an awareness of the personal cost in attitude and conduct of the availability of the benefits of membership in their city or country. He realized, and was devoting his talents to making known, that courageous, innovative, prudent action with service to the common good as the motive, discovers, exercises, and makes the most of a person's endowments and that the achieving of nationhood and the promotion of citizens' freedom through republican institutions was the way for coming into personhood.

Subsequently, despite irregular appearances and setbacks, an awareness of the right of every person to security and opportunity for expression of his talents has found, as servicable instruments, the developing institutions of participatory democracy. The ideal end always lacks that factor which only the not-yet-experienced progress toward it can contribute. The reality is one's value system in operation; but there is an interim period during which there is a work to be done by an intermediate structure and process, never to be confused with the end process, but necessary for it even though different from it. A premature grasp for the end as if already achieved is symbolized in the violence which this impatience induces and provokes. An intelligent willing, infused with—or tempered by—a renunciation of a claim of certainty (hence a "hunger and thirst" after the unattained in the presence of that of which the inadequacy of the present makes it appear in itself as nothing of value except as it serves as an instrument fully functioning in that quest), such is the crucible generating living toward truth. Pocock has written of:

> the dilemma which Joseph Levenson has described as that between "value" and "history"; what ought to be is not what is going to happen but nonetheless it requires to be affirmed.[189]

With subtle analysis John Knox has set forth clearly the danger of disregard and inappropriate treatment of the different degrees of magnitude of truth being apprehended:

> there are at least three perils to which the learned are particularly subject: one is pride in oneself and one's powers; another is confidence in the ability of the mind to master all truth and control all things; and the third is the habit of analyzing and classifying to the exclusion of any vision of things in their concreteness, wholeness, and simplicity. *Wisdom* is always humble and in a sense naive . . . the really important truth is *revealed* truth; it is not discovered by us, but disclosed to us. Such truth is not less than our minds, so that we can seize, organize, secure, and be served by it; it is *more* than our minds so that we can only pray for it, place ourselves in the way of receiving it, seek to serve it. If we are to know it, God must make it known.[190]

The political arena, also, as Wolin has pointed out, has its own penumbral phenomena:

> Political life does not yield its significance to terse hypotheses but is elusive, and hence meaningful statements about it often have to be allusive and intimative. Context becomes supremely important, for actions and events occur in no other setting. Knowledge of this type tends, therefore, to be suggestive and illuminative rather than explicit and determinate, borrowing from M. Polanyi, we shall call it "tacit political knowledge." The acquisition of tacit political knowledge is preeminently a matter of education of a particular kind and it is on this ground that the issue needs to be joined with the political methodist.[191]

462

Chapter Fifteen

SOME CHARACTERISTICS OF A TRULY SCIENTIFIC POLITICAL SCIENCE

What would characterize a truly scientific political science?

The search for truth—the growing point of science—is open-ended to the intentional experience, expressed as faithfully observed, directed toward no other allegiance or influence than a working understanding in inter-personal relations. The inquiry into the generation, increase, establishment, maintenance, decline or loss of influence in human relations, requires, as its frame of reference, attention to mankind as an organismic whole and each individual participating as a uniquely potential factor in the generating of power. Any less inclusive system, any restrictive parameter taken as life-or-death authority, involves structures of fiction annealed by violence and innerly driven on by insecurity and instability and heavily relying on secrecy and deception.

The processes and phases relevant to power may be deliberately observed through experimental explorations on various scales: individual, group, institutional—both public and private: experiments structured in terms of diverse models of control by one, the few, the many, or true consensus of all concerned. The data would consist of participant observations of human behavior—observations themselves untinged by any such assumptions as those of inherent "good" or "evil" in human nature, or of the presence or absence of patterns in "history."

The intellectual processes would consist of projects of inquiry taking the form of responsibly participatory actions unbiased with respect to but giving due weight to political and economic systems, or religious, racial or cultural presumptions.

Reflecting on the experience of Quakers in attempting to provide services as conciliators, Mike Yarrow, seeking for clues for future procedure, wrote:

One might postulate a more formalized "Quaker Conciliation Service" ready to prevent or allay conflict wherever it might occur in the world.

463

My own experience is that Quaker conciliation is best left to the more spontaneous reactions of individuals and groups with subsequent gathering in of resources as needed, rather than to a special bureau which might come to operate without the religious conditioning of Quaker "leading." We have attempted to describe this leading in the historical precedents and case studies. It is a combination of sympathy for suffering human beings and and practical wisdom as to possibilities, coupled with a religious impulse, a sense that the work is important in the sight of God. None of these elements can be called forth at the sounding of an alarum bell. They depend ultimately on the right type of persons having the call to undertake the conciliation, either from their own experience or laid upon them by the group. The religious leading is both corporate and individual.[1]

The poet Robert Frost once proclaimed:

I bid you to a one-man revolution.[2]

Here, also, Machiavelli gives substantial support and clear guidance:

It is in this world of great importance to know oneself, and to be able to measure the forces of one's spirit and of one's position;[3]

those defenses alone are good, are certain, are durable, that depend on yourself and your own abilities;[4]

a wise prince takes care to base himself on what is his own;[5]

I do not give advice to anyone, nor take advice from anyone, except this general advice: that each man do what his spirit dictates to him, and with boldness;[6]

I assert once more, indeed, it is very true, according to what we see in all the histories, that men are able to assist Fortune but not to thwart her. They can weave her designs but cannot destroy them. They ought, then, never to give up as beaten, because, since they do not know her purpose and she goes through crooked and unknown roads, they can always hope, and hoping are not to give up, in whatever fortune and whatever affliction they may be;[7]

no man without inventiveness was ever great in his profession;[8]

since my purpose is to write something useful to him who comprehends it, I have decided that I must concern myself with the truth of the matter as facts show it rather than with any fanciful notion;[9]

I shall keep on taking counsel with myself and shall try to act in such a way that, since I tell the truth, nobody will be able to complain.[10]

464

Machiavelli sought to arouse men to the realization that Fortune

leaves the other half [of our actions], or almost, under our control,[11]

that

> To believe that without effort on your part God fights for you, while you are idle and on your knees, has ruined many kingdoms and many states,[12]

and that history is rightly studied only insofar as guidance from it is being sought and applied in order not to repeat past errors and for the purpose of seeking help in solving current problems.[13] Idle and unattentive reading, as Machiavelli learned from Dante,

> does not produce knowledge when we hear but do not remember[14]

and, as Machiavelli indicated in *Mandragola,* is likely to give rise to idle talking which promotes confusion and defeats carefully devised plans.[15] On the other hand, rightly pursued, the study of history is of inestimable value for the directing of human affairs.[16]

The process for growth in wisdom, Machiavelli described in his chapter entitled "How Flatterers Can Be Avoided":

> There is no other way for securing yourself against flatteries except that men understand that they do not offend you by telling you the truth; but when everybody can tell you the truth, you fail to get respect. Hence a prudent prince uses a third method, choosing for his government wise men and to them alone giving free power to tell him the truth, but on such things only as he asks about, and on nothing else. But he asks them about everything and listens to their opinions; and then he decides for himself, at his own pleasure, on the basis of their advice; and with each of them he so bears himself that every adviser realizes that the more freely he speaks, the better he is received. Except these advisers, the prince listens to no one; he follows up the thing decided on and is firm in his decision . . . A wise prince, then, seeks advice continually, but when it suits him and not when it suits somebody else; moreover, he deprives everyone of courage to advise him on anything if he does not ask it. But nevertheless he is a big asker and then, on the things asked about, a patient listener to the truth. Further, if he learns that anybody for any reason does not tell him the truth, he is angry.[17]

A basic guideline has been well formulated by Halford E. Luccock:

> the mind must be a court open to the testimony of those most competent to give witness.[18]

The perspective and motive power has received clear expression in religious terms:

The belief that the world is ruled by a God who is righteousness alive is the most important conviction which can be held in the mind of men. The belief that God who is living righteousness is also the God of suffering love has in it the power to make all things new. These two beliefs were the precious inheritance of the man of Patmos;[19]

Christ became poor to make men rich and call men to be God's people;[20]

God designed human nature to be fulfilled neither under complete freedom nor under control, but under constant remaking through sharing responsibility. No human will is good enough to be imposed on the hidden possibilities of other individuals or groups . . . And what is to be a responsible person, which is God's intention for all of us? He is one who is *able to respond,* on the one hand to God who has new meanings still to disclose that are not yet realized by us, and on the other hand to people who require help peculiar to their own characters. What spoils such ability to respond is "self," keeping first place where it is a trespasser, and so preventing us from the experience of being worked through, "controlled," by a will greater than our own which is concerned with the unknown worth of each and all of us;[21]

Any human being who is loyal to the final mystery of infinite preparation and is ready with his best to answer the call of conscience and leave the conclusions for the Creator to draw is the most creative force in the world scene;[22]

the Quaker mission to the czar at the time of the Crimean War, though it did not stop the war, was not considered futile by Friends. The biographers of Joseph Sturge says, "Humanity does not progress to greater perfection merely or chiefly by achieved success, but rather by moral effort put forth and repeated again and again in the midst of apparent failure."[23]

That George Washington was motivated by the same perception, the quotation engraved on New York City's Washington Arch gives evidence:

Let us raise a standard to which the wise and just will repair. The event is in the hands of God.

The science of power progresses through the expressed and applied wisdom of responsibly observing participants. For men born of the earth and living thereon, "responsible" involves behavior and conduct intentionally within terms of time and space. Presumptions that problems can be resolved or dispelled, or

466

that the "kingdom of heaven" for some can be ushered in by resort to cataclysmic violence or an Armageddon-enlisted ally against one's fellow men, lures to suicidal annihilation for all through distracting from the true direction for the search and blinds to the perception and recognition of clues for constructive and creative reconciliation as they appear. Machiavelli labored in the hope that men could learn from experience to grow in freedom through the application of prudence. May not human beings develop the capacity to immunize themselves against the primal disease of which the symptom is the impulse to try to control others or to submit to control by them? May they come to perceive and to affirm each his rightful place in compassionate, courageous, personally creative, mutual endeavor for the common good?

In a sense and to a degree not traditionally emphasized, Machiavelli held true to Jesus's insight that through recognition and guidance by the light of experience-derived truth men grow in worth and freedom. Likewise, Jesus, as later Machiavelli, manifested an indispensable risk-taking action in the affirmation of higher purpose. It was not to "the world" that Jesus directed his attention nor was it for its organizations that he spent his energies:

I have not come to judge the world, but to save the world.[24]

His energy concentrated in sensitivity to those who in feeling their need were willing to accept his help and in the quality of his help so that his response befitted the transformation of need into growth: for the other, the restoration of the sense of health and well-being; for Jesus, the receiving of "the food" which was his own.[25] It was through such service that he would come to be "lifted up"[26] and men gain the light of truth and the awareness of freedom.[27] And with Machiavelli, the way of concerning himself

with the truth of the matter as facts show it[28]

involved exercising power divested of blinding greed,[29] knowing oneself[30] (above, p. 122), employing courageously one's own concrete resources (above, pp. 321–322)—in praising Castruccio, he wrote:

Nobody was ever bolder about entering into dangers, or more wary about getting out of them. He used to say that men ought to try everything, not to be afraid of anything; and that God is a lover of strong men—[31]

and, as he wrote in "Preface" to the *Discourses*:

doing without any hesitation the things that I believe will bring benefit common to everybody.[32]

467

To generate the attitudes, practices and institutions competent for managing constructively the forces which their advancing technology releases and makes available, men, especially as individuals dealing directly with each other, will find adequately refreshing enlightenment in more perceptive responsiveness to Machiavelli's love of the homeland (now viewed as the earth as a whole), Jesus' love of his fellowmen as friends through sharing with and serving whom one comes to win awareness of his own self, and the open-ended exploration toward justice through living into truth. Through courageously living into ambiguities, but nourished by occasional glimpses of sovereign truth, people already are establishing in freedom the state.

APPENDIXES

Appendix 1

ABBREVIATION OF PRINCIPAL WORKS CITED IN THE NOTES

A.W. Niccolo Machiavelli, *The Art of War* in *Machiavelli, The Chief Works and Others,* trans. Allan Gilbert (Durham, N.C.: Duke University Press, 1965). 3 vols. (Hereafter referred to as *MG*). Copyright © 1965 Alan Gilbert.

D. Niccolo Machiavelli, *Discourses on the First Decade of Titus Livius, MG.*

"G.A." Niccolo Machiavelli, "The (Golden) Ass," *MG.*

H.F. Niccolo Machiavelli, *The History of Florence, M.G.*

Lett.fam. Niccolo Machiavelli, *Letere Familiari,* ed. Edoardo Alvisi (Florence: Sansoni, 1883).

M.G. Niccolo Machiavelli, *The Chief Works and Others,* ed. Allan Gilbert, cit, supra.

N.E.B. The New English Bible: The Old Testament (Oxford University Press; Cambridge University Press, 1970); *The New Testament* (Oxford University Press; Cambridge University Press, 1961).

I.B. The Interpreter's Bible, A Commentary in Twelve Volumes, ed. Nolan B. Harmon (New York: Abingdon Press, 1955). 12 vols.

Opp.MC. Niccolo Machiavelli, *Tutte le opere storiche e letterarie,* eds. Guido Mazzoni and Mario Casella (Florence: G. Barbera, 1929).

Pocock. J.G.A. Pocock, *The Machiavellian Moment, Florentine Political Thought and the Atlantic Republican Tradition,* (Princeton: Princeton University Press, 1975). Copyright © 1975 by Princeton University Press. Scattered excerpts reprinted with permission of Princeton University Press.

P. Niccolo Machiavelli, the *Prince, MG.*

"T.A." Niccolo Machiavelli, "Tercets on Ambition," *MG.*

"T.F." Niccolo Machiavelli, "Tercets on Fortune," *MG.*

Ridolfi. Roberto Ridolfi, *The Life of Niccolo Machiavelli,* trans., Cecil Grayson (Chicago: The University of Chicago Press, 1963).

Tommasini. Oresta Tommasini, *La vita e gli scritti di Noccolo Machiavelli nella, loro relazione col Machiavellismo* (Rome: Prof. P. Maglione Succ. di E. Loescher, 1941.) 2 vols. (the second in two parts).

"F.D." Niccolo Machiavelli, *First Decennale, MG.*

"S.D." Niccolo Machiavelli, *Second Decellane, MG.*

"Remodeling." Niccolo Machiavelli, "A Discourse on Remodeling the Government of Florence," *MG.*

"Ghiribizzi." Niccolo Machiavelli, "Ghiribizzi scritti in Raugia al Soderino," *Opp.MC*.

"Lingua." Niccolo Machiavelli, "Discorso o Dialogo intorno alla Nostra Lingua," *Opp.MC*.

"L.C." Niccolo Machiavelli, "Life of Castruccio Castruacani."

"Money." Niccolo Machiavelli, "Words to be Spoken on the Law for Appropriating Money."

Pansini. Anthony J. Pansini, *Niccolo Machiavelli and the United States of America* (Greenvale, N.Y.: Greenvale Press, 1969).

Appendix 2

NOTE REFERENCES

CHAPTER ONE

1. I Kings 3:9 (New English Bible unless otherwise indicated, hereafter, *N.E.B.*).
2. Eccles. 8:16–17.
3. Matt. 2:12.
4. Ibid., 16.
5. John 8:31–32.
6. I Cor. 1:19–21.
7. Letter to the Ten, 6 Sept. 1506, in Pansini, p. 1074.
8. Letter to the Ten, 28 Sept. 1506, *ibid.*, p. 1084.
9. Draft of letter to Soderini, Jan. 1512–(1513), *MG.*, 2, 896 *(Lett. fam.,* 116).
10. Letter to Vettori, 9 Apr. 1513, *M.G.*, 2, pp. 900–901 *(Lett. fam.,* 120).
11. Letter to Vettori, 29 Apr. 1513, ibid., p. 906 *(Lett. fam.,* 128).
12. Letter to Vettori, 20 Dec. 1514 *(No. 2)*, ibid., p. 958 *(Lett. fam.,* 155).
13. *P.,* chap. 15, *MG.*, 1, 57.
14. *D.*, 1, 18, *MG.*, 1, 240; letter to Vettori, 20 June 1513, *MG.*, 2, 911 *(Lett. fam.,* 124).
15. *D.*, 1, 58, *ibid.*, pp. 313–14.
16. *A.W.*, 7, *MG.*, 2, 721.
17. John Humphreys Whitfield, *Discourses on Machiavelli* (Cambridge: W. Heffer & Sons, 1969), p. 163.
18. Count Carlo Sforza, *Living Thoughts of Machiavelli* (London: Cassell & Co., 1942), p. 10.
19. Max Kemmerich, *Machiavelli* (Wien: Karl Konig, 1925), pp. 126–27.
20. Arnoldo Mondadori, *Machiavelli,* I Giganti della letteratura, mondiale (Verona: Mondadori, 1968), p. 125.
21. "Ghiribizzi," *Opp. MC.,* p. 879.
22. Letter to Vettori, 25 Feb. 1513–(1514), *MG.*, 2, 941 *(Lett. fam.,* 144).
23. *D.*, 3, 6, *MG.*, 1, 441.
24. "G.A.," 5, 11, 115–17, *MG.*, 2, 764.
25. *D.*, 2, 29, *MG.*, 1, 408.
26. *H.F.*, 6, 13, *MG.*, 3, 1299.

27. *A.W.*, 4, *MG.*, 2, 657.

28. *P.*, chap. 25, *MG.*, 1, 92.

29. *P.*, Dedication, ibid., p. 10.

30. *P.*, chap. 15, ibid., p. 57.

31. *D.*, 1, Preface, ibid., p. 190.

32. *D.*, 1, 3, ibid., p. 201.

33. Tommasini, 2, 3.

34. Letter to Vettori, 10 Dec. 1513, *MG.*, 2, 929 *(Lett. fam.,* 137).

35. Whitfield, op. cit. pp. 3–4.

36. *D.*, 3, 1, *MG.*, 1, 419.

37. "Legation 13. An Official Mission to the Court of Rome, The Papal Court," Letter to the Ten of Liberty and Balia, 18, 4 Nov. 1503, *MG.*, 1, 144; *D.*, 1, 3, ibid., 1, 201.

38. *P.*, chap. 15, *MG.*, 1, 57.

39. Konrad Lorenz, *On Aggression,* trans. Marjorie Kerr Wilson (New York: Harcourt Brace & World, 1963), p. 233. Copyright © 1963 by Dr. G. Borotha-Schoeler Verlag, Wien; English translation copyright © 1966 by Konrad Lorenz. Reprinted by permission of Harcourt Brace Jovanovich, Inc.

40. W. E. H. Lecky, *History of European Morals,* II, 189, as quoted by Arthur John Gossip, "Exposition," John 7:45–52, *I.B.,* 8, 590. Copyright renewal © 1980 by Abingdon. Used by permission.

41. *Webster's New World Dictionary.*

42. Shakespeare, *A Midsummer Night's Dream,* act 5, sc. 1.

43. Kurt Goldstein, *The Organism, A Holistic Approach to Biology Derived from Pathological Data in Man,* American Psychology Series, ed. Henry E. Garrett (New York: American Book Company, 1939); also, id., *Human Nature in the Light of Psychopathology* (New York: Shocken Books, 1963).

44. Jer. 31:28–30.

45. Ezek. 18:20.

46. Matt. 10:30–31; Luke 12:6–7.

47. Matt. 25:40.

48. Matt. 18:12–14; Luke 15:3–7.

49. Luke 15:8–10.

50. I Cor. 2:11.

51. "Ghiribizzi," *Opp. MC.,* p. 879.

52. Draft of letter to Soderini, *MG.,* 2, 896–7 *(Lett. fam.,* 116).

53. *D.,* 3, 6, *MG.,* 1, 429.

54. 2, 28, ibid., p. 406.

55. Ibid., p. 405.

56. *P.,* chap. 17, ibid., p. 63 and n.4; *D.,* 3, 6, ibid., p. 429; 41, ibid., p. 519; 47, ibid., p. 527.

57. *P.,* chap. 19, ibid., p. 67.

58. *D.,* 3, 6, ibid., pp. 429–30.

59. Ibid., p. 438.

60. 3, ibid., p. 425; 1, 16, ibid., p. 236.

61. *P.,* chap. 19, ibid., p. 74.

62. *D.,* 3, 6, ibid., p. 430.

63. Deut. 10:14.

64. Ps. 24:1.

65. I Cor. 10:26.

66. Ibid., 4:7.

67. Luke 2:10.

68. I John 4:8, 9, 11, 16, 18.
69. Ibid.
70. Acts 17:27 28.
71. John 10:10.
72. Matt. 6:25, 32–34, 7:7–8, 11; John 14:2–3.
73. Matt. 5:3, 7:12; Luke 18:10–14.
74. Luke 10:30–36.
75. John 8:31–32.
76. Matt. 6:12, 14–15.
77. Luke 10:25–37; Matt. 7:12, 25:24–40, 45, 10:42.
78. Tommasini, 2, 574.
79. *A.W.*, 1, *MG.*, 2, 579.
80. *D.*, 1, 1, *MG.*, 1, 194.
81. *P.*, chap. 17, ibid., p. 62.
82. Isa. 9:6.
83. Acts 3:15.
84. Matt. 6:25–34, 25:40, 45.
85. John 8:32.
86. Kurt Goldstein, "On Emotions: Considerations from the Organismic Point of View," *Journal of Psychology*. 31 (1951), p. 49.

CHAPTER TWO

1. *D.*, 3, 30, *MG.*, 1, 496.
2. *D.*, 3, 27, ibid., pp. 491–92.
3. *D.*, 1, 12, ibid., p. 228.
4. *H.F.*, 8, 17, *MG.*, 3, 1406–1407.
5. *D.*, 2, 4, *MG.*, 1, 339; *P.*, chap. 26, ibid., p. 96.
6. *D.*, 1, 10, ibid., p. 220.
7. "Remodeling," ibid., p. 114.
8. *D.*, 1, 9, ibid., p. 218; 18, ibid., pp. 242–43; 3, 1, ibid., p. 421.
9. *A.W.*, 2, *MG.*, 2, 622, 623.
10. *H.F.*, 5, 8, *MG.*, 3, 1242.
11. *D.*, 3, 41, *MG.*, 1, 519; 1, 18, ibid., pp. 241–43.
12. "Lingua," *Opp. MC.*, pp. 770–71.
13. *D.*, 3, 47, *MG.*, 1, 526; cf., *H.F.*, 2, 22, *MG.*, 3, 1106.
14. *H.F.*, 3, 7, *MG.*, 3, 1150.
15. "The Natures of Florentine Men," *MG.*, 3, 1438.
16. Letter to Vettori, 16 Apr. 1527, *MG.*, 2, 1010 *(Lett. fam.*, 225).
17. Exod. 32:32.
18. Rom. 9:2–5 [*N.E.B.* alternative reading].
19. Matt. 8:20.
20. Mark 3:21, 31–35; Matt. 10:35–38; Mark 10:29–30; Matt. 12:46–50; Luke 18:29–30.
21. Matt. 26:39.
22. Mark 8:35, 36–37.
23. John 3:3.
24. Garrett Mattingly, "Machiavelli," in J. H. Plumb *The Horizon Book of the*

Renaissance, ed. Richard M. Ketchum (New York: American Heritage Publishing Co., 1961), p. 64. © 1961 American Heritage Publishing Co., Inc. Reprinted by permission from English language edition of *The Horizon Book of the Renaissance* by J. H. Plumb.

25. Gen. 4:9.
26. Meeting for business, Westbury Quarterly Meeting, Religious Society of Friends (Quakers), Autumn 1940.
27. James Henry Breasted, *The Dawn of Conscience* (New York: Charles Scribner's Sons, 1934), p. 299.
28. Gen. 15:5–21.
29. Ibid., 18:22–33.
30. I Sam. 8:5.
31. Ibid., 7–22.
32. Breasted, op. cit., pp. 120–23, 255, 270–71.
33. Micah 6:8.
34. Deut. 30:2–3, 6, 11–14.
35. Jer. 29:12–14.
36. Ibid., 31:31–32, 33–34.
37. Ezek. 36:23–24, 26–28, 11:17–20.
38. Isa. 57:15.
39. Ibid., 49:6, 66:18.
40. Flavius Josephus, *The Works of Flavius Josephus comprising the Antiquities of the Jews. A History of the Jewish Wars and Life of Flavius Josephus, Written by Himself,* trans. William Whiston (Philadelphia: David McKay, n.d.), 17, 10, 538.
41. Shirley Jackson Case, *Jesus, A New Biography,* p. 204, as quoted in Kirby Page, *How Jesus Faced Totalitarianism,* from *Living Prayerfully* (New York: Fellowship of Reconciliation, n.d.), p. 4.
42. Matt. 4:8–10.
43. Matt. 20:25–28; Mark 9:35, 10:42–45.
44. Ps. 75:7.
45. Matt. 7:1–5; Luke 6:37; Rom. 2:1.
46. Matt. 13:24–30.
47. Ibid., 47–49.
48. Mark 10:17–18.
49. Ibid., 27.
50. Ibid., 29–37.
51. Ibid., 5:44–45.
52. Ibid., 6:12.
53. Ibid., 7:12.
54. Rom. 14:4, 10–12, 2:1.
55. Ibid., 12:19; Deut. 31:35.
56. Jas. 4:11–12.
57. Matt. 5:23–24, 6:12, 14–15, 7:1–2; Rom. 2:1; I John 4:20–21.
58. Matt. 11:12.
59. Matt. 10:34–36, 38–39; Luke 18:29.
60. George Arthur Buttrick, "Exposition," Rom., *I.B.,* 7, 373–74. Copyright renewal © 1979 by Abingdon. Used by permission.
61. Gerald R. Cragg, "Exposition," Rom. 4:16, *I.B.,* 9, 445. Copyright © 1982 by Abingdon. Used by permission.
62. Mark 2:6–12, 15–17, 23–28, 3:1–6, 5:1–17, 7:1–8, 11:27–28, 12:10–27, 14:3–4, 47–48, 61, 15:5.
63. Mark 10:32–34; Luke 9:51.
64. Mark 11:1–10.

65. Ibid., 15–19.
66. Ibid., 11:27–12:44.
67. John 11:50.
68. Rom. 8:6.
69. Cragg, op. cit., p. 511.
70. Robert H. Strachan, "The Gospel in the New Testament," *I.B.*, 7, 15.
71. Claude Joseph Goldschmid Montefiore, *Some Elements of the Religious Teaching of Jesus* (London: Macmillan & Co., 1919) as quoted by Arthur John Gossip, "Exposition," John 6:30–34, *I.B.*, 8, 566.
72. Acts 25:10–11.
73. Matt. 6:10.
74. Rom. 12:2; Gal. 6:14.
75. Johann Wolfgang von Goethe, *Faust,* sc. 3, trans. Bayard Taylor (Boston: Houghton Mifflin, 1898), p. 51.
76. Aristotle, *Politics,* trans. Benjamin Jowett (New York: Colonial Press, 1899), 1, 2.
77. Ibid., p. 5.
78. *D.*, 1, 3, *MG.*, 1, 201; Legation 13. 18, ibid., p. 144; *D.*, 1, 17, ibid., p. 240; 37, ibid., p. 272; 3, 30, ibid., pp. 495–98; *P.*, 8, ibid., pp. 35–39; 17, ibid., p. 62.
79. "T.A.," 11. 73–81, *MG.*, 2, 737.
80. *D.*, 1, 9, *MG.*, 1, 218.
81. *P.*, chap. 23, ibid., p. 88; "T.F.," 11, 84–85, *MG.*, 2, 747.
82. *D.*, 2, 13, *MG.*, 1, 357–58; 1, 11, ibid., p. 225.
83. *D.*, 1, 25, ibid., p. 252.
84. *P.*, chap. 18, ibid. p. 65.
85. Ibid., p. 64.
86. Ibid., p. 65; chap. 19, ibid., p. 73.
87. *D.*, 2, Preface, ibid., p. 323.
88. *D.*, 2, 27, ibid., p. 404.
89. *H.F.*, 2, 31, *MG.*, 3, 1117.
90. *D.*, 3, 21, *MG.*, 1, 477; 1, 37, ibid., p. 272.
91. *D.*, 1, 5, *MG.*, 1, 206.
92. *D.*, 1, 37, ibid., p. 274.
93. *H.F.*, 4, 18, *MG.*, 3, 1207.
94. *D.*, 1, 37, *MG.*, 1, 272.
95. *P.*, chap. 17, ibid., p. 62; chap. 9, ibid., p. 42.
96. "T.A.," 11. 55–63, *MG.*, 2, 736.
97. "An Exhortation to Penitence," *MG.*, 1, 171–74.
98. *New York Times,* 7 June 1981, p. 12; 10, 376, 900, *World Almanac 1985*, p. 608.

CHAPTER THREE

1. Pocock, J.G.A. *The Machiavellian Moment, Florentine Political Thought and the Atlantic Republican Tradition* (Princeton: Princeton University Press, 1975), p. 71.
2. Luke 9:55–56 (alternative reading).
3. Matt. 9:13; Mark 2:17.
4. Matt. 11:19; Luke 7:34.
5. Matt. 26:51–56; Luke 9:54–55, 22:49–53; John 18:10–11.
6. Matt. 27:38; Mark 15:27; Luke 23:33.
7. John 1:16.

8. Matt. 5:6.

9. I Cor. 2:11.

10. Lynn Harold Hough, "Exposition," Rev. 17:1–6, *I.B.*, 12, 598. Copyright renewal © 1985 by Abingdon Press. Used by permission.

11. *P.*, chap. 6, *MG.*, 1, 26.

12. *D.*, 3, 30, ibid., p. 496.

13. *P.*, chap. 6, ibid., p. 27.

14. *D.*, 3, 30, ibid., p. 497.

15. Matt. 23:8–10.

16. Mark 10:18; Luke 18:19; Matt. 19:17.

17. *The Columbia History of the World*, eds. John A. Garraty and Peter Gay (New York: Harper & Row, 1972), p. 208.

18. *P.*, chap. 18, *MG.*, 1, 66–67; chap. 21, ibid., p. 81.

19. *D.*, 1, 11, ibid., p. 223–12, p. 227.

20. *D.*, 2, 2, ibid., p. 331.

21. *D.*, 3, 33, ibid., p. 503.

22. *A.W.*, Preface, *MG.*, 2, 566–67.

23. *A.W.*, 6, ibid., p. 691; 4, ibid., p. 661.

24. *A.W.*, 4, ibid., p. 661.

25. *P.*, chap. 8, *MG.*, 1, 38.

26. Ibid., p. 36.

27. Sydney Anglo, *Machiavelli, A Dissection* (New York: Harcourt, Brace & World, 1969), pp. 110–11. Copyright © 1969 by Sydney Anglo. Reprinted by permission of Harcout Brace Jovanovich, Inc.

28. Cragg, "Exposition," Rom. 10:2, *I.B.*, 9, 554.

29. *D.*, 3, 6, *MG.*, 1, 438.

30. Ibid., p. 442.

31. *H.F.*, 8, 1, *MG.*, 3, 1383–84.

32. Lorenz, op. cit., pp. 109–38.

33. *D.*, 3, 1, *MG.*, 1, 419; *H.F.*, 5, *MG.*, 3, 1242.

34. D., 3, 49, *MG.*, 1, 527; 1, 33, ibid., pp. 265–66.

35. 1, 58, ibid., p. 317.

36. *P.*, chap. 3, ibid., pp. 16–17.

37. *D.*, 3, 49, ibid., p. 528.

38. "Lingua," *Opp. MC.*, pp. 770–71.

39. "Remodeling," *MG.*, 1, 113–14.

40. *A.W.*, 2, *MG.*, 2, 622, 623; *Mandragola*, act 2, sc. 3, ibid., pp. 788–89.

41. *D.*, 3, 28, *MG.*, 1, 492–93.

42. *H.F.*, 7, 1, *MG.*, 3, 1337.

43. *D.*, 3, 41, *MG.*, 1, 519; *H.F.*, 5, 8, *MG.*, 3, 1242.

44. Letter to Vettori, 16 Apr. 1527, *MG.*, 2, 1010 (*Lett. fam.*, 225).

45. Jacob Burkhardt, *Die Renaissance in Italien*, p. 66, as quoted by Tommasini, 2, 425.

46. Draft of letter to Soderini, *MG.*, 2, 896 (*Lett. fam.*, 116).

47. *P.*, chap. 15, *MG.*, 1, 57; *D.*, 1, 58, ibid., pp. 313–14.

48. Ferdinand Schevill, *History of Florence from the Founding of the City through the Renaissance* (New York: Harcourt Brace & Co., 1936), pp. 434–37.

49. *P.*, chap. 6, *MG.*, 1, 26–27.

50. Schevill, op. cit., pp. 453–54.

51. Ibid., pp. 347–48, 438.

52. Ibid., p. 461.

53. Tommasini, 1, 235.
54. Ridolfi, p. 99.
55. *D.,* 3, 3, *MG.,* 1, 425; 9, ibid., p. 453.
56. 1, 9, ibid., pp. 217–20.
57. Tommasini, 2, 646.
58. *D.,* 3, 15, *MG.,* 1, 468.
59. 1, 9, ibid., p. 218; 18, ibid., pp. 242–43; 3, 1, ibid., p. 421; 15, ibid., p. 468.
60. 30, ibid., pp. 495–96.
61. 3, ibid., p. 425; 1, 16, ibid., pp. 236, 238.
62. 3, 4, ibid., p. 426.
63. 1, 16, ibid., p. 236.
64. *H.F.,* 5, 7, *MG.,* 3, 1242.
65. *D.,* 3, 27, *MG.,* 1, 489.
66. Ibid., p. 490.
67. 1, 17, ibid., pp. 239–40.
68. 18, ibid., p. 243; 9, ibid., p. 219.
69. 55, ibid., p. 309.
70. 3, 28, ibid., p. 493; 1, 33, ibid., pp. 264–65.
71. *P.,* chap. 6, ibid., pp. 26–27.
72. *D.,* 1, 26, ibid., pp. 253–54.
73. *P.,* chap. 8, ibid., p. 38.
74. *D.,* 3, 22, ibid., pp. 480–81.
75. *P.,* chap. 7, ibid., p. 31; letter to Vettori, 13 Jan. 1514–(1515), *MG.,* 2, 962, (*Lett. fam.,* 159).
76. *D.,* 3, 34, *MG.,* 1, 506–507; 28, ibid., pp. 492–93; *H.F.,* 7, 1, *MG.,* 3, 1337.
77. *D.,* 2, 2, *MG.,* 1, 329.
78. Ibid., pp. 332–33; 1, 16, ibid., p. 236.
79. *A.W.,* 1, *MG.,* 2, 572.
80. *D.,* 3, 12, *MG.,* 1, 461.
81. 1, 9, ibid., p. 218.
82. Letter to Vettori, 16 Apr. 1527, *MG.,* 2, 1010 (*Lett. fam.,* 225).
83. *D.,* 1, 9, *MG.,* 1, 218; *H.F.,* 4, 1, *MG.,* 3, 1187.
84. *D.,* 1, 9, *MG.,* 218–19 with reference to Livy, *History of Rome,* trans. Rev. Canon Roberts (London: J. M. Dent, 1912), 1, 8, 11.
85. Livy, op. cit., 1, 48, pp. 56–57.
86. "Remodeling," *MG.,* 1, 112–15; Ridolfi, p. 183 and n. 28.
87. Tommasini, 2, 429, 435.
88. *P.,* chap. 6, *MG.,* 1, 24–25; chap. 14, ibid., pp. 56–57; *D.,* 1, 19, ibid., p. 245.
89. *P.,* chap. 14., ibid., p. 55; *D.,* 3, 22, ibid., pp. 480–81.
90. Friedrich Meinecke, *Machiavellism, the Doctrine of Raison d'Etat and its Place in Modern History,* trans. Douglas Scott (New Haven: Yale University Press, 1957).
91. *D.,* 1, 9, *MG.,* 1, 219.
92. Ibid.
93. Letter to Vettori, 13 Jan. 1514–(1515), *MG.,* 2, 962 (*Lett. fam.,* 159); *P.,* chap. 7, *MG.,* 1, 27–34; chap. 13, ibid., pp. 52–53, 54–55.
94. *P.,* chap. 6, *MG.,* 1, 25, 26; *D.,* 1, 10, ibid., p. 223; chap. 19, ibid., pp. 244, 245.
95. *P.,* chap. 6, ibid., p. 25; chap. 26, ibid., p. 93; *D.,* 3, 20, ibid., p. 476; *A.W.,* 7, *MG.,* 2, 722; letter to Vettori, 26 Aug. 1513, *MG.,* 2, 925 (*Lett. fam.,* 134).
96. *P.,* chap. 6, *MG.,* 1, 25; chap. 26, ibid., p. 93; *D.,* 1, 1, ibid., p. 192.
97. *P.,* chap. 6, ibid., p. 27; chap. 13, ibid., p. 53; *D.,* Dedication, ibid., p. 189.
98. Letter to Vettori, 10 Dec. 1513, *MG.,* 2, 929 (*Lett. fam.,* 137).

99. *P.*, Dedication, *MG.*, 1, 10–11; chap. 26, ibid., pp. 92–96; letter to Vettori, Aug. 1513, *MG.*, 2, 926–27 (*Lett. fam.*, 135); "Pastoral: The Ideal Ruler," *MG.*, 1, 97–100.

100. Letter to Vettori, 15 Mar. 1525–(1526), *MG.*, 2, 994–95 (*Lett. fam.*, 204); Tommasini, 2, 785–86.

101. "L.C.," *MG.*, 2, 533–59.

102. *H.F.*, 1, 4, *MG.*, 3, 1038–39.

103. 1, 31, ibid., pp. 1071.

104. 3, 16–17, ibid., pp. 1165–68.

105. *D.*, 1, 9, *MG.*, 1, 218–19.

106. 3, 1, ibid., p. 421.

107. Draft of letter to Soderini, *MG.*, 2, 897.

108. "T.F.," 11. 100–20, ibid., p. 747.

109. 11. 181–83, 190–92, ibid., p. 749; *P.*, chap. 25, *MG.*, 1, 92.

110. Plutarch, as quoted by Samuel Angus, *The Mystery Religions and Christianity* (New York: Chas. Scribners, 1925), p. 311 as quoted by Gossip, "Exposition," John 1:14–18, *I.B.*, 8, 476.

111. *D.*, 1, 18, *MG.*, 1, 242–43.

112. 1, 17, ibid., p. 240.

113. *H.F.*, 4, 1, *MG.*, 3, 1187.

114. *D.*, 1, 9, *MG.*, 1, 218; 18, ibid., pp. 242–43; 3, 1, ibid., pp. 421–22.

115. *H.F.*, 3, 10, *MG.*, 3, 1154.

116., *P.*, chap. 17, *MG.*, 1, 63; chap. 19, ibid., p. 67; ibid., p. 74; *D.*, 1, 16, ibid., 236; 28, ibid., p. 405; ibid. p. 406; 3, ibid., pp. 424–25; 6, ibid., p. 429; ibid., pp. 429–30; ibid., p. 430; ibid., p. 438; 3, 41, ibid., p. 519; letter to Giovanni de'Medici as indicated by Tommasini, 1, 600–601.

117. *D.*, 3, 48, *MG.*, 3, 526; letter of 27 Aug. 1501 in *Opp. P.*, vol. III, p. 160ff. as quoted in Ridolfi, pp. 38–39; "S.D.," 11. 181–92, *MG.*, 3, 1461.

118. D., 2, 27, *MG.*, 1, 404.

119. *D.*, 3, 6, ibid., pp. 438, 442; *H.F.*, 8, 1, *MG.*, 3, 1383–84.

120. 1, 10, *MG.*, 1, 220.

121. *H.F.*, 2, 32, *MG.*, 3, 1120.

122. 8, 1, ibid., pp. 1383–84.

123. *D.*, 1, 9, *MG.*, 1, 218.

124. Ibid.

125. *P.*, Dedication, ibid., p. 10.

126. *D.*, 3, 43, ibid., p. 521; "Clizia," Prolog, *MG.*, 2, 823.

127. *D.*, 1, 11, ibid., p. 226; Preface, ibid., p. 191.

128. *D.*, 1, 39, *MG.*, 1, 278; *H.F.*, Preface, *MG.*, 3, 1031; *D.*, 2, Preface, *MG.*, 1, 324; 3, 43, ibid., pp. 521, 522; see also Leo Strauss, *Thoughts on Machiavelli* (Seattle: University of Washington Press, 1969), pp. 80–81; "Clizia," Prolog, *MG.*, 2, 823.

129. *D.*, 2, 30, ibid., p. 412.

130. *H.F.*, 5, 1, *MG.*, 3, 1232; "G.A.," chap. 5, 11. 88–105, *MG.*, 2, 763.

131. *H.F.*, 3, 5, *MG.*, 3, 1145–48.

132. Anglo, op. cit., p. 175.

133. Ibid., p. 241.

134. *H.F.*, 5, 1, *MG.*, 3, 1233.

135. *D.*, 1, Preface, *MG.*, 1, 190–91.

136. 2, Preface, ibid., p. 324.

137. *D.*, 3, 30, ibid., p. 497.

138. *P.*, chap. 14, ibid., pp. 56–57; *D.*, 1, 10, ibid., p. 221.

139. *H.F.,* Preface, *MG.,* 3, 1031; 5, 1, ibid., p. 1233.

140. *H.F.,* Preface, ibid., p. 1031.

141. *A.W.,* Preface, *MG.,* 2, 566–67.

142. *D.,* 2, Preface, *MG.,* 1, 321.

143. 5, ibid., pp. 340–41.

144. *D.,* 2, 5, ibid., p. 340.

145. *P.,* chap. 17, ibid., p. 63.

146. *H.F.,* Preface, *MG.,* 3, 1032–33.

147. *A.W.,* 2, *MG.,* 2 622, 622–23.

148. *D.,* 2, Preface, *MG.,* 1, 321.

149. 1, 10, ibid., p. 221. Cf. Machiavelli's own method in writing about the Medici, as indicated in *MG.*'s introductory note to *H.F., MG.,* 3, 1028.

150. Tommasini, 2, 125; letter to Guicciardini, 17 May 1521, *MG.,* 2, 972 (*Lett. fam.,* 179).

151. "T.F.," 11. 190–93, *MG.,* 2, 749.

152. Martin Fleischer. "A Passion for Politics, The Vital Core of the World of Machiavelli" in *Machiavelli and the Nature of Political Thought,* ed. Martin Fleisher (New York: Atheneum, 1972), pp. 146–47 (hereafter referred to as *Machiavelli . . . Thought*).

153. *D.,* 3, 6, *MG.,* 1, 429.

154. *P.,* chap. 15, ibid., p. 57.

155. Anglo, op. cit. pp. 254–61.

156. Strauss, op. cit. pp. 107–10, 121, 139–40.

157. *D.,* 3, 31, *MG.,* 1, 498.

158. *A.W.,* 1, *MG.,* 2, 579.

159. *D.,* 1, 1, *MG.,* 1, 194; 5, ibid., p. 206; 37, ibid., p. 272; *H.F.,* 4, 18, *MG.,* 3, 1207; "T.A.," 11. 73–81, *MG.,* 2, 737.

160. *D.,* 1, 3, *MG.,* 1, 201; 9, ibid., p. 218; ibid. p. 219; *P.,* chap. 17, ibid., p. 62; chap. 18, ibid., p. 65; chap. 23, ibid., p. 88; "T.A.," 11. 55–63, *MG.,* 2, 736.

161. *D.,* 1, 9, *MG.,* 1, 217–20; 3, 15, ibid., p. 468; 16, ibid., pp. 236, 238; 17, ibid., pp. 239–40; 18, ibid., pp. 242–43; 26, ibid., pp. 253–54; 3, 1, ibid., p. 421; 3, 3, ibid., p. 425; 15, ibid., p. 468; 22, ibid., pp. 480–81; 30, ibid., pp. 495–97; *P.,* chap. 7, ibid., p. 31; chap. 8, ibid., p. 38; letter to Vettori, 15 Jan. 1514–(1515), *MG.,* 2, 962.

162. *P.,* chap. 18, *MG.,* 1, 64–67; *D.,* 1, 25, ibid., p. 252; 2, 13, ibid., pp. 357–58.

163. *D.,* 1, 9, ibid., pp. 218, 220; 16, ibid., pp. 236; 238; 17, ibid., pp. 239–40; 18, ibid., p. 243; 19, ibid., p. 245; 26, ibid., pp. 253–54; 3, 3, ibid., p. 425; 4, ibid., p. 426; 22, ibid., pp. 480–81; 27, ibid., pp. 489, 490; 30, ibid., pp. 496–97; 42, ibid., p. 520; *P.,* chap. 6, ibid., pp. 26–27; chap. 7, ibid., p. 31; chap. 8, ibid., p. 38; chap. 13, ibid., pp. 52–53; chap. 14, ibid., pp. 55—57; letter to Vettori, 31 Jan. 1514–(1515), *MG.,* 2, 962, (*Lett. fam.,* 159); *H.F.,* 5, *MG.,* 3, 1242; 8, 22, ibid., p. 1413; "Money," ibid., p. 1442.

164. *D.,* 3, 27, *MG.,* 3, 490; 1, 9, ibid., p. 219; 18, ibid., p. 243; 55, ibid., pp. 309–10; 3, 28, ibid., p. 493; *P.,* chap. 8, ibid., pp. 36, 38.

165. *D.,* 3, 6, *MG.,* 1, 429.

166. Felix Gilbert, *Machiavelli and Guicciardini, Politics and History in Sixteenth Century Florence (Princeton: Princeton University Press, 1965), p. 154.*

167. *P.,* chap. 7, *MG.,* 1, 31; 8, ibid., pp. 37, 38; *D.,* 1, 9, ibid., pp. 218–20; 16, ibid., p. 236; 18, ibid., pp. 242–43; 33, ibid., pp. 264–65; 3, 1, ibid., p. 421; 3, ibid., pp. 424–35; 22 ibid., pp. 479–81; 27, ibid., pp. 489, 490; 28, ibid., p. 493; 30, ibid., p. 406.

168. *A.W.*, 4, *MG.*, 2, 662.
169. *D.*, 3, 6, *MG.*, 1, 430.
170. 33, ibid., p. 502.
171. *A.W.*, 1, *MG.*, 2, 581.
172. Ibid., pp. 585–86.
173. *D.*, 2, 20, *MG.*, 1, 382.
174. 3, 31, ibid., p. 500; *A.W.*, 1, *MG.*, 2, 584–85, 587; 7, ibid., pp. 722, 724; *H.F.*, 2, 5–6, *MG.*, 3, 1086; 26, ibid., pp. 1111–12; 5, 9, ibid., p. 1244.
175. *P.*, chap. 17, *MG.*, 1, 64.
176. Chap. 13, ibid., pp. 52–53; chap. 7, ibid., p.33.
177. 13, ibid., p. 54; *D.*, 1, 21, ibid., pp. 246–47; *A.W.*, 1, *MG.*, 2, 584, 587.
178. *D.*, 1, 43, *MG.*, 1, 286.
179. "A Provision for Infantry," Preamble, ibid., p. 3.
180. *A.W.*, 1, *MG.*, 2, 583–84.
181. Pocock, pp. 88–89.
182. *D.*, 2, 19, *MG.*, 1, 379, 380; *H.F.*, 5, 21, *MG.*, 3, 1261.
183. *D.*, 1, 6, *MG.*, 1, 209–11; Herbert Butterfield, *The Statecraft of Machiavelli* (New York: Macmillan, 1967), pp. 43–44.
184. Harvey claflin Mansfield, Jr., "On the Impersonality of the Modern State, A Comment on Machiavelli's Use of *Stato*," *American Political Science Review*, 77, 4, 855.
185. *D.*, 1, 7, *MG.*, 1, 211.
186. 3, 16, ibid., pp. 468–69; 1, 37, ibid., p. 272.
187. 1, 4, ibid., p. 203.
188. *H.F.*, 3, 1, *MG.*, 3, 1140–41.
189. *D.*, 1, 4, *MG.*, 1, 202–203.
190. Pocock, "Custom and Grace, Form and Matter: An Approach to Machiavelli's Concept of Innovation," in *Machiavelli . . . Thought*, p. 174.
191. *D.*, 2, 4, *MG.*, 1, 337.
192. Alfredo Bonadeo, *Corruption, Conflict, and Power in the Works and Times of Niccolo Machiavelli* (Berkeley: University of California Press, 1973), pp. 39–40.
193. Ibid., p. 64.
194. Ibid., pp. 70–71.
195. Lorenz, op. cit., p. 190.
196. Ibid., p. 251.
197. Ibid., p. 268.
198. Ibid., p. 271.
199. Ibid., pp. 272–73.
200. *D.*, 1, 16, *MG.*, 1, 236, 238; 3, 3, ibid., pp. 424–25.
201. 3, 27, ibid., p. 489.
202. 30, ibid., pp. 495–96.
203. *H.F.*, 5, 8, *MG.*, 3, 1242; *D.*, 3, 1, *MG.*, 1, 419; 49, ibid., pp. 527–28.
204. *D.*, 3, 1, *MG.*, 1, 421.
205. 2, 23, ibid., p. 390.
206. *A.W.*, Dedicatory Preface, *MG.*, 2, 566; *H.F.*, 2, 5, *MG.*, 3, 1085; *A.W.*, 1, *MG.*, 2, 571–72.
207. *D.*, 3, 31, *MG.*, 1, 500.
208. *A.W.*, 7, *MG.*, 719–20.
209. *D.*, 1, 4, *MG.*, 1, 202.
210. "Money," *MG.*, 3, 1442; *D.*, 3, 42, *MG.*, 1, 520; *P.*, chap. 18, *MG.*, 1, 64–67; Legation 11.40, An Official Mission to Duke Valentino, 8 Nov. 1502, *MG.*, 1,

482

132; letter to Guicciardini, 1 Jan. 1525–(1526), *MG.*, 2, 991, (*Lett. fam.*, 202); letter to Guicciardini, 15 Mar. 1525–(1526), ibid., p. 995, (*Lett. fam.*, 204).

211. *H.F.*, 8, 22, *MG.*, 3, 1413.

212. 5, 21, ibid., p. 1261.

213. *P.*, chap. 3, *MG.*, 1, 16–17.

214. Chap. 14, ibid., pp. 55–56.

215. *D.*, 1, 21, ibid., p. 247.

216. *A.W.*, 2, *MG.*, 2, 619.

217. 1, ibid., p. 576.

218. Ibid., p. 578.

219. Ibid., pp. 584–85.

220. *H.F.*, 6, 1, *MG.*, 3, 1284; *D.*, 2, 6, *MG.*, 1, 341.

221. *P.*, chap. 16, *MG.*, 1, 60–61.

222. *D.*, 2, 6, ibid., pp. 341–43; *A.W.*, 5, *MG.*, 2, 672–73.

223. *H.F.*, 5, 8, *MG.*, 3, 1242; Livy, *History* 9.1.10 as quoted in *P.*, chap. 26, *MG.*, 1, 94 and *D.*, 3, 12, ibid., p. 461.

224. *D.*, 2, 21, *MG.*, 1, 385.

225. 1, 39, ibid., p. 278; 2, Preface, ibid., p. 324; 3, 43, ibid., pp. 521, 522; *H.F.*, Preface, *MG.*, 3, 1031; "Clizia," Prolog, *MG.*, 2, 823.

226. *H.F.*, 5, 1, *MG.*, 3, 1232; "G.A.," 5, 11. 88–105, *MG.*, 2, 763.

227. "G.A.," 3, 11. 79–84, *MG.*, 2, 757.

228. Letter to Giovanni Vernacci, 25 Jan. 1517–(1518), ibid., p. 969 (*Lett. fam.*, 168).

229. "G.A.," chap. 3, 11. 100–102, 118–20, ibid., p. 758.

230. Letter to Vettori, 10 Dec. 1513, ibid., p. 929 (*Lett. fam.*, 137).

231. Draft of letter to Soderini, ibid., p. 896 (*Lett. fam.*, 116).

232. "T.F.," 11. 176–77, ibid., p. 739; *D.*, 2, 1, *MG.*, 1, 324; *A.W.*, 1, *MG.*, 2, 624; *P.*, chap. 25, *MG.*, 1, 89–90; Draft of letter to Soderini, *MG.*, 2, 897.

233. *P.*, chap. 25, *MG.*, 1, 89–90; "T.F.," 11. 25–30, ibid., p. 745.

234. *D.*, 2, 30, *MG.*, 1, 412.

235. "S.D.," 1. 45, *MG.*, 3, 1458.

236. *D.*, 2, Preface, *MG.*, 1, 324.

237. 29, ibid., p. 406.

238. "T.F.," 11. 112–14, *MG.*, 2, 747; *D.*, 2, 1, *MG.*, 1, 324; Draft of letter to Soderini, *MG.*, 2, 897.

239. "T.F.," 1. 83, *MG.*, 2, 747.

240. "S.D.," 11. 181–89, *MG.*, 3, 1461.

241. *D.*, 1, 37, *MG.*, 1, 272.

242. Draft of letter to Soderini, *MG.*, 2, 896–97 (*Lett. fam.*, 116).

243. *D.*, 3, 9, *MG.*, 1, 452; Draft of letter to Soderini, *MG.*, 2, 897.

244. "G.A.," chap. 1, 11. 88–90, *MG.*, 2, 752.

245. *H.F.*, 5, 34, *MG.*, 3, 1281–82.

246. "T.F.," 11. 82–84, *MG.*, 2, 747.

247. *P.*, chap. 8, *MG.*, 1, 38; chap. 18, ibid., pp. 66–67; chap. 21, ibid., p. 81; *D.*, 1, 11–12, ibid., pp. 223–228; 15, ibid., 234; 2, 2, ibid., 331; 3, 33, ibid., p. 503; *A.W.*, Preface, *MG.*, 2, 566–67; 4, ibid., p. 661; 6, ibid., p. 691; 7, ibid., p. 723.

248. *D.*, 2, 20, *MG.*, 1, 392; *A.W.*, 1, *MG.*, 2, 585–86; ibid., p. 622; letter to Vettori, 16 Apr. 1527, ibid., p. 1010 (*Lett. fam.*, 225); "Lingua," *Opp. MC.*, pp. 770–71.

249. *P.*, chap. 3, *MG.*, 1, 16–17; *D.*, 1, 33, ibid., pp. 265–66; 58, ibid., p. 317; 3, 1, ibid., p. 419; 49, ibid., pp. 527, 528; *H.F.*, 5, 8, *MG.*, 3, 1242.

250. *P.*, chap. 18, *MG.*, 1, 64–67; *D.*, 1, 11, ibid., p. 225; 25, ibid., p. 252; 2,

13, ibid., pp. 357–58; 3, 12, ibid. p. 461.

251. *P.*, chap. 18, ibid., pp. 64–67; chap. 19, ibid., p. 73; *D.*, 1, 11, ibid., p. 225; 2, 13, ibid., pp. 357–58; 3, 42, ibid., p. 520.

252. *P.*, chap. 6, ibid., pp. 25–26; 8, ibid., p. 36; *D.*, 1, 9, ibid., p. 219; 18, ibid., p. 243; 27, ibid., p. 255; 33, ibid., pp. 264–65; 55, ibid., p. 309; 3, 28, ibid., p. 493.

253. *P.*, chap. 14, ibid., pp. 56–57; 1, 10, ibid., p. 221; *A.W.*, Preface, *MG.*, 2, 566–67; 7, ibid., p. 726.

254. *P.*, chap. 16, *MG.*, 1, 60–61; *D.*, 2, 6, ibid., pp. 342–43; *H.F.*, 6, 1, *MG.*, 3, 1284.

255. *D.*, 1, 37, *MG.*, 1, 274; Anglo, op. cit., pp. 102–13.

256. *D.*, 1, 6, *MG.*, 1, 209.

257. *H.F.*, 3, 7, *MG.*, 3, 1149.

258. *D.*, 3, 24, *MG.*, *1, 485–86.*

259. *A.W.*, 1, *MG.*, 2, 578.

260. Ibid., pp. 573–74.

261. Ibid., p. 575.

262. Ibid., p. 577.

263. *D.*, 2, 19, *MG.*, 1, 381.

264. *D.*, 1, 18, *MG.*, 1, 242.

265. *H.F.*, 3, 1, *MG.*, 3, 1141.

266. Pocock, p. 88.

267. *A.W.*, 2, *MG.*, 2, 623.

268. *D.*, 2, 2, *MG.*, 1, 330–32; 19, ibid., p. 381.

269. 4, ibid., p. 339; 5, ibid., p. 341.

270. *H.F.*, 4, 14, *MG.*, 3, 1202.

271. *A.W.*, 5, *MG.*, 2, 671–72.

272. *P.*, chap. 17, *MG.*, 1, 63.

273. 19, ibid., pp. 67, 74; *D.*, 1, 28, ibid., pp. 405, 406; 3, 6, ibid., pp. 426, 429, 430, 438.

274. *D.*, 3, 42, ibid., p. 520.

275. *P.*, chap. 18, ibid., p. 65.

276. *H.F.*, 2, 14, *MG.*, 3, 1096.

277. 4, 14, ibid., p. 1202.

278. *D.*, 1, 3, *MG.*, 1, 201.

279. G. F. Young, *The Medici* (New York: Modern Library, 1930), p. 71.

280. Ridolfi, p. 2.

281. Ibid., pp. 2–3.

282. Ibid., p. 8.

283. Ibid., p. 9.

284. *D.*, 1, 12, *MG.*, 1, 228.

285. Letter to Guicciardini, 17 May 1521, *MG.*, 2, 972 *(Lett. fam.,* 179).

286. *Mandragola,* act 4, sc. 6, *MG.*, pp. 810–11; act 5, sc. 1, ibid., p. 815.

287. *H.F.*, 1, 9, *MG.*, 3, 1046.

288. 23, ibid., p. 1061.

289. 8, 17, ibid., pp. 1406–1407.

290. 2, 10, ibid., p. 1092.

291. 1, 25, ibid., p. 1063.

292. 23, ibid., p. 1062.

293. 8, 11, ibid., pp. 1398–99.

294. Letter to the Ten, 18 Aug. 1510 as quoted in Ridolfi, p. 116.

295. *D.*, 1, 27, *MG.*, 1, 254–55.

296. 3, 1, ibid., p. 422.

297. 1, Preface, ibid., p. 190.

298. "Amerigo Vespucci," *Encyclopaedia Britannica*, 15th ed.

299. Felix Gilbert, op. cit. p. 158, n.19.

300. *A.W.*, 4, *MG.*, 2, 662.

301. *D.*, 3, 6, *MG.*, 1, 430.

302. 24–25, ibid., pp. 485–86; 1, 18, ibid., p. 242; 2, 2, ibid, pp. 330–32; *H.F.*, 3, 1, *MG.*, 3, 1141.

303. Gal. 6:16; I Cor. 10:17–18; Col. chaps. 1 and 2.

304. Young, op. cit., p. 186.

305. Ibid., p. 196.

306. Orestes Ferrara, *Machiavel*, trans. Francis de Miomandre (Paris: Champion, 1928), p. 168.

307. *D.*, 2, 2, *MG.*, 1, 329; ed. n. *MG.*, 3, 1027–28.

308. "Remodeling," *MG.*, 1, 113–114; *A.W.*, 2, *MG.*, 2, 622; *D.*, 3, 28, *MG.*, 1, 492–93; *Mandragola*, act 2, sc. 3, *MG.*, 788–89.

309. *D.*, 2, Preface, *MG.*, 1, 322–23.

310. 1, 55, ibid., p. 307.

311. *H.F.*, 3, 5, *MG.*, 3, 1146.

312. 5, 1, ibid., p. 1233.

313. *P.*, chap. 26, *MG.*, 1, 93.

314. "T.A.," 11. 121–59, 178–86, *MG.*, 2, 738–39.

315. Carnival Songs, 3, "By the Blessed Spirits," 11. 1–27, *MG.*, 2, 880.

316. *P.*, chap. 26, *MG.*, 1, 94–95.

317. *A.W.*, 7, *MG.*, 2, 724–25.

318. *D.*, 1, 18, *MG.*, 1, 243; 9, ibid., p. 219; 32, ibid., p. 264; 33, ibid., pp. 264–65; 55, ibid., p. 309.

319. 55, ibid., p. 309.

320. "Remodeling," ibid., p. 107.

321. *H.F.*, 2, 34, *MG.*, 3, 1125.

322. "Remodeling," *MG.*, 1, 110.

323. Ibid., pp. 112–15.

324. *D.*, 1, 5, ibid., pp. 204–205; for the analysis with respect to a princedom, see 16, ibid., p. 237.

325. 3, 9, ibid., pp. 452–53.

326. 1, 20, ibid., p. 246.

327. 3, 34, ibid., p. 507.

328. 1, 4, ibid., p. 203.

329. 1, 49, ibid., p. 296.

330. 2, 7, ibid., p. 211.

331. 1, 4, ibid., p. 203.

332. 58, ibid., p. 316.

333. *A.W.*, 2, *MG.*, 2, 622; *H.F.*, 7, 33, *MG.*, 3, 1378.

334. *D.*, 1, 58, *MG.*, 1, 316–17.

335. 2, 2, ibid., p. 329.

336. 1, 16, ibid., p. 236.

337. 58, ibid., p. 318.

338. 3, 28, ibid., pp. 492–93; *A.W.*, 2, *MG.*, 2, 622.

339. "Lingua," *Opp. MC.*, pp. 770–71.

340. Tommasini, 2, 945.

341. William MacDougal, *The Group Mind,* Preface to Second Edition (New York: Putnam, 1928), p. iii.

342. John Dewey, *The Public and Its Problems* (New York:Henry Holt, 1927), p. 201.

CHAPTER FOUR

1. "L.C.," *MG.,* 2, 554.

2. Letter to Vettori, 10 Dec. 1513, *MG.,* 2, 929 (*Lett. fam.,* 137).

3. Letter to Vettori, 9 Apr. 1513, ibid., pp. 900–901 (*Lett. fam.,* 120).

4. Draft of letter to Soderini, *MG.,* 2, 895–97 (*Lett. fam.,* 116); letter to Vettori, 29 Apr. 1513, ibid., pp. 905–906 (*Lett. fam.,* 128); letter to Vettori, 20 Dec. 1514 (*No. 2*), ibid., p. 958 (*Lett. fam.,* 155); *P.,* chap. 15, *MG.,* 1, 57; *D.,* 1, 18, ibid., p. 240; 58, ibid., pp. 313–14.

5. *D.,* 1, 1, *MG.,* 1, 194.

6. "Ghiribizzi," *Opp. MC.,* p. 879.

7. Letter to Vettori, 20 June 1513, *MG.,* 2, 911 (*Lett. fam.,* 124).

8. Letter to Guicciardini, 30 Aug. 1524, ibid., p. 978 (*Lett. fam.,* 186).

9. Letter to Vettori, 10 Dec. 1513, ibid., p. 929 (*Lett. fam.,* 137).

10. Draft of letter to Soderini, *MG.,* 2, 895 (*Lett. fam.,* 116).

11. Ridolfi, pp. 163–64.

12. *P.,* Dedication, *MG.,* 1, 10.

13. Letter to Vettori, 10 Dec. 1513, *MG.,* 2, 930 (*Lett. fam.,* 137).

14. *D.,* Dedication, *MG.,* 1, 188–89.

15. 1, Preface, ibid., p. 190.

16. *A.W.,* Preface, *MG.,* 2, 567.

17. Ibid.

18. *P.,* chap. 6, *MG.,* 1, 26.

19. Chap. 23. ibid., pp. 87–88.

20. Chap. 17, ibid., p. 64; *A.W.,* 1, *MG.,* 2, 587.

21. Chap. 24, *MG.,* 1, 89.

22. *D.,* 2, 10, ibid., pp. 350–51.

23. 3, 10, ibid., p. 456.

24. *A.W.,* 1, *MG.,* 2, 584.

25. Ibid., p. 587.

26. 4, ibid., p. 657; *H.F.,* 6, 13, *MG.,* 3, 1299.

27. Letter to Vettori, 10 June 1514, *MG.,* 2, 945, (*Lett. fam.,* 148).

28. *D.,* 1, preface, *MG.,* 1, 190.

29. 2, Preface, ibid., p. 324.

30. *P.,* chap. 25, ibid., p. 92; "T.F.," 11. 73–75, *MG.,* 2, 746.

31. *A.W.,* 3, *MG.,* 2, 626.

32. 1, ibid., p. 573.

33. 7, ibid., p. 726.

34. *H.F.,* Preface, *MG.,* 3, 1031.

35. Letter to his son, Guido, 2 Apr. 1527, *MG.,* 2, 1006 (*Lett. fam.,* 222).

36. *D.,* 3, 46, *MG.,* 1, 525.

37. Letter to Vettori, 5 Apr. 1527, *MG.,* 2, 1008.

38. *D.,* 2, 29, *MG.,* 1, 408.

39. 15, ibid., pp. 359–60.

40. *P.*, chap. 25, ibid., p. 90.

41. *A.W.*, 4, *MG.*, 2, 656.

42. *D.*, 1, 32, *MG.*, 1, 263.

43. 51, ibid., p. 299.

44. Legation 11.40, 8 Nov. 1502 (*second letter*), quoting from a conversation with a friend, ibid., p. 132.

45. *D.*, 1, Preface, ibid., p. 190.

46. 18, ibid., p. 240.

47. *H.F.*, 4, 7, *MG.*, 3, 1194; 6, 13, ibid., p. 1299; letter to Vettori, 18 Mar. 1512–(1513), *MG.*, 2, 899 (*Lett. fam.*, 119); 4 Feb. 1513–(1514), ibid., p. 937 (*Lett. fam.*, 142); *P.*, chap. 25, *MG.*, 1, 90, 92.

48. Draft of letter to Soderini, *MG.*, 2, 896; Legation to Julius II, Letter to the Ten, 28 Sept. 1506, Pansini, p. 1084; *D.*, 1, 18, *MG.*, 1, 240; letter to Vettori, 20 Dec. 1514, *MG.*, 2, 958 (*Lett. fam.*, 155).

49. *P.*, chap. 15, *MG.*, 1, 57.

50. Carnival Songs, 3, "By the Blessed Spirits," 1. 45, *MG.*, 2, 880.

51. Plato, *The Republic*, trans. Benjamin Jowett (New York: Colonial Press, 1901), 2, 52.

52. "*G.A.*," chap. 7, 11. 106–32 through chap. 8, 1. 151, *MG.*, 2, 769–72.

CHAPTER FIVE

1. Letter to Vettori, 16 Apr. 1527, *MG.*, 2, 1010 (*Lett. fam.*, 225); "Lingua," *Opp. MC.*, pp. 770–71.

2. Schevill, op. cit., pp. 218–19.

3. Nicolai Rubinstein, *Florentine Studies, Politics and Society in Renaissance Florence* (Evanston, Illinois: Northwestern University Press, 1968), p. 451.

4. Ibid., pp. 420–21.

5. Ibid., p. 450.

6. Schevill, op. cit., p. 274.

7. Rubinstein, op. cit., p. 374.

8. Felix Gilbert, op. cit., p. 220.

9. Rubinstein, op. cit., p. 450.

10. *D.*, 3, 43, *MG.*, 1, 521, 522; "Clizia," Prolog, 2, 823; Leo Strauss *Thoughts on Machiavelli* (Seattle: University of Washington Press, 1969), pp. 80–81.

11. *D.*, 2, 4, ibid., pp. 335–37.

12. 3, ibid., p. 328.

13. 3, 43, ibid., p. 522.

14. 2, 5, ibid., p. 341.

15. 1, 55, ibid., p. 309; *P.*, chap. 26, ibid., p. 93.

16. *D.*, 2, 4, ibid., p. 339.

17. *A.W.*, 2, *MG.*, 2, 623; *D.*, 2, 2, *MG.*, 1, 332.

18. Strauss, op. cit., p. 81.

19. Ridolfi, p. 2.

20. *H.F.*, 3, 1, *MG.*, 3, 1140–41.

21. *D.*, 1, 9, *MG.*, 1, 218–19; 19, ibid., pp. 244–45.

22. 49, ibid., p. 296.

23. Rubinstein, "Florentine Constitutionalism and Medici Ascendancy in the Fifteenth Century," op. cit., pp. 454–58.

24. Ridolfi, p. 2; Rubinstein, op. cit., p. 456.

25. Donald Weinstein, "The Myth of Florence," in Rubinstein, op. cit., pp. 43–44.

26. Felix Gilbert, op. cit., p. 254.

27. Ridolfi, pp. 1–2; Tommasini, 1, 78–80; Charles Benoist, *Le Machiavelisme, II, MAchiavel* (Paris: Plon, 1934), pp. 1–4.

28. *H.F.,* 2, 14, *MG.,* 3, 1096.

29. Ibid., p. 1097.

30. 1, ibid., pp. 1140–41.

31. Tommasini, 1, 286.

32. Ridolfi, pp. 1–2.

33. Ibid., p. 2.

34. Tommasini, 1, 479–84; Ridolfi, pp. 112–13.

35. Ridolfi, pp. 34–35.

36. Ibid., p. 2.

37. Ibid., p. 258 n. 9.

38. Ibid., p. 34.

39. Ibid.

40. Ibid., p. 42.

41. Ibid., p. 46.

42. Ibid., pp. 74–75, 238, 268 n. 10, 274–75 n. 40; Tommasini, 1, 217 nn. 4, 6.

43. Tommasini, 1, 219.

44. Ibid., p. 208 and n. 5.

45. Letters to Giovanni Vernacci: 18 Aug. 1515, *MG.,* 2, 963 *(Lett. fam.,* 160); 19 Nov. 1515, ibid., pp. 963–4 *(Lett. fam.,* 161); 15 Feb. 1515–(1516), ibid., p. 964; *(Lett. fam.,* 162); 10 Oct. 1516, ibid., p. 965 *(Lett. fam.,* 163); 8 June 1517, ibid., pp. 965–66 *(Lett. fam.,* 164).

46. Letter to Vettori, 10 Dec. 1513, *MG.,* 2, 927–29 *(Lett. fam.,* 137).

47. Ferrara, op. cit., pp. 44–45; Ridolfi, p. 2.

48. Tommasini, 1, 100; Ridolfi, p. 16.

49. Ridolfi, p. 2.

50. Ibid., n. 4.

51. Ibid., p. 2.

52. Ibid., p. 113; Tommasini, 1, 216.

53. Ibid., p. 2.

54. Letter to Vettori, 16 Apr. 1514, *MG.,* 2, 943 *(Lett. fam.,* 145).

55. Letter to Vettori, 10 June 1514, ibid., p. 945 *(Lett. fam.,* 148).

56. Tommasini, 1, 556.

57. Ibid., p. 217.

58. Letter to Vettori, 18 Mar. 1512–(1513), *MG.,* 2, 899 *(Lett. fam.,* 119).

59. Ridolfi, p. 2; Benoist, op. cit., p. 3; L. Gautier Vignal, *Machiavel* (Paris: Payot, 1929), p. 16.

60. Tommasini, 1, 477–84; Ridolfi, pp. 2 n. 4, 112–13.

61. Ferrara, op. cit., p. 47.

62. Ibid., p. 46.

63. Vignal, op. cit., p. 72; Ridolfi, pp. 36–37, 39.

64. Ridolfi, p. 59; letter to the Ten, 10 Dec. 1502; Pansini, p. 982; 14 Dec. 1502, ibid., p. 984; 23 Dec. 1502, ibid., p. 987 [date given in *MG.,* 1, 141].

65. Letter to the Ten, 22 Nov. 1503, ibid., p. 1037; 25 Nov., 1503, ibid., p. 1042.

66. Letter to the Ten, 22 Nov. 1506, Pansini, p. 1087.

67. Letter to the Ten, 18 Aug. 1510, Ridolfi, p. 117.

68. *D.*, 3, 25, *MG.*, 1, 486; 3, 16, ibid., p. 469; "Portraits of the Affairs of Germany," Pansini, p. 649; "Ritratto delle Cose della Magna," *Opp. MC.*, p. 740.

69. *D.*, 1, 37, ibid., p. 272; 2, 19, ibid., p. 378.

70. 3, 25, ibid., p. 488.

71. *A.W.*, 1, *MG.*, 2, 571–72.

72. Letter to Vettori, 10 Dec. 1513, ibid., p. 930 *(Lett. fam.,* 137).

73. Letter to Vettori, 18 Mar. 1512–(1513), ibid., p. 899 *(Lett. fam.,* 119); 10 June 1514, *MG.*, 2, 945 *(Lett. fam.,* 148); 4 Dec. 1514, *MG.*, 2, 947 *(Lett. fam.,* 152).

74. Letter to Giovanni Vernacci, 15 Feb. 1515–(1516), ibid., p. 964 *(Lett. fam.,* 162); 8 June 1517, *MG.*, 2, 966 *(Lett. fam.,* 164); 25 Jan. 1517–(1518), *MG.*, 2, 969 *(Lett. fam.,* 168).

75. *D.*, 3, 25, *MG.*, 1, 487–88.

76. 2, Preface, ibid., p. 323; 1, 37, ibid., p. 272; "T.A.," 11. 12–66, *MG.*, 2, 735–36.

77. *D.*, 1, 3, *MG.*, 1, 201.

78. Ridolfi, p. 3; Tommasini, 1, 78; 2, 730.

79. Letter to Guido Machiavelli, 2, Apr. 1527, *MG.*, 2, 1006–1007 *(Lett. fam.,* 222).

80. Letter to Giovanni Vernacci, 15 Feb. 1515–(1516), ibid., p. 964 *(Lett. fam.,* 162); 8 June 1517, *MG.*, 2, 966 *(Lett. fam.,* 164); 5 Jan. 1517–(1518), *MG.*, 2, 968 *(Lett. fam.,* 167); 15 Apr. 1520, *MG.*, 2, 970 *(Lett. fam.,* 169).

81. Letter to Lodovico Alamanni, 17 Dec. 1517, ibid., p. 967 *(Lett. fam.,* 166).

82. *D.*, 3, 1, *MG.*, 1, 422.

83. Letter to Guicciardini, 17 May 1521, *MG.*, 2, 972 *(Lett. fam.,* 179).

84. "An Exhortation to Penitence," *MG.*, 1, 170–74.

85. Ridolfi, p. 253.

86. Ibid., p. 250, and quoting the letter from Piero Machiavelli, Niccolo's son, to his maternal uncle, Francesco Nelli, ibid., p. 330 n. 25.

87. *D.*, 3, 30, *MG.*, 1, 496.

88. Tommasini, 2, 659n.

89. *Opp. MC.*, pp. 770–78.

90. Tommasini, 2, 683, n.8.

91. *D.*, 3, 1, *MG.*, 1, 419.

92. Tommasini, 2, 634 n.3.

93. *D.*, 1, 9, *MG.*, 1, 217–20; 18, ibid., pp. 242–43; 3, 1, ibid., pp. 420–21.

94. Tommasini, 2, 646 and n.3.

95. *P.*, chap. 6, *MG.*, 1, 26.

96. Tommasini, 2, 622.

97. J. H. Plumb, *The Horizon Book of the Renaissance* (New York: American Heritage Publishing Co., 1961), p. 243.

98. Ibid., p. 214.

99. *The Columbia History of the World,* eds. John A. Garraty and Peter Gay (New York: Harper & Row, 1972), p. 510.

100. Tommasini, 2, 655 and n.6.

101. John Knox, "Exegesis," on Rom. 1:16, *I.B.*, 9, 391.

102. Tommasini, 2, 287–88.

103. Kemmerich, op. cit., p. 11.

104. *Mandragola,* act 3, sc. 2, *MG.*, 2, 794–95; Tommasini, 2, 398–99, 676 n.2, 677–78 and n.5; letter to Bartolomeo (Cavalcanti?), Nov. 1526, *MG.*, 2, 1004 *(Lett. fam.,* 219B).

105. *P.*, chap. 15, *MG.*, 1, 57.

106. Tommasini, 2, 694.

107. Draft of Letter (to Ricciardo Bechi) 9 Mar. 1497–(1498), *MG.*, 2, 887 *(Lett. fam.*, 3).

108. *D.*, 1, 11–15, *MG.*, 1, 223–34.

109. *P.*, chap. 18, ibid., p. 66.

110. *D.*, 1, 45, ibid., p. 288.

111. Draft of letter (to Riciardo Bechi) 9 Mar. 1497–(1498), *MG.*, 2, 889.

112. *D.*, 1, 45, *MG.*, 1, 288–89.

113. *P.*, chap. 6, ibid., p. 27.

114. *D.*, 1, 12, ibid., pp. 226–27.

115. *P.*, chap. 15, *Opp. MC.*, p. 30.

116. *P.*, chap. 15, *MG.*, 1, 57.

117. *A.W.*, 1, *MG.*, 2, 572.

118. *P.*, chap. 6, *MG.*, 1, 27; Pocock, pp. 193–94.

119. *D.*, 1, 11, ibid., pp. 224–25; 2, 2, ibid., p. 331.

120. Carnival Songs, 3, "By the Blessed Spirits," 1. 45, *MG.*, 2, 880.

121. Letter to Guicciardini, 17 May 1521, ibid., p. 972.

122. *D.*, 2, 2, *MG.*, 1, 331; 3, 1, ibid., p. 422; *A.W.*, 2, *MG.*, 2, 623.

123. Legation to the Court of Rome, letter to the Ten, 20 Nov. 1503, Pansini, p. 1032.

124. *D.*, 1, 12, *MG.*, 1, 228.

125. Ibid.

126. "Lingua," *Opp. MC.*, pp. 770–71.

127. *D.*, 3, 41, *MG.*, 1, 519.

128. 47, ibid., p. 526.

129. Letter to Vettori, 10 Apr. 1527, *MG.*, 2, 1010 *(Lett. fam.*, 225).

130. *D.*, 2, 2, *MG.*, 1,331.

131. Ibid.

132. "An Exhortation to Penitence," ibid., pp. 171, 174.

133. Ibid., p. 173; *D.*, 1, 12, ibid., p. 228; 3, 1, ibid., p. 422.

134. "An Exhortation To Penitence," ibid., pp. 173, 174.

135. *D.*, 3, 1, ibid., p. 422; letter to Guicciardini, 17 May 1521, *MG.*, 2, 972 *(Lett. fam.*, 179).

136. *D.*, 2, 2, *MG.*, 1, 331.

137. 1, 12, ibid., p. 228.

138. 2, 2, ibid., p. 331.

139. 3, 30, ibid., p. 496.

140. 1, Preface, ibid., p. 191; 2, 2, ibid., p. 331; 3, 1, ibid., p. 422; *A.W.*, 2, *MG.*, 2, 623.

141. Friedrich Meinecke, *Machiavellism, the Doctrine of Raison d'Etat and its Place in Modern History,* trans. Douglas Scott (New Haven: Yale University Press, 1957), p. 40.

142. Ibid., p. 31.

143. Ibid., p. 29.

144. Strauss, op. cit., p. 41.

145. Ibid., p. 49.

146. Ibid., p. 51.

147. Guiseppe Prezzolini, *Niccolo Machiavelli, the Florentine,* trans. Ralph Roeder (New York: Brentano's, 1928), p. 167.

148. Prezzolini, *Machiavelli,* trans. Gioconda Savini of *Machiavelli anticristo* (Rome, 1954) (New York: Farrar, Straus & Giroux, 1967) author's n., p. i.

149. Prezzolini, "The Christian Roots of Machiavelli's Moral Pessimism," *Review of National Literatures,* 1, no. 1 (Spring, 1970), p. 27.

150. Ibid., p. 29.

151. Ibid., p. 37.

152. Prezzolini, *Machiavelli, the Florentine,* p. 177.

153. Kemmerich, op. cit., p. 182.

154. Mansfield, "Party and Sect in Florentine History," in *Machiavelli . . . Thought,* p. 238.

155. Ibid., p. 240.

156. Ibid., p. 241–42.

157. Ibid., pp. 244–45.

158. Ibid., pp. 257–58.

159. *D.,* 1, 12, *MG.,* 1, 228; 3, 1, ibid., p. 422.

160. Matt. 4:8–10, 20:25–28; Mark 9:35, 10:42–45.

161. *Novissima Encyclopedia Monografica Illustrata,* s.v. "Machiavelli," Alfredo Oxilia (Firenzi: "NEMI," 1932), p. 32.

162. Draft of letter to Bechi, 9 Mar. 1497–(1498), *MG.,* 2, 888 *(Lett. fam.,* 3).

163. Ferrara, op. cit., pp. 55, 168, 244.

164. Pocock, pp. 117–18.

165. "Remodeling," *MG.,* 1, 110.

166. Whitfield, op. cit., pp. 89–91, 107–108; *Machiavelli* (New York: Russell and Russell, 1965), pp. 87–91.

167. *P.,* chap. 12, *MG.,* 1, 48.

168. Chap. 6, ibid., p. 27.

169. *D.,* 3, 30, ibid., p. 497.

170. "F.D.," 11. 154–65, *MG.,* 3, 1448.

171. *D.,* 1, 11, *MG.,* 1, 226.

172. 45, ibid., pp. 288–89.

173. Letter to Guicciardini, 17 May 1521, *MG.,* 2, 972 *(Lett. fam.,* 179).

174. Tommasini, 1, 399.

175. Ferrara, op. cit., p. 150.

176. Ibid., p. 57.

177. Vignal, op. cit., pp. 10, 58.

178. Tommasini, 1, 452.

179. "Advice to Raffaello Girolami When He Went as Ambassador to the Emperor," *MG.,* 1, 116–19.

180. Ferrara, op. cit., p. 86. Probably the letter referred to by Ridolfi, p. 56 n.9, dated 11 Oct. 1502; Tommasini, 1, 263.

181. Ibid., p. 116.

182. Ridolfi, p. 92.

183. Letter to the Ten, 12 Jan. 1502, Pansini, p. 999.

184. Ridolfi, p. 49.

185. Ibid., p. 66.

186. Ibid., pp. 72–73.

187. Schevill, op. cit., p. 462.

188. Legation 11.44, 13 Nov. 1502, *MG.,* 1, 133.

189. 27, 27 Oct. 1502, ibid., p. 128.

190. 36, 3 Nov. 1502, ibid., p. 129.

191. 82, 26 Dec. 1502, ibid., p. 142.

192. "Letter V," 3 Nov. 1502, Pansini, p. 964.

193. "Letter VII," 8 Nov. 1502, ibid., p. 967.

194. Legation 11.44, 13 Nov. 1502, *MG.,* 1, 133–34; Ridolfi, p. 55.

195. 53, 26 Nov. 1502, *MG.,* 1, 137.

196. 82, 26 Dec. 1502, ibid., p. 142; Ridolfi, p. 62.

197. Legation 11.13, 15 Oct. 1502, *MG.,* 1, 126.

198. Ridolfi, pp. 38–39.

199. Ibid., p. 102.

200. Ibid., p. 105.

201. Ibid., p. 116.

202. Ibid., p. 125.

203. *P.,* chap. 3, *MG.,* 1, 17.

204. Ridolfi, p. 127.

205. *Postilla ms. de'Frammenti storici,* as quoted by Tommasini, 1, 523.

206. *D.,* 2, 10, *MG.,* 1, 349–51.

207. *A.W.,* 7, *MG.,* 2, 719–20.

208. *D.,* 2, 30, *MG.,* 1, 409–12.

209. "Ghiribizzi," *Opp. MC.,* p. 879.

210. *D.,* 1, 1, *MG.,* 1, 194.

211. 2, 27, ibid., p. 404.

212. *P.,* chap. 17, ibid., p. 64; chap. 24, ibid., p. 89.

213. Letter to Vettori, 25 Feb. 1513–(1514), *MG.,* 2, 941 *(Lett. fam.,* 144).

214. *A.W.,* 2, *MG.,* 622; "Remodeling," *MG.,* 1, 113–14; *D.,* 3, 28, ibid., pp. 492–93; *Mandragola,* act 2, sc. 3, *MG.,* 2, 788–89.

215. *A.W.,* 2, *MG.,* 2, 622.

216. "Advice to Girolami," *MG.,* 1, 116.

217. *D.,* 1,1, ibid., p. 194.

218. 18, ibid., p. 240; 58, ibid., pp. 313–14.

219. Letter to Vettori, 20 Dec. 1514 *(No. 2), MG.,* 2, 958 *(Lett. fam.,* 155); 29 Apr. 1513, ibid., pp. 905–906 *(Lett. fam.,* 128).

220. *P.,* chap. 15, *MG.,* 1, 57.

221. *D.,* 2, Preface, ibid., p. 324; 1, Preface, ibid., pp. 190–92; *A.W.,* 7, *MG.,* 2, 726.

222. *H.F.,* Dedication, *MG.,* 3, 1030.

223. *P.,* chap. 11, *MG.,* 1, 45.

224. Chap. 12, ibid., p. 50.

225. *D.,* 1, 12, ibid., p. 228.

226. *H.F.,* 8, 17, *MG.,* 3, 1406–1407.

227. 1, 9, ibid., p. 1046; 2, 10, ibid., p. 1092.

228. 1, 23, ibid., p. 1062; 25, ibid., p. 1063; 8, 10–11, ibid., 1395–98.

229. *A.W.,* 7, *MG.,* 2, 724–25.

230. Legation 11.44, 13 Nov. 1502, *MG.,* 1, 133–34.

231. "F.D.," 11. 535–50, *MG.,* 3, 1457.

232. Tommasini, 1, 312.

233. Ibid., p. 354.

234. "A Provision for Infantry," Preamble, *MG.,* 1, 3.

235. Ridolfi, p. 96; Tommasini, 1, 367 and n.3.

236. *Opp. P.,* vol. v, p. 398, as quoted in Ridolfi, p. 107.

237. Ridolfi, p. 107.

238. Schevill, op. cit., p. 469.

239. *A.W.,* 1, *MG.,* 2, 585.

240. *P.,* chap. 12, *MG.,* 1, 47.

241. 13, ibid., p. 52.

242. Ibid., p. 54; pp. 54–55; 7, ibid., p. 33.

243. *D.,* 3, 33, ibid., p. 502.

244. 31, ibid., p. 500.

245. 1, 43, ibid., p. 286.

246. *A.W.*, 4, *MG.*, 2, 662; 1, ibid., pp. 585–86.

247. 1, ibid., p. 581.

248. Ibid., pp. 591–92.

249. Ibid., Preface, p. 566.

250. Ibid., pp. 584–85.

251. Ibid., pp. 583–84, 584, 587.

252. 2, ibid., p. 619.

253. 7, ibid., p. 722.

254. *H.F.*, 1, 5–6, *MG.*, 3, 1085–87.

255. 2, 26, ibid., pp. 1111–12.

256. 5, 9, ibid., pp. 1244–45.

257. Ferrara, op. cit., p. 123.

258. Ibid., p. 351; Ridolfi, p. 89.

259. Ridolfi, p. 80.

260. Ibid., p. 109.

261. Tommasini, 1, 438–39.

262. Ferrara, op. cit., pp. 244, 55, 168.

263. Mattingly, op. cit., pp. 61–62.

264. Letter to Vettori, 10 Dec. 1513, *MG.*, 2, 930.

265. *H.F.*, 1, 25, *MG.*, 3, 1063.

266. Ridolfi, p. 185.

267. *H.F.*, Dedication, *MG.*, 3, 1029.

268. Ridolfi, p. 18; Tommasini, 1, 93.

269. Ridolfi, p. 19.

270. Ibid., pp. 47–50.

271. Ibid., pp. 53–54.

272. Tommasini, 1, 222.

273. Schevill, op. cit., p. 461.

274. Ibid., p. 464.

275. Tommasini, 1, 227.

276. Ibid., p. 223.

277. "On the Method of Dealing with the Rebellious Peoples of the Valdichiana," *MG.*, 1, 162.

278. Ibid., p. 162.

279. Tommasini, 1, 238.

280. Ridolfi, p. 66.

281. Ibid., p. 75; Legation 13. "Letter XIII," 16 Nov. 1503, Pansini, p. 1024; 56, "Letter XXI," 23 Nov. 1503, ibid., p. 1039; 57, "Letter XXII," 24 Nov. 1503, ibid., p. 1040.

282. Ridolfi, p. 75 n.41.

283. Ibid., p. 75.

284. Ibid., pp. 75, 80–81; *P.*, chap. 7, *MG.*, 1, 33.

285. Ibid., p. 81.

286. Ibid., p. 82.

287. "F.D.," 11. 541–49, *MG.*, 3, 1457.

288. Ridolfi, p. 82.

289. Ibid., pp. 86–87.

290. Ibid., p. 87.

291. Ibid., p. 88.
292. Ibid., p. 96.
293. Ibid., p. 97.
294. Letter to Vettori, 16 Apr. 1513, *MG., 2, 902 (Lett. fam.,* 122); Ridolfi, pp. 143, 157.
295. Ridolfi, p. 203.
296. Ibid., pp. 42, 60; Ferrara, op. cit., p. 62.
297. Ridolfi, p. 46.
298. Tommasini, 1, 113–14.
299. "Articles for a Pleasure Company," *MG., 2,* 865–68.
300. Tommasini, 1, 172.
301. Ridolfi, p. 72.
302. Ibid., p. 60.
303. Ibid., pp. 42, 59, 112–13.
304. Ibid., p. 59.
305. Ibid., pp. 59, 75, 117.
306. Ibid., p. 39.
307. Ibid., p. 86.
308. Ibid., pp. 57–58.
309. Ibid., p. 56.
310. Ibid., p. 132.
311. Ibid., pp. 74–75.
312. Ibid., pp. 48–50.
313. Tommasini, 1, 215–16.
314. Ferrara, op. cit., p. 86; Ridolfi, p. 56.
315. Ridolfi, p. 56; Tommasini, 1, 263.
316. Ridolfi, p. 78.
317. Ibid., pp. 77–78.
318. Tommasini, 1, 305.
319. Ridolfi, p. 84.
320. Tommasini, 2, 67–68; Ridolfi, pp. 135–36.
321. Ridolfi, p. 138.
322. Tommasini, 2, 70–71.
323. Ridolfi, p. 101.
324. Ferrara, op. cit., pp. 127–28.
325. Vignal, op. cit., p. 134.
326. Ridolfi, pp. 99–100.
327. Ibid., p. 101.
328. Tommasini, 1, 410.
329. Ibid., p. 410.
330. Ridolfi, pp. 103–104.
331. Ibid., p. 104.
332. Ibid., p. 105.
333. Ibid., p. 117.
334. Letter of 3 Aug. 1510, in *Lett. fam.,* p. 200 ff. as quoted by Ridolfi, p. 117.
335. Ridolfi, p. 129; Ferrara, op. cit., pp. 167–68.
336. Letter to Vettori, 13 Mar. 1512–(1513), *MG., 2,* 898, *(Lett. fam.,* 117).
337. 18 Mar. 1512–(1513), ibid., pp. 898–99 *(Lett. fam.,* 119).
338. Ibid., p. 899.
339. Ridolfi, pp. 139–40.

340. Letter to Vettori, 9 Apr. 1513, *MG.*, 2, 900–901 *(Lett. fam.,* 120).

341. 16 Apr. 1513, ibid. pp. 901–903 *(Lett. fam.,* 122).

342. 29 Apr. 1513, ibid., pp. 903–910 *(Lett. fam.,* 128).

343. Ridolfi, pp. 161, 163.

344. Ibid., p. 161.

345. Tommasini, 2, 78.

346. Letter to Vettori, 10 Dec. 1513, *MG.*, 2, 929 *(Lett. fam.,* 137).

347. 31 Jan. 1514–(1515), ibid., pp. 962–63 *(Lett. fam.,* 159).

348. Quoted from Guasti, *I Manoscritti Torrigiani* . . . , Florence, 1878, p. 67 by Ridolfi, p. 162; Tommasini, 2, 105, n.3.

349. Ridolfi, p. 163.

350. Ibid., p. 298 n.30.

351. Ibid., p. 163.

352. Ibid., p. 164.

353. Ibid., p. 163.

354. Letter to Vettori, Aug. 1513, *MG.*, 2, 926–27 *(Lett. fam.,* 135).

355. Tommasini, 2, 103–104.

356. Ridolfi, p. 164.

357. Ibid.

358. Ridolfi, p. 139.

359. Letter to Vettori, 18 Mar. 1512–(1513), *MG.*, 2, 900 *(Lett. fam.,* 119).

360. 16 Apr. 1514, ibid., p. 941 *(Lett. fam.,* 145).

361. 31 Jan. 1514–(1515), ibid., pp. 960–63 *(Lett. fam.,* 159).

362. Ibid., pp. 961–62.

363. Ibid., pp. 362–63.

364. Ferrara, op. cit., pp. 187–88.

365. Ridolfi, p. 169.

366. Letter to Vettori, 10 Dec. 1513, *MG.*, 2, 929 *(Lett. fam.,* 137).

367. 5 Apr. 1527, ibid., pp. 1007–1008 *(Lett. fam.,* 223); 14 Apr. 1527, ibid., p. 1009 *(Lett. fam.,* 224); 16 Apr. 1527, ibid., p. 1010 *(Lett. fam.,* 225); 18 Apr. 1527, ibid., p. 1011 *(Lett. fam.,* 227); Ridolfi, pp. 240–41.

368. Anglo, op. cit., p. 87; Ridolfi, pp. 168–70; Ferrara, op. cit., pp. 287–90; Vignal, op. cit., pp. 226–27; Tommasini, 2, 90.

369. Anglo, op. cit., p. 87.

370. Tommasini, 2, 90.

371. Ibid., 1, 300.

372. Ridolfi, p. 121.

373. Tommasini, 1, 528; Ridolfi, p. 121.

374. Tommasini, 1, 528.

375. Ibid., p. 531.

376. Ridolfi, p. 168.

377. Ibid., p. 300 n.10.

378. Ibid., pp. 202–203, 247.

379. Ibid., p. 170.

380. Ibid., *D.,* Dedication, *MG.,* 1, 188–89.

381. Ridolfi, p. 180.

382. Ibid., p. 176.

383. Ibid., p. 177.

384. Felix Gilbert, op. cit., p. 112.

385. Ridolfi, p. 178.

386. Ibid., p. 179.
387. Ibid., p. 181; Tommasini, 2, 253.
388. Tommasini, 2, 429, 435.
389. Ridolfi, pp. 180–81.
390. Ibid., p. 182.
391. Ibid.
392. Ibid., p. 198; Tommasini, 2, 214 and n.1.
393. Ridolfi, p. 200.
394. Ibid., p. 201.
395. Ibid.
396. Ibid., p. 202.
397. Ibid., pp. 202–203.
398. Ibid., p. 203.
399. Ibid.
400. Ibid., p. 246.
401. Ibid., p. 247.
402. Ibid., p. 248.
403. Ibid., p. 250.
404. Tommasini, 1, 560; Ridolfi, p. 127.
405. Ridolfi, p. 187.
406. Letter to Vettori, 10 Dec. 1513, *MG.*, 2, 930.
407. Ridolfi, pp. 187, 189.
408. Ibid., p. 189.
409. Ibid.
410. Ibid., pp. 189–92.
411. Ibid., p. 200.
412. Tommasini, 1, 248–49.
413. Ibid., p. 385; Ridolfi, p. 208.
414. Ridolfi, p. 225.
415. Letter to Guicciardini, 30 Aug. 1524, *MG.*, 2, 978 *(Lett. fam.,* 186).
416. Ridolfi, pp. 208–10.
417. Ibid., pp. 210–11.
418. Ibid., p. 212.
419. Ibid., pp. 212–13.
420. Ibid., p. 213.
421. Orestes Ferrara, *The Private Correspondence of Niccolo Machiavelli* (Baltimore: Johns Hopkins Press, 1929), p. 42.
422. Ridolfi, p. 213.
423. Ibid., p. 214.
424. Ibid., p. 213.
425. Ibid., p. 215.
426. Ibid.
427. Ibid.
428. Ibid., pp. 215–16; letter to Guicciardini, 3 Aug. 1525, *MG.*, 2, 978–80 *(Lett. fam.,* 192).
429. Letter to Guicciardini, 2 June 1526 *(third letter), MG.*, 2, 1000 *(Lett. fam.,* 211).
430. 17 Aug. 1525, ibid., pp. 981–82 *(Lett. fam.,* 196); (after 21 Oct. 1525), ibid., pp. 984–87 *(Lett. fam.,* 199); 19 Dec. 1525, ibid., pp. 988–89 *(Lett. fam.,* 200).
431. 17 Aug. 1525, ibid., p. 981; (Sept. 1525), ibid., pp. 983–84 *(Lett. fam.,* 198); 3 Jan. 1525–(1526), ibid., p. 990 *(Lett. fam.,* 202).

432. Ridolfi, p. 216; Tommasini, 2, 793.
433. Letter to Guicciardini, 19 Dec. 1525, *MG.*, 2, 989 *(Lett. fam.,* 200).
434. Tommasini, 2, 842; Ridolfi, p. 222.
435. Ridolfi, pp. 224 25.
436. Tommasini, 2, 785.
437. Ibid., p. 248.
438. Ridolfi, p. 226; Tommasini, 2, 868.
439. Letter to Guicciardini, 15 Mar. 1525–(1526), *MG.*, 2, 994–95 *(Lett. fam.,* 204);* Ridolfi, p. 226.
440. Tommasini, 2, 848.
441. Ridolfi, p. 227.
442. Ibid.
443. Ibid., p. 229; Tommasini, 2, 854, 856.
444. Ridolfi, pp. 233, 324 n.4.
445. Ibid., pp. 234–35; Tommasini, 2, 866.
446. Ridolfi, p. 235.
447. Ibid.; Tommasini, 2, 873.
448. Tommasini, 2, 887; Ridolfi, p. 243.
449. Ridolfi, pp. 229, 233.
450. Tommasini, 2, 894.
451. Ridolfi, p. 231.
452. Letter to Vettori, 16 Apr. 1527, *MG.*, 2, 1010.
453. Ridolfi, p. 246.
454. Ibid., p. 247.
455. Ibid., p. 250.
456. Ibid., pp. 227, 238; Tommasini, 2, 848.
457. Ridolfi, p. 239.
458. Letter to Guido, 2 Apr. 1527, *MG.*, 2, 1006 *(Lett. fam.,* 222).
459. Ridolfi, p. 237.
460. Schevill, op. cit., pp. 376–77.
461. Ibid., pp. 377–78.
462. Ibid., pp. 385–87.
463. Ibid., p. 388.
464. Ibid., p. 389.
465. Ibid., pp. 351–52, 395–96.
466. *H.F.*, 2, 21, *MG.*, 3, 1104; Tommasini, 2, 514.
467. Schevill, op. cit., p. 276.
468. Ibid., pp. 344–45.
469. Ibid., pp. 404–405; Tommasini, 1, 90; 2, 546; Young, op. cit., p. 194.
470. Tommasini, 1, 90.
471. Vignal, op. cit., p. 173.
472. Schevill, op. cit., p. 406.
473. Ibid., p. 453.
474. Ridolfi, pp. 15, 19–20.
475. Ibid., pp. 131, 177.
476. Ibid., p. 129.
477. Letter "To an unidentified lady" (Sept. 1512), *MG.*, 2, 890–95 *(Lett. fam.,* 115);* Ridolfi, pp. 131, 289 n.29.
478. Ridolfi, p. 131.
479. Ibid., p. 131.

480. Ibid., p. 133.

481. Ibid., p. 134.

482. Tommasini, 2, 67–70; Ridolfi, pp. 135–36.

483. Ridolfi, pp. 135–36.

484. Ibid., pp. 136–38.

485. Ibid., pp. 138–39; letter to Vettori, 13 Mar. 1512–(1513), *MG.*, 2, 898 *(Lett. fam.,* 117).

486. 18 Mar. 1512–(1513), ibid., p. 899 *(Lett. fam.,* 119); Ridolfi, p. 140.

487. Ridolfi, p. 139; Carnival Songs, 3, "By the Blessed Spirits," *MG.*, 2, 880.

488. Letter to Vettori, 13 Mar. 1512–(1513), ibid., p. 898.

489. 18 Mar. 1512–(1513), ibid., p. 899 *(Lett. fam.,* 119); 9 Apr. 1513, ibid., p. 901 *Lett. fam.,* 120; 16 Apr. 1513, ibid., pp. 902–903 *(Lett. fam.,* 122); 10 Dec. 1513, ibid., pp. 927–31 *(Lett. fam.,* 137); 10 June 1514, ibid., p. 145 *(Lett. fam.,* 148); 20 Dec. 1514 *(No.* 3), ibid., p. 960 *(Lett. fam.,* 158); 31 Jan. 1514–(1515), ibid., pp. 962–63 *(Lett. fam.,* 159).

490. "A Third Sonnet to Giuliano," *MG.*, 2, 1015; Ridolfi, p. 140.

491. Letter to Vettori, 29 Apr. 1513, *MG.*, 2, pp. 903–10 *(Lett. fam.,* 128); 20 June 1513, ibid., pp. 910–13 *(Lett. fam.,* 124); 10 Aug. 1513, ibid., pp. 915–21 *(Lett. fam.,* 131); 20 Dec. 1514 *(Letter No.,* 1), ibid., pp. 948–56 *(Lett. fam.,* 154); *(No.* 2), ibid., pp. 956–59 *(Lett. fam.,* 155).

492. *H.F.,* 1, 23, *MG.,* 3, 1061–62.

493. Vignal, op. cit., pp. 186–87, 205, 212.

494. Tommasini, 2, 103–104.

495. Ridolfi, pp. 148–49.

496. Letter to Vettori, 10 Dec. 1513, *MG.*, 2, 930 *(Lett. fam.,* 137).

497. Ridolfi, p. 163; Vignal, op. cit., p. 207.

498. Ridolfi, p. 163; Young, op. cit., p. 290; Tommasini, 2, 131.

499. Tommasini, 2, 131–32.

500. Letter to Vettori, Aug. 1513, *MG.*, 2, 926–27 *(Lett. fam.,* 135).

501. *P.,* Dedication, *MG.,* 1, 10–11.

502. Tommasini, 2, 136.

503. Schevill, op. cit., p. 476.

504. Tommasini, 2, 926; 1, 11–13.

505. Ibid., p. 926 and n.5.

506. Schevill, op. cit., p. 474; Ridolfi, p. 163.

507. Schevill, op. cit., pp. 474–75.

508. Tommasini, 2, 131; Schevill, op. cit., p. 476; Ridolfi, p. 163.

509. Tommasini, 2, 131–32; Schevill, op. cit., p. 476.

510. Ridolfi, p. 173.

511. Ibid., p. 176; Vignal, op. cit., p. 229.

512. Young, op. cit., pp. 297, 785 n.5.

513. Schevill, op. cit., p. 476; Young, op. cit., p. 177.

514. Schevill, op. cit., p. 476.

515. Young, op. cit., p. 785 n.5.

516. Ridolfi, p. 121.

517. Ibid., p. 177.

518. Ibid., p. 173.

519. Ibid., p. 179.

520. Ibid., p. 180.

521. Ibid., p. 181.

522. Ibid., p. 182; Tommasini, 2, 254–55.

523. Ibid.
524. Vignal, op. cit., p. 229.
525. Ridolfi, p. 183.
526. Tommasini, 2, 199–200.
527. "Remodeling," *MG.*, 1, 101–115; Tommasini, pp. 199–201; Vignal, op. cit., pp. 229–30.
528. "Remodeling," ibid., p. 113.
529. Schevill, op. cit., p. 478.
530. Ridolfi, p. 201.
531. Ibid.
532. Ibid., p. 202.
533. Ibid.
534. Ibid., pp. 202–204.
535. Young, op. cit., pp. 313, 319.
536. Ridolfi, op. cit., p. 205.
537. Ibid., pp. 211–12.
538. Ibid.
539. Ibid., pp. 212–14.
540. Ibid., p. 217.
541. Ibid., p. 342.
542. Ibid., p. 202.
543. Ibid., pp. 243–45.
544. Ibid., p. 246.
545. Ibid., pp. 247, 329 n. 16.
546. Ibid., pp. 247–48.
547. Ibid., pp. 248, 250.
548. *H.F.*, 2, *MG.*, 3, 1104.
549. Preface, ibid., p. 1031.
550. 5, 1, ibid., p. 1233.
551. Letter to Guicciardini, 10 Aug. 1524, *MG.*, 2, 978 *(Lett. fam.,* 186).
552. *H.F.*, Preface, *MG.*, 2, 1029–30.
553. Editor's Foreword, ibid., p. 1028; Ridolfi, pp. 198–99; Tommasini, 2, 342–43.
554. *H.F.*, Editor's Forword, *MG.*, 3, 1028.
555. Dedication, ibid., p. 1029.
556. Editor's Preface, p. 1027; 3, 3, ibid., p. 1153; 20, ibid., p. 1172; 29, ibid., p. 1186; 4, 16, ibid., p. 1204; *D.*, 1, Preface, *MG.*, 1, 190.
557. *H.F.*, 7, 6, *MG.*, 3, 1346.
558. Ibid., p. 1345.
559. Ibid., p. 1346.
560. "Remodeling," *MG.*, 1, 102.
561. Ibid., p. 107.
562. *H.F.*, 7, 3, *MG.*, 3, 1340.
563. "Remodeling," *MG.*, 1, 102–103.
564. *H.F.*, 8, 36, *MG.*, 3, 1434.
565. Ridolfi, p. 76.
566. "F.D.," 11. 16–27, *MG.*, 3, 1445.
567. Tommasini, 1, 90; ibid., 546; Schevill, op. cit., pp. 404–405; Young, op. cit., p. 194.
568. Young, op. cit., p. 295.
569. Ibid., pp. 286–87.
570. "Two Sonnets to Giuliano," *MG.*, 2, 1013–14; Ridolfi, 136–38.

571. Letter to Vettori, 13 Mar. 1512–(1513), ibid., p. 898 *(Lett. fam., 117)*; 18 Mar. 1512–(1513), ibid., p. 899 *(Lett. fam., 119)*; 16 Apr. 1513, ibid., pp. 902–903 *(Lett. fam., 122)*; Ridolfi, pp. 140–42.

572. Ridolfi, p. 161.

573. Letter to Vettori, 10 Dec. 1513, *MG.*, 2, 929 *(Lett. fam., 137)*; Ridolfi, p. 152.

574. Ridolfi, p. 163.

575. Letter to Vettori, Aug. 1513, *MG.*, 2, 926–27 *(Lett. fam., 135)*.

576. "A Pastoral: The Ideal Ruler," *MG.*, 1, 96–100.

577. *P.,* Dedication, ibid., pp. 10–11.

578. Young, op. cit., p. 319.

579. Schevill, op. cit., p. 477.

580. Letter to Guicciardini, 15 Mar. 1525–(1526), *MG.*, 2, 994–95 *(Lett. fam., 204)*.

581. Ridolfi, p. 234.

582. Tommasini, 2, 546.

583. *H.F.,* 8, 9, *MG.*, 3, 1395.

584. Letter to Guicciardini, 19 Dec. 1525, *MG.*, 2, 989 *(Lett. fam., 200)*; Ridolfi, p. 221.

585. Ridolfi, p. 231; Young, op. cit., p. 329.

586. Letter to Guicciardini, 5 Nov. 1526, *MG.*, 2, 1002 *(Lett. fam., 219)*; Ridolfi, p. 233.

587. Letter to Bartolomeo (Cavalcanti?) Nov. 1526, *MG.*, 2, 1004 *(Lett. fam., 219B)*.

588. Letter to Guicciardini, 16 Apr. 1527, ibid., p. 1010 *(Lett. fam., 225)*; Ridolfi, p. 241.

589. Young, op. cit., pp. 330–33.

590. Ridolfi, p. 246.

591. Ibid., p. 247.

592. Ibid., p. 250.

593. Meinecke, op. cit., pp. 51, 54.

CHAPTER SIX

1. *H.F.,* 5, 1, *MG.*, 3, 1232.

2. Schevill, op. cit., p. 363.

3. *D.,* 1, Preface, *MG.*, 1, 190–91.

4. Ibid., p. 191; 3, 6, ibid., p. 428.

5. Letter to Vettori, 10 Dec. 1513, *MG.*, 2, 929 *(Lett. fam., 137)*.

6. *Mandragola,* act 3, sc. 2, *MG.*, 2, 795.

7. *H.F.,* 6, 29, *MG.*, 3, 1322.

8. Draft of letter to Soderini, Jan. 1 1512–(1513), *MG.*, 2, 896 *(Lett. fam., 116)*.

9. Letter to Vettori, 9 Apr. 1513, *MG.*, 2, 900–901 *(Lett. fam., 120)*.

10. Letter to Vettori, 10 Dec. 1513, *MG.*, 2, 929 *(Lett. fam., 137)*.

11. *P.,* Dedication, *MG.*, 1, 10.

12. Chap. 15, ibid., p. 57; letter to Vettori, 10 Dec. 1513, *MG.*, 2, 930 *(Lett. fam., 137)*.

13. *D.,* 1, Preface, *MG.*, 1, 190–92; 2, Preface, ibid., p. 324.

14. *A.W.,* Dedication, *MG.*, 2, 567.

15. Ibid., pp. 571–72.

16. 7, ibid., p. 720.

17. Ibid., p. 726.

18. *H.F.*, Preface, *MG.*, 3, 1031; 5, 1, ibid., p. 1233.
19. Letter to Guicciardini, 17 May 1521, *MG.*, 2, 971.
20. Tommasini, 2, 655–56 and n.6; 39 n.1; 287–88.
21. *MG.*, ed. ii. on *P.*, chap. 1, *MG.*, 1, 11.
22. Pocock, p. 92.
23. Tommasini, 2, 655–56 and n.6.
24. John 16:33.
25. I John 5:3.
26. *Il Principe,* xv, *Opp. MC.*, p. 30.
27. "T.F.," 11. 25–30, *MG.*, 2, 745.
28. "T.A.," 11. 176–77, ibid., p. 739; Draft of letter to Soderini, *MG.*, 2, 897; *P.*, chap. 25, *MG.*, 1, 89–90; *A.W.*, 2, *MG.*, 2, 624; "Money," *MG.*, 3, 1443.
29. *P.*, chap. 25, *MG.*, 1, 80.
30. "T.F.," 11. 13–15, *MG.*, 2, 745.
31. "S.D.," 1. 45, *MG.*, 3, 1458; *D.*, 2, 30, *MG.*, 1, 412.
32. Ridolfi, pp. 136, 139.
33. Letter to Vettori, 18 Mar. 1512–(1513), *MG.*, 2, 899.
34. *H.F.*, 4, 7, *MG.*, 3, 1194; 6, 13, ibid., p. 1299.
35. *D.*, 1, Preface, *MG.*, 1, 190.
36. Letter to Guicciardini, 30 Aug. 1524, *MG.*, 2, 978 *(Lett. fam.,* 186).
37. *D.*, 3, 31, *MG.*, 1, 500; "S.D.," 1. 190–192, *MG.*, 3, 1461; "Lingua," *Opp. MC.*, pp. 770–71; *A.W.*, 2, *MG.*, 2, 622; 4, ibid., p. 662; "Remodeling," ibid., pp. 113–114; "Advice to Girolami," *MG.*, 1, 116.
38. *H.F.*, 7, 1, *MG.*, 3, 1337.
39. 3, 6, ibid., pp. 1145–48.
40. 7, 1, ibid., pp. 1336–37.
41. Tommasini, 1, 309.
42. "Lingua," *Opp. MC.*, pp. 770–771.
43. *D.*, 3, 41, *MG.*, 1, 519; 1, 18, 241–43; *P.*, chap. 7, ibid., p. 28; *H.F.*, 5, 8, *MG.*, 3, 1242.
44. Cicero, *Philippica,* XI, 12 as quoted in Tommasini, 2, 196 n.7.
45. *P.*, chap. 7., *MG.*, 1, 34.
46. *D.*, 3, 41, ibid., p. 426; letter to Vettori, 29 Apr. 1513, *MG.*, 2, 908 *(Lett. fam.,* 128), Legation 13.18, 4 Nov. 1503, *MG.*, 1, 144.
47. *D.*, 3, 47, ibid., p. 526; *H.F.*, 2, 22, *MG.*, 3, 1106.
48. *P.*, chap. 8, ibid., p. 38; chap. 18, *MG.*, 1, 87.
49. *D.*, 1, 18, ibid., pp. 242–43; "Remodeling," ibid., pp. 112–14.
50. *P.*, chap. 18, ibid., p. 67; "Remodeling," ibid., p. 113.
51. *D.*, 2, 2, ibid., p. 329.
52. 1, 9, ibid., p. 218.
53. 3, 41, ibid., p. 519.
54. Schevill, op. cit., p. 343.
55. Gino Capponi, *Ricordi,* as quoted by Tommasini, 2, 522 and n.1.
56. *H.F.*, 3, 7, *MG.*, 3, 1150; "The Nature of Florentine Men, of Francesco Valori," ibid., p. 1438; letter to Vettori, 16 Apr. 1527, *MG.*, 2, 1010 *(Lett. fam.,* 225).
57. Mattingly, op. cit., pp. 57–58.
58. *D.*, 1, Preface, *MG.*, 1, 190; "Lingua," *Opp. MC.*, pp. 770–71.
59. *D.*, 1, 9, *MG.*, 1, 218.
60. "Remodeling," ibid., p. 110.
61. *H.F.*, 2, 34, *MG.*, 3, 1125.

62. "Remodeling," *MG.*, 1, 115.
63. *D.*, 3, 28, ibid., p. 492; *H.F.*, 7, 1, *MG.*, 3, 1337.
64. *D.*, 1, 9, *MG.*, 1, 218.
65. *D.*, 1, 12, ibid., p. 228; *P.*, chap. 7, ibid., p. 31; letter to Vettori, 31 Jan. 1514–(1515), *MG.*, 2, 962 *(Lett. fam., 159).*
66. *D.*, 1, 12, *MG.*, 1, 228–29.
67. 3, 1, ibid., p. 422.
68. *A.W.*, 2, *MG.*, 2, 622; *D.*, 3, 28, *MG.*, 1, 492–93; *Mandragola*, act 2, sc. 3, *MG.*, 2, 788–89.
69. "T.F.," 11. 61–63, 109–120, 190–93, *MG.*, 2, 746–47.
70. "A Description of the Method Used by Duke Valentino . . .," *MG.*, 1, 169.
71. Legation 13.18, 4 Nov. 1503, ibid., pp. 143–44.
72. 22, 6 Nov. 1503, ibid., p. 145.
73. 64, 28 Nov. 1503, ibid., p. 157.
74. 74, 3 Dec. 1503, ibid., p. 160.
75. *Mandragola*, Canzone after Act 2, *MG.*, 2, 793.
76. *A.W.*, 1, *MG.*, 2, 587, 584–87; *D.*, 1, 21, *MG.*, 1, 246–47.
77. *D.*, 1, 9, *MG.*, 1, 218–20; 18, ibid., pp. 242–43.
78. *H.F.*, 1, 9, *MG.*, 3, 1154; *D.*, 1, 9, *MG.*, 1, 218; 58, ibid., p. 317; "Remodeling," ibid., pp. 112–15.
79. *H.F.*, 3, 1, *MG.*, 3, 1141.
80. *A.W.*, 1, *MG.*, 2, 585–86.
81. Kemmerich, op. cit., pp. 138–40.
82. Tommasini, 2, 3.
83. 1, 556; 2, 455.
84. Ridolfi, pp. 274–75 n.40.
85. Tommasini, 1, 217–19 n.6; Ridolfi, pp. 264–75 n.40.
86. Letter to Vettori, 10 June 1514, *MG.*, 2, 945 *(Lett. fam., 148);* to Giovanni Vernacci, 15 Feb. 1515–(1516), ibid., p. 964 *(Lett. fam., 162);* id., 5 Jan. 1517–(1518), ibid., p. 968; id., 25 Jan. 1517–(1518), ibid., p. 969 *(Lett. fam., 168).*
87. Letter to Vettori, 10 Dec. 1513, ibid., p. 930 *(Lett. fam., 137).*
88. "Remodeling," *MG.*, 1, 113–114; *D.*, 1, Preface, ibid., pp. 190–92; 2, Preface, ibid., p. 324; 3, 28, ibid., pp. 492–93; *A.W.*, Dedication, *MG.*, 2, 567; 2, ibid., p. 622; 7, ibid., p. 726; *H.F.*, Preface, *MG.*, 3, 1031; *Mandragola*, act 2, sc. 3, *MG.*, 2, 788–89.
89. *D.*, 3, 17, *MG.*, 3, 471.
90. *A.W.*, 7, *MG.*, 2, 721.
91. *P.*, chap. 15, *MG.*, 1, 57; *D.*, 1, Preface, ibid., pp. 190–92; 58, ibid., pp. 313–14.
92. Ibid., p. 331; *A.W.*, 2, *MG.*, 2, 623.
93. *H.F.*, 3, 1, *MG.*, 3, 1141.
94. *D.*, 1, 9, *MG.*, 1, 218; 18, ibid., pp. 242–43; "Remodeling," ibid., pp. 107, 113–15.
95. *D.*, 1, 17, *MG.*, 1, 240; *H.F.*, 4, 1, *MG.*, 3, 1187.
96. Ferrara, op. cit., p. 116.
97. Tommasini, 1, 311–12.
98. *MG.*, 3, ed. n. p. 1444.
99. Letter to Vettori, 13 Mar. 1512–(1513), *MG.*, 2, 898 *(Lett. fam., 117);* 18 Mar. 1512–(1513), ibid., 898–99 *(Lett. fam., 119);* 9 Apr. 1513, ibid., pp. 900–901 *(Lett. fam., 120);* 29 Apr. 1513, ibid., pp. 903–10 *(Lett. fam., 128);* 20 June 1513, ibid., pp. 910–13 *(Lett. fam., 124);* 10 Aug. 1513, ibid., pp. 915–21 *(Lett. fam., 131);* 26 Aug. 1513, ibid., pp. 922–26 *(Lett. fam., 134);* Aug. 1513, ibid., pp. 926–27 *(Lett. fam.,*

135); 10 Dec. 1513, ibid., pp. 927–31 *(Lett. fam.,* 137); 16 Apr. 1514, ibid., pp. 941–43 *(Lett. fam.,* 145); 20 Dec. 1514 *(Lett. fam.,* 1), ibid., pp. 948–56 *(Lett. fam.,* 154); *(No. 2),* ibid., pp. 956–59 *(Lett. fam.,* 155); 31 Jan. 1514–(1515), ibid., pp. 962–63 *(Lett. fam.,* 159).

100. Draft of letter to Soderini, Jan. 1512–(1513), ibid., p. 895 *(Lett. fam.,* 116).

101. *P.,* Dedication, *MG.,* 1, 10.

102. *D.,* 1, Preface, ibid., p. 190.

103. *A.W.,* Preface, *MG.,* 2, 567.

104. Letter to Vettori, 10 Dec. 1513, ibid., p. 929 *(Lett. fam.,* 137).

105. Charles Benoist, *Machiavel* (Paris: Plon, 1934), p. 161.

106. Editor's foreward to *P., MG.,* 1, 9.

107. Strauss, op. cit., pp. 80–81.

108. Whitfield, *Discourses . . .,* pp. 107–108.

109. *H.F.,* 3, 1, *MG.,* 3, 1141.

110. Felix Gilbert, "The Venetian Constitution in Florentine Political Thought," in *Florentine Studies,* ed. N. Rubenstein, p. 464.

111. Titus Livius, *The History of Rome,* I, i.xxxii, p. 38.

112. *D.,* 3, 1, *MG.,* 1, 419–23.

113. Tommasini, 2, 613.

114. Strauss, op. cit., pp. 29–30.

115. Ridolfi, pp. 257–58 n.7.

116. Tommasini, 2, 658–59 n.2.

117. Livius, op. cit., Preface, I, 2.

118. Ibid., Preface, pp. 1–2; I.vii, p. 9; xvi, pp. 19–20; xix–xxi, pp. 23–25; xxii, p. 26; xxxvi, p. 44; xlv, p. 53.

119. Ibid., xxxii, p. 38.

120. Ibid., vii, p. 11.

121. Ibid., xlviii, pp. 56–57.

122. Ridolfi, pp. 201–202.

123. Livius, op. cit., I, iv.x, p. 233.

124. *D.,* 3, 43, *MG.,* 1, 522.

125. Livius, *History,* Preface, op. cit., p. 1.

126. *H.F., MG.,* 3, 1030.

127. Tommasini, 2, 163 and n.1.

128. "Remodeling," *MG.,* 1, 101–15.

129. *D.,* 1, 9 and 18, ibid., pp. 217–220, 241–43.

130. *MG.,* ed. n., ibid., p. 101.

131. Tommasini, 2, 516–17.

132. *A.W.,* 1, *MG.,* 2, 584–85.

133. Vignal, op. cit., p. 211.

134. Ridolfi, pp. 178–79.

135. "G.A.," chap. 2, 1.49; *MG.,* 2, 754.

136. Vignal, op. cit., p. 232 n.1.

137. *Mandragola,* act 1, sc. 3, *MG.,* 2, 783.

138. Livius, op. cit., I, i.lviii–lix, pp. 66–67.

139. Carnival Songs, "By the Devils Driven Out From Heaven," 11. 1–7, *MG.,* 878.

140. Shakespeare, *Hamlet,* act 2, sc. 2.

141. Kemmerich, op. cit., p. 188.

142. Ridolfi, pp. 172–73.

143. *Novossima Encyclopedia Monografica Illustrata,* s.v. "Machiavelli," Adolfo

Oxilia, op. cit., p. 37.

144. Tommasini, 2, 401–403.
145. Ferrara, op. cit., pp. 311–12.
146. Ridolfi, p. 182.
147. *H.F.*, Dedication, *MG.*, 3, 1029.
148. Tommasini, 2, 522.
149. Ibid., p. 482.
150. Felix Gilbert, op. cit., pp. 160, 171–76.
151. Tommasini, 2, 489–90, 508 n.1., 556 n.4.
152. Ibid., p. 53 and n.2; *D.*, 2, 8, *MG.*, 1, 344–45; *H.F.*, 1, 1, *MG.*, 3, 1034–35; *D.*, 3, 31, *MG.*, 1, 500; 32, ibid., p. 502; 43, ibid., pp. 521–22; Tommasini, 2, 291–92 and n.5.
153. Burckhardt, op. cit., as quoted in Tommasini, 2, 425.
154. A. Schmidt, *Niccolo Machiavelli und die allgemeine Staatslehre der Gegenwart* (Karlsruhe, 1907), p. 91, as quoted in Tommasini, 2, 941 n.3.
155. Tommasini, 2, 943; Ridolfi, p. 196.
156. Quinet, *Les Revolutions d'Italie*, p. 270 as quoted in Tommasini, 2, 556 n.4.
157. Tommasini, 2, 556.
158. *MG.*, 3, ed. foreword to *H.F.*, 1028.
159. Tommasini, 2, 291.
160. "A Description of the Method Used by Duke Valentino in Killing Vitellozzo Vitelli, Oliverotto Da Fermo, and Others," *MG.*, 1, 163–69; Ridolfi, p. 64.
161. "On the Method of Dealing with the Rebellious Peoples of the Valdichiana," *MG.*, 1, 161–62.
162. Tommasini, 1, 264.
163. Ridolfi, p. 180.
164. Ridolfi, p. 181.
165. Tommasini, 2, 429–30.
166. "Ritratto di Cose di Francia" and "Ritratto delle Cose della Magna," *Opp. MC.*, pp. 731–43.
167. "Advice to Girolami," *MG.*, 1, 118.
168. Kemmerich, op. cit., p. 107.

CHAPTER SEVEN

1. *P.*, chap. 15, *MG.*, 1, 57–58 and n.3.
2. Draft of letter to Soderini, January 1512–(1513), *MG.*, 2, 897 *(Lett. fam.*, 116); "T.F.," 11. 100–20, ibid., p. 747.
3. *P.*, chap. 25, *MG.*, 1, 90.
4. Draft of letter to Soderini, *MG.*, 2, 896.
5. *D.*, 3, 6, *MG.*, 1, 441.
6. *P.*, chap. 8, ed. n. 5, ibid., p. 38.
7. Meinecke, op. cit., p. 149.
8. Fleisher, "Introduction" in *Machiavelli . . . Thought*, p. 10.
9. Lynn Harold Hough, "Exposition," *Rev.* 2:18–29, *I.B.*, 7, 557.
10. Federico Chabod, "Synthesis and Condemnation of Italian History," in *Machiavelli, Cynic, Patriot, or Political Scientist?*, ed. De Lamar Jensen (Lexington, Mass.: Heath & Co., 1960), p. 51.

11. Lord Morley, *Machiavelli* (London, 1887), p. 23, as quoted by Tommasini, 2, 944, n.2.

12. *D.*, 1, Preface, *MG.*, 1, 191; 11, ibid., p. 226; 39, ibid., p. 278; 58, ibid., p. 315; 3, 43, ibid., p. 521.

13. *P.*, chap. 19, ibid., p. 72.

14. *A.W.*, 1, *MG.*, 2, 579.

15. *D.*, 1, 3, *MG.*, 1, 201.

16. *H.F.*, 5, 11, *MG.*, 3, 1246–47.

17. *D.*, 2, 29, *MG.*, 1, 408.

18. *P.*, chap. 18, ibid., pp. 64–67.

19. Chap. 6, ibid., p. 26.

20. *D.*, 3, 22, ibid., p. 480.

21. *H.F.*, 8, 22, *MG.*, 3, 1413; "Money," ibid., p. 1442; *D.*, 3, 42, *MG.*, 1, 520; Legation 11.40. An Official Mission to Duke Valentino, 8 Nov. 1502 (*Second Letter*), *MG.*, 1, 132; letter to Guicciardini, 25 Mar. 1525–(1526), *MG.*, 2, 995 (*Lett. fam.*, 204).

22. *P.*, chap. 14, *MG.*, 1, 55, 55–57; *D.*, 1, 19, ibid., p. 245.

23. *D.*, 2, 21, ibid., p. 385.

24. *P.*, chap. 9, ibid., p. 42.

25. *D.*, 1, 18, ibid., p. 243; 9, ibid., p. 219; 55, ibid., p. 309.

26. 55, ibid., pp. 307, 309–10; *P.*, chap. 26, ibid., pp. 94–95.

27. Meinecke, op. cit., pp. 72–73.

28. *D.*, 2, 19, *MG.*, 1, 379; 1, 6, ibid., pp. 209–11; 3, 16, ibid., p. 469.

29. Felix Gilbert, "Venetian Constitution . . . ," in *Florentine Studies*, ed. Rubinstein, p. 494.

30. "Money," *MG.*, 3, 1439–42.

31. *D.*, 3, 39, *MG.*, 1, 516.

32. Anglo, op. cit., p. 190.

33. Legation 11.40, 8 Nov. 1502, *MG.*, 1, 132; "Money," *MG.*, 3, 1442.

34. *D.*, 3, 42, *MG.*, 1, 520.

35. 1, 44, ibid., p. 287.

36. 2, 13, ibid., pp. 357–58; 1, 11, ibid., p. 225.

37. *D.*, 1, 25, ibid., p. 252.

38. 2, 27, ibid., p. 404.

39. *P.*, chap. 18, ibid., pp. 64–67; 19, ibid., p. 73.

40. "T.A.," 11. 37–40, *MG.*, 2, 736.

41. "T.F.," 11. 88–89, ibid., p. 747.

42. *H.F.*, 5, 1, *MG.*, 3, 1233.

43. 3, 5, ibid., pp. 1145–46.

44. 13, ibid., p. 1159.

45. Ibid., p. 1160.

46. 6, 17, ibid., p. 1304.

47. *D.*, 3, 40, *MG.*, 1, 518.

48. "Lingua," *Opp. MC.*, pp. 770–71.

49. Tommasini, 2, 53 and n.3; *D.*, 2, 8, *MG.*, 1, 344–45; *H.F.*, 1, 1, *MG.*, 3, 1034–35; *D.*, 3, 31, ibid., p. 500; 32, *MG.*, 1, 502; 43, ibid., pp. 521–22; Tommasini, 2, 291–92 and n.5.

50. *D.*, 1, 11, *MG.*, 1, 225; 18, ibid., p. 241; 3, 33, ibid., pp. 502–503.

51. Ibid.

52. *P.*, chap. 6, ibid., p. 25; chap. 26, ibid., p. 93; *D.*, 1, 9, ibid., p. 219; 2, 8, ibid., p. 346; 3, 30, ibid., p. 496.

53. *D.*, 2, 2, ibid., p. 331.

54. Ibid., pp. 330–32; 4, ibid., p. 339; *A.W.*, 2, *MG.*, 2, 623.

55. *P.*, chap. 26, *MG.*, 1, 93, 96; *H.F.*, 5, 1, *MG.*, 3, 1233; "F.D.," 1. 18, ibid., p. 1445.

56. Letter to Guicciardini, 17 May 1526, *MG.*, 2, 998 *(Lett. fam.*, 207).

57. *P.*, chap. 26, *MG.*, 1, 92–96.

58. Letter to Guicciardini, 17 May 1526, *MG.*, 2, 998 *(Lett. fam.*, 207).

59. Letter to Vettori, 10 Aug. 1513, *MG.*, 2, 919 *(Lett. fam.*, 131).

60. 26 Aug. 1513, ibid., p. 925.

61. Tommasini, 2, 291 and n.5.

62. *A.W.*, 7, *MG.*, 2, 725, 722.

63. Mondadori, op. cit., p. 130.

64. Ridolfi, p. 89.

65. *A.W.*, 4, *MG.*, 2, 662.

66. *D.*, 3, 6, *MG.*, 1, 430.

67. *A.W.*, 1, *MG.*, 2, 581, 585–86; *D.*, 1, 21, *MG.*, 1, 247; 2, 20, ibid., p. 382.

68. *D.*, 3, 31, *MG.*, 1, 500; *A.W.*, 1, *MG.*, 2, 581, 584–85, 587.

69. *D.*, 3, 33, *MG.*, 1, 502; *H.F.*, 2, 5–6, *MG.*, 3, 1086; 26, ibid., pp. 1111–12; 5, 9, ibid., p. 1244.

70. *A.W.*, 1, *MG.*, 2, 576.

71. *P.*, chap. 26, *MG.*, 1, 94.

72. *D.*, 3, 12, ibid., p. 461.

73. Livius, *History*, II, ix.i, p. 159.

74. *H.F.*, 5, 8, *MG.*, 3, 1241—42.

75. 6, 1, ibid., p. 1284; *D.*, 2, 6, *MG.*, 1, 341.

76. *A.W.*, 1, *MG.*, 2, 587, 584–87; *D.*, 1, 21, *MG.*, 1, 246–47.

77. *D.*, 2, 6, *MG.*, 1, 342.

78. *P.*, chap. 16, ibid., pp. 60–61.

79. *D.*, 1, 37, ibid., p. 272; 2, 6, ibid., p. 341; 19, ibid., p. 378; 3, 16, ibid., p. 469; 25, ibid., p. 486; "Portraits of the Affairs of Germany," Pansini, p. 649; *H.F.*, 6, 1, *MG.*, 3, 1284.

80. *A.W.*, 1, *MG.*, 2, 578; "Lingua," *Opp. MC.*, pp. 770–71.

81. *H.F.*, 4, 14, *MG.*, 3, 1201–1202; *A.W.*, 5, *MG.*, 2, 671–72.

82. *D.*, 3, 24, *MG.*, 1, 485–86.

83. *A.W.*, Preface, *MG.*, 2, 566.

84. *D.*, 3, 24–25, *MG.*, 1, 485–88.

85. 24, ibid., pp. 485–86; *A.W.*, 1, *MG.*, 2, 573–75, 578–80.

86. *D.*, 2, 6, *MG.*, 1, 342–43; *A.W.*, 5, *MG.*, 2, 672–73.

87. *A.W.*, 1, *MG.*, 2, 575–78.

88. *D.*, 2, 6, *MG.*, 1, 343.

89. *A.W.*, 2, *MG.*, 2, 623.

90. *H.F.*, 3, 1, *MG.*, 3, 1141.

91. *D.*, 2, 2, *MG.*, 1, 330–32.

92. Ibid., p. 331; *A.W.*, 2, *MG.*, 2, 623.

93. *A.W.*, 2, *MG.*, 2. 623.

94. Hough, "Exposition," Rev. 21:6, *I.B.*, 12, 533.

95. *P.*, chap. 8, *MG.*, 1, 38; 18, ibid., pp. 66–67.

96. *D.*, 1, 12, ibid., pp. 226–27.

97. 12–15, ibid., pp. 226–34.

98. 3, 41, ibid., p. 519; 47, ibid., p. 526.

99. Letter to Vettori, 16 April 1527, *MG.*, 2, 1010 *(Lett. fam.*, 225); *H.F.*, 3, 7, *MG.*, 3, 1150; "The Natures of Florentine Men, Of Francesco Valori," ibid., p. 1438.

100. Carnival Songs, 3, "By the Blessed Spirits," 11. 37–54, *MG.*, 2, 880.

101. *D.*, 1, 55, *MG.*, 1, 307, 309–10.

102. Ibid., p. 307; 2, Preface, ibid., p. 323; *P.*, chap. 25, ibid., p. 93; "T.A.," 11. 110–11, 118–86, *MG.*, 2, 737–39; Carnival Songs, 3, "By the Blessed Spirits,"n 11. 1–34, ibid., p. 880; letter to Vettori, 26 Aug. 1513, ibid., p. 926 *(Lett. fam.*, 134); *H.F.*, 5, 1, *MG.*, 3, 1233.

103. *P.*, chap. 11, *MG.*, 1, 45; chap. 26, ibid., p. 93.

104. "F.D.," 11. 523–40, *MG.*, 3, 1456–57; letter to Vettori, 10 Aug. 1513, *MG.*, 2, 919 *(Lett. fam.*, 131); 20 Dec. 1514 *(Letter No. 1)*, ibid., pp. 952–53 *(Lett. fam.*, 154).

105. Letter to Vettori, 26 Aug. 1513, *MG.*, 2, 925 *(Lett. fam.*, 134); *P.*, chap. 26, *MG.*, 1, 94–95; *A.W.*, Preface, *MG.*, 2, 567; 1, 582; 2, ibid., pp. 608, 619–20, 624, 625; 7, ibid., pp. 722–23, 724–25.

106. "F.D.," 11. 548–49, *MG.*, 3, 1457.

107. "T.A.," 11. 109–14, *MG.*, 2, 737.

108. *A.W.*, 6, ibid., p. 694.

109. 7, ibid., p. 724.

110. *D.*, 3, 48, *MG.*, 1, 526.

111. Tommasini, 1, 30 n.2.

112. Ibid., 2, 627, n.1.

113. Ibid., p. 786 n.2.

114. Letter to Guicciardini, 17 May 1521, *MG.*, 2, 973 *(Lett. fam.*, 179).

115. *D.*, 1, 11, *MG.*, 1, 225.

116. "L.C.," *MG.*, 2, 536; Tommasini, 2, 437–38.

117. Draft of Letter to Soderini, Jan. 1512–(1513), *MG.*, 2, 897; "T.F.," 11. 112–20, ibid., p. 747; *D.*, 1, 17, *MG.*, 1, 240; 18, ibid., pp. 242–43.

118. *D.*, 2, 13, *MG.*, 1, 357–58.

119. *P.*, chap. 15, ibid., p. 57.

120. Letter to Vettori, 20 Dec. 1514 *(No. 2)*, *MG.*, 2, 958 *(Lett. fam.*, 155).

121. Ed. Preface, *MG.*, 1, 9.

122. Ridolfi, pp. 251–54.

123. *P.*, chap. 18, *MG.*, 1, 65; *D.*, 1, 13, ibid., pp. 357–58.

124. *D.*, 1, 9, ibid., pp. 218–19; 18, ibid., pp. 242–43.

125. "A Provision for Infantry," Preamble, ibid., p. 3; *P.*, chap. 12, ibid., p. 47; *D.*, 4, 4, ibid., p. 202; 3, 31, ibid., p. 500.

126. Legation 11.44, 13 Nov. 1502, ibid., pp. 133–34; 53, 26 Nov. 1502, ibid., p. 137; "Provision for Infantry," Preamble, ibid., p. 3; *P.*, chap. 12, ibid., pp. 47–51; 13, ibid., p. 54; *D.*, 3, 31, ibid., p. 500; *A.W.*, Preface, *MG.*, 2, 566–67; 1, ibid., pp. 585–87.

127. *P.*, chap. 12, *MG.*, 1, 47; *D.*, 1, 4, ibid., p. 202; 3, 31, ibid., p. 500.

128. *A.W.*, Preface, *MG.*, 2, 566–67.

129. *D.*, 3, 41, *MG.*, 1, 519; 46, ibid., p. 526.

130. Letter to Vettori, 16 Apr. 1527, *MG.*, 2, 1010 *(Lett. fam.*, 225); *H.F.*, 3, 7, *MG.*, 3, 1150.

131. *H.F.*, 4, 1, *MG.*, 3, 1187.

132. Tommasini, 2, 399.

133. *D.*, 3, 49, *MG.*, 1, 527–29.

134. Legation to Julius the Second, Letter VIII, 6 Sept. 1506, Pansini, p. 1074; Letter XIX, 25 Sept. 1506, ibid., p. 1084; Draft of letter to Soderini, *MG.*, 2, 897 *(Lett.*

fam., 116); letter to Vettori, 9 Apr. 1513, ibid., pp. 900–901 *(Lett. fam.*, 120); 29 Apr. 1513, ibid., p. 906 *(Lett. fam.*, 128); 20 Dec. 1514 *(No. 2), MG.*, 2, 956–9 *(Lett. fam.*, 155); *P.*, chap. 15, *MG.*, 1, 57; *D.*, 1, 18, ibid., p. 240; 58, ibid., pp. 313–14.

135. Strauss, op. cit., p. 123.

136. *D.*, 1, 21, *MG.*, 1, 247; 23, ibid., p. 250; 29, ibid., p. 258; 56, ibid., p. 311; 2, 12, ibid., p. 354; 21, ibid., p. 384; 3, 6, ibid., p. 445; 42, ibid., p. 520; 43, ibid., p. 521; *A.W.*, 2, *MG.*, 2, 601.

137. *Discorsi*, 1, xlix, *Opp. MC.*, p. 120; *D.*, 1, 49, *MG.*, 1, 296; Strauss, op. cit., p. 123.

138. *Discorsi*, 1, xvi, *Opp. MC.*, p. 83; *D.*, 1, 16, *MG.*, 1, 235; Strauss, op. cit., p. 123.

139. *A.W.*, 2, *MG.*, 2, 622–23; *D.*, 2, Preface, *MG.*, 1. 321; 1, 10, ibid., p. 221.

140. Legation 11.44, 13 Nov. 1502, *MG.*, 1, 133.

141. Letter to the Ten, Legation to Duke Valentino, Letter XXVII, 12 Jan. 1502–(1503), Pansini, p. 1001.

142. Letter to Vettori, 29 Apr. 1513, *MG.*, 2, 905, 906 *(Lett. fam.*, 128).

143. 26 Aug. 1513, ibid., p. 924 *(Lett. fam.*, 134).

144. *H.F.*, 3, 13, *MG.*, 3, 1159–61.

145. 1, ibid., pp. 1140–41.

146. Letter to Guicciardini, 30 Aug. 1524, *MG.*, 2, 978 *(Lett. fam.*, 186).

147. "Advice to Girolami," *MG.*, 1, 116–19.

148. Legation to Julius the second, Letter VIII, 6 Sept. 1506, Pansini, p. 1074.

149. Legation 11.27, 27 Oct. 1502, *MG.*, 1, 129.

150. *P.*, chap. 23, ibid., pp. 87–88.

151. *D.*, 3, 35, ibid., pp. 508–509.

152. "Advice to Girolami," ibid., p. 116.

153. M. deSalzmann, *Footnotes to the Gurdiieff Literature* (Armonk, NY: The Society for Experimental Studies, 1983), p. 4.

154. Draft of letter to Soderini, *MG.*, 2, 896.

155. "Advice to Girolami," *MG.*, 1, 117.

156. *D.*, 2, 19, *MG.*, 1, 378–79.

157. Ibid., p. 23.

158. "Money," *MG.*, 3, 1443; "Lingua," *Opp. MC.*, pp. 770–71; *A.W.*, 2, *MG.*, 2, 622; *D.*, 3, 28, *MG.*, 1, 492–93; *Mandragola*, act 2, sc. 3, ibid., pp. 788–89; "Remodeling," *MG.*, 1, 113–14.

159. Tommasini, 1, 238, 589–90.

160. pp. 217–19; Ridolfi, pp. 238, 326 nn. 22–24.

161. Tommasini, 1, 594, 596 n.2.

162. Plumb, op. cit., p. 243.

163. Ridolfi, p. 90; Schevill, op. cit., p. 368; Rubinstein, op. cit., pp. 442–55.

164. Ridolfi, pp. 1–2.

165. Letter "To a Lady," Sept. 1512, *MG.*, 2, 890–95.

166. Ridolfi, pp. 133–34.

167. Draft of letter to Soderini, *MG.*, 2, 895–97 *(Lett. fam.*, 116).

168. Tommasini, 1, 589–90.

169. Ibid., p. 597.

170. Ibid., p. 600; 2, ibid., p. 95 and n.2.

171. "Remodeling," *MG.*, 1, 107–15; Ridolfi, pp. 183, 201; *D.*, 1, 55, *MG.*, 1, 309; *H.F.*, 3, 1, *MG.*, 3, 1141.

172. Ridolfi, pp. 135–36.

173. Ibid., p. 162.
174. Ibid , pp. 202–203.
175. Tommasini, 2, 793.
176. *P.,* Dedication, *MG.,* 1, 10–11; chap. 26, ibid., pp. 92–96.
177. "Remodeling," ibid., pp. 113–15.
178. Carnival Songs, 3, "By the Blessed Spirits," 11. 34–54, *MG.,* 3, 880.
179. "A Pastoral: the Ideal Ruler," *MG.,* 1, 97–100.
180. Ridolfi, p. 226.
181. Mondadori, op. cit., p. 125.
182. "S.D.," 11. 190–92, *MG.,* 3, 1461.
183. Young, op. cit., pp. 366, 372.
184. Ridolfi, p. 202; Young, op. cit., p. 322.
185. Schevill, op. cit., p. 491.
186. Ibid., p. 514.
187. Young, op. cit., p. 735.
188. J. R. Hale, "The End of Florentine Liberty: the Fortezza da Basso," in *Florentine Studies,* ed. Rubinstein, pp. 530–31.
189. Vignal, op. cit., p. 284.
190. *D.,* 3, 37, *MG.,* 1, 512; "G.A.," chap. 5, 11. 103–105, *MG.,* 2, 763.
191. *P.,* chap. 15, *MG.,* 1, 57–58.
192. Chap. 17, ibid., p. 62; *D.,* 1, 3, ibid., p. 201; 3, 40, ibid., p. 518; "T.A.," 11. 55–81, *MG.,* 2, 736–37.
193. *P.,* chap. 15, *MG.,* 1, 58.
194. *D.,* 1, 18, *MG.,* 1, 240; 58, ibid., pp. 313–14; letter to Vettori, 20 June 1513, *MG.,* 2, 911 *(Lett. fam.,* 124); "S.D.," 11. 181–92, *MG.,* 3, 1461.
195. Benoist, op. cit., p. 224.
196. *P.,* chap. 8, *MG.,* 1, 36–38; *D.,* 1, 18, ibid., p. 64; 3, 40, ibid., p. 518.
197. *D.,* Preface, ibid., pp. 190–92; 1, 58, ibid., pp. 313–14; *A.W.,* 7, *MG.,* 2, 721.
198. "Belfagor: the Devil Who Married," *MG.,* 2, 869–77.
199. *Mandragola,* ibid., pp. 776–821.

CHAPTER EIGHT

1. *D.,* 1, 3, *MG.,* 1, 201; 9, ibid., p. 218; 17, ibid., p. 240; 37, ibid., p. 272; 2, Preface, ibid., p. 323; 28, ibid., p. 404; 30, ibid., pp. 495–98; *P.,* chap. 8, ibid., pp. 35–39; 17, ibid., p. 62; 18, ibid., pp. 64–65; 23, ibid., p. 88; "T.A.," 11. 55–63, 73–81, *MG.,* 2, 736–37; "T.F.," 11. 84–85, ibid., p. 747; 11. 190–92, ibid., p. 749.
2. *D.,* 1, 9, *MG.,* 1, 217–20; 16, ibid., pp. 236, 238; 17, ibid., pp. 239–40; 18, ibid., pp. 242–43; 26, ibid., pp. 253–54; 33, ibid., pp. 264–65; 55, ibid., p. 309; 3, 1, ibid., p. 421; 3, ibid., p. 425; 4, ibid., p. 426; 15, ibid., p. 468; 22, ibid., pp. 480–81; 27, ibid., pp. 489–90; 28, ibid., p. 493; 30, ibid., pp. 495–96; *P.,* chap. 6, ibid., pp. 25–27; 8, ibid., p. 38; 9, ibid., p. 42; *H.F.,* 5, 8, *MG.,* 3, 1242; 8, 1, ibid., pp. 1383–84.
3. *D.,* 1, 9, *MG.,* 1, 218; 16, ibid., p. 236; 2, 2, ibid., p. 331; 3, 3, ibid., pp. 424–25; 22, ibid., pp. 480–81.
4. 49, ibid., pp. 527–29.
5. *P.,* chap. 9, ibid., p. 41.
6. *D.,* 1, 5, ibid., pp. 204–205.
7. 16, ibid., p. 237.
8. *P.,* chap. 26, ibid., pp. 92–93.

9. *A.W.*, 7, *MG.*, 2, 724.

10. Isa. 2:2–4; Ezek. 24:22–31; Mic. 4:1–8.

11. Strauss, "Machiavelli and Classical Literature," *Review of National Literatures, Italy: Machiavelli "500,"* 1, no. 1 (Spring 1970), p. 25.

12. Ridolfi, pp. 87–91.

13. *P.,* chap. 25, *MG.,* 1, 92; "T.F.," 1. 75, *MG.,* 2, p. 746; Draft of letter to Soderini, ibid., p. 896 *(Lett. fam.,* 116).

14. *D.,* 2, Preface, *MG.,* 1, 324.

15. *A.W.,* 1, *MG.,* 2, 573.

16. 3, ibid., p. 626.

17. 1, ibid., p. 591.

18. 7, ibid., p. 726.

19. 4, ibid., p. 662; 1, ibid., pp. 585–86, 581; *D.,* 2, 20, *MG.,* 1, 382; "Lingua," *Opp. MC.,* pp. 770–71; Legation 11. 14, 16 Oct. 1502, *MG.,* 1, 127.

20. *D.,* 3, 33, *MG.,* 1, 500.

21. 6, ibid., p. 430.

22. 1, 9, ibid., pp. 218, 220; ibid., pp. 241–43; 3, 1, ibid., p. 421; 41, ibid., p. 519; 47, ibid., p. 526; "Lingua," *Opp. MC.,* pp. 770–71; *H.F.,* 2, 22, *MG.,* 3, 1106; 7, ibid., p. 1150; 5, 8, ibid., p. 1242; "The Natures of Florentine Men, Of Francesco Valori," ibid., p. 1438; letter to Vettori, 16 Apr. 1527, *MG.,* 2, 1010 *(Lett. fam.,* 225).

23. "Remodeling," *MG.,* 1, 113–14; *A.W.,* 2, *MG.,* 2, 622; *D.,* 3, 28, *MG.,* 1, 492–93; *H.F.,* 7, 1, *MG.,* 3, 1337; "Lingua," *Opp. MC.,* pp. 770–71; *Mandragola,* act 2, sc. 3, *MG.,* 2, 788–89.

24. *D.,* 1, 31, *MG.,* 1, 412–13; *Opp. MC.,* pp. 770–71.

25. *H.F.,* 2, 22, *MG.,* 3, 1105–1106.

26. Schevill, op. cit., pp. 218–19.

27. Ridolfi, pp. 20–21.

28. Ibid., p. 96.

29. Schevill, op. cit., pp. 438, 467.

30. Tommasini, 1, 151–54; Ridolfi, p. 29.

31. *Postilla ms. de Frammenti storici,* as quoted in Tommasini, 1, 523.

32. Ridolfi, pp. 32–41.

33. Legation 11.44, letter to the Ten, 13 Nov. 1502, *MG.,* 1, 133–34; 53, 26 Nov. 1502, ibid., p. 137.

34. Ridolfi, pp. 80–81.

35. Ibid., p. 88.

36. "A Provision for Infantry," Preamble, *MG.,* 1, 3.

37. Ridolfi, pp. 87–88, 91, 97, 107.

38. Ibid., pp. 89–90.

39. "F.D.," 11. 496–98, *MG.,* 3, 1456.

40. 11. 541–49, ibid., p. 1457.

41. Ridolfi, p. 81.

42. Ibid., pp. 107–108.

43. *A.W.,* 1, *MG.,* 2, 585.

44. *P.,* chaps. 12–13, *MG.,* 1, 47–53; chap. 7, ibid., p. 33.

45. Ibid., p. 54; *D.,* 1, 21, ibid., pp. 246–47; 43, ibid., p. 286; 3, 31, ibid., p. 500; 33, ibid., p. 502; *A.W.,* 1, *MG.,* 2, 573–79, 581, 583–85; *H.F.,* 2, 5–6, *MG.,* 3, 1086; 26, ibid., pp. 1111–12; 5, 9, ibid., p. 1244.

46. *A.W.,* 1, *MG.,* 2, 587.

47. Ridolfi, pp. 212–15.

48. Ferrara, op. cit., p. 351; Ridolfi, p. 89.

49. *H.F.*, 2, 34, *MG.*, 3, 1125.

50. "Remodeling," *MG.*, 1, 110, 115; *P.*, chap. 9, ibid., p. 41.

51. *D.*, 1, 4, ibid., p. 203; 49, ibid., p. 296; 58, ibid., pp. 316–17; 2, 2, ibid., pp. 329, 332–33; 3, 34, ibid., p. 507; *A.W.*, 2, *MG.*, 2, 622; *H.F.*, 7, 33, *MG.*, 3, 1378; "Money," ibid., p. 1443.

52. *H.F.*, Preface, *MG.*, 3, 1030.

53. *D.*, 1, 32, *MG.*, 1, 263–64.

54. 1, 6, ibid., pp. 209–11; 2, 19, ibid., pp. 378–79, 380; *H.F.*, 5, 21, *MG.*, 3, 1261.

55. "A Provision for Infantry," *MG.*, 1, 3.

56. Ibid.

57. *P.*, chap. 12, ibid., p. 47; *D.*, 1, 4, ibid., p. 202; 3, 31, ibid., p. 500; *A.W.*, 2, *MG.*, 2, 619.

58. *D.*, 3, 49, ibid., pp. 527–28.

59. 3, 9, ibid., pp. 452–53; 1, 20, ibid., p. 246.

60. 1, 5, ibid., pp. 204–205; 16, ibid., p. 237.

61. *P.*, chap. 3, ibid., pp. 12–13.

62. *D.*, 1, 55, ibid., p. 309; 3, 28, ibid., p. 493.

63. 1, 18, ibid., p. 243; 9, ibid., p. 219.

64. 1, 2, ibid., pp. 200–201; 1, 9, ibid., p. 218; "Remodeling," ibid., pp. 113–15.

65. *A.W.*, 2, *MG.*, 2, 619.

66. *D.*, 3, 1, *MG.*, 1, 419, 421, 422; 11, ibid., p. 459; 37, ibid., p. 512.

67. 3, 11, ibid., p. 457.

68. 1, ibid., pp. 419, 422.

69. Ibid., p. 421.

70. 22, ibid., p. 481; 1, ibid., p. 419.

71. Ridolfi, pp. 135–36.

72. Ibid., pp. 202–203.

73. *D.*, 3, 6, ibid., p. 428.

74. *H.F.*, 3, 12–16, *MG.*, 3, 1158–66.

75. *A.W.*, 6, *MG.*, 2, 703.

76. "T.A.," 11. 176–77, ibid., p. 739; *D.*, 2, 1, *MG.*, 1, 324; *A.W.*, 2, *MG.*, 2, 624; "Money," *MG.*, 3, 1443; *P.*, chap. 25, *MG.*, 1, 89–90.

77. Draft of letter to Soderini, *MG.*, 2, 896; *D.*, 2, 29, *MG.*, 1, 407–408.

78. *D.*, 2, 30, *MG.*, 1, 412.

79. "L.C.," *MG.*, 2, 533–34.

80. *D.*, 3, 31, *MG.*, 1, 498.

81. *A.W.*, 2, *MG.*, 2, 624.

82. Letter to Vettori, 10 Dec. 1513, *MG.*, 2, 927.

83. *D.*, 2, 29, *MG.*, 1, 407–408.

84. *D.*, 3, 9, *MG.*, 1, 452.

85. "S.D.," 1. 45, *MG.*, 3, 1458.

86. Letter to Giovanni Vernacci, 15 Feb. 1515–(1516), *MG.*, 2, 964 (*Lett. fam.*, 162); 8 June 1517, ibid., p. 966 (*Lett. fam.*, 164); 5 Jan. 1517–(1518), ibid., p. 968 (*Lett. fam.*, 167); to Vettori, 10 Dec. 1513, ibid., p. 929 (*Lett. fam.*, 137).

87. To Vernacci, 25 Jan. 1517–(1518), ibid., p. 969.

88. "G.A.," chap. 3, 11. 76–87, ibid., p. 757; 11. 100–102, 118–20, p. 758.

89. *A.W.*, 7, ibid., p. 726; *D.*, 2, Preface, *MG.*, 1, 324.

90. *P.*, chap. 25, *MG.*, 1, 90.

91. *D.*, 2, 29, ibid., p. 408.

92. *P.*, chap. 6, ibid., p. 25.

93. *H.F.*, 1, 9, *MG.*, 3, 1196.

94. 3, 5, ibid., p. 1148.

95. *D.*, 3, 31, *MG.*, 1, 498.

96. 2, 30 ibid., p. 412.

97. *P.*, chap. 25, ibid., p. 90; *D.*, 3, 9, ibid., p. 452; Draft of letter to Soderini, *MG.*, 2, 897 (*Lett. fam.*, 116); "T.F.," 11. 115–20; ibid., p. 747; "S.D.," 11. 181–92, *MG.*, 3, 1461.

98. *P.*, chap. 25, *MG.*, 1, 92; *D.*, 2, 10, ibid., p. 350; 3, 10, ibid., p. 456; Draft of letter to Soderini, ibid., p. 896 (*Lett. fam.*, 116); letter to Vettori, 20 Dec. 1514 (*Letter No. 1*), ibid., p. 954.

99. Letter to Vettori, 18 Mar. 1512, ibid., p. 899 (*Lett. fam.*, 119).

100. "G.A.," chap. 4, 11. 4–12, ibid., pp. 758–59.

101. *P.*, Dedication, *MG.*, 1, 11.

102. Ibid., p. 10; chap. 26, ibid., pp. 92–96; letter to Vettori, 10 Dec. 1513, *MG.*, 2, 929–30 (*Lett. fam.*, 137); *D.*, Dedication, *MG.*, 1, 188; Preface, ibid., pp. 190–92; *A.W.*, Preface, *MG.*, 2, 567.

103. Ferrara, op. cit., p. 245.

104. Ibid., p. 295.

105. Ibid., p. 321.

106. *A.W.*, 7, *MG.*, 2, 726.

107. *P.*, chap. 26, *MG.*, 1, 96.

108. *D.*, 1, Preface, *MG.*, 1, 190–91; 2, Preface, ibid., p. 324; *A.W.*, Preface, *MG.*, 2, 566–67; 7, ibid., p. 726; *H.F.*, Preface, *MG.*, 3, 1031; 5, 1, ibid., p. 1233.

109. "Portraits of the Affairs of France," Pansini, pp. 639–48; *Opp. MC.*, pp. 731–39.

110. "Portraits of the Affairs of Germany," Pansini, pp. 649–57; *Opp. MC.*, pp. 740–43.

111. Tommasini, 2, Prefazione, xxiv, n.

112. *D.*, 1, 9, *MG.*, 1, 217–20.

113. 17–18, ibid., pp. 238–43; 55, ibid., p.309; 3, 1, ibid., pp. 421–22.

114. 3, 6, ibid., p. 428.

115. 3, 28, ibid., p. 492.

116. *A.W.*, 2, *MG.*, 2, 622.

117. *D.*, 1, 4, *MG.*, 1, 203; 3, 28, ibid., p. 493.

118. 1, 46, ibid., p. 291; 3, 28, ibid., pp. 492–93.

119. "Lingua," *Opp. MC.*, pp. 770–71; "Remodeling," *MG.*, 1, 113–14.

120. *A.W.*, 1, *MG.*, 2, 585–86; *D.*, 1, 43; *MG.*, 1, 286; 3, 33, ibid., p. 502.

121. Jacob Bronowski, "The Ascent of Man," a television broadcast series.

122. *P.*, chap. 25, *MG.*, 1, 90.

123. Chap. 26, ibid., p. 94.

124. *D.*, 1, 1, ibid., p. 194; *A.W.*, 1, *MG.*, 2, 579.

125. "Ghiribizzi," *Opp. MC.*, p. 879; Pansini, p. 1152.

126. *P.*, chap. 23, *MG.*, 1, 87–88.

127. *D.*, 2, 29, ibid., p. 408; 14, ibid., pp. 359–60; 1, 32, ibid., p. 263; 52, ibid., p. 299; *A.W.*, 4, *MG.*, 2, 656; Legation 11.40, 8 Nov. 1502, *MG.*, 1, 132.

128. *D.*, 1, 28, *MG.*, 1, 405.

129. 3, 6, ibid., p. 430.

130. "Exhortations to Penitence," ibid., p. 173.

131. *D.*, 3, 6, ibid., p. 442.

132. *H.F.*, 8, 1, *MG.*, 3, 1383–84.

133. J. Harley Cotton, "Exposition," Heb. 2:6–9, *I.B.*, 11, 611.

134. *D.*, 1, 26, *MG.*, 1, 254; Tommasini, 2, 716–17 and n.; "Remodeling," *MG.*, 1, 107.

135. Letter to Vettori, 16 Apr. 1527, *MG.*, 2, 1010 (*Lett. fam.*, 225).

136. Tommasini, 2, 759, 576 n.4, 945.

137. Ibid., p. 945.

138. Legation 11.14, 16 Oct. 1502, *MG.*, 1, 127.

139. *D.*, 3, 31, *MG.*, 1, 498.

140. 1, 10, ibid., p. 222; Tommasini, 2, 717.

141. *A.W.*, 2, *MG.*, 2, 623.

142. *D.*, 3, 31, *MG.*, 1, 500; "A Provision for Infantry," ibid., p. 3; *P.*, chap. 11, ibid., p. 47.

143. *A.W.*, Preface, *MG.*, 2, 567; Tommasini, 1, 364–65 and n.1.

144. "Exhortation to Penitence," *MG.*, 1, 173.

145. Tommasini, 2, 582, 586.

146. Aristotle, op. cit., 1, 5.

147. *D.*, 4, 43, *MG.*, 1, 521; 1, 55, ibid., p. 309; 2, 4, ibid., p. 339; *P.*, chap. 26, ibid., p. 93.

148. Legation 11.44, 13 Nov. 1502, ibid., pp. 133–34; letter to Vettori, 31 Jan. 1514–(1515), *MG.*, 2, 962 (*Lett. fam.*, 159); *P.*, chap. 7, *MG.*, 1, 28–29, 33; chap. 13, 52–53, 54–55.

149. *P.*, chap. 26, *MG.*, 1, 94.

150. "Remodeling," ibid., p. 107.

151. *H.F.*, 3, 1, *MG.*, 3, 1141.

152. *A.W.*, Preface, *MG.*, 2, 567; 1, ibid., p. 571; 7, ibid., p. 726; *H.F.*, Preface, *MG.*, 3, 1031; 5, 1, ibid., p. 1233.

153. Tommasini, 2, 425.

154. Ridolfi,p. 89.

155. *D.*, 1, 20, *MG.*, 1, 246; *A.W.*, 2, *MG.*, 2, 622.

156. *D.*, 2, 19, *MG.*, 1, 378–79.

157. *P.*, chap. 16, ibid., pp. 60–61.

158. *D.*, 2, 6, ibid., pp. 341–43; *H.F.*, 6, 1, *MG.*, 3, 1284.

159. *P.*, chap. 16, *MG.*, 1, 60; *D.*, 2, 6, ibid., pp. 341–43.

160. *H.F.*, 4, 14, *MG.*, 3, 1202.

CHAPTER NINE

1. Tommasini, 2, 482.

2. *D.*, 1, 4, *MG.*, 1, 202–203; *H.F.*, 3, 1, 1140–41.

3. *D.*, 1, 18, *MG.*, 1, 242; 2, 2, ibid., p. 332; 4, ibid., p. 339; *A.W.*, 2, *MG.*, 2, 622–23; *H.F.*, 3, 1, *MG.*, 3, 1141.

4. *D.*, 2, 2, *MG.*, 1, 331; *A.W.*, 2, *MG.*, 2, 623.

5. *D.*, 2, 2, *MG.*, 1, 332.

6. Tommasini, 2, 658–59 and n.2.

7. Ibid., p. 652.

8. *D.*, 1, 12, *MG.*, 1, 228–29; 3, 1, ibid., p. 422.

9. Tommasini, 2, 613–14, 634.

10. *D.*, 3, 1, *MG.*, 1, 419–23.

11. *A.W.*, Preface, *MG.*, 2, 566–67; 7, ibid., p. 726.
12. *D.*, 1, 12, *MG.*, 1, 228; 3, 1, ibid., p. 422.
13. Ibid.
14. Ibid.
15. 1, 11–12, ibid., pp. 223–27.
16. 1, 11, ibid., p. 225.
17. Hough, "The Message of the Book of Revelation," 17:1–6, *I.B.*, 12, 599.
18. Matt. 4:3–4; Luke 4:2–4.
19. Matt. 4:5–7; Luke 4:9–12.
20. Matt. 4:8–10; Luke 4:5–8.
21. John 2:4.
22. Matt. 12:46–50; Mark 3:31–35; Luke 18:28–30; John 7:3–8.
23. Luke 10:29–37; 17:11–19.
24. Matt. 8:20, 16:15–28, 17:12–13, 20:17–28, 26:26–35; Mark 8:31–38; Luke 9:21–27, 44–45, 57–58.
25. Matt. 26:39, 42; Mark 14:35–36; Luke 22:42.
26. Matt. 26:51–56; Luke 22:49–53; John 18:10–11.
27. Matt. 27:46; Mark 15:34.
28. John 19:30; Luke 23:46.
29. R. H. Strachan, "The Gospel in the New Testament," *I.B.*, 7, 12.
30. John 10:10.
31. Tommasini, 2, 655–56 and n.6.
32. Ibid., pp. 287–88, 39 and n.1.
33. "Exhortation to Penitence," *MG.*, 1, 173.
34. "L.C.," *MG.*, 2, 558; Tommasini, 2, 723, n.1.
35. Matt. 16:23; Mark 8:33; Matt. 19:17; Mark 10:18; Matt. 23:8–12.
36. Matt. 7:1–5; Luke 6:37, 42.
37. Deut. 10:16–19.
38. Mark 12:29–31.
39. Luke 10:27–37.
40. Matt. 6:12; Luke 11:4.
41. Luke 4:17–22.
42. W. M. Macgregor, *The Making of a Preacher* (London: Student Christian Movement Press, 1945), p. 70, as quoted by Morgan P. Noyes, "Exposition," 2 Tim. 3:17, *I.B.*, 11, 507.
43. Matt. 11:12 (alternative reading in *N.E.B.*); Tommasini, 2, 657 ("567," *sic*)—658 and n.
44. Paul W. Hoon, "Exposition," I John 2:4–5, *I.B.*, 12, 231.
45. Matt. 8:13, 9:29, 17:20; Mark 1:15, 5:36; Luke 8:50; Mark 9:23, 11:24; John 1:7.
46. Bos, *Psychologie de la croyance* (Paris, 1902), p. 7, as quoted in Tommasini, 2, 760 n.1.
47. Matt. 6:12, 14–15, 18:35; Mark 11:25; Luke 11:4.
48. Matt. 5:17.
49. John Short, "Exposition," I Cor. 1:18–25, *I.B.*, 10, 30. Copyright renewal © 1981 by Abingdon. Used by permission.
50. *A.W.*, 1, *MG.*, 2, 579.
51. Matt. 20:25–28.
52. Luke 2:10.
53. Luke 12:32, 35.
54. John 14:27, 30–31.
55. I John 4:18–21.

56. Mark 16:15–16.
57. Rom. 1:16.
58. Heb. 7:25.
59. Rev. 22:17.
60. *P.*, chap. 15, *MG.*, 1, 57.
61. *D.*, 1, 18, ibid., p. 240.
62. Matt. 26:51–52; John 18:10–11.
63. *P.*, chap. 17, *MG.*, 1, 64.
64. Matt. 11:12 (alternative reading in *N.E.B.*).
65. Mark 13:33, 14:38.
66. Luke 12:35, 40, 49.
67. Ibid., 21:34, 36; Matt. 24:42, 26:41.
68. Matt. 21:31.
69. Ibid., 23:3–4.
70. Luke 10:37.
71. Matt. 25:34–40.
72. Ibid., 6:10–12.
73. Ibid., 14–15.
74. Ibid., 5:16.
75. Ibid., 7:12.
76. Ibid., 24–29.
77. John 21:25.
78. Ibid., 5:8.
79. Acts 17:28.
80. I Cor. 8:1.
81. John Knox, "Exposition," Luke 11:14–19, *I.B.*, 8, 206.
82. Matt. 5:44–45, 48.
83. Ibid., 26:51–54; John 18:10–11.
84. Luke 9:54–56.
85. II Cor. 11:23–33.
86. I Cor. 9:24–26; Gal. 2:2, 5:7; I Tim. 6:12; II Tim. 4:7–8.
87. I Cor. 9:26.
88. Rom. 13:12–14; II Cor. 6:7, 10:3–6; Eph. 6:10–18; I Thess. 5:8.
89. Jas. 1:22.
90. Ibid., 2:17.
91. *D.*, 2, 2, *MG.*, 1, 331.
92. Ibid.
93. Roland H. Bainton, *Christian Attitudes Toward War and Peace. A Historical Survey and Critical Re-evaluation* (New York: Abingdon Press, 1960), pp. 67–68. Copyright © 1960 by Abingdon Press. Used by permission.
94. Ibid., pp. 72–73.
95. *Columbia History,* p. 231.
96. *P.*, chap. 15, *MG.*, 1, 57–58.
97. Ibid., n.3.
98. Deut. 30:11–14, 19–20.
99. Jer. 29:12–14, 31:31, 33–34.
100. Ezek. 11:17–20, 36:23–24, 26–28.
101. Isa. 57:15.
102. Walter Russell Bowie, "Exposition," Luke 3:21, *I.B.*, 8, 78.
103. Matt. 5:17–18.
104. Isa. 11:10, 42:1–4, 49:6; Jer. 16:19–21; Hos. 2:23; Mal. 1:11.

515

105. Matt. 8:10–13.

106. S. MacLean Gilmour, "Exposition," Acts 28:28, *I.B.*, 8, 7.

107. Acts 8:26–39.

108. Ibid., 10–11:18.

109. Ibid., 14:46–49; Rom. 11.

110. Ibid., 10:34.

111. *D.*, 1, 11, *MG.*, 1, 224–25; 15, ibid., p. 234.

112. Letter to Vettori, 16 Apr. 1527, *MG.*, 2, 1010 *(Lett. fam.,* 225).

113. *P.*, chap. 15, *MG.*, 1, 57.

114. *D.*, 1, 18, ibid., p. 240; 58, ibid., pp. 313–14.

115. Letter to Vettori, 20 June 1513, *MG.*, 2, 911 *(Lett. fam.,* 124); 20 Dec. 1514 *(No. 2),* ibid., p. 958 *(Lett. fam.,* 155); letter to Guicciardini, 30 Aug. 1523, ibid., p. 978 *(Lett. fam.,* 186).

116. Harnack, *Mission und Ausbreitung des Christentums,* p. 214 as quoted in Tommasini, 2, 572 n.1.

117. John 10:10.

118. Eph. 3:20.

119. Mark 10:29–30; Luke 18:29–30.

120. Matt. 6:25, 32–33, 8; Luke 12:22–23, 29–31.

121. Matt. 5:17–18.

122. Deut. 30:11–14, 19–20; Jer. 29:12–14, 31:31, 33:34; Ezek. 11:17–20, 36:23–24, 26–28; Isa. 57:15.

123. Matt. 5:43, 48, 6:1, 4, 6, 8, 9, 14–15, 18, 26, 32, 23:9; Luke 11:2.

124. Matt. 23:8–12.

125. *Columbia History,* pp. 230–32.

126. Ibid., p. 382.

127. Ibid., pp. 388–90, 421.

128. *H.F.*, 1, 25, *MG.*, 3, 1063.

129. Tommasini, 2, 586 and n.2; Ferrara, op. cit., p. 351.

130. Tommasini, 2, 748–58.

131. Matt. 18:12–13; Luke 15:4–7.

132. Luke 15:8–10.

133. Ibid., 11–32.

134. Matt. 13:25–30.

135. Ibid., 47–49.

136. Ibid., 5:43–45.

137. I John 4:16, 19.

138. John 15:26.

139. Amos N. Wilder, "Exegesis," on I John 1:3–5a, *I.B.*, 12, 230–31.

140. Mark 14:62 (alternative reading *N.E.B.*).

141. Luke 17:20.

142. Ibid., 21 (alternative reading *N.E.B.*).

143. I Cor. 10:16–17, 12:12–13; Rom. 12:4–5; Eph. 1:22–23, 4:12; Col. 1:28.

144. Phil. 3:20 (Moffatt translation).

145. Tommasini, 2, 594.

146. Ibid., pp. 571, 589.

147. *D.*, 2, 2, *MG.*, 1, 331.

148. Tommasini, 2, 572, n.1.

149. Ibid., p. 575; I Kings 19:12; Isa. 11:10, 42:1, 49:6; Jer. 16:19, 31:29–31, 33–34; Ezek. 18:20; Hos. 2:23; Mal. 1:11.

150. Acts 22:28.

151. Ibid., 23:6, 26:5; Phil. 3:5.

152. Acts 8:1, 3, 9:21, 26, 26:9–11; Phil. 3:6.

153. Acts 22:25–29, 23:27, 25:11.

154. Ibld., 25:11.

155. Morgan P. Noyes, "Exposition," I Tim. 3:9, *I.B.*, 11, 418.

156. Tommasini, 2, 588.

157. Bainton, op. cit., pp. 73–75.

158. Ibid., p. 70.

159. *Columbia History*, pp. 230–31; Tommasini, 2, 584–85.

160. *Webster's New World Dictionary*, "Saint Cyprian."

161. Tommasini, 2, 650.

162. Ibid., pp. 580–81.

163. Ibid., pp. 600, 610–11.

164. H. Ch. Lea, *A History of the Inquisition of the Middle Ages* (New York, 1, 213), quoted in Tommasini, 2, 601 n.1.

165. Bainton, op. cit., pp. 111, 114.

166. *Columbia History*, p. 389.

167. Tommasini, 2, 610–15; Bainton, op. cit., pp. 115–16; *Columbia History*, pp. 389–90.

168. *Columbia History*, p. 390; Bainton, op. cit., p. 115; Tommasini, 2, 616–17.

169. Tommasini, 2, 634–45, 658–59 n.2.

170. George H. Sabine, *A History of Political Theory* (New York: Holt, Rinehart and Winston, 1961), p. 280.

CHAPTER TEN

1. W. Windelband, *A History of Philosophy, with especial reference to the formation and development of its problems and conceptions,* trans. James H. Tufts (New York: Macmillan, 1919), p. 42.

2. E. Troeltsch, *Politische Ethik und Christentum* (Göttingen, 1904), pp. 22, 25 as quoted in Tommasini, 2, 729.

3. Tommasini, 2, 729.

4. Meinecke, op. cit., p. 35.

5. I Sam. 8:5, 20.

6. Ibid., 7–22.

7. Jer. 31:31–34.

8. Matt. 20:24–28.

9. Sherman Johnson, "Exegesis," on Matt. 5:44, *I.B.*, 7, 303.

10. *Epistle to Diognetus*, 5:5 as quoted by Elmer H. Homrighausen in "Exposition," I Pet. 1:2, *I.B.*, 12, 89; I John 2:15–17.

11. *D.*, 1, 11, *MG.*, 1, 226; Preface, ibid., pp. 191; 39, ibid., p. 278; 2, Preface, ibid., p. 324; 3, 43, ibid., pp. 521–22; Preface, *MG.*, 3, 1031.

12. *H.F.*, 5, 1, *MG.*, 3, 1232; "G.A.," 5, 11. 88–105, *MG.*, 2, 763; Martin Rist, "Exegesis," and Lynn Harold Hough, "Exposition," Rev. 20:12–13, *I.B.*, 12, 524–28.

13. Ezek. 18:23.

14. Luke 15:7.

15. I John 4:7–9, 16, 20–21.

16. Acts 17:27–28.

17. John 14:16–17.

18. Sabine, op. cit., p. 273.

19. Egidius Colonna, *De ecclesiastica potestate,* ed. R. Scholz as *Aegidius Romanus D . . . e . . . p . . .* (Weimar, 1929), II, 7, p. 75 as quoted in Sabine, op. cit., p. 275.

20. Sabine, op. cit., p. 281.

21. Ibid., pp. 280–81.

22. Matt. 26:64 (alternative translation, *N.E.B.*).

23. A. E. Taylor, *The Faith of a Moralist* (London: Macmillan & Co., 1930), 1, 188–89, as quoted by R. H. Strachan, "The Gospel in the New Testament," *I.B.,* 7, 11–12.

24. Strachan, ibid.

25. I John 4:19.

26. John 14:16.

27. Prezzolini, "Christian Roots . . . ," op. cit., p. 29.

28. Meinecke, op. cit., pp. 36, 39.

29. Tommasini, 2, 634 and n.3.

30. *D.,* 3, 1, *MG.,* 1, 419.

31. 2, 2, ibid., p. 328.

32. Matt. 23:33, 36–38; Luke 13:34–35.

33. Luke 19:41–42.

34. Letter to Vettori, 26 Aug. 1513, *MG.,* 2, 926 *(Lett. fam.,* 134).

35. Ridolfi, p. 224.

36. Letter to Guicciardini, 17 May 1526, *MG.,* 2, 998 *(Lett. fam.,* 207).

37. Matt. 11:12 (alternative reading in *N.E.B.).*

38. James W. Clarke, "Exposition," II Thess. 1:5–10, *I.B.,* 11, 319–21.

39. Ridolfi, pp. 212–14.

40. Ibid., pp. 227–28.

41. Ibid., p. 229.

42. Mansfield, op. cit., p. 207.

43. Luke 2:10.

44. Ibid., 12:32, 35.

45. Letter to Vettori, 5 Apr. 1527, *MG.,* 2, 1008 *(Lett. fam.,* 223).

46. *A.W.,* 7, ibid., p. 718; 4, ibid., p. 658.

47. *P.,* chap. 17, *MG.,* 1, 64.

48. *D.,* 3, 49, ibid., pp. 527–29.

49. Letter to Guicciardini, 19 Dec. 1525, *MG.,* 2, 989 *(Lett. fam.,* 200).

50. *D.,* 1, 18, *MG.,* 1, 240; 58, ibid., pp. 313–14.

51. Letter to Vettori, 20 June 1513, *MG.,* 2, 911 *(Lett. fam.,* 124).

52. "S.D.," 11. 181–86, 190–92, *MG.,* 3, 1461.

53. Matt. 6:33.

54. Luke 8:50.

55. Heb. 11:1; James W. Clarke, "Exposition," I Thess. 5:23–28, *I.B.,* 11, 315.

56. Theodore M. Greene, "Christianity and its Secular Alternatives," in Henry P. Van Dusen, ed. *The Christian Answer* (New York: Charles Scribner's Sons, 1945) p. 76 as quoted by Morgan P. Noyes, "Exposition," I Tim. 3:6, *I.B.,* 11, 416.

57. Jas. 2:17.

58. *D.,* 1, Preface, *MG.,* 1, 191–92; 2, Preface, ibid., p. 324; *A.W.,* 7, *MG.,* 2, 726.

59. Alfred E. Barnett, "Exegesis," on II Pet. 3:11–13, *I.B.,* 12, 203.

60. Elmer G. Homrighausen, "Exposition," II Pet. 3:14, ibid., p. 204.

61. *D.,* 1, 9, *MG.,* 1, 218.

62. 2, 28, ibid., p. 405.

63. "Lingua," *Opp. MC.,* pp. 770–71; letter to Vettori, 16 Apr. 1527, *MG.,* 2, 1010 *(Lett. fam.,* 225).

64. Luke 9:23, 14:27.

65. *D.*, 3, 47, *MG.*, 1, 526.

66. 1, 51, ibid., p. 299; 52, ibid., pp. 300–302; 3, 12, ibid., pp. 459–62; *A.W.*, 4, *MG.*, 2, 662.

67. John Knox, "Exposition," Luke 14:26, *I.B.*, 8, 259.

68. Luke 14:26–27, 33.

69. Matt. 11:19; Luke 7:34.

70. *P.*, chap. 15, *MG.*, 1, 57.

71. *D.*, 2, Preface, *MG.*, 1, 321; 2, 10, ibid., p. 221; *A.W.*, 2, *MG.*, 2, 622–23.

72. *D.*, 1, 26, *MG.*, 1, 254; "Remodeling," ibid., p. 107; *P.*, chap. 8, ibid., p. 36.

73. *D.*, 2, 2, ibid., p. 331; 3, 1, ibid., p. 422; letter to Guicciardini, 17 May 1521, *MG.*, 2, 972.

74. *D.*, 1, 12, *MG.*, 1, 228; *H.F.*, 1, 23–25, *MG.*, 3, 1062–64; 2, 10, ibid., p. 1092; 8, 11, ibid., pp. 1398–99.

75. *D.*, 1, 12, *MG.*, 1, 228; 3, 1, ibid., p. 422; *Mandragola, MG.*, 2, 776–821.

76. *D.*, 1, 6, *MG.*, 1, 209; 2, 19, ibid., p. 380.

77. 2, 2, ibid., p. 332; 19, ibid., p. 381; *A.W.*, 2, *MG.*, 2, 623.

78. *H.F.*, 5, 1, *MG.*, 3, 1232; "G.A.," chap. 5, ll. 88–105, *MG.*, 2, 763.

79. *P.*, chap. 15, *MG.*, 1, 57.

80. Ibid.

81. "S.D.," ll. 190–92, *MG.*, 3, 1461.

82. Luke 12:6–7; Matt. 10:29–31.

83. Luke 15; Matt. 18:10–14.

84. Matt. 25:40, 34–40; Luke 10:29–37.

85. John 3:3–8.

86. Eph. 4:23–24.

87. Col. 3:8–10.

88. Gal. 6:15.

89. Robert H. Wicks, "Exposition," Phil. 2:1–5, *I.B.*, 11, 47.

90. Draft of letter to Soderini, Jan. 1512–(1513), *MG.*, 2, 896–97 *(Lett. fam.,* 116).

91. *P.*, chap. 25, *MG.*, 1, 90.

92. 26, ibid., p. 94.

93. *A.W.*, 1, *MG.*, 2, 579.

94. *D.*, 1, 3, *MG.*, 1, 201; 1, ibid., p. 194; "T.F.," l. 85, *MG.*, 2, 747.

95. *A.W.*, 7, *MG.*, 2, 721.

96. "Ghiribizzi," *Opp. MC.*, p. 879.

97. *P.*, chap. 25, *MG.*, 1, 92.

98. Letter to Vettori, 25 Feb. 1513–(1514), *MG.*, 2, 941 *(Lett. fam.,* 144).

99. Ibid.

100. *A.W.*, 7, *MG.*, 2, 721.

101. *D.*, 1, 1, *MG.*, 1, 194.

102. *A.W.*, 4, *MG.*, 2, 657.

103. *H.F.*, 6, 13, *MG.*, 3, 1299.

104. *D.*, 2, 29, *MG.*, 1, 408.

105. Letter to Vettori, 5 Apr. 1527, *MG.*, 2, 1008 *(Lett. fam.,* 223).

106. Letter to Guido, 2 Apr. 1527, *MG.*, 2, 1006 *(Lett. fam.,* 222).

107. *P.*, chap. 24, *MG.*, 1, 89.

108. *A.W.*, 1, *MG.*, 2, 587.

109. *D.*, 3, 6, ibid., p. 438.

110. *A.W.*, 4, *MG.*, 2, 662; 1, ibid., pp. 581, 584–85, 585–86, 587; *D.*, 3, 31, *MG.*, 1, 500; 33, ibid., p. 502; *H.F.*, 2, 5–6, *MG.*, 3, 1086; 26, ibid., 1111–12; 5, 9, ibid., p. 1244.

111. Letter to Vettori, 20 Dec. 1514 *(No. 3), MG.,* 2, 960 *(Lett. fam.,* 156).
112. "Lingua," *Opp. MC.,* pp. 770–71; *D.,* 3, 47, *MG.,* 1, 526.
113. Matt. 6:25–34.
114. Ibid., 14.
115. Ibid., 7:1–5; Luke 6:37.
116. Matt. 7:12.
117. Ibid., 25:34–40; Luke 10:29–37.
118. *Columbia History,* pp. 398–99; Sabine, op. cit., pp. 273–74.
119. *D.,* 3, 1, *MG.,* 1, 422.
120. 2, 2, ibid., p. 331; 3, 1, p. 422.
121. Tommasini, 2, 746 n.3.
122. Letter to Guicciardini, 19 Dec. 1525, *MG.,* 2, 989 *(Lett. fam.,* 200).
123. "S.D.," 11. 181–92; *MG.,* 3, 1461.
124. Matt. 25:13, 24:42, 26:41; Mark 14:38; Luke 21:36.
125. Mark 13:33, 37.
126. Luke 12:35.
127. Matt. 13:9; Mark 4:9.
128. *A.W.,* 1, *MG.,* 2, 579.
129. "G.A.," chap. 5, 11. 115–18, 124–27, ibid., p. 764.
130. *D.,* 1, 1, *MG.,* 1, 194.
131. 3, 6, ibid., pp. 429–30.
132. 1, 43, ibid., p. 286.
133. 2, 2, ibid., p. 329.
134. *H.F.,* 2, 34, *MG.,* 3, 1124.
135. Matt. 7:25–32; Luke 12:6–7.
136. *A.W.,* 1, *MG.,* 2, 579.
137. *P.,* chap. 26, *MG.,* 1, 95.
138. *A.W.,* 2, *MG.,* 2, 622.
139. *D.,* 2, 6, *MG.,* 1, 341–43.
140. "Lingua," *Opp. MC.,* pp. 770–71.
141. Matt. 20:25; Luke 11:46.
142. Mark 7:29.
143. Luke 19:18–19.
144. Mark 5:34.
145. *D.,* 3, *MG.,* 3, 31, 500; 32, p. 502.
146. John 3:3, 5–8; "Lingua," *Opp. MC.,* pp. 770–71.
147. John 14:16–17; "S.D.," 11. 190–92, *MG.,* 3, 1461.

CHAPTER ELEVEN

1. Ferrara, op. cit., p. 244.
2. Sabine, op. cit., pp. 315–16.
3. Ibid., pp. 274–75.
4. Ibid., pp. 280–82.
5. Hough, "Exposition," Rev. 8:3, *I.B.,* 12, 427.
6. Samuel Eliot Morison, Henry Steele Commager, William E. Leuchtenburg, *The Growth of the American Republic* (New York: Oxford University Press, 1969), 1, 77 (hereafter referred to as Morison, *et al.*)
7. Alfred Owen Aldridge, *Man of Reason, The Life of Thomas Paine* (New York: Lipincott, 1959), p. 169.
8. Aristotle, op. cit., p. 5.

9. Kemmerich, op. cit., p. 172.

10. *D.*, 2, 4, *MG.*, 1, 335–39; Tommasini, 2, 44–45.

11. *D.*, 3, 1, ibid., p. 419; 17, ibid., p. 471; Tommasini, 2, 44–45.

12. Meinecke, op. cit., pp. 39–41.

13. *D.*, 2, 2, *MG.*, 1, 331.

14. Matt. 4:17, 10:7.

15. Matt. 6:8; Luke 12:30.

16. Deut. 10:14; Exod. 9:29; Ps. 24:1; I Cor. 10:26.

17. Matt. 6:14.

18. Ibid., 7:1–2, 5; Luke 6:37, 42.

19. Luke 10:25–37, 25:34–40, 45.

20. Matt. 7:12; Luke 6:31.

21. Matt. 6:25, 32–34, 7:7–8, 11; John 14:2–3.

22. Nicholas Berdayev, *Freedom and the Spirit*, p. 268 as quoted by Gossip in "Exposition," John 12:24–26, *I.B.*, 8, 663.

23. *D.*, 2, 28, *MG.*, 1, 405, 406; 3, 4, ibid., p. 426; 6, ibid., pp. 430, 438; *P.*, chap. 19, ibid., p. 74.

24. "Money," *MG.*, 3, 1443.

25. *P.*, chap. 25, *MG.*, 1, 90; "T.F.," 11. 13–15, 25–30, *MG.*, 2, 745; "S.D.," 11. 181–92, *MG.*, 3, 1461.

26. "Lingua," *Opp. MC.*, pp. 770–71.

27. Henry J. Cadbury, *Jesus: What Manner of Man* (New York: Macmillan, 1947), pp. 26–27 as quoted by John Knox, "Exposition," Luke 10:13–14, *I.B.*, 8, 187.

28. *D.*, 1, 3, *MG.*, 1, 201.

29. 3, 12, ibid., p. 460.

30. *P.*, chap. 15, ibid., p. 57.

31. Herbert Butterfield, "Machiavelli's Historical Method and Statecraft," in De Lemar Jensen, *Machiavelli* . . . , etc., op. cit., p. 58.

32. *D.*, Preface, *MG.*, 1, 191; 1, 11, ibid., p. 226; 39, ibid., p. 278; 58, ibid., p. 315; 3, 43, ibid., p. 521.

33. *H.F.*, 5, 1, *MG.*, 3, 1232; "G.A.," chap. 5, 11. 76–105, *MG.*, 2, 763.

34. *D.*, 1, 58, *MG.*, 1, 316.

35. 9, ibid., p. 218; *H.F.*, 4, 1, *MG.*, 3, 1187.

36. Sherman E. Johnson, "Exegesis," on Matt. 14:17, *I.B.*, 7, 430.

37. Letter to Vettori, 25 Feb. 1513–(1514), *MG.*, 2, 941 *(Lett. fam.*, 144); *D.*, 1, 1, *MG.*, 1, 194.

38. *D.*, 1, 6, *MG.*, 1, 209, 211.

39. *A.W.*, 2, *MG.*, 2, 622.

40. "Ghiribizzi," *Opp. MC.*, p. 879; *P.*, chap. 24, *MG.*, 1, 89.

41. *D.*, 3, 6, *MG.*, 1, 430; 2, 28, ibid., pp. 405, 406; 3, 6, ibid., p. 438; *P.*, chap. 19, ibid., p. 74.

42. Draft of letter to Soderini, *MG.*, 2, 895–96 *(Lett. fam.*, 116).

43. *D.*, 1, Preface, *MG.*, 1, 190.

44. 1, 28, ibid., p. 240; 58, ibid., pp. 313–14; letter to Vettori, 20 June 1513, *MG.*, 2, 911 *(Lett. fam.*, 124).

45. *P.*, chap. 15, *MG.*, 1, 57.

46. "Lingua," *Opp. MC.*, p. 770; letter to Vettori, 16 Apr. 1527, *MG.*, 2, 1010 *(Lett. fam.*, 225); "Remodeling," *MG.*, 1, 113–14.

47. *D.*, 2, 2, *MG.*, 1, 331–32; 3, 24, ibid., pp. 485–86; *A.W.*, 2, *MG.*, 2, 622–23; *H.F.*, 3, 1, *MG.*, 3, 1140–41.

48. *D.*, 1, 11, *MG.*, 1, 226; 1, Preface, ibid., p. 191; *P.*, chap. 25, ibid., pp. 89–92; "S.D.," 11. 181–92, *MG.*, 3, 1461.

49. "Lingua," *Opp. MC.*, pp. 770–71.
50. Letter to Vettori, 16 Apr. 1527, *MG*, 2, 1010 (*Lett. fam.*, 225).
51. Tommasini, 2, 482.
52. *H.F.*, 1, 1, *MG.*, 3, 1034–35; Tommasini, 2, 489–90, 503 n.1.
53. "Lingua," *Opp. MC.*, pp. 770–71.
54. Vignal, op. cit., p. 213.
55. Ibid., p. 225.
56. *D.*, 1, 9, *MG.*, 1, 218; 4, ibid., p. 203; 49, ibid., p. 295; *H.F.*, 4, 1, *MG.*, 3, 1187.
57. *D.*, 3, 28, *MG.*, 1, 492–93.
58. 34, ibid., pp. 505–507.
59. 49, ibid., p. 527.
60. 1, 4, ibid., p. 203.
61. 11–12, ibid., pp. 223–27; 2, 2, ibid., p. 331.
62. 2, 2, ibid., p. 331.
63. Cragg, "Exposition," Rom. 10:2, *I.B.*, 9, 554–55.
64. "T.F.," 11. 13–15, *MG.*, 2, 745; "S.D.," 11. 181–192, *MG.*, 3, 1461.
65. "Lingua," *Opp. MC.*, pp. 770–71; *A.W.*, 2, *MG.*, 2, 622.
66. Rom. 13:1–6.
67. Acts 22:25–29, 16:17.
68. Ibid., 23:17–31.
69. Ibid., 25:10–11.
70. *P.*, chap. 25, *MG.*, 1, 90, 92; chap. 26, ibid., p. 94.
71. *D.*, 1, 3, *MG.*, 1, 201; 17, ibid., p. 240; 37, ibid., p. 272; 3, 30, ibid., pp. 495–98; *P.*, chap. 8, ibid., pp. 35–39; chap. 17, ibid., p. 62.
72. *P.*, chap. 23, ibid., p. 88; *D.*, 1, 3, ibid., p. 201; "T.F.," 11. 84–85, *MG.*, 2, 747.
73. *H.F.*, 5, 11, *MG.*, 3, 1246–47.
74. Letter to Vettori, 18 Mar. 1512–(1513), *MG.*, 2, 899 (*Lett. fam.*, 119); *H.F.*, 6, 13, *MG.*, 3, 1299.
75. *D.*, 2, 1, *MG.*, 1, 324–27.
76. *P.*, chap. 25, ibid., p. 90; *D.*, 2, 29, ibid., p. 408.
77. *D.*, 2, 30, ibid., p. 412; *P.*, chap. 25, ibid., pp. 90, 92; "S.D.," 11. 181–92, *MG.*, 3, 1461.
78. "T.F.," 11. 13–15, *MG.*, 2, 745.
79. *D.*, 1, 9, *MG.*, 1, 218–20.
80. 18, ibid., pp. 242–43; 3, 1, ibid., pp. 421–22.
81. 3, 16, ibid., pp. 468–70.
82. 31, ibid., p. 500; *A.W.*, 1, *MG.*, 2, 583–87; *P.*, chaps. 13–14, *MG.*, 1, 54–55.
83. *D.*, 1, 9, *MG.*, 1, 218; "Remodeling," *MG.*, 1, 112–15.
84. 1, 2, ibid., p. 196; 9, ibid., pp. 218–19; 18, ibid., pp. 242–43.
85. Draft of letter to Soderini, *MG.*, 2, 897 (*Lett. fam.*, 116); "T.F.," 11. 100–20, ibid., p. 747; 11. 190–92, ibid., p. 749; *D.*, 1, 17, *MG.*, 1, 240; 18, ibid., pp. 242–43.
86. John 1:14.
87. *D.*, 1, 2, *MG.*, 1, 196.
88. 18, ibid., p. 242.
89. Ibid., p. 243.
90. 16, ibid., 236; 3, 3, ibid., pp. 424–25; *P.*, chap. 6, ibid., pp. 26–27.
91. *D.*, 2, 2, ibid., p. 331; 3, 1, ibid., p. 422.
92. *H.F.*, 3, 1, *MG.*, 3, 1141; *A.W.*, 2, *MG.*, 2, 623.
93. Jer. 31:31, 33–34.
94. Matt. 7:12.

95. Thomas Jefferson, as quoted by John Dewey, *Living Thoughts of Thomas Jefferson* (New York: Longmans, Green, 1940), p. 87.

96. Ibid., pp. 44–45

97. Ibid., p. 67.

98. Ralph Waldo Emerson, "Politics," in *Man or the State? A Group of Essays by Famous Writers,* ed. Waldo R. Browne (New York: Huebsch, 1919), p. 66.

99. Henry David Thoreau, "On the Duty of Civil Disobedience." ibid., p. 89 (hereafter referred to as, "Civil Disobedience").

100. Dr. Frederick James Eugene Woodbridge, as quoted by Paul Wolfe, "Conversations with the Old Man," *American Scholar,* 14, 1, Winter, 1944–45, p. 44.

101. John Dewey, *Freedom and Culture* (New York: Putnam, 1939), p. 130.

102. *P.,* chap. 17, *MG.,* 1, 64.

103. *D.,* 3, 6, ibid., p. 441.

104. 1, ibid., p. 587.

105. 2, ibid., p. 622.

106. *D.,* 3, 33, *MG.,* 1, 502–503.

107. *A.W.,* 2, *MG.,* 2, 619.

108. *D.,* 2, 29, *MG.,* 1, 408.

109. *H.F.,* 6, 13, *MG.,* 3, 1299.

110. *A.W.,* 4, *MG.,* 2, 657.

111. *D.,* 2, 10, *MG.,* 1, 350.

112. 3, 10, ibid., p. 456.

113. *P.,* chap. 9, *MG.,* 1, 42.

114. *D.,* 3, 49, ibid., p. 527.

115. 12, ibid., p. 460.

116. 38, ibid., p. 515.

117. 2, 19, ibid., p. 380.

118. Eugene F. Mulcahy, Superintendent of Schools, Teaneck, New Jersey, *New York Times,* 24 July 1983.

119. Matt. 20:25–27.

120. Luke 10:35–37.

121. Matt. 10:42, 25:40.

122. *D.,* 1, 37, *MG.,* 1, 272; 5, ibid., p. 206; 2, Preface, ibid., p. 321; 27, ibid., p. 404; 3, 21, ibid., p. 477; *H.F.,* 2, 31, *MG.,* 3, 1117; 4, 18, ibid., p. 1207.

123. "T.A.," 11. 55–66, 73–81, *MG.,* 2, 736–37; *P.,* chap. 17, *MG.,* 1, 62.

124. *D.,* 1, 3, *MG.,* 1, 201; 9, ibid., p. 218; *P.,* chap. 9, ibid., p. 42; chap. 23, ibid., p. 88.

125. *D.,* 1, 37, ibid., p. 272; 3, 25, ibid., p. 486.

126. "G.A.," chap. 5, 11. 79–81, *MG.,* 2, 763.

127. *H.F.,* 2, 32, *MG.,* 3, 1120.

128. George Herbert Mead, "The Genesis of the Self and Social Control," in *Selected Writings,* ed. Andrew J. Reck (New York: Bobbs:Merrill, 1964), pp. 286–88 (hereafter referred to as "Genesis . . . Self.").

129. Matt. 6:14–15; Mark 11:25–26; Luke 6:37.

130. Tommasini, 2, 576.

131. Ibid., pp. 760–61.

132. *D.,* 1, 9, *MG.,* 1, 218.

133. "Remodeling," *MG.,* 1, 110.

134. *D.,* 1, 49, ibid., p. 296.

135. 2, 2, ibid., p. 329.

136. 1, 16, ibid., p. 236.

137. Francis Wrigley Hirst, *Life and Letters of Thomas Jefferson* (New York: Macmillan, 1926), p. 31.

138. Strauss, *Thoughts* . . . , pp. 13–14.

139. *D.*, 1, 9, *MG.*, 1, 217–20; 3, 1, ibid., pp. 421–22.

140. Justice Oliver Wendell Holmes, as quoted by Alistair Cooke in a television broadcast.

141. Letter to Guicciardini, 17 May 1526, *MG.*, 2, 998 *(Lett. fam.,* 207).

142. *P.,* chap. 26, *MG.*, 1, 96.

143. Chap. 12, ibid., p. 50.

144. Chap. 26, ibid., p. 93; *H.F.*, 5, 1, *MG.*, 3, 1233.

145. "F.D.," 11. 16–30, ibid., p. 1445.

146. Ridolfi, p. 118.

147. Schevill, op. cit., p. 468.

148. *P.,* chap. 12, *MG.*, 1, p. 50; *H.F.*, 5, 1, 1233.

149. *D.*, 2, Preface, *MG.*, 1, 321; *A.W.*, 2, *MG.*, 2, 622.

150. Tommasini, 2, 729.

CHAPTER TWELVE

1. *A.W.*, 2, *MG.*, 2, 622–23.

2. Hough, "Exposition," Rev. 7:14, *I.B.*, 12, 422.

3. *D.*, 1, 18, *MG.*, 1, 240; 58, ibid., pp. 313–14; letter to Vettori, *MG.*, 2, 911 *(Lett. fam.,* 124); "S.D.," 11. 181–92, *MG.*, 3, 1461.

4. *A.W.*, 1, *MG.*, 2, 585–86; *D.*, 3, 31, *MG.*, 1, 500; 33, ibid., p. 502.

5. *D.*, 1, 57, *MG.*, 1, 313.

6. Short, "Exposition," I Cor. 1:18–25, *I.B.*, 10, 32.

7. Gal. 3:23–29.

8. Rom. 7:7–8:4.

9. Matt. 4:8–10, 19:17; Mark 10:18.

10. I Sam. 8:5–22.

11. Matt. 6:19–34; Luke 12:22–32.

12. Rom. 14.

13. "Lingua," *Opp. MC.*, pp. 770–71; *D.*, 3, *MG.*, 526.

14. *A.W.*, 2, *MG.*, 2, 622, 623; *D.*, 3, 31, *MG.*, 1, 500; 33, ibid., p. 502; 1, 12, ibid., pp. 226–27.

15. *D.*, 1, 3, *MG.*, 1, 201; Tommasini, 2, 941, n.1.

16. *D.*, 1, Preface, *MG.*, 1, 190.

17. *A.W.*, 7, *MG.*, 2, 726; *D.*, 2, Preface, *MG.*, 1, 324.

18. *D.*, 1, 18, *MG.*, 1, 240; 58, ibid., pp. 313–14; letter to Vettori, 20 June 1513, *MG.*, 2, 911 *(Lett. fam.,* 124).

19. Letter to Vettori, 10 Dec. 1513, *MG.*, 2, 929 *(Lett. fam.,* 137).

20. *A.W.*, 2, *MG.*, 2, 622.

21. 1, ibid., p. 587; *P.,* chap. 17, *MG.*, 1, 64.

22. *D.*, 3, 6, *MG.*, 1, 441.

23. *A.W.*, 2, *MG.*, 2, 619; *D.*, 3, 31, *MG.*, 1, 500; 33, ibid., p. 502.

24. *P.,* chap. 25, ibid., p. 92; "Ghiribizzi," *Opp. MC.*, p. 879; letter to Vettori, 25 Feb. 1513–(1514), *MG.*, 2, 941 *(Lett. fam.,* 144); *D.*, 3, 44, *MG.*, 1, 522.

25. Letter to Vettori, 20 June 1513, *MG.*, 2, 911 *(Lett. fam.,* 124); chap. 25, *MG.*, 1, 90, 91; "S.D.," 11. 181–92, *MG.*, 3, 1461.

26. *A.W.*, 7, *MG.*, 2, 721.

27. Ibid., p. 722; *D.*, 3, 31, *MG.*, 1, 500; 33, ibid., p. 502.

28. *D.*, 3, 1, *MG.*, 1, 419.

29. Ps. 24:1.

30. 1 Cor. 10:26, 28.

31. *D.*, 3, 6, *MG.*, 1, 429–30, 430; 2, 28, ibid., pp. 405, 406.

32. "G.A.," chap. 7, 11. 106–33—chap. 8, 11. 1–151, *MG.*, 2, 769–72.

33. "T.F.," 11. 112–20, ibid., p. 747; Draft of letter to Soderini, ibid., pp. 896, 897 *(Lett. fam.,* 116).

34. *D.*, 3, 44, *MG.*, 1, 522; *P.*, chap. 25, ibid., p. 92; *D.*, 3, 6, ibid., p. 441; "Ghiribizzi," *Opp. MC.*, p. 879.

35. *D.*, 3, 40, ibid., p. 519.

36. Meinecke, op. cit., pp. 55–56.

37. Letter to Vettori, 16 Apr. 1527, *MG.*, 2, 1010 *(Lett. fam.,* 225).

38. *D.*, 3, 47, *MG.*, 1, 526; *A.W.*, 2, *MG.*, 2, 622; "Lingua," *Opp. MC.*, pp. 770–71.

39. Erich von Däniken, *Gold of the Gods*, trans. Michael Heron, (New York: Putnam, 1972), p. 198.

40. John 15:14–15.

41. *D.*, 1, 9, *MG.*, 1, 218; 3, 1, ibid., pp. 420–21; *H.F.*, 5, 8, *MG.*, 3, 1242.

42. *D.*, 3, 37, *MG.*, 1, 512; *P.*, chap. 19, ibid., p. 72; "G.A.," chap. 5, 11. 103–105, *MG.*, 2, 763.

43. Matt. 13:24–30.

44. Ibid., 47–49.

45. *D.*, 3, 17, *MG.*, 1, 512.

46. *P.*, chap. 6, ibid., p. 25; *A.W.*, 2, *MG.*, 2, 624; "T.F.," ibid., pp. 745–49.

47. Rom. 14:4, 10–12.

48. Jas. 4:11–12.

49. Deut. 32:34–35.

50. Rom. 12:19.

51. *D.*, 1, 3, *MG.*, 1, 201; 9, ibid., pp. 218, 220; 10, ibid., p. 220; 16, ibid., p. 236; 17, ibid., p. 240; 18, ibid., pp. 242–43; 2, 13, ibid., pp. 357–58; 2, 27, ibid., p. 404; 28, ibid., pp. 405, 406; 3, 1, ibid., p. 421; 3, ibid., p. 425; 6, ibid., pp. 429, 430, 438, 442; 16, ibid., pp. 468–69; 22, ibid., pp. 480–81; 27, ibid., p. 489; 30, ibid., pp. 495–96; 48, ibid., p. 526; *P.*, chap. 14, ibid., p. 55; chap. 25, ibid., p. 92; chap. 26, ibid., pp. 92–96; "T.F.," 11. 100–120, *MG.*, 2, 747; 11. 190–92, ibid., p. 749; Draft of letter to Soderini, ibid., p. 897 *(Lett. fam.,* 116); letter to Vettori, 16 Apr. 1527, ibid., p. 1010 *(Lett. fam.,* 225); *H.F.*, 2, 32, *MG.*, 3, 1120; 3, 10, ibid., 1154; 4, 1, ibid., p. 1187; 5, 8, ibid., p. 1242; 8, 1, ibid., pp. 1383–84.

52. John 4:34.

53. Ibid., 17:1, 4, 6.

54. Matt. 26:39, 42; Mark 14:36; Luke 22:42.

55. Matt. 26:52; Luke 22:49–51.

56. John 18:11.

57. *D.*, 3, 33, *MG.*, 1, 502.

58. *A.W.*, 7, *MG.*, 2, 724.

59. 1, ibid., p. 587.

60. *D.*, 3, 31, *MG.*, 1, 500.

61. *A.W.*, 7, *MG.*, 2, 722.

62. *D.*, 1, 43, *MG.*, 1, 286.

63. Legation 11.44, 13 Nov. 1502, *MG.*, 1, 133–34; 53, 26 Nov. 1502, ibid., p. 137; "A Provision for Infantry," Preamble, ibid., p.3; Ridolfi, pp. 80, 81, 87–88, 89, 91, 97, 107; "F.D.," 11. 496–98, *MG.*, 3, 1456; 11. 541–49, ibid., p. 1457; Ridolfi,

pp. 107–108; *A.W.*, 1, *MG.*, 2, 573–79, 581, 583–84, 584–85, 585–86; *P.*, chap. 12, *MG.*, 1, 47–chap. 13, ibid., pp. 53–54; *D.*, 1, 4, ibid., p. 202; 21, ibid., pp. 246–47; 43, ibid., p. 286; 3, 33, ibid., p. 502; *H.F.*, 2, 5–6, *MG.*, 3, 1085; Ridolfi, pp. 212–15; Ferrara, op. cit., p. 351.

64. Rom. 10:4.
65. Fred D. Gealy, "Exegesis," on II Tim. 1:7, *I.B.*, 11, 465.
66. Rev. 19:11.
67. Gal. 3.
68. Gen. 2:7, 22.
69. Matt. 1:22–25.
70. Luke 1:26–38.
71. John 3:1–22.
72. Rom. 8:29.
73. I Sam. 2:11.
74. I Cor. 2:11.
75. Rom. 7:19–25.
76. Matt. 6:14–15.
77. Matt. 5:5 (King James version).
78. Letter to Vettori, 29 Apr. 1513, *MG.*, 2, 906 *(Lett. fam.,* 128); *D.*, 1, 58, *MG.*, 1, 313–14.
79. *D.*, 2, 2, *MG.*, 1, 331.
80. 3, 1, ibid., p. 422.
81. I Kings 19.12 (King James version and *N.E.B.*).
82. Luke 8:30, 35.
83. Exod. 3:14; John 8:58; Rev. 1:18.
84. *D.*, 1, Preface, *MG.*, 1, 191; 10, ibid., p. 221; 39, ibid., p. 278; 2, Preface, ibid., p. 324; 3, 43, ibid., p. 521; "Clizia," Prolog, *MG.*, 2, 823; *H.F.*, Preface, *MG.*, 3, 1031.
85. "S.D.," 11. 181–92, *MG.*, 3, 1461.
86. *D.*, 1, Preface, *MG.*, 1, 191.
87. 3, 48, ibid., p. 526; "S.D.," 11. 181–92, *MG.*, 3, 1461.
88. *D.*, 3, 30, *MG.*, 1, 496.
89. 1, Preface, ibid., p. 191.
90. 2, Preface, ibid., p. 321.
91. 5, ibid., pp. 340, 340–41; *P.*, chap. 17, ibid., p. 63; *H.F.*, Preface, *MG.*, 3, 1031, 1032–33.
92. *A.W.*, 2, *MG.*, 2, 622, 622–23; *D.*, 1, 10, *MG.*, 1, 221; 2, Preface, ibid., p. 321.
93. I Cor. 1:27–29.
94. *A.W.*, 2, *MG.*, 2, 622; "Lingua," *Opp. MC.*, pp. 770–71; "Remodeling," *MG.*, 1, 113–14; *D.*, 3, 41, ibid., p. 519; *H.F.*, 5, 8, *MG.*, 3, 1242.
95. *D.*, 1, 12, *MG.*, 1, 228; 16, ibid., 236; 2, 2, ibid., pp. 329, 332–33; *A. W.*, 2, *MG.*, 2, 622; *H.F.*, 7, 33, *MG.*, 3, 1378; "Lingua," *Opp. MC.*, pp. 770–71.
96. *A.W.*, 4, *MG.*, 2, 622; 1, ibid., pp. 585–86; *D.*, 2, 20, *MG.*, 1, 382; 3, 6, ibid., p. 430; 33, ibid., p. 502; 31, ibid., p. 500; "F.D.," 1. 18, *MG.*, 3, 1445; *P.*, chap. 17, *MG.*, 1, 63 and n.4; chap. 26, pp. 93, 96; *H.F.*, 5, 1, *MG.*, 3, 1233; letter to Guicciardini, 17 May 1526, *MG.*, 2, 998 *(Lett. fam.,* 207).
97. *D.*, 1, Preface, *MG.*, 1, 190; 9–10, ibid., pp. 218–21; 18, ibid., pp. 242–43; 3, 1, ibid., p. 421; 15, ibid., p. 468.
98. 1, 18, ibid., p. 240.
99. 58, ibid., pp. 313–14; letter to Vettori, 29 Apr. 1513, *MG.*, 2, 905–906 *(Lett. fam.,* 128).

100. Letter to Vettori, 26 Aug. 1513, ibid., p. 924 *(Lett. fam.,* 134).

101. 16 Apr. 1527, ibid., p. 1010 *(Lett. fam.,* 225).

102. *H.F.,* 3, 7, *MG.,* 3, 1150; "The Natures of Florentine Men. Of Francesco Valori," ibid., p. 1438.

103. "Lingua," *Opp. MC.,* pp. 770–71.

104. *D.,* 1, 9, *MG.,* 1, 218; *H.F.,* 4, 1, *MG.,* 3, 1187.

105. *D.,* 3, 48, *MG.,* 1, 526; "S.D.," 11. 181–92, *MG.,* 3, 1461.

106. Letter to Vettori, 16 Apr. 1527, *MG.,* 2, 1010 *(Lett. fam.,* 225).

107. *D.,* 1, 9, *MG.,* 1, 218–19; 16, ibid., pp. 236, 238; 3, 3, ibid., pp. 424, 425; 27, ibid., p. 489; 30, ibid., pp. 495–96.

108. 2, 28, ibid., pp. 405, 406; 3, 6, ibid., pp. 429–30, 438.

109. 1, 10, ibid., p. 220; 3, 6, ibid., pp. 438, 442; *P.,* chap. 19, ibid., p. 74; *H.F.,* 2, 32, *MG.,* 3, 1120; 8, 1, ibid., pp. 1383–84.

110. *D.,* 1, 11, *MG.,* 1, 225, 227.

111. 1, 3, ibid., p. 201; Legation 13.18, 4 Nov. 1503, ibid., p. 144.

112. Exod. 32:32.

113. Rom. 9:3.

114. Mark 8:36.

115. Matt. 5:17–18.

116. Exod. 9:29.

117. Deut. 10:14.

118. Ps. 24:1.

119. I Cor. 10:26.

120. Matt. 10:29–31; Luke 12:6–7, 10:29–37; Matt. 25:40.

121. *A.W.,* 1, *MG.,* 2, 579.

122. *H.F.,* 3, 7, *MG.,* 3, 1149.

123. 10, ibid., p. 1154.

124. *D.,* 1, 18, *MG.,* 1, 240; 58, ibid., pp. 313–14.

125. *P.,* chap. 15, ibid., p. 57.

126. *D.,* 1, 9–10, ibid., pp. 217–21.

127. 18, ibid., pp. 242–43.

128. 2, 19, ibid., pp. 379, 380; 1, 6, ibid., pp. 209–11; 3, 16, ibid., pp. 468–69; *P.,* chap. 3, ibid., pp. 16–17; chap. 16, ibid., pp. 60–61; *H.F.,* 3, 1, *MG.,* 3, 1140–41; 6, 1, ibid., p. 1284; *D.,* 2, 6, *MG.,* 1, 342–43.

129. *D.,* 1, 3, *MG.,* 1, 201; 37, ibid., p. 272; 2, 19, ibid., p. 378; 16, ibid., p. 469; 25, ibid., p. 486.

130. *P.,* chap. 23, ibid., p. 88; "T.F.," 11. 84–85, *MG.,* 2, 747.

131. *D.,* 3, 48, *MG.,* 1, 526; "S.D.," 11. 181–92, *MG.,* 3, 1461; *D.,* 2, 27, *MG.,* 1, 404.

132. *H.F.,* 4, 14, *MG.,* 3, 1202; 6, 1, ibid., p. 1284.

133. *D.,* 3, 24, *MG.,* 1, 485–86; 2, 2, ibid., p. 332; 4, ibid., p. 339; 19, ibid., p. 381; 1, 18, ibid., p. 242; *A.W.,* 1, *MG.,* 2, 573–74, 578; 2, ibid., pp. 621–23.

134. *D.,* 3, 6, *MG.,* 1, 429–30; 2, 28, ibid., pp. 405, 406; *P.,* chap. 19, ibid., p. 74.

135. Matt. 3:2, 4:17 (cf. Luke 14:21).

136. "T.F.," 11. 13–15, *MG.,* 2, 745; "S.D.," 11. 181–92, *MG.,* 3, 1461.

137. *P.,* chap. 6, *MG.,* 1, 26–27.

138. Ridolfi, pp. 251–54.

139. *H.F.,* 3, 7, *MG.,* 3, 1149.

140. 10, ibid., p. 1154.

141. *D.,* 1, 17, *MG.,* 1, 240; *H.F.,* 4, 1, *MG.,* 3, 1187.

142. *D.,* 1, 18, *MG.,* 1, 242–43; 1, 9, ibid., p. 220; *H.F.,* 2, 32, *MG.,* 3, 1120; 8, 1, ibid., pp. 1383–84; "T.F.," 11. 118–20, *MG.,* 2, 747; 11. 190–92, ibid., p. 749.

143. *D.*, 1, 3, *MG.*, 1, 201; 9, ibid., pp. 217–20; 3, 1, ibid., p. 421; *H.F.*, 5, 8, *MG.*, 3, 1242.

144. *H.F.*, 3, 1, *MG.*, 3, 1140–41.

145. *A.W.*, Preface, *MG.*, 2, 566–67.

146. 1, ibid., pp. 571–72.

147. *D.*, 3, 24, *MG.*, 1, 485–86.

148. *A.W.*, 1, *MG.*, 2, 575–78.

149. 2, ibid., pp. 622–23; *D.*, 2, 2, *MG.*, 1, 332; 4, ibid., pp. 335–37; 5, ibid., p. 341.

150. *H.F.*, 3, 1, *MG.*, 3, 1140–41.

151. *D.*, 1, 12, *MG.*, 1, 228–29; 3, 1, ibid., p. 422.

152. Tommasini, 2, 658–60 and n.2.

153. Shakespeare, *A Midsummer Night's Dream,* act 5, sc. 1.

154. *D.*, 1, 18, *MG.*, 1, 240.

155. 58, ibid., pp. 313–14.

156. 3, ibid., p. 201.

157. 9, ibid., pp. 218–20; 18, ibid., pp. 240–43; 3, 30, ibid., p. 496.

158. 1, 4, ibid., p. 202.

159. *A.W.*, Preface, *MG.*, 2, 566–67.

160. "Lingua," *Opp. MC.*, pp. 770–71.

161. *A.W.*, 2, *MG.*, 2, 622; *H.F.*, 7, 33, *MG.*, 3, 1378.

162. *P.*, chap. 12, *MG.*, 1, 47; *D.*, 1, 4, ibid., p. 202; 21, ibid., pp. 245, 247; 3, 31, ibid., p. 500; 33, ibid., p. 502.

163. *P.*, chap. 23, ibid., p. 87.

164. *D.*, 1, 4, ibid., p. 203.

165. 1, 3, ibid., pp. 201–202.

166. 3, 6, ibid., p. 447.

167. 1, 3, ibid., p. 201; *P.*, chap. 17, ibid., p. 62; "T.A.," 11. 55–63, *MG.*, 2, 736.

168. "An Exhortation to Penitence," *MG.*, 1, 172–73.

169. *D.*, 1, 9, ibid., pp. 218–19; 18, ibid., pp. 242–43; 3, 3, ibid., p. 425; 2, 13 ibid., pp. 357–58, 358; 3, 40, ibid., p. 518.

170. 2, 28, ibid., pp. 405, 406; 3, 6, ibid., p. 438; *P.*, chap. 19, ibid., p. 74; *D.*, 3, 6, ibid., p. 430; 4, ibid., p. 426.

171. *D.*, 3, 42, ibid., p. 520; *P.*, chap. 18, ibid., p. 65.

172. Letter to Vettori, 20 June 1513, *MG.*, 2, 911 (*Lett. fam.*, 124); *D.*, 1, 18, *MG.*, 1, 240; 58, ibid., pp. 313–14.

173. "S.D.," 11. 181–92, *MG.*, 3, 1461.

174. *P.*, chap. 18, *MG.*, 1, 65; chap. 15, ibid., pp. 58–59; *D.*, 1, 12, ibid., p. 227; 2, 2, ibid., p. 331.

175. "L.C.," *MG.*, 2, 555; "G.A.," chap. 5, 11. 115–27, ibid., p. 764; *D.*, 2, 2, *MG.*, 1, 331.

176. Rom. 8; I John 4.

177. *D.*, 1, 9, *MG.*, 1, 218–19.

178. 3, 1, ibid., p. 421.

179. 1, 18, ibid., p. 242; 1, 17, ibid., p. 240; *H.F.*, 4, 1, *MG.*, 3, 1187.

180. *H.F.*, 3, 10, *MG.*, 3, 1154.

181. 7, ibid., p. 1149.

182. Matt. 6:12, 14–15.

183. Mark 2:7; Luke 5:21.

184. "Ghiribizzi," *Opp. MC.*, p. 879; *P.*, chap. 17, *MG.*, 1, 64; chap. 13, ibid., p. 54; chap. 24, ibid., p. 89; *D.*, 3, 31, ibid., p. 500; 33, ibid., p. 502; *A.W.*, 1, *MG.*,

2, 584–87; 2, ibid., p. 619; *D.*, 3, 6, *MG.*, 1, 441; 2, 29, ibid., p. 408.

185. Matt. 7:5; Luke 6:42.
186. Wicks, "Exposition," Phil. 3:13, *I.B.*, 11, 881.
187. Wicks, "Exposition," Phil 1:21, ibid., p. 37.
188. Rupert Brooke, "Safety," *Collected Poems* (New York: Dodd, Mead, 1915) as quoted by Cragg, "Exposition," Rom. 15:13, *I.B.*, 11, 641.
189. Phil. 1:9.
190. John 3:8.
191. Time-Life Film, "Psyche," TV, 17 June 1976.
192. Aristotle, op. cit., p. 5.
193. *D.*, 1, 3, *MG.*, 1, 201; 9, ibid., p. 218.
194. *D.*, 1, 9, *MG.*, 1, 218; "Remodeling," *MG.*, 1, 111–115.
195. "Lingua," *Opp. MC.*. pp. 770–71.
196. Rom. 8:29, 9:29.
197. J. H. Hale, "The End of Florentine Liberty: the Fortezza da Basso," in Rubinstein, *Florentine Studies,* pp. 508, 526, 529, 531.
198. *D.*, 1, 58, *MG.*, 1, 316.

CHAPTER THIRTEEN

1. *P.,* chap. 15, *MG.*, 1, 57.
2. *D.*, Preface, ibid., p. 190; "Lingua," *Opp. MC.*, pp. 770–71.
3. *D.*, 1, 9, *MG.*, 1, 218.
4. 18, ibid., p. 240; letter to Vettori, 20 June 1513, *MG.*, 2, 911 *(Lett. fam.,* 124).
5. "Lingua," *Opp. MC.*, pp. 770–71; *D.*, 2, 19, *MG.*, 1, 379; *A.W.*, 2, *MG.*, 2, 622, 623; *H.F.*, 7, 33, *MG.*, 3, 1378.
6. *D.*, 1, 1, *MG.*, 1, 194.
7. *P.,* chap. 17, 64; chap. 24, ibid., p. 89; *A.W.*, 7, *MG.*, 2, 721.
8. *A.W.*, 2, *MG.*, 2, 622–23; "Lingua," *Opp. MC.*, pp. 770–71.
9. *D.*, 3, 33, *MG.*, 1, 502.
10. Ferrara, op. cit., p. 240.
11. Fleisher, op. cit., p. 116.
12. Neal Wood, "The Value of Asocial Sociability: Contributions of Machiavelli, Sidney and Montesquieu," in *Machiavelli . . . Thought,* pp. 291–92.
13. Ibid., pp. 292–93.
14. Pocock, p. 484.
15. Wood, op. cit., p. 298.
16. Ibid., p. 299.
17. Pocock, p. viii.
18. Ibid., p. 85.
19. Ibid., p. 317.
20. Antonio Pace, *Benjamin Franklin and Italy* (Philadelphia: The American Philosophical Society, 1958), p. 2.
21. Ibid., p. 5.
22. Ibid., p. 8.
23. Clinton Rossiter, *Seedtime of the Republic* (New York: Harcourt Brace, 1953), p. 359 and reference to J. Adams *Works* (Boston: Little & Brown, 1851), 4, 17, 57.
24. John Adams, *Diary and Autobiography, Works,* 1, 179.
25. Ibid., p. 362.

26. Ibid., V, 95.

27. Ibid., p. 11.

28. Ibid., p. 179.

29. Ibid., p. 183.

30. Ibid., IV, 406.

31. Ibid., p. 408.

32. Ibid., p. 410.

33. *Novanglus*, ibid., p. 57.

34. *Works*, IV, 430–31; (for Gilbert's translation, *D.*, 1, 55, *MG.*, 1, 309).

35. *Works*, IV, 431.

36. David Hawke, *A Transaction of Free Men, The Birth and Course of the Declaration of Independence* (New York: Chas. Scribner's, 1964), p. 41.

37. James Madison, "Commonplace Book, 1759–1773," in *The Papers of James Madison*, I, 13 and n. 31, p. 26.

38. Ibid., VI, 63, 86.

39. Rossiter, *Alexander Hamilton and the Constitution* (New York: Harcourt, Brace & World, 1964), pp. 119–20. Copyright © 1964 by Clinton Rossiter. Reprinted by permission of Harcourt Brace Jovanovich, Inc.

40. Broadus Mitchell, *Alexander Hamilton, Youth to Maturity*, 1755–1788 (New York; Macmillan, 19579, p. 28; p. 486, n. 74.

41. John C. Miller, *Alexander Hamilton, Portrait in Paradox* (New York: Harper, 1959) pp. 10, 12–13.

42. Ibid., p. 228.

43. Ibid., p. 227.

44. Rossiter, *Alexander Hamilton,* p. 182.

45. Ibid., p. 122.

46. Ibid., pp. 123–24.

47. Ibid., pp. 124–25.

48. *D.*, 2, Preface, *MG.*, 1, 324.

49. Morison, *et al.* 1, 75.

50. Dumas Malone and Basil Rauch, *Empire for Liberty, The Genesis and Growth of the United States of America* (New York: Appleton-Century-Crofts, 1960), 1, 78.

51. James Parton, letter of 24 Oct. 1956, as editor of *American Heritage* magazine.

52. Paul A. W. Wallace, *The White Roots of Peace* (Philadelphia: University of Pennsylvania Press, 1946), p. 30.

53. Thomas H. Henry, *Wilderness Messiah, The Story of Hiawatha and the Iroquois* (New York: William Sloane, 1955), p. 226.

54. Max Savelle, *Seeds of Liberty* (New York: Knopf, 1948), pp. 328–29.

55. Lewis H. Morgan, *League of the Ho-de-No-San-Nee or Iroquois* (New York: Dodd, Mead, 1904), App. B, p. 205, nn. 38–39.

56. Ibid.

57. Garry Wills, *Inventing America, Jefferson's Declaration of Independence* (Garden City, New York: Doubleday, 1978), pp. 207–208.

58. Hawke, op. cit., p. 150.

59. Carl Lotus Becker, *The Declaration of Independence, A Study in the History of Ideas* (New York: Harcourt, Brace, 1922), pp. 25–27.

60. *D.*, 1, 9, *MG.*, 1, 218.

61. Benjamin R. Barber, "The Compromised Republic," in *The Moral Foundations of the American Republic,* ed. Robert H. Horwitz (Charlottesville: University Press of Virginia, 1977), pp. 29–30 (hereafter referred to as *Moral Foundations*).

62. *D.*, 2, 19, *MG.*, 1, 379.

63. 2, 4, ibid., pp. 338–39.
64. Ibid., pp. 335, 339.
65. Ibid., p. 338.
66. Ibid., pp. 337–38.
67. Adams, *Works*, V, 183.
68. Stanley Pargellis, "The Theory of Balanced Government," in *The Constitution Reconsidered*, ed. Conyers Read (New York: Columbia University Press, 1938), p. 39.
69. Adams, *Works*, V, 183.
70. *A.W.*, 1, *MG.*, 2, 573–74, 578.
71. Arthur T. Prescott, *Drafting the Federal Constitution* (University of Louisiana, State University Press, 1941), p. 515.
72. Ibid., p. 524.
73. Pocock, p. 528.
74. *D.*, 1, 58, *MG.*, 1, 314.
75. *A.W.*, 1, *MG.*, 2, 577.
76. "Lingua," *Opp. MC.*, pp. 770–71; "Remodeling," *MG.*, 1, 113–14; *A.W.*, 2, *MG.*, 2, 622; letter to Vettori, 16 Apr. 1527, ibid., p. 1010 (*Lett. fam.*, 225).
77. *P.*, chap. 3, *MG.*, 1, 16–17; *D.*, 31, ibid., p. 419; 1, 58, ibid., p. 317; 33, ibid., pp. 265–66; 3, 49, ibid., pp. 527, 528; *H.F.*, 5, 8, *MG.*, 3, 1242.
78. *D.*, 2, 2, *MG.*, 1, 329.
79. 1, 9, ibid., p. 218.
80. *H.F.*, 2, 34, *MG.*, 3, 1125; "Remodeling," ibid., pp. 110, 115.
81. *Declaration of Independence*.
82. *Constitution of the United States*, Preamble.
83. *D.*, 1, 5, *MG.*, 1, 204–205.
84. *D.*, 3, 1, ibid., 1, 419.
85. Pocock, p. 518.
86. Ibid., p. 517.
87. Ibid., pp. 523–24.
88. Ibid., p. 527.
89. Ibid., p. 534.
90. *H.F.*, 4, 7, *MG.*, 3, 1194; 6, 13, ibid., p. 1299; *D.*, 2, 29, *MG.*, 1, 408.
91. Luke 4:5–8.
92. Gal. 4:8–10.
93. Col. 2:8.
94. *P.*, chap. 25, *MG.*, 1, 90; *D.*, 2, 10, ibid., p. 350; 2, 29, ibid., p. 408; 3, 10, ibid., p. 456; *A.W.*, 4, *MG.*, 2, 657; "G.A.," chap. 5, 11, 115–27, ibid., p. 764; *H.F.*, 6, 13, *MG.*, 3, 1299.
95. Mark 12:31; Luke 10:27–28.
96. Luke 10:30–37.
97. Matt. 25:31–46.
98. Matt. 16:24–26; Mark 8:35–38; Luke 9:23–25.
99. Luke 22:69.
100. Fleischer, op. cit., p. 11.
101. Martin Diamond, "Ethics and Politics: the American Way," in *Moral Foundations*, p. 41.
102. Sforza, op. cit., pp. 4–5.
103. Whitfield, *Discourses*, p. 135.
104. *D.*, 1, 12, *MG.*, 1, 228.
105. Sforza, op. cit., p. 6.
106. Whitfield, *Discourses*, pp. 33–35, 146, 152, 156.

107. Ibid., p. 146.
108. Ibid., p. 35.
109. Ibid., pp. 104–108.
110. Ibid., p. 161.
111. Ibid., p. 160.
112. *D.*, 2, 4, *MG.*, 1, 335–39; *A.W.*, 1, *MG.*, 2, 571.
113. *D.*, 2, 4, *MG.*, 1, 339.
114. Gordon S. Wood, "The Democratization of Mind in the American Revolution," in *Moral Foundations*, p. 110.
115. *H.F.*, 2, 38, *MG.*, 3, 1133.
116. Whitfield, *Discourses*, p. 139.
117. Luke 10:27–28.
118. *D.*, 2, 28, *MG.*, 1, 405, 406; 3, 6, ibid., p. 429.
119. "Lingua," *Opp. MC.*, pp. 770–71; *D.*, 3, 1, *MG.*, 1, 419.
120. "T.F.," 11. 61–63, 82–86, *MG.*, 2, 746–47.
121. *D.*, 3, 12, *MG.*, 1, 459–62.
122. 2, 12, ibid., pp. 354–55.
123. *A.W.*, 4, *MG.*, 2, 662.
124. Matt. 7:4–5; Luke 6:41–42.
125. Matt. 6:12; Luke 11:4.
126. *D.*, 1, 1, *MG.*, 1, 194.
127. *A.W.*, 4, *MG.*, 2, 662.
128. *D.*, 2, 12, *MG.*, 1, 355.
129. *A.W.*, 4, *MG.*, 2, 662.
130. *P.*, chap. 16, *MG.*, 1, 60–61.
131. Rom. 8:29.
132. Matt. 5:44.
133. Ibid., 26:52.
134. Ibid., 7:1.
135. Ibid., 5:38–48.
136. Ibid., 6:12, 14–15.
137. Ibid., 7:12.
138. Rom. 8; Luke 8:35; John 1:29, 8:3–11.
139. Matt. 25:40, 45, 7:24–27; Luke 6:46–49, 10:36–37.
140. Matt. 6:10, 11:12; Luke 17:20–21.
141. Tommasini, 2, 655 and n.6.
142. Matt. 26:64.
143. John 12:27, 47.
144. Ibid., 11:50.
145. Ridolfi, p. 177.
146. Fleisher, op. cit., pp. 121–22.
147. Ibid., pp. 123–25.
148. Ibid., p. 129.
149. Ibid., p. 141.
150. Joseph Cropsey, "The United States as Regime and the Sources of the American Way of Life," in *Moral Foundations*, p. 91.
151. Pocock, pp. 40–41.
152. Ibid., pp. 193–94.
153. Ibid., p. 203.
154. Ibid., p. 212.
155. Ibid., p. 213.
156. Matt. 10:34–39; Mark 10:28–30; Luke 14:26–27, 21:12–17.

157. Neal Wood, in *Machiavelli . . . Thought*, p. 290.

158. Ibid., p. 283.

159. Ibid., pp. 287–88.

160. Ibid., p. 288.

161. Ibid., pp. 290–91.

162. Robert H. Horwitz, "John Locke and the Preservation of Liberty: A Perennial Problem of Civic Education," in *Moral Foundations,* pp. 132–33.

163. *H.F.,* 3, 7, *MG.,* 3, 1149.

164. 6, 1, ibid., p. 1284.

165. 4, 14, ibid., pp. 1201–1202.

166. 5, 21, ibid., p. 1261.

167. *D.,* 1, 18, *MG.,* 1, 242; 2, 4, ibid., p. 339; 19, ibid., p. 381; 3, 24, ibid., p. 486; *A.W.,* 1, *MG.,* 2, 573–75, 577, 578; 2, ibid., p. 623; *H.F.,* 3, 1, *MG.,* 3, 1141.

168. *A.W.,* 6, *MG.,* 2, 700; *H.F.,* 4, *MG.,* 3, 1202.

169. *H.F.,* 3, 10, *MG.,* 3, 1154.

170. *P.,* chap. 6, *MG.,* 1, 26–27.

171. Letter to Vettori, 31 Jan. 1514–(1515), *MG.,* 2, 962 *(Lett. fam.,* 159); *P.,* chap. 7, *MG.,* 1, 28–29; chap. 13, ibid., pp. 52–53.

172. *D.,* 3, 3, *MG.,* 1, 425; 9, ibid., p. 453; 30, ibid., p. 497.

173. *D.,* 3, 3, *MG.,* 1, 419.

174. Draft of letter to Soderini, Jan. 1512–(1513), *MG.,* 2, 897 *(Lett. fam.,* 116); "T.F.," 11. 100–20, ibid., p. 747.

175. *H.F.,* 4, 1, *MG.,* 3, 1187.

176. *D.,* 1, 18, *MG.,* 1, 242.

177. Ridolfi, pp. 176–77.

178. *H.F.,* 4, 1, *MG.,* 3, 1187.

179. *D.,* 1, 18, *MG.,* 1, 242–43.

180. 9, ibid., p. 218.

181. *H.F.,* 2, 32, *MG.,* 3, 1120.

182. "T.F.," 11. 181–83, 190–92, *MG.,* 2, 749.

183. *D.,* 2, 17, *MG.,* 1, 367–72; *A.W.,* ed.n., *MG.,* 2, 563.

184. *H.F.,* 3, 7, *MG.,* 3, 1149.

185. *D.,* 2, 21, *MG.,* 1, 385.

186. *P.,* chap. 26, ibid., p. 94; *D.,* 3, 12, ibid., p. 461; *P.,* chap. 3, ibid., pp. 16–17; *A.W.,* 2, 576; *H.F.,* 5, 8, *MG.,* 3, 1241–42.

187. *D.,* 2, 1, *MG.,* 1, 326–27; 2, 19, ibid., 2, 378–79; *P.,* chap. 16, ibid., pp. 60–61; *A.W.,* 1, *MG.,* 2, 576.

188. *D.,* 3, 33, *MG.,* 1, 502; 31, ibid., p. 500.

189. *P.,* chap. 26, ibid., p. 96.

190. Ridolfi, p. 228.

191. Letter to Guicciardini, 17 May 1526, *MG.,* 2, 998 *(Lett. fam.,* 207).

192. *H.F.,* 4, 14, *MG.,* 3, 1202.

193. John Maynard Keynes, *The Economic Consequences of the Peace* (New York: Harcourt, Brace and Howe, 1920).

CHAPTER FOURTEEN

1. Isa. 2:2, 3b–4.

2. Ibid., 24:21–22, 23; 32; 34–35.

3. Dan. 2:44.

4. Matt. 4:8–10.

5. Ibid., 5:3, 7:12; Luke 18:10–14.

6. Matt. 18:1–4, 10–14, 20:24–28, 25:34–40.

7. Ibid., 26:51–52.

8. John 18:36.

9. Matt. 6:10.

10. Whitfield, *Discourses*, p. 3.

11. *D.*, 1, 37, *MG.*, 1, 272; 2, 19, ibid., p. 378; 3, 16, ibid., p. 469; 25, ibid., p. 486; *A.W.*, 1, *MG.*, 2, 572.

12. *D.*, 2, 19, ibid., p. 378.

13. Pocock, pp. 492–93.

14. Ibid., pp. 498–99.

15. "The War Against the Poor," *New York Times,* ed., 27 Dec. 1981.

16. *D.*, 3, 25, *MG.*, 1, 486.

17. I. deSola Poole, "The Public and the Polity," *Contemporary Political Science: Toward Empirical Theory* (New York, 1967), p. 26, emphasis added, as quoted in Sheldon Wolin, "Political Theory as a Vocation," *Machiavelli . . . Thought*, p. 31.

18. Draft of letter to Soderini, *MG.*, 2, 896–97 *(Lett. fam.,* 116); "Ghiribizzi," *Opp. MC.*, p. 879; *D.*, 2, 29, *MG.*, 1, 408.

19. *D.*, 3, 6, *MG.*, 1, 430.

20. *P.*, chap. 17, ibid., p. 64; 24, ibid., p. 89; *A.W.*, 1, *MG.*, 2, 584, 585–86, 587.

21. *A.W.*, 7, *MG.*, 2, 721.

22. Letter to Guido, 2 Apr. 1527, *MG.*, 2, 1006 *(Lett. fam.,* 222).

23. *A.W.*, 4, ibid., p. 662; "Lingua," *Opp. MC.*, pp. 770–71; *D.*, 3, 33, *MG.*, 1, 502; 47, ibid., p. 526; 41, ibid., p. 519.

24. *A.W.*, 2, *MG.*, 2, 622–23; "Lingua," *Opp. MC.*, pp. 770–71.

25. Robert R. Wicks, "Exposition," Phil. 2:12, *I.B.*, 11, 63.

26. Whitfield, *Discourses*, p. 79.

27. Halford E. Luccock, "Exposition," Mark 12:37, *I.B.*, 7, 851.

28. *D.*, 1, 37, *MG.*, 1, 272; 2, 19, ibid., p. 378; 3, 16, ibid., p. 469; 25, ibid., p. 486; *A.W.*, 1, *MG.*, 2, 572.

29. *A.W.*, 1, *MG.*, 2, 575–76, 578.

30. *D.*, 3, 25, *MG.*, 1, 487.

31. *A.W.*, 1, *MG.*, 2, 575–76, 578, 580.

32. Ibid., p. 578.

33. Ibid., p. 579; *D.*, 1, 1, *MG.*, 1, 194.

34. Matt. 25:40, 45.

35. John Donne, *Devotions,* XVII, A Meditation, *Devotion upon Emergent Occasions* (Ann Arbor, Mich.: University of Michigan Press, 1959), p. 109.

36. Aldredge, op. cit., p. 169.

37. Emma Lazarus, "The New Colossus."

38. John F. Kennedy, Address in West Berlin as quoted by C.H. Mike Yarrow, *Quaker Experiences in International Conciliation* (New Haven: Yale University Press, 1978), p. 65 (hereafter referred to as *Quaker Experiences*). Used by permission.

39. Luccock, "Exposition," Mark 10:39, *I.B.*, 7, 814.

40. "S.D.," 11. 184–92, *MG.*, 3, 1461.

41. Fleischer, op. cit., p. 133.

42. *D.*, 1, Preface, *MG.*, 1, 190; 2, 2, ibid., p. 329.

43. Whitfield, *Discourses*, pp. 33–35, 146, 152.

44. *A.W.*, 2, *MG.*, 2, 622–23; "Lingua," *Opp. MC.*, pp. 770–71; *D.*, 1, 16, *MG.*, 1, 236.

45. *P.*, chap. 15, *MG.*, 1, 57.

46. Draft of letter to Soderini, *MG.*, 2, 896–97 *(Lett. fam.*, 116).

47. *D.*, 2, 28, *MG.*, 1, 405, 406; 3, 4, ibid., p. 426; 6, ibid., pp. 430, 438; *P.*, chap. 19, ibid., p. 74.

48. *A.W.*, 7, *MG.*, 2, 721.

49. "Ghiribizzi," *Opp. MC.*, p. 879; *P.*, chap. 25, *MG.*, 1, 92; letter to Vettori, 25 Feb. 1513–(1514), *MG.*, 2, 941 *(Lett. fam.*, 144); *D.*, 2, 29, *MG.*, 1, 408; *H.F.*, 6, 13, *MG.*, 3, 1299.

50. *D.*, 1, 18, *MG.*, 1, 240; letter to Vettori, 29 Apr. 1513, *MG.*, 2, 905–906 *(Lett. fam.*, 128); 20 Dec. 1514 *(No. 2)*, ibid., p. 958 *(Lett. fam.*, 155).

51. *P.*, chap. 15, *MG.*, 1, 57.

52. Robert Orr, "The Time Motif in Machiavelli," in *Machiavelli . . . Thought*, p. 206.

53. Ibid., p. 208.

54. Pocock, p. 113.

55. Ibid., p. 153.

56. Ibid., pp. 154–55.

57. Ibid., p. 157.

58. *D.*, 1, 58, *MG.*, 1, 314.

59. Whitfield, *Discourses*, p. 163.

60. Sforza, op. cit., p. 10.

61. *D.*, 1, 9, *MG.*, 1, 218; 18, ibid., pp. 242–43; "T.A.," 11, 160–65, *MG.*, 2, 739.

62. *D.*, 1, 9, *MG.*, 1, 218.

63. Morison, *et al.*, op cit., 2, 257–61.

64. Matt. 10:34–36, 38–39; Luke 18:29–30.

65. *H.F.*, 3, 1, *MG.*, 3, 1140–41.

66. Bonadeo, op. cit., pp. 64, 70–71.

67. *D.*, 1, 9, *MG.*, 1, 218; 17, ibid., p. 240; 18, ibid., pp. 242–43.

68. Barbara Lupo and John Collins, Co-directors, Clergy and Laity Concerned, letter of May, 1983.

69. Petra Kelly, Green Party member of West German Parliament, "Meet the Press," TV Broadcast, 10 June 1983.

70. Yarrow, *Quaker Experiences*, pp. 37–38.

71. Ps. 24:1.

72. Deut. 10:14.

73. Matt. 6:25, 32–34, 7:7–8, 11; John 14:1–3.

74. I Cor. 10:26, 4:7.

75. "Lingua," *Opp. MC.*, pp. 770–71; *A.W.*, 2, *MG.*, 2, 622.

76. Barber, "The Compromised Republic: Public Purposelessness in America," in *Moral Foundations*, p. 35.

77. Pocock, p. 75.

78. *D.*, 1, 18, *MG.*, 1, 243; 9, ibid., p. 219; 55, ibid., p. 309.

79. Brayton Polka, "Commentary, on Pocock, 'Custom & Grace, Form and Matter: An Approach to Machiavelli's Concept of Innovation,' " in *Machiavelli . . . Thought*, p. 181.

80. *D.*, 1, 3, *MG.*, 1, 201; 9, ibid., p. 218; 17, ibid., p. 240; 37, ibid., p. 272; 2, Preface, ibid., p. 323; 27, ibid., p. 404; 3, 30, ibid., pp. 495–98; *P.*, chap. 8, ibid., pp. 35–39; chap. 17, ibid., p. 62; chap. 18, ibid., p. 64; chap. 23, ibid., p. 88; "T.A.," 11. 55–63, 73–81, *MG.*, 2, 736–37; "T.F.," 11. 84–85, ibid., p. 747; "Exhortation to Penitence," *MG.*, 1, 171–74.

81. *D.*, 3, 37, *MG.*, 1, 512.

82. *H.F.*, 2, 32, *MG.*, 3, 1120.

83. *D.,* 1, 58, *MG.,* 1, 316, 316–17.

84. 1, 4, ibid., p. 203; 1, 58, ibid., p. 317.

85. 1, 39, ibid., p. 278; 3, 43, ibid., p. 521; "Clizia," Prolog, *MG.,* 2, 843.

86. *P.,* Dedication, *MG.,* 1, 10; chap. 26, ibid., pp. 92–96; letter to Vettori, 10 Dec. 1513, *MG.,* 2, 929–30 *(Lett. fam.,* 137); *D.,* Dedication, *MG.,* 1, 188; Preface, ibid., pp. 190–92; *A.W.,* Preface, *MG.,* 2, 567; 7, ibid., p. 726.

87. *D.,* 2, 28, *MG.,* 1, 405, 406; 3, 4, ibid., p. 426; 6, ibid., pp. 429, 430, 438, 442; *P.,* chap. 19, ibid., p. 74.

88. Draft of letter to Soderini, *MG.,* 2, 897 *(Lett. fam.,* 116); *D.,* 1, 17, *MG.,* 1, 240; 18, ibid., pp. 242–43; "T.F.," 11. 100–120, *MG.,* 2, 747; 11. 181–83, 190–92, ibid., p. 749.

89. *H.F.,* 4, 14, *MG.,* 3, 1202; *A.W.,* 5, *MG.,* 2, 671–72.

90. *H.F.,* 3, 7, *MG.,* 3, 1149.

91. 1, ibid., pp. 1140–41; *D.,* 1, 6, *MG.,* 1, 209–11; 2, 19, ibid., p. 379; 3, 16, ibid., pp. 468–69.

92. *D.,* 1, 6, *MG.,* 1, 209; 18, ibid., p. 242; 2, 2, ibid., pp. 330–32; 4, ibid., p. 339; 5, ibid., p. 341; 3, 24, ibid., pp. 485–86; *A.W.,* 1, *MG.,* 2, 573–74, 575, 578; 2, ibid., p. 623; *H.F.,* 3, 1, *MG.,* 3, 1141.

93. Phil. 2:6–8.

94. Wicks, "Exposition," Phil. 3:12, *I.B.,* 11, 88.

95. Pocock, p. 37.

96. Pocock, "Custom, Grace, Form & Matter," p. 169.

97. Orr, p. 193.

98. Aristotle, op. cit., p. 2.

99. Orr, p. 202; *D.,* 2, 30, *MG.,* 1, 411–12; *D.,* 3, 31, ibid., p. 498.

100. "L.C.," *MG.,* 2, 554.

101. Matt. 18:12–14; Luke 15:3–32.

102. Matt. 25:40, 45; John 5:17.

103. Matt. 6:25–34; Luke 12:22–31.

104. Matt. 6:25, 32–34.

105. I Cor. 10:26.

106. I John 4:10.

107. Ibid., 18.

108. *D.,* 2, 28, *MG.,* 1, 405, 406; 3, 6, ibid., pp. 426, 429, 430, 438; *P.,* chap. 19, ibid., p. 74.

109. *D.,* 3, 33, ibid., p. 502; 31, ibid., p. 500.

110. Matt. 6:14–15.

111. Col. 3:13–15.

112. Pocock, p. 375.

113. Ibid., p. 457.

114. John 14:30–31.

115. Wilbert F. Howard, "Exegesis," on John 14:29–30, *I.B.,* 8, 714.

116. Pocock, pp. 537–38.

117. I Cor. 2:11.

118. Shakespeare, *Hamlet,* act 3, sc. 2.

119. *D.,* 1, Preface, *MG.,* 1, 190.

120. 3, 1, ibid., p. 419.

121. 1, 12, ibid., p. 228.

122. 3, 30, ibid., p. 496.

123. Pocock, p. 63.

124. "Lingua," *Opp. MC.*, pp. 770–71.

125. Sheldon Wolin, "Political Theory as a Vocation," in *Machiavelli . . . Thought,* p. 63.

126. *D.,* 1, Preface, *MG.,* 1, 190.

127. Pocock, p. 336.

128. *D.,* 3, 41, *MG.,* 1, 519; 47, ibid., p. 526; "Lingua," *Opp. MC.*, pp. 770–71.

129. *D.,* 2, 2, *MG.,* 1, 331.

130. Francis W. Beare, "Exegesis," Col. 1:21–23, *I.B.,* 11, 173; Rom. 8:19–22.

131. Pocock, pp. 386–87.

132. William Carey McWilliams, "On Equality as the Moral Foundation for Community," in *Moral Foundations,* p. 191.

133. Brestead, op. cit., pp. 299–300; Jer. 31:31, 33–34; Ezek. 36:23–24, 26–28; Heb. 8:8–12.

134. Matt. 6:10; Luke 11:2.

135. Luke 17:20–21; Matt. 10:6–7.

136. Pocock, p. 45.

137. "Civil Disobedience," pp. 88–89.

138. Yarrow, op. cit., p. 99.

139. Whitfield, *Discourses,* p. 163.

140. Ibid., p. 170.

141. Ibid., pp. 166–67.

142. Mark 14:62.

143. Matt. 24:30; Luke 21:27.

144. Mark 9:1.

145. Yarrow, op. cit., p. 99.

146. Ibid., p. 48.

147. Ibid., pp. 164–65.

148. Ronald J. Fisher, "Third-Party Consultation: A Method for the Study and Resolution of Conflicts," *Journal of Confict Resolution,* 16, No. 1, March, 1972, p. 85, quoted in Yarrow, op. cit., pp. 283–84.

149. Yarrow, op. cit., p. 76.

150. Adam Curle, letter to Mike Yarrow, 17 Aug. 1976, quoted in Yarrow, op. cit., p. 265.

151. Yarrow, op. cit., p. 101.

152. Ibid., pp. 74–75.

153. Curle, *Making Peace* (London, Tavistock Publications, 1971), p. 240, as quoted in Yarrow, op. cit., pp. 265–66.

154. *Journey Through a Wall* (Philadelphia: American Friends Service Committee, 1964), p. 61, as quoted in Yarrow, op. cit., p. 85.

155. Yarrow, op. cit., p. 64.

156. Roland Warren, "Quaker Peace Work in Tense International Situation," *International Affairs Reports from Quaker Workers,* 10, no. 1, Jan. 1963, p. 7, as quoted in Yarrow, op. cit., pp. 102–103.

157. Yarrow, op. cit., p. 252.

158. Ibid., pp. 256–57.

159. Ibid., p. 250.

160. Ibid., p. 257.

161. Ibid., pp. 174–75.

162. *P.,* chap. 25, *MG.,* 1, 90.

163. Ibid.

164. *D.*, 1, 18, ibid., p. 240; letter to Vettori, 20 June 1513, *MG.*, 2, 911 *(Lett. fam.*, 124).

165. *P.*, chap. 15, *MG.*, 1, 57.

166. *D.*, 1, Preface, ibid., p. 190.

167. John 10:10.

168. Ibid., 14:6.

169. *D.*, 3, 6, *MG.*, 1, 430; *P.*, chap. 26, ibid., p. 96; letter to Guicciardini, 17 May 1526, *MG.*, 2, 997–98 *(Lett. fam.*, 207).

170. *D.*, 1, 12, *MG.*, 1, 228.

171. "Lingua," *Opp. MC.*, pp. 770–71.

172. *A.W.*, 2, *MG.*, 2, 622.

173. Pocock, p. 193.

174. Wicks, "Exposition," Phil. 3:4–16, *I.B.*, 11, 80.

175. Pocock, pp. 98–99.

176. The Declaration of Independence.

177. Mead, "Genesis . . . Self," pp. 285–88.

178. John Dewey, *The Public and Its Problems,* (New York: Henry Holt, 1927), chaps. 1–2, pp. 1–74.

179. Raymond T. Stamm, "Exegesis," on Gal. 5:14, *I.B.*, 10, 556.

180. *P.*, chap. 24, *MG.*, 1, 88.

181. Ibid., p. 89.

182. *A.W.*, 1, *MG.*, 2, 585–86.

183. *D.*, 1, 12, ibid., p. 228; *P.*, chap. 7, ibid., p. 31.

184. *D.*, 2, 2, ibid., pp. 329, 332–33; 1, 16, ibid., p. 236.

185. 3, 33, ibid., p. 502; 31, ibid., p. 500; *A.W.*, 1, *MG.*, 2, 585–86; 4, ibid., p. 662.

186. *D.*, 1, 43, *MG.*, 1, 286.

187. 1, 9, ibid., pp. 218, 220; 3, 1, ibid., p. 421.

188. Pocock, p. 218.

189. Ibid., p. 243.

190. Knox, "Exposition," Luke 10:21, *I.B.*, 8, 190.

191. Wolin, op. cit., in *Machiavelli . . . Thought,* p. 45.

CHAPTER FIFTEEN

1. Yarrow, op. cit., p. 264.

2. Luccock, "Exposition," Mark 10:35–45, *I.B.*, 7, 612.

3. "L.C.," *MG.*, 2, 554; *A.W.*, 5, ibid., p. 671.

4. *P.*, chap. 24, *MG.*, 1, 89.

5. Chap. 17, ibid., p. 64.

6. "Ghiribizzi," *Opp. MC.*, p. 879 [for the Italian, see chap. 1, n.21].

7. *D.*, 2, 29, *MG.*, 1, 408; 2, 14, ibid., pp. 359–60.

8. *A.W.*, 7, *MG.*, 2, 721.

9. *P.*, chap. 15, *MG.*, 1, 57.

10. Letter to Guicciardini, 10 Aug. 1524, *MG.*, 2, 978 *(Lett. fam.*, 186).

11. *P.*, chap. 25, *MG.*, 1, 90; *D.*, 2, 29, ibid., p. 408.

12. "G.A.," chap. 5, 11. 115–17, *MG.*, 2, 764.

13. *D.*, 1, Preface, *MG.*, 1, 190–91; 2, Preface, ibid., p. 324; 3, 6, ibid., p. 428; *A.W.*, Dedicatory Preface, *MG.*, 2, 566–67; 7, ibid., p. 726; *H.F.*, Preface, *MG.*, 3, 1031–32; 5, 1, ibid., p. 1233.

14. Letter to Vettori, 10 Dec. 1513, *MG.*, 2, 929 *(Lett. fam.,* 137).

15. *Mandragola,* act 3, sc. 2, *MG.,* 2, 795.

16. *P.,* chap. 14, *MG.,* 1, 56–57.

17. Chap. 23, ibid., pp. 86–87.

18. Luccock, "Exposition," Mark 8:27, *I.B.,* 7, 765.

19. Hough, "Exposition," Rev. 17:7–13, *I.B.,* 12, 599.

20. Stamm, "Exegesis," on Gal. 5:15, *I.B.,* 10, 558.

21. Wicks, "Exposition," Phil. 3:3, *I.B.,* 11, 76.

22. 3:21, ibid., p. 103.

23. Stephen Hobhouse, *Joseph Sturge, His Life and Work* (London: Dent, 1919), p. 146, as quoted in Yarrow, op. cit., p. 298.

24. John 12:47.

25. Ibid., 4:32.

26. Ibid., 8:28.

27. Ibid., 32.

28. *P.,* chap. 15, *MG.,* 1, 57.

29. *S.D.,"* 11. 184–92, *MG.,* 3, 1461.

30. "L.C.," *MG.,* 2, 554.

31. Ibid., p. 555.

32. *D.,* 1, Preface, *MG.,* 1, 190; 9, ibid., p. 218.

Appendix 3

CHRONOLOGY

Events in Machiavelli's Life	*Relevant External Events*
1469, 3 May Birth	Christopher Columbus (1446?–1506). Lorenzo de'Medici (1449–1492). Vasco da Gama (1469–1524).
	Lorenzo de'Medici (born 1 Jan. 1449),[1] upon the death of his father, Piero (2 Dec. 1469),[2] responsible head of government of Florence and of Medici enterprises.
1475.	Birth of younger brother, Totto.
1478, 26 Apr.	Pazzi Conspiracy: murder of Lorenzo's brother, Giuliano, followed by war of Papacy and Naples against Florence.
1480.	Peace with Naples. Capture of Otranto by Turks. Peace with Papacy. Reorganization of Florentine government into instrument for Lorenzo.
1489.	Savonarola's arrival in Florence.
1492.	Death of Lorenzo. Beginning of Columbus' four voyages of discovery of America (1492–1506).[3] Election of Roderigo Borgia as Pope Alexander VI.

1494.	Invasion of Italy by Charles VIII. Expulsion of Medici from Florence. Revolt of Pisa. Savonarola in control.
1496, 11 Oct. Death of mother.	Beginning of war to recover Pisa.
1497, 2 Dec. Letter written on behalf of the Machiavelli families in defense of their property claims against the Pazzi.	
1498, 23 May	Execution of Savonarola. Piero Soderini's election as Gonfalonier of Justice. Rounding of Cape of Good Hope by Vasco da Gama (same age as Machiavelli).
19 June. Confirmation of appointment as First Secretary of Signory; also, Chancellor and Secretary to the Ten (in charge of war and foreign affairs).	
14 July. Attached also to the Ten of Liberty.	
20 Nov. First mission: to Piombino.	
? "Rules for a Society of Pleasure"	
? "Carnival Songs"	
1499, 24 Mar.–? To Piombino.	
May. "Discourse before the Ten on Pisan Affairs."[4]	
13 July–1 Aug. To Catherine Sforza.	Suspicion regarding loyalty of Paolo Vitelli, commander of Florentine forces against Pisa.
Involvement in condemnation of Vitelli.[5]	
1 Oct.	Execution of Vitelli.
	Voyage to America by Amerigo Vespucci, a Florentine merchant.[6]

542

Nov.–Dec.	Conquest of Romagna by Cesare Borgia with French aid.
1500, 10 May. Death of father.	Mutiny of troops sent by France to aid Florence in reconquest of Pisa.
16 June–July? With two Florentine Commissioners to army in field before Pisa.	
1501, 18 July–14 Jan. First mission to France.	
Death of sister (married to Francesco Vernaccia).[7]	
Feb., June, July, Oct. Several missions to Pistoia.	
Aug. Marriage to Marietta Corsini.	
1502	Rumors that Vitellozzo Vitelli, in pay of Cesare Borgia, was stirring revolt in Arezzo.
May. To Arezzo.	
Birth of daughter, Primerana.	Revolt in Arezzo and Valdichiana.
	Request by Cesare Borgia that Florence send negotiators to him.
22 June–? As secretary to Bishop Soderini, on mission to Cesare Borgia.	Borgia's criticism of Florence's government as not inspiring confidence and request that he and his army be employed by the city.
Aug. and Sept. To Arezzo.	
20 Sept.	

	Election of Piero Soderini as Gonfalonier for life.[8]
6 Oct–23 Jan. 1503. To Caesar Borgia. Biagio Buonaccorsi's letters about Marietta's discontent with Machiavelli's prolonged absence.	
31 Dec. Borgia's conversation with Machiavelli immediately after the seizure of his enemies.	Caesar Borgia's coup at Sinigaglia.
1503, 26 Apr. To Siena.	
1 June–18 Aug. "On the Method of Dealing with the Rebellious Peoples of Valdichiana."[9]	
17 Aug.	Death of Alexander VI; illness of Caesar Borgia.
22 Sept.	Accession of Pius III.
17 Oct.	Death of Pius III
24 Oct.–16? Dec. To Rome.	
1 Nov.	Accession of Julius II. Fall of Caesar Borgia.
8 Nov. Birth of second child, Bernardo.[10]	
1504, 20 Jan.–? Mar. Second mission to France.	
? Apr. To Piombino.	
? Commencement of *Mandragola*.[11]	
Oct. Birth of second son, Lodovico.	

8 Nov. Dedication of "Decen-nale" to Alamanno Salviati, vic-tor over the Arezzo rebellion.[12]

1505, 9 Apr.–? To Gianpaolo Baglioni of Peruggia.

4 May–? To Mantua.

16 July–? To Siena.

21 Aug.–? To army before Pisa.

30 Dec. Authorization by Sig-noria for Machiavelli's to begin recruiting for the militia.[13] Con-ferring, by Council of Eighty, of commission on Borgia's ex-lieutenant, don Michele,[14]

Dec.–Mar. 1506. To various
1506. parts of the territory in prepara-tion for setting up a new military organization.

Feb. First printing of "Decen-nale."

15 Feb. First parade of militia.

? Reception of dead sister's son, Giovanni Vernaccia, to be raised with his family.

Review of candidates for militia.

14 June. Death of an infant.[15]

25 Aug.–26 Oct. To Julius II's court on campaign against Bo-logna.

2 Oct. "Ordinance for National Militia." (Infantry)

6 Dec. Creation of the Nine Officers of the Florentine Ordinance and Militia.

1507, 12 Jan. Election as Secretary of the Nine Officers . . .

14 Mar.–17 Apr. To Florentine territories conscripting soldiers.
18 May. To Piombino.
9–14 Aug. To Siena.

1507–1515. "Tercets on Ingratitude."[16]

17 Dec.–16 June, 1508. To
1508 Emperor Maximilian.

Friendship with Francesco Vettori. Interest in Swiss.

17 June. Second "Report on German Affairs."

16 Aug.–? To interior of state.

10 Dec.   League of Cambrai against Venice.

1509. Jan. In camp.

10 Mar. To Piombino.

Possible   performance   of "Clizia."[17]

20 May. With commissioners negotiating with Pisan envoys for first stages of surrender of Pisa.[18]

1509, 4 June.   Surrender of Pisa.

8 June. Entry into Pisa with the Commissioner and his battalions.

"Tercets on Ambition."[19]

10 Nov.–2 Jan. 1510. To
1510 Emperor at Mantua and Verona.

"Discourse on Affairs of Germany and the Emperor."

?   various poems.

5 Jan. Bequest to Machiavelli by his brother Totto (when ordained as a priest) of his share of the paternal inheritance.[20]

15 Feb. Death of a child.[21]

12 Mar.–3 June. To interior of the state.

?   Birth of a child.[22]

20 June–19 Oct. Third mission to France. "Picture of France." "On the Nature of the French."

13–29 Nov. To the interior of the state.

3–29 Nov. To the interior of the state.

1511 5 Jan.–15 Feb. To various parts of the state.

Feb. Death of the child born in 1510.[23]

547

5 May. To Monaco.	Papal League against France.
19 Aug. Birth of child.[24]	
10 Sept.–2 Nov. Fourth mission to France. "Picture of the French."	
	Papal interdict against Florence (15 Sept.–1 Dec.)
3–4 Nov. To Pisa.	
5–12 Nov.	Council of Pisa.
22 Nov. Drafting of Machiavelli's first will.	
2 Dec. Mission for raising troops in and beyond the territory.	
15 Dec.	Renewal of papal interdict against Florence.
"Note on the Choice of a Commander of the Infantry."	
1512 23–30 Mar. "Provision for National Militia" (Cavalry).	
11 Apr.	French victory at Ravenna but death of Gaston de Foix. Recovery of power by Julius II through diplomacy.
"Picture of Germany."[25]	
6 May–23 Aug. To Pisa, etc.	
21 Aug.	Spanish invasion of Tuscany.
28–29 Aug.	Defeat of militia. Sack of Prato and massacre.
30 Aug. Soderini's escape conducted by Machiavelli and Vettori.	Expulsion of Gonfalonier Piero Soderini.

1 Sept.	Restoration of Medici and termination of the liberties of the Florentines.
7 Nov. Dismissal from office.	
10 Nov. Exile from Florence for a year but confinement to Florentine territory and posting of bond of 1,000 gold florins.	
17 Nov. First of several suspensions (for government's convenience) of prohibition from entering the Palace of the Signoria.	
1513 the *Prince*.[26]	
Jan. Letter from P. Soderini and draft of reply.	
19 Feb. Imprisonment and torture on charge of conspiracy.	
20 Feb.	Death of Julius II.
Three sonnets from prison to Giuliano de'Medici.	
1513, 11 Mar. Release from prison. Six days in Florence "recovering force" and hoping for reconsideration by the Medici.	Election of Giovanni de'Medici as Pope Leo X.
"Hymn of the Blessed Spirits."[27]	
13 Mar.–31 Jan. Correspondence with Vettori.	

–1514 (Winter) "Serenade."[28]
–1519. "A Pastoral: The Ideal Ruler."[29]

−1519. *Discourses on the First Ten Books of Livy*[30]

"Andria" translated from Terrence.

Aug.–? Birth of second daughter, who died three days later.

10 Dec. Letter to Vettori describing his way of life.

1514–1517?

"Second Decennale."[31]

? "Dialogue on the Languages Used by Dante, Boccacio, and Petrarch."

? "Tercets on Fortune."

? "Belfagor: The Devil Who Married."

1514, 4 Sept. Birth of fourth son, Piero.[32]

1515. May. Vettori returned to Florence.

Lorenzo de'Medici elected Captain General of the Florentines.

Letters to his nephew: 15 Aug., "almost lost the memory of myself."

13 Sept.

Battle of Marengo.

19 Nov. Letter to nephew: "only relatives and friends left. I count only on them."

1516, 15 Feb. Readiness to "grasp good fortune when it should come, and have patience, should it not come."

Mar.

Death of Giuliano de'Medici to whom Machiavelli had dedicated the *Prince*.

Sept. the *Prince* finished, rededication to Lorenzo de'Medici.

1517, 15 Feb. Letter to G. Vernaccia: Machiavelli's hospitality.

Invitation to the Rucellai circle.

Oct.

The posting by Martin Luther of his 95 theses against indulgences.

"The (Golden) Ass" (unfinished).[33]

1518, 4 Mar.–Apr. To Genoa in interest of some Florentine merchants.

Printing of the completed *Mandragola*.[34]

7 Sept.

Arrival in Florence of Lorenzo de'Medici and his French wife, Madeline de la Tour d'Auvergne, a relative of Francis I.

1519, 12 Jan.

Death of Emperor Maximilian.

4 May.

Death of Lorenzo de'Medici (to whom Machiavelli had dedicated *The Prince* and of whom is Michaelangelo's statue, *Il Pensieroso*) within a month after the death of[35] his wife, four days after bearing[36] Catherine de'Medici, later queen of France.

	More liberal leadership of Florence under government by Cardinal Giulio de'Medici.
2 June.	Election of Charles V as emperor.
2 Nov.	Burial of Cosimo Rucellai.[37]

1519–20.

"Discourse on the Reform of the Government of Florence."

The Art of War

1520, 10 Mar. Introduction of Machiavelli to Cardinal Giulio de'Medici.

9 July–8–10 Sept. To Lucca as representative of some Florentine merchants.

"Description of the Government of the City of Lucca."

Aug. "Life of Castruccio Castracani of Lucca."

8 Nov. *Florentine History* commissioned by Cardinal de'Medici.

? "Discourse on Florentine Affairs after the death of Lorenzo."[38]

Performance of *Mandragola* in Florence, Rome, elsewhere.

1521, 8 May.   Alliance between Pope Leo X and Emperor Charles V.

11–19 May. To Capri. "Orator" (highest diplomatic title he received) on behalf of the Signoria.

? "On the methods Adopted by the Duke Valentino When Murdering"[39]

? "On the Manner of Raising Money for the Country."[40]

? "Discourse to the Balia of Florence."

Aug. Printing of *"The Art of War* in Florence.[41]

Performance of *Mandragola* in Monteloro.[42]

1 Dec.   Death of Pope Leo X.

1522, 9 Jan.   Accession of Pope Adrian VI.

13, 16 Feb. Performance of *Mandragola* in Venice.

At request of Cardinal de'Medici, submission of suggestions for reform of the government of Florence.[43]

June.   Involvement of leaders among Machiavelli's young auditors in anti-Medicean conspiracy supported by former Gonfalonier Soderini.[44]

8 June. Death of Machiavelli's brother, Totto.

15 June. Closing of Rucellai Gardens.

23 Oct. "Advice to Raffaello Girolami When He Went as Ambassador to the Emperor."

27 Nov. Second (and last) will.[45]

1523.   Giovanni Verrazzano explored the Atlantic coast of North America.[46]

14 Sept.   Death of Pope Adrian VI.

18 Nov.   Election of Cardinal Giulio de'Medici as Pope Clement VII.

?   "An Exhortation to Penitence."[47]

1524. Printing of *Mandragola*.

1525. 13 Jan. Performance of "Clizia" in Florence.[48]

24 Feb.   French disaster at Pavia. Francis I taken
15 Mar. Machiavelli's suggestion to Guicciardini that Giovanni de'Medici might be supported by Italy's liberator.[49]   prisoner.

1 Apr.   Papal alliance with the Emperor.

May–June. Completion of first part of *History of Florence:* presentation to Clement VII in Rome; renewal of commission.

Clement's interest in Machiavelli's proposal for a militia in Romagna checked by Guicciardini's reluctance in endorsing it.

10 (11?) June–26 July. To Romagna.

Correspondence between Machiavelli and Guicciardini; between Machiavelli and Vettori.

Aug. Restoration of Machiavelli's eligibility for holding government office in Florence.

17 Aug.–16 Sept. To Venice on Behalf of the Consuls of the Wool Guild.

6 Sept. News from Nerli that Machiavelli's name had been included in list of those eligible for public office.[50]

? Birth of son, Totto.[57]

1526, Performance of *Mandragola* in Venice.

4 Apr. Consultant on fortifications of Florence.

10 (?) Apr.–26. To Rome.[52]

Chancellor of Fortifications of Florence; his son, Bernardo, his assistant.

17 May.

League between King of France, the Pope, the Florentines, the Venetians.

6 July–30 (?) Oct. "In the field with the Camp of the League in Lombardy."

555

30 Nov.	Death of Giovanni de'Medici. "Delle Bande Neri," son of Catherine Sforza.
30 Nov.–5 Dec. To Guicciardini at Modena and Bologna.	
1527, 3 Feb.–18 Apr. To Guicciardini at Parma and Bologna.	
26 Apr.	Florentine revolt against Medici.
2 May. Machiavelli, along with Guicciardini and troops, to Rome in pursuit of the Germans.	
6 May.	Sack of Rome by German forces.
?–22 May. To Andrea Doria, Commander of papal fleet, at Civita-Vecchia.	
16 May.	Restoration in Florence of the constitution of Savonarola. Exile of Medici.
17 May.	
? Machiavelli's return to Florence.	
10 June.	Conferring of Machiavelli's old post on a member of the Medicean administration.
20 June. Attack of sickness.	
21 June. Death.	
22 June. Burial in Santa Croce.	
1531, Publication of *Discourses on Livy*.	

1532, Publication of *The Prince,* "The Life of Castruccio Castracani of Lucca," *The History of Florence.*

1537, Publication of "Clizia."

1541, Feb. Performance of "Clizia" in Rome.[53]

1552, Death of his wife, Marietta.

NOTES

1. Schevill, *History of Florence,* p. 374.
2. Ibid., p. 377.
3. Morrison, Commager, Leuchtenburg, *The Growth of the American Republic,* 1, 18–22.
4. Ridolfi, *The Life of Niccolo Machiavelli,* pp. 25, 263 n.3.
5. Ibid., pp. 28–29.
6. Morrison, et. al., op. cit., I, 22.
7. Ridolfi, op. cit., p. 42; Tommasini, 1, 208.
8. *MG.,* 1, 125 n.2; Schevill, op. cit., p. 461.
9. Ridolfi, pp. 52, 269 n.25; *MG.,* 1, 161.
10. Ridolfi, p. 274, n.40.
11. Tommasini, 2, 384–85.
12. Ridolfi, pp. 82, 276 n.16.
13. Tommasini, 1, 354.
14. Ridolfi, p. 87.
15. Ibid., p. 326 n.22.
16. *MG.,* 2, 740.
17. Ibid., p. 774.
18. Ridolfi, p. 107.
19. *MG.,* 2, 735.
20. Ridolfi, pp. 113, 286, n.24; Tommasini, 1, 216.
21. Ridolfi, p. 36 n.22.
22. Ibid., p. 117.
23. Ibid.
24. Ferrara, *Machiavel,* p. 159.
25. Ridolfi, p. 283 n.18.
26. Pocock, p. 154; Anglo, *Machiavelli, a Dissection,* p. 84.
27. *MG.,* 2, 878.
28. *MG.,* 1, 1016.
29. *MG.,* 1, 97.
30. Whitfield, *Discourses,* p. 116; Anglo, op. cit., p. 84.

31. *MG.*, 3, 1444.
32. Tommasini, 1, 219.
33. *MG.*, 2, 750.
34. Ridolfi, pp. 173, 303, n.20.
35. Schevill, op. cit., p. 476.
36. Tommasini, 2, 136.
37. Ridolfi, 304, n.30.
38. Ibid., pp. 183, 308 n.28.
39. *MG.*, 1, 161; Anglo, op. cit., p. 36.
40. *MG.*, 3, 1439.
41. Ridolfi, p. 198.
42. Tommasini, 2, p. 385.
43. Ridolfi, p. 202.
44. Ibid., p. 202–203.
45. Pansini, pp. 1229–32.
46. *The Columbia History of the World*, p. 662.
47. *MG.*, 1, 170.
48. Tommasini, 2, 414, n.4.
49. Ridolfi, p. 226.
50. Tommasini, 2, 793.
51. Ridolfi, pp. 238, 326 n.22.
52. Tommasini, 2, 783, 847 and n.2.
53. Ibid., p. 922.

Appendix 4

Sequence of Excerpts from Machiavelli, the Chief Works and Others

Pages in Gilbert, Chief Works	Chapter in This Text	Footnote Reference	Page in This Text
	"A Provision For Infantry"		
3	III	179	79
	V	234	162
	VIII	55	269
	The Prince		
10	I	29	6
	III	125	69
	VIII	102	275
12–3	VIII	61	270
16–7	III	213	86
		36	56
17	V	203	158
24–5	III	88	64
25	VIII	92	274
26	IV	18	123
	VII	19	237
	III	11	48
	V	95	141
26–27	III	71	61

27	V	113	143
31	III	75	62
34	VI	45	210
36	III	26	51
38	III	73	61
		25	51
1	VIII	5	264
42	VII	24	238
	XI	113	352
47	V	240	163
	VII	127	251
47–53	VIII	44	268
48	V	167	153
52	V	241	163
52–3	III	176	78
54	III	177	78
	V	242	163
	VIII	45	269
55	III	89	65
	VII	22	238
55–6	III	214	86
56–7	IV	138	71
57	X	80	319
	I	13	3
		38	7
	III	47	58
		154	176
	IX	60	291
	X	70	319
		79	319
	XII	125	378

	XIV	51	436
		165	458
		9	430
	XV	28	467
	V	105	142
		116	143
57–8	VII	1	233
	IX	96	295
58	VII	193	260
	IX	97	295
60–1	III	221	88
62	I	81	15
	II	95	36
63	I	56	11
	III	145	73
64	X	47	315
64	III	175	78
	IV	20	124
	IX	63	291
	XI	102	350
	XV	5	464
	II	85	34
64–7	VII	39	241
65	III	275	98
	II	86	34
		84	34
66–7	III	18	49
67	I	57	12
72	VII	13	236
74	I	61	12
86–7	XV	17	465
87–8	IV	19	124
	VIII	126	279
	XII	163	385
88	II	81	34
	XIV	180	460

89	IV	21	124
	X	107	322
	XIV	181	460
	XV	4	464
89–90	III	233	91
	XV	11	465
90	XIV	162	457
	VII	3	234
	VIII	90	274
	X	91	321
	XIV	163	458
	IV	40	127
	VIII	97	275
92	I	28	6
	IV	30	125
	VIII	13	266
		98	275
	X	97	321
92–3	VIII	8	264
93	III	313	110
94	VIII	123	279
	X	92	321
		149	282
94–5	III	316	111
96	XIII	189	426
	VIII	107	277

"Remodeling The Government of Florence"

102	V	560	200
102–3	V	563	200
107	III	320	112
	V	561	200
	VIII	150	282
110	V	165	152
	III	322	112
	VI	60	212
	VIII	50	269

	III	278	99
	VIII	1	263
	XI	28	339
	XII	111	377
		156	382
		167	385
	I	32	6
	V	77	140
	VII	15	236
202	III	209	85
	XII	158	384
202–3	III	189	82
203	III	328	113
		187	81
	XII	164	385
	III	331	114
204–5	VIII	6	264
	III	324	113
	XIII	83	407
206	II	91	35
209	III	256	93
209–11	III	183	81
211	III	185	81
		330	13
217–20	III	56	59
	V	93	141
218	III	59	59
		114	68
	VI	59	212
	XIII	79	407
	XIV	62	438
	II	8	18
	III	81	64
	VI	64	212
	II	80	34
	III	123	69
	VI	52	211
219	III	91	65
		92	65
220	II	6	18

	III	120	68
221	III	149	74
222	VIII	140	281
223–7	III	19	50
226	V	171	153
	III	127	69
228	V	137	145
	III	284	101
	V	124	144
		125	144
		225	161
	VI	65	212
	II	3	18
	XIII	104	412
228–9	VI	66	214
236	III	336	114
	XI	136	357
	III	63	60
237	VIII	7	264
239–40	III	67	60
240	III	112	67
	I	14	3
	IV	46	127
	V	218	160
	X	50	315
	XII	98	376
		154	382
	XIV	164	458
242	III	264	96
242–3	III	111	67
	XIII	176	424
		179	425
243	XI	89	348
	III	68	60
	VIII	63	270
	XIV	78	442
246	III	326	113

247	III	215	86
252	II	83	34
	VII	37	240
253–4	III	72	61
254	VIII	134	280
	X	72	319
254–5	III	295	104
263	IV	42	127
263–4	VIII	53	269
272	II	94	36
	III	241	92
	V	69	139
274	III	255	93
	II	92	35
278	III	128	69
286	III	178	79
	X	132	324
	XII	62	371
287	VII	35	240
288	V	110	143
288–9	V	172	154
291	VIII	118	278
296	III	329	113
	XI	134	356
	V	22	133
299	IV	43	127
307	III	310	109
309	III	69	60
	VIII	62	270
	III	319	111
313	XII	5	364

313–14	I	15	4
	XII	99	376
		155	382
314	XIII	74	406
316	III	334	114
316–7	III	334	114
317	III	35	55
318	III	337	115
321	III	142	72
72			
		148	73
322–3		309	109
323	II	87	35
	V	76	140
324	III	136	71
		236	91
	IV	29	125
	VIII	14	266
	XIII	48	399
328	V	12	131
329	III	77	63
		335	114
	VI	51	211
	X	133	324
	XIII	78	407
	XI	135	357
330–2	III	268	97
331	III	20	50
	IX	147	301
	V	122	144
		130	145
		131	145
		138	145
	VII	53	243
	IX	92	294
332–3	III	78	63
335–7	V	11	131

335	XIII	64	404
337–8	XIII	66	404
338	XIII	65	404
339	II	5	18
	V	16	132
	XIII	113	414
	III	269	97
340	III	144	72
340–1	III	143	72
341	V	14	132
341–3	III	222	90
349–51	V	206	159
350	XI	111	351
350–1	IV	22	124
354–5	XIII	122	415
		128	416
357–8	II	82	34
	VII	36	240
359–60	IV	39	127
379	III	182	80
380	XI	117	353
381	III	263	95
382	III	173	78
385	III	224	89
	VII	23	238
390	III	205	85
404	II	88	35
	V	211	160
	VII	38	240
	III	118	68
405	I	55	11
	VIII	128	279

406	I	54	11
	III	237	91
407–8	VIII	83	273
408	I	25	5
	IV	38	127
	VIII	91	274
	X	104	322
	XI	108	350
	XV	7	464
412	III	234	91
	VIII	78	272
		96	275
412–3	VIII	24	267
419	I	36	7
	V	91	141
	VIII	68	271
	XIII	84	407
	III	33	55
421	III	204	85
	VIII	69	271
422	III	296	105
425	I	60	12
	III	61	60
425	III	52	62
	VI	46	210
428	VIII	73	272
		114	279
429	III	153	76
	I	53	11
429–30	I	58	12
		131	324
430	I	62	12
	III	301	107
	VIII	129	279
438	III	29	52
	I	59	12

441	I	23	5
	VII	5	234
	XI	103	350
442	III	30	52
447	XII	166	77
452	VIII	84	273
	III	243	92
452–3	III	325	113
456	IV	23	124
	XI	112	351
457	VIII	67	271
459–62	XIII	121	415
460	XI	29	339
		115	352
461	III	80	63
468–9	III	186	81
471	VI	89	218
477	II	90	35
480	VII	20	237
480–1	III	74	62
481	VIII	70	271
485–6	III	258	94
486	V	68	139
	XIV	16	432
487–8	V	75	140
488	V	70	139
489	III	65	60
490	III	66	60
491–2	II	2	18

492	VIII	115	278
	VI	63	212
492–3	XI	57	343
	III	41	56
493	III	70	60
495–6	III	60	61
496	II	1	17
	V	87	140
		139	145
	XIV	122	449
497	V	169	153
	III	137	71
498	III	157	76
	VIII	95	275
		139	281
		80	273
500	III	207	85
		142	281
		174	78
502	III	170	77
502–3	XI	106	350
503	III	21	51
505–7	XI	58	343
506–7	III	76	62
507	III	327	113
508–9	VII	151	254
512	XII	42	369
	XIV	81	442
515	XI	116	352
516	VII	31	239
518	VII	47	243

519	II	11	19
	V	127	145
520	XII	171	386
	III	274	98
	VII	34	240
521	V	10	130
	III	126	69
522	VI	124	223
	V	13	132
525	IV	36	126
526	II	36	20
	V	128	145
	X	65	318
	III	117	68
	VII	110	248
527	XI	59	343
		114	352
527	III	34	55
527–9	X	48	315
528	III	37	56

"The Life of Castruccio Castracani of Lucca"

533–4	VIII	79	272
554	IV	1	121
	XIV	100	445
	XV	3	464
555	XV	31	467

The Art of War

566	III	206	85
566–7	III	141	72
		22	51
	XII	159	384
567	IV	17	123
	VI	14	207
	IV	16	123

573

571–2	VI	15	207
	XII	146	381
	V	71	139
572	V	117	143
	III	79	63
573	IV	32	125
	VIII	15	266
573–4	III	260	95
575	III	261	87
576	III	217	95
577	XIII	75	406
	III	262	95
578	III	259	94
		218	87
579	I	79	15
	VII	14	236
	IX	50	290
	X	93	321
		128	323
581	III	171	78
583–4	III	180	79
584	IV	24	124
584–5	III	219	87
	V	250	164
585	V	239	·162
585–6	III	172	78
	VI	80	216
	XIV	182	460
587	IV	25	124
	VIII	46	269
	X	108	322
	XI	104	350
591	VIII	17	266

591–2	V	248	164
619	III	216	86
	VIII	65	271
	XI	107	350
622	III	40	56
	VIII	116	278
	XI	105	350
	II	9	18
	III	333	114
	V	215	160
	XII	161	385
	III	147	73
	XII	92	375
623	III	267	96
	VIII	141	281
624	VIII	81	273
626	VIII	16	266
	IV	31	125
656	IV	41	127
657	I	27	6
	IV	26	124
	X	102	322
	XI	110	351
661	III	24	51
662	III	168	77
		300	107
	XIII	123	415
		127	416
		129	416
671–2	III	271	97
691	III	23	51
694	VII	108	248
700	XIII	168	424
718	X	46	315
719–20	III	208	85
	V	207	159

720	VI	16	207
721	I	16	4
	X	100	321
	XIV	21	433
	XV	8	464
722	V	253	164
	XII	61	371
724	VII	109	248
	XII	58	371
	VIII	9	265
724–5	III	317	111
725	VII	62	244
726	IV	33	126
	VI	17	207
	VIII	18	266
		89	274
		106	277
736	VII	40	241
	II	96	36
737	II	79	34
	VII	107	248
738–9	III	314	110
739	III	232	90
	VI	28	208
	VIII	76	272

"Tercets on Ingratitude or Envy"

745	VI	30	209
		27	208

"Tercets on Fortune"

746–7	XIII	120	415
747	III	246	92
		239	91

		108	66
		238	91
	VII	41	241
749	III	1ь1	75
	III	109	66

"The (Golden) Ass"

752	III	244	92
754	VI	135	225
757	III	227	90
	VIII	88	274
758	III	229	90
758–9	VIII	100	275
763	XI	126	354
764	I	24	5
	X	129	324
	XV	12	465
769	VI	76	215

Mandrogola

783	VI	137	226
793	VI	75	215
795	VI	6	206

"By The Devils Driven Out From Heaven"

878	VI	139	226

"By The Blessed Spirits"

880	III	315	111
	V	120	144

"Letters"

887	V	107	143
888	V	162	151
889	V	111	143
895	IV	10	123
896	III	231	90
	VIII	77	272
	I	9	3
	III	46	57
	VI	8	206
	VII	154	254
896–7	I	52	11
	III	242	92
897	III	107	66
	VII	2	233
898	V	488	190
899	V	338	177
	VI	33	209
	VIII	99	275
900	V	359	179
900–1	VI	9	206
	I	10	3
	IV	3	122
905	VII	142	252
906	I	11	3
911	IV	7	122
	X	51	315
919	VII	59	244
924	VII	143	252
	XII	100	376
925	VII	60	244
926	X	34	313

926–7	V	500	193
927	VIII	82	273
929	III	230	90
	IV	2	121
	I	34	8
	V	366	180
	XII	19	366
	IV	9	122
	XV	14	465
	V	346	177
	VI	104	219
930	V	496	192
		72	139
		406	183
	VI	87	218
	IV	13	123
973	VII	114	250
978	V	551	198
	VI	36	209

	VII	146	252
	XV	10	464
	IV	8	122
989	V	433	185
		584	203
	X	122	323
994–5	V	580	202
998	X	36	313
	XIII	191	426
	VII	56	244
1002	V	586	203
1004	V	587	203
1006	IV	35	126
	V	458	188
	X	106	322
	XIV	22	433
1008	IV	37	126
	X	45	322
		105	315
1010	II	16	20
	V	129	145
		452	187
	VIII	135	280

"History"

1028	V	554	199
1029	V	267	169
	555	199	
1029–30	V	552	198
1030	VI	126	223
	VIII	52	269
1031	III	139	72
	IV	34	126
	III	140	72
1032	VIII	148	282

1032–33	III	146	73
1046	III	287	102
1061	III	288	102
1061	III	292	103
1063	III	292	137
1063	III	291	102
1092	III	290	102
1096	III	276	98
1105–6	VIII	25	267
1117	II	89	35
1120	III	121	69
	XIV	82	443
1124	X	134	324
1125	III	321	112
	VI	61	212
	VIII	49	269
1133	XIII	115	414
1140–1	III	188	81
	V	30	136
1141	VI	79	216
	III	265	96
	VI	93	218
	VIII	151	282
1145–6	VII	43	242
1146	III	311	109
1148	VIII	94	275
1149	III	257	93
	XIII	163	423
1150	II	14	20

1154	III	115	68
1159	VII	44	242
1160	VII	45	242
1187	III	113	68
	XIII	178	425
1194	IV	47	127
	VI	34	209
	XIII	90	411
1196	VIII	93	274
1201–2	VII	81	246
	XIII	165	423
1202	III	270	97
		277	98
1207	II	93	35
1232	III	130	70
	VI	1	205
1233	III	312	109
	VII	42	242
	III	134	70
1241–2	VII	74	246
1242	II	10	19
	III	64	60
		223	89
1246–7	VII	16	236
	XI	73	345
1261	III	212	86
	XIII	166	424
1281–2	III	245	92
1284	III	220	88
1299	I	26	5
	X	103	322
	XI	109	350

1304	VII	46	242
1322	VI	7	206
1337	III	42	56
	VI	38	209
1345	V	558	200
1346	V	557	199
		559	200
1383–4	III	31	53
1395	V	583	202
1398–9	III	293	104
1406–7	III	289	102
1413	III	211	86
	VII	21	237
1434	V	564	200

"The Natures of Florentine Men"

1438	II	15	20

"Words To Be Spoken On The Law For Appropriating Money"

1439–41	VII	30	239
1442	III	210	85
1443	XI	24	338

"First Decennale"

1445	V	566	201
1448	V	170	153
1456	VIII	39	268
1457	V	287	171
	VII	106	248
	VIII	40	268

"Second Decennale"

1458	III	235	91
	VIII	85	273
1461	III	240	92
	X	52	316
	VII	182	259
	X	81	320

BIBLIOGRAPHY

Adams, John. *Diary and Autobiography,* Vol. 1 of *Works.* 10 Vols. Boston: Little & Brown, 1851.

Aldridge, Alfred Owen. *Man of Reason: The Life of Thomas Paine.* New York: Lippincott, 1959.

Anglo, Sydney. *Machiavelli: A Dissection.* New York: Harcourt, Brace & World, Harvest Book, 1969.

Aristotle. *Politics.* Translated by Benjamin Jowett. Rev. ed. New York: Colonial Press, Willey Book Co., 1899.

Bainton, Roland H. *Christian Attitudes Toward War and Peace: A Historical Survey and Critical Re-evaluation.* New York: Abingdon Press, 1960.

Becker, Carl Lotus. *The Declaration of Independence: A Study in the History of Ideas.* New York: Harcourt, Brace, 1922.

Benoist, Charles. *Machiavel.* Vol. 2 of *Le Machiavelisme.* 3 Vols. Paris: Librarie Plon, 1934.

The Bible. New English Bible: Old Testament. New York: Oxford University Press, 1970. New Testament. New York: Oxford University Press. 1961.

Bonadeo, Alfredo. *Corruption, Conflict, and Power in the Works and Times of Niccolo Machiavelli.* Berkeley: University of California Press, 1973.

Breasted, James Henry. *The Dawn of Conscience.* New York: Charles Scribners & Sons, 1934.

Browne, Waldo R., ed. *Man or the State? A Group of Essays by Famous Writers.* New York: B.W. Huebsch, 1919.

Buttrick, George Arthur, ed. *The Interpreter's Bible.* 7–12. New York: Abingdon Press, 1955.

Butterfield, Herbert. *The Statecraft of Machiavelli.* New York: Collier Books, 1967.

Dewey, John. *The Public and Its Problems.* New York: Henry Holt & Co., 1927.

————. *The Living Thoughts of Thomas Jefferson.* New York: Longmans, Green & Co., 1940.

————. *Freedom and Culture.* New York: Putnam, 1959.

Donne, John. "Devotions, XVII, A Meditation." *Devotion upon Emergent Occasions,* Ann Arbor, Mich.: University of Michigan Press, 1959.

585

Ferrara, Orestes. *Machiavel.* Translated by Francis de Moimandre. Paris: Librairie Ancienne Honorè Champion, 1928.

———. *The Private Correspondence of Nicolo Machiavelli.* Baltimore: Johns Hopkins Press, 1929.

Fleischer, Martin, ed. *Machiavelli and the Nature of Political Thought.* New York: Atheneum, 1972.

Garraty, John A. and Gay, Peter. *The Columbia History of the World.* New York: Harper & Row, 1972.

Gilbert, Felix. *Machiavelli and Guicciardini: Politics and History in Sixteenth-Century Florence.* 3 Vols. Princeton: Princeton University Press, 1965.

Goethe, Johann Wolfgang von. *Faust.* Translated by Bayard Taylor. Boston: Houghton Mifflin, 1898.

Goldstein, Kurt. *The Organism: A Holistic Approach to Biology Derived from Pathological Data in Man.* New York: American Book Co., 1939.

———. *Human Nature in the Light of Psychopathology.* New York: Schocken Books, 1963.

———. "On Emotions: Considerations from the Organismic Point of View," *Journal of Psychology,* 31 (1951): 37–49.

Hawke, David. *A Transaction of Free Men: The Birth and Course of the Declaration of Independence.* New York: Charles Scribner's, 1964.

Henry, Thomas H. *Wilderness Messiah: The Story of Hiawatha and the Iroquois.* New York: William Sloane, 1955.

Hirst, Francis. *Life and Letters of Thomas Jefferson.* New York: Macmillan, 1926.

Horwitz, Robert H., ed. *The Moral Foundations of the American Republic.* Charlottesville: University Press of Virginia, 1977.

Jensen, De Lamar, ed. *Machiavelli: Cynic, Patriot, or Political Scientist?* Lexington, Mass.: D.C. Heath & Co., 1960.

Josephus, Flavius. *Works.* Translated by William Whiston. Philadelphia: David McKay, n.d.

Kemmerich, Max. *Machiavelli.* Wien: Verlag Karl Konig, 1925.

Keynes, John Maynard. *The Economic Consequences of the Peace.* New York: Harcourt, Brace and Howe, 1920.

Livius, Titus. *The History of Rome.* Translated by Rev. Canon Roberts. 3 Vols. New York: E.P. Dutton & Co., 1926.

Lorenz, Konrad. *On Aggression.* Translated by Marjorie Kerr Wilson. New York: Harcourt, Brace & World, 1963.

MacDougal, William. *The Group Mind.* 2nd ed. New York: Putnam, 1928.

Machiavelli, Niccolo. *Machiavelli: The Chief Works and Others.* Translated by Allan Gilbert. 3 Vols. Durham, N.C.: Duke University Press, 1965.

———. *Tutte le Opere Storiche e Letterarie.* Edited by Guido Mazzoni e Mario Casella. Firenze: G. Barbera Editore, 1929.

Madison, James. *The Papers of James Madison.* 10 Vols. Chicago: University of Chicago Press, 1962.

Malone, Dumas and Rauch, Basil. *Empire for Liberty: The Genesis and Growth of the United States of America*. 2 Vols. New York: Appleton-Century-Crofts, 1960.

Mansfield, Harvey Claflin, Jr. *Machiavelli's New Modes and Orders: A Study of the Discourses on Livy*. Ithaca, N.Y.: Cornell University Press, 1979.

————. "On the Impersonality of the Modern State: A Comment on Machiavelli's Use of *Stato*," *American Political Science Review*, 77, no. 4 (December 1983), 849–857.

Mead, George Herbert. "The Genesis of the Self and Social Control," in *Selected Writings*, edited by Andrew J. Reck. New York: Bobbs-Merrill Co., 1964.

Meinecke, Friedrich. *Machiavellism: The Doctrine of Raison D'Etat and Its Place in Modern History*. Translated by Douglas Scott. New Haven: Yale University Press, 1957.

Miller, John C. *Alexander Hamilton: Portrait in Paradox*. New York: Harper, 1959.

Mitchell, Broadus. *Alexander Hamilton, Youth to Maturity 1755–1789*. New York: Macmillan, 1957.

Mondadori, Arnoldo, ed. *Machiavelli*. Milano: Periodici Mondadori, 1968.

Morgan, Lewis H. *League of the Ho-de-No-San-Nee or Iroquois*. New York: Dodd, Mead, 1904.

Morrison, Samuel Eliot, Commager, Henry Steele and Leuchtenburg, William E. *The Growth of the American Republic*. 2 Vols. New York: Oxford University Press, 1969.

Oxilia, Adolfo. *Machiavelli*. Firenze: Ditta Alfani e Venturi, 1932.

Pace, Antonio. *Benjamin Franklin and Italy*. Philadelphia: The American Philosophical Society, 1958.

Page, Kirby. *How Jesus Faced Totalitarianism*. New York: Fellowship of Reconciliation, n.d. (reprint from *Living Prayerfully*. New York: Farrar and Rinehart, n.d.)

Pansini, Anthony J. *Niccolo Machiavelli and the United States of America*. Greenvale, New York: Greenvale Press, 1969.

Parel, Anthony, ed. *The Political Calculus: Essays on Machiaveli's Philosophy*, Toronto, Canada: University of Toronto Press, 1972.

Plato. *The Republic*. Translated by Benjamin Jowett. Rev. ed. New York: Colonial Press, Willey Book Co., 1901.

Plumb, J.H. *The Horizon Book of the Renaissance*. New York: American Heritage Publishing Co., 1961.

Pocock, J.G.A. *The Machiavellian Moment: Florentine Political Thought and the Atlantic Republican Tradition*. Princeton: Princeton University Press, 1975.

Prescott, Arthur T. *Drafting the Federal Constitution*. University, La.: Louisiana State University Press, 1941.

Prezzolini, Giuseppe. *Niccolo Machiavelli: The Florentine*. Translated by Ralph

Roeder. New York: Brentano's, 1928.

———. *Machiavelli: A study of the life, work, influence and originality of an obscure civil servant who has become our contemporary.* New York: Farrar, Straus & Giroux, Noonday Press, 1967.

———. "The Christian Roots of Machiavelli's Moral Pessimism." *Review of National Literatures.* 1, No. 1 (Spring 1970): 26–37.

Read, Conyers, ed. *The Constitution Reconsidered.* New York: Columbia University Press, 1938.

Ridolfi, Roberto. *The Life of Niccolo Machiavelli.* Translated by Cecil Grayson. Chicago: The University of Chicago Press, 1963.

Rossiter, Clinton. *Seedtime of the Republic.* New York: Harcourt, Brace, 1953.

———. *Alexander Hamilton and the Constitution.* New York: Harcourt, Brace & World, 1964.

Rubinstein, Nicolai, ed. *Florentine Studies: Politics and Society in Renaissance Florence.* Evanston, Ill.: Northwestern University Press, 1968.

Sabine, George H. *A History of Political Theory.* 3rd ed. New York: Holt, Rinehart and Winston, 1963.

Savelle, Max. *Seeds of Liberty.* New York: Knopf, 1948.

Schevill, Ferdinand. *History of Florence from the Founding of the City through the Renaissance.* New York: Harcourt, Brace and Co., 1936.

Sforza, Count Carlo. *The Living Thoughts of Machiavelli.* London: Cassell, 1942.

Strauss, Leo. *Thoughts on Machiavelli.* Seattle, Wash.: University of Washington Press, Washington Paperbacks, 1958.

———. "Machiavelli and Classical Literature," *Review of National Literatures* 1, no. 1 (Spring 1970): 7–25.

Tommasini, Oreste. *La Vita e gli Scritti di Niccolo Machiavelli nella loro relazione col Machiavellismo.* 2 Vols. (the second in two parts). Roma: Prof. P. Maglione Succ. di E. Loescher, 1940–2.

von Däniken, Erich. *The Gold of the Gods.* New York: Putnam, 1972.

Vignal, L. Gautier. *Machiavel.* Paris: Payot, 1929.

Wallace, Paul A.R. *The White Roots of Peace.* Philadelphia: University of Pennsylvania Press, 1946.

Whitfield, John Humphreys. *Machiavelli.* New York: Russell & Russell, 1965.

———. *Discourses on Machiavelli.* Cambridge: W. Heffer & Sons, 1969.

Willis, Garry. *Inventing America: Jefferson's Declaration of Independence.* Garden City, N.Y.: Doubleday, 1978.

Windelband, Dr. W. *A History of Philosophy with especial reference to the Formation and Development of its Problems and Conceptions.* Translated by James Hayden Tufts. New York: Macmillan, 1919.

Yarrow, C. Mike. *Quaker Experiences in International Conciliation.* New Haven: Yale University Press, 1978.

Young, G.F. *The Medici.* New York: The Modern Library, 1930.

Index

Julius II, Pope
M.'s appraisal of, 104

Leadership. *See also* Fiction
failure of, 1, 43–48, 453–454
Lenin, Nicolai
disappearance of the state, 453
Locke, John
individualism, 357
life, liberty and property, 402
separation of powers, 405
Lorenz, Konrad
militant enthusiasm, 83–84
scientific method, 7–8
Luther, Martin
Christian freedom, 17
publication of "Ninety-five Theses," 105

Machiavelli, Bernardo (father)
Livy's *History*, preparation of index to
place names in, 100, 137
Machiavelli, Niccolo
activism, 4–7. *See also* Activism
aim
fulfillment of conditions for, 346–347
literary purpose, 6–7, 65, 205–232
army (standing), opposition to, 94–96,
405
conservation, 272
contemporaneity, 234–235, 363
founder of political science, 2–4, 225,
231, 235, 263
human capacity, faith in, 259–261, 272–
278, 316
the individual, concept of, 278–283
New World political experiences, parallels
in, 403–412
"polit-," a word root without negative implications for M., 454
and political innovation, 437–439
religion, 100–105
atheism, alleged, 145–151
the Bible, 60, 140
renewal, 7
self-appraisal, 121–128
self-reliance, 121–128
state, concept of, 272, 278, 407, 411–412,
460–461
virtu! 208–210, 215–27, 308, 414, 417–
418, 419–421, 444–445
war. *See also* Force
doubts about effectiveness of, 422, 427

"Machiavellian": origin of, 203–204
Madison, James
army (standing), opposition to, 405
interest in M., 397
youthful response, 399
Medici, family
geneological table of, 213
M.'s evaluation of, 197–203
Medici, Cosimo de',
emergence to leadership, 58
Medici, Lorenzo de', "The Magnificent"
achievements, 105
emergence to leadership, 58
Montesquieu
contributions from M., 393–394
separation of powers, 405

Nansen, Fritjof
judgment on international relations, 333,
440
Nation-forming
impact on M., 18–20
Nation-state
evaluation of adequacy, 35–39
limited availability of nationhood, 37–38
myth of national security, 32–33
pertinent questions, 39
tension between individualism and regula-
tion, 39–40
unaddressed human needs, 37
vulnerabilities, 37
Natural right
pursuit of happiness, 10
Necessity
and fortune, 92
New World experience
re-inforcing M.,'s directives, 399–414

Order
ancient concepts of universal, 429–430
M.'s militant pluralism, 430–433
perennial civic qualities, 433–439
Organismic approach, 9, 440
Organismic behavior, 440
Organismic process: inner development,
459–460

Paine, Thomas
apostle of freedom, 435, 443
Common Sense, 414
Paul
precursor of science of politics, 2

592

Penn, William
  democratic process, institution of, 400
  "Holy Experiment," 39
  law-giver, 357
Political science
  aim, 379–380
  experimental approach, 463–464
  fictions, need to identify, 9
  founders, 1–4, 12, 231, 263
  individual as agent, 464–468
  intentional behavior, 463–468
  M.'s insights, 235–261
  precursors of science of politics, 2
  process, 383–384
  responsible participation, 463–464
  traditional concepts, need for re-examination of, 40
Power relative to force, 23–32, 47–53. *See also* Fiction, Force
  alternative to territorial state, 30–31
  blindness, political, 35, 68, 91–92
  Borgia, Cesare, 78
  Cain, 22
  Ikhnaton, 22
  James, 28
  Jesus, 26–27, 28–31
  Moses, 23
  Paul, 27–28, 30, 31
  Samuel, 23–24
  self-reliance, 410–412
Principle of proportionate duty, 339, 453
Property
  and the collective, 53
  and land ownership, 106–107
  Locke and Jefferson, 402–403
  M.'s perspective, 350–351
  origin of, 445–447
    David, 13
    Jesus, 14
    Machiavelli, 14–15
    Moses, 13
    Paul, 13
  right to resources, 14, 53–54, 78

Questions, basic: 1, 12–13, 15, 32, 33, 41, 43, 129, 235, 283, 285, 307, 336, 337, 361, 366, 371, 442, 443, 463

Reason, participation-derived
  consensus, factors enhancing, 381–390
  history (new), 363
  liberation, resources for, 366–381

personal character (new), 363–366
Religion. *See also* Fiction
Religion, political use of, 49–52, 92, 100–105, 116–117, 146–147
  Augustus, 49
  church-state relation, 31–32, 105
  versus individualism, 105
  renewal, principle of, 7
Renewal
  decision-making, 449–462
Republican government
  and individualism, 108–116
  M.'s preference for, 111–115, 343, 356–357

Savonarola
  accession to power, 58
  influence on M., 152–154
  rise and fall, 100
Science, method of, 7–8
Science of politics
  founding of, 2–4, 125, 231, 261
  Ecclesiastes, precursor, 1
  Herod, precursor, 2
  Paul, precursor, 2
  Pilate, precursor, 2
  Solomon, precursor, 1
Self-reliance as source of power, 410–412
Similarities of political challenges
  M.'s and our times, 457–462
Soderini, Piero
  accession to power in Florence, 58
Solomon
  precursor of science of politics, 1
State as association, 407
State, components of, 263–271
  administration of justice, 269–270
  aggressive posture, 269
  appropriate form of government, 270–271
  citizen army, 267–269
  commitment to more inclusive relationships, 235–236
  consent of the governed, 269
  effective leader, 263–264
  foresight *versus* fortune, 233–234
  fraud, 240–243
  fusion of good arms and good laws, 251
  human nature, firm understanding of, 260–261, 263
  impressionable youth, 264–266
  necessity transcending good and evil, sense of, 236–238

594